EFFECTIVE EXPERT TESTIMONY

THIRD EDITION

EFFECTIVE EXPERT TESTIMONY

THIRD EDITION

David M. Malone

Trial Run, Inc.

Paul J. Zwier

Emory University School of Law

NITA®

NATIONAL INSTITUTE FOR TRIAL ADVOCACY

Address inquiries to:

Reprint Permission
National Institute for Trial Advocacy
1685 38th Street, Suite 200
Boulder, CO 80301-2735
Phone: (800) 225-6482
Fax: (720) 890-7069
E-mail: permissions@nita.org

ISBN 978-1-60156-340-8
FBA 1340

Library of Congress Cataloging-in-Publication Data

Malone, David M., 1944- author.

 Effective expert testimony / David M. Malone, Trial Run, Inc.; Paul J. Zwier, Emory University School of Law. -- Third edition.

     pages cm

   ISBN 978-1-60156-340-8

1. Evidence, Expert--United States. I. Zwier, Paul J., 1954- author. II. Title.

   KF8961.M35 2014

   347.73'67--dc23

                          2013045193

Printed in the United States.

To Dorinda, Ryan, and Patrick,
who have always encouraged my teaching and writing.

D.M.M.

This edition of the book is dedicated to my dear friend and co-author,
David M. Malone, who passed way before his time.

P.Z.

CONTENTS

Preface xiii

Chapter One: Introduction: Some Reflections on Experts

Chapter Two: Finding Experts

  2.1   Where to Find an Expert 5

       2.1.1 "Inside" Expert 6

       2.1.2 "Outside" Expert 7

  2.2   Where to Find an Outside Expert 9

  2.3   Maintaining Confidentiality 10

  2.4   Expert Fees 11

Chapter Three: Caring for an Expert

  3.1   Top Ten Things to Avoid in Dealing with Experts 15

       3.1.1   Number Ten: "Hold Up on that Project from Last Week." 15

       3.1.2   Number Nine: "Hi, I've Got a Trial Next Month and ...." 16

       3.1.3   Number Eight: "Harry's Rent-an-Expert Is Way under
               Your Proposed Budget." 16

       3.1.4   Number Seven: "I'm Not Sure What We'll Need or
               When We'll Need It." 16

       3.1.5   Number Six: "I'll Just Send (.pdf) All the Paper . . . ." 17

       3.1.6   Number Five: "I Know You Called a Few Weeks Ago,
               but I've Been so Busy." 17

       3.1.7   Number Four: "Oh, I'm Sure that Check Is in
               the Mail Right Now." 18

       3.1.8   Number Three: "Let's Use My People on This, OK?" 18

       3.1.9   Number Two: "Is There Some Way You Can Cut
               a Few Bucks Off What We Budgeted?" 19

       3.1.10 Number One: "Did I Forget to Tell You the Fact that . . . ?" 19

Chapter Four: Timelines for Working with Experts

4.1   The Plaintiff's Expert Timeline.. 21

4.2   The Defendant's Expert Timeline 22

4.3   Report Requirements for All Experts.. 22

4.4   Rebuttal Disclosure.. 23

Chapter Five: Nondeposition Discovery against Experts

5.1   What Should You Tell the Expert? 30

5.2   Dealing with the Consulting Expert 31

5.3   Consulting v. Nonconsulting... 31

5.4   Protective Orders... 33

5.5   Beauty Contests... 33

5.6   Communications with the Expert... 34

        5.6.1   Under the Federal Rules—Keeping Drafts and
                   Communications with Counsel 34

                 5.6.1.1   The Applicable Rules before 2010......................... 34

                 5.6.1.2   2010 Changes.. 36

Chapter Six: Preparing to Depose the Expert

6.1   Expert Discovery 41

6.2   Location of the Deposition 44

6.3   Preparing for the Deposition.. 45

        6.3.1   Brainstorming on Themes and Facts 46

        6.3.2   Creating a Timeline 47

        6.3.3   Reviewing Documents 47

Chapter Seven: Deposing the Expert: Strategies

7.1   Deposing Experts: Strategies.. 51

7.2   *Daubert* and Deposition Strategy 59

Chapter Eight: Deposing and Defending the Expert: Tactics

8.1   Deposing Experts: Tactics 61

8.2   Rule 803(18): Learned Treatises as Nonhearsay....................... 66

8.3   Expert Witness: Preparation... 67

8.4   Conclusion 76

Chapter Nine: Direct Examination of Experts

9.1   Analyzing Expert Testimony 77

9.2   Preparing the Expert for Direct Examination 79

9.3   Expert Direct Examinations.. 80

9.4   Outline of Testimony... 84

     9.4.1   Introduction 85

     9.4.2   Tickler 85

     9.4.3   Qualifying the Expert 86

     9.4.4   Tender 90

     9.4.5   Opinions 91

     9.4.6   Bases.. 92

     9.4.7   Anticipating Cross-Examination 95

     9.4.8   Save a Point for Redirect and or End Strong 96

Chapter Ten: Experts and Exhibits

10.1   Exhibits and Evidentiary Foundations... 115

     10.1.1   Evidentiary Hurdles for Illustrative or Summary Exhibits 115

     10.1.2   Hearsay Hurdles for Exhibits 116

10.2   Foundations for Specific Exhibits... 118

     10.2.1   Photographs.. 118

     10.2.2   From Photographs to Videos to Computer Graphics 119

10.3   The Role of the Pretrial Conference... 123

10.4   Staying Organized During Pretrial 124

10.5   The Lawyer as Protector of Fairness: Edit and Critique
Experts' Exhibits 125

     10.5.1   Misleading Icons and Labels 125

10.6   Opposing Graphic Evidence at the Pretrial Conference........................ 127

10.7   Handling Documents at Trial: Dancing with Documents 128

10.8   Choosing the Medium and the Occasion.. 132

10.9   The Next Level of Persuasion with Exhibits 133

Chapter Eleven: Cross-Examination of an Expert Witness: Control

11.1   Form of Question 139

11.2   Control Techniques for the "Run-On" Witness..................................... 142

     11.2.1   Repeat the Question 142

     11.2.2   Use a "Reverse Repeat" 143

11.2.3 Cross-Examine the Witness with Your Eyes.................................. 143

11.2.4 Other Control Techniques 144

11.2.5 Do Not Go to the Judge Too Early, if at All 144

Chapter Twelve: Cross-Examination of an Expert Witness: Impeachment

12.1 Impeachment with a Prior Inconsistent Statement.............................. 145

12.2 Impeachments by Omission.. 149

12.3 Using Learned Treatises under Cross-Examination.............................. 153

12.4 Use the Expert's Report to Assert Control... 156

12.5 Cross on Financial or Other Bias 156

12.6 Impeachment by Prior Bad Acts... 159

**Chapter Thirteen: Cross-Examination of an Expert Witness:
Organizational Choices**

13.1 Putting It All Together 163

13.2 Bill v. Woodframe Construction Company 164

13.3 Constructive v. Destructive Cross-Examination 169

13.4 Primacy v. Recency 172

13.5 Storytelling v. Fact-Gathering 176

13.6 Substance v. Impeachment... 177

13.7 Applying Control Techniques to Cross-Examination of Experts.......... 179

        13.7.1 Enlistment and Narrowing of Issues................................. 180

13.8 Macro v. Micro Cross-Examination 182

13.9 Demystify the Dispute—Analogies 185

13.10 Corralling the Expert 187

13.11 Eighth-Grade Science Norms... 190

13.12 Expert Testimony on Reconstruction and Recreations........................ 191

        13.12.1 The Recreation of Damage to the Roof of the Subaru........ 192

        13.12.2 The Model of the Moose 193

        13.12.3 The Roof Pillars that Were Not Roof Pillars.................... 194

        13.12.4 Conclusions from the Moose Case for Direct and
                    Cross-Examination 194

**Chapter Fourteen: Cross-Examining an Expert Witness in an International
Commercial Arbitration**

14.1 Dissimilarities in Skills and Techniques of Cross-Examination
        between an International Commercial Arbitration and Trial 198

        14.1.1 General Discovery.. 198

14.1.2 Expert Reports.. 198

14.1.3 General Approach.. 199

14.1.4 Researching the Expert's Qualifications..................... 201

14.1.5 Background of the Tribunal 202

14.1.6 Damages v. Other Issues 202

14.1.7 Time Constraints.. 203

14.2 Trial Advocacy Cross-Examination Skills and Techniques
for International Commercial Arbitrations............................ 203

14.2.1 Basic Techniques.. 204

14.2.2 Additional Techniques 205

14.2.3 Tribunal-Appointed Experts...................................... 206

14.2.4 Witness Conferencing.. 206

14.3 Summary.. 207

Chapter Fifteen: *Daubert* Trilogy

15.1 *Daubert:* The Gathering Clouds...................................... 209

15.2 *Daubert*: The Supreme Court, Gatekeepers,
and Expert Reliability 211

15.3 Post-*Daubert* Issues 213

15.4 *Daubert*: To *Kumho* and Beyond 216

Chapter Sixteen: Examining the Reliability of Expert Testimony

16.1 Hearsay Exceptions and Admissibility of Bases.................... 219

16.2 Confrontation Clause Challenges to
Expert Bases in Criminal Cases.. 220

16.3 Interviews, Market Information, or Research Produced by
the Expert Herself to Test Her Opinion 221

16.4 *Daubert* Challenges to the Reliability of the Expert's Opinion............... 221

16.4.1 Publication and Peer Critique 222

16.4.2 Error Rate that Can Be or Is Known 223

16.4.3 Acceptance in the Relevant Scientific Field................ 223

16.4.4 Testability or Replicability... 223

16.4.5 Preparation or Creation for a Purpose Other
Than Litigation 224

16.4.6 Adequacy to Explain Important Empirical Data 225

16.4.7 Basis in Quantitatively Sufficient Data...................... 226

16.4.8   Basis in Qualitatively Acceptable Data 227

16.4.9   Methodological Consistency 236

16.4.10 Consistency in This Application 236

16.4.11 Recognition in a Body of Literature 237

16.4.12 Adequacy of the Expert's Credentials 237

16.4.13 Derivation from Mainstream Approaches 238

Chapter Seventeen: Conclusion

Appendix A: Selected Federal Rules of Evidence

Article VII: Opinions and Expert Testimony, Rules 701–06............................. 245

Article VIII: Hearsay, Rule 803(18) 247

Appendix B: Federal Rule of Civil Procedure 26 Title V. Disclosures and Discovery:

Rule 26. Duty to Disclose; General Provisions Governing Discovery 249

Appendix C: Selected Cases Supreme Court of the United States

Daubert v. Merrell Dow Pharmaceuticals, Inc. 263

General Electric Co. v. Joiner 279

Kumho Tire Company, Ltd. v. Carmichael 293

Melendez-Diaz v. Massachusetts 309

Bullcoming v. New Mexico 347

Williams v. Illinois 373

Bell Atlantic Corp. v. Twomby 427

Appendix D: Court of Appeals Cases

Antitrust Experts... 461

Index... **463**

PREFACE

One only needs to pick up any one of a dozen specialty journals for various areas of trial law, and there, in the back pages, is evidence of the explosive growth of the market for expert witnesses. The advertisements prove the market is thriving. Nowadays, we have experts for airline crashes on land and others for crashes on water; we have experts for the adequacy of restraint systems to keep passengers in cars and others who show how passengers were injured by those restraint systems; we have experts for computer manufacturing and others for computer use, keyboard injuries, e-mail security, or chat room stalkers; we could even hire expert historians to tell us why politicians in the South or North behave the way they do. Entire divisions of the largest accounting firms are devoted to providing "litigation support" for the lawyer's case—support that goes far beyond forensic accounting and economics. While we may long for the simpler days, we also wonder where all these experts have come from and whether we are required to employ them to provide competent counsel.

The law itself is substantially responsible for this explosion of specialists in court. Tort law requires expert testimony that the doctor accused of malpractice fell well below the standard of care in treating the plaintiff; product liability cases require experts to explain the complicated technology, designs, and manufacturing processes; any slip-and-fall, toxic tort, or automobile accident case raises questions of causal nexus and extent of damages, which probably cannot be answered by a lay jury without help from experts. Federal Rule of Evidence 702 may allow such expert proof, but our complicated society virtually demands it. In the criminal law arena, the state is required to provide proof beyond a reasonable doubt to deprive someone of his or her liberty. The prosecution has more and more experts to draw on to help it meet its burden. In addition to experts in traditional fields of blood, fingerprints, voice recognition, chemistry, and blood alcohol, new experts include analysts of DNA, hair, fiber, and mental health experts opining on PTSD, spouse abuse syndrome, memory retrieval, and the validity of functional MRIs for determining truth speaking.

Recognize that our entire legal system is upside-down; we choose people to resolve a dispute because they know nothing about the facts involved—ignorance is a qualification for a juror to be a "peer" of the parties to the suit. This ignorance theoretically protects the parties from being subjected to bias or prejudice and from being held to impossibly high standards of conduct by "experts" on the jury (such as the board that administers the dreaded "oral exams" to hopeful doctoral candidates).

To counter the jurors' built-in ignorance, it is little wonder the state or plaintiffs call experts to educate and inform the jurors, forcing the defendants to then present their own experts to correct the state's or plaintiff's errors and omissions. With complex subjects where the entire case may rise or fall on the experts' opinions, all parties increasingly demand high-quality work from the experts. The experts, in turn, spend more time on the cases and charge more in fees, so the consequences of failure increase further. Those experts with superior skills in analysis, explication, and persuasion come to be more in demand, and fees rise further until it is much more profitable for an engineer, economist, or psychologist to spend her time testifying rather than building, assisting, or treating. The professional testifying expert is born.

Yet we lawyers are not so naive that we fail to recognize that the burgeoning need for experts and the commensurate increase in their compensation have created biases that put the reliability of the experts' opinion in question. That very same professionalization can make experts depend too heavily for their livelihood on the side they consistently represent from case to case. Their objectivity suffers, and they become so sophisticated in matters of discovery that their reports become too "lawyerly" and their deposition answers lose their spontaneity and candor. Even at trial, experts have come to "know the game," so they become aggressive advocates and tailor their methodologies to achieve the results sought. Trial judges, who deal with these experts day in and day out, may start to stereotype the expert as "bought and paid for," perhaps ruing the day experts were ever invited into the courtroom.

These are problems that trial lawyers must confront when they deal with experts: the courts hold them in disdain; the parties are offended by their expense; and the jurors are resentful because the experts arrogantly claim superior knowledge. How can the trial lawyer deal with these biases, resolve them, and lead the court and jurors to welcome the experts as helpful, credible, and persuasive? That is the question that prompted the authors to attempt to create a useful and practical guide to expert witnesses.

Since the second edition of this book was published, federal statutory law and federal case law regarding experts has continued to evolve. For example, in an attempt to try to control litigation costs, Federal Rule of Civil Procedure 26 now provides limits on what the litigator can discover pretrial about what the hiring attorney told or showed her expert. While Rule 26 has long specified that the expert is to submit to the opposing side a written report containing the things the expert considered in reaching her opinions, the new restrictions on discovery of communications between the attorney and the expert make it more difficult to find out whether the lawyer was too aggressive when forming the report and the expert's opinions. More and more states are adopting the federal rules in this regard. As a consequence, we have expanded our coverage of these issues in chapter six. In addition, we now have a better idea of how the court will look at the *Daubert* and *Kumho Tire* gate-keeping criteria, and as a consequence, in chapters seven and eight we have expanded our coverage of the strategy and tactics of both taking and defending depositions with

Federal Rule of Evidence 702 in mind. Moreover, we have teamed up with Lexis Nexis to provide links to their *Daubert* tracker. Their Web site provides links to the latest cases, organized by the type of expert testimony that was provided in the case. We still include our own Appendix D, where we analyze the latest Supreme Court opinions dealing with reliance by experts on evidence given by others and whether in criminal cases such evidence violates the defendant's confrontation clause rights; this includes other updates on experts and the criminal law. We also analyze recent attempts by the courts to respond to criticism that convictions be based on valid science.

In chapter fourteen, we have added a discussion of how to conduct direct and cross-examinations of experts in an international commercial arbitration setting to highlight the different attitudes toward experts held by arbitrators from civil law jurisdictions.

It is fair to ask the source of our expertise. The two authors first met a number of years ago at a NITA trial advocacy program for the Federal Trade Commission in Washington, DC. Dave Malone was a senior trial attorney at that agency and had faced and presented experts in every case he had handled (in one case examining or cross-examining fifty-two experts). His experience in thirty years of practice included experts of all sorts: construction, antitrust econometrics, drug patents, savings and loan failures, products liability, and others. When they met, Paul Zwier was an academic and a trial advocacy teacher—an enthusiastic NITA teacher—and an occasional expert witness himself. Since their first meeting two decades ago, Zwier has studied the role of the trial attorney in shaping the testimony of expert witnesses and the role of the rules of evidence and ethics in governing the relationship of the experts to lawyers, juries, and courts. He is a law professor at Emory University School of Law, where he teaches torts, evidence, and an advanced international negotiation and mediation seminar, and directs the litigation skills curriculum. His interest in experts and advocacy has turned out to be a lasting one.

Over the years, the authors have taught together in literally hundreds of NITA litigation programs, dealing with what they have come to call "the care and feeding of experts." This book is the result of their experience in the "NITA classroom laboratory," where they have worked with lawyers—young and old, green and experienced, women and men—as they conducted depositions or examined and cross-examined expert witnesses of all types. Dedicated and skilled NITA teaching colleagues have continuously and generously provided their insights, their examples, and their enthusiasm. From the different perspectives of practice and scholarship, the authors have explored and enjoyed what the painter Edgar Degas termed "the charm and delight of the conversation of specialists." Degas believed "one could understand nothing" of such specialists' musings; however, the authors believe expert testimony can be understood by the well-prepared lawyer and translated and presented so that it is interesting and persuasive to the jury. We hope readers sense our enthusiasm for the topic and share some of our charm and delight.

Special thanks are owed to Wendy Velez, NITA project manager for this new edition, as well as to Eric Sorensen, who provided careful and thoughtful editorial guidance. Special thanks are also owed to all our teaching friends, inside and outside NITA, who continue to support our writing and teaching and who are a boundless source of inspiration and energy. Insightful ideas in this book were borrowed by us and handed on; errors and omissions were born with us and remain our responsibility.

[In the process of editing this edition, my co-author, Dave M. Malone passed away. He was a mentor and dear friend. He will be greatly missed. He is the heart and soul of this book and what I know about experts. The legal profession has lost an amazing teacher, and writer, who worked daily to try to improve the skills of legal advocates. His commitment to such training was grounded in the belief that it is the individual lawyer/advocate who is the key to our oral adversarial system—that for the system to deliver on its promise to manage disputes with justice and promote the rule of law, the advocate must have both the substantive understanding of the law and the skills and ethics to make it work. PZ]

National Institute for Trial Advocacy

CHAPTER ONE

INTRODUCTION: SOME REFLECTIONS ON EXPERTS

Experts represent a unique opportunity for the trial attorney. They can have a dispositive effect on trial, and therefore, they must be presented well and challenged with care. The satisfaction attorneys get from dealing with experts derives from the ability to use their skills in their field to challenge the experts' skills in their field, and there is the additional pleasure that comes from the adrenalin charge an attorney gets from the competition with a bright and intelligent expert who has chosen a different path.

Many trial attorneys consider the direct and cross-examination of experts to be the most rewarding part of their craft. The attorney must understand enough to participate intelligently in the courtroom and be prepared to match his wits and knowledge against those of a professional in the field. This high level of civilized combat is certainly what attracts many attorneys to focus on the expert portion of trial practice.

The attorney in expert practice has the opportunity to learn about brand new fields outside the law, and he can learn it from acknowledged authorities. Whether they want to or not, the experts educate the attorney about their fields at deposition, preparation, and trial. And the attorney, in turn, can use their testimony to educate the judge and jurors. For a brief moment, the attorney will be as expert as they—maybe even more expert. For trial lawyers, part of the charm of experts is the excuse experts provide to learn something new.

However, experts present a challenge for the trial attorney. If the attorney does not learn the expert's field (at least in some narrow way so he can be on an equal footing), the examinations, direct or cross, will be complete failures—confusing to the trier of fact, unproductive, and perhaps even supportive of the opposing attorney's case. The dilemma is that the attorney must become an expert, but not so expert that he loses his ability to communicate with the jurors. Michael Tigar gives a wonderful example of this problem. He describes one of his first cases that had an expert accountant who was detailing the distinction between ordinary income and capital gains. During the trial, the bailiff reported to him that he had heard one juror say to another, "Who is this Captain Gains?" and the other juror replied, "I don't know; I think we'll hear from him tomorrow." The point is that the experts and the lawyers were having a wonderful conversation, but the jurors did not enjoy or understand it.

The trial attorney's task is to retain something of the expert's aura of authority in the testimony, but insure the expert effectively communicates to the fact-finder as well. That task begins with the decisions on whether to hire an expert (nontestifying or testifying), how to use that expert, how to prepare and present that expert, and how to meet the expert presented by the other side. All along its length, this path is marked by special rules designed by courts and legislatures to attempt to extract meaning from experts without letting them dazzle the jury to the point of blindness.

To many seasoned trial judges, however, experts have lost their charm. Maybe they have heard an expert orthopedist define orthopedics too many times, or a chemist describe how one determines whether a powdery substance is cocaine. Usually, the judge just wants to move the testimony along and will apply pressure that further burdens the trial lawyer's ability to make the testimony interesting and persuasive.

Additionally, the trial judge serves as a gatekeeper, deciding whether the testimony is admissible; whether it is "relevant and reliable," in the words of the *Daubert* court. The trial judge must also make an epistemological determination about whether the expert's testimony will help the jurors resolve the issues in the case. If the judge is skeptical of either the plaintiffs' or defendants' expert case, the judge may wield the skeptic's epistemological scalpel and prevent the expert witness from testifying at all.

In some sense, the expert must accomplish the impossible because the attorneys want the expert to tell them what happened and to prove it to their satisfaction in the face of centuries-long philosophical difficulties with defining "knowing" and "cause and effect." The philosophical problem is: "Even if I know what happened many times in the past under similar circumstances—in a statistical sense—how do I know what happened in this particular case?" However, the rules of evidence attempt to authorize the philosophically impossible: they give the jury the power to make decisions about what is known and what should be believed.

A reasonable concern may be that the attorneys themselves do not fully understand the expert's field, so they attempt to protect the decision-making process by seeking even more certainty than the expert would require in her day-to-day work or that they would require if they better understood the expert's work. *Daubert* can be seen as an attempt by the Supreme Court to encourage trial judges to impose legal standards on the admissibility of expert testimony. Ironically, lawyers demand more certainty of expert witnesses, who attempt to provide what are admittedly opinions, than they do of percipient witnesses, who claim they "know the facts." Experts, like all witnesses, provide only a piece of the puzzle—they do not guarantee to provide the answer.

The relationship between the expert's degree of confidence and the burden of proof remains substantially undetermined. With a statistical expert, for example, is confidence at the 95 percent level equivalent to "beyond a reasonable doubt"? Would 90 percent confidence not be sufficient in a criminal case, but still be adequate in a civil case? Indeed, if the expert states she always demands a 95 percent level of confidence, is that level required for her testimony even in a civil case? One can only wonder what the judge's reaction would be if an expert said from the stand, "I hold this opinion with a 51 percent degree of confidence." It is likely the court would rule that such an opinion was insufficiently reliable to be admitted; that is, no reasonable juror could find—by a preponderance or beyond a reasonable doubt—that such an opinion represented the truth. But the answer seems less clear if the expert claims accuracy at the 75 percent confidence level. At least one judge, Hon. Alex Konzinski, has said that he would not allow a plaintiff's expert to opine a causal relationship between the drug Bendectin and limb reductions unless there was epidemiological proof showing that exposure to Bendectin raised by a factor of two the likelihood that a child would be born with a limb reduction. As applied in the area of social science, filled with confounding variables and restrictions on human subject testing, this standard may be difficult to meet, especially for early litigants. Does *Daubert,* as applied to *Kumho Tire*-experienced-based experts, go too far in constraining what the jury may consider because it excludes expert testimony that may be particularly useful to a jury even though its reliability has not been proven to the judge? The skeptic's bias may unfairly invade the juror's province of finding facts and assessing credibility.

Yet recent studies of the judge's gatekeeping role don't seem to indicate a higher rate of dismissal in *Daubert* jurisdictions than in jurisdictions applying the old *Frye* test.[1] Perhaps judges are still in the process of learning their new roles (might it take twenty years?) or perhaps the defense lawyers have not yet learned to use the new rules to their full defensive advantage. Or perhaps the legal profession itself is advantaged financially by a system promoting expert testimony, and lawyers on both sides tacitly agree to use them, despite the unreliability of their methods. In any event, *Daubert* has not yet delivered on its promises to provide a better tool for insuring that experts opinions are reliable.

The rules regarding experts permit the expert to testify in the form of an opinion. The law of evidence generally disfavors opinion testimony, allowing lay witnesses to

---

1. GEORGE FISHER, EVIDENCE,. Foundation Press, 805–10 (3d ed. 2013) (reviewing a number of studies, including 1) a Rand Institute report in 2002 that seemed to suggest an initial uptick in dismissals in the Third Circuit after *Daubert, see* LLOYD DIXON & BRIAN GILL, CHANGES IN THE STANDARDS FOR ADMITTING EXPERT EVIDENCE IN FEDERAL CIVIL CASES SINCE THE *DAUBERT* DECISION xvi (2001); Edward K. Cheng & Albert H. Yoon, *Does* Frye *or* Daubert *Matter? A Study of Scientific Admissibility Standards,* 91 VA. L. REV. 471, 473 (2005); *and* Eric Helland & Jonathhan Klick, *Does Anyone Get Stopped at the Gate? An Empirical Assessment of the* Daubert *Trilogy in the States* (University of Pennsylvania Law School, Institute for Law and Economics, Research Paper 09-12 at 13 (March 2009). Fisher concludes that it has taken a while for judges to get the message that they are to start taking a more aggressive role in policing against junk science. *Cf.* JAMES LANGENFELD AND CHRISTOPER ALEXANDER, DAUBERT AND OTHER GATE-KEEPING CHALLENGES OF ANTITRUST EXPERTS, http://www.americanbar.org/content/dam/aba/administrative/litigation/materials/sac_2012/18-1_b_daubert_and_other_gatekeeping_challenges_with_appendix_antitrust.authcheckdam.pdf (where authors conclude there are more dismissals of plaintiff expert testimony in antitrust cases).

give an opinion only when her opinion is rationally related to the witness's experience, helpful to clearly understanding the witness's testimony or to determining a fact in issue, and is not based on *technical* or *specialized* knowledge.

If the opinion is based on *technical* or *specialized* knowledge, then the witness must first be qualified to give that opinion and must demonstrate a method that is reliable. Whether an opinion is based on *specialized* or *technical* knowledge is not always that clear. A prosecution witness might offer an opinion, for example, that the white powdery substance the defendant sold him was cocaine, based on the witness's experience with cocaine. Or a prosecution witness might want to give an opinion that the defendant was drunk when he got behind the wheel of a car. Is this specialized knowledge or an opinion based on personal experience that a lay witness can give?

Under the "collective facts doctrine," once she has established an adequate foundation, a lay witnesses can opine that a person was sad, angry, anxious, or drunk, or that the weather was dry and the sky was blue, based on experience common to living in a society. Where the prosecution offers a witness who will testify that a substance was cocaine, based on taste and personal consumption, the line between personal knowledge and *specialized* knowledge is blurred. (In chapter fifteen, we will give a brief discussion of a major case (*United States v. Ganier*) that tries to define the distinction between personal and specialized knowledge in the context of a computer specialists offering testimony about the search capabilities of a computer.)

In practice, the distinction between personal and specialized knowledge can have real consequences. If the witness is giving an expert opinion in both a civil and criminal case, the opposing side needs to be put on notice of that fact. In the civil setting, the expert needs to be listed pretrial as an expert witness and provide a report that shows the things the expert relied on in arriving at her opinion. In a criminal trial, similarly, the defendant needs an opportunity to challenge the witness pretrial if that witness will give an expert opinion. In both types of cases, the law allows the opposing party to depose the expert and move to strike his opinion testimony as being unreliable or irrelevant. Absent this opportunity to challenge the expert's opinion pretrial, the particular witness may not be allowed to give his opinion.

The attorneys must satisfy the court that the expert testimony is admissible while also recognizing that beyond the threshold of admission lies the realm of persuasion. In dealing with experts, one must be conversant with both areas. From here forward, except for in chapter fourteen, it will be assumed the attorney has made the decision to use an expert in the case—a decision that requires careful analysis of the case and selection of the legal theory and theme most likely to inform and persuade—and, therefore, the material in this guide will deal with admissibility and persuasion of expert opinion testimony.

CHAPTER TWO

FINDING EXPERTS

When searching for an expert, the trial attorney has many choices not only about where to find an expert, but then how to maintain client confidences and manage the experts fees in a way that protects the client's litigation budget.

Regarding finding an expert, the choices are usually three: the client may have impressive experts on his own staff, the local university may be able to provide an entirely competent expert who is very accessible (and perhaps already possesses knowledge of the local industry in question) at a very reasonable price, and prestigious universities like Harvard (or Yale, or Princeton, or Stanford, or M.I.T.) have many smart people. Your search for an expert should start with seeking advice from people you trust, and only as a last resort should you depend on the self-serving notices in expert directories and on Web sites. After you have identified a potential expert, you will have time to search the Web to insure that the expert is who she says she is as well as research her experience and qualifications to insure against surprises from the opponent.

2.1 Where to Find an Expert

Moving from the realm of charm to the practicalities of the lawsuit, the first decisions you must make are whether an expert is needed and, if so, how to find one. In addition to the distinction we discussed earlier between personal experience and technical and specialized knowledge, if expertise is required, then what type of expert you need depends on the substantive law of the case and practice in the forum. If the lawsuit involves damages in a wrongful death case in a jurisdiction that does not allow claims for loss of consortium or hedonic damages, you will not be looking for an expert in those areas. (You might use lay witnesses to give opinions about how much enjoyment a plaintiff experienced before the accident from a particular activity—like playing the piano or swimming or riding his bike). In a negligence case involving medical malpractice where the jurisdiction requires expert testimony on the question of informed consent, you obviously need an expert who will be able to give an opinion on that issue. And in a product defect case based on strict liability, expert testimony on the manufacturing of products and negligence might be allowed but would not be required. Therefore, for the purpose of further discussion, assume that the case and jurisdiction allow or require expert testimony.

But now arises your first quandary: how do I gather enough information to make an intelligent choice on a proper expert?

One possibility is to hire a graduate student to research the field, present the important questions, and identify appropriate and available experts. Graduate students are a wonderful resource because their knowledge is so fresh and their hourly rates are so reasonable. Indeed, some attorneys add a graduate student to their trial team early in the process so the graduate student's knowledge is available when all of the expert decisions are made. (From an evidentiary point of view, the graduate student on the trial team is a nontestifying expert, and her participation under most circumstances is not discoverable.)

Seven Different Ways to Find Experts

1. Client
2. Colleagues
3. Similar cases
4. Publications
5. Local schools
6. National schools
7. Internet

2.1.1 *"Inside" Expert*

Consider the advantages of first "going inside" to find an expert witness. One clear advantage of looking inside the client's organization for an expert (nontestifying or testifying) is that this expert is already on the client's payroll and therefore does not represent an incremental cost to the client. There are obviously implicit costs as the attorney makes demands on the employee's time that were not present before, but those costs will in no way compare in total to the costs of an expert from a nationally known educational institution who must first educate herself on the subject matter and who is charging as much as $1000 or more per hour.

Where Do I Find an Expert?	
Inside	**Outside**
—inexpensive	—superior
—available	—experienced
—cooperative	—dedicated
—controllable	—objective
—knowledgeable	—cooperative
—familiar	—respected

Inside experts are also more available for the simple reason that if the case is important to the client, the client can direct the inside expert to make herself available. In contrast, outside experts have independent schedules—teaching and consulting—that constrain their availability. The attorney must work within their calendars. Inside experts are generally cooperative because they come with a vested interest in the client's success.

Where to Find an Inside Expert

Research and Development Division
Production Department
Accounting
Marketing
General Counsel's Office

An additional benefit of using the inside expert is that they often know what choices were available at the time the decisions were made on the issue in litigation, such as choices in design, in accounting approach, or of medical treatment.

The danger with using an inside expert who is experienced with the particular process or product is the expert may be a fact witness; when deciding whether an inside expert should be employed, remember she will be a liability if she participated in the activities that the lawsuit is reviewing. For example, the senior accountant who created the accounting system that is now under scrutiny may have the most knowledge about it, but she is likely to be a fact witness on whom the opposition focuses. Subordinates to that accountant share in the same disability, although to a lesser extent. The same is clearly true for engineers who helped design the faulty O-ring or gas tank configuration. In addition, the inside expert's vested interest may be labeled as bias by the opposing counsel, which should cause you some concern when you consider the jurors' view of the inside expert's objectivity. Additionally, in the pretrial stage, you must always be sensitive to the dilemma in which such witnesses find themselves because they want to protect their job as well as help the client.

In other words, the spirit of cooperation brought to the work by the inside expert also represents a danger to the trial attorney because the expert may be more malleable and less critical in her analysis than you really desire.

2.1.2 "Outside" Expert

Choosing an inside expert to help prepare for trial does not mean that other experts must be excluded. Commonly, trial attorneys rely on a client's employees to provide day-to-day help as nontestifying experts, while using outside experts to provide greater objectivity and credibility when presenting their case to the judge and jurors. This perceived objectivity in the testifying expert is particularly important. The fact that an expert, who has an independent status and reputation to protect, is willing to support the attorney's version of facts and proof in the client's case gives that expert a substantial advantage in front of the jury. The expert who can say, "I could have said 'no' to this case, as I have said "no" to other cases," brings strong objectivity to her testimony at trial.

Outside experts often have additional advantages. For example (without intending to slight all those people who are expert in their fields and who have chosen to work for a single employer), it remains a fact that outside experts normally present superior academic credentials and broader experience in their field. They have had the opportunity to compare and contrast relevant activities at many different operations and that has provided them with insights that are unavailable to the inside expert. For example, one of the strongest witnesses for the plaintiffs in the *Pennzoil* case[1] was an expert witness who had served on the board of directors of a number of companies that had been taken over. This expert could testify to the intent of the parties and the reasonableness of the positions that the parties were taking. As another example, Dr. F. M. Scherer, a leading industrial organization economist, brought substantial credibility to testimony in favor of a proposed acquisition in the beer industry when he was able to say on cross-examination that he had come forward to testify voluntarily—without pay—because he was familiar with this industry from years of study and thought that the government's position challenging the acquisition was untenable. In fact, one of the advantages of outside experts is that their dedication often comes from an altruistic motive or from some desire to contribute to the public good. You must also be aware, however, that at least part of the outside expert's dedication derives from her compensation. So if the engagement becomes unprofitable, more difficult, or more time-consuming than originally anticipated, the expert may find ways to reduce her time commitment in favor of work on other more interesting (or more profitable) projects.

A final advantage of outside experts is they have gained a reputation (hopefully positive) in their field. The client may be impressed by this reputation and therefore be more willing to pay the rates that the expert requests; after all, if a Harvard professor is willing and available to support a client's position, it may be worth the extra money.

Where to Find an Outside Expert

Local universities
National universities
Similar cases
Partners in the firm
Friends in practice
Internet
Expert services

---

1. Texaco Inc. v. Pennzoil Co., 784 F.2d 1133, 1157 (2d Cir. 1986) (where Texaco's interference in the purchase by Pennzoil of Getty Oil eventually resulted in a jury verdict against Texaco of over seven billion dollars, plus punitive damages).

2.2   Where to Find an Outside Expert

When looking for an outside expert, you have many resources. A telephone call to the appropriate department at a local university will very often result in a list of people either at that school or at others nearby who are qualified to help in the lawsuit. Local university faculty can be especially effective when the party is local, when the jury pool is local, and when the opposition is not local. A judge or jury may very well entertain a predisposition to believe the local expert. All things being equal, do not ignore such an advantage. One jury consultant has stated that one of the most widely trusted people in America is the high school science teacher. In many ways, the attorney wants an expert who is going to be a good teacher, but who is not so esoteric that she will spark an anti-intellectual bias. Compared to a tenured full professor at an elite university, a high school science teacher can be much more accessible. Depending on the issue, the concepts may be quite complex, but a high school teacher may be more used to explaining things to less sophisticated students.

It may be that that teacher represents the last person in the scientific hierarchy the average juror could understand. It is not recommended that a high school science teacher be used as an expert; rather it is recommended that the expert adopt some of the demeanor of the high school science teacher.

On the other hand, there is nothing like a good Harvard professor to make the judge or jury think that the attorney has brains on his side. Association with any institution that has a national reputation makes the experts larger than life and their opinions more respected.

Academics: Local or National?	
Local Institutions	**National Institutions**
—home team appeal	—Harvard professors are smart
—availability	—Harvard professors are really smart
—community roots	—client respect
—contrast with opposition	—experience
—lower cost	—contacts

Harvard professors seem smart—really smart—but it goes beyond appearance; they really are smart. They are on boards and have experiences that are broad, international, and impressive. There is a reason they were picked by Harvard, and that reason makes them more credible to the judge or jury. The appearance of seeming smart may be enough for some jurors, but the reality of being smart is what helps you prepare your case and have confidence in the experts' opinions.

When looking for outside experts, another obvious source is your own experience in similar cases or the experience of others—other lawyers in the practice and colleagues in the bar. Call them up, have lunch with them, ask about their experience, ask for their recommendations, ask for transcripts, and use this information along with the expert's credentials to make a choice. When talking to attorneys who have worked with experts, remember that qualifications are only part of the decision criteria. You should also look for an expert with whom you can work long hours on the road under stressful circumstances on matters that you have come to take personally. Being able to maintain a good working relationship is important.

There are expert directories both in print and on the Internet. They are suspect to the same extent that an advertisement claiming to offer the "best plumber" is suspect. Consider the source of the information—it signals a person who makes her living supporting litigation. This fact can mean the expert will be more open to attack on her objectivity and credibility—or on her very expertise. For example, because these experts are spending so much time testifying, they may have lost touch with the practice of designing products, treating patients, or doing accounting. More direct work within their field would let them know where the field is going, what the latest research shows, or what it is like to be actively working in a hospital emergency room. The same considerations apply to the printed expert services, which are reminiscent of publications like *Who's Who in American High Schools*. The criteria for inclusion in such services must be more than a willingness to pay a fee; otherwise, there is no value to the apparent recommendation being provided.

Finding Experts on the Internet

www.legalcom.com
www.experts.com
www.internetcourt.com/experts/framewit.html
www.emory.edu/medweb.html
www.acs.org

2.3   Maintaining Confidentiality

When searching for an expert, inside or outside, you must be sensitive not only to the need for confidentiality, but also to the potential for conflicts. With an inside expert, conflicts are not normally a problem. Confidentiality can routinely be handled by reminding the employee/expert of the importance of the case to the client/employer and by advising her of the serious consequences to the lawsuit and the client if the content of preliminary discussions with the expert is revealed in employee lunchrooms, at professional gatherings, or in casual discussions with other experts whom she might encounter. With the outside expert, you should probably adopt a more aggressive stance. Before you make substantive disclosures to the expert, ask about the possibility of conflicts arising from past engagements or other clients of the expert. Give the expert a fee for an appropriate number of hours, so she is fairly compensated for the preliminary time, even if it does not lead to a further engagement. It is reasonable to ask her at that initial meeting to sign a confidentiality agreement.

2.4   Expert Fees

An unpleasant, but necessary fact of life is that you will have to discuss fees—usually in the first meeting—with the expert. The starting point is to ask the expert what she has charged in her last two or three engagements, both by the hour and in total for the entire project. In a sense, the framework is the same for any negotiation where information is key. If the expert has consulted out of the goodness of her heart, it would be silly to offer a lot of money when she is willing to do it for much less. At the same time, once you find out what her fees have been, you may be able to negotiate down, depending on the complexity of the matter and the issues that are at stake. One thing to keep in mind during the negotiations with the potential expert is that the expert should not enter the engagement feeling that the attorney has taken advantage of her by squeezing every last dime from her fee. She should not feel ill-used—and certainly should not feel ill-used right from the outset.

Several attorneys have adopted the practice of having their expert contract directly with the client. They believe this somehow provides more protection for the expert's preliminary of communications work product among the client, the expert, and the attorney. After all, these direct communications without counsel participation will lack attorney-client protection, as well as make work-product protections based on the fact that the communication involve the lawyer's mental impressions less defensible. Others believe it is sufficient to have the expert contract with the attorney, and in fact, this may be preferable, as it may give the attorney some additional control over the expert and her work. Case law does not support the conclusion that the expert's work will receive more protection from discovery if the expert has contracted directly with the client, and indeed, there should be no greater protection because the choice of signatory parties to the expert's engagement contract is purely a matter of form and not of substance. The attorney is, after all, the agent of the client, and a contract entered by the agent with the authority of the principal should have the same effect as the contract entered by the principal—here, the client. Of course, if the expert the attorney is engaging is already an employee of the client, then there is some greater suggestion that work done on behalf of the client—in furtherance of the investigations of what went on and what happened—ought to be protected, even though the attorney was not involved. In fact, in some jurisdictions (like California), there is a privilege—entitled "self-criticism"—that protects the ability of the client to investigate and to make reports that are self-critical.

Federal Rule of Civil Procedure 26(a)(2)(B) states with regard to the disclosure of expert testimony:

> Unless otherwise stipulated or ordered by the court, this disclosure must be accompanied by a written report—prepared and signed by the witness—if the witness is one retained or specially employed to provide expert testimony in the case or one whose duties as the party's employee regularly involve giving expert testimony.

The concept is that even the inside expert has an obligation to prepare an expert report if she will testify. While the language of Rule 26(a)(2)(B) is less than clear on this point, the concept is simple enough: the parties cannot evade the obligation to make expert disclosures, including an expert report, simply by designating a regular employee as their expert and then claiming that she was not "retained or specially employed" for that purpose.[2] While the courts have differed, the better ruling is if the employee does not regularly provide expert testimony for the party, then she is "retained or specially employed" for the purpose, and if she does regularly provide expert testimony, she is covered by the later language of the rule, which refers to employees "whose duties 'regularly involve giving expert testimony.'"

At deposition, it is appropriate to inquire about the fees being paid to the opponent's expert. Nevertheless, the disclosure of those fees at trial will probably not have as great an impact as often supposed. For example, if the proponent's expert is paid substantially more per hour than the opposing expert, jury studies indicate that the jurors may conclude that expert is worth more. Conversely, if the proponent's expert is paid substantially less, but makes a good case that she is testifying in substantial part because of her belief in the cause the attorney's party represents, the jurors may admire her public-spirited approach and take her lower fees as evidence of that objectivity. In other words, while you should ask about the expert's fees at deposition and be prepared to introduce such information at trial, do not build your cross-examination around them or pin your hopes on them.

When discussing fees with the expert witness, remember to consider not only the hourly rate, but also the total fee for the project. A Harvard professor may appear to be very expensive on an hourly basis, but because of her familiarity with the subject or greater facility with the science, she may be able to arrive at a defensible opinion in only a third of the time needed by another expert. In such a case, that Harvard expert may be a bargain. Additionally, you must keep in mind the budget that is likely to be imposed by the client; it is recommended that the client be a part of, or consulted closely during, the fee-negotiation process. The client will pay the bills and should therefore have a say in the items that make up the bills.

---

2. In fact, the exemption seems directed primarily for treating physicians who will be called to testify on behalf of the plaintiff. Treating physicians morph into testifying experts only when the opinions they will give go beyond the scope of the work usually done by a treating physician. *Goodman v. Staples, the Office Superstore, LLC,* 644 F.3d 817 (9th Cir. 2011).

As an additional matter relating to fees (although slightly out of chronological sequence), handle the expert's bills as quickly as possible when they are presented, either paying them directly or arranging for prompt payment by the client. You do not want your matter to become an unpleasant one for the expert. If the expert develops the belief that she will always be paid late, she may develop the practice of working on the matter only at times that are convenient for her, perhaps between other matters. Additionally, you will have lost any favor with her that would have allowed you to ask for expedition or special treatment.

As a practical matter, make sure the client is involved in discussions about how much an expert might cost so the client is not caught by surprise when the bill is passed their way. If the client has set parameters, then you may choose how best to spend the budgeted amount. If you have $25,000 for a project, you can hire an expert at $250 an hour for 100 hours or you can hire somebody less expensive and change the scope of the project. You could also reduce the average rate and the hours spent by the expert by using graduate students more.

Finally, the fee agreement will need be disclosed in discovery, along with the report. Federal Rule of Civil Procedure 26(a)(2)(B)(vi) provides that the report must contain "a statement of the compensation to be paid for the study and testimony in the case."[3]

---

3. Note that California has a privacy restriction on discovery of medical malpractice expert witness compensation in other unrelated cases. *See* Allen v. Superior Court, 151 Cal. App. 3d 447 (1984).

CHAPTER THREE

CARING FOR AN EXPERT

The relationship among the trial attorney, the consulting expert, and the testifying expert is extensive and intensive. The expert depends (with some trepidation) on you to keep her properly informed, fairly treated, and reasonably compensated. You must recognize that an expert who is unhappy for any reason may be less motivated to put your requests at the top of her list of things to do. Casual empiricism suggests a list of actions you must avoid so you can foster the necessary close relationship with experts.

Dave and Paul's Ten Best Lines for Driving the Expert Crazy

10. "Hold up on that project from last week."
9. "Hi, I've got a trial next month and . . . ."
8. "Harry's Rent-an-Expert is way under your proposed budget."
7. "I'm not sure what we'll need or when we'll need it."
6. "I'll just send all the paper . . . ."
5. "I know you called a few weeks ago, but I've been so busy."
4. "Oh, I'm sure that check is in the mail right now."
3. "Let's use my people on this, OK?"
2. "Is there some way you can cut a few bucks off what we budgeted?"
1. "Did I forget to tell you the fact that . . . ?"

3.1 Top Ten Things to Avoid in Dealing with Experts

3.1.1 Number Ten: "Hold Up on that Project from Last Week."

Experts, whether they are inside or outside, have obligations other than your lawsuit. There are demands on their time and on their support staff, which make it impossible for them to start, stop, and start again at your every whim.

Before you authorize an expert to start a project, you must decide with the client when you will try to have the project completed. The project will cost more, and the expert will become more frustrated and less responsive if she has to be interrupted because the possibility of settlement has increased by 3 percent, the judge has extended the pretrial period by three weeks, or the expert's deposition has been delayed by three months. If the project is in the budget and the expert has already told you that she has set aside the time to complete it, your relationship with the expert will be best served by going forward.

3.1.2 Number Nine: "Hi, I've Got a Trial Next Month and . . . ."

If six weeks is all you have between the time you recognize you need an expert and the time you envision putting a jury in the box, then you may be forced to give the expert only six weeks. But if you only have six weeks because you delayed seeking an expert in the hopes the trial would go away, the other side would cave, or the technical issues would magically resolve themselves so the monetary and other costs in dealing with an expert would not have to be faced, then you are being unfair to the client and the expert. It is unlikely, with six weeks or less advance time, that you will find the best expert for your client; it may not even be likely that you will find a good expert. As soon as you perceive the need for an expert to testify or to consult in the client's case, you should begin your search. During this search, you may schedule the various activities of the expert even if you do not plan to commit to all of them—it depends on the progress of your preparation. If you do have to hire an expert late in the process, be frank about what caused the delay and subsequent short time frame and be realistic in your demands on the expert.

3.1.3 Number Eight: "Harry's Rent-an-Expert Is Way under Your Proposed Budget."

There are many reasons to hire an expert; this is not one. If all you can say about the expert is she is the least expensive, then you should review your standards and expert list and find one who has some other redeeming feature. It is a rule of reality that the cheapest expert normally will be worth what you pay; in other words, there is a reason why she is the least expensive. It may be she has cut her staff to the bone (so you can expect a longer lag time between requests and production); it may be she tries to juggle too many engagements to increase her revenue by volume (so you become a case number and not a name), or it may just be the only way she can get clients is by charging bargain basement prices (not a sign of quality, either in women's handbags or trial experts). However, it may just be she is charging under the market to gain experience and build an expert practice, but you should investigate her credentials and capabilities thoroughly in such a case to find other reasons to make her his expert.

3.1.4 Number Seven: "I'm Not Sure What We'll Need or When We'll Need It."

As has been mentioned before, today's experts have many obligations beyond your lawsuit—obligations to other cases, obligations to other clients, and obligations to other aspects of their careers. They cannot ordinarily subordinate their entire schedules to the case, which is what you are asking when you refuse to provide them with any reasonable guidelines on your needs for their participation. If you do not tell them with some reasonable certainty what you will be expecting of them, you can expect that they will not be able to deliver what you need. In addition, everyone is helped by deadlines—dates when work is due serve to motivate the expert to accomplish tasks that can be tedious and uninteresting. In other words, treat the expert as you would have your client treat him. As soon as possible, outline the next six months for the expert; tell her what is likely to happen and when. You do not need to guarantee it, but you should do the best that you can. When you first engage the expert, tell her that you will in good faith keep her informed about the progress of the matter, including changes in deadlines, changes in schedules, and changes in obligations. Assure the expert that you will not only tell her about changes to the discovery schedule or issues in the case because of motions practice or other discovery, but you will also discuss with her the impact such events will likely to have on her obligations. The expert's reputation, like yours, is at risk when the expert testifies, and the expert's ability to prepare should not be diminished because you did not properly communicate changes to the schedule or otherwise.

3.1.5 Number Six: "I'll Just Send (.pdf) All the Paper . . . ."

While the expert lives in fear of being kept ignorant of important facts, she also lives in fear that she will be overwhelmed by a mountain of unorganized paper and digital data that she will be expected to comb through for relevant material. The expert's time is not well spent in creating an index to materials that should have been indexed by temporary clerks or paralegals. The expert must have access to all information that is even potentially relevant to her analysis, but she will be unable to complete her analysis in any sufficient way if she is overwhelmed with useless paper and digital files. Have your staff index the materials and then provide the index to the expert. Or have your staff organize the materials physically in one or several file rooms and then arrange for the expert to inspect, review, and sample those files. From the index or from the review of files, the expert can select the materials she would first like to review, and then she can make notes on materials that she will review later if she needs more information.

3.1.6 Number Five: "I Know You Called a Few Weeks Ago, but I've Been so Busy."

Just as you would expect your client or other witnesses to return your calls so you can have the information you need to go forward with your trial preparation, the expert looks to you as her primary line of communication, the person who can provide her with the information she needs to do her job. If you do not return your expert's telephone calls in a timely manner, she feels cut off and unsupported.

Worse, she feels you do not value her time and advice, and she may be less willing to devote her energies to the case. Additionally, the expert's calls may be an attempt to advise the you of changes in her schedule or important developments in her analysis. It is important to return the expert's phone calls so she knows what her next steps will be. Finally, if for some reason you will be out of touch for some time (an out-of-town trial that may last several weeks, for example), make certain the expert knows in advance and has alternative channels of communication available.

3.1.7 Number Four: "Oh, I'm Sure that Check Is in the Mail Right Now."

The expert has bills to pay, staff to compensate, and other obligations that require a cash flow, of which you are a part. While it may make your bills to the client look more reasonable in the short term, deferring the expert's bills will eventually catch up with you because you will be forced to submit three or four at one time. For no long-term gain, you run the risk of creating a long-term problem—antagonizing the expert to the point where your case is the last one she wants to work on. When it comes to paying the account receivable, treat the expert as you would have your client treat you. Pay the bills promptly, pay them cheerfully, review them fairly, and do not let them become a point of contention that might adversely affect the expert's support of the client's case. Use these same arguments to persuade your client to handle the expert's bills promptly. Make sure the client understands the importance of keeping the expert functioning as a happy and productive team member. The expert will work more efficiently and more enthusiastically if she is treated professionally; that includes not only having her bills paid on time, but accompany that payment with only reasonable questions about their content and amount. Remind the client that if the expert becomes disenchanted with this particular engagement, she may work less efficiently, assign less experienced staff, or put the case at the bottom of her pile of projects. None of these options advances the client's cause.

3.1.8 Number Three: "Let's Use My People on This, OK?"

The expert will be more comfortable using and relying on her own staff. She knows their credentials, and she knows their capabilities. They know her needs, and they know the form in which she would prefer to receive their inputs. Your people do not. Even though having your people bill their support of the expert on this project may add to your gross monthly revenue, it is probably less efficient and will ultimately result in higher bills for the client. Furthermore, the expert may feel as though she has lost control of the project, and she may be reluctant to rely on the work product of the attorney's people. Finally, if the expert is ever questioned about the reliability and the basis for her testimony and she must disclose the subordinates who gathered the materials or performed some of the underlying tasks, she has more credibility if she relied on people from her office rather than on your clerks.

3.1.9 Number Two: "Is There Some Way You Can Cut a Few Bucks Off What We Budgeted?"

The attorney has already put the expert to the task of preparing and defending a detailed budget of the projects she reasonably anticipates for the engagement. The amounts inserted in the budget have been debated and submitted to the client, who finally approved the charges. At that point, the expert could reasonably believe that the particular projects would result in defined revenues that would cover her costs and give her a reasonable profit. If you attempt to renegotiate the budget to impress your client with your sharp pencil, you will certainly not achieve any substantial savings, and you may provoke substantial inefficiencies. Instead of devoting what remains of her budgeted time to a project that had its expenses trimmed, the expert is likely to reduce that time, her staff, or her efforts on that project. She is not in this engagement to lose money or to break even. Once you have agreed on a project budget, look on it as a set of mutual promises and try to keep your part of that bargain.

3.1.10 Number One: "Did I Forget to Tell You the Fact that . . . ?"

As previously mentioned, the greatest fear of experts is that they will remain ignorant of a material fact either through the attorney's neglect or through the attorney's intentional omission. At trial, where the court believes that the ignored fact is dispositive, the expert's testimony can be excluded. For example, in a case involving responsibility for construction delay, the expert testified that it was the fault of the subcontractor who was supposed to provide sand to the concrete contractor. The expert testified that problems at the sand quarry prevented the sand subcontractor from meeting his obligations. On cross-examination, the expert was shown a photograph clearly depicting a pile of sand at the sand quarry that absolutely demonstrated that sand was available and the expert was wrong. The court found this factual ignorance so offensive that it struck the expert's direct examination and refused to allow the party to present a substitute expert. There is no fact—no matter how damaging—that should be left undisclosed to the expert.

CHAPTER FOUR

TIMELINES FOR WORKING WITH EXPERTS

Trial attorneys often postpone selecting a testifying expert until the complaint and answer have been filed and discovery is underway, perhaps thinking they are saving money by limiting the expert's contact with the case. From either the plaintiff or defense side, this strategy is risky because the subsequently hired expert is limited by the pleadings, which she did not help compose. By participating in the case early—especially analyzing the issues—the expert can help shape the case, limit discovery, and achieve efficiencies—benefits that exceed the additional cost, if any, of having the expert on the team early.

4.1   The Plaintiff's Expert Timeline

As the plaintiff, the timing of the decisions relating to experts is driven by the need to state an adequate case in the complaint and to craft discovery in a useful way. Because the plaintiff's attorney controls the content of the complaint and the time he files it, he can normally postpone the filing until he is satisfied that he has adequate expert support. For Rule 11 purposes, the technical support for the complaint may be provided by inside experts because it is reasonable for counsel to rely on statements of his client to satisfy those early due diligence obligations. All of this suggests that after the attorney and the client have made the preliminary decision to sue in a manner that appears to require expert testimony, the attorney should then contact the potential inside expert (or an outside expert if inside experts are not available) and discuss the case in whatever detail possible at that stage of his understanding.

The purposes here are twofold—first, to insure that you, as plaintiff's attorney, are not crafting a case that a reasonable expert cannot support; and second, to satisfy yourself that you have a case to prosecute. If, at this early stage, the expert voices concern about the scientific, technical, or other "specialized" underpinnings of the case—concern that makes her feel unable to testify in support—both Rule 11 and common sense dictate that you should conduct further investigation and legal research. In a complex commercial matter, this pre-complaint due diligence stage probably extends two months or so from the first client contact; in an especially complicated matter such as a patent antitrust case, it might extend six months. On the other hand, in an emergency where you may have to seek a temporary restraining order, the due diligence standards are somewhat lower and the need for speed is greater. In such situations, the expert due diligence period may be as short as a few days. On average, you should probably plan to invest a month to satisfy yourself that the case will have adequate expert support before filing a complaint.

4.2   The Defendant's Expert Timeline

From the perspective of defense counsel, if you have anticipated that a lawsuit will be filed against your client, you should have begun the search for an expert witness already. You know the facts, you know the law, you can anticipate the shape of the complaint that is likely to be filed (probably as well or better than the plaintiff can), and you have the information to identify at least a nontestifying expert to provide support. If there will be a need for extensive testing or for access to the product in question—the one alleged to have failed, for example—then the expert should identify what she will need to start conducting the tests in an expeditious manner. Additionally, that expert must help you identify important evidence that must be preserved, either in your client's possession or, more importantly, in the possession of the plaintiff-to-be. Rule 16 conferences define one time marker: the federal judge in charge of the case may require counsel to report on the number of experts they are going to call and the time it is going to take to do discovery in the case. Other courts impose a schedule on experts by setting the trial date—once that date is set, the Federal Rules of Civil Procedure impose a series of deadlines by which expert reports, reply reports, and supplementary reports must be received.

4.3   Report Requirements for All Experts

Unless otherwise agreed to or directed by the court, Rule 26(a)(2)(B) requires both parties to provide a written report signed by the experts. The report should be submitted at least ninety days before the case is set for trial, or thirty days if it is a rebuttal report. The expert's report should contain the following:

(i)   a complete statement of all opinions the witness will express and the basis and reasons for them;

(ii)   the facts or data considered by the witness in forming them;

(iii) any exhibits that will be used to summarize or support them;

(iv)   the witness's qualifications, including a list of all publications authored in the previous 10 years;

(v)   a list of all other cases in which, during the previous 4 years, the witness testified as an expert at trial or by deposition;[1] and

---

1. The "identification of 'cases' at a minimum should include the courts or administrative agencies, the names of the parties, the case number, and whether the testimony was by deposition or at trial." Nguyen v. IBP, Inc., 162 F.R.D. 675, 682 (D. Kan. 1995).

(vi) A listing of any other cases in which the witness has testified as an expert at trial or by deposition within the preceding four years.[2]

Reports from experts are due from every witness who "is retained or specially employed to provide expert testimony in the case . . . ." Since *Daubert* and *Kumho*,[3] these reports must be drafted to meet relevance and reliability requirements of Federal Rule of Evidence 702. In other words, these reports should contain (among other relevant indicia of reliability):

- tests done to verify the opinions given in the report;

- information on the general acceptance in the relevant scientific community of any methodology used;

- any peer review of the methodology employed;

- information on a known or knowable error rate from the methodology employed;

- whether the methodology was originally developed for the purpose of litigation; or

- any other indicia of reliability on which the proponent of the expert intends to rely.

4.4   Rebuttal Disclosure

Rule 26(a)(2)(C) allows thirty days after the receipt of an expert report for the submission of a report intended "solely to contradict or rebut" the earlier report. Remember, Rule 26(a)(2) relates only to expert evidence. Rule 26(a)(3) relates to all evidence and additionally mandates the disclosure of witnesses, documents, and depositions intended to be used at trial except those intended solely for impeachment. Counsel might be tempted to argue that contradiction and rebuttal evidence under Rule 26(a)(2)(C) is actually impeachment evidence under Rule 26(a)(3), and such expert evidence does not need to be disclosed. This argument ignores the introductory language to Rule 26(a)(3), which states, "In addition to the disclosures required by Rule 26(a)(1) and (2) . . . ." Any other interpretation would threaten to excuse the production of any responsive expert evidence because it could be argued that by accepting the responsive evidence, the opposing expert would be impeached. Such interpretations go too far.

Pursuant to Rule 803(18), the interrelationship between the two provisions should also be examined in the context of using learned treatises during the cross-examination of the opposing expert. On preliminary analysis, it would seem an expert's testimony that a writing is a learned treatise should not have to be disclosed under

---

2. Fed. R. Civ. P. 26(a)(2)(B).
3. *See* discussion *infra*, chapter fourteen.

Rule 26(a)(2)(C), because that testimony is laying the foundation for impeachment of the opposing expert under Rule 803(18). Therefore, as impeaching evidence, it would seem to be excused from production pursuant to Rule 26(a)(3). However, as reliable commentators point out, "[i]t is important to remember that statements in learned treatises come in for their truth . . . they are not limited to impeaching credibility, but can be used for the truth of the matters stated."[4] Even if Rule 26(a)(3) is tortuously read as limiting the disclosures required under Rule 26(a)(2)(C) rather than expanding them as its introductory language indicates, the statements in learned treatises are not "solely impeaching," and therefore seem to be clearly within the mandatory disclosure requirements of Rule 26(a)(2)(C). It remains to be seen whether trial courts will require such advance disclosure when they are faced with technical obligations that seem to be at odds with normal expert practice in which such "learned treatise cross-examination" is typically considered a form of impeachment. If the proponent of the 803(18) statements disclaims any substantive purpose, claiming only impeachment, would that constitute failure to provide notice under Rule 26(a)(2)(C)? It is perhaps unlikely the proponent would be so foolish, but the logic of the rule would seem to dictate failure to disclose should prohibit later use of the learned treatise in this way. Finally, a federal court may interpret the rules of civil procedure like it does the rules of evidence—to insure that justice is done. Whether justice is done may vary on the particular circumstances of what the expert has opined and on how devastating the learned treatise is in its rebuttal of the point.

Another example of superficial conflict between these two rules occurs when an expert not intended to testify at trial submits an affidavit or provides testimony in a *Daubert* hearing that challenges the methodology employed by the opposing expert. Because the challenging, nontestifying expert has not filed a report, she has not made the disclosures required by Rule 26(a)(2)(C); nor has she made any disclosures required by Rule 26(a)(3) (but such disclosures might be excused because the testimony is "solely for impeachment"). The problem seems to evaporate, however, when you recall that Rule 26(a)(2)(C) applies only to experts whose testimony is intended to be used at trial, and Rule 26(a)(3) applies only to evidence the party expects to present at trial. Since the Rule 104 hearing is not a "trial," these obligations, conflicting or otherwise, may not apply. As a practical matter, these arguments about the requirements of affirmative discovery concerning experts, their opinions, and their foundations are based on a closer and more precise reading of the rule than most judges are enforcing. Judges are uncomfortable sanctioning parties for failure to make extensive voluntary disclosures when all of the tools of normal discovery were available and used. One of those tools is the ability of counsel to depose the expert, which protects them by way of face-to-face interrogation of the expert. In case after case, courts reject requests for sanctions for failure to make

---

4. Stephen A. Saltzburg, Michael M. Martin, & Daniel J. Capra, Federal Rules of Evidence Manual (7th ed. 1998).

National Institute for Trial Advocacy

proper voluntary disclosures because they conclude the failure was harmless in light of the extensive depositions that occurred.

There is tremendous advantage to be gained by having the expert (nontestifying or testifying) available to advise you as you prepare your discovery and respond to the opposing attorney's discovery. To keep matters as clean as possible, it is better to talk through the discovery plans—what documents you intend to ask for, what interrogatories you intend to propound, what depositions you think you will be taking—with the testifying expert, rather than advise her of those plans in writing. Especially in states not adopting the federal Rule 26 protections, once again, unless there is some supervening need, written communication with the testifying expert merely creates additional material that you may then wish you could protect from discovery. With respect to the consulting expert (a term used to mean the nontestifying expert—an expert you have firmly decided will never take the stand), that expert should be included fully in all discovery decisions that potentially impact the expert case. Indeed, the consulting expert can provide first drafts of document requests and interrogatories that seek information that might eventually be presented to the testifying expert. Because better practice requires they precede all other discovery, document requests should occur early, and thus you will require the consulting expert's participation even earlier. (Again, do not forget the consulting expert at this stage may be a graduate student—or at least someone who has not yet attained the highest ranks in the expert field. You are not selling their personal credibility; you are not expecting them to persuade the opposition, the judge, or jury; you are merely taking advantage of their superior knowledge to help keep yourself informed and your case on track at these early stages.)

In the typical case, you will begin to receive documents in response to your request for production within two months of the complaint being filed, and the consulting expert—this time with the help of graduate students, if necessary—can organize and index the documents and perform a preliminary evaluation of their utility. Ultimately, the testifying expert must determine what material she will review. Nevertheless, the index, which allows the testifying expert to select information for review, can in the first instance be created by the consulting expert, by graduate students, or by paralegals under the direction of the consulting expert (be sure, however, to advise them to make the index exhaustive). That same team can logically draft follow-on document requests and supplemental interrogatories based on their review of the initial responses. This way you have expert advice in this process without burdening the testifying expert with this ministerial task. Use conference calls with the testifying expert to get her input on further discovery. However, carefully control such calls so they do not transmit substantive information—information "considered" by her and therefore discoverable—unless you intend to do so. In those conversations, let the testifying expert tell you what she needs; especially in states not following the federal Rule 26 restrictions on communications between lawyer and expert, you do not want to tell her what you and the consulting expert think unless you do not care if those conversations are discovered in detail.

Under the current Federal Rules of Civil Procedure, experts may not be deposed until their written reports have been received. This amendment had little effect on actual practice, however, because it was normal for experts to be deposed toward the very end of the discovery period. Indeed in some courts, such as the "rocket docket" of the Eastern District of Virginia, the standing orders require experts to be deposed as the last discovery act.

At first blush, it seems some advantage can be gained by filing the expert report early in the pretrial period because that filing will trigger an obligation on the part of the opposing attorney to prepare and to file a rebuttal report within thirty days or be forever precluded. There are several problems with this tactic of early filing, however. First, the expert may not be ready to reduce her opinions and their bases to a formal report without the benefit of the information to be learned during the discovery period, especially when the opposing attorney could wait until ninety days before trial before having to supply his affirmative expert report. Indeed, one can only salivate when considering the opportunity to cross-examine an expert at trial who reached her final opinion before viewing any of the discovery. Second, the requirement to file a rebuttal report within thirty days relates only to a report that "is intended solely to contradict or rebut" the other party's report—it is a simple matter to create a report that does more than "solely rebut." Therefore, the tactical advantage sought to be gained by filing an expert's report early may be evanescent, and the disadvantage of formalizing the expert's report too early may be substantial.

In the complex case with a two-year pretrial period, it is normal and logical for the experts to file their reports after all other discovery has been completed and then to be deposed as the final act in the discovery process. Whenever the affirmative reports and rebuttal reports are filed, a party is obliged to amend or supplement any Rule 26(a) disclosures, which include the disclosures under Rule 26(a)(2)(A) of the expert's identity, Rule 26(a)(2)(B) of the expert's report, and Rule 26(e)(2) of the expert's rebuttal report, as well as any information provided by the expert in deposition that subsequently is found to be materially incorrect, misleading, or incomplete. By operation of Rule 26(e)(1), such supplementation or correction must be done in a timely manner before trial or at some other time as the court allows or the parties have agreed. Failure to supplement may result in imposition of sanctions, which commonly takes the form of precluding the supplemental additional fact or opinion at trial.[5]

In the complex case where a two-year pretrial period would not be unusual, these expert activities can nevertheless fill the time as the attorney works with the consulting expert to structure his affirmative discovery, to respond to his opponent's discovery, and to analyze the documents received and the documents on hand to

---

5. *See, e.g.,* Cummins v. Lyle Indus., 93 F.3d 362 (7th Cir. 1996).

find support. Nevertheless, in a rocket docket jurisdiction the same complex case may be squeezed into a four- or six-month pretrial period in which a ninety-day interval between expert reports and trial is impossible. Under such expedited procedures, document discovery will be accelerated, interrogatory discovery will be limited, depositions will be fewer in number and shorter in duration, and expert reports will likely be due within two or three months of the complaint or perhaps within thirty days of trial. Rebuttal will be foreshortened, and all of the time periods relating to discovery and preparation—including expert discovery and preparation—will be accelerated. Nevertheless, the sequence of events remains relatively fixed.

Below is a timeline that shows the Federal Rules of Civil Procedure requirements for expert reports and rebuttal reports, moving forward from the when the parties set the discovery schedule and then moving back from the trial date to when reports and rebuttal are due.

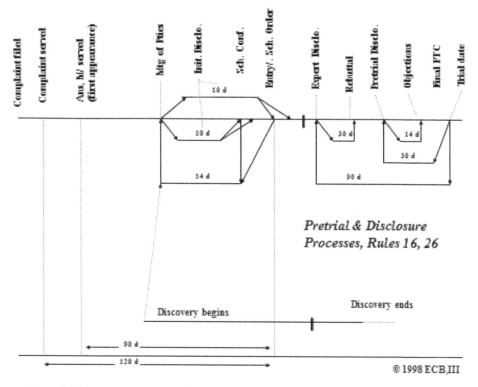

Pretrial & Disclosure
Processes, Rules 16, 26

© 1998 ECB,III

As a final note on timing, there are many state jurisdictions and state judges who do not require expert reports and the sequence of disclosure and discovery relating to them. Those judges or jurisdictions have chosen not to adopt the federal approach, and, for good or ill, if you are prosecuting or defending a case in such a jurisdiction, the factor driving the discovery schedule will likely be the dates on which the expert and the opposing expert can be available for deposition. You will have to schedule the other discovery so that the expert gets the information she needs before she is first questioned under oath. That information may come from documents, interrogatories, or deposition of fact witnesses. (Some state courts, such as New York, refuse discovery by deposition of expert opinions unless local court rules say otherwise. In situations where no report is required, expert cases can truly be "trial by ambush.")

In circumstances where the plaintiff may have a choice of forum, consider whether one of the courts follows the old rules while the other applies the new rules on disclosure, and then decide whether there is some strategic or tactical reason to avoid the expert report process. As you look at what the rules are in the available forums, be sure to check for the court's position on opting out, the court's rules on discovery embedded in the local district rules, and, finally, any standing orders issued by particular judges that may affect discovery. Of course, where you have not yet filed your complaint, you cannot accurately predict whether you will be in front of the judge whose standing order may apply, and you may have to live with that uncertainty. For example, some federal district court judges in Chicago use Rule 16 conferences to set the discovery rules, engage in preliminary evaluations of the facts and the law, and encourage the parties to settle the cases early; other federal judges, knowing most filed cases will settle from their own weight sometime before trial, prefer not to get involved at all until as late in the process as possible, preferably after all discovery has been completed, including expert discovery with no disputes that require court intervention. Therefore, it is impossible to state with certainty the precise schedule any lawsuit will follow through pretrial. The schedule is affected by the rules, by the judge, by the complexity of the case, by the sophistication and reasonableness of the counsel and parties, by the availability of the information, and by the determination of the parties who either want to pursue the lawsuit in court or to resolve it through compromise and settlement.

Further discussion of expert reports, their creation, and use is contained in the next chapter, "Nondeposition Discovery against Experts."

National Institute for Trial Advocacy

Chapter Five

Nondeposition Discovery against Experts

Because experts play such an important role in the resolution of disputes, the courts must exercise extra care when performing their role as gatekeepers. The discovery of the expert's opinions, bases, and credentials provides the advocate and the court with an opportunity to examine the expert's biases and prejudices as well the reliability of her methods. Changes to the Federal Rules of Procedure in 2000, largely echoed by the states, expanded the scope of discovery until it included almost everything a testifying expert had considered in any way. Discovery was also expanded by the teachings of the *Daubert, Joiner,* and *Kumho Tire* cases, which teach counsel in deposition to question on indicia of reliability (as discussed in chapters thirteen through fifteen, *infra*). The unintended consequence was that the pretrial costs of discovery of experts greatly increased. As a result, as we will see, in 2010 the Federal Rules of Civil Procedure were amended to limit opponent discovery of drafts of expert reports to see if this might help cut down on wasteful discovery of what each side "fed" to their own witnesses.

As a result, this chapter will take a look at both the reasons for the broad scope of discovery behind the 1993 amendments and the new changes. You need to be aware that if the state in which your case is being heard has patterned their civil procedure rules on the federal expansive approach, but not incorporated the 2010 amendments to the Federal Rules of Civil Procedure into its procedural rules, the discovery of expert attorney communications, including drafts, remains very broad. Additionally, under the new federal rules, we will see that while discovery of communications between attorney and expert and drafts are generally out of bounds, there are some important exceptions.

Of course, the expert's mandatory report is the most prominent communication from the expert, and even with the new rules restricting disclosure of drafts, the attorney's participation in the creation of that report and in the preparation of the expert for testimony raises questions of both ethics and expert independence. If the expert's testimony is to be most effective, you must keep in mind not only the specific discovery rules, but also the professional responsibility rules in all of your communications to and from the testifying expert. In addition, you must understand the differences between testifying and nontestifying experts to insure how to best learn the nontestifying expert's potential case theories without exposing client confidences to the other side. Because of the exceptions to limitations on disclosure of communication between lawyer and expert, the distinction between testifying and nontestifying experts remains important under the new rules.

5.1   What Should You Tell the Expert?

What should you tell the expert about the case as she prepares her opinion? From the beginning, it is important to recognize that the rules allow for the discovery of data that will be considered in the expert's report under Rule 26(a)(2)(B). (It is essential to understand the word "considered" was used intentionally by the drafters of the rule amendment in response to years of problems with courts debating whether certain materials that were reviewed, but not relied on by experts should have been discoverable. The term "considered," at least in theory, lays that debate to rest. As one court has said, the word "considered" means "touched,"[1] so the material will be discoverable even if the expert says, "I never read it; I never thought about it; I never relied on it; all I did was touch it.")

Prior to 2010, and in state jurisdictions not adopting the new Rule 26, this breadth meant that discovery of the conversations between the attorney and the expert during her hiring was appropriate for the opposing party. If the attorney in his zeal to win the expert over provided selective information to the expert or couched the information in such strong and slanted terms so as to bias the expert, then the discovery of this would give the opposing attorney the means to dismantle the expert. As an example (albeit a rather crude one), imagine the delight of the opposing attorney as he contemplates cross-examination when he discovers an engagement letter that states the expert was hired to provide an opinion that the defendant's steering gear was manufactured in a safe, non-negligent, state-of-the-art manner and was therefore unlikely to lead to the accident in question. He would also be delighted if the engagement letter stated that the expert would look only at a particular set of data. In either event, the expert's freedom to exercise her expertise—her collection of knowledge, experience, training, and judgment—had been constrained by the attorney, and such a constraint puts her credibility squarely at issue. While these examples are obvious in their inappropriateness, they serve to illustrate a serious concern: Attorneys should avoid tainting the expert witness by forcing particular opinions or conclusions on her or by limiting the materials she can consider. Instead, a lawyer should say, for example, "What do you need to see to reach an opinion in a case like the one I just described?" The expert normally will say, "Well, I'm not sure. Let me start with the complaint and answer, and I'll get back to you." If she does not get back to the lawyer, he must get back to her and make sure she has what an expert in her field needs.

---

1. Trigon Ins. Co. v. United States, 204 F.R.D. 277 (E.D. Va. 2001).

What Should You Keep in Mind before Talking to the Expert?

— Remember Rule 26(a)(2)(B): "The report must contain . . . the facts or data considered . . . ."
— Protect the testifying expert from taint
— Protect confidential information
— Treat the nontestifying expert like a testifying expert (until the lawyer is sure that the consulting expert will not be used as a future testifying expert)
— Use protective orders to minimize risk
— Guard communications to and from the expert

5.2 Dealing with the Consulting Expert

Once you have decided that a particular expert will remain a consulting expert and never be converted into a testifying expert, you may safely treat that nontestifying expert as a member of the trial team and include him in trial team discussions, brainstorming sessions, and analyses of evidence. (Under Rule 26(b)(4)(D), there is the possibility that the party seeking discovery could subject a nontestifying, consulting expert to documentary discovery or deposition by "showing exceptional circumstances under which it is impracticable for the party to obtain facts or opinions on the same subject by other means.") Review of cases where a consulting expert has been subjected to such discovery suggests those "exceptional circumstances" occur where the consulting expert was a percipient or fact witness in the matter in litigation. For example, a geologic expert might actually go to the site of the landslide while it was still occurring, and through her eyes gather information on which she may rely as a nontestifying expert. It is her role as eyewitness, or fact witness, that subjects her to discovery; there is nothing about her role as consulting expert that makes it impracticable for the other party to prepare for trial without access to her.

5.3 Consulting v. Nonconsulting

By treating the consulting expert exactly like the testifying expert (until a firm decision is made that the consulting expert will never be converted to a testifying expert), you preserve the option of using the consulting expert as a testifying expert at trial. If you believe that protecting the materials the expert has considered is not sufficiently important for you to limit your communications with the experts, you might choose to ignore this distinction completely (except you still must monitor contacts between the consulting expert and the testifying expert).

The temptations are very real here. For example, consider the situation where you consult with a damages expert after talking with a consulting expert, who is a client employee. To save money, the consulting, nontestifying expert could do significant work with a large amount of data and generate a report that would be extraordinarily useful to the testifying expert. However, it is highly doubtful that data could be shared with the testifying expert without opening up the possibility of discovery of the materials the nontestifying expert considered. This is true even though Rule 26(b)(4)(C) limits disclosure of communications between lawyer and expert. That is because Rules 26(b)(4)(C)(ii) and (iii) make express exceptions for disclosure of facts or data provided by the attorney to the testifying expert and or for assumptions provided to the testifying expert by the attorney.[2] Nontestifying experts may be providing such communications to the testifying expert, and especially where provided in writing, their discovery is likely to be ordered under these exceptions.

Indeed, the nontestifying expert herself may be subjected to deposition because she has, in effect, become a basis for the testifying expert's opinions.[3] As part of their analysis on this question, the courts ask whether the opposing party needs such discovery through document production or deposition to conduct a full and fair cross-examination of the testifying expert.[4] In summary, discovery against a nontestifying, consulting expert may be had where that expert is a unique source of information (e.g., an eyewitness to relevant events) or has contributed information to the testifying expert, which in fairness must be made available for inquiry by the opposing party.[5]

If these circumstances are not present, you may proceed with some confidence to treat the consulting expert as immune from discovery and to include her in the activities of the trial team. As a practical matter, these questions may be moot if each side recognizes it has nontestifying experts who have served as consultants and who may have been made privy to confidential information. Because the opposing attorney does not want to be forced to reveal his consultant or the consultant's findings, he may avoid seeking the identity and findings about your consulting expert. Nevertheless, the safer course is to treat a nontestifying expert just like the testifying expert until you have made a firm decision that the nontestifying expert shall never see the shadowy light of the courtroom.

---

2. The general rule has usually been that providing otherwise privileged materials to a testifying expert, who then considers them in forming an opinion, will generally waive the privilege. Yeda Research & Dev. Co., Ltd. v. Abbott GmbH & Co. KG, No. CIV.A. 10-1836 RMC, 2013 WL 2995924 (D.D.C. June 7, 2013). But what if an expert is a testifying expert as to certain issues and a consulting expert as to others? According to a 2013 District of Columbia district court opinion, "every court to address this 'multiple hats' problem has concluded that an expert's proponent still may assert a privilege over such materials, but only over those materials generated or considered uniquely in the expert's role as consultant." *Id.* at *7 (internal citations omitted) (collecting cases). And the scope of privilege must be "narrowly construed against the expert's proponent . . . ." *Id.* (internal citation omitted). As a result, any ambiguity is construed in favor of production. *Id.* (internal citations omitted).
3. Trigon Ins. Co. v. U.S., 204 F.R.D. 277 (E.D. Va. 2001).
4. Franks v. National Dairy Corp., 41 F.R.D. 234 (W.D. Tex. 1966).
5. FED. R. CIV. P. 26(b)(4)(B) provides the basis for getting discovery of attorney work product for "fairness" reasons. United States v. 23.76 Acres of Land, 32 F.R.D. 593 (D. Md. 1963). *See* Terre Haute Warehousing Serv., Inc. v. Grinnell Fire Prot. Sys., Inc., 193 F.R.D. 561 (S.D. Ind. 1999).

National Institute for Trial Advocacy

5.4   Protective Orders

There are times when you cannot know how the information held by either the consulting expert or the testifying expert will be treated. If the consulting geologic expert did watch a landslide as it scraped houses into the valley, you might want to know if that fact would persuade the court to order the consulting expert to sit for a deposition. If the testifying expert was currently working on an engagement for a different client in which the analysis was similar to your case and she had obtained confidential information from that client, you will want to know if the court is likely to order disclosure of that confidential information from the other engagement. Indeed, in either of these circumstances, the answer to the question of disclosure might affect your decision to hire those experts.

Pursuant to Rules 26(b)(4)(B) and (C) and Rule 26(c), a motion in limine for a protective order provides the vehicle by which you can obtain a ruling from the court on either of these questions. The "related engagement" question is a bit convoluted; after all, the confidences sought to be protected by the order are not the client's confidences, but rather the confidences of a nonparty, someone not before the court. In such an instance, you can appropriately advise the nonparty that the question of discoverability of her confidences is going to be presented, and she may, through her own counsel, make whatever showing to protect that information. If the expert's analysis of the information for the nonparty is similar to the one that the expert is using in your case, the court will likely require some limited disclosure—perhaps under a strict confidentiality agreement—rather than completely precluding disclosure.[6] A cross-examiner may make his best points by demonstrating the expert has altered the analysis from case to case, apparently to achieve a different result. Such is the stuff of great cross-examinations, and discovery should not be completely precluded.

There may be times when an attempt to protect an expert against discovery offends some larger policies embedded in the law. For example, there are cases where courts have rejected settlement agreements that incorporate provisions making the expert opinions nondiscoverable in related litigation because those provisions offend public policy.

5.5   Beauty Contests

On a related topic, a potential for conflict of interest can arise when an expert on a case related to yours participates in a "beauty contest"—that is, she interviews to be hired for your case. How can you form a relationship in that interview process that will insure confidentiality? The first and most obvious step involves actually putting a contract or a nondisclosure statement into writing at the first meeting. The contract would clearly define the relationship, including the confidentiality

---

6. *See* comments to FED. R. CIV. P. 26(b)(4)(C).

obligations, and would put the onus of attacking the confidentially of the relation-ship on the party seeking discovery. Of course, you should keep track of retained experts who defected or had a falling out with either the client or the attorney. Such an expert may seek to auction her services to the opposing party. If opposing coun-sel approaches the defector, the initial retaining party should immediately move to disqualify both the expert and the opposing counsel.[7]

5.6 Communications with the Expert

Regardless if the case has testifying or nontestifying experts, you can increase the protection of confidential information by providing the expert with very little writ-ten material that you have authored. What, however, should be the lawyer's response to an expert who asks what she should do with her notes and drafts?

5.6.1 Under the Federal Rules—Keeping Drafts and Communications with Counsel

5.6.1.1 The Applicable Rules before 2010

Federal Rule of Civil Procedure 26(b)(3) states that to obtain protected trial-preparation materials, the party seeking the discovery must show "substantial need" and "undue hardship" in obtaining the information from another source. When ordering discovery of such materials when the required showing has been made, the court "must protect against disclosure of the mental impressions, conclusions, opin-ions, or legal theories of an attorney or other representative of a party concerning the litigation."[8] The work-product doctrine as codified in Rule 26(b)(3) is limited by subsection (b)(4), which provides for discovery of information obtained by or through testifying experts. The Advisory Committee Notes state that the expert dis-closure provisions "reject as ill-considered the decisions which have sought to bring expert information within the work-product doctrine."[9]

In 1993, amendments to Rule 26 extended the scope of expert discovery to include a written expert report and disclosure of all information that was considered by the expert in forming his or her opinions. Rule 26(a)(2)(B) provides in relevant part:

The [expert] report must contain:

(i)   a complete statement of all opinions the witness will express and the basis and reasons for them;

---

7. *See* American Prot. Ins. Co. v. MGM Grand Hotel-Las Vegas, Inc., 1983 U.S. Dist. LEXIS 11007, 1983 WL 25286 (D. Nev. 1983).
8. FED. R. CIV. P. 26(b)(3)(B).
9. FED. R. CIV. P. 26(b)(4)(A), Advisory Committee Notes to 1970 Amendments.

(ii) the facts or data considered by the witness in forming them;

(iii) any exhibits that will be used summarize or support them;

* * *10

Rule 26(a)(2)(B) requires that the expert "consider" the information. The Advisory Committee Notes explain that given the disclosure obligation, "litigants should no longer be able to argue that materials furnished to their experts to be used in forming their opinions—whether or not ultimately relied upon by the expert—are privileged or otherwise protected from disclosure."[11]

Before 2010 and in those state jurisdictions that have not adopted these changes, if the expert, accountant or otherwise, asked whether she may destroy notes that are merely scraps and jottings—page numbers and scratch-paper additions and subtractions, memos "to self—re-read complaint"—as has always been her practice, there seemed little harm in destruction, since the likelihood that these scraps and jottings would have been potential evidence is very low.

If, however, the expert asked whether she may continue her practice of destroying, erasing, or otherwise discarding and keeping from discovery drafts of her report—even incomplete, partial, early drafts—then your answer to her must be "no," regardless of her practice with other attorneys in other cases. The rule of thumb is straightforward: If you can imagine any reasonable circumstances where the material in question might serve as evidence—for impeachment, to understand the report, to evaluate the expert's thought process in making assumptions, to inquire into the attorney's involvement, to examine decisions to include or exclude bases and opinions—then it may not be destroyed without running the risk of sanction for spoliation and perhaps for obstruction of justice. Neither you nor the expert through your implicit approval of past destruction practice may destroy evidence or hinder the opposition in its search for evidence. Again, under states who do not follow the new Rule 26, advise the expert to accept the discoverability of the information she puts in her drafts. With this in mind, forewarn the expert about taking the time, even in her long-hand notes, and especially in drafts, to choose her words with care. To the extent you can inform the expert ahead of her drafting about any applicable legal language the opinion must employ or any *Daubert* criteria that her methodology should consider, then a lot of the unfair uses that might otherwise occur from discovery of her drafts can be diminished. This is an especially important conversation to have with someone who has never testified before.

---

10. FED. R. CIV. P. 26(a)(2)(B).
11. FED. R. CIV. P. 26(a)(2)(B), Advisory Committee Notes to 1993 Amendments.

5.6.1.2 2010 Changes

Communications, Drafts, and Help

In 2010, Rules 26(b)(4)(B) and (C) were amended. These amendments are meant to restrict wasteful time and effort on disclosure of expert drafts and attorney expert communications. Before you get too comfortable, however, remember there are exceptions relating to communications between lawyer and expert about expert compensation and facts or data provided by counsel as well as for communications of the assumptions the lawyer gives to the expert by the attorney. These exceptions still place at risk many of the communications between consulting and testifying experts. Because of these exceptions, the better practice is still not to destroy drafts.[12]

Preparing and providing the report present two problems worth special discussion. The first (and more easily handled problem) derives from the continuing requirement after 2010 that the report be "prepared by" the expert witness. From the Advisory Committee's notes, you know that in some instances you may help the expert prepare the report. For example, where the expert is a tool-and-die maker whose expertise does not extend to authoring written descriptions of complex processes, it seems appropriate and unobjectionable for you to help the expert organize the report and perhaps even take dictation of a process or methodology and reduce it to writing for the expert's approval and adoption. However, the Harvard professor of economics would not normally need such help.

It seems inappropriate for an attorney and expert to exchange multiple drafts of the "expert's" report. This process sometimes even begins with the initial draft coming from the attorney, with the back-and-forth redlined versions eventually yielding to a final "report of the expert." There seems no reason to call this the "expert's report"; it would be more appropriate to call it the "attorney's report." Some courts, when encountering such intrusive and extensive participation by the attorney, have stricken the report, precluded the expert from submitting a new report, and prevented the expert from testifying.[13] If you suspect your opponent of authoring the

---

12. FED. R. CIV. P. 26 advisory committee's note, 2010 amend. The note indicates an intent to exclude facts or data containing attorney mental impressions, but to still require disclosure of facts or data considered by the expert in arriving at her opinion.

At the same time, the intention is that "facts or data" be interpreted broadly **to require disclosure of any material considered** by the expert, from whatever source, **that contains factual ingredients**. The disclosure obligation extends to any facts or data "considered" by the expert in forming the opinions to be expressed, not only those relied on by the expert.

See Innovative Sonic Ltd. v. Research in Motion, Ltd., 2013 WL 775349, at *2 (citing Rule 26(b)(4)(C) advisory committee's notes, 2010 amend., subdiv. (b)(4)). (The court held that that such privilege is not absolute and can be waived. In particular, if the information is provided to a testifying expert for use in forming his or her opinions, "otherwise-protected information and materials [would become] subject to discovery.")

13. Butera v. District of Columbia, 235 F. 3d 637, 661–62 (D.C. Cir. 2001). *Cf.* Marbled Murrelat v. Pacific Lumber Co., 880 F. Supp. 1343, 1360, n. 37, 1363–64 (N.D. Cal. 1995) (where the court did not strike the opinion, but found that the report lacked credibility).

National Institute for Trial Advocacy

"expert" report (because, for example, you have a word-for-word expert report your opponent used in a separate, but similar case), you may produce drafts that support your suspicion.

But won't the rule changes that protect against discovery of communications between counsel and expert as well as of the expert report drafts make discovery unlikely anyway? The answer to this problem is logically found in analyzing how free of the attorney's taint are the expert's substantive thoughts, methods, and opinions that make up the ultimate report. At deposition (as discussed in chapters seven and eight, *infra*), it is clearly fair to question the expert on the process by which the expert's report was produced. The attorney deposing under the Federal Rules of Civil Procedure (or the state equivalent) will expect objections to discovery of communications between attorney and expert concerning the preparation of the report and the drafting process. Yet the deposing attorney should be able to ask whether facts or data or assumptions were provided by counsel or consulting expert working with counsel. If the attorney's extensive participation is discovered and the supplied facts or data or assumptions reveal substantive changes at the attorney's direction—or if the expert admits to performing calculations that were discarded after the new facts, data, or assumptions were provided—authorship of the report might be in question. In such a case, the court may be persuaded to limit or even exclude the expert's testimony—or at least limit or exclude the testimony related to infected portions of the report. If, on the other hand, no "infected" facts, data, or assumptions are produced and the expert's deposition testimony about the preparation of the report discloses no taint, then there is really no basis for the argument that the expert or the report should be excluded.

This discussion suggests that if you find it necessary to participate legitimately in the preparation of the report—not by suggesting substantive approaches and changes, but by correcting grammar, word choice, organization, or other nonsubstantive elements of the report—then you should retain the various drafts and be prepared to turn them over during discovery, even if not required to do so. If your changes are indeed nonsubstantive, the disclosure should do little harm (other than to the expert's ego, whose poor grammar has been exposed). As a practical matter, if you hold the work sessions with the expert leading up to the creation of the final report on the telephone or face-to-face without exchanging notes and drafts, and if you sketch the organization of the report on a whiteboard (which you erase, change, and erase again as work continues), you can avoid the difficulties of deciding which drafts to keep and whether all of them have been kept or turned over. (This is not an invitation for you to find ways to alter the substantive content of expert reports without risking discovery; it is a reminder that when you have appropriate communication with the expert, you and your expert have no obligation to create a paper (or computerized) trail of evidence of those proper communications that must be safeguarded and eventually disclosed.)

In summary of this point, it may not be just the expert machinist who requires some assistance in preparing an expert report—other experts, even ones you would think would be competent authors, may need help organizing their report to meet the legal requirements of the substantive law of the case and the procedural rules of the forum. But again, do not see this limited role as presenting an opportunity to shape the substance of the expert's testimony; that substance must continue to originate with and be the choice of the expert. Remember that even under the new rules there are exceptions for facts, data, or assumptions that come from the attorney. As a result, even in federal litigation under the 2010 amendments, destruction of drafts is inadvisable.

One final practice tip with regard to drafts. Some lawyers report their experience with such notes in these terms: "What goes around, comes around." If you intend to spend a significant amount of discovery time seeking these types of notes from your opponent, be certain that your own expert has not also engaged in such drafting and memorandum writing. Many lawyers have found the pursuit of such materials is not worth the effort because the material is often marginally useful and the lawyer ends up being obligated to produce his expert's draft materials to the opposing attorney. Nevertheless, unless you and your opponent have explicitly discussed whether such materials will be produced and have agreed they will not be sought, you may have to propound such discovery defensively and prepare for production.

Other Disclosures

As noted previously, Rule 26(a)(2)(B) requires the expert to prepare and sign a report for pretrial submission to the other party. The report should contain:

(i) a complete statement of all opinions the witness will express and the basis and reasons for them;

(ii) the facts or data considered by the witness in forming them;

(iii) any exhibits that will be used summarize or support them;

(iv) the witness's qualifications, including a list of all publications authored in the previous 10 years;

(v) a list of all other cases in which, during the previous 4 years, the witness testified as an expert at trial or by deposition; and

(vi) a statement of the compensation to be paid for the study and testimony in the case.

The second (and certainly the more subtle) question that arises with Rule 26(a)(2)(B) expert disclosures concerns how much of the "opinions the witness will express and the basis and reasons for them" includes the indicia of reliability that you, as the proponent, intend to present in support of the admissibility of the expert's testimony. The *Daubert*-type criteria are required as part of the foundation for admissibility—they are a portion of the proponent's affirmative burden. If pretrial you know that you intend to demonstrate the internal and external consistencies of the expert's methodology to persuade the judge the opinion testimony is admissible (as well as to persuade the jury the testimony is worthy of substantial weight), then it does not seem unfair to require you to disclose consistency information as part of the "basis and reasons" for the opinions. The consistency is certainly part of the "basis and reasons" you believe the jury should use to accept the opinions, and parsing this rule's language much further seems an empty exercise.

Suppose, however, you see no problems with reliability; perhaps the expert is in a field, like antitrust economics, in which experts have been testifying for decades without *Daubert*-type challenges. There might be no mention of indicia of reliability in the expert report. When your opponent raises a *Daubert* challenge by a motion in limine or voir dire during trial and you respond by proffering evidence of internal and external consistencies, can your opponent complain that these factors were not disclosed in the expert report and cannot fairly be considered by the court? The answer must be no; otherwise, the least well-founded challenge to the reliability of the testimony (and therefore the challenge least anticipated in the creation of the expert report) would be the most likely to succeed because rebuttal to the challenge might be precluded.

In other words, if the expert's methodology is of a type that clearly meets all four original *Daubert* criteria[14]—for example, where the expert is a physicist talking about the operation of a nuclear reactor, you would not expect her to list in her report the evidence that indicates nuclear physics methodologies are generally accepted in the relevant scientific community; that they have been subjected to peer review in appropriate publications; that there is a known error rate for the involved calculations; and that the procedures are testable and have been tested repeatedly. You certainly anticipate that you will hear testimony on these points, but you do not expect challenges on them. If they are challenged, the court should be perfectly free to receive evidence on them, even though they were not included in the expert report. As a counter-example, if you intend for the expert to try to demonstrate that an innovative approach is reliable (as was the actual case with Dr. Done and his colleagues in the *Daubert* matter), then it seems reasonable to require you to give some advance notice in the expert's report that innovative testimony will be presented so the other side can adequately prepare to challenge it.

Considering the *Daubert*-type criteria question in its larger context, you should not require the expert to anticipate and discuss every possible cross-examination challenge in the expert report—evidence the expert's methodology can survive such

---

14. For simplicity, we here consider the original four criteria—peer review, known or knowable error rate, general acceptance in the relevant field, and testability—because we understand from *Daubert* itself that the actual list of criteria of reliability is as unlimited as the fields of human knowledge.

challenges does not logically comprise the "basis and reasons" for the opinions. Any other interpretation of the rule would require all experts to state in their reports that, for example, they were not under the influence of hallucinogenic substances when they came to their conclusions. Where the proponent of the expert is introducing the information or issue as part of the basis or reason for the expert's opinion testimony, then disclosure in the report is appropriate and should logically be required as courts deal with this question of expert reports and the disclosure of *Daubert*-type criteria. On the other hand, if the opponent only injects the issue to challenge the admissibility or weight, then whether the issue was mentioned in the report seems irrelevant.

Chapter Six

Preparing to Depose the Expert

You should begin preparing for the deposition of the opponent's expert by reviewing the expert report and the "voluntary disclosures" required under Rule 26. Here, graduate students can provide inexpensive, talented support. Despite tantalizing anecdotal evidence, the curriculum vitae is least likely to provide effective cross-examination material, and the information it contains can be easily checked outside the deposition. However, it remains important to check whether the expert actually obtained claimed degrees and credentials—a surprisingly high percentage of experts still exaggerate their accomplishment. Conferences with consulting and testifying experts are a rich source of questions for the deposing expert at the deposition. Two timelines—one showing the historical events giving rise to the lawsuit and the other showing the history of the opposing expert's involvement from first contact through the anticipated completion of the work—are important tools during preparation and at the deposition itself.

6.1 Expert Discovery

As your thoughts turn to discovery of the facts and opinions held by the opponent's experts, do not overlook the discovery devices that are available in addition to depositions. Most federal courts routinely require Rule 26(a) voluntary disclosures, which provide some information about the expert, along with expert reports, which provide much more information about the expert's opinions and bases (if they are done properly). Of course, you will normally not get those expert reports until perhaps ninety days before trial, and therefore you cannot rely on them to guide other discovery efforts or trial preparation. Interrogatories are a poorly conceived device for obtaining useful information for two simple reasons: 1) there is no practical opportunity for follow-up questioning, in which incomplete or less useful answers can be clarified; and 2) the responses, while signed by a party, are prepared by attorneys. More properly, you should recognize that just as one party's word processor creates the interrogatory set, the other party's word processor creates the response to that interrogatory set. With regard to requests for admissions, their usefulness is minimal before the expert deposition, but they can be particularly useful to pin down specific opinions, assumptions, and bases if more specificity is needed for trial.

Again turning to graduate students and their role as nonconsulting experts, one technique you can use is to assign the students the role of preparing the expert report of the opponent. The student will research the facts and case from the perspective of the opposing party and can then provide you with questions, learned texts, and treatises the opposing expert may use in preparing her report. Be sure to read these texts and treatises so that you have some in expertise in the field when questioning the opposing expert in deposition.

When it comes time to review the transcripts of prior testimony, which have been identified through the 26(a) disclosures, graduate students are invaluable because they provide an inexpensive source of sophisticated labor. Although the federal rules mandate that a party must disclose its expert's trial or deposition testimony, you are not limited to researching beyond that four-year period—the availability of computerized legal research makes it simple. (The mandated contents of the report are a "floor," not a "ceiling," for disclosures.) Later at deposition, feel free to ask the expert about testimony given beyond those four years just as you should feel free to ask about publications authored beyond the ten-year period stated in Rule 26. Before deposition, you are clearly free to direct your graduate students or other assistants to investigate earlier testimony and earlier publications and to read them all with the issues of the present case in mind. If you have been so fortunate to find other counsel who have opposed this expert in their cases, they may be able to provide you not only with transcripts, but also with copies of exhibits prepared by that expert—or at least used by the expert—that will foreshadow the expert presentation you are likely to face at deposition and trial. All of this discovery is conducted "outside the rules," to the extent that it is not governed by rule-imposed deadlines or limitations.

Graduate students or other assistants, operating under the loose direction of the attorney or the consulting expert, can also create a complete résumé for the opposing expert even before one is received through the discovery process. Publications by the expert, available in specialized libraries, normally provide substantial biographical detail; Web sites maintained by educational institutions often proudly boast of the credentials of their faculty; and prior testimony is likely to contain sworn statements or adopted exhibits that detail the expert's credentials. Thus, before you obtain a formal curriculum vitae from the expert, your informal discovery may provide you with even more complete information. All of that information can then be run down by graduate students to determine its truthfulness and accuracy. As a result, the trial lawyer's dream of unmasking the expert as never having graduated from Hometown U as claimed may still become reality, but the foundation for such deadly cross-examination will have been laid months earlier before formal discovery even began. (To avoid the nightmare of having the same cross-examination happen to your expert witness, have your graduate students conduct the same kind of search on the credentials of experts you are considering or perhaps have already hired.)

You can also use online research to find additional instances in which the opposing expert has testified and to find additional cases where the same expert issues have arisen. For example, LexisNexis has a number of ways to search cases to get information dealing with

- the opposing expert's actual testimony;

- who she usually testifies for;

- whether her testimony has ever been refused;

- other experts who may have given opinions on the same subject; and

- multiple copies of résumés that may have been submitted electronically as exhibits to dispositive motions.

In addition, you can search (or have your litigation team search) news articles about the expert as well as other public-record information, including where she lives, property she owns, and professional licensing information that might be available online. Finally, LexisNexis has a verdict and settlement reporting feature that may also contain information on a given expert or area of expertise. Google searches may reveal Web pages that contain résumés or other publication information not provided in discovery. From such information, you can often identify material you can use on cross-examination— résumé changes or exaggeration of credentials, the identity of other experts who disagree with the approach being taken, the existence of literature from reliable authorities that contradicts assumptions or approaches the opposing expert uses, and even data problems that challenge the opposing expert's ability to come to the conclusions she is presenting. (As an example, in the *Daubert* case itself, the expert in question, Dr. Done, was amalgamating data from several studies that had been found by experts in other cases to be insufficient as a basis for epidemiological analysis. Done's ability to reach valid conclusions based on the agglomeration of otherwise inadequate data became the central issue in the appeal of the *Daubert* case. These individual prior cases might have been discovered by computer searches directed at the issues rather than at Dr. Done.) LexisNexis has a "*Daubert* tracker" feature that can greatly help provide updated information relating to *Daubert* issues that have been raised in the subject area of the experts' field of specialty. For instance, you can find cases that will not only help you to prepare to defeat a *Daubert* motion, but also to prepare you to gain admissions from the opposing expert in deposition that may keep the expert from testifying.

Clearly, if you have already committed to having a testifying expert, you will spend substantial time with that expert learning the areas of her field that are relevant to the case and understanding the adversary's position before taking the opposing expert's deposition. Your own expert can provide invaluable help reducing the opposing expert's advantages, shaping the case, and preparing for all phases of discovery.

Rule 703—Bases of Opinion Testimony by Experts

An expert may base an opinion on facts or data in the case that the expert has been made aware of or personally observed. If experts in the particular field would reasonably rely on those kinds of facts or data in forming an opinion on the subject, they need not be admissible for the opinion to be admitted. But if the facts of data would otherwise be inadmissible, the proponent of the opinion may disclose them to the jury only if their probative value in helping the jury evaluate the opinion substantially outweighs their prejudicial effect.

6.2 Location of the Deposition

If possible, hold the deposition in the expert's own office or building. The deposition may be interrupted from time to time as the expert's regular work intrudes, but you will have the opportunity to learn more about the expert, her approach to matters, and her other interests. The titles of books on the expert's shelves, the identity of her colleagues down the hall, the photographs of handshaking politicians on the wall—all of these give some additional clues to the personality and allegiances of this witness. They may not amount to much—if anything at all—but once again, why give up a possible advantage, no matter how small?

An additional reason to hold the deposition at or near the expert's office is that her files will be more accessible, and you may have the opportunity to see and use underlying materials at the deposition for which you would otherwise have to wait. Certainly, the normal exchange of expert interrogatory responses and underlying data may provide a good deal of material before the deposition, but you are not interested only in what the expert and the opposing counsel have concluded are the underlying support. For example, it is quite enjoyable and profitable to review the material that the expert considered, but rejected because it did not support the expert's opinion. If you are in the expert's office, you are more likely to obtain such materials. On the other hand, if you are insecure about your own level of knowledge, there are advantages to seeing after your own comfort and convenience. Controlling where the expert sits, what she looks at during the deposition (what view she has from the conference room window), and protecting the session from interruption can all lead to a more complete and accurate understanding of what the expert has to say.

A party who identifies an expert as a likely witness at trial will normally be obligated to present that expert for deposition within the jurisdiction of the forum court or at the expert's normal place of business. By agreement (including the expert's agreement), the expert deposition may be held almost anywhere. If faced with a dispute, the forum court is likely to defer to the expert's convenience, especially if the expert is only occasionally a witness and is normally engaged in the practice of her profession. In other words, it is appropriate for you, as the deposing attorney, to choose your preferred location for the expert's deposition and to negotiate to gain that location, but you are limited in your ability to insist on it.

6.3   Preparing for the Deposition

There is a lot you can do to prepare yourself to take an expert deposition. On the deposing side, begin your preparation two or three weeks before the expert deposition by immersing yourself in the relevant information—the data, the reports, the statistics, the engineering data, the depositions of the fact witnesses, the opposing expert's writings, the expert's teachings, the findings of the graduate students—all the information that may provide grist for the deposition mill. In discussions with the consulting expert and assistants (graduate students or others), raise possible lines of deposition inquiry and expert response so you not only practice following up, but also become familiar with the "scientific, technical or other specialized knowledge" that is the subject of the expert's opinion. In further preparation, review your legal theories, which have probably by this point been sharpened by motions to dismiss and motions for summary judgment.

When you are on the defense side of a case, analyze the elements of the affirmative defenses. In addition, research the law of evidence to determine whether there are any particular standards that must be met by the opinion of the opposing expert. For example, in a medical malpractice case, must the opinion include knowledge of the local standard of care, or in a legal malpractice case, must the opinion display knowledge of the level of practice within a particular legal specialty like antitrust counseling or products liability prosecutions? There may be cases where the methodology to be employed by the expert is dictated by statute or prior cases. In a patent case where she is computing damages due to infringement, the expert may be required to state them in terms of reasonable royalties that were lost by the patent-holding party.[1]

With a lay witness, reviewing legal theories would be sufficient for that portion of deposition preparation, but with an expert, you must also review the "scientific, technical, or other specialized" theories being offered by both your own expert and the expert to be deposed. Herein lies a great part of the challenge and charm: for a short time during the deposition, your goal is to be as expert as the expert in the narrow slice of her field that involves the case. While you are indeed adopting the persona of the ignorant (but interested) student as you depose the expert, that ignorance is largely feigned. You must be sensitive to the nuances of the expert's opinions, to those small changes in assumptions or facts that result in major changes in conclusions, and to those studied choices of words that try to mask or avoid weaknesses or unfavorable alternatives. You are seeking to become attuned to the relevant science to the point where you can identify when the expert has substituted

---

1. *See* Georgia Pacific Corp. v. U.S. Plywood Corp., 318 F. Supp. 1116, 1121 (S.D.N.Y. 1970), *modified*, 446 F.2d 295 (2d Cir. 1971), *cert. denied*, 404 U.S. 870 (1971).

judgment for knowledge, assumptions for facts, faith for understanding, or opinion for truth. The consulting expert is your greatest ally in this preparation; the testifying expert may be less useful because of concerns of exposing her to worries about unfavorable theories and marginally provable fact. When developing this very narrow, but intense understanding of the relevant science, you must position yourself to unmask what is nonscience—those factors of judgment and discretion, of bias and prejudice, of interest and ignorance that allow the opposing expert to disagree with the proponent's expert while wrapping that disagreement in a cloak of apparent scientific certainty.

6.3.1 *Brainstorming on Themes and Facts*

One device you can use to get to that level of preparation is brainstorming the case with your graduate students, associates, and consulting experts. Brainstorming is the process of encouraging a group to call out, without argument or disagreement, facts that are good or bad for the case; scientific approaches that are helpful or harmful; areas of expert strength or weakness; data that are supportive or unsupportive; or themes that are attractive or unattractive. It is often helpful to brainstorm around a blackboard or easel to capture the contributions of the group and to discover connections, themes, and theories that will provide you with a unifying theory of attack or identify areas of in which you are ignorant.

The purpose in avoiding argument or critical comment about contributions in a brainstorming session is twofold. First, the recipient of a negative comment will be reluctant to voice his thoughts on the next point; second, even an ignorant comment may spark an insight by another member of the group—a valuable insight that may be lost if the original ignorant comment is suppressed. Therefore, until the ordering or ranking portion of the session has been reached, the person facilitating the brainstorming session must actively work to avoid negative comments from all members and to encourage universal participation. One additional way to help structure the brainstorming session is to impose a time limit. The time limit will provide assurance to the more compulsive types in the group that the creative process will eventually come to an end and will allow them to participate with an eye toward more structured analysis.

After the brainstorming has been completed, organization begins. One way to organize the facts, opinions, data, and approaches is to place the material on a timeline. The timeline can be constructed according to when key facts occurred in the case; it can be constructed to reveal when the opposing expert reached her opinions in relation to when she acquired these facts. Timelines are also useful for telling you what you know and what you do not know. Look at the timeline and ask what caused the events to occur; ask what facts, approaches, and opinions do not appear or were not used by the expert or by the party on the other side. Policies and procedures—which may have been in place, but not followed—may not show up on the timeline, but the timeline should signal you to ask whether those policies and procedures existed. ("Timeline," as used here, refers to a horizontal array of information organized chronologically from left to right.)

6.3.2 Creating a Timeline

During deposition preparation, prepare a timeline and redraft it until you are comfortable that it displays known and relevant information organized correctly by date. Reduce this timeline to a size that can be kept available during the deposition, so when the expert refers to events, you can locate them on the timeline easily, add them to the timeline if necessary, and determine their relationship to the other historical incidents that make up the dispute being litigated. Post hoc ergo propter hoc, "after which therefore because of which," is indeed a logical fallacy (just because bullfrogs come out after it rains does not mean it rained bullfrogs); however, causes do precede effects (bullfrog (cowfrog) eggs precede bullfrogs), and until the chronological relationship of events is understood, the cause-and-effect relationship may remain undiscovered. One additional reason to prepare a timeline is it can be used as a jumping-off point for creating a story album—how to tell the jurors about what happened, why it happened, and how it compares with their intuitions and experience in a way that will appeal to their common sense. Preparing a two-paragraph, chronological statement that answers the question "What is this case about?" encourages you to focus on the forest and not on a selected tree or two.

In addition, use a timeline to better understand the expert's relationship to the case. For instance, when the expert was hired in relationship to when the complaint was filed—and the damages claims made in it—might suggest some theories: if hired well before the case was filed, was the expert also being used in other related litigation? Or in another example, did the opposing expert issue her supplementary report before or after your expert issued his report? Who suggested the need for a supplement? Was her initial report authored before she had all the relevant data? Why was this the case?

6.3.3 Reviewing Documents

As further preparation for taking the opposing expert's deposition, you must review and become intimately familiar with the important documents in the case—those that support your client's position and those that challenge it. Especially where you are working with documents recording scientific information—laboratory notes, chemical analysis, engineering diagrams, critical path flow charts, econometric calculations, medical charts—there is extraordinary comfort in having at the deposition a well-annotated copy of the document in question, where the annotations are a result of careful review by you and your consulting expert. Such review begins with the consulting expert explaining the document to you line by line, entry by entry, number by number, describing sources for each entry and providing meaning to each entry. As the consultant guides you through the document, annotate his copy in way that eventually allows you to explain the document in the same detail as the consultant. At deposition, your goal is not to disclose your thorough knowledge of the documents, but rather to use that thorough knowledge to recognize instances where the opposing expert has inadequate or mistaken knowledge of the document and may be relying on it with potentially illogical foundations to their conclusions.

When the entire case is presented to the jury, there will likely be no more than a dozen or so documents that will sway the jury's verdict—in part because it is too difficult to consider more documents than that and to keep them separate; in part because the jurors will be satisfied to select one document from a group as representative of the case and will use it while ignoring the others; and in final part because, when lawyers tend to overcomplicate cases, jurors act to reduce them once again to their proper dimensions. (In other words, some cases are as simple as "who hit who first?") In the deposition preparation, you must deal with more than the ultimate dozen or so documents—you might not be able to identify which dozen those are, but you should not overcomplicate your preparation or the deposition by attempting to master (and then to question) all aspects of all documents. Clearly, "all documents" will not be the subject of cross-examination at trial. Life is too short!

Expert Depositions in a Nutshell

- Opinions
- What did you do; why did you do it; how did you do it; what result did you get; what effect did that have on your opinion?
- Learned treatises
- What assumptions did you make?
- What did you not do?
- Curriculum vitae

As a final step in preparing to take the deposition of the opposing expert, you must determine your goal. There are times when you will be taking the expert's deposition purely for discovery—to learn the opinions and bases, the methodology, and conclusions that she is preparing to state at trial. When such pure discovery is the goal, remind yourself that open questions are your sharpest tool: who, what, when, where, how, why, tell us, describe, explain. These questions force the expert to speak in more than monosyllables and, in the best of deposition worlds, encourage the building of a rapport between you and the opposing expert as you play your role of ignorant, but interested student.

Another goal—not inconsistent with pure discovery, but normally pursued after the discovery portion of an expert deposition—is theory testing: laying before the opposing expert different portions of the expert's explanations and opinions to learn before trial the opposing expert's avenues of challenging your expert case or to gain admissions or concessions and narrow the issues. For example, you could ask the opposing expert:

> Professor Jones, am I correct then that you have no fault with the use of a critical path methodology in determining the cause for the construction delay? Instead, your only disagreement with the plaintiff's expert involves the proper reading of the blueprints to determine the number of structural steel units that should have been purchased?

In a medical malpractice case where the question is whether the plaintiff's epilepsy was caused by a motorcycle accident, you might ask the opposing expert:

> Doctor, your opinion is that the plaintiff's epilepsy is idiopathic—of unknown origin. Of the factors that are potential causes of epilepsy, which factor do you believe is the most likely cause of the plaintiff's epilepsy, even though you cannot select one as the cause?

Or you might ask:

> If the cause of the plaintiff's epilepsy is not idiopathic—and please accept that for the moment, at least hypothetically—then will you agree that the most likely cause was traumatic head injury?

A third reasonable goal in taking the deposition of an opposing expert is to test cross-examination—that is, to try part or even all of an interrogation that challenges the expert in her credentials or opinion testimony. The benefit is that you can learn about defenses the expert may have during cross-examination and then try to avoid those defenses during trial. The detriment is the expert is alerted to that possible line of cross and will be more prepared to meet it. If, however, you have weighed these possible results and determined that the line of cross is too tenuous to use without some confirmation that it will work, then you have little to lose by testing it during deposition. (One way to determine this is to do a dry run and practice your theory on that ever-present graduate student and see whether it works). In addition, the purpose of the cross could be to persuade opposing counsel to settle the case by demonstrating the weakness of his expert. Finally, in the best of all worlds, the deposition cross can lead to a motion for summary judgment, which may dispose of the case.

Occasionally, counsel will seek to punish an opposing expert during the deposition by extending its length or increasing its heat, as though the witness has committed some crime by daring to appear for the other side or daring to hold contrary opinions. The theory seems to be the witness will rethink her decision to testify because the deposition was so unpleasant and cross-examination is yet to come. A strong argument exists that deposition questioning designed with this goal in mind is improper and perhaps unethical because it is not the role of counsel to delay the proceeding; to sanction witnesses; or to take a position merely to harass, annoy, or embarrass the witness.

Using the deposition of the opposing expert to confirm known facts serves the purpose of limiting the dispute—at least the dispute between the experts—and perhaps facilitating a settlement or accelerating the end of the trial. Creating a record at the expert deposition of facts on which the expert relies as true for the purposes of her analysis makes it virtually impossible for the opposing party to contest those facts during motions practice or at trial. (Indeed, a close reading of Rule 801(d)(2), especially sections C and D, has persuaded a number of courts that a party's expert makes party statements when she speaks at deposition. As a technical matter, facts accepted as true (and admitted as such) by the opposing expert at her deposition need not be the subject of requests for admission under Rule 36 because they would already be opposing party statements (admissions) by operation of Rule 801(d)(2).)

CHAPTER SEVEN

DEPOSING THE EXPERT: STRATEGIES

Open questions seeking new information remain the recommended approach for expert depositions. While experts possess some advantages over lay witnesses at trial, you often can turn those apparent advantages to your own use. Experts often feel constrained by factors beyond the lawsuit, such as a need to maintain their mainstream position in their profession, which can be used to bring them back from extreme positions. The deposition of the opposing expert provides an opportunity to discover "reliable authorities" that may provide material to be used at trial as evidence under Rule 803(18). By making the expert think of you as an ignorant, but very interested student, you will encourage her to teach you what you need to know.

7.1   Deposing Experts: Strategies

The single best piece of advice on deposing the opposing expert is: "Do not assume you know any answers the expert will give." When Albert Einstein was asked, "What do you consider the most powerful force in the universe?" anyone at all familiar with Einstein and his work might reasonably have guessed that his answer would be "gravity" or "mass times the speed of light squared," or, if one were of a particularly philosophical bent, "the human mind." All are consistent with general knowledge about Einstein, and yet all would be incorrect assumptions. Einstein's actual answer: "Compound interest." The *interesting* thing about this Einsteinian answer is it tells more than just what Einstein saw as a potent force—it tells about Einstein himself, about his sense of humor, his perspective on himself, his work in relation to common people and their problems, and his ability to differentiate between the abstractions of a relativistic universe and the unavoidable financial realities of everyday life. By asking Professor Einstein at deposition, "What do you consider the most powerful force in the universe?" instead of, "Is it your opinion that gravity is the most powerful force in the universe?" you create an opportunity to see into Einstein's mind. "The human mind is dark to those of us who attempt to look into it and to most of us who attempt to look out from it."[1] How presumptuous of attorneys to believe they can accurately predict the answers to complex

---

1. Carl Gustav Jung.

questions as analyzed by experts with opposing viewpoints, when those who study the human mind suggest people cannot even understand their own motivations.

As you approach the opposing expert for her deposition, recognize that as an expert, she has some substantial advantages that she brings to the process—advantages you can sometimes diminish or turn to your advantage at deposition and trial.

Experts' Advantages

♦ They are experts.
♦ They are not intimidated by the process.
♦ They can hide behind their expertise.
♦ Trial work is more lucrative than office or classroom work.
♦ They are more highly educated than lawyers.
♦ They like to teach.

One of the expert's primary advantages is she has superior knowledge in her field—superior to you, superior to her own counsel, and superior to everyone involved in the case. If the direct and cross-examination at trial had as its purpose to allow the jurors to decide whether the lawyer or the opposing expert were the better geologist, endocrinologist, or mathematician, there would be little contest (and little purpose to holding the trial at all). But that is not the purpose of the trial or of the expert's testimony at the trial. Instead, she is there to offer her specialized help to the trier of fact who will attempt to resolve a dispute that touches upon some small portion of her field of expertise. And in that small portion for a very short time while you and the expert face one another, you may be equally expert. You can improve your chances of holding your own by carefully choosing the areas of confrontation on cross-examination. You have no obligation to examine the expert on every facet of her knowledge or even in any facets that support her opinions in the case. Working in your own arena, you are entitled to ask questions limited to those areas in which the expert is factually ignorant, mistaken, or poorly prepared. If you have been able to identify such areas through deposition and other discovery, you have negated the expert's advantage of superior knowledge in her field.

A second advantage possessed by the expert is that she is not intimidated by the discovery and trial process. Either she has gone through it before and understands that it is normally not fatal, or she has discussed the process with the counsel presenting her, and because she is educated and intelligent, she recognizes her limited exposure to inconvenience, embarrassment, or ridicule. While the lay witness approaches cross-examination with some trepidation (except for business people with the phrase "assistant to" in their titles who seem to believe they are the embodiment of all business acumen), the expert generally looks forward to the challenge, relishes the intellectual exchange, and often prefers the excitement of the courtroom to the perceived drudgery of the classroom, laboratory, or doctor's office. (There are some experts in the field of actuarial economics or forensic economics who are wary of the process because they have learned how public the deposition can be. They have learned that what they say in one case can come back to haunt them in another. These experts are not intimidated by the deposition process, but they can become overly cautious and overly concerned about choosing the right words, with the result that they can appear hesitant and evasive.)

The fact that many experts are not intimidated by the deposition or trial process, however, is not an unmitigated advantage to them. That same fear or concern in lay witnesses serves to make those witnesses more cautious about allowing the deposing attorney to develop a rapport or to encourage them to speak freely. "Unintimidated" experts, on the other hand, may lose sight of the deposing attorney's goal, which is to find means to diminish the expert's credibility or to challenge the bases for the expert's opinions. Because they think they understand the process, because they think they cannot be seriously challenged, because they think they are safe within their own field, experts at deposition may be more willing to provide explanations and lengthy answers, to volunteer information, and to educate their ignorant, but interested student. Therefore, if the deposing attorney can remember to smile, nod, lean forward, maintain eye contact, and ask open questions in his genuine search for illumination from the expert, the expert may allow her teaching instincts and her passion for her subject to outweigh the caution that her counsel has been advising for the previous three months.

Another advantage possessed by an expert when she appears in the legal field is that her compensation for preparation and expert testimony is normally much greater than anything she can earn back in the classroom, laboratory, or doctor's office. Sometimes in deposing a lay witness, the attorney can look across the table and, by a raised eyebrow or tilted chin, communicate that he is willing to stay at the deposition table for the next four days if she is not more forthcoming in her answers to his questions. With an expert, however, such a message is met with only a smile as she rapidly calculates how many payments on her BMW those four additional days of testimony represent. The deposing attorney can turn this to his advantage because the willingness of the expert to stay in the deposition longer results in the expert being willing to provide more complete answers and explanations. The expert's counsel cannot successfully shut off the flow of information by reminding the expert that volunteered facts or opinions extend the deposition, because extending the deposition may seem like a fine idea to the expert. There is also a certain athletic quality to deposition where the lawyer should have an advantage: stamina. This is the ability to listen and to do the hard work of "corralling" the expert about her opinion. Although the expert may be willing to stay, she may not be as able to go the distance as well as the deposing attorney.

Experts may also derive some comfort from their belief that if they encounter a question they do not want to answer, they can hide behind their expertise by using jargon, by insisting on hyper-technical definition of terms, or by discussing the premises and conditions they claim to see as being built into the question to a point where the examiner has forgotten what the question was and has literally lost his ability to determine whether it was ever answered at all. For example, when asked whether the assumed shape of the curve showing the receipt of profits for a project was more an ascending ramp than a descending ramp, an econometrician might answer:

> Well, counsel, that question presumes more information than is readily available on the few facts you seem to be implying, and without engaging in substantial efforts at crafting a regression equation that produced a large enough R to give us some comfort, an acceptable degree of confidence, perhaps at the 95 percent level, we will be unsure whether we are dealing adequately with problems of heteroskedasticity or multicolinearity.

This use of jargon to avoid answering the question can be dealt with and turned into some advantage for the lawyer. The expert, in using such jargon, is counting on the lawyer's unwillingness to show his ignorance by asking for explanations. She presumes (with some good reason for many trial attorneys) his ego will keep him from admitting that he is unable to determine whether she has answered his question and he will therefore go blindly forward. But because you will take the role of the interested, but admittedly ignorant student, you will feel no shame in admitting your ignorance, and when faced with jargon and other expert-speak, you will say: "I'm sorry. I don't understand that last answer. Can you help me? What do you mean by regression analysis? What do you mean by R? What do you mean by large enough R? What do you mean by heteroskedasticity? Why should we be concerned about that in your analysis?" You will continue with this line of questioning until you have called on the expert to define all of the terms. By doing so, you will have demonstrated that you have the patience and intent to cure your apparent ignorance with detailed questions. Whether the expert has been intentionally trying to dissemble by hiding behind the jargon of her expertise or has merely forgotten that English is the language in which she is normally expected to converse, the lesson will eventually become clear to her: this is the attorney's arena, she will answer the questions, and neither the attorney's ignorance nor his desire to get on with life will prevent him from slicing through her attempts at obfuscation.

In a survey conducted a few years ago, psychological researchers attempted to identify the greatest fear of American adults—a fear that caused them to wake up from nightmares in a cold sweat. The researchers anticipated (a mistake had they been dealing with experts) that they would learn adult Americans feared most the death of a loved one (spouse or child), their own death, or destruction of their home or possessions. Instead, they found the single greatest fear of American adults was public speaking. The normal American may worry for ways about her need to make a presentation to a committee at work, the parent-teacher association, or the library board. (Trial lawyers, of course, relish the opportunity to speak in public and abuse it as often as possible; therefore, counsel's own experience as a trial attorney should not be taken as indicative in any way of the experience or concerns of human beings.)

Expert witnesses, like trial lawyers, have largely overcome the fear of public speaking. They have put themselves in a position in their professions that requires them to make public presentations—not only in the trial courtroom, but more routinely in the classroom or before professional organizations. While some may still get the sweaty palms and a racing pulse adrenalin can produce, many of the experts you encounter in the courtroom are as comfortable as you at presenting their viewpoints from the stand. In sum, they like to teach. The fact that experts like to teach may give them an advantage at trial, but if you can successfully encourage them to teach at the deposition with you in the role as student, the experts will ultimately give more information than their counsel would prefer. Giving the expert a whiteboard to use to explain her analysis at deposition may also encourage her to drop into a teaching role. Instead of remembering that you are seeking material to use to diminish her credibility and undermine her opinion, she may come to think it is her responsibility and obligation to teach you—to repeat, to simplify, to analogize, and to instruct until she is confident that you understand even the most esoteric and sophisticated aspects of her methodology and conclusions. As a result, her advantage has been turned to yours.

This is particularly true when you ask an expert about what methods she might choose in arriving at an opinion in this case. The expert may start to teach about all the methods that might have been used, or tests to perform to change her confidence in the results, before realizing that she didn't use those methods or tests in this case. While your own expert might have provided you with information on these additional methods and tests, a given expert might disclose new or better methods not used that your own expert might now use in her supplemental opinion.

Experts' Vulnerabilities
- ♦ It is the lawyer's arena.
- ♦ They cannot resist teaching.
- ♦ You know how to use Federal Rule of Evidence 803(18).
- ♦ Their time is finite, and the universe is infinite.
- ♦ They must rely on assumptions.
- ♦ They are concerned about consistency.
- ♦ They worry about facts they do not know.

Experts have other vulnerabilities you should exploit at deposition. An important one is that their time to devote to this particular engagement is finite, while the universe of information is infinite. Therefore, the expert must always admit that there is more she could have done and more she could know. While she may claim it is only a remote possibility that her opinion would be changed if she knew those unknown facts or had done those undone tasks, you may be able to present a sufficient number of such facts and tasks to persuade the jurors that the expert has left her job unfinished. As an example, at deposition of a damages expert in a wrongful death action, you ask the expert to identify all the people she has talked with as she gathered information to use in calculating the future income stream, which she then reduced to present value. She answers she has talked to the decedent's superiors at work, others in the same field of work, professors who were familiar with the decedent's potential, and other experts who studied the decedent's field of employment to determine the likelihood of its economic growth. You ask if there were any others she spoke with, and in various forms you ask again and again. She finally states clearly and without condition that she has identified everyone she spoke with, but she has not identified the decedent's husband. With this deposition foundation, you are prepared at cross-examination at trial to make this apparently undone task seem significant and inexcusable:

Q: Professor Delaney, I understand from your direct examination that you spent approximately 217 hours working for plaintiff's counsel in this matter.

A: Yes, I believe that's correct.

Q: And of those 217 hours, I imagine you spent, what, perhaps twenty-four hours—that is, three work days—talking with Sheila Foley's husband? That would be three days out of about twenty-six?

A: No, I didn't. I . . . .

Q: Well, is it fair to say you spent at least one day talking with Carl Foley?

A: Well, no, what I'm trying to say is . . . .

Q: Well, if not one day of conversation, then I presume you had some substantial correspondence with Mr. Foley. Letters back and forth, asking him for information, is that right?

A: No, I talked to Sheila Foley's bosses and coworkers and professors. I talked to people in her computer science field . . . .

Q: So, Professor Delaney, the simple fact is that in all of those hours—those 217 hours—you spent trying to figure out how much money the plaintiff should get from the hospital, you never even spent five minutes talking to her husband about her plans to work or have a family or make other decisions about her life? Is that correct?

A: I never talked to him.

Q: Well, Professor Delaney, who decided you wouldn't talk to Sheila Foley's husband? You or the attorneys you were working with?

Another problem for experts that makes them vulnerable to cross-examination is some information, necessary for their work in the case, is simply not knowable. As an example, Professor Delaney in the wrongful death case is attempting to calculate the present value of the future income stream. Part of that calculation involves future interest rates, future inflation rates, and future discount rates. While these can be estimated, they cannot be known. A typical approach for an expert in such a position is to look at those same values for a similar past period; if she is projecting income for a twenty-year period in the future, she may take the average inflation rate (or discount rate or interest rate) for the immediate past twenty years. But this is not the same as knowing. The average is almost certain to be incorrect when compared to the actuality (twenty years from now), and any reasonable expert will always admit this. Nevertheless, they have little choice but to assume the past average (or some other proxy) will be a sufficiently close approximation to the future actual rate that the figures generated will be reasonably close to accurate. There is no other way to do the calculation.

In such a situation, the expert cannot logically be faulted for relying on assumptions; indeed your own expert may have to rely on assumptions, albeit different and (from your perspective) more reasonable assumptions. Of course, you may have already decided that you are not going to present an expert—this is normally more an option when representing the defendant than when representing the plaintiff—because you do not want to lend credence to the "pseudoscience" being hawked by the plaintiff. For example, presenting an expert to challenge plaintiff's expert witness who seeks to testify about the emotional distress damages the plaintiff suffers in a sexual discrimination case may lend too much weight to those damages.

When challenging an expert, remember that there are many ways to diminish the opposing expert's testimony without putting your own expert on the stand. Therefore, if you are concerned with giving credence to the science represented by the opposing expert by presenting an expert in that questionable field yourself, you may instead consider challenging the accuracy of the facts the opposing expert is relying on; the reasonableness of alternative assumptions she could have made; the sources of data she did not consult; the learned treatises that do not support her conclusions; her sketchy record of publications; or the dependence of her conclusion on the honesty and truthfulness of those who have reported the facts to her. In other words, the psychologist testifying in the case alleging sexual harassment depends to an extraordinary extent on the truthfulness of statements made by the claimed victim as that victim purports to describe her experiences; the child abuse expert must rely on the truthfulness and memory of young children as they are encouraged to describe unpleasant experiences; the damages expert testifying for the plaintiff in a patent infringement case must accept as accurate the plaintiff's statements regarding the success with which he would have marketed the product had the infringement not occurred.

In the *Texaco-Pennzoil* case, the defendant wanted to avoid a damages presentation of its own because it did not want to give credence to the plaintiff's liability case, and when the jury found it liable, it left them with no alternative to the plaintiff's gargantuan damage figure. However, this problem can be ameliorated in several ways: by presenting alternatives in the cross-examination of the opposing expert; by identifying other assumptions and introducing through that opposing expert recalculations based on those other assumptions; by identifying information the expert did not take into consideration and then asking the expert to agree that such information might well reduce her damage calculations; by pointing out to that expert instances in which a conclusion crucially depended on the truthfulness of a single witness; or by other circumstances, which put the experts figures in doubt, thereby providing the jurors with an alternative figure or an indication of the direction of appropriate change.

One tie-in between expert testimony and the overall theme of the case is whether the expert has made an unreasonable assumption. The unreasonableness of that assumption can affect not only the credibility of the expert on the damages calculations, but also the overall credibility of the opponent's case. The trial lawyer can eventually argue if the expert is wrong about damages or if her assumptions are fanciful, what else is she making up to support the story she is telling?

Unlike lay witnesses, experts bear the burden of belonging to a profession; they feel themselves to be part of a larger whole, and while they may wish to stand out as superior when compared to their colleagues, they have no desire to stand out because they are outliers—that is, because they are espousing such extreme positions that few, if any, of their colleagues agree with them. Thus, as much as they are able while fulfilling the terms of their engagement (which require them to support their principal's case), they will try to remain consistent with the mainstream beliefs and approaches in their field. For example, you may be more apt to get an agreement that the texts and treatises your expert relies on are authoritative (for purposes of Federal Rule of Evidence 803(18)) if he asks about them in general before you highlight to the expert that her opinion disagrees with those sources. In fact, if the expert believes you are examining her credentials by asking about her familiarity with authoritative texts, she may be more willing to demonstrate she has a broad knowledge of authoritative literature in the field—much more willing than she would have been if you had foreshadowed your intention of reviewing that literature to determine whether she was being consistent with it.

A further aspect of the expert's desire to appear consistent is her constant concern that she not say anything in the case that contradicts something she has said in another case or in some of her own publications. As a result, while you are focusing on three pages of transcript and four pages of two articles that you have identified as possibly useful on cross-examination, she is worrying about all twenty-three of her articles and the four cases in which she has given both deposition and trial testimony, and she is wondering whether she should have her graduate student assistant review them all again or perhaps cancel her vacation and review them herself.

7.2   *Daubert* and Deposition Strategy

In situations where you received a copy of the opposing expert's report and her report fails to contain the facts or data sufficient to support the opinion under *Daubert*, you are presented with some strategic choices. One choice is to "sandbag" the expert, and not depose at all, waiting to challenge the expert when the expert's opinion is offered. This approach is tempting where you will not be presenting expert opinion of your own, so the opposing expert will not be tipped off to the potential *Daubert* challenges that exist in her opinion. After all, it is the duty of the expert to put into the report the information she relies on in reaching her opinion, and it is her duty to supplement her report, if necessary, before trial.

However, the downside of this approach is that most courts want evidentiary issues handled pretrial and to learn ahead of time if there are *Daubert* challenges in the works. It is also in the court's discretion to let the expert supplement her report if the court believes the interests of justice are served by it[2] In the end then, the court may grant leave to supplement and the sandbagging attempt will fail.

A second approach could be to bring a motion in limine or a summary judgment motion, again arguing under *Daubert* that the expert's opinion is insufficient. Of course, under this approach, the expert is put on notice and any further testing or supplementing that might be done, will be done, and affidavits of those results will be produced.

The best approach is to depose the expert and try to both expose insufficiencies and learn whether the expert has any answers to these insufficiencies. The strategy here is to discover what might be done to test the data, or improve the sufficiency of the data, or develop a known or knowable error rate, or determine if the methodology used was peer reviewed. If this work has been done—or peer review occurred, but has not been provided—you discover why it has not been done, or whether the results from the missing tests showed that the data was insufficient to support the data, or who did the peer review. This last approach is particularly effective when your expert has done the missing tests or analysis or has a methodology that has been peer reviewed. (The opposing expert's failure to provide that information earlier may also preclude some or all of her testimony.)

The last approach is based on the belief that it is better to know whether the expert will be able eventually to provide sufficient support than not to know what the expert's answer will be. It favors discovery over sandbagging so you can better know whether the opposing expert will be able to withstand a *Daubert* challenge.

---

2. Fed. R. Evid. 102.

CHAPTER EIGHT

DEPOSING AND DEFENDING THE EXPERT: TACTICS

The seven most useful answers are still pertinent,[1] and the expert must be cautioned to tell the truth, briefly, unless *Daubert* requires otherwise.

In taking the opposing expert's deposition—especially today when the time available for experts' depositions is limited by rule, court order, expense, or all three—extract the opinions and bases as early in the deposition as possible. Ask the expert to describe her methodology and bases in detail and articulate fully all the indicia of reliability you deem pertinent. The funnel technique, which moves from wide-open questions seeking new information to confirmation of known information and to testing of one's theories, is especially valuable with experts. As mentioned earlier, if you assume the role of an ignorant, but interested student, you may encourage the opposing to lecture about their opinions and methods.

Once you have completed the "discovery" part of the deposition, integrate the newly discovered information into a series of challenges to the expert's testimony. Depending on the number and type of opinions the expert says she is willing to give, these challenges can be regarding reliability of the method used for arriving at each opinion (whether peer reviewed, generally accepted, or possessing a known error rate, or testable), the sufficiency of the data consulted, and whether the method or methods were consistently applied. In addition, if time allows challenges can be made to fit between the qualifications of the expert and each opinion she is offering, or looking for bias in who hired the expert and the terms and conditions of that hiring.

8.1   Deposing Experts: Tactics

Many attorneys start the deposition of the opposing expert with a detailed examination of the expert's background.[2] Other attorneys spend a great deal of time taking the expert through a chronological recitation of how they were hired, what

---

1. *See infra* Chart.
2. Some attorneys call this a curriculum vitae even when they are referring to it in front of the jury. Casual empiricism suggests many jurors no longer speak Latin; some attorneys avoid the problem with Latin by referring to this as a résumé; indeed, French is not Latin. "List of credentials" may derive from Latin (or French or Greek), but it is currently English and, therefore, to be preferred.

they were shown, what they were asked to do, and what they did before reaching their opinion. There are several disadvantages with both of these approaches. In these days of limited time for depositions and increasing expense, especially for expert depositions, you should postpone questioning about those areas that are less likely to be informative, less likely to lead to material for cross-examination, and have a greater tendency to antagonize the expert and keep the expert from becoming the teacher. Additionally (especially with respect to the credentials), this material is easily checked by graduate student assistants outside of the cumbersome and expensive deposition or discovery process. Finally, in her preparation by opposing counsel, the expert was told: "They'll probably spend the first hour or so, maybe two, asking about your résumé, when we first contacted you, and what we told you. That's fine; it gets us almost all the way to lunch before we have to deal with any hard stuff." If you behave as predicted, you increase the expert's confidence in both herself and her counsel.

Instead, choose another topic, an important topic—one that the expert is most concerned about and one that must concern you as well. Ask the most important question first. In other words, ask the expert for her opinions. Her opinions are what distinguish her from the opposing expert. Her opinions are information you absolutely must know to prepare for trial. Her opinions are something she would much rather talk about after she has settled into the process and has become accustomed to your techniques and tempo. Her opinions are not what she wants to talk about immediately. So ask for her opinions first. Begin the opposing expert's deposition by asking her for all of her opinions. Ask her to list them all before going back to ask her to explain any individual opinion or give the bases for the opinion. The learning theorists say this provides the glass into which the expert will pour her opinion or the framework in which the expert will organize her presentation.

Such a preview of the structure of the deposition provides comfort on a number of levels. It provides you comfort because you can keep track of where you are—you can proceed in terms of importance by covering those things that are most important to you before getting to things that are of lesser importance. It provides comfort to the expert because it allows her to time the information she gives and to organize it to efficiently teach the lawyer what she knows and how she arrived at her opinions. This statement of opinions at the outset essentially becomes her teaching notes, so she can proceed in an organized fashion if you impress her as a student whom she wants to educate. Of equal importance, however, is the fact that you must learn the expert's opinions at the deposition, even if you learn nothing else; you could forego learning about aspects of her credentials or publications, her familiarity with your expert, or the details of her initial engagement if you are forced to leave some questions unasked. Of course, you go in armed with the expert report, which in theory contains the expert's opinions and identifies information being used. The danger of leaving the deposition with opinions undisclosed has therefore been somewhat reduced. Nevertheless, it is dangerous to rely on the opposing counsel and his expert to present a report with an adequate and informative statement of her opinions; because you choose the order of examination at the deposition, you should ask the expert for her opinions first and check to insure that those opinions are no more and no less than the opinions disclosed in the expert report.

Therefore, here is question number one at the expert deposition:

1. "What opinions have you reached in this matter?"

After obtaining the expert's statement of each of her opinions and taking the normal steps to satisfy yourself that the expert's knowledge of those opinions has been exhausted ("Are those all your opinions? You stated four opinions. Are there any more?" "Is there anything that would help you recall whether there are other opinions?" "Did you make any notes on your opinions?"), go back to the first (or most important, or most interesting) opinion, restate it for the expert, ask her to agree that it is her opinion, and then ask for the bases for that opinion. When questioning about the bases, the next five questions are recommended. (The first four are useful when having any witness describe any process.) Indeed, they are the same four or five questions you would use on direct examination to have an expert describe how she came to her opinions.

2. What did you do?

3. Why did you do that?

4. How did you do that?

5. What result did you get?

6. What significance does that result have to your conclusion?

Ask these same five questions to obtain the basis for each opinion. Ask the expert whether she has any additional bases. Are these all the bases? Did she make any notes on her bases? These questions make certain you have exhausted the expert's knowledge on relevant points.

There are many checklists on the market that claim to anticipate and to cure all problems that you might encounter in expert depositions. Some are interesting. Nevertheless, there is no real substitute for careful preparation, thoughtful questioning, attentive listening, and intensive follow-up. If you read your questions to insure you cover everything on your list while deposing an expert witness, the danger is you will become wedded to that list and not respond to the cues, the body language, the voice tone, and the pauses that signal the need for follow-up not contained in your notes. When used properly, reasonable checklists can stimulate your memory or imagination, but you must always be aware of the danger that they will become a crutch, keeping you from creative leaps and useful insights. If the deposition on oral examination could be reduced to a checklist, it would be called "deposition on written interrogatories."

Nevertheless, in the spirit of offering a quick and pithy checklist to provide for those in need, take the six questions above ("What are your opinions?" and the five follow-up questions) and these four following questions. Together they comprise a reasonably effective ten-question deposition:[3]

7. What are the reliable authorities in this field?

8. What assumptions did you make in your work?

9. What tasks did you not do?

10. Is this your current and accurate list of credentials?

One caveat: an ambush strategy may tempt you to examine an expert's report for things she has left out—a key area of necessary qualifications, the absence of evidence that she can meet the *Daubert* standard, or no mention of requisite legal standard. You may think it better to choose not to depose on these areas at the deposition and bring these omissions up at a pretrial hearing. (Some courts will require the lawyer to bring up *Daubert* objections pretrial to preserve them for appeal.) You may decide to surprise your opponent with a *Daubert* challenge rather than put him on notice of the witness's failing in time for the expert to supplement her report for trial. You may think that at the pretrial stage it will be too late for the plaintiff to rebut the challenge and the witness may be barred from testifying, which may allow you to succeed on a motion to dismiss. Note, however, the parties are allowed to supplement testimony with affidavit testimony at Rule 104 conferences—just as one can in a summary judgment motion. In addition, today most judges will not take the time to hold a hearing. They will instead order the parties to fully disclose the experts and present the depositions as their basis for opposing or supporting expert opinions. If you have support for your expert, you should present that support during your expert's deposition (prepare a direct examination, complete with things considered, reliability of methodology, consistency of application, and sufficiency of data.) When opposing, you should prepare a cross that demonstrates the unreliability of the opponent expert's methodology (lack of peer review, or lack of known error rate, for example, lack of consistency in application, and insufficient data). If the court allows the parties to supplement the expert's testimony with additional affidavits, then it is probably a better strategy to ask the witness about gaps in her opinion before she has a chance to talk with her counsel. Trial by ambush often does not work. It is better if to test your theories in the deposition so you will not be surprised by the response when it is too late to rebut. If, however, the court will not allow such supplementation, then your silence on such *Daubert* points at the deposition may be appropriate.

---

3. These ten questions are not intended to present the be-all and end-all of thorough deposition questioning of an opposing expert. They are not intended to capture all the nuances of subtle and sophisticated questioning of an expert, which may reveal hidden biases, untold assumptions, or imperfect calculations. They are intended to illustrate the main areas that must be covered in any expert deposition (with questions 1 through 9) or that can be covered (with question 10).

National Institute for Trial Advocacy

To recap, where the court will treat the deposition as the basis for the *Daubert* ruling, conduct the deposition as though it was a deposition to preserve the expert's testimony for trial. The proponents of the expert's testimony have an affirmative burden to put on sufficient evidence to establish the reliability of their expert case. If they do not do so, you might choose not to ask questions on those essential points and then move for preclusion, dismissal, or summary judgment.[4]

Here is another list of useful questions:

Expert Depositions

(All Things Considered)

♦ Who in the field agrees with you?

♦ Who in the field disagrees with you?

♦ What did you review and choose not to rely on?

♦ Who selected the documents you reviewed?

♦ Did you ask for anything you did not receive?

♦ Peer reviewed publication

♦ Error rate

♦ Acceptance in the field (*Frye*)

♦ Testability or

♦ Relevance (fit)

♦ Reliability (scientific foundation)

♦ Foundation for learned treatises

♦ Prior testimony (and rejections)

♦ Sources of income, percentages

Sometimes you go into the deposition of an expert already having discovered all that can be discovered about what the expert has done and not done to insure the reliability of her methodology. Your background work with your own expert (or with grad student research or on the Internet) put you in a position to move into a theory testing mode and forgo the discovery tactics described above. In these situations, the tactics of the deposing lawyer are very similar to those of a cross-examining lawyer. Instead of asking open-ended questions, you, as the deposing lawyer, will ask leading questions. First, get the expert to agree on definitions of key terms for measuring the success of a given method. Second, assert what the expert has done or not done and see if the expert will admit first that she did and not have perfect data and second that she did not have the ideal circumstances for collecting the data. After the expert admits that she lacks the full data, you can ask if her opinion lacked the testability features that might have been otherwise used to determine if there were other causes or whether there were confounding variables. Your purpose will

---

4. *See* Celotex v. Catrett, 477 U.S. 317 (1986).

be to see whether you can get the expert to admit that the data in a particular case was "insufficient" and that the reliability of the opinion was less than ideal, unique in some way, and therefor substantially compromised.

8.2   Rule 803(18): Learned Treatises as Nonhearsay

Federal Rule of Evidence 803(18) is, on its face, merely another exception to the rule excluding hearsay statements. In practice, however, it has become a powerful tool for cross-examining and impeaching expert witnesses. Rule 803(18) permits the introduction of relevant material from written sources that have been demonstrated as being reliable, either by the testimony of the proponent's expert, testimony of the opposing expert, or through judicial notice. The deposition provides an excellent opportunity to find out whether the opposing expert will concede the existence of reliable authorities in the field, which can be obtained and reviewed for use on cross-examination. The beauty of this approach to cross-examination is that the author of the materials, although functioning as a source of expert information in the case, is never hired, paid, deposed, or cross-examined. Indeed, she may not even earn a royalty on her book because the book itself does not come into evidence, but is merely read in pertinent part (and then can be returned to the library).

At the deposition, ask the expert what sources she consults when she has a question in her field and wants a second opinion; if she is a teacher, ask about materials she directs students to; ask about publications by colleagues in her company or college department—especially if she considers them useful. Her counsel may have warned her about the phrase "reliable authority," so she may shy away from providing useful answers to questions that use that language, but other language such as "useful," "well researched," or "important" will be sufficient at trial. Putting the language aside, if the expert admits to using a publication in her own work, she can hardly argue at trial that the work was not a "reliable authority." A question that is always useful at expert or lay depositions may be particularly appropriate in the learned treatise context: "How would you find out?" Ask where the expert would look for other approaches, where she checks her approach, where she looks for additional issues or to find more sources of help. If she needed help in understanding, where would she go? Did she cite sources in her last article because she thought their science was sound? Such a foundation should logically be sufficient under Rule 803(18).

Then, on cross at trial, you can call her attention to a portion of a text that favors you, reminding the expert that at deposition she considered the writing to be sound or authoritative. When read on the record, the material comes in as substantive evidence, whether she agrees or not.

The *Daubert* decision and its progeny have changed expert deposition practice substantially. When supporting expert testimony, you must demonstrate the reliability of the methodology; when challenging expert testimony, you have new authority to question the methodology. All of this adds new importance to the question of why an expert did a particular study or took particular steps because that "why" provides the connection (or exposes the lack of connection) between what the expert did and the results and their utility. When examining the reliability of methodology, you are looking for the reasonable causal nexus between what was done and the conclusion reached. When the logic of that connection is lacking (as when the astrologer opines the angle between Saturn and Jupiter makes Sagittarians prone to impulsiveness in matters of love), the court is likely to find that the reliability of the methodology has not been shown. Where an analysis of the logic is beyond the capability of a nonexpert court (as when dealing with questions of subatomic physics), you may profitably utilize proxies for an understanding of the causal relationships. Thus, *Daubert* suggests that the lawyers and trial courts look at whether an approach has been subjected to peer review through publication—presuming those peers will understand the process and point out errors when they read about it; or you should look at whether there is a known or knowable error rate—presuming that if it is known, the court can decide whether it is too high even without knowing what causes the errors, and if it is unknown, the court can reject that methodology as insufficiently proven to this point.

Daubert and the issues deriving from it are discussed in detail in chapters thirteen and fourteen, *infra*; the point here is the deposition is the opportunity to gather information for *Daubert* challenges or to prepare your own expert to defend the reliability of her methodology.

8.3   Expert Witness: Preparation

Just as with lay witnesses, you must prepare the expert witness for her deposition. Although most expert witnesses have had substantial public speaking experience—either in the classroom, at professional meetings, or even in the courtroom—they still may suffer from some anxiety at the thought of giving a deposition in front of lawyers in a very formal and artificial environment. Therefore, as with lay witnesses, spend some preparation time to reduce the witness's anxiety about the process so the witness is able to perform to her potential. To reduce the witness's anxieties, simplify the witness's task: explain to her that the only task she has at the deposition is to tell the truth, briefly. "Telling the truth, briefly" means providing accurate answers to questions after they are understood (and clarified if necessary) and stating those accurate answers in as short a way as possible without unnecessary adverbs, adjectives, parentheticals, footnotes, asides, qualifications, and other unrequested information.

Many expert witnesses are at first so frustrated by this direction that they abstain from volunteering additional information. Counsel will hear statements like, "Why can't I just tell them what I know? Won't that shorten the whole process?" Or, "I know where they're going. Why don't I just tell our side of this case?" In fact, the more volunteered information the expert includes, the longer the deposition will be.

When persuading expert witnesses that volunteering will not shorten their deposition experience, keep in mind the story of Sir Richard Francis Burton and John Hanning Speke, two noted explorers from the United Kingdom (Burton was Welsh, Speke was English) who are credited with following the Nile to its source at Lake Victoria. (Richard Francis Burton gained considerable fame for the discovery of the source of the Nile as Lake Tanganyika, although subsequent disclosures reveal he turned back before the source was found and left John Hanning Speke to continue the trip up the White Nile to its eventual source in Lake Victoria. Speke, in fact, was seriously wounded by natives during these trips, apparently being shot with arrows in both arms and legs and pierced through his body with a spear. Nevertheless, he continued.) Each time the Burton-Speke party reached a fork in the river in their travels, they had to establish a base camp and send part of their party to explore what seemed the less likely branch of the river. When that less likely branch was found to end in a backwater (so that it obviously was not the source of the Nile), that portion of the party returned to the base camp, they all packed up and then continued their exploration on the other branch of the river.

This is exactly how attorneys have learned to ask questions. Every time the witness uses an adjective or adverb or supplies additional unrequested information, the attorney feels compelled to ask about those forks in the testimony. For example, if the question is, "What color is your car?", the witness should answer, "Green." If instead the witness, expert or lay, responds, "I have a green Buick," then the attorney is faced with a fork: should he ask about why the color green was chosen, why a Buick was chosen, or does he already know enough to recognize the Buick does not lead him into any relevant waters? You need to find a way to use the Burton-Speke story or your own examples to persuade the expert witness that she does not want to help turn her deposition into the exploration of the Nile River. You do not want to spend weeks and months at this deposition—you want to spend hours, or perhaps a day. In the diagrams on the accompanying page, note the similarity between a map of the Nile and a "map" of a typically volunteered answer to the question, "What color is your car?" You might think about using those diagrams to make that point with your witness.

At this point in the litigation, you have already gone over with the expert where she fits into the case and how she supports your theories in the case. For plaintiffs in particular, the expert may be tasked with providing legally necessary support for certain essential elements in the case through her testimony. For example, a causation witness must testify at the deposition that she believes to a reasonable degree of certainty in her field that there is a causal relationship between the plaintiff's injury and the alleged conduct of the defendant. You should be careful to strike a balance in your "do not volunteer" instructions—you do not the expert to show any hesitancy; you do want her to testify fully and completely about her opinions on the causation elements or the elements on which you have the affirmative burden of proof. One way to test this distinction between volunteering unnecessary facts and volunteering essential facts is to use role-playing. In role-playing, you can teach your witness how she is to distinguish between inappropriate volunteering and contributing those essential elements she needs to contribute.

Role-playing takes a fair amount of time. It involves analyzing where the questions are likely to come from the opposing counsel and asking the follow-up questions the opposing counsel is likely to ask once the answers are given. During role-play, you should fully explore the answers your expert is giving to questions that touch on the essential elements of the case, and you should display a skeptical attitude toward the answers the witness gives so the rehearsal can truly prepare the expert for the skepticism of the opposing counsel. The practice sessions can show the expert the dangers of unnecessary volunteering and encourage the expert to be as forceful and direct as possible in those areas where her testimony is crucial to the case.

Fig. 1 – Map of the Nile

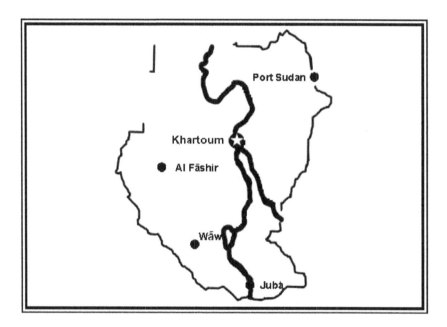

Fig. 2 – Car-тоum

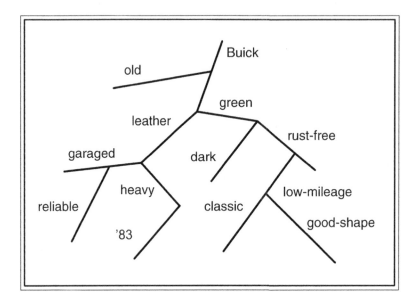

You should use role-playing to diagnose what type of expert witness you have. Is she a "master of the universe" type, where she comes off in an arrogant way, an overly confident way, and a way that shows she has lost her objectivity as she becomes involved in the case? Or on the other hand, is she overly hesitant, too concerned with making a mistake, and worried she may have said things in earlier testimony that will be used against her either in this case or in her professional arena? As you gauge where this expert falls in the spectrum between the "master of the universe" and the "nervous" witness, your job is to bring her to the middle—confident where she needs to be confident and careful where she needs to be careful.

When role-playing with the witness, be aware it can be confusing to the witness to have you, whom she has come to rely on as her guide through this process, adopt a cross-examination mode—more strident tone of voice, more piercing eye contact, more insistent demeanor—as you assume the role of opposing counsel at deposition. If you have adequate support, consider asking one of your colleagues to assume the role of opposing counsel; sit right alongside the witness as you will at the deposition, providing physical and moral support. Indeed, you should sit on the same side of the witness and keep the same side at the deposition so she becomes accustomed to having you there as her support. That way at the deposition, where the room and some of the people will be different, at least the important things—your physical and supportive relationship with her—will be the same. If you must conduct the role-playing deposition yourself, do not do it from your chair alongside the witness—that is the chair for her supporter—instead, leave that chair, sit down across the table where the opposing counsel will be, and conduct the cross-examination from there. As soon as you have finished the moot examination, make it clear that you are leaving the adopted role of the opposing counsel and that you are once again her supporter. Come back to your chair on her side of the table, turn partially to face her in this more friendly position, and remind her that you are in your normal role as her counsel.

As you prepare the expert witness to be examined at deposition, you should also review important documents—but here "important" has a slightly different meaning. The expert has some responsibility to explain to the opposition the interpretation and significance of the various documents she has considered as part of her analysis. Although she may consider many of those documents much less important than the core she intends to use in her trial testimony, nevertheless, she must be able to demonstrate a familiarity and comfort with them as opposing counsel asks her to explain them. Therefore, you will have to spend more time on documents with the expert than you do with lay witnesses. Have the expert explain the documents to you until you fully understand them. Then have her explain them again. The expert should make notations—even if they are decipherable only by her—on her copies of the documents if she feels making such notations will make her more comfortable and less likely to forget the relationship between various figures, entries, numbers, formulas, or other documentary content. Although you should recognize such notations may be discovered at the deposition as opposing counsel sees the expert referring to them, the presence of such notes is not improper, and the expert should have little concern about using them. Understand, however, that these are minimal notes, not major dissertations or caveats written in margins or along the bottom of several succeeding pages.

If the expert is asked at deposition if she reviewed documents in preparing for the deposition, her answer will obviously be "yes." Almost invariably, the opposing counsel will ask her to identify the documents she reviewed. If you know those documents have already been turned over to opposing counsel as part of the voluntary disclosure of expert materials, or as attachments to the expert report, or in the remainder of documentary discovery, there seems little harm in allowing the expert to identify the documents she reviewed. It is going to come out in any event, and there is no need to tie up any expert in some procedural battle between you and opposing counsel. If this matter has not been settled in the your jurisdiction, and if you still have the possibility of protecting attorney work product even though it has been revealed to the expert and is therefore considered by her, then you must make your objections at the deposition and direct the witness not to answer the question or the attorney work-product immunity from production will be lost.

The introduction of the word "considered" to the expert discovery vocabulary in Federal Rule of Civil Procedure 26(a)(2)(B) has created a significant distinction between the law relating to lay witness preparation and the law relating to expert witness preparation; with respect to the lay witness, documents that were reviewed, but did not refresh the witness's recollection—either because they were not effective in refreshing recollection or because the witness's recollection was already sound and did not need recollection—are not subject to production simply because they were reviewed. Unless the author of the document is counsel and therefore subject to protections of Rule 26(b)(4)(C), with the exceptions we discussed earlier, they may be subject to production because they were called for under requests for documents or subpoenaed or for other reasons, but their review in preparation for the deposition does not in and of itself make them produceable. However, that is no longer the case with expert witnesses. By reviewing the document in preparation for deposition, the expert may put that document in the category of all the other documents she has "considered," and as considered material it must be produced, subject only to the exceptions in jurisdictions that still permit some protection of materials that were considered, but are also attorney work product.

In addition, Federal Rule of Evidence 612 comes into play where you use documents to prepare to give deposition testimony. Your opponent is entitled under Rule 612 to examine any document used to refresh a witness's testimony with respect to the substance of their testimony. If your expert admits to having had her testimony refreshed, then the work-product protection is waived.

When you or your colleague has been questioning your expert in the manner of opposing counsel at the deposition during role-playing, you are trying to provide the expert with an opportunity to answer questions in a deposition context. Therefore, you probably used open questions—questions beginning with who, what, where, when, why, how, tell us, describe, or explain. By asking the questions the opposing attorney would ask at a deposition, you force your expert to craft an answer and to provide content to it. This is good practice for the expert and is an appropriate way to proceed in role-playing. As has been mentioned, this is also your opportunity to talk to the witness about the need for her to explain each of her opinions fully so the judge can understand it if the record of the deposition is used to support a dispositive motion.

Nevertheless, because of the way most attorneys ask questions at deposition, you and your expert can expect the overwhelming majority of questions asked will be closed: "did you," "do you," "have you," "were you," "was there," and the like. The expert needs guidance on how to answer these closed questions. While your advice to the expert has been to state her opinions fully and completely, it may not be appropriate to attempt those full and complete explanations in response to questions that call simply for "yes" or "no," or for some small bit of information like the color of her car or the name of her graduate student assistant. When faced with those closed or small questions, the expert must be authorized to give specific and equally narrow answers, so despite her desire to be heard and understood on her core issues, she accepts as proper the one- or two-word answers that dispose of the question. Therefore, review with the expert the same "seven answers to most deposition questions" that you provide lay witnesses.

The Seven Answers to Most Deposition Questions

♦   Yes.
♦   No.
♦   Green.
♦   I don't know.
♦   I don't remember.
♦   I don't understand the question.
♦   I need a break.

The first and second answers to most deposition questions for expert or lay witnesses will be "yes" and "no." If the questioning attorney has framed the question so it is properly answered with a "yes" or "no" answer, the expert is entitled to answer it "yes" or "no," and she has no responsibility to create a better question in her head and provide that better answer. Indeed, an attempt to improve the questioning attorney's performance will only lead to a longer deposition.

Unless the matter is one where the expert has a burden—concerns the reliability of her method, the consistency of application, and sufficiency of her data—the third best answer to most deposition questions is "green":

Q: What color is your car?

A: Green.

The witness should not answer: "My car is a green Buick." The questioner did not ask what kind of car the witness had, but on learning that it is a Buick, the questioner may feel compelled to ask both about the decision to buy a green car and the decision to buy a Buick. By referring back to the Nile diagram of the answer, "I have an old green Buick," the attorney can see that single question can present so many forks that the question, which could have been answered with the word "green," is now taking up fifteen minutes or half an hour of deposition time.

The fourth answer to most deposition questions is "I don't know." This answer is particularly hard for experts to give in deposition simply because they are experts, and as experts, they believe they are under some obligation to know everything that touches on the subject matter of their expertise. After all, they are thinking no self-respecting expert is ignorant, and the answer "I don't know" discloses ignorance. The expert must be assured in preparation that she is not obligated to know everything; in fact, there are things not related to her analysis that she legitimately does not know; there are matters she did not investigate and therefore does not know; and there may be other testimony or information in the case she has not yet reviewed and therefore does not know. The best answer in such circumstances is "I don't know." For proof, simply consider the alternatives. If the expert professes knowledge when she has none, nothing but trouble is ahead of her. Therefore, she must be authorized to state "I don't know" when that is the most accurate answer.

Answer four has an important caveat. When the question concerns the subject of her confidence in her results, and therefore relates to whether her method has an error rate or is testable, the expert should be prepared with an answer other than "I don't know." The expert might convert these questions into a statement of her confidence in her opinion or that she holds her opinion to a reasonable degree of certainty in her field.

A closely related answer at deposition is "I don't remember." This answer is distinguished from "I don't know" because it suggests the witness once had the information being sought, but can no longer remember. If that is true, this is the best answer for the witness, lay or expert. If the expert says that she does remember some information that she does not, she will not be able to deal intelligently with the follow-up questions that are sure to come. The way to avoid those embarrassing follow-up questions is to admit without embarrassment, "I don't remember."

No witness, lay or expert, is obligated to answer a question she does not understand. Most attorneys carefully instruct witnesses on this precise point as they approach the deposition. However, they often forget to tell the witness what to do when the witness does not understand the question. Tell the expert witness she is not obligated to answer any question she does not understand, and if she is asked a question she does not understand, she should say, "I'm sorry. I don't understand your question." Tell her to resist (what for an expert is an understandable temptation) suggesting ways in which the question could be fixed so she could understand and answer it. The likelihood is if she attempts such repairs, she will simply create more forks in the river—forks the questioner would never discover for himself, which he will feel compelled to explore, and which will further extend the deposition. On the other hand, if opposing counsel asks what word or concept in his question she does not understand, tell her not to be too cute, but to answer specifically, without volunteering optional meanings.

The seventh best answer to most deposition questions is simply "I need a break." If the expert witness for some reason believes that she cannot continue the deposition or if she is not comfortable without taking a break—a break to talk to her attorney, a break to call the office, a break to check on matters at home, a break to use the facilities, a break merely to walk up and down the hall, or a break to stretch and to reflect—then she should say, "I need to take a break." She can say it to opposing counsel, or she can say it in an aside to her attorney; but she should say it on the record. If she says it to you, her attorney, you should say, "We're taking a break," and then you should stand and take the witness out of the room for a break. Almost inevitably, opposing counsel will object, especially if the break occurs while a question is pending. It is much better deposition practice to answer the question before taking a break. In an aside with the witness, you might ask if she feels she must take the break before answering the question because there is something about the answer that concerns her—for example, the possibility of a privilege being involved. However, if the witness insists that she have a break before she provides an answer, then you have little choice other than to take that break. You must be available to provide counsel to the witness for matters of privilege or confidentiality, personal or professional, and your relationship with her depends on her continued confidence in your ability to protect her interests and meet her concerns.

In one sense, there is an eighth answer available at deposition to expert witnesses. An expert may be frustrated by what may fairly be characterized as trick questions, such as questions that ask whether she considered three factors that are completely irrelevant to any legitimate analysis. For example, an expert in diamond appraisal may be asked whether she considered prior ownership in assessing the value, or whether she spoke with the woman who was wearing the diamond when it was last photographed, or whether she had ever considered whether there was any relationship between the two words "carat" and "carrot." Instead of growing increasingly upset with such questions, she should be prepared to come back to her "core" positions, if they are at all responsive. She might say:

> Those matters need not be considered, because my opinion depends on the factors I have mentioned already, including cut, clarity, color, and carats; the demand in the market for diamonds of this particular quality and size; and the availability of such diamonds within a reasonable distance from the location of the purchaser. These items are so important, so overwhelmingly important, that other matters, such as you mention, are either relatively trivial or, like the ones you mention, completely irrelevant from a gemologists point of view. Cut, clarity, color and carats; demand and availability; that's what you need, and that's all you need.

Thus, instead of trying to defend whether the suggested additional factors can ever play a role and sometimes must be considered, she emphasizes her core positions and brings the discussion back to a focus with which she is comfortable. In a car accident case, a reconstruction expert, when asked whether he considered the location where the hubcap was found, in a field off the road, might say:

> The debris field was wide; nevertheless, the locations of the cars' frames and engines, the heaviest parts, in relation to the skid marks provided us with sufficient and persuasive data from which to reconstruct the movement of the cars before and after the impact. The location of the hubcap alone could not alter the conclusions we drew from the much more important information about the location of the tons of components we considered, all of which showed that your client's car crossed the center line and then struck the plaintiff's car.

Thus, instead of debating whether this or that small piece of evidence, perhaps aberrational, refuted her conclusions, the expert returns the focus to the mass of much more persuasive evidence that supports her opinions.

During preparation, press the expert to identify the "four pillars" that support her opinions (or the three or five). As long as those pillars remain intact on deposition and cross-examination, she need not worry greatly about bits and pieces of less important evidence, and she should not risk her credibility by trying to argue that, yes, she implicitly considered this, and yes, she implicitly considered that. She should instead consider whether the challenge in the question goes to her core concepts, the pillars, or the question is an attempt to get her to make some minor difference seem like a major theoretical or methodological dispute. It is when the expert tries to explain everything, the location of every hubcap and license plate screw, the behavior of every diamond-buyer in the market, that she risks overreaching and inconsistencies. Her theme might well be summed up by having her practice saying, "I don't know, and it really doesn't matter, why the hubcap wound up in the middle of the field; but I have spent 300 hours determining why the cars wound up trying to occupy the very same spot on US-91 at 3:00 p.m. on September 30, and the answer is that your client crossed the center line."

In addition, work with your expert to determine a place where the expert is being conservative. By identifying a conservative assumption, the expert can use it as a safe harbor, or a "run to" should she get pressed on specific topics where the sufficiency of the data is less than optimal.

8.4 Conclusion

Witness preparation of an expert can no longer be conducted by the "seat of the pants." If an expert is being deposed to rebuff a *Daubert* challenge, the seven "best answers" do not apply. But if the expert is a "master-of-the-universe" type and an egoist, likely to get herself into trouble by her arrogance and verbosity, then she needs "preparation" that involves some drilling to help her keep her answers short. Tailor your preparation advice to the case, the purpose of the deposition, and the personality of the deponent.

CHAPTER NINE

DIRECT EXAMINATION OF EXPERTS

9.1   Analyzing Expert Testimony

In analyzing the admissibility of expert testimony, Professor Imwinkelreid has provided a useful framework in an article entitled, "The Bases of Expert Testimony: The Syllogistic Structure of Scientific Testimony."[1] In that article, Professor Imwinkelreid suggests each expert presents a dichotomy when appearing in court; the major premise of that dichotomy, which in broad terms coincides with the requirements of Rule 702, consists of those characteristics the expert brings to the case: scientific field, credentials, credibility, experience, judgment, intelligence, personality, values, research, related engagements—all those things make the witness the expert that she is. Imwinkelreid's minor premise, roughly coinciding with the requirements of Rule 703, consists of all of the information the case provides to the expert: the facts, the data, the hypothetical, the character and credibility of the other witnesses, and the legal standards.

When trying to determine how to approach an expert witness, either for the purpose of organizing and simplifying direct examination or for the purpose of marshaling a challenge for cross-examination, this dichotomy is a powerful analytical tool. Imwinkelreid considers one of the most famous and well-publicized disputes in relatively recent times between Whittaker Chambers—columnist, author, and admitted former communist spy—and Alger Hiss—intellectual, lawyer, and government executive and advisor.

In 1948, the United States was experiencing one of its darkest episodes as Senator Joseph McCarthy conducted a witch hunt for communists in and out of the government. In this effort, McCarthy had the assistance of the famous House Un-American Activities Committee and a young congressman from California, Richard Nixon. Whittaker Chambers brought to the attention of the House Committee his role about twenty years earlier as a member of a communist cell

---

1. Edward J. Imwinkelreid, 67 N.C.L. Rev.1 (1988). Professor Imwinkelreid's views on experts are interesting not only because of his eloquence as a writer and his powers of evidentiary analysis, but also because he eventually helped the plaintiffs present briefs to the U.S. Supreme Court in *Daubert* and was permitted to file an amicus curiae brief in *Kumho Tire*. His insights into useful approaches to offering, analyzing, and challenging expert testimony therefore have special weight.

working in the United States to gather intelligence for the Soviet Union. In his congressional testimony, Chambers went on to identify Alger Hiss as a fellow traveler who supplied government information to him, Chambers, to send on to the Soviets. Hiss vigorously denied these charges and appeared before the Committee to confront his accuser.

The country sided with Hiss, entranced by his Ivy League background, Jimmy Stewart good looks, and previously untarnished reputation for integrity and public service. Chambers stuck by his accusations. Alger Hiss challenged Whittaker Chambers to repeat those accusations in an unprivileged forum (his committee testimony being privileged), and Chambers did in two radio broadcasts within the next few weeks. The country continued to support Hiss; much of the committee apparently supported Hiss; but Richard Nixon believed Chambers and pledged he would continue his investigation until he was proven right. After the radio broadcasts, Hiss sued Chambers, and at trial Chambers repeated his charges. He also repeated the story of an incident he had reported to the Committee. He claimed he had photographed secret papers Hiss had given him for the Soviets and then kept those microfilmed images in a hollowed-out pumpkin in his garden; these became famous as the "Pumpkin Papers." The Committee's staff found the papers in the pumpkin, and on examination, it was discovered the typography on those papers exactly matched a typewriter found hidden in the back of a closet in Alger Hiss's home. (Defenders of Hiss, loyal to the end, maintained this showed the true depravity of his detractors—that they would stoop so low as to manufacture a typewriter that exactly matched Hiss's typewriter so that fraudulent papers could be created.)

While Chambers gave this and the remainder of his testimony at trial, Hiss's lawyers were not idle, and when Whittaker Chambers finished his direct and cross-examination, the Hiss attorneys called to the stand a man who had been sitting in the front row of the spectator section of the courtroom. He was revealed to be a psychologist, and he stated he had watched Whittaker Chambers throughout his entire testimony—he had carefully observed his body language, his speech pattern, his pauses, his intonation, his eye movements—and based on such observations, he was able to determine Whittaker Chambers's truthfulness. "What is your opinion about whether Whittaker Chambers is telling the truth?" asked Hiss's attorneys. "In my opinion," responded the psychologist, "Whittaker Chambers is a compulsive liar who is incapable of telling the truth, and he is not telling the truth now."

So the time came for cross-examination of the psychologist by Whittaker Chambers's counsel. The attorneys challenged the psychologist by demanding that he admit the science of psychology was not sufficiently advanced to allow it to identify compulsive lying; it was an uncertain, soft science and could not be relied on to provide accurate results. In retrospect, it is obvious the attorneys were challenging the major premise from Imwinkelried's dichotomy: what the expert brought to the case. They were challenging the field of psychology itself, the expert's reason for being, and the utility of a psychologist in these circumstances. In short, their challenge was to the field of psychology and could not have been framed in a manner more likely to arouse the psychologist's defenses. Imwinkelreid's mode of analysis suggests Chambers's attorneys should have considered the alternative approach of a challenge to the minor premise: here the questions could have ceded the ability of psychologists under the proper conditions and with adequate time and appropriate tools—such as written tests, statements, or controlled and comparative studies—to determine the willingness or ability of a patient to tell the truth; and then they could have gone on to demonstrate item by item that this case did not provide the field of psychology with an adequate basis for such analysis. Instead, Hiss's attorneys unfairly asked the psychologist to observe a person in the artificial arena of a courtroom, acting under the extreme stress of direct and cross-examination, sitting isolated in a witness chair, under the eyes of courtroom spectators and the national press and public—and then conclude from the sweat on his upper lip or his raised eyebrows that he was incapable of telling the truth. In these circumstances, the minor premise attack seems much more likely to obtain some support from the witness. (A federal indictment of Hiss interrupted the civil lawsuit, and he was convicted of perjury and jailed from 1950 to 1954.)

Inwinkelreid's dichotomy is particularly useful to you as you are getting ready to move from the deposition setting to the trial setting. With the dichotomy in mind, you may be able to structure direct examination more clearly to highlight the expert's qualifications to give testimony and to display the extensive information available to the expert on which she bases her testimony. Armed with the deposition transcript of the expert, you can identify potential major premise attacks and differentiate them from the minor premise attacks as a final step in the preparation for both the direct and the cross-examination at trial.

9.2 Preparing the Expert for Direct Examination

You need to again prepare your expert witness before she gives her testimony at trial. Here, the focus needs to be on the different audience for her testimony. The expert needs to turn her attention from persuading a lawyer and the opposing client to teaching the jurors in a way that will make the testimony understandable and consistent with the jurors' common sense. Many lawyers use a preparation process similar to what they have used in deposition preparation, which includes reminding the witness where she fits into the theory of the case; reminding the witness of the documentary evidence that she will need to refer to, including the three or four most important documents she has prepared or will be shown to support her opinion; and taking her through a rehearsal of the actual direct examination and cross-examination, giving her the confidence that comes from already having been put through the process. This also reminds her of answers she has given in her deposition to protect her from impeachment.

Now you should work hard with your expert to come up with those teaching devices (geared to an eighth-grade ability) that will help the jurors follow and understand the expert's testimony. Create visual aids with the expert. Have the expert do dry runs at using a white board, demonstrating key parts of the testimony and describing analogies that are consistent with what you know about the jurors' life experiences.

One additional issue to raise with the expert is where she ought to look—where her eyes ought to be during the direct examination. Some experts "mug" to the jury too much. Her eyes should be on you while you are asking a question on direct examination, and she should play to the jurors only when the focus of the testimony is on teaching them about the opinions she has in the case. Smiling at the jurors or rolling her eyes while the cross-examiner asks a question gives the impression the expert is insincere and does not take the proceeding seriously enough. She should be polite and patient in her answers on cross-examination. Tell the expert it is not her job to win the case. Explain that there is no need for her to try to repeat testimony—you will do that if it is appropriate when you makes your closing argument. The most important thing for her to do is to maintain her appearance of objectivity and to focus her energies on teaching the jurors about the case and about her opinion.

In video-recorded depositions to preserve expert testimony, have the expert use the actual visual exhibits and then perhaps splice in close-ups of those exhibits in the video you present at trial; at appropriate moments, place the actual exhibit in front of the jurors, next to the screen or television. This mixed-media presentation of the exhibits that the expert is using in the deposition makes the expert's recorded testimony seem more real allows the jurors to better follow the deposition testimony. After the testimony is over, provide the jurors with individual copies of the visual exhibits; if you do it during the testimony, the jurors may look at the exhibits instead of listen to the expert witness. The courtroom foam board showing the exhibits can be moved around, used with other witnesses, and left on the easel during other parts of your case to give the exhibits more substance and reality in the judge's and jurors' minds.

Include the expert in site photographs or videos of demonstrations and views. Such photographic evidence not only shows the jurors what the site looks like or how the test or experiment was done (crash tests, accident reconstructions, product experiments), but it also shows the expert was right there, sleeves rolled up, involved in the gathering of genuine, honest-to-goodness evidence that you cannot find in a classroom or library. Such credibility enhancement is so valuable that you should actively look for these opportunities to involve his expert.

9.3 Expert Direct Examinations

On Mother's Day on the dusty streets of downtown Chicago near the corner of LaSalle and Washington, a young clerk stood behind the counter at Burger King.[2]

---

2. Based on United States v. Tranowski, 659 F.2d 750 (7th Cir. 1981).

It had been a slow day. A customer walked in, a man in his twenties, and he ordered a Whopper (hold the onions), two colas, and fries. The clerk bagged the food, and the customer handed over a five-dollar bill. The clerk took the bill, but remembered what his manager had said in a staff meeting just a few days earlier, that someone was passing counterfeit five-dollar bills in the downtown area and the police had warned them to be careful. This bill looked a little funny, so the clerk said to the customer, "Wait, I have to get change from the back," and he took the five-dollar bill back to the manager's office.

The manager agreed the bill looked suspicious, so he and the clerk went back to the counter to ask some questions of the customer. The customer saw them coming with the five-dollar bill, and grabbing the Whopper, drinks, and fries, he took off running, through the front door and down the street. The clerk followed with the manager on his heels, and they chased the customer under the elevated tracks, through alleys, across streets, and even through a neighborhood soccer game. The soccer players thought that running with adults through the streets of Chicago would be more fun than playing soccer, so they joined the chase until finally after a mile or more, they lost the customer after he ran through an alley and disappeared between buildings. They recovered the drinks and fries; the Whopper was lost forever.

But one of the soccer players was struck by the appearance of the customer and could not get the thought out of his mind that he had seen the man before. His questions were not answered, however, until a few days later when he was in the neighborhood drugstore buying a candy bar, and the images clicked into place. "Mr. Schultz," he said, turning to the pharmacist who ran the store, "you know the man that comes in here every Saturday morning and buys the *Tribune* and a box of powdered doughnuts?" "Sure," replied Schultz. "That's Stanley Tranowski. He lives around the block in the little house with the cedars in the front." Persuaded that Tranowski was the man they had been chasing several days earlier, the soccer player went to the neighborhood precinct house, where the police were very interested to hear about Stanley Tranowski.

Within the hour, police, soccer player, clerk, and manager were on the steps of the Tranowski home. They knocked. Stanley answered. "That's him!" said the clerk, soccer player, and manager. "Hello, Stanley," said the police.

About three months later, the Assistant U.S. Attorney for the Northern District of Illinois presented this story through the evidence of his witnesses in federal court. The jury looked with conviction at Stanley Tranowski, but his defense case had yet to be heard. As the first and only defense witness, defense attorney called Walter Tranowski, Stanley's brother. "Mr. Tranowski, where were you on May 24 of this year?" asked Stanley's attorney. Walter answered, "That was Mother's Day Sunday, and I spent it with my brother, Stanley, and my mother. I went over to pick Mom and Stanley up early, and we went out for breakfast. Then we took a ride, and in the afternoon, we had to take Mom to a wake for one of her friends. Afterward, we went to a Rustler Steak House for dinner. We didn't get home until late in the day." "Could Stanley have been at the Burger King at LaSalle and Washington at about 12:30 that day?" "No," said Walter, "he was with me all day, and I can prove it. Here's a picture," he said, handing over a photograph he had in his pocket. "I took this picture on that Mother's Day at about 12:30 or 1:00 in the afternoon in front of Mom's house. See, there's Mom, that's Stanley, and, oh, that's Jerry, our dog. So you can see Stanley couldn't have been at a Burger King. This shows he was with us."

Persuasive testimony indeed, complete with family pet. However, the Assistant U.S. Attorney was not finished. In rebuttal, he called the only type of expert witness one could imagine using in a case such as this involving counterfeit money, Whoppers, soccer, pharmacists, and pets—an astrophysicist, Dr. Smithson.

Dr. Smithson took the stand and told the jury she was a professional astrophysicist employed by the Chicago Planetarium. Her current project, she said, was to measure the mountains on the moon. Many had been measured, but many remained unmeasured. She was asked how she did this while sitting there on the shores of Lake Michigan, and she gave the following explanation:

> From tables compiled over hundreds of years and now verified to great accuracy by computer, we know all the angles that occur at any given time between the sun, the moon, the earth, and each of the other planets. Therefore, when I look at the moon and the mountains on it, I know the angle at which the sun is striking those mountains. I measure the length of the shadows, which the sun casts, and using that length plus the sun's angle and simple trigonometry, I can calculate the height of the mountain that casts the shadow.

The prosecutor asked whether she could calculate the length of the shadow if she was given the angle of the sun and height of the mountain.

Smithson:	Of course. It is a simple formula, and you can solve it no matter which factor is unknown.
Prosecutor:	Could you solve it for the angle of the sun if you knew the length of the shadow and the height of the mountain?
Smithson:	Yes, of course. It's exactly the same problem.
Prosecutor:	And if you knew the angle of the sun, what else would you know?
Smithson:	Well, you would obviously know the location of the sun or, more properly, the location of the moon with respect to the sun, and that would give you information about the date on which your observation was made.

Prosecutor:	Let me hand you Defense Exhibit 17 in evidence and ask if you have seen this before.
Smithson:	Yes, that's a photograph showing Stanley Tranowski, his mother, and Jerry, their dog. You gave that to me last month and asked if I could do some calculations.
Prosecutor:	Were you able to do those calculations?
Smithson:	Yes, I was.
Prosecutor:	What did you do?
Smithson:	Well, with you and a police officer and a surveying crew, we went out to the Tranowski house. We determined how the house was oriented according to the point of the compass, and we also determined that there was negligible slope to the property, at least that portion of it shown in the photograph.
Prosecutor:	Did you do anything else?
Smithson:	Oh, yes. We measured Jerry, the dog. We had him sit as he is sitting in the picture, and we measured him from the ground to the top of his head. He was very cooperative. Nice dog.
Prosecutor:	And what were you able to do with these measurements and calculations?
Smithson:	You can see from the photograph that Jerry's shadow is the only complete shadow in the picture. That was fortunate because it allowed us, since we knew Jerry's height and can measure the length of his shadow in the photograph, to determine the angle of the sun at the time the photo was taken. From that information, performing essentially the same calculations as I do every day as an astrophysicist at the planetarium, I consulted the tables for information on the date.
Prosecutor:	Then, are you able to tell us the date on which this photograph was taken?

And she said, looking confidently at the jury and then disdainfully at Stanley Tranowski:

> No. But I can tell you the date on which it wasn't taken. The sun is in the same place in the sky twice a year on its apparent journey south and on its apparent return journey north. Therefore, I can tell you that this photo was taken either on February 11 of this year or on October 23 of last year, but it was not taken on Mother's Day.

The jury looked at Stanley Tranowski and said, "Guilty." And in the subsequent trial of Walter Tranowski for perjury, the jury said, "Guilty," again.

In the next section, the introduction, structure, and evidentiary foundation of this expert examination will be examined in detail. At this point, however, it is of singular importance to note the prosecuting attorney, through his creativity and planning, presented an expert witness who was guaranteed to entertain and interest the jurors—the hallmarks of an expert who will be able to persuade.

9.4   Outline of Testimony

Your task is to persuade the jurors to believe your expert and to accept her opinions over those of some opposing expert. To begin, put one principle above all others: interesting expert testimony persuades jurors. By definition, the subject of an expert's testimony is not well known to the average juror. Work hard to maintain their interest so that they will be sufficiently persuaded to make a "leap of faith," accepting the expert's opinions as true even if they do not understand all the technical, methodological details.

A well-organized direct examination contributes greatly toward creating the necessary interest. Logically organized material encourages the jurors to conclude that the opinions supporting the case were logically developed.

For every case, you should organize your expert's direct examination following this outline of testimony:

1. Introduction
2. Tickler
3. Qualifications
4. Tender
5. Opinions
6. Bases for the opinions
7. Anticipating cross-examination
8. Save a Point for Redirect and or End Strong

9.4.1 Introduction

During the first few minutes of your expert's testimony, you should establish a rapport between the witness and the jurors. For example, you should show the jurors that your expert is a real person—a neighbor, perhaps. Note the following exchange, as it might have happened in the case of "Jerry, the Dog":

Q: What is your profession, Dr. Smithson?

A: I am a professional astronomer here in Chicago with the Chicago Planetarium.

Q: And where do you live?

A: I live just outside the city on Sherman Avenue in Evanston near Northwestern University. I've lived here for twenty-three years.

Another way to establish rapport is to associate the expert with a local, well-respected institution. By doing this, you emphasize the fact that you have not brought in a "hired gun."

If the expert has no local ties, you will want to demonstrate that she comes from a prestigious institution or is so well recognized as a leading expert in the field that where she comes from is irrelevant. Mentioning these associations in the introduction immediately shows the jurors that this witness is special and worth consideration. One way to do this in an unpretentious way is to prepare the expert to answer your question of what astronomers do by using examples that might be interesting to our proverbial "eighth grader."

9.4.2 Tickler

Make your introduction brief, so you can spend most of your time persuading the jurors. Capture their attention by immediately explaining the expert's relevance to the case. The following question from "Jerry, the Dog" demonstrates this point:

Q: Dr. Smithson, have you come to court today prepared to state your expert opinion on whether this photograph [*holding up exhibit*] was taken on Mother's Day, as Walter Tranowski swore under oath?

A: Yes, I am prepared to state my opinion as to whether the photograph was taken on Mother's Day.

This device, called the "tickler," enables skilled attorneys to "tickle" the jurors' imaginations by stating the theory of the case almost as soon as the witness takes the stand. The tickler also suggests to the jurors that the expert agrees with that theory.

To insure this approach succeeds, alert your expert in advance that you will ask the question in just this way and that you do not want her opinion at that point. Neither the court, counsel's opponent, nor the jurors would be ready for it.

At this point, the jury will have heard your theory of the case twice—first in your own words in the opening statement and again in your "tickler" question to the expert. Repeating theory and themes effectively nudges the jurors toward the conclusion that your theory is correct.

9.4.3 Qualifying the Expert

As you move from the tickler to your witness's qualifications, create a transition that explains how these qualifications are relevant to the case the jurors must decide.

> Q: Before we get to that opinion, Doctor, I would like to ask you about your training and education that qualify you to form such an opinion.

You are now ready to address your expert's qualifications. Credentials give weight to the expert's opinions. However, human nature being what it is, jurors are not automatically interested in someone else's education and job history. Persuade them that it is in their interest to pay attention to these credentials. Continue the qualifications with the approach that began in the tickler: establish a connection between the expert and the case. Show the jurors that these background facts have a direct relationship to the expert's opinions and to their decision.

Consider how this might have been done in the case of "Jerry, the Dog":

> Q: Dr. Smithson, as part of your studies for your doctorate in astronomy, what courses did you take that related directly to your work in this case on the photograph?
>
> A: Well, I had several. One course was concerned entirely with solar system measurements and geometry, and I used that information extensively when I did the calculations relating to the dating of this photograph.
>
> Q: What is solar system geometry, Dr. Smithson?
>
> A: Solar system geometry is the study of the mathematical relationships among the locations of the sun, the planets, the moons, and other objects in the solar system. Studying these relationships allows us to predict solar or lunar eclipses; track comets; and guide rockets, the space shuttle (once upon a time), and planetary probes.
>
> Q: And in analyzing this photograph, did you have to consider the location of the sun and planets?
>
> A: Yes, I did—at least the sun, the moon, and the planet Earth, and, of course, the Tranowski's house.

Q: Now, Dr. Smithson, what professional position did you hold before you came to the planetarium here in Chicago?

A: I was a consultant for Rand McNally, the mapmakers. In fact, I still am a consultant at Rand McNally—part-time.

Q: Did your work at Rand McNally relate to the work you undertook in this case to put a date on this photograph?

A: Yes. In fact, it related very closely to this work. At Rand McNally, I helped to verify precise locations by measuring sun, star, and planetary angles. When you know the date, you can use the angles of those bodies to determine your location here on earth with great accuracy.

Q: And how does that relate to the work you did here, Dr. Smithson?

A: In the present case, I knew the location and some of the angles, and I wanted to determine the precise date. It is essentially the same calculation, just solving it for the date instead of the location.

Q: Dr. Smithson, let's turn to your work at the planetarium . . . .

The phrasing of these questions told the jurors before they heard the answer that the expert's work and education related to "Jerry, the Dog" in a direct and understandable way. That motivated them to pay attention to her qualifications and any other aspect of this expert's background that was pertinent to the testimony.

During this phase of testimony, you will present the expert's list of credentials. Have it marked by the clerk and authenticated by the witness, and then offer it in evidence. Although it is hearsay, the court will normally receive it because it is efficient to do so.

Do not recite the résumé. Select some of the most relevant books, articles, jobs, or speeches, and have the witness explain to the jury their relevance to the case. Back to "Jerry, the Dog":

Q: Doctor, have you written any articles relating to the question of how the angle and direction of the sun can be used to establish the day of the year?

A: Yes. In fact, I have written several papers that relate to that type of calculation.

Q: Would you tell us how they relate?

A: Of course. These articles deal with special situations encountered as we try to gain information about our solar system. One of them describes the geometry and mathematics needed to calculate the size of features, like rocks or hills, on Mars by using the shadows they cast plus the angle and elevation of the sun.

Q: Doctor Smithson, would using a diagram help you describe the work in that article?

A: Yes, it would. In fact, we have one that was printed with that article.

Q: All right. With the court's permission, will you step down to the easel and continue your answer, using this exhibit?

A: Yes, of course. If you know the size of the feature and the length of the shadow, you could just reverse the usual process and calculate the angle and elevation of the sun. From that information, you can calculate the date, or, actually, the dates, since the sun is at a particular angle and elevation twice in each earth year.

Note that although you are still concentrating on qualifications, you already have your witness giving opinions and testimony linking her expertise to issues of the case, which moves the jurors along the path of persuasion.

If your jurisdiction discourages or prohibits qualifying a witness in open court, remember the jurors can also consider qualifications as bases for expert testimony. Simply postpone and slightly reword your questions to accomplish everything you need to display the expert's credentials. For example:

Q: Dr. Smithson, we have now looked at several of the bases for your opinion that this photograph was not taken on Mother's Day. Are there others?

A: Yes, one further basis. I carefully reviewed all of the literature on similar calculations, including my own article in *Astronomy Magazine*, and determined that my approach was correct.

Q: How did your article in *Astronomy Magazine* affect your conclusion the photo was not taken on Mother's Day?

A: That article dealt with the measurement of the size of features on Mars, using shadows and the angle and elevation of the sun . . . .

Bases are qualifications, and qualifications are bases. Think of qualifications as the portion of the expert's bases you show the court, preliminarily, to satisfy the judge that it makes sense to allow your expert's opinion testimony. Whether presenting qualifications or bases, your questions are intended to impress the jurors with the reliability of his expert's work in the case so that they will give weight to these opinions. Of course, you should have your expert explain the demanding work of preparing an article for publication in a peer-review journal, because some jurors may not know what publishing in a peer-reviewed journal entails.

During your persuasive qualification of your expert, your opponent may offer to stipulate to this foundation to limit testimony. If the court encourages you to accept the stipulation, you can still make an effort to get the qualifications into the record at that point simply by responding:

> Direct Examiner: Your Honor, I appreciate the offer to stipulate to the qualifications and expertise of Dr. Smithson, and I accept it. I would like the court's permission to briefly touch on a few elements of Dr. Smithson's education and experience as a professional astronomer so the jurors can decide how much weight to give her testimony.

As illustrated, respond by emphasizing the jurors' responsibility to determine the weight to give testimony, expert or nonexpert. And if you attorney say, "Briefly," be brief! Do not abuse the court's good graces. If the court expresses its impatience with the length of the qualifications, simply ask about the important qualifications during the bases part of your examination.

Some, like noted trial lawyer Michael Tigar, suggest organizing the direct examination in a way that moves you quickly through qualification:

> Q: Have you prepared a list that will summarize your experience, education, and training?
>
> A: Yes, I have.
>
> Q: I show you Exhibit 15. What is this?
>
> A: It is the list that I have prepared.
>
> Direct Examiner: I move to admit Exhibit 15 into evidence.

Then show the exhibit on the overhead and highlight the three most important qualifications in this case.

This approach has the advantage of brevity. However, it does not seem to play a significant role in satisfying the burden of persuasion that belongs you and your expert. While most courts will allow you to introduce the résumé or list of credentials without question (even though it is technically hearsay), the more important question remains whether the credentials, when presented in this way, fulfill any role beyond satisfying the judge that the expert may be heard.

9.4.4 Tender

After laying the foundation under Federal Rule of Evidence 702 to qualify your expert to offer opinion testimony, you are then ready to make what is traditionally called the "tender" of the witness. The tender is the formal presentation to the court of the expert and her qualifications. A properly phrased tender concisely summarizes the expert's testimony up to this point. It aims to signal to the court and your opponent that you have completed qualifying your witness as an expert and are ready for the opponent's voir dire of the witness and the court's ruling whether the witness may testify as an expert. A formal tender, when permitted by the court, also reminds the jurors of the relevance of the expert's testimony.

Depending on where you practice, a tender of the witness may be permitted or even required. The following example in the case of "Jerry, the Dog" demonstrates a formal tender:

Direct Examiner:	Your Honor, I tender Dr. Smithson to the court as an expert in the field of astronomy and astronomical mathematics and submit that she is qualified by reason of her education, experience, and training to provide expert opinion testimony on the question of whether Walter Tranowski took the photograph in question on Mother's Day.

The formal language of this tender, while sounding somewhat stilted, actually accomplishes five objectives:

1. It signals the court that you have finished the qualifications, and it is now time for the court to rule whether your expert may give opinion testimony.

2. It reminds the jurors of the relevance of the expert's testimony.

3. It gives you another opportunity to present your theory of the case.

4. It defines the scope of the expert's testimony so the court can decide whether the testimony is within the expert's qualifications.

5. It signals that it is time for voir dire by opposing counsel.

Even if the court frowns on formal tenders, you can usually signal the court that you have completed the qualifications and are ready to proceed:

Direct Examiner:	Your Honor, we have now completed the portion of Dr. Smithson's testimony dealing with her credentials as an expert astronomer. May we proceed?

9.4.5 *Opinions*

Make the presentation of the opinion dramatic. Draw the jurors' attention to it. Set it apart from what led up to it and from what follows it. Pause, then do something as simple as clearing the board of graphics. Get a different notebook from the lectern or simply change position in the courtroom before resuming the questioning. Remember the jurors know from your "tickler" question that your expert will render an opinion on the subject in question, and they should be prepared to hear it. Ask for your expert's opinion in formal language to call attention to it and to assure the judge you have followed the legal formalities.

In the case of "Jerry, the Dog," the expert witness examination might proceed as follows:

Q: Dr. Smithson, we have now reviewed your qualifications as an expert to present your opinion on whether this photograph of Mom, Stanley, and Jerry, the dog was taken on Mother's Day. Now, let us get to that opinion itself.

Do you have an opinion that you hold with a degree of certainty reasonable in the field of astronomy as to whether Walter Tranowski did indeed photograph Mom, brother Stanley, and Jerry, the dog on Mother's Day?

A: Yes, I do.

Q: And what is that opinion, Doctor?

A: This photograph was not taken on Mother's Day. It may have been taken on February 11, or it may have been taken on October 23 of last year, but it was not taken on Mother's Day.

The formal language used here calls attention to the opinion and gives it weight. The terminology, "reasonable degree of certainty," is also required in virtually identical language in many jurisdictions.

Where the expert will give more than one opinion:

1. Determine which opinions are major and which are subsidiary. State them consistently with the theory.

2. Highlight the major opinions by mounting them on a board, poster, or flip chart.

3. Put all the major opinions on the board, projector, or pad simultaneously to serve as an outline of the opinion testimony for the jurors to follow.

4. Introduce the major opinions with the same language, "an opinion that you hold with a degree of certainty reasonable in the field," to alert the jurors an important opinion is coming.

5. For the minor opinions, use less formal language, and introduce them in a more conversational way. This leaves the most emphasis where you want it—on the major opinions. The following bit from "Jerry the Dog" illustrates this:

   Q: Dr. Smithson, in your opinion, how accurate is your calculation that shows the photograph was not taken on Mother's Day?

   A: Well, actually, I don't think I could be off by more than fifteen minutes on the time on those days the picture was taken. There is really very little chance my calculation of the day could be wrong by more than two days either way.

   Q: Now, you have told us you used charts of the sun's angles at various times of year. Do you consider the charts to be a reliable source of that information?

   A: Oh, yes. These charts have been prepared by the most reliable scientists in our field, and they have been published and used for so many years as the basis for calculations like this that any errors would have been discovered and corrected long ago.

6. When eliciting multiple opinions, each with more than one basis, use graphics for the bases and color-code the opinions and the bases: everything on the board that has a green strip relates to the green-coded opinion. If you have outlined your expert's major opinions on a board, list bases and minor opinions under the major opinions they support.

7. As you complete the discussion of the opinion and its bases, restate the opinion to reinforce it with the jurors and signal that you have finished discussing that opinion.

   Q: Now Dr. Smithson, have we discussed all of your bases for concluding that Walter Tranowski did not take this photograph of Mom, Stanley, and Jerry, the dog on Mother's Day?

   A: Yes, we have.

   Q: All right. Let's turn then to your second opinion . . . .

When the witness answers "yes," move the strip for that opinion to the side, and move another opinion strip to the center of attention. This transition introduces the next opinion.

9.4.6 Bases

After you have introduced all of the major opinions, go back to the first and tell the witness (and implicitly the jurors) that you want to outline the process by which the expert arrived at that opinion. Be sure to remove references to the other major opinions from his graphics board. Question in the following format:

Q: What did you do?

Q: Why did you do that?

Q: How did you do that?

Q: What result did you get?

Q: What is the significance of that result?

This is how these questions might have been used in the case of "Jerry, the Dog":

Q: Dr. Smithson, what did you do in measuring the angles in the photograph?

A: Well, working with an enlargement so I could be as accurate as possible, I calculated the angle of the sun in the sky.

Q: Why did you do that?

A: I did that to locate the sun in the sky in terms of its apparent travel from east to west and its location north-south.

Q: How did you calculate that angle?

A: I constructed a line from the end of Jerry's shadow to the highest part of Jerry's head, which cast that shadow. That line would therefore be aimed directly toward the sun, which was causing the shadow.

Q: On this enlargement of the photograph of Jerry, the dog, will you show us what you did?

A: Yes. Here's the end of Jerry's shadow on the ground, and here is the top of Jerry's head, which is casting that shadow. With a straight-edge, I drew a line from the end of the shadow to the top of Jerry's head and beyond. I also drew a baseline from the end of the shadow along the ground where Jerry was sitting. The angle between the baseline and the line toward the sun gave the angle of the sun in the sky. I also measured Jerry, the dog on a visit to that house and used that measurement and the length of the shadow to confirm my calculations of the angle.

Q: What result did you get?

A: Measurement of the angle showed it to be 57 degrees, 18 minutes, 32 seconds.

Q: What significance does that measurement of 57 degrees, 18 minutes, 32 seconds have in your conclusion that this photograph was not taken on Mother's Day?

A: That provides me with one half of the information I need to locate the sun precisely. I need the angle up from the horizon, which is called the "angle of ascension," and I need the angle down from the North Pole, which is called the "angle of declination." Once I have those two numbers, I can determine the date because the sun is only in that particular location on two days each year—once on its apparent trip north in the summer, and once on its trip back south as winter comes.

As always, visually support the expert's testimony with graphics. Additionally, with an expert you will normally want to ask a question such as:

Q: What significance does that result have in coming to your opinion that Stanley Tranowski did not take this photo of Mom, Walter, and Jerry, the dog on Mother's Day?

Having outlined the process for arriving at a major opinion, go back and recreate the analysis leading to the opinion. Consider this example:

Q: [*In front of board with several opinions on it.*] Dr. Smithson, you have told us you have opinions on each of these subjects. Let me clean this board off, and let's go back to the first opinion you stated, that Walter Tranowski's photograph was not taken on Mother's Day.

    Doctor, let's now discuss your bases for that opinion. Could you outline them for us, and then we'll come back and discuss them in more detail?

A: Yes. My first basis was the determination of the angle of the walls of the house and the precise location of the house in terms of its latitude, so I could have a reference point. I actually visited the house for that purpose.

Q: If I put "house angle" up here, will that help keep track of that point?

A: Yes, I should think so. My next basis is the measurements I made from the photograph itself. Measurements of the angle and the length of shadows and figures.

Q: I'll put "measurements from photograph" up, OK?

A: Yes. Next, I made measurements of Jerry, the dog because Jerry was the only figure in the photograph who cast a completely visible shadow.

Q: OK. [*Puts up measurements of Jerry, the dog.*] Did you have any other bases for your opinion that this photograph was not taken on Mother's Day?

A: Yes, one last one. That is the astronomical charts that allowed me to take those measurements and determine the days when the photograph could have been taken.

As your expert testifies, follow with visual reinforcement to increasingly involve and persuade the jurors of the importance and logic of his expert's testimony. Where the court allows, it is even more interesting if the expert makes the notes at the board.

9.4.7 Anticipating Cross-Examination

In any case, you can anticipate at least two likely lines of challenge to your expert's testimony. One questions the expert's assumptions; the other questions all the things the expert did not do—materials not reviewed, people not interviewed, and calculations not made. Prepare the jurors for these likely approaches to cross-examination by bringing at least some of the questions up yourself, thereby defusing any possible negative impact your opponent's questions might otherwise have with the jurors.

Regarding assumptions, ask your expert whether she had to make any assumptions. Then ask why she made those assumptions and whether those assumptions are more reasonable than other assumptions that could have been made.

Also ask your expert whether contrary assumptions would have substantially affected the final opinion. This establishes that the expert's opinions are not particularly sensitive to the assumptions made and that those opinions remained consistent throughout the entire range of reasonable assumptions. Note how this technique would work in the case of "Jerry, the Dog":

Q: Dr. Smithson, in making your measurements and calculations from the photograph to come to your conclusion that it was not taken on Mother's Day, did you have to make any assumptions?

A: Yes, I did.

Q: What assumptions did you make?

A: Well, I had to assume Jerry, the dog did not grow substantially between the time the photograph was taken and the time that I measured him.

Q: Why did you make that assumption?

A: Because if he had grown substantially, then the angle in the photograph would be different from the angle that I calculated.

Q: Did you do anything to determine how much Jerry, the dog would have to have grown to have a substantial effect on your calculations?

A: Yes. In a sitting position, he would have to have grown about three inches before it made a one-week difference in my calculations of the date the picture was taken.

Q: Doctor, if Jerry, the dog had grown three inches, could the photograph have been taken on Mother's Day?

A: No. In that case, the photo would have been taken either on April 13 or August 31, but still not on Mother's Day.

Q: Did you make any other assumptions as you made your calculations about the date of this photograph?

A: Yes, I had to assume the ground right around Jerry, the dog was reasonably level.

Q: Why did you have to make that assumption?

A: If the ground was too steeply sloped, then the shadow would look longer or shorter than it actually was, and my calculations would be incorrect.

Q: Do you have an opinion on whether that assumption was reasonable?

A: Yes, I believe that it was reasonable because I actually looked at the yard where the picture was taken, and it was pretty level.

Q: Did you do anything to determine what effect sloped ground would have had on your calculation of the date?

A: Yes, I did. The ground would have had to slope away from Jerry at more than seven degrees before my date calculations were altered by more than one week. You can see, even from the picture alone [*indicating*] that it does not slope that much.

Q: If your calculations were off by one week, could the photograph have been taken on Mother's Day?

A: No.

9.4.8 Save a Point for Redirect and or End Strong

One effective of way of taking back the jurors to expert's side of the case after cross-examination is to save a point for redirect. For example, you might save a redirect to show the witness's opinions are not sensitive to things your expert did not do, and it was reasonable not to do them.

National Institute for Trial Advocacy

Q: Dr. Smithson, did you speak with any Tranowski family member during your work on this matter?

A: No, I did not. Well, actually, I did talk to Jerry, the dog and petted him a bit, but he didn't say anything back.

Q: Perhaps that was on advice of counsel. But let me ask you, Doctor, since you were measuring the family dog and you were concerned about the location of the wall and the slope of the yard, wouldn't it have been useful to talk to someone in the family?

A: No, it really would not have helped at all to talk to the family members. My calculations and my opinion are based on objective information, height and length and measurable angles. Whatever someone tells you about whether the ground is sloped or walls are angled, they cannot change the objective, measured facts.

Q: Dr. Smithson, you have told us you based your calculations on information from the nautical almanac. Did you use any other sources to check your calculations?

A: No, I did not.

Q: Why didn't you?

A: Well, these calculations are so straightforward that it is really not a question of using the right sources. In fact, the nautical almanac is what is used by astronomers in observatories all around the world—and by sailors all around the world also. That's where it gets its name. There simply is no better authority.

Not only does this provide the expert the opportunity to defend her opinions in a friendly atmosphere, but you have also shown the jurors you are not afraid to ask the hard questions and to deal with what might be seen after a cross-examination as weaknesses in your case. The ability and of both you and your expert to face these questions head-on gives jurors added reason to believe your witness.

Of course, you might choose to conduct this same line of questioning as part of the direct and rely on the jurors to remember these points all through the cross. In any event, after you have finished your questioning in anticipation of cross-examination, take the opportunity to ask a final question, which presents your theory of the case one more time:

Q: Dr. Smithson, we have talked about assumptions you did make; we have talked about things you did and things you didn't do. Does reconsideration of any of those subjects lead you to change your expert opinion that Walter Tranowski did not take this picture of Mom, Stanley, and Jerry, the dog on Mother's Day?

A: No, it does not; that is still my opinion.

The effective direct examination of the expert witnesses is the result of careful planning by you and your expert. You must coordinate your presentation of expert opinion testimony and its necessary legal foundation with the use of supporting exhibits and graphics.

A persuasive presentation weaves testimony about the expert's qualifications and the bases for her opinions into a supporting background fabric for the opinion testimony. Relating this testimony to the jurors' task while creating rapport between the jurors and the expert creates a bond between witness and jurors that promotes persuasion. The skillful use of repetition and visuals reinforces with the jury your theory of the case.

You can adapt the techniques shown to the presentation of any expert's testimony in every case. Integrating these techniques into your trial presentation will insure that in every case you present persuasive expert testimony. Two examples follow: one involves the direct examination of an economic damages expert in a gender discrimination case, and the second is an examination of a neurologist who gives an opinion that a plaintiff's claim that his epilepsy was caused by a collision between his motorcycle and the defendant's car is not supported by medical science.

Direct Examination of a Neurologist, Dr. Rosenberg

Introduction

Q: Dr. Rosenberg, What is your profession?

A: I am a doctor of medicine, and I specialize in neurology. I am a neurologist.

Q: What is a neurologist?

A: A neurologist is a medical doctor who specializes in problems of the nervous system, including, of course, the brain and spinal cord.

Q: Where do you live and work?

A: I live and work here in Nita City, Nita, and I have been practicing here for thirteen years.

Tickler

Q: Dr. Rosenberg, have you come to court today prepared to state your expert opinion as a neurologist on the cause of Jackie Fulbright's epilepsy?

A: Yes.

Q: Before we get to your opinion on the cause of Jackie Fulbright's epilepsy, please describe your education, training, and experience that qualify you to give your opinion. Let's start with your education. Would you review that for us, please?

Qualifications

A: Of course. I went to Harvard Medical School and graduated twenty years ago, and then I obtained an internship in neurology at the Mayo Clinic from 1994 through 1995.

Q: Tell us about your internship and practice after your internship.

A: My two-year internship was at the Mayo Clinic, which is one of the world's leading centers in internal medicine. It helped me to secure my residency in neurology at Columbia Presbyterian Hospital, in New York City. My residency lasted from 1995 to 1998. I then went into the army, and was stationed as a staff neurologist at Walter Reed Medical Center, in Washington DC, from 1998 to 2000.

Q: When did you come to Nita?

A: I came to Nita in 2001 and have been in private practice here since moving here. I'm also a Clinical Instructor in Neurology at Nita Medical School. I have been on the faculty since 2004.

Q: Are you board certified in neurology?

A: Yes, I studied for and became board certified in my first year after my residency in 1998.

Q: On your first attempt?

A: Yes.

Q: What does it mean to be board certified?

A: It means that you have been examined by a board—a panel—of the leading neurologists who certify that you have the skills and training to be a specialist in neurology.

Q: Tell us about your work in private practice.

A: I work with patients with a wide range of neurological ailments. Some have strokes, some have spinal cord injuries, some have head trauma, some have cancer or various diseases that affect the brain or nervous system, and some have epilepsy. I also do research as part of my responsibilities at Nita Medical School. I keep up on the latest studies and procedures and develop new and better procedures and treatments of my own. I also have to remain current on the latest research to make sure that Nita Medical School graduates will practice at the highest level when they become doctors.

Q: After your experience in working with patients and your research in neurology for over twenty years, what particularly qualifies you to give an opinion in this case?

A: Over the years I have examined hundreds of patients with various forms and degrees of severity of epilepsy. I have also specialized in the current science surrounding epilepsy and written about and conducted my own research on the causes and treatment of epilepsy. I have also testified about my opinions before a number of courts. While I have worked with both plaintiffs and defendants, I would say most of my clients have been defendants. Because I have testified often, I have learned how to look carefully for biases and faulty assumptions and remove them from my analysis and from competing opinions to develop an accurate model. I have also studied and written my own papers on epilepsy.

Q: How many times have you testified before in court?

A: I have been received as an expert in court in approximately fifty cases. The great majority of the cases in which I am involved settle short of trial.

Tender

[*In jurisdictions that require or allow tender.*]

Q: Your Honor, based on his education, training, and experience in the field of neurology, and especially on his years of work in treating and studying epilepsy, I tender Dr. Rosenberg to the court as an expert in neurology, and in particular, in identifying the causes of epilepsy.

Methodology

[*This may be a separate step, especially useful for a defendant medical expert, as it creates the opportunity for the expert to give an explanation of how doctors routinely are called in to review files and give second opinions for the purposes of diagnosis and treatment.*]

Q: Dr. Rosenberg, we have now reviewed your qualifications. With the court's permission, would you please come on down to the flip pad and take us through what you needed to do to help you come to the conclusions you came to in this case. We would like to hear your methodology, the basic steps you took in doing your analysis to form an opinion like the one you formed in this case.

A: All right. First, it is not at all uncommon for neurologists to rely on the medical charts of some other emergency room doctor or treating physician. Both Dr. Barron [*the plaintiff's treating physician*] and I have done so in this case. So I examined the history taken by the emergency room doctor, the hospital records, the CAT-scan records, x-rays, and MRI's, and I also looked at the depositions of the parties and the report of Dr. Barron.

Things Considered

◆   History of Patient
◆   Hospital Records
◆   Tests
  - CAT Scans
  - X-rays
  - MRIs
◆   Depositions
◆   Report of Dr. Barron

Opinions

[*One approach is to get the entire opinion up front. Here, that approach might be particularly useful to help the jurors understand the testimony.*]

Q: Do you have an opinion as to the cause of Jackie Fulbright's epilepsy?

A: Yes.

Q: What is that opinion?

A: Mr. Fulbright's epilepsy is idiopathic; that is, it has no known cause.

Q: What about the motorcycle accident as a cause?

A: No, that was not the cause. While I cannot tell you what was the cause, I can tell you that I do not think that the motorcycle accident was the cause.

Q: Let's break down what you found in the examination of the record in this case that leads you to your conclusion that Mr. Fulbright's epilepsy is of unknown origin. First, to be clear, why do you say that Mr. Fulbright's epilepsy has not been caused by the motorcycle accident?

A: Unfortunately, we just do not know, so we cannot be certain what was the cause. And this is very difficult to hear, because it is human nature to want to attribute a causal relationship between an event and an affect. However, the motorcycle accident seems much too remote in time to have been the cause of Mr. Fulbright's epilepsy.

Q: Dr. Rosenberg, what do you mean it is hard for us to hear? Can you give us an example?

A: I see patients all the time that want desperately to know, why them? Why they got a particular disease, or why they had a stroke. They ask me, "Was it the way I ate, the way I drank, the fall I took, or in my genes?" And sometimes—in fact, in most times—with epilepsy, we have to say that medical science just does not know. Epilepsy can be caused by a chemical imbalance in the brain, by a brain injury at birth, by some sort of brain tumor that may be too small to diagnosis at the time, or even abuse of alcohol or drugs, although we certainly don't think that is the case here. The point is, we often cannot pinpoint the cause, and that is the case in Mr. Fulbright's situation. It is hard for patients and their families, to accept, but sometimes epilepsy is not anyone's fault—not the patient's and not anyone else's.

Anticipating Cross

Q: Why not just look at the last time he hit his head and use that as the likely cause?

A: Well, if we did that, the most likely cause would be his being tackled on the football field, the day he had his first grand mal seizure. But medical science has shown us that the last potential cause is often not the cause, because there are other causes, and because there is not a sufficient enough connection in the science of neurology to determine whether that tackle was the precipitating cause.

Q: Is there a criterion you use in determining whether a trauma, like a football tackle, caused epilepsy?

A: Yes, my area of science has determined that for us to say that a head trauma caused epilepsy, there need to be four things present: 1) prolonged unconsciousness, 2) clinical evidence of brain injury beyond loss of consciousness, 3) skull fracture, and 4) bloody spinal fluid. None of these were present with the football tackle, so while it might have been a cause, we just can't say for sure.

Q: What about with the motorcycle accident three weeks before the football incident: Does an analysis of those factors lead you to conclude that was the cause of his epilepsy?

A: No, I don't believe we can say that was the cause either. This "four factors" test is simply not satisfied.

Q: Do you have an opinion held to a reasonable degree of certainty in the field of neurology whether the motorcycle accident caused Mr. Fulbright's epilepsy?

A: Yes, I do.

Q: What is that opinion?

A: That we cannot say it caused his epilepsy. We simply have to conclude that Mr. Fulbright's epilepsy is idiopathic, having an unknown origin.

Q: So take us through your list of things you considered and match it with your four criteria. Tell us what did you do, what did you find, and what does it mean? Let's start with the emergency room report after the motorcycle accident.

A: OK. We are looking here at emergency room records for Mr. Fulbright's emergency room visit after the motorcycle accident . . . .

Save a Point for Redirect

Q: On cross-examination you were asked about your opinion that Mr. Fulbright's epilepsy is idiopathic. How confident are you in that opinion?

A: Look, I deal with patients and families all the time who are struggling to determine whether they might have been the cause of someone's epilepsy. I don't give such opinions lightly. On the one hand, patients and families need to take responsibility for their actions if either was the cause of the epilepsy in question. On the other hand, they should not unduly blame themselves for what a loved one in experiencing, especially where the cause if not known. We simply most often don't know enough to say what caused a person like Mr. Fulbright to get epilepsy. Was it his playing football? Was the coach to blame for not taking him out of practice? Was it in his genes and his parents to blame? We simply don't know. And any doctor that says otherwise is simply not basing his opinion on science, but on emotion.

Direct Examination of Plaintiff's Damages Expert in Gender Discrimination Case

Introduction

Q: Ms. Jones, what is your profession?

A: I am an accountant. I specialize in determining the amount of economic damages plaintiffs may have suffered due to discrimination in their employment.

Q: Where to you live?

A: I live in Atlanta, Georgia.

Tickler

Q: Ms. Jones, are you here today as an expert witness to provide your opinion on how much economic loss Ms. Employee suffered as a result of Firm Inc.'s discrimination against her in her employment with the Firm?

A: Yes.

Q: Before we get to your opinion on how much she lost, please tell the jury first about your education, training, and experience that qualifies you to form that opinion.

Qualifications

Q: What was your major in college?

A: I majored in accounting.

Q: Where did get your degree in accounting?

A: My degree in accounting was from Emory University.

Q: What did you do after getting your degree?

A: I studied for and passed my CPA exam?

Q. "CPA"—that stands for . . . ?

A. Certified public accountant. If you don't pass this seven-part test, you cannot be responsible for examining the books and records of public companies. Only a CPA can issue a report on an company's financial statements that certifies that they are prepared in accordance with generally accepted accounting principles, known as GAAP, and that she has utilized generally accepted auditing standards, called GAAS. It is quite important to pass this examination, and I worked hard to make certain that I did. It is a test of your overall proficiency as an accountant.

Q: Did you pass it on the first try?

A: Yes, I passed all parts my first try, which is quite unusual. Typically, accountants pass three or four parts the first time and then come back to try for the remainder. It make take three times for some people, and a lot just give up.

Q: Where did you go to work after you became a CPA?

A: I went to work as an accountant for "Big Accounting Firm."

Q: Tell us about your progress with Big Accounting Firm?

A: I started out as a member of an auditing team, as most accountants do, and specialized in conducting audits of firms like Firm Inc. From that experience, I learned about how firms like Firm Inc. are structured, their different classes of employees and partners, and their executive pay structure and compensation packages, among other things. Eventually, I headed a number of audit teams myself, and I learned a great deal about the financial workings of corporations. Then I joined our litigation support group, and I am now a partner in that group, heading up of a team of financial, accounting, and economic specialists to provide support for firms in employment disputes. I help design damages models to accurately measure damages that may have been sustained by a claimant. I have been a partner and have been doing this type of litigation support for approximately eighteen years.

Q: From your experience in litigation support, with a specialty in employment disputes, what credentials in addition to your being a CPA qualify you to give in opinion in this case?

A: Over the years I have done more than a hundred damages models in employment cases. I have worked for both plaintiffs and defendants. Because I have represented parties on both sides of these kinds of disputes, I have learned how to make conservative and defensible models and look for biases and faulty assumptions and remove them from my calculations or from the calculations made by opposing experts to get an accurate model. I have also researched the effects of employment discrimination on the compensation, tenure, and advancement of high-level employees and how discrimination is likely to effect the career prospects of similarly situated employees in the years following the discrimination.

Q: Have you testified before in court?

A: Yes, I have been accepted as an expert by courts in approximately twenty-five cases. The great majority of the cases I'm involved in settle short of trial.

Tender

[*In jurisdictions that require tender, or in any federal court where the judge's practice is for lawyers to make a tender.*]

Q: Your Honor, I tender Ms. Jones to the court as an expert in calculating damages in employment disputes; we submit that she is qualified by reason of her education, experience, and training to provide expert opinion on the amount of damage Ms. Employee sustained as a result of the wrongful termination of Ms. Employee's employment with Firm Inc.

Methodology

[*Treating this as a separate step is especially useful for damages experts, because it creates the opportunity to give a summary of the calculation that the expert will lead the jury through. Such a summary calculation can anchor the testimony in an exhibit that most jurors can follow. See chapter ten.*]

Q: Ms. Jones, we have now reviewed your qualifications. Please, with the court's permission, come down from the stand so that you can use the flip chart and take us through the calculation you did in this case. Describe the basic components of your damage calculation.

A: To accurately measure damages, we need to know what Ms. Employee would have made had she not been denied partnership. [*Wage, first year as partner.*] Then we need to determine the number of years she would likely have worked as a partner at the firm. [*Number of years working.*] Next, we need to grow or increase those wages year-to-year to represent how she would have likely progressed in her pay status. [*Wage growth.*] Then we need to subtract from each year's pay the amount that she will likely make in other employment. Finally, we need to discount the net amount of her shortfall in each future year so we know what it is worth in today's dollars. [*Discount rate.*] That will give us a present value of the total of economic damages she would have incurred had she not been wrongfully terminated.

Wage First Year	
Number of Years Working	
Growth of Wages (approx.)	
Subtraction for Other Employment (adjusted straight line growth)	
Discount for Present Value	
(Interest in Safe Security Minus Inflation)	
Total Loss	

Opinions

[*One approach is to get the total opinion up front, so that it can then be mentioned naturally as you are discussing the bases for the expert's opinion and the other parts of her direct examination.*

  Now, Ms. Jones, as you came to your opinion that Ms. Employee's total economic loss was $2 million 700 thousand dollars, what factors did you consider?

Others worry that when the figure is large, the jurors may get sticker shock, and they propose that it is better to get the component parts out one at a time and then let the jurors do the calculation for themselves, adding and subtracting to their "own" conclusion as to the amount of loss. This way the jurors take "ownership" of the calculation and try to get the right answer, just as a middle-school student might do when completing a calculation begun by the teacher. This may be somewhat risky, however, considering the number of mathematical errors that the average American makes on tax returns and jury verdict forms.]

Q: Would it be useful to first get your opinion for each of these parts of your model and then have you show us the basis of each part of your overall opinion?

A: Yes, I think that is a good idea.

Q: Do you have an opinion as to the amount of wages she would have earned if she had not been wrongfully terminated?

A: Yes.

Q: What is that opinion?

A: She would have earned $425,000 in her first year as partner.

Q: How did you determine that figure?

A: In this case, I looked at the average amount paid to the men who made partner in the year that Ms. Employee was denied partner.

Q: What did you find?

A: I found that the three males who made partner were paid $400,000, $420,000, and $455,000. I added the figures together and divided by three to get the average salary.

Anticipate Cross

Q: Did you do any analysis to determine whether this figure was too high or too low?

A: Actually, from what I understand from the record, Ms. Employee had above-average ability to draw in new clients, like the highest-paid male who made partner, and she might actually have made closer to the $455,000 figure. I used the average, a lower number, to be conservative.

Q: So take the $425,000 and show us where you use it in the summary calculation.

A: It goes right here.

Wage First Year	425k
Number of Years Working	
Growth of Wages (approx.)	
Subtraction for Other Employment (adjusted straight line growth)	

Discount for Present Value	
(Interest in Safe Security Minus Inflation)	
Total Loss	

Q: Now, what did you do next?

A: I needed to determine a fair number of years to run the wages going forward.

Bases

Q: What assumptions did you make?

A: Well, her colleagues indicate that she is very talented. I therefore assumed that she would likely return to the market working someplace else; the question is to determine the number of years she will work before she is back to the wage level that she would have had if there had been no discrimination. Based on other work I've done in similar cases, I've determined that the market place will allow her to catch up, to overcome the discrimination effect, in about seven years. This gives Ms. Employee some time to find the right employer to recognize her abilities, which usually takes about two years, and then to regain her confidence and reach the level of her "true wage worth," in the competitive marketplace.

Q: What did you do to determine this seven-year figure.

A: I've looked at all employees in Ms. Employee's profession, and in similar professions, in this job market who have either won awards in lawsuits or reached settlements after allegations of discrimination, and I measured their wages in their new job against wages in their old job. I had a sample size of 100 similarly situated professionals. I determined that their wages caught up, on average, in approximately ten years.

Q: So how did you use that ten years figure in your calculations?

A: Well, here I need to talk about some of the other variables that come into play to help me determine what wages she would have earned in each of the ten years. I needed to determine the growth rate of wages—the wages she would have likely earned in other employment—and then discount these wages to their present value.

Q: Have you prepared a chart to show us how the ten years and these other factors—the growth in wages, the subtractions you made for other employment, and the discounting you did—combine to affect your opinion?

A: Yes, I have.

Q: Let's turn to that chart [enlarged exhibit or PowerPoint slide]. Please explain to us how the chart is organized. Let's start with the top column headings, and then describe the row headings along the left hand side of the chart.

Years	YR-2	YR-1	YR-0	YR+1	YR+2	YR+3	YR+4	YR+5	YR+6	YR+7
Wage in each year	425k	475k	500k	525k	550k	575k	600k	625k	650k	675k
Other Employment	0	0	0	200k 325k	300k 250k	400k 175k	500k 100k	600k 25k	625k 25k	675k 0
Discount Rate Applied to Wag				2.5% 317k	2.5% 237.5k	2.5% 162k	2.5% 91k	2.5% 20k	2.5% 17k	0
Accumu-lated Loss Wages	425k	900k	1.4m	1.717k	1.954k	2.1m	2.191m	2.21m	2.227m	0

Total Income lost as a result of discrimination $2,227,000.

[*The chart in this example would have been prepared outside of court. The expert may also fill in the various boxes in the courtroom and might use different colors for key figures. Or the expert could "reveal" the chart figures, on PowerPoint or by removing blank cell covers, to show the chart filled in.*]

Wage First Year	425k
Number of Years Working	7 years
Growth of Wages (approx.)	25k
Subtraction for Other Employment (adjusted straight line growth)	100k* a year
Discount for Present Value	2.5%
(Interest in Safe Security Minus Inflation)	
Total Loss	$2,270,000

Anticipate Cross

Q: Now as part of your analysis in coming to your opinion, did you read the expert report and deposition of the defendant's accounting expert?

A. Yes, I studied that material quite carefully.

Q. Then you read the portion where he challenges your figures because he says that your discount rate does not reflect the risks that a particular firm like Firm Inc. will still be in existence seven years from now: perhaps it would be bought out, downsized, or may it lost its competitive edge and didn't compete well enough to survive. How did you consider that possibility?

A: Well, Firm Inc. had survived and in fact grown substantially in revenues and total employees for thirty years before this year. Furthermore, many of the years that it survived successfully were years of low economic growth, much worse than now. Therefore, there is substantial reason to believe that Firm Inc. will be around for at least the ten years that we are talking about and probably for much longer. Even if it merges with another firm during that time, there is reason to believe that valuable employees—young partners with bright futures—would survive and thrive.

Q: So do you have an opinion that you hold with a reasonable degree of certainty in your field of accounting and damages projections about the amount in today's dollars that is needed to fairly make up for the fact that Ms. Employee was discriminated against by Firm Inc.

A: Yes, I do.

Q: What is your opinion?

A: My opinion on her economic damages is $2,227,000 dollars; I have put it right here on the chart.

CHAPTER TEN

EXPERTS AND EXHIBITS

Experts require effective exhibits because expert testimony requires explanation. The entire premise of expert testimony is that the expert presents information to the jurors that is beyond their ken; therefore, exhibits and experts must work together. You must know the law of evidence with regard to exhibits, must know the role the pretrial conference plays in getting documents admitted, must be able to make strategic choices about the way you create exhibits, and must see and contest the impermissible choices the opponents may make creating their exhibits. Finally, you must know the strategies for using, displaying, and handling exhibits in openings, examinations of witnesses, and closing arguments.

The purpose of expert testimony is to help the jurors understand a *process*—like the conversion of gasoline into energy to move a car; a *relationship*—like that between a tainted vaccine and the disease it causes; or a *phenomenon*—like an avalanche in the Rocky Mountains. The jurors must find the expert credible and must understand at least the structure of the methodology the expert has employed; only then are they comfortable enough to rely on the expert's testimony. The jurors do not have to be trained to the point that they can independently replicate the expert's studies, experiments, or clinical investigations, but on the other hand, the expert testimony cannot present Edgar Degas's "conversation of specialists," where one understands nothing. Therefore, exhibits used to illustrate the expert's opinion must be especially helpful, especially interesting, and especially memorable.

10.1 Exhibits and Evidentiary Foundations

10.1.1 Evidentiary Hurdles for Illustrative or Summary Exhibits

Even before trial, an expert has a head start in preparing exhibits to support her testimony. Essential portions of the expert's Rule 26(b) report should provide themes for *illustrative* or *summary* visual exhibits. Yet while the expert's report may be required in discovery, it is unlikely to be exciting. It contains more information than the jurors need to remember because it is intended 1) to reveal all of the expert's bases and opinions, 2) to serve as a vehicle for pretrial discovery, and 3) to provide a basis for the court's rulings on the admissibility of the expert's testimony.

However, an outline of the report will provide a list of its most important points; from that list, you can probably identify essential opinions and bases that in turn will suggest interesting graphic exhibits. If this outline approach does not suggest effective exhibits, create a new list of high-level opinions with the expert and brainstorm on ways to visualize them. Remember, we normally are looking for evocative pictures, not arrays of data.

Getting the exhibit in evidence depends on what kind of exhibit it is. The requisite foundation for illustrative exhibits with experts is merely that the exhibits will assist the expert in giving her testimony. When you reach the appropriate point in the expert's direct examination, ask the expert, "Have you prepared any exhibits to help you explain this to us?" (Notice the phrase is "to us," not "to the jury." To avoid separating yourself from the jurors or suggesting that you are better informed than they, do not ask the expert, "Can you explain this to the jury?") For variety, you may also ask, "Can you show us what you mean?" or "Is there some way we can see that?" or any other question that cues your expert it is time for pictures.

Some lawyers make the mistake of trying to admit merely illustrative exhibits as summaries. The evidentiary hurdle for summaries is higher than for illustrative exhibits. Summaries, or charts, are only permitted for efficiency purposes and only where the underlying data is voluminous; it must indeed save the court time and not mislead the court. Federal Rule of Evidence 1006, which deals with summaries, requires that originals or duplicates of the underlying data be made available to the opposition at a reasonable time and place. If a party offers a computer simulation as a summary, Rule 1006 allows opposing counsel to argue that the proponent be required to turn the summary over to him well in advance of trial and in a format (computer language or otherwise) his expert can read and manipulate. Of course, the proponent may contest that this exchange allows free-riding on his expert's work. (It may have cost tens of thousands of dollars to create the simulation, but once in a system, it can be easily manipulated by simply changing a few key pieces of data or lines of code.) Yet the need to provide the opportunity to attempt to rebut the factual assumptions the computer simulation employs may require the early exchange of the simulation and the data. If the court is concerned that the opponent of a computer simulation has not been given a chance to rebut it, then the court may reject it.[1] Therefore, be sure to label and argue your illustrative exhibits appropriately.

10.1.2 Hearsay Hurdles for Exhibits

Another tool for opposing exhibits is grounded in evidence rules concerning hearsay. Exceptions to the rules that exclude hearsay in exhibits (and other statements) are contained in Rules 803 and 804, and they are construed strictly and conservatively. Since the codification of the Federal Rules of Evidence, no new exceptions

---

1. *See* the discussions of things to look for in the opponent's exhibits at the pretrial conference, *infra*.

have been created in the federal system, and the existing exceptions have consistently been interpreted to reject expansion. In general, the courts have proclaimed the exceptions will be strictly construed so that even circumstances that come close to satisfying an exception will not be approved under that exception or under the "catch-all" exception now contained in Rule 807 (previously Rules 803(24) and 804(b)(5)). There is a genuine concern that these exceptions be kept within their traditional bounds, so that they do not swallow the rule. The catch-all exception, especially, is intended to allow courts to exercise discretion when faced with circumstances beyond the contemplation of the drafters of the original rules—not for circumstances that come close to satisfying an established exception, but fail for technical reasons. (To take advantage of the Rule 807 exception, the proponent needs to give the opponent notice at pretrial that he will use Rule 807 as a basis for the admissibility of the proffered evidence.)

Exhibits used with experts often present hearsay problems because they present, summarize, or otherwise use out-of-court statements. (Of course, if the statements are nonhearsay opposing party statements (admissions), there is no problem.) While exhibits may be specially prepared and offered as summaries of complex or voluminous underlying data or material—accounting, economic and scientific graphs, or video demonstrations and recreations being prime examples—the summary exhibit incorporates all the hearsay deficiencies contained within the underlying data. You cannot eliminate hearsay problems merely by incorporating the underlying hearsay data into another exhibit. As a corollary, when evaluating an opponent's exhibits, be sure to consider the adequacy of foundation for all data underlying summary exhibits.

Your evaluation starts with Rule 703:

> If experts in the particular field would reasonably rely on those kinds of facts or data in forming an opinion on the subject, they need not be admissible for the opinion to be admitted.

The first level of response to a hearsay objection is to say an expert may rely on hearsay. However, even though an expert may rely on inadmissible bases customarily used in her field, newly revised Rule 703 precludes presentation of such inadmissible bases to the jurors, unless the proponent can show that the probative value outweighs the prejudicial impact. This is essentially the reverse of the familiar test in Rule 403. Where the proponent survives this balancing test under Rule 703, the opponent should at least get a limiting instruction from the court that specified data on the exhibit is only there to help the jurors know the bases on which *this* expert relied to reach her particular opinion; that these facts are contested; and that the expert's exhibit is not itself evidence of these facts. When presenting an expert's illustrative exhibit that contains hearsay, a safe exhibit should not represent the hearsay evidence as fact, but instead it should clearly represent the evidence under the heading "reasons" or "bases." (A difficult case is presented where all of the expert's bases are inadmissible for hearsay or other evidentiary reasons, but are normally used by experts in the field. Exclusion of the bases leaves the expert with no apparent basis for her opinion, but admission might overwhelm the jurors with inadmissible material.)

Keep in mind that another basis for admissibility of exhibits during expert testimony is if they merely present *market reports or commercial publications* (stock data from the *Wall Street Journal*) that meet the admissibility requirements of Rule 803(17).

Exhibits can be useful in a number of additional evidentiary situations, even where the exhibit will not actually be entered into evidence. An exhibit may be used to impeach an opposing expert, or *to refresh recollection*, or as *past recollection recorded*; in such uses, it is read to the expert and into the record, but the document itself is not received or provided to the jurors during their deliberations. The concept is identical for all exhibits intended to refresh memory or to stand in place of a witness's testimony (and for learned treatises under Rule 803(18), which may supplement or contradict an expert's testimony). Since the material is essentially being offered either as a substitute for or in contrast to the expert's testimony, it is received orally, just like the expert's testimony, so the jurors are not led to place inappropriate weight on a testimonial substitute merely because it is on paper. (Note again that as an illustrative aid to that oral testimony, an overhead or other presentation might be shown to the jurors and again in closing argument, but it will not be received into evidence.)

It is also vital that you know the rule of completeness so that you can effectively respond when your opponent uses your exhibits, especially parts of the expert's report or deposition, to try to impeach your expert. If part of the expert's report or deposition is accepted into evidence, the opposing lawyer may (at the judge's discretion) offer other portions that the jurors, in fairness, should consider at the same time. Rule 106, the "rule of completeness," is intended to prevent an advocate from misleading the jurors by presenting only a portion of an exhibit. The proper functioning of the rule permits the opponent to request the court to authorize the admission of additional portions at the same time, so the jurors have the complete context. In practice, courts often respond to such requests by stating, "Well, you have cross-examination." Of course, the opponent had cross-examination without Rule 106, so such a ruling completely ignores the important purpose of the rule. If the document in question is a formal deposition, you may also cite Federal Rule of Civil Procedure 32(a)(4), a rule of completeness for deposition extracts, to provide additional comfort and guidance to the court.

10.2 Foundations for Specific Exhibits

10.2.1 Photographs

A photograph is admissible on evidence that it fairly and accurately depicts a relevant scene at a relevant time. The focus in analyzing the foundation for photographic evidence is whether the relevant view seen by the expert is fairly and accurately depicted in the photograph. Therefore, it does not matter whether the exhibit was *photographed* (or recorded by whatever process) at a relevant time (any more than a chart prepared for an accountant's testimony must have been prepared at the same time the sales and revenues were earned). Although the possibility of forgery may have increased with modern computerized photo manipulation tools, that is logically a challenge for cross or voir dire on the exhibit.

10.2.2 From Photographs to Videos to Computer Graphics

If each individual "frame" of a graphic exhibit is fair and accurate, whether there are thousands that comprise a motion picture or one that comprises a still photograph, the exhibit is admissible unless there is something about the motion— perhaps the speed—that renders the series unfair (under Rule 403), even though the individual frames, taken one at a time, would not be. For example, a video of a plane crash, when played at normal speed, accurately shows the events; if the video was shown at slow speed, however, it might give the appearance the pilot had more time to control the plane and thus avoid the accident than was the actual case. Similarly, any cropping of photographs, stills, or movies might place undue emphasis on certain portions of the picture or scene—just as omitting portions of a document might result in an unfair or incomplete understanding of the document. If the jurors do not see everything relevant in the picture, they may think the missing thing was not there. When an expert has testified a depiction is fair and accurate, the burden of proving lack of foundation shifts to the opponent, who must present evidence that the depiction is unfair itself or has been presented or altered in some unfair way.

As a matter of evidence and trial procedure, you, as the proponent attorney, need to know when the admissibility of a photograph, movie, or computer simulation is opposed on the basis that the expert lacks a foundation for testifying. For example, an expert may be vague in establishing that she had a similar view; or that the actors and their actions were similar to those of the parties involved; or the expert cannot say the facts entered in the mathematical model used to create the computer simulation are relevant to anything at issue in the case; and then the admissibility question is handled under Rule 104(b). The relevancy is conditioned on a fact, and you only need to provide evidence that would support a reasonable jury's finding that the expert had the perspective to say the photo, video, or computer simulation is fair and accurate for it to be admissible. The rest of the challenge goes to weight. Under Rule 104(c), determinations of preliminary matters regarding admissibility shall be conducted out of the hearing of the jurors when interests of justice require it.

The court may still be less comfortable in admitting computer simulations as readily as it admits photos. It is very hard to cross-examine a video or computer simulation once the jurors have seen it. Some lawyers would go so far as to say you can only counteract a memorable video or computer simulation with one of your own—where you show the jurors what the event would look like by importing your own facts and perspective. Some courts agree the video or computer simulation may be too powerful and will not let in a computer simulation or video unless the court is convinced of its accuracy and reliability—a standard higher than "a reasonable jury could find . . . ." (They seem to analyze a computer simulation like an expert opinion on cause and effect, based on a mathematical model, or like a *Daubert v. Merrell Dow* problem.) Remember that under *Daubert*, the court acts as a gatekeeper, determining as a foundational matter whether the model controls for all the important variables and has been subjected to other tests of relevance and reliability of scientific modeling (*see* discussion of *Daubert* in chapters thirteen and fourteen.)

Other courts treat videos and computer simulations like photos. They hear arguments that refer to four rules of federal evidence:

- Rule 403 (evidence that is unduly prejudicial and misleading to the jury is excluded) is one of the main rules of discussion along with

- Rule 102 (the rules are to be construed to secure fairness, eliminate unjustifiable expense and delay, and promote the growth of the law of evidence to the end that the truth may be ascertained),

- Rule 104(b) (evidence conditioned upon a showing sufficient to support a finding that the fact does exist), and finally,

- Rule 611(a) (provides that the court should exercise reasonable control over the mode and order of interrogating experts and presenting evidence so as to make the interrogation and presentation effective to ascertain the truth and avoid wasting time). Under FRE 611(a), if a picture can be admissible because it avoids needlessly wasting time, then a computer simulation should also be admissible. And many courts do appreciate technology that produces substantial time savings in trials.

With video and other digital recordings, the technology employed in making the record, in creating the visual exhibit, is not an element of the foundation itself, but it may be relevant in persuading the court that the depiction is not fair and accurate because the process was subject to abuse—and was, in fact, abused. Therefore, unless there is some showing that videos or other digital media that has been used can be more easily altered than still photos or photographic motion pictures, the analysis of admissibility will be the same for either technology. If there is a challenge to admissibility based on a claim of alteration, then differences in the ability to alter the pictures would be relevant. (Videos that incorporate computer simulations require a more complex analysis. Because the computer simulation may be so easily manipulated once the mathematical data has been entered, the court does have cause to be more skeptical of the entire video. See the discussion below.)

Photographs and videos of a reenactment are not inadmissible simply because they portray a reenactment; if they are "fair and accurate" and the scene is relevant, they are admissible. In other words, if there is evidence that the signing of the Declaration of Independence looked "just like" it looks in a photograph or video and the scene is relevant to the case, it will be admissible. This rule flows from the basic evidentiary requirement that recorded evidence be a fair depiction—if the expert (or some other witness) can testify that the reenactment is relevant. For example, the actors in the video—those who are portraying the participants in the events at suit—are not themselves vouching for the accuracy of their actions or the resulting scene; that depends on the testimony of the sponsoring expert or witness that depiction is fair and accurate. The analysis of a computer-generated reenactment is conceptually a bit more difficult often because there is no one who can testify directly about the fairness and accuracy of the scene shown. For example, you may use a computer recreation may be used to show the locations and movements of all the vehicles relevant to a traffic accident, perhaps from an overhead perspective unavailable to any person at the time of the accident. Here, the "fairness and accuracy" of the computer recreation depends on the testimony of the expert, normally an expert who is familiar with or participated in the preparation of the reenactment. If that expert can identify bases for the computer inputs (for example, testimony from still other witnesses) and she (or another expert) is able to testify the methodology (the computer programs) used to generate the recreation from that data is reliable, then the fairness and accuracy of the computer-generated evidence will have been established. The key to admissibility is demonstrate that the methodology employed in creating the conclusions shown in the exhibit is reliable, as was emphasized for the expert's methodology overall by the Supreme Court in *Daubert v. Merrell Dow Pharmaceuticals.* Again, the court would reason that if the methodology—here, the computer program—is shown to be reliable, if the data input are shown to be reliable, and if the scene is relevant (it is the accident scene in the suit), then the visual recreation or reenactment will be admissible, even though no human being had ever actually seen the events depicted.

Computer-generated simulations or reenactments are admissible if they are fair and accurate depictions, but you will have to meet the possibility of improper manipulation (because of computer technology). Because the technology is now available to alter photographs and videos at a very fine level (that is, by changing individual pixels, the small elements that form the picture when combined in groups of hundreds of thousands), as the proponent of the visual evidence, you should certainly recognize the skepticism the jurors or court may feel toward important visual evidence. While the jurors do not have the opportunity to rule on accepting the evidence into the record, they certainly decide whether to give the evidence any weight in its deliberations. Such concerns may persuade you to ask at least a few questions to the expert to demonstrate there has been no tampering. These questions should be in the form of: "Has anyone had an opportunity to manipulate either the data or the program?"; or better: "How do you know that the data are accurate or were accurately manipulated?", so that the expert gets to answer the hard question during her direct. One thing to note in criminal cases is who actually inputted the data into the computer simulation. If the person inputting the data from a crime scene is a police officer, confrontation clause questions might be raised if the police officer never testifies about how he got his measurements and how he insured that those measurements were fed into the computer accurately.

Anyone who viewed the actual scene at a relevant time can testify about the fairness and accuracy of the visual evidence. There is no requirement that the foundational witness be a party to the lawsuit or the party's expert; alternatively, it is not necessary that the witness be uninvolved in the lawsuit. The only requirement for a foundational witness is that she must have been able to perceive the relevant scene at a relevant time (or in the case of computer-generated evidence, she be competent to testify about the reliability of the program and data used). Test the foundational witness's competence to lay the foundation for visual evidence in the same way you test her ability to testify directly about the scene she saw.

If she can say, "Then I saw the plane crash on the runway," she should also be allowed to say, "This picture of a plane crash fairly and accurately shows the angle that the plane hit the runway." If she can say, "Increasing the velocity vectors will increase the post-accident separation in this program," then she should be allowed to say, "This computer depiction correctly shows the two cars' locations after the crash." In the computer context, if the foundational expert would be allowed to testify that in her opinion, the processes would have certain results, then she will also be allowed to testify that a visual exhibit showing those results is fair and accurate. For example, if the actual scene was not witnessed (or could not be witnessed—for example, the scene is a view of the inside of an operating nuclear reactor), foundation testimony will need to include technical testimony to connect the data input with the graphic output, using reliable methodology (consistent with *Daubert*). Statistical calculations performed by computer, DNA comparisons shown on charts, or chemical analyses displayed in summary charts all have to be founded on testimony about the reliability of the methodology used to manipulate and display the data.

Again, the use of illustrative aids to testimony may be an attempt to evade these foundation requirements for the admissibility of certain exhibits. Exhibits that are intended merely to illustrate an expert's testimony are as admissible in regard to that testimony—and no more. If an expert presents an exhibit to "show what she is talking about," like a graph or sketch or diagram, and her testimony is then excluded or rejected, the illustrative exhibit must likewise be excluded or rejected. "Illustrative" exhibits have no substantive probative value of their own, but derive their probative value entirely from the testimony they illustrate. "Demonstrative" exhibits, in contrast, normally have independent substantive value (for example, a demonstration of the effect of mixing two chemicals provides independent information to the trier-of-fact, which may be used to support findings). Demonstrative exhibits may be solely demonstrative, they may be illustrative *and* substantive, but they are never merely illustrative.

Exhibits divulged or obtained as part of mandatory "voluntary" disclosures under Rule 26(a) are supposed to include materials that a party "may use to support its claims or defenses." Nevertheless, the initial disclosures by the attorneys are likely to be incomplete and give rise to time-consuming challenges—or, equally likely, the opponents may try to bury each other in discovery as broad as that which occurred before the disclosure procedure was adopted.

Nevertheless, opposing party statements are contained in discovery productions: the act of producing an exhibit in an initial voluntary disclosure or in response to a document request or an interrogatory constitutes a party statement regarding portions of the foundation for the exhibit. For example, if a document request calls for the production of "all documents that show profits earned between June 2008 and May 2009," then the return of twelve documents constitutes an opposing party statement of two facts: the twelve documents are relevant to profits in that period, and the opposing party has no access to any other documents that are relevant to profits during that time. In discovery, therefore, never ask for "documents sufficient to show" because you will not the benefit of this second admission.

Parties will often provide documents in response to an interrogatory, as they are allowed to do by the rules. That response constitutes a party statement that those documents answer the interrogatory, i.e., they are relevant to the subject. By providing exhibits in an initial voluntary disclosure, the party at the very least is stating that exhibits are relevant to the party's claims or defenses, that technically, they are all of the documents that the party has that are relevant to its claims or defenses. However, it is likely to be very difficult to persuade a court to apply the language of the voluntary disclosure rule quite so strictly that it would completely preclude any "subsequently discovered" exculpatory materials.

10.3   The Role of the Pretrial Conference

Typical pretrial standing orders, or local rules, require exhibits to be identified, exchanged, and offered by the final pretrial conference. Most judges nowadays do not want to take trial time to hear argument about foundation for exhibits; they therefore require exchange and objection to occur prior to trial, and they will not hear objections later that could have been made pretrial. Objections based on relevance and the various policies embodied in Rule 403—such as cumulativeness, confusion, unfair prejudice, and wasting time—will often be deferred until trial because the judge feels she needs the advantage of context to make a proper ruling. Nevertheless, be sure to state such objections pretrial so they are not waived.

Motions in limine are used to get advance rulings of admissibility, as well as advance rulings of inadmissibility. Under *Daubert*, when it is difficult to forecast whether a particular judge will find a foundation to be adequate for an expert's testimony, a request for an in limine ruling may be essential, and that request should include the expert's exhibits also. The presentation supporting that request for a ruling may include live testimony under the procedures of Rule 104(c). It is a common misunderstanding, based on a mistranslation of the phrase "in limine" (which means "at the threshold" of the courtroom or chambers or trial), that such motions are only useful "to limit" the evidence. If you have an exhibit that you anticipate will be challenged and it is sufficiently important to the flow of your case that you do not want to wait until trial to find out whether it is going to be admitted, ask for an in limine ruling. Of course, if the court has scheduled an "exhibit day" during the pretrial sessions, you can get your ruling at that time. However, there are judges who prefer to postpone routine exhibit rulings until they come up at trial. When you are in front of one of these judges, a request for in limine rulings on important exhibits is appropriate.

10.4 Staying Organized During Pretrial

Use an "exhibit book" or "trial notebook" during pretrial and trial arguments on the expert's and all of your exhibits. For the exhibit day, if you are dealing with 200 to 300 exhibits, put copies in one or two notebooks in numerical order. Note with care which exhibits the expert needs to have admitted for her to refer to as a basis of her opinion. If your opponent has conceded the admissibility of the exhibit, indicate that fact at the top in some bright color. For those exhibits for which admissibility has not been conceded, write "OPRAH" vertically at the top of the first page of each exhibit. OPRAH stands for "original writings," "privilege," "relevance," "authentication," and "hearsay." Then consider how you would respond to any objection on any of those elements of foundation and make a note opposite the element.

Objections to exhibits made and overruled at pretrial should be renewed at trial. Unless the judge states on the record or in a written order that she will not allow exhibit offers to be renewed at trial if she has sustained an objection to the exhibit during pretrial, renew the exhibit offer at trial to avoid waiver. You might state the offer or objection when the jury is out, during a bench conference, or in the morning or evening housekeeping session, but be sure to do it in the presence of the reporter so it is on the record. It is true some judges get testy about attorneys restating objections or offers that the judge thought were completely and properly handled at pretrial; if the judge seems perturbed, explain that you are concerned about having an adequate record and do not intend to reargue the ruling; rather, you are just making certain your position is not waived.

If the offer in evidence is not explicitly limited, then it is general. There are times when an exhibit is offered for a limited purpose, such as showing that a statement has been made, regardless of its truth, thereby avoiding a hearsay objection. If that is your purpose, then you might say, "Your Honor, we offer Plaintiff's Exhibit 13 in evidence for the limited purpose of showing the store claimed to offer 50 percent off on the gas barbecue grills that day." When such a limited offer is made, the jury will normally be instructed, in this example, that they are to consider the exhibit only to show the statement was made, not for the truth of the statement itself. Remember to record any limited admissibility ruling the court makes, so you can guard against the general offer and the impermissible general use by the opponent and the opponent's expert.

10.5 The Lawyer as Protector of Fairness: Edit and Critique Experts' Exhibits

Oil Imports Have Doubled

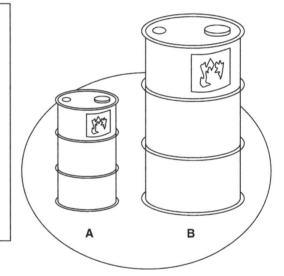

- Have oil imports doubled from A to B?

- Barrel B is *twice* as high.

- But Barrel B is *twice* as wide, also, and therefore has *twice* the radius.

- Therefore, Barrel B is *8 times* as great.

10.5.1 Misleading Icons and Labels

Be sure to guard against misleading icons in not only your opponent's graphics, but your own as well. Misleading icons are symbols that unfairly exaggerate relevant information, such as the extent of change or difference, in a graphic. Because they are misleading, the court will reject the exhibit. For example, an oil barrel graphic that doubles in height and width to show a doubling in oil imports from one year to the next is misleading because doubling both dimensions gives the "doubled" icon eight times the volume of the un-doubled icon. The visual impact can be enormously misleading.

In another example, a graph showing yearly sales volumes (and perhaps even entitled "Yearly Sales Volumes") is misleading if the last amount shown is for less than a year (a problem that can be thought of as an "apple-orange problem"). On a much more subtle level, a bar graph showing growth in profits from $10 million to $13 million will show the second bar as 1.3 times as high as the first, but if the Y-axis is labeled to begin at $9 million, the first bar will be one unit high (showing $1 million over the baseline), and the second bar will be four units high, or *four* times the height of the first.

Graphics that are misleading because of icon, label, axis/baseline, "apple-orange," or other problems are likely to be excluded under Rule 403. Once the proper objection is made, misleading graphics will be rejected until they are corrected; therefore, if the error is not discovered or disclosed until trial, there may be no opportunity to correct the problem and the evidence may be lost. Of course, if there is some reason to believe the error was known, but objection was withheld intentionally, the court might find waiver of the objection.

Insure that your graphics do not distract or detract from the seriousness and credibility of the evidence. Just as you would not dress your key expert in a yellow suit with a clown wig, keep your backgrounds professional and pick font size and colors that match or complement the evidence.

That being said, don't be afraid to experiment with different displays, changing variables, and axes until you achieve the emphasis and message you want. Just as you would instruct a witnesses to speak up to help the jurors understand and better hear her point, you will want graphics that contain information about multiple variables to provide sufficient emphasis to the data on the particular variable that is most important, such as the illegal profit, the white blood cell count, or the decline in garbage tonnage. Simplify the display by eliminating variables that are not relevant or significantly explanatory. Try different colors (or a single color against black and white "other" data). You should not be satisfied with the exhibit until a layperson, looking at it for the first time, is able to state the point you want to make with the data you are relying on. Graphic evidence must have immediate visual impact to be effective.

Adjust the expert's mode of presenting data and numbers so the important numbers and comparisons will stand out. To show comparisons such as differences over time, growth, or response to variables, present a graphic exhibit that displays the two conditions side by side. If the changes are displayed in a series of graphics in a way that the jurors do not see them simultaneously, the jurors must rely on their memories for the quantity and even location (from 1,573 to 1,945; this row, that column, that door, this window, or right lung, lower lobe). This is the problem described by master graphic philosopher Edward Tufte of Yale as "one damn thing after another." Instead, display the before and after (or healthy and sick or unmodified and modified) views on the same graphic, at the same time, side by side, with the differences colored, highlighted, or circled so they appear visually.

Do not mistake "big documents" for "graphic evidence." A blowup of a document, especially of a text document, is merely a *big text document*; it does not tell a story visually. Pictures, charts, graphs, videos, or computer animations make effective visual exhibits if the viewer has an immediate reaction that supports the theme of the case. To cite an extreme example, an accounting worksheet or table, filled with rows and columns of numbers, has little visual impact (unless the theme is boredom), but if the final number in the far right column, bottom row, stands out because it is written **$15,000,000** in red, then the viewer's immediate reaction to the exhibit is that somebody lost a lot of money. Having isolated the elements needed to promote visual impact, you should ask why the other elements are necessary—all those other rows and columns of numbers have become nothing more than background. Perhaps they should be *dimmed*, as computer programs do with commands that are unnecessary or unavailable at a particular time.

Even enlarged exhibits that *are* pictures are not effective if the relevant details are lost among other items in the scene. By direct analogy to the accounting worksheet discussed above, a pictorial scene may contain the relevant information, but not display it effectively because of the clutter caused by other items in the scene. To avoid any charges of unfairness or tampering, present the entire picture without enhancement, then present alongside the original an enhancement that circles the relevant item and dims the remaining scene, or circles the relevant item and "calls it out" with an arrow to an enlargement of that portion to the side—or which in some other way attracts attention to the important component and leaves the remainder as background. The advantage of visual exhibits is that through the eyes of the viewer they reinforce particular information.

10.6   Opposing Graphic Evidence at the Pretrial Conference

When opposing graphic evidence, look for changes in scale or perspective that might exaggerate or unduly emphasize the point being made. Remember the magician's trick: stacking objects one in front of another creates the illusion they are close to each other and that there is little or no space between them to hide things—the reality, however, is that things may have indeed been hidden. Also, even a graphic can be tilted to cause the jurors to see some things more easily than others. For example, does the graphic present a misleading "bird's eye view" that no one had and suggest the defendant could see all the danger points without obstruction?

When opposing, look carefully at the labels used on exhibits and consider whether that label is appropriate for the particular use at trial. Do the labels argue? Not allowed on opening. Do they lead? Not allowed on direct examination. Do the labels mischaracterize? Not allowed on direct or cross. Do the labels represent as evidence things not entered into evidence? Not allowed on closing.

Look at your opponent's method of emphasis in the exhibits. Do words or data contained in the exhibit shout at the jurors? The exhibits should only be allowed to "speak" to the jurors, analogous to limits a court would put on the way experts speak on the stand. After all, the jurors are instructed to take the evidence as a whole and presenters should not be allowed to unduly emphasize one part of the evidence over all the rest. Advertisers know how to do this; the opposing expert may also. Especially check for boxes with black text on bright yellow or orange background (like yield signs), which may unduly emphasize some information in a document over its context.

At pretrial, in limine—if not before—you will want to know what your opponent will be using in opening. If the opposing expert has created some super graphic or computer simulation as illustrative evidence, she may attempt to use the computer simulation in opening, which could be devastating to your case. You will want to see ahead of time not only all of your opponent's charts and exhibits, but also anything that moves or has animation. Remember, once the jurors see a scene or reenactment—either on a board, on a screen, or in a box (TV)—it will be very hard for them to unlearn it. Insist on previewing any animation so you can object if you doubt the foundation. (Remember to use Rule 611 (the court controls the mode of the presentation of evidence) and Rule 1006 (if the computer simulation is offered as a summary) to insure the court recognizes its obligation to insure you have been given a fair chance to see, understand, and respond to the underlying data.)

10.7   Handling Documents at Trial: Dancing with Documents

Be sure to let the judge know what you are about to do. Assuming the documents have been premarked, as is the case in most courts, there is no need to get the court reporter to mark a document separately. The memory trigger for handling documents can start with "Your Honor, I have in my hand a document that has been premarked for identification as Exhibit 13." The judge then can look at her list of documents and see what is coming.

Make the "three-step exhibit circuit" when presenting an item of evidence at trial. When you are ready to present an exhibit to the expert, open your folder of copies of that exhibit and take three copies in hand. Ask the court for permission to approach the expert (if you have not presented documents to this expert before and if you are allowed to leave the lectern). First, on your way to the expert, you should place one copy on opposing counsel's table saying, "Counsel" audibly so it is apparent to all that you have given him a copy. Second, you should say, "Your Honor, would you like a copy?" Third, hand the expert a copy, saying, "Ms. Hobart, I'm handing you Plaintiff's Exhibit 13 for identification." The first step prevents opposing counsel from interrupting your examination about the exhibit by asking for time to find his copy or by insisting he needs to compare his copy with the one the expert is using. The second step makes certain the judge is following the examination with her copy of the document; if the judge has her copy, she'll say, "Thank you, I have it." If the judge does not have her copy, she will take one from you and say, "Thank you." The third step makes it clear on the record that the expert has a copy of this particular exhibit in front of her, without you needing to make any artificial statements such as, "Your Honor, I would like the record to reflect that I am handing the expert . . . ."

Have the expert lay the foundation for the exhibit before asking questions about its contents and substance. Until the court has ruled that there is a proper basis for admitting the exhibit in evidence, its substance and content should not be put into the record or discussed in front of the jurors. Of course, with some exhibits, you must refer to the contents in a limited way to identify the contents as relevant. For example, someone would have to identify a photograph of the accident scene as a fair and accurate depiction of the relevant scene at a relevant time. Testimony on the contents beyond that would be inappropriate until the exhibit is received, so do not ask the expert before the exhibit is received "Is that how the plaintiff's body looked as it protruded through the windshield of the defendant's truck?"

Offer the exhibit in evidence. After you have completed the foundation for the exhibit, say, "Your Honor, I offer Plaintiff's Exhibit 13 in evidence." Nothing more complex is required. It is not necessary to say, "Your Honor, we move the admission of Plaintiff's Exhibit 13," or anything to that effect. The simple "I offer" is sufficient. In olden times or in very formal jurisdictions, counsel sometimes says, "I offer Plaintiff's Exhibit 13 for identification in evidence and ask that the identifying mark be stricken," but since there is not real possibility of ambiguity about what is happening, this is mostly excess verbiage.

During direct examination, bring your expert off the stand to work with the visual exhibits. Getting the expert out of her chair in the witness box allows her to move around, to talk with more animation, and to teach the jurors more naturally. On direct examination, use visual exhibits to provide an opportunity for the expert witness to come down and interact. Say, "Your Honor, may the witness come down to use an exhibit in explaining this point?" Schedule the use of exhibits for times when the jurors' (or judge's) attention and may be low: midmorning, right before lunch, late afternoon. Rehearse with the expert to make sure she does not inadvertently get in the way of the exhibit or misuse it.

In contrast, during cross-examination keep the opposing expert in her seat and resist her attempts to get in front of the jurors with an exhibit. On cross-examination, watch for attempts by the well-prepared opposing expert to maneuver you into letting her come down and explain something with visual exhibits. Beware the opposing expert who says on cross-examination: "Well, counsel, if I could just come down and show you what I mean on an exhibit I used earlier," or "Counsel, it might help the jury and judge if I just showed them a diagram that I have in my exhibit case." Respond to those requests with something like: "Let's just talk about this point for a moment, and then we can decide if we need the exhibit," or "Let me ask something else here, and then perhaps we'll come back to that area if we have time." Of course, whether you actually do come back to that area later depends on a host of factors, chief among which is whether you ever want to come back to that area.

Distribute the jurors' copies of a complicated exhibit after your expert has testified about it. If the testimony about an exhibit will take a few minutes—for example, when there are several portions of the exhibit to discuss—hold the jurors' copies until the testimony is completed so they will watch the overhead or blow-up and hear the testimony. If they receive their copies too early, they will busy themselves with reviewing the exhibits and miss portions of the oral testimony. If the exhibit is relatively straightforward and the testimony is short, you could distribute the copies before the testimony.

Consider the advantages and disadvantages of three different display options: the evidence camera-to-screen option, the computer-to-screen option, or the computer or video recorder-to-box or monitor. The evidence camera, or "Elmo," to screen option is the most versatile display option—and the easiest to operate. You only need to know how to turn on the camera's power, place the exhibit (document, picture, or object) under the lens, push the focus button, and move the exhibit to show what you want to show. The camera will then show a picture of the exhibit on a display screen. It also has a zoom button that allows you to focus on details. This option is a great backup if any of the other options goes wrong. As long as you have made a backup copy of your exhibits, you can simply put them under the evidence camera and turn on the machine.

A second option is the computer-to-display screen option. Many courtrooms today have projection systems that will project images from computer programs onto a large screen. PowerPoint and other trial evidence and presentation software can access slides or files containing exhibits, pictures, and videos—with a sweep of a bar code or the click of a mouse or an Internet connection—and, if hooked up properly to a compatible projector, project the exhibit for all the court to see. Of course, you need to make certain the jurors can see the details of the exhibit, simulation, and/or the size of the lettering. To do so, you will need to know about the lighting of the courtroom and the capabilities of the projector. Regarding size of lettering, some lawyers use the following formula to determine whether an audience will be able to read the screen: $D \times 0.05 = H$. D is the distance in feet to the farthest person in the room. H is the height in inches of letters or symbols on the screen, board, or flip chart. Thus, if the farthest person is thirty feet away from the screen, $30 \times .05 = 1.5$, and one-and-a-half inches is the smallest lettering you should use. (Actually, this seems too small to the authors; we would go with 0.1 as the multiplier, arriving at three inches in this example.)

A third option is the computer/video-to-monitor. Again, depending on the number of and size of monitors in the courtroom, the "box" method may be the best. If the monitors each have good sound systems (and sound is important), the monitor may be the best option. In addition, the box does give the display the look and feel of a TV newscast, which may enhance the credibility of the showing. If the judge and expert also have monitors, it allows them to preview and lay the foundation without premature publication to the jury.

Whatever the option, remember these ten tips for visuals:

1. Like billboard advertisers, shoot for one picture and no more than seven words per line;

2. Use professional colors and graphic devices such as boxes and borders;

3. Avoid overly slick displays, especially if you want the jurors to later handle and discuss the exhibit in the jury room;

4. Do not talk to the visual;

5. Stand alongside the visual and face the audience;

6. Do not show the visual before you or your expert begins talking about its subject;

7. To improve the jurors' and judge's focus, point to the appropriate places as you speak or reveal and cover (old-fashioned pointers are better than laser pointers because up to a third of the males in the courtroom cannot see red; therefore, the laser pointer is useless to them);

8. Think of the three "T"s—touch, turn, and talk. (And on direct, make it the expert who is doing the "T"s; if on cross, opening, or closing, you should do the "T"s);

9. With flip charts, do not talk and write simultaneously; and

10. For special emphasis and drama, pause mid-sentence, turn, face the chart or screen, and write or reveal without speaking, then turn back and reestablish eye contact.

Try to present your exhibits (and overall story) in chronological order. The exceptions to this approach may overwhelm the rule; nevertheless, your first approach to organization and the exhibits with the story should be chronological. First, chart out the story; then arrange the witnesses to cover the period of the story (with overlapping coverage); then rearrange the witnesses after determining their availability; and finally, arrange the exhibits—first chronologically and then distributed among the witnesses as necessary to lay the foundations. Some courts require the exhibits to be numbered in the order in which they are offered; the only practical way to do that is to number them as they are offered (have your backup number the copies for opposing counsel and your files simultaneously). If the documents are prenumbered and then introduced out of numerical order, find some opportunity in opening—or at the time the first document is admitted—to explain to the jurors that the numbers have nothing to do with the importance of the document—the numbers are just a way to keep track of sheets of paper and other items, and they should not be concerned about the number sequence.

Jurors' notebooks should contain your important documents, not all your documents. If the fourteen documents that win the case are buried among 312 other documents, the jurors will not give them proper attention; in other words, the impact of the most important documents will be diluted by the presence of the other documents. During your opening statement, tell the jurors that your will give them copies of the most important documents for them to place in their own notebooks; then, when you do give them a document, it will come with your implicit "certificate of importance." If, at the end of the trial, your fourteen or twenty-seven documents are aligned against your opponent's 327, you can argue that your opponent has tried to confuse the issues and the evidence, has refused to focus on the actual dispute, and has cluttered the record with irrelevancies not only in his documents, but also, undoubtedly, in his testimonial proof. If, however, the court insists all documents be placed into the juror's notebooks, ask your expert on the stand the following questions: "Which of these three documents was more important to you in coming to your conclusions?" "Which of these photographs did you find most useful in understanding the causes of the fire?" "Which of these charts provides the best summary of the performance of this industry during the 2000s?" Then, in closing, you can recall that testimony for the jurors and invite them to make a note of those more important documents.

Remember to preview and keep within the sightlines in the courtroom when presenting visual evidence. It is very frustrating for a juror or judge to be presented with a chart, document, or photograph that is just a little bit too far away or on too much of an angle to read easily, or is obscured by a glare from the window. Before the trial, check out the courtroom sightlines at several times during the day so you can see how the light changes. Put a colleague in the jury box and another on the witness stand, then determine where to place the easel or screen to allow clear viewing. Do not block your opponent's sightlines of the exhibits or put the jurors or expert behind the exhibits, but if there is no reasonable way to arrange the exhibits without blocking your opponent, tell the court and ask the court's permission to locate the exhibit so the jurors and expert can see it, inviting opposing counsel to move around to the front of the exhibit to participate in the examination. You want the judge to see the exhibit also, but reasonable judges understand that the expert and the jurors come first in this choreography. If you cannot work out an arrangement that allows the judge to see the exhibit from her bench, then make sure the judge understands and provide her with an additional copy of the exhibit, perhaps larger than previous copies, so she can follow the examination. Of course, if the expert is doing something to the exhibit or on the exhibit, then the choreography must allow the judge to observe the testimony.

10.8   Choosing the Medium and the Occasion

You should be allowed to use exhibits in opening statement if you have a good-faith basis for believing they will be admitted in evidence. In some jurisdictions

(Minnesota, for example), the use of visual exhibits in opening statement is generally forbidden, apparently on the theory that the jurors should not be exposed to material that has not been admitted into the record. Certainly, during the presentation of evidence, exhibits are not shown to the jurors until they are offered and received in evidence; however, testimony is routinely referred to in openings, even though no expert has yet taken the stand. If the opening is indeed supposed to present a preview of the evidence, that preview should include the visual evidence as well. If there is visual evidence that presents an unusually serious danger of unfair prejudice, it could be considered on motion in limine, and the court could reject it at that time or reserve a ruling until the foundation is heard at trial and direct that the particular exhibit not be used in the opening statement. There is no reason for a blanket rule that excludes all visual exhibits from opening when rulings on particular exhibits are available.

During opening and throughout the trial, timelines are essential exhibits. Events happen in the flow of time chronologically and often can be understood only against a background of a timeline. (Some call timelines anchors because they will anchor the jurors to the key events if they can place the events when they occurred.) Timelines are not vertical lists of events with dates attached; they are horizontal calendar bars into which events have been inserted. If the jurors are presented with a timeline exhibit early in the case, they will be able to follow the flow of events more easily and therefore understand the facts more clearly. If your version of events depends on showing confusion, disorganization, or lack of coordination—such as where you are trying to show absence of conspiracy or plan in defending a RICO case or a failure to respond appropriately to an emergency in prosecuting a personal injury case—then your goal would be to display many events on a timeline, emphasizing the lack of chronological relevance among them. When you create a timeline exhibit in front of the jurors, event by event, you invite their participation; as a result, they become invested in the exhibit and protective of it, resisting and resenting efforts by opposing counsel and opposing experts to dismiss it or to change it without sufficient basis.

10.9   The Next Level of Persuasion with Exhibits

Every exhibit has not only a legal foundation, but also a persuasive foundation—a set of questions for the expert that will explain the events and persuade the jurors on a key issue in the case. Often, lawyers get to the exhibit too early and miss the underlying importance of the factual context of the exhibit. For example, an exhibit may merely corroborate an important event, like a telephone call where goods were ordered. The exhibit must not diminish the importance of the expert witness's memory of doing the test or discovering the key result. Sometimes the context is independently persuasive. For example, you should not interrupt a police officer who is describing the scene of an accident just when she is about to tell about the condition of your client. Nor should you interrupt your expert when she is about to state her causation opinion with a question like, "Now, Dr. Done, did you prepare a diagram that shows the shape of molecules known to cause birth defects and the shape of Bendectin?" That will distract the jurors from Dr. Done's opinion that Bendectin caused birth defects because you are preoccupied by the legal technicalities of admissibility. Or you may miss the chance to get a point told twice by going to the exhibit too early. If an expert can describe an event orally, with drama, then you can go back over it with more detail a second time with a document or graphic. Finally, even the technical foundation should not be rushed. If a document is a business record, let the jurors in on the persuasive nature of the Federal Rules of Evidence. By asking about the importance of records to a particular business, who looks at them, and why they need the records to be accurate, you will lay this "persuasive" foundation in a narrative fashion so the jurors understand why business records would be accurate. The technical, by-the-rules leading questions can be asked for the benefit of the court just before the document is offered: "Was Exhibit 3 prepared in the ordinary course of business by someone with knowledge at or near the time of the events it records, and was the document kept as a part of a regularly conducted business activity?" "Yes." Again, in these situations, do not go to the legal foundation until you have laid the persuasive foundation.

Do not ask to "publish" admitted documents to the jury; ask instead to be allowed to show the document or piece of evidence to the jurors. This is not a big deal, just a minor quibble. Each time you use specialized, legalistic language, you remind the jurors that you are a lawyer, and they are not. Since your goal is to communicate, to relate, to teach, you should use language your audience is familiar with, not language that requires constant interpretation and translation. Observe the "do not walk and talk" rule. In the theater, when one character is delivering an important line or monologue, the other actors refrain from any activity that would distract the audience's attention; otherwise, they are guilty of "upstaging" the actor during the scene or "walking on his lines." In court, when you are handling your own exhibits, remember this same rule. You can walk and talk when you are not saying anything important—for example, when you are merely doing the exhibit circuit and delivering copies of the exhibit to the opponent, the court, and the expert. However, when you are asking substantive questions about an exhibit, stand still; when your expert is speaking about an exhibit, stand still; when you have just handed an important exhibit to the jurors and you want them to see the clarity with which it makes your point, stand still. If you don't, your motion around the courtroom will make the audience think they need to watch, that something more interesting than the exhibit might be about to happen.

Magnetic cards that stick up on a whiteboard are a very effective way to present words, category titles, and essential quotes. The process of adding, subtracting, and rearranging words and phrases is neat, quick, and simple. You can emphasize the subject of particular testimony, give a heading to a listing of factors, or add a picture to a speaker's words without detracting from your own performance by relying on your own (possible) poor public penmanship. You can also color code the magnetic cards, so related ideas are immediately associated with one another. In theory, Velcro stick-ups should work just as well, but they do not because they are not actually magic like magnetic cards. Magnetic tape with an adhesive back can be used to stick just about anything on a coated steel board.

With magnetic or Velcro cards or small items of real evidence, you or your expert should hold them while you examine the expert about them. The jurors look from you to the expert and back while they listen to the questions and answers. You will present a memorable picture if you are holding a foam board card that reads, "Nicotine is addictive," while you question the expert about label warnings; or a card that reads, "No reliable studies," while you cross-examine on bases for expert testimony; or a piece of rusted metal from the actual building in question while you ask the architect questions about the adequacy of corrosion protection of the steel embedded in the foundation. In other words, you should do something with your visual evidence in addition to putting it in front of the jurors' eyes. Talk about it; walk with it; handle it; hand it to the expert as she steps from the expert box, and ask her to put it up on the magnetic board or to hold it in the same position it had in the building. When that line of questioning is finished and you ask the court for two minutes to check your notes, ask if the document or item of real evidence can be passed to the jurors for their examination. (If the document is not already in their notebooks, this is when you could pass out copies so the testimony is not interrupted.)

Use multiple easels to display different exhibits simultaneously. There are times when you need to show two boards so the jurors can appreciate the difference or the progression—the comparison—without going through Tufte's "one damn thing after another." In fact, putting a visual exhibit on easel A, then a different one on B, then a new one on A, and so on keeps the show going while allowing the audience (judge and jurors) to see where they have been. If you project a computer graphic on a screen between the two easels, then a little coordination results in a multi-media tour de force.

Television sets are sometimes more effective than big-screen projection, and sometimes they are not. Jury analysts once reported that jurors tend to believe what they see on television because of their association of television with a reliable newscaster and other trusted commentators. Additionally, televisions can be seen in normal room lighting. Conversely, big screens are often associated with *Star Wars, Indiana Jones, Pocahontas*, and other fables and fictions. However, television is very common and can become part of the background noise at home, while big-screen movies promise excitement and entertainment. So here is a guide to choosing among static boards, displays on television, and projections on a big screen:

- if motion is not important to the point being made, use boards on easels;
- if the segment depends on motion, such as a deposition or demonstration, and it is short, use the televisions because they are bright, easy on and off, and very reliable; and

- if the exhibit needs motion, but is longer, use the big screen projection so background distractions are reduced and the main points are clearly shown.

Remember that with any of these presentation modes, the material must be high-interest; the jurors would prefer to see live cross-examination, experts defending their opinions to the death, and battles between real flesh and blood lawyers who succeed by their wits and wiles, just like on *The Practice, Law and Order, Boston Legal,* and *The Good Wife.*

You cannot alter an opponent's graphics. You cannot not mark or edit your opponent's admitted graphic evidence or have your expert alter it. You may, however, make your own copy and mark it, or overlay your opponent's original with an acetate sheet, have your expert or the opponent's expert mark the sheet, and offer the marked copy or graphic in evidence. Assuming the markings are relevant, the marked copy is as admissible as the original exhibit and should be considered by the judge or jury along with that original. There is much satisfaction in turning an opponent's graphic evidence against him by pointing out errors or inconsistencies or by highlighting portions that support your case, especially if your opponent's expert can be enlisted in the effort. You can attack expert's exhibits with the same tools you use to attack expert testimony. As presented elsewhere (see chapters 11 and 12), you can often attack expert testimony by identifying things the expert did not do, information the expert did not consider, and assumptions the expert had to make. To the extent the expert's exhibits reflect or illustrate the opinions that suffer from these weaknesses, they may be turned to the advantage of the cross-examiner. For example, if the expert has calculated the present value of a future income stream, which required him to make assumptions about future interest rates and inflation rates, an exhibit that shows the calculation embodies whatever assumptions the expert made about those variables. Using the expert's deposition testimony on the range of assumptions that were reasonable and the same computerized formula that generated the expert's results shown on the chart, you should first have the expert "guide" you through duplicating the expert's result (displaying it side by side with the expert's own chart to show they are identical); then you should have the expert help you enter your chosen, reasonable alternative assumptions. The resulting chart should present the alternative assumptions next to the different results (e.g., the expert's 4.7 percent next to his $2 million, and your alternative 5.5 percent next to your $43.18). Use the opposing expert to lay the foundation for each of these additional exhibits, which are merely variations on his own, by leading him through the appropriate testimony. During such examination, it is important to emphasize through repetition that you and the expert are following the same methodology as she did in creating her original exhibit.

If you create a new exhibit during expert cross-examination, number it and offer it in evidence. It may be merely illustrative if it has no intrinsic substantive value, but only illustrates the expert's testimony (or his cross-examination), or it may be substantive if the expert has allowed you to lay the foundation for new substantive information, which is contained or displayed in the exhibit (perhaps from a "learned treatise" that you have used pursuant to Rule 803(18)). Regardless of its status, you should get it numbered and admitted—even if it is for a limited purpose—so you can refer to it during later examinations and closing argument.

Give your own expert the ammunition to counter attempts to create new "cross-examination exhibits." During preparation for testimony at trial, explain to your expert that opposing counsel may try to create new exhibits or alter the expert's own exhibits. Tell your expert that when it is true, she can disagree with the cross-examiner's new exhibits by saying: "That's not my methodology, but I can explain further," or "That's not what I did, but I will be happy to show you my approach." The cross-examiner must rely on the hostile expert to lay the foundation for the new exhibit. Therefore, if the expert understands that, she can say, "I think your new exhibit is misleading." The court may not receive the exhibit or the jurors may not give it any weight. Of course, you need to educate the expert needs about trigger words like "misleading, "incomplete," or "confusing," which are more effective than others in frustrating such cross-examination.

Observe the "gold and dross" rule. Many attorneys carry their documents around the courtroom as though they were as important as a brown-bag lunch—papers bunched in fist, arm swinging at side, eyes on the expert or court. That is a fine way to carry an opponent's exhibit—the implicit message being that the exhibit is not worth any more attention or care than that; those exhibits are the dross, the metallic impurities that are discarded during the smelting of gold. But with your own exhibits, treat each sheet as though it was engraved on gold foil, as though it had substantial weight, as though each time you look at it you are once again impressed with its significance. Hold your exhibit in two hands as you carry it across the courtroom and return it to the table or folder as though you care about keeping it organized and undamaged. With your most important exhibits (just a few), keep your copies in envelopes and put them back into those envelopes after you ask your questions. Then, during closing argument, you can take them out of the envelopes again, and the jurors will remember that these are important materials.

In the closing, review only the important visual and documentary exhibits, not all the exhibits. Avoid overwhelming the jurors, especially after they have just sat through the typically overlong presentation of the entire case. Once again, select the exhibits that make a difference, just as you select certain testimony to emphasize. Where you have used a series of exhibits at trial (for example, to show growth, change, or other comparisons), consider whether you could present the first and last exhibits in the series to help the jurors remember the scope of the change or difference. Remember that merely illustrative exhibits are often excluded from the jury room; if you highlight those illustrative exhibits in your closing, the jurors could be disappointed or confused when the illustrative exhibits are not available to them during deliberations.

With regard to PowerPoint or other presentation software during closing argument, remember that less is more, or it soon becomes "one damn slide after another." The technology of presentations software is seductive because it is fun to create and because it allows you to share your notes with the jurors during your closing. Yet you need to stay in touch with the jurors' nonverbal cues about their interest and skepticism. If you are too wedded to your prepared presentation, you are likely to lose your jury. Also, the power of the screen means the jurors will likely stop paying attention to you and watch the screen. Because they will also need time to read the screen, you will be tempted to speak "over the top" of their reading. To avoid both the competition with the screen and the boredom of too many slides, mix your medium. Start with talking to the jurors directly, then use timelines and charts—and only a few slides of your most important pictures and documents with call-outs. And when it comes time to wrap up, turn the technology off, retake center stage, look at the jurors, and talk to them. Again, regarding technology, less is more on closing.

We have briefly mentioned this before, but one last technique to consider with the right type of expert is whether to use a video of your expert in the lab to enliven your presentation. Such a video can be used as an illustrative exhibit on direct—this would give the jurors a chance to see the expert actually conducting his experiments. For example, if a termite expert was pulling up stoops and crawling under foundations to determine what kind of termite was causing damage, then the best way to convince the jurors is to take them to the scene with the expert so they can see how the expert did her job. Or if a part of the autopsy is particularly important, have the forensic pathologist create a video showing how he uses his examination of the body to determine the path of the bullet.

CHAPTER ELEVEN

CROSS-EXAMINATION OF AN EXPERT WITNESS: CONTROL

A credible opposing expert represents a substantial threat to your case. You must exercise close control to prevent cross-examination from becoming a vigorous restatement of the expert's direct. Control begins with properly formed leading questions devoid of argumentative adjectives and adverbs, and continues using repetition, reverse repetition, eye contact, pleas for reciprocal fairness, and (as a last resort) instructions from the court.

Witness control is important for cross-examination of lay witnesses; for experts, it is even more important. You should review the principles of cross-examination generally and look at how those principles are applied to cross-examination of an expert.

11.1   Form of Question

Cross-examination is not a time to do discovery. You should cross-examine only to the extent necessary to make your point for closing argument. The reason to take this limited view of cross, particularly with an expert, is that the expert will repeat and improve her story during the cross-examination and therefore make it easier for the jurors to understand. In other words, the expert will be able to fill the gaps left from direct by responding to new questions in a way that makes her case even better. Where the witness is articulate and persuasive, as is often the case with the expert witness, it is all the more important to control the witness on cross-examination.

Whenever you cross-examine an expert witness, refine the form of your question so that it displays as little curiosity as possible (but use a tone that conveys incredulity). This first rule is sometimes stated: always lead the witness. Yet a further refinement is in order. There are three forms of questions that are available for use in court. The first form, which shows the most curiosity from the questioner, is a question that starts with the following: "who," "what," "when," "where," "how," "why," "tell us," "describe," "explain." These questions are most often used on direct examination, and they ask the witness to tell the jurors in her own words what she knows. Because the witness becomes the center of attention, the witness can develop rapport, establish her credibility by speaking to the jurors, and teach the jurors what she knows.

The second form of question, which start with verbs, may or may not be objectionable leading questions. For example, "Do you see the person in the courtroom who you saw hold up the clerk?" does not unduly suggest the answer, although it does suggest the person is in the courtroom. Nevertheless, the question focuses everyone on a particular point of importance to the examiner—the identity of the criminal. However, it is still not completely controlling. Suppose, however, you ask the witness: "There is a person sitting next to defense counsel wearing a green tie and a yellow jacket. That's the same man you saw hold up the clerk, isn't it?" Here, you would be leading the witness, and you would greatly diminish the witness's credibility by reducing her role to that of merely confirming that what you say is true. This is the third type of question, and it is what we want to use for cross of an expert for maximum control.

Look carefully at this third form of question. It is more in the nature of a statement than a question because its syntax is "noun-verb" instead of the inverted "verb-noun," which is normally used to signal a question. The examiner tells the witness what happened and thereby tells the jurors what happened. The question bounces off the witness and into the minds of the jurors. As a further example:

Q: Dr. Done, you reviewed the epidemiological studies on Bendectin?"

A: Yes.

Q: The studies you examined showed no significant difference in the rate of birth defects in the children of women who took Bendectin?

A: That is right.

Of course, there are no guarantees an expert like Dr. Done will not volunteer longer answers or try to be cute at the end of a statement form of the question and ask, "Is that a question?" (If the judge insists you ask a question, follow up your statement with the words "Right?" or "Correct?", but after a couple of these, you should be able to go back to the simple statement form.) It is clear to everyone in the courtroom that your statement invites the witness to correct you if the witness disagrees, and therefore, it is understood and accepted as a question. The effect on many witnesses of using this noun-verb form of question is to train the witness to follow along with your logic without interrupting with long explanations.

The second rule of expert cross-examination is: keep the questions short. You will maintain better control of expert (and lay) witnesses by keeping the question short, so the witness has fewer words to quibble with. Some commentators suggest you keep your questions to seven words or fewer: "Doctor, you are not an epidemiologist?[1] You didn't graduate from Harvard? You went to a foreign medical school? Your medical degree is from Guadalupe?"

The shorter the question, the less time the witness has to think of an escape route or to quarrel with the attorney. Short questions also allow the jurors to appreciate the ultimate point as it develops, so they discover it or anticipate it for themselves. ("Oh, it sounds like this doctor is not nearly as well qualified as the doctor this attorney presented yesterday.") When jurors come to their own conclusion on such a point, they will hold that conclusion more firmly than if they feel it is merely an argument from the lawyer.

Now consider the third rule that maximizes control: use only facts and not conclusions, adjectives, or wiggle words. For example, compare the following two approaches. First:

Q: Dr. Done, you take the unwarranted and unreasonable position that Bendectin causes birth defects?

A: Well, I disagree that it is unwarranted and unreasonable because
. . . .

Ten minutes later, Dr. Done will still be testifying.

Second:

Q: Now, Dr. Done, you say that Bendectin causes birth defects?

A: Yes.

Q: You've looked at existing epidemiological studies?

A: That's right.

Q: Their conclusions don't support you?

A: That's true.

---

1. Question marks are used in writing these "statement-questions" to remind the reader that you are questioning the witness and need to obtain an answer. However, the normal inflection for questions in social conversation, where the voice rises in pitch at the end of the sentence, is not used for cross-examination questions; instead, the voice drops at the end, just as it would on a declarative statement such as, "I went to the store." As a mnemonic device to aid in recalling the sound of such a question, think of the motif of Beethoven's Fifth Symphony, "dum, dum, dum, DUM" and say, "You bought some milk. You stole the drugs. You are a crook. You killed the dog." Then extend the length of the sentence (trying to keep it under seven words), but maintain the delivery: "You never went home that day. You told him you needed to work late. You said, 'I love you,' and hung up the phone." All of these statement-questions should end with a slight drop in the pitch of the voice to emphasize there is really no question about the truth of the facts stated. Or, again, for variation or as an advanced technique, try incredulity, where your tone is more like what you would use when you say, "You have got to be kidding me that you believe that."

While you would be sorely tempted at this point to say, "So, how can you con-clude that Bendectin causes birth defects?", the danger is Dr. Done will be ready with an answer:

> Because I find support in the animal studies showing birth defects in animals that were injected with Bendectin. I also know the shape of a key molecular component of Bendectin is very close to the shape of a molecule we know is related to birth defects in humans, and I have also amalgamated and reanalyzed all of the data, which allows me to be confident enough to draw my recent conclusions.

Again, it is better to lead Dr. Done into your point by keeping your questions leading, short, and factual.

Q: Dr. Done, let's talk about animal studies.

Q: Many scientists are cautious about them?

Q: Drugs can affect animals and humans differently?

Q: The effects of drugs on animals may be unreliable to predict a drug effect on humans?

Q: You worked at the FDA? You never approved a drug as safe, based solely on animal studies?

Your goal is to avoid all the excuses for the witness to talk beyond simply agreeing with the point you are making. If in response to such a question, the witness adds an answer beyond a simple "yes" or "no," you can follow up using a number of other control techniques that will demonstrate the witness is not playing fair.

11.2 Control Techniques for the "Run-On" Witness

11.2.1 Repeat the Question

Where a witness expands an answer to a tightly constructed, single fact, short question, one way to reassert control is to repeat the exact same question. The effect in the courtroom is really quite amazing because this technique points out to the jurors that the witness really is not playing fair—the question did not call for a further explanation. For example, if the cross-examiner asks, "Dr. Done, no epidemiological studies connect Bendectin to birth defects?", and Dr. Done volunteers, "No, but that doesn't matter because I have developed additional methodologies for analyzing the existing data, which I think are quite effective," simply then say, "Dr. Done, no studies connect Bendectin to birth defects?" If the expert runs on again, the jurors will see his avoidance as advocacy and discount his credibility. And if Dr. Done runs on again, you can start to take the gloves off some more.

11.2.2 Use a "Reverse Repeat"

The reverse repeat sometimes surprises the witness into answering shortly and directly. Do not interrupt because it appears rude and suggests you are afraid of what Dr. Done has to say. Even though it is difficult, it is probably better to wait until the witness finishes answering, unless the answer is unfairly prejudicial and inadmissible. After the expert has finished, use a "reverse repeat": "Wait, now, Dr. Done, are you saying that there *are* epidemiological studies that show a statistically significant correlation between Bendectin and birth defects?" Note also that the language of the reverse repeat is more specific and defined than the global terms used in the initial question. You have, in effect, raised the bar through this question. To defend his position now, the expert needs not just to identify "studies that connect" the original question, but "epidemiological studies" that "show a statistically significant correlation." So in the initial global question, you try to exclude the universe of studies; in the reverse repeat question, you force the expert witness to identify a very specific type of study you know does not exist. The result of his denial in response to the reverse repeat is that the trier of fact assumes there are no "studies that connect," just as you wanted to prove with your initial question.

A further example may clarify this point of rhetorical art. The question is, "There are no good violinists from New Jersey," and the witness waffles, "Well, I have certainly seen and heard a number of quite competent violinists as I traveled through New Jersey and other northeastern states." You then ask the reverse repeat, "Doctor, are you saying that there are violinists born and trained in New Jersey who have won international acclaim for their musicianship and who have gone on to become first violinists with the symphony orchestra in any major American city?" You know there are no such people because you have added qualifications that your research revealed no one possesses, just as you knew there were no "statistically significant epidemiological studies." If the reverse repeat is simply a repetition in a different syntax, it will receive the same unwanted answer; it must add qualifications, which seem fair and relevant to the jurors and, at the same time, force the witness to give the answer you want.

11.2.3 Cross-Examine the Witness with Your Eyes

Another technique to gain and maintain control is to pause and look the witness in the eye from "center stage" before starting the examination. This focuses the attention of the courtroom on the witness and impliedly says, "I dare you to look me in the eye and lie." Second, if you take a position center stage and the witness must look you in the eye, then the witness cannot look at the jurors without appearing to be avoiding you. This may make the witness forget she is trying to persuade the jurors as she focuses instead on you, the source of the attack. Third, intense eye contact with the witness will give you more clues that the witness may not be going along with the question. If the witness starts to shake her head, to look at her lawyer, or to flip through her report, then you can see you are about to lose her. At that point, it is better to withdraw the question, so the witness will not have the chance to debate your point, than to plow ahead and face the possible harmful answer.

11.2.4 Other Control Techniques

If the witness still persists in volunteering, you might decide it is necessary to take on the witness even further. One technique is to raise your hand before you start the question, take a few steps toward the witness (where allowed), and preface your question by saying: "Now, ma'am, stay with me on this. Try to give me a 'yes' or 'no' here, OK? Will you do that?" (The "ma'am" works well for one of the authors, who can be an "aw, shucks" kind of guy, but does not work at all for the other. The "ma'am" may be too Jimmy Stewart for some attorneys who should instead just use "Dr. Smith.") Then proceed right to your next question.

Or counsel might try to play "Let's Make a Deal": "Dr. Smith, I'll make a deal with you. First, you answer my question, and then you can explain whatever you want in addition." Of course, if the witness accepts that invitation to insert additional information, be careful to avoid the "deer in the headlights" look. Do not position yourself in a way that forces you to look at her while she is answering. If you believe the jurors have already figured out that she has become an advocate and does not deserve your full attention, you might go back to your notes and flip through them, or look at your watch and show some impatience, or even, in the most extreme cases, turn half away from the witness, look at the clock, and then turn back when she is finished, saying, "Are you done? OK, now let's get back to the facts."

Another control technique is to preface the question with a statement that describes the purpose of cross-examination. For example, you might say: "Now, Dr. Smith, you understand your lawyer has already had a chance to ask you all the questions he thought you needed to answer on direct, so would you just listen to my question and answer it," or, "When I'm done, your lawyer can go back and ask you more questions, but now you need to listen to my question and try to answer me."

11.2.5 Do Not Go to the Judge Too Early, if at All

Most experienced trial lawyers say they never ask the judge for help. They are concerned that if they ask, they may not get it, or they are afraid that asking for help shows they lost control of the witness; or they are afraid of looking whiny or like a crybaby ("Judge, make her answer my question"). If, however, you have been patient and reasonable, there may be no need to make the request because the judge will jump in and tell the witness to answer the question that has been asked. In any event, seek the court's help infrequently and only when the answer you seek is necessary to allow you to continue with other portions of your cross.

CHAPTER TWELVE

CROSS-EXAMINATION OF AN EXPERT WITNESS: IMPEACHMENT

Once again, the danger posed by clever opposing experts is they are more likely to recognize attempts at impeachment from a distance and to take steps to avoid any damage. Nevertheless, thorough fact investigation through pretrial discovery and successful depositions can provide material for impeachments by prior inconsistent statements, by omission (of the pertinent facts from a prior statement), by chart cross-examination, by learned treatises, for financial or other bias or prejudice, and for bad character. (Challenges to the reliability of expert testimony may take the form of impeachment—for example, challenging the reliability of the methodology because it is apparently internally inconsistent—but the interesting part of such cross-examination is the substance of the challenge, not the form as impeachment; therefore, the discussion of reliability challenges will be postponed until the detailed treatment of *Daubert* and *Kumho* in chapters fifteen, sixteen, and seventeen.)

12.1   Impeachment with a Prior Inconsistent Statement

Much cross-examination consists of impeachment (or attempted impeachment). Not only will you attempt to impeach a witness for bias, prejudice, lack of perception, prior bad acts, and past crimes, but every once in a while the witness says something at trial that is contradicted by an earlier statement in a letter, report, or sworn testimony. When this happens, determine the significance of the inconsistency. If the inconsistency is trivial or easily explainable, then do not interrupt your prepared cross to point the inconsistency out to the jurors. In other words, resist your "instinct for the capillary" and use your cross for more important matters. However, if you have a number of individually minor inconsistencies, these may add up to a showing that the witness is not credible on any one thing, just as a major inconsistency or contradiction would. Next, determine whether you believe the earlier statement is true. If it is not true, are you still tempted to use it because it shows the witness simply does not know what happened or has little regard for the truth? But if the witness is saying in court the opposite of what she said earlier—and what you think is true—then you need to demonstrate the truth of the earlier statement by taking the jurors and court through four important steps remembered as "commit, credit, confront, and contrast." These steps (the "four Cs") will keep you organized in the face of the lying witness and help you demonstrate what you know.

Your first job is to let the judge know what is coming, because whenever you pick up a piece of paper, the judge's immediate reaction is to think the paper may be hearsay. While prior inconsistent statements are not hearsay under Rule 801, the judge does not know your purpose or the nature of the document you have in your hand; thus, the first step in any impeachment is to "commit" the witness to her previous in-court testimony. There are two basic ways to do commitments. First, you can do it the "old-fashioned way."

> Q: Did you tell this jury today that you believe the data were sufficient to support a statistically reliable conclusion?
>
> A: That's right.

Note a number of things from this old-fashioned approach to commitment. You must distance yourself from the witness's in-court statement by using a fairly incredulous tone of voice. Instead of saying, "Is it your testimony?", say, "tell," "say," "claim," or "is it your story?" By using these words, you makes it sound like you do not believe what the witness said. It also tells the judge and jurors something else is coming that will prove the witness's statement is untrue.

Yet, some lawyers feel using tone and word choice to evoke incredulity is still too subtle. Some are worried that by repeating the testimony, the jurors will more likely remember it the way the witness now says it happened. One alternative approach is to use a reverse commitment, asserting the truth of the earlier statement and the opposite of what the witness said in court, so that the jurors hear the cross-examiner's version as the set-up. (The witness might even agree with the cross-examiner, so that impeachment will not be necessary):

> Q: The data were insufficient for statistical accuracy, weren't they?
>
> A: No, no, that's not correct. The data were generally sufficient.
>
> Q: But, they were insufficient to allow any conclusions as to cause and effect?
>
> A: No, I disagree.

This last statement is now the statement you impeach (for example, with deposition testimony that data were insufficient). The advantage to this approach is the words the jurors hear from you are always your version of the story, and you are not repeating the witness's lies or misstatements. The witness's final disagreement is what is impeached with the earlier statement.

Under either the old or new approach, however, you need to next move to the second "C," crediting (or accrediting) the out-of-court, inconsistent statement, demonstrating circumstances that make that statement more likely true. For example:

Q: You wrote an early report to your lawyer in this case?

A: Yes.

Q: He wanted your help in determining the cause of the birth defects?

A: Yes.

Q: You told him the truth?

A: Yes.

Q: You wrote it up in a letter to him, which you signed?

A: I don't remember precisely, but that sounds right.

Counsel: Your Honor, I have here a document, which has previously been marked Defense Exhibit 117 for identification. May I approach the witness?

Court: Yes.

Q: I'm showing you Exhibit 117. You are the Dr. Smith referred to here?

A: That's right.

Q: Exhibit 117 is entitled "Draft Report of Dr. James Smith"?

A: Yes.

Q: It contains three pages?

A: Yes.

Q: This is your signature here, at the bottom?

A: Yes.

Q: And the letter is dated August 24?

A: Yes.

Q: August 24, that was three weeks after you were hired?

A: Yes.

This cross-examination displays the circumstances surrounding the creation of the early statement that make it more likely to be true. Of course, if the accrediting document is a deposition, letter, or the witness's final report, then the questions will reflect what makes those documents important and credible.

One difficulty that can arise is that if you take too long with the accrediting portion of the impeachment, the jurors can lose track of the earlier in-court statement. Some lawyers prefer to go directly to the impeaching statement, and if the witness is quarrelsome, do the accrediting questions as counterpunches. For example, some prefer:

Q: Dr. Smith, the data were not sufficient for statistical purposes, were they?

A: No, they were sufficient.

Q: They were not sufficient because there were not enough data points, right?

A: No, I disagree.

Q: Well, Dr. Smith, you wrote an early report that said [*picks up the statement and reads*]: "Additional data sources will be needed to permit valid statistical analysis."

A: I don't recall that.

Q: Well, let's take a look. Your Honor, I have here a document entitled "Draft Report of Dr. Smith." I'd like it marked as Exhibit 117. May I approach the witness? Dr. Smith, let me hand you a copy of Exhibit 117.

A: Yes.

Q: That is your signature at the bottom?

A: Yes.

[*Other accrediting questions.*]

Q: Now read along and tell me if I read this right.

The advantage to the second approach is that you get the contrast out up front, you have the accreditation, and then you get to reread the impeaching statement. And, of course, there are other variations on this theme. You can commit, accredit, and then recommit or reverse commit just before you confront, or you can use the blackboard or flip chart and list the in-court testimony under the heading "Claim Today" and the early statement under "Previous Claim." This technique is particularly effective if you have a number of inconsistencies, which individually may not sound like much, but, when taken together, show the witness either is confused or lying. For example:

SUBJECT	CLAIM TODAY	PREVIOUS CLAIM
Adequacy of data	Perfectly adequate	Inadequate
Additional data	Available	Unavailable
Statistical certainty	Greater than 95%	Unacceptable
Additional work	Unnecessary	Desirable
Calculated risk multiple	2.7–3.5	Less than 2.0

This kind of presentation is sometimes called a "chart cross-examination." It is especially effective where the significance of an individual inconsistency is not especially clear to the jurors,[1] but they can appreciate the fact of inconsistencies, which all show a bias to the other side. Of course, if there are inconsistencies going both ways, the chart would emphasize those inconsistencies that result in a change in favor of the expert's client; perhaps another chart, on less substantive topics, would show changes going both ways to support the argument that the expert is confused in her analysis or is trying to satisfy everyone.

12.2   Impeachments by Omission

Experts often add information to their in-court testimony. They had a chance to say the same thing in their witness statement or deposition, but they did not do so. The challenge for the cross-examiner in this situation is to show these key facts would have been included earlier *if they had been true*, so their omission form the earlier statement indicates they are untrue. The cross-examination suggests that intervening conversations with the lawyers or their clients, who they want to help, have caused the expert to shade the truth (or flat-out lie) now that the case has come to trial.

Again, you must be careful that you are not going after a capillary or using a gun to kill a gnat. If the omission shows an expert witness is improving her in-court story to help her side, then impeachment by omission can be as devastating as impeachment by prior inconsistent statement. Using as an example an expert witness (of sorts), a law-enforcement officer, she may improve her identification of a witness on the stand by testifying as follows:

---

1. For example, the trier-of-fact is unlikely to know, without education from counsel, of the significance of the relative risk numbers. In analyzing risks, statistical epidemiologists and their followers use relative risk figures to indicate the importance of a particular variable as a cause of the effect being studied. In the Bendectin cases, for example, the control group of non-Bendectin patients would show a relative risk of birth defect as 1.0 by definition, since it is the control group; assume the Bendectin patient group showed a relative risk of 1.7, that is, an increase of 0.7. The courts have accepted the argument that causation has not been shown by a preponderance of the evidence because the possibility that the defect was caused by non-Bendectin factors (1.0) is at least as great as the possibility that it was caused by Bendectin (0.7). By this logic, the relative risk associated with the suspect variable must always exceed 2.0 for a plaintiff's case to be successful. Therefore, the expert's earlier statement, shown in the chart, that the relative risk was less than 2.0 is fatal to the plaintiff's case.

Q: How did she appear at that time?

A: I saw a 5'5" white female, approximately 125 pounds. She had short brown hair—almost like a man—was wearing glasses, and had several earrings in each ear. She was wearing a tan trench coat, belted at the waist, knee-high brown leather boots, and she was carrying a brown leather shoulder bag on her right shoulder.

You question as follows:

Q: Special Agent O'Rourke, you're a special agent with the FBI?

A: Yes.

Q: You have been trained in making witness identifications?

A: Yes.

Q: Special Agent O'Rourke, you would agree that some identifications by witnesses are better than others?

A: I don't know what you mean.

Q: Well, all things being equal, an identification that included the gender of the suspect would be better than an identification that didn't mention the gender?

A: Yes.

Q: And an identification that included something distinctive about the suspect's hair would be better than one that didn't have anything about the hair?

A: Yes, though hair can be cut.

Q: Yes, but it is difficult to grow it in a short period of time, wouldn't you agree?

A: Yes.

Q: That's why you will often note cut of hair, if you know it? And certainly its color? If you know it?

A: Yes.

Q: And distinctive footwear? In these days after the O.J. trial, we all realize that noting distinctive footwear can make an identification better?

A: I guess.

Q: And distinctive jewelry should also be noted, if you see it?

A: I guess.

Q: And a report should include what a person is carrying? And perhaps how they are carrying it, because that can tell you something about whether they might be right-handed or left?

A: It might.

Q: Noting that they are carrying something can also make an identification better than an identification that does not note whether the witness is carrying anything?

A: Yes.

Q: Now Officer, today you claim that over a year from the night you saw the suspect on Front Street, the suspect was (I wrote this down when you testified because I wanted to get it right) 5'5"white female, approximately 125 pounds. [Suspect] had short brown hair—almost like a man—was wearing glasses, and had several earrings in each ear. [Suspect] was wearing a tan trench coat, belted at the waist, knee-high brown leather boots, and . . . was carrying a brown leather shoulder bag on her right shoulder?

[Note the word "claim." Even in the commitment stage, you should not adopt the witness's version of the events. You should never put in the gender of your client nor use your client's name when confirming the witness's story.]

A: Right.

Q: Officer, you made a report the morning after you saw the suspect?

A: Right.

Q: You have been trained in making reports?

A: Yes.

Q: At Quantico, Virginia, the FBI's special training facility?

A: Yes.

Q: You were taught about the importance of making reports?

A: Yes.

Q: That you must be accurate?

A: Yes.

Q: That they must be complete?

A: Yes.

Q: That other officers will use the report to try to find and arrest a suspect?

A: Yes.

Q: And the more important details you include, the better?

A: Yes.

Q: That often the U.S. Attorney might review these reports for accuracy? And to evaluate whether to even bring the case?

A: I guess.

Q: I have in my hand Exhibit 34 for identification, a document entitled "Report of Officer O'Rourke." [*To the court.*] May I approach the witness?

Court: Yes.

Q: Officer, Exhibit 34 is a copy of your report of what you saw at 2:00 a.m. on November 14 of last year?

A: Yes.

Q: Let me give you this pen. Would you please circle for me where you identified the suspect as female?

A: Well, it says 5'5", 125 pounds.

Q: It doesn't say female, does it?

A: No.

Q: In fact, you mention a trench coat, but where do you say the trench coat is belted?

A: It is not there.

Q: Now about earrings, circle for me where you say the suspect was wearing earrings.

A: I don't.

Q: That's right; it's not there, is it?

A: No.

Q: And where do you say that the suspect has short hair?

A: I don't.

Q: Well, you do say it was brown, right?

A: I think so.

Q: Well, circle it for me, will you?

A: It's not there.

Q: And how about footwear; where do you say the witness was wearing knee-high boots?

A: I guess I didn't mention it.

Q: It is not there?

A: Right.

Q: So how many items are circled because you included them in the report, Officer?

A: None.

Now imagine as you are asking the above questions, the jurors are watching you prepare a chart like this:

Good Identification	Claimed Today	If Seen, Should Be Reported	Was In Fact Reported
Sex	Y	Y	N
Hair cut	Y	Y	N
Hair color	Y	Y	N
Jewelry	Y	Y	N
Footwear	Y	Y	N
Carrying anything?	Y	Y	N

In your closing argument, you could bring back this chart, and cross out the "Claimed Today" column.

12.3   Using Learned Treatises under Cross-Examination

If you understand how to cross-examine a witness who has made a prior inconsistent statement (see above), then you understand how to cross-examine a witness who has said something inconsistent with a learned treatise. The steps are much the same with some minor variations. First commit the witness to the in-court statement that will be contradicted.

Q: Dr. Done, your position is that animal studies and similarities in molecular structure between Bendectin and a known agent of birth defects can lead a cautious scientist to conclude fairly that Bendectin causes birth defects?

A: Yes.

Some may argue this in-court commitment through repetition of the expert's testimony is unnecessary. It gives too much credence and emphasis to the opposing expert's position. As discussed earlier, some attorneys suggest that it is better to start the topic by stating their version of the issue to be discussed. For example, you might say:

> Q: Dr. Done, animal studies and molecular structure alone are not sufficient by themselves to conclude that Benedectin causes teratogenic birth defects, right?

The next step is to accredit the learned treatise. Rule 803(18) provides a number of ways to lay the evidentiary foundation for using a learned treatise. The best is to have the expert herself admit on cross that the writing is authoritative. You can do this using the expert's deposition or by way of a request for admission, although the request for admission approach does tip off opposing counsel. Even where the opposing expert or party refuses to recognize the writing as authoritative, your own expert may testify to its authoritative nature. If your expert has not yet testified, you can make an offer of proof to the court, based on your expert's anticipated testimony, and ask the court to permit the text to be read into evidence. Finally, the court itself could take judicial notice that the text is authoritative.

Certain well-known texts and treatises are often referred to in court. For example, *The Physician's Desk Reference* or *The Merck Manual of Diagnosis and Treatment* might be recognized by the court without other foundation. The important point is that you should "trumpet" the proffer of the treatise as authoritative. You would almost welcome a hearsay objection, just to give the court the opportunity to rule that the text is authoritative and admissible for the jurors' consideration.

Where the author has impressive degrees, it might also be worth a few questions to contrast the qualifications of the author with those of the opposing expert. For example:

> Q: Let me show you XYZ Treatise. You see in the biographical section of the introduction that the author is Professor I. M. Pressive?
>
> A: Yes.
>
> Q: It says she teaches at the Harvard Medical School?
>
> A: Yes.
>
> Q: That she has been doing research for twenty years. Is that true?
>
> A: Yes.
>
> Q: That she has been recognized by the American Academy of Scientists?
>
> A: Yes.

If the attorney wants to be certain the jury appreciates the point, he might go on:

Q: And Dr. Done, you don't teach or do research at Harvard?

A: No.

Q: And you haven't been recognized by the American Academy of Scientists for your work?

A: No.

This "extra accrediting" does slow down the actual impeachment, however, so it is probably better to postpone it until after the confrontation segment. The next part of the cross is to confront the expert with the contradictory section of the text. For example, you might present to the jurors—through blowup, overhead, evidence camera, or PowerPoint® slide—the paragraph you want the jurors and expert to read. Then, using call-outs, highlighting, or zoom, ask the witness:

Q: Now, Dr. Done, read along with me and tell me whether I read this right.

A: OK.

Q: Chapter 1, page 10, first full paragraph:

Without other epidemiological support, it is simply bad science for a researcher to conclude he or she knows that a particular drug is the cause of a disease or condition by merely studying the drug's molecular structure or the results of animal studies. There are too many differences between animals (even chimpanzees) and humans for scientists to be able to safely conclude drugs that are safe on animals, or not safe on animals, are similarly safe or not safe on humans, without substantive confirming information.

Q: Did I read that right?

A: Yes, but I don't agree.

Q: But you agree that Professor Pressive wrote that statement in her book?

It is important to try to control the expert's tendency to want to explain away the difference. Keep it safe by asking narrow, very well-tailored questions. Go for what the text says; do not try to get a confession. Just ask whether you read the portion correctly. And be prepared to repeat your question (or to reverse repeat it) to retain or maintain control.

12.4 Use the Expert's Report to Assert Control

Another key to maintaining control is to use the expert's own report, especially when you intend to challenge the expert in her area of expertise. In her answers, listen to whether she improves on the opinions or bases she gave in her report. If the improvement is significant, you may attempt a classic impeachment by omission because the expert is required by the rules of procedure to provide in her report the bases for her opinions and to supplement her opinions if she does substantial additional work or makes material changes in her opinions or bases. As the expert becomes more of an advocate, she may be tempted to "improve" on her analysis. She may have also gained some idea of where you might attack by analyzing your expert's report and thinking about the questions you asked at her deposition. If you exhausted her reasoning and studies at the deposition, if you clarified both the exact nature of her expertise and the limits of what she has been asked to do, and if she has not supplemented her report, then the expert should be readily impeachable if she tries to surprise you in court with new—or altered—opinions or bases.

12.5 Cross on Financial or Other Bias

Most often, where there are experts on both sides of an issue, there is reduced benefit from showing how much the experts are being paid. You gain little benefit by showing the opposing expert is being paid $250 an hour, when the attorney's own expert is making about the same. In fact, some lawyers believe jurors may be impressed by high fees, saying to themselves, "That expert must really know her stuff if she gets paid $600 an hour." If your expert is superior in education or area of expertise, you will normally profit more from cross on those matters instead of fees. It is too easy for an experienced expert to defend herself against clumsy challenges for bias.

> Q: Dr. Winsome, you are getting paid $250 an hour for your testimony here today?
>
> A: Attorney Losesome, I'm being paid for my time just like you are.

So lawyers often leave the topic alone.

Yet, sometimes there is a real point to make about the relationship between the expert and the lawyer (or client) on the other side. Consider the following situation with Dr. Rosenberg, expert for the defendant, in a motorcycle accident case. Where your expert is the treating physician, you can present a genuine contrast between your expert and the defendant's expert on the issue of bias. When you have this opportunity, however, watch out for two things:

First, timing—save the point for the end or for a time when the expert is already resisting you. If you lead with financial bias, you have essentially called the witness a liar whose opinion is for sale. She is not going to cooperate with any constructive examination that might narrow the issues, show agreement on basic facts, or demonstrate her support of your expert. It is better to wait to see if she turns into an advocate who will not give you concessions on the most basic matters. If she does become an advocate, you can then introduce financial bias to explain what motivates this witness.

Second, if you do cross on financial bias, make it more than a one-shot affair. Do not just stop at what she makes an hour. Do some research and background work in your deposition so you can do an examination like the following:

Q: Dr. Rosenberg, you are a neurologist?

A: Yes.

Q: But you also spend a good deal of time testifying in court?

A: Some.

Q: Correct me if I'm wrong, but you testify approximately twenty-five times a year, don't you?

A: Something like that.

Q: And each time you testify, you prepare a report?

A: Yes.

Q: And you charge $1,000 per page for the report?

A: Yes.

Q: And then you are often deposed?

A: I'd say about half the time that I testify.

Q: You testify at trial twenty-five times a year.

A: Yes, approximately.

Q: You are often deposed even when there is no trial?

A: Yes, that's right.

Q: Because many of the cases settle before they get to trial?

A: Yes.

Q: And there's also a report prepared every time you are deposed?

A: Yes.

Q: So would it be fair to say you also testify in a deposition about twenty-five times a year?

A: I guess.

Q: And you charge $1,500 a day to testify at a deposition?

A: Yes.

Q: And you charge $2,000 a day to testify at trial?

A: Yes.

Q: So that is [*putting the figures on the blackboard*] let's see, $1,500 times twenty-five equals $37,500 plus $2,000 times twenty-five equals $50,000 or [*pausing and looking at the jurors to check the math*] a total of $87,500 a year for testimony?

A: I guess.

Q: And then fifty reports on top of that, at $1,000 per page per report? And the reports average what, five pages?

A: That's about right.

Q: So that's fifty times five, times $1,000 equals $250,000?

A: Yes, that's the math.

Q: Totaling $337,500 in a year?

A: Well, that much testimony is a lot of work.

Q: And that is just in this one year?

A: Yes.

Q: Now, Doctor, you testify primarily for defendants?

A: I don't know.

Q: Well, isn't it true you estimate that you work for defendants about 80 percent of the time?

A: OK.

Q: But now, Doctor, you have never come into a courtroom and testified that an injured person should recover any money for the injuries they have suffered?

A: That's, uh, that's correct.

By making the hourly or daily rate into a "lifestyle" issue—an issue that supports the kids going to college, buys expensive suits, or pays country club dues—the bias of the expert is more dramatically shown. The pressure on the expert from wanting to do well for a particular side in litigation to maintain and "grow" the business can provide a juror with reason to reject that expert and to favor your expert.

Of course, it is important to realize even a treating physician can have some bias. The treating physician can lose perspective because she "cares for the patient"—that is, she is emotionally invested in the matter on a personal level. Furthermore, if there is any question about the adequacy or competency of treatment, the treating physician may feel a judgment against the defendant drug company or hospital will exonerate her for her own treatment decisions.

12.6   Impeachment by Prior Bad Acts

There are two areas of evidence law that you need to consult when considering whether to cross an expert witness on prior bad acts. The first area is contained in Federal Rules of Evidence 404(b) and 405, which read:

Rule 404(b). Other Crimes, Wrongs, or Acts

(1) *Prohibited Uses.* Evidence of a crime, wrong, or act is not admissible to prove the a person's character in order to show that on a particular occasion the person acted in accordance with the character

(2) *Permitted Uses; Notice in Criminal Case.* This evidence may be admissible for another purpose, such as proving motive, opportunity, intent, preparation, plan, knowledge, identity, absence of mistake, or lack of accident. On request by a defendant in a criminal case, the prosecutor must:

(A) provide reasonable notice of the general nature of any such evidence that the prosecutor intends to offer at trial; and

(B) do so before trial—or during trial if the court, for good cause, excuses lack of pretrial notice.

Rule 405. Methods of Proving Character

(a) By Reputation or Opinion. When evidence of a person's character or character trait is admissible, it may be proved by testimony about the person's reputation or by testimony in the form of an opinion. On cross-examination of the character witness, the court may allow an inquiry into relevant specific instances of the person's conduct.

(b) By Specific Instances of Conduct. When a person's character or character trait is an essential element of a charge, claim or defense, the character or trait may also be proved by relevant specific instances of the person's conduct.

It is not easy to predict whether evidence is admissible under Rule 404(b). The advisory committee's notes reveal only that "[t]he determination must be made whether the danger of undue prejudice outweighs the probative value of the evidence in view of the availability of other means of proof and other facts appropriate for making decisions of this kind under Rule 403." The rule does seem to be one of inclusion rather than exclusion, so it seems the court should exercise its discretion to favor admissibility.[2]

When the court evaluates whether there is sufficient evidence of the prior bad act to provide the requisite foundation for asking the questions, it examines whether the lawyer has a good-faith belief that the information is true. Then, under *Huddleston v. United States*,[3] "other acts" are admissible if, using a preponderance of the evidence standard, there is evidence sufficient to support a jury's finding the defendant committed a similar act and the other act is probative of a material issue other than the defendant's character. While no preliminary inquiry under Rule 104(a) is necessary, the notice provisions contained in the body of Rule 404 suggest it is prudent in a criminal matter to be certain of the sufficiency of evidence of prior bad acts before surprising a witness with it on cross. If the prior bad act evidence is of a criminal conviction, you must consider the second area of evidence law regarding impeachment through prior criminal acts, Rule 609. It reads:

Rule 609. Impeachment by Evidence of Conviction of Crime.

(a) **In General.** The following rules apply to attacking a witness's character for truthfulness by evidence of a criminal conviction:

   (1) for a crime that, in the convicting jurisdiction, was punishable by death or by imprisonment for more than one year, the evidence:

   (A) must be admitted, subject to Rule 403, in a civil case or in a criminal case in which the witness is not a defendant; and

   (B) must be admitted in a criminal case in which the witness is a defendant, if the probative value of the evidence outweighs its prejudicial effect to that defendant; and

   (2) for any crime regardless of punishment, the evidence must be admitted if the court can readily determine that establishing the elements of the crime required proving—or the witness's admitting—a dishonest act or false statement.

(b) **Limit on Using the Evidence After 10 Years.** This subdivision (b) applies if more than 10 years have passed since the witness's conviction or release from confinement for it, whichever is later. Evidence of the conviction is admissible only if:

   (1) its probative value, supported by specific facts and circumstances, substantially outweigh its prejudicial effect; and

   (2) the proponent gives an adverse party reasonable written notice of the intent to use it so that the party has a fair opportunity to contest its use.

---

2. *See, e.g.*, United States v. Long, 574 F.2d 761, 766 (3d Cir. 1978).
3. 485 U.S. 681 (1988).

An impeachment with such evidence with an expert does not differ from an impeachment with a lay witness.

Q: Dr. Jones, you once lived in Nita City, Nita?

A: Yes.

Q: In fact you lived there in June, YR-5?

A: Yes.

Q: And on June 30, YR-5, in federal court Nita City, you were convicted of falsifying a record filed with the United States Patent Office?

A: Well, that was a mistake. The forms were confusing.

Q: Were you convicted?

A: Yes. Yes, I was.

Q: Lying to the government is a federal crime?

A: Yes.

Q: A felony?

A: Yes.

Q: You received three years probation, didn't you?

A: Yes.

Under Rule 403, the court must consider whether the probative value of the evidence is substantially outweighed by the danger of unfair prejudice.

If written evidence of a prior bad act is admitted, the cross-examining lawyer can read it to the jurors. If the evidence is of a criminal act, the cross-examiner is often limited to reading only the bare bones information of crime, date, and sentence. If prior crimes or acts are too remote in time under Rule 609, their probative value may be substantially weakened so that, on balance, they should be excluded. If the act is a crime more than ten years old, and therefore outside the allowable limits of Rule 609, then the cross-examiner may still try to use it by satisfying the balancing test under Rule 609(b), described above, or under Rule 404(b), regarding absence of mistake or lack of intent. Rule 404(b) does not contain the time restraints of Rule 609(b). The court will have to conduct a balancing test under Rule 403 to determine its admissibility, and the opposing party should be given notice that such a conviction may be used.

CHAPTER THIRTEEN

CROSS-EXAMINATION OF AN EXPERT WITNESS: ORGANIZATIONAL CHOICES

You must organize your expert in way that allows the jurors to understand your theme. From all the points that you could make with the expert, select the points you must make to support your closing argument. There are a number of different organizational choices that might not only support a good closing but also provide a high-impact cross. Organizational choices include constructive and destructive cross-examination, "primacy and recency," storytelling and fact gathering, and substance versus impeachment. As with lay cross-examination, cross of an expert often will start with a strong point that sets a different tone in the courtroom. Examine on less certain (but still necessary) points in the middle, and save an impressive point for an exit line. Often, the two opposing experts in a case will be in agreement on 90 percent of the expert issues; demonstrating the extent of that agreement on cross-examination enhances your own expert. In planning expert cross-examination, it is often helpful to distinguish between "minor point" cross-examination, and "major point" cross-examination and to remember the way in which an eighth-grade science teacher explains concepts to his students.

13.1 Putting It All Together

The art of cross-examination consists of taking the techniques described above and constructing a cross that has a clear purpose or theme so the jurors will "get" the point you are making about the witness and decide how they feel and think about the witness, even before your closing. In other words, you want to control the witness by preventing the witness from retelling her story; you want to avoid becoming argumentative and asking "the one question too many"; and you want to keep the witness cooperative enough so the witness will admit those facts that she must admit—all while making certain the jurors get the point.

Organize the cross in a way that attains all of the above goals. The next important step in planning any cross is to move beyond technique, to look at the case theory and ask which points could be made with any particular witness. Next, you need to edit the number of points you can make until you have identified the points you must make to have the evidence available for your closing argument in the case. Because jurors object to repetition and watching attorneys spend their time on trivial matters, an often-stated rule is that the examiner should cross-examine only to the extent necessary to make his closing argument.

Irving Younger taught that the cross-examiner should never have more than three points on cross, that two were better than three, and one was best of all. This does not mean you ask three or fewer questions; it means you ask the number of questions needed to establish your point with a witness, but you limit the number of points you make to no more than three. Beyond three points, the jurors may lose interest and the expert witness may find a way to beat you. If you can succeed on three points, you may be well positioned to argue the expert is not credible in general.

Yet, even when you have edited the number of points down to only those you need, you still needs to organize your points in the most persuasive way. To demonstrate this point, here is a simplified illustration from an actual case.

13.2   *Bill v. Woodframe Construction Company*

On July 17, YR-3, the plaintiff, Jason Bill, was injured when the lift-assistance spring attached to his garage door pulled out from the wood frame of the door and the spring bracket struck him in the face as he stood on a ladder while attempting to install a garage door opener bracket above the spring bracket. Bill had loosened the spring bracket approximately 1/4" to slide that bracket down slightly, so the door opener bracket could be installed just above the spring bracket over the door. Bill brings suit against Woodframe Construction Company, which installed the garage door and spring assembly in Bill's new home, and alleges the screws holding the spring bracket were only 1-1/4" long and had been installed through 3/8" wallboard into standard construction grade pine planks. The screw penetration into the wood was therefore not more than 3/4", since the bracket itself was 1/8" thick. Installation instructions packaged with the door, manufactured by Geronimo Garage Doors, Incorporated, specify the use of a 2" wood screw of a particular thread and thickness. In its answer, Woodframe raises the affirmative defense of contributory negligence and assumption of risk, alleging if Bill had not ignored the warnings on the door, specifically advising homeowners to have adjustments made only by qualified garage door installation companies because the lift-assist springs were under high tension, the 1-1/4" screws would have continued to hold the bracket, and his face would not have been near the bracket if and when it ever pulled out.

During discovery, Woodframe provided the written report of Dr. Nels Interwood, an expert both in wood, screw, and nail fasteners and in instances of the failure of the connection between wood and nails or screws. In pertinent part, his report states as follows:

Report of Nels Interwood, PhD

After examining the garage, which was the site of the accident, I collected the samples of the wallboard material, the wood planking materials behind the wallboard, and the paint on the surface of the wallboard from areas adjacent to—but at least two feet removed from—the site at which the spring bracket had been installed. At that time, the spring bracket and spring assembly were hanging loose, affixed to the garage doorjamb only by the end brackets, and the screws that had held the spring bracket were not present. (It was reported to me those screws had been thrown out of the bracket at the time of the accident as the spring unwound and rapidly turned the bracket with it.) The statement of job materials provided by the crew of Woodframe Construction Company indicates those screws were No. 10, 1-1/4" screws with a 1/4" shoulder, which is the unthreaded portion immediately below the head.

Measurements of all components were taken, and measurements were made indicating the location from which wallboard and wood samples were removed. The entire frame-header assembly was subsequently removed by agents of the garage door manufacturing company and of the plaintiff, Mr. Bill, along with the untensioned spring assembly—with bracket—for testing in a laboratory. I have observed video recordings of those tests, and I have received and reviewed the data generated by those tests. All of the information mentioned in this paragraph forms a part of the bases for my expert opinions provided in this report.

Diagram of Wood Screw

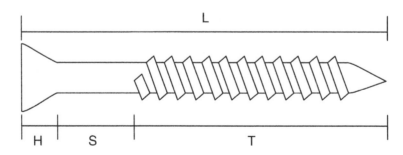

Head = .125 in.

Shoulder = .25 in.

Thread + Tip = .875 in.

Total length = 1.25 in.

Based on my experience, training, and education in wood science, strength of materials, and wood-fastener applications, and on the measurements, tests, and analyses I have conducted or have observed using the materials described in the preceding paragraph, I have come to the following conclusions, which I hold with a degree of certainty appropriate to the field of engineering and materials science the following conclusions:

The wood employed in the frame and header was adequate for the application, being composed of adequately dried and proper lengths of 2×12" and 2×6" yellow pine, the most typical construction material for this type of application.

The wood screws used to install the spring bracket were shorter than specified by the door/spring manufacturer, but it is my experience manufacturers of such items often overdesign such components because of the very low cost of specifying longer or heavier screws or other reinforced components.

The bracket screws appeared to be properly inserted into the wood frame, without stripping of the wood in the screw hole, as observed on cross-sectional microscopic examination, which was photographed and preserved for trial use. There was no evidence any oversized pilot hole was drilled to facilitate insertion of the screws, as is sometimes done by less experienced installation crews in this industry. (In fact, there was no way to determine whether a pilot hole had been drilled at all, which definitely shows it could not have been oversized.) Because the 1/4" shoulder of the screw is unthreaded, it does not contribute to the holding force of the screw connection, regardless of whether it is embedded in wood or in wallboard. Routinely, wallboard is removed to permit installation directly against the wooden header beam, although that was not the case here.

The failure of the spring bracket system was due to the partial withdrawal of the bracket retention screws by the homeowner during the attempted installation of the overhead door motor assembly, which was completely separate from—and unattached to—the lift-assist spring assembly. These screws had, according to the homeowner, been withdrawn approximately 1/4", which was a sufficient distance to loosen them in their screw holes. The system was stable before the homeowner undertook adjustment himself, which is further indication that his adjustment caused the failure.

Because the screws themselves can be viewed as elongated cones and, therefore, as creating elongated conical holes, even the slightest withdrawal will result in disengagement of the threads along the entire length of the screw regardless of how long the screw is. Thus, even if the screws had been an inch longer, the 1/4" withdrawal by the homeowner would still have severely compromised the integrity of the screw-wood connection.

At his deposition in December YR-1, Dr. Interwood repeated the conclusions from his report, and made the following additional statements:

Q: Can you describe this screw and your diagram more exactly?

A: Yes, certainly. This is a standard, 1-1/4" number 10 wood screw, Phillips head, made of stainless steel, which appears to have been used, inserted once, and withdrawn once.

Q: What do you mean by standard?

A: Standard means it has the normal components of a wood screw of this particular size and a normal head shape, which is flat, as opposed to pan head or round, or some other configuration.

Q: What do you mean by 1-1/4"?

A: Well, that's the length of the screw from tip to head, total length.

Q: Not just the threaded portion or the threaded portion and shoulder together?

A: No, total length. The threaded portion is approximately—well, exactly—7/8"; the shoulder is 2/8"; the head is 1/8", so the entire length is 10/8", or 1-1/4".

Q: What does the number 10 mean?

A: That is a code relating to the number of threads per inch, turns per inch of length. Numbers 8 and 10 are standard for construction work of this type.

Q: Why do you think it was inserted only once?

A: Because I can look at the markings from the screwdriver on the portion of the head that takes the force on insertion, and they are not severe. It hasn't been put in and taken out a number of times. Same thing for withdrawal—not much scratching or rounding of the internal shoulders of the screwdriver slots.

Q: Is that significant to you?

A: Yes, because if the screw had been inserted, withdrawn, and inserted again a number of times, the threads that were impressed into the wood were likely to have become worn down, and they would not have held the screw as well.

Q: Couldn't you look at those impressed threads directly, since you had access to the wood?

A: No. Well, I could look at the wood, but remember, these screws had been explosively expelled from the wood under the force of the tensioned spring. Since the garage door weighed several hundred pounds, that spring was capable of exerting that kind of force, and the screws were pulled very rapidly out of their holes by the bracket and spring assembly. So the wood in the holes where the threads of the screws meshed with the wood, that was pretty much torn up.

Q: In your report, on page thirteen, you describe the screws as "elongated cones."

A: Yes, I see that.

Q: Does your diagram depict that?

A: Well, not really. After I had written the report, I asked my assistant to make an accurate drawing of the screw, according to its three axis views, and when I looked at the diagram after I had submitted the report, I saw it was accurate and perhaps my description was less accurate. The tip of the screw is certainly conical, and that is essentially what I meant to describe in my report.

Q: The tip is conical, but the remainder of the screw is, what, cylindrical?

A: Yes, cylindrical, that's correct. So, on even the slightest withdrawal, the tip loses contact with the wood and provides no holding power.

Q: How long is the tip?

A: Let's see. The diagram puts the tip at 2/8".

Q: Then the remaining threaded portion, up to the unthreaded shoulder, is 5/8"?

A: Yes, that's right.

Q: That's 5/8" then of threaded screw, which does not lose its contact with the wood if it is withdrawn?

A: If I understand where you are going, if the screw is fully embedded in wood, including the shoulder, then a withdrawal of 1/4" would expose the shoulder, but would not expose any of the threaded portion of the screw.

Q: Doctor Interwood, let's take our morning break at this point for fifteen minutes, OK?

After the deposition was resumed, a number of additional matters were developed, including information that showed two months after he was retained in this matter—but before he had written his report—Dr. Interwood was retained by the same attorneys as a testifying expert in the defense of an entire series of product failure cases in which alleged damages exceed $42 million.

Finally, on direct examination at trial Dr. Interwood testifies in a way that is generally consistent with his report. At one point, he makes the following statement:

> A: If you draw—that is, withdraw—a screw from the wood in which it is embedded, you destroy the contact that screw had with the wood, with the threads impressed into the wood of the screw hole. That greatly weakens the holding power of the screw-wood connection, and it is therefore hardly surprising these bracket screws would fail. The homeowner should never have touched them, much less have removed them as far as he did. That was just irresponsible and showed a complete lack of understanding of the connection system. In my opinion as an expert, the homeowner's actions caused the spring bracket to come loose; he brought this on himself.

With all of this as background, let us consider the organizational choices facing the cross-examiner. He needs to decide 1) between *constructive* and *destructive* examination; 2) between *primacy* and *recency*; 3) between *storytelling* and *fact-gathering*; and 4) between *substance* and *impeachment*. Other less major choices must also be made "on the fly" (such as the decision whether to discipline a witness immediately for adding some nonresponsive information at the end of an otherwise permissible answer), but these are normally matters of style and the moment, and they cannot be planned in advance very well. An analysis of each of the major choices follows.

13.3 Constructive v. Destructive Cross-Examination

Constructive cross-examination enlists the support of the opposing expert, seeking her agreement that certain fundamental facts, principles, or limitations are correct. The appropriateness of a particular methodology that is generally accepted in the field, the unavailability of Bureau of Labor Statistics data for certain time periods, the inability to determine a nuclear particle's mass and velocity at the same time, or her own decision not to conduct certain additional tests—these are the kinds of areas in which a reasonable expert (or an unreasonable one who nevertheless recognizes the danger of denying the truth of matters that can be proved) is likely to agree, thereby saving energy for more important battles. Constructive examination depends on the credibility of the opposing expert; you want the jurors to believe her when she says that you are right about something or that your expert is right about something. Such agreement makes the "something" equivalent to a universal truth—no one disagrees, so the jurors can accept it.

Destructive cross-examination attempts to diminish the credibility of the expert. Therefore, as a matter of logic you must conduct constructive cross-examination before destructive cross-examination; otherwise, you are first saying to the jurors, "Don't believe this expert," and then trying to say to them, "Believe her just on those helpful points." It is easier to argue: "She is right on these few helpful points, but look at the inconsistencies and irregularities of the remainder of her analysis." Start friendly, get what you can, then go into a more dramatic cross-examination mode. Move from a friendly tone to using a tone of voice you use when you are incredulous about what someone is saying. With Dr. Nels Interwood, there are some constructive points to be made based on his report and deposition:

Q: Dr. Interwood, I think we can agree on a few things at the outset here. First, you agree the wood used as framing for the garage door assembly was suitable for that use?

A: Yes, it was suitable. "Adequate" is the word I think I used.

Q: It had been properly seasoned or dried?

A: Yes.

Q: The workmen who framed the house, they had chosen the proper lengths of lumber to frame the garage door opening?

A: Yes. It was all long enough, without joints, so there was no sag, which would have, well, could have affected the strength of the screw connection through the bracket.

Q: Doctor, you are not an expert in garage springs, are you?

A: No, no. I know wood and screws and nails. Not springs.

Q: And yet you know the spring on that door was capable of exerting a force of several hundred pounds on the bracket and the screws holding the bracket?

A: Well, yes, because the spring is designed to assist in lifting the door. Since the door weighs several hundred pounds, and we want the person or opener mechanism to have to exert only twenty-five or twenty pounds of force, the spring must make up the difference, so to speak. So that spring can exert close to 300 pounds of force.

Q: And Dr. Interwood, one more thing on which we can agree: the wood where the bracket screws were inserted, that wood was pretty much torn up after the bracket came off the wall?

A: Yes, yes, and that's important because we could not look at the thread marks inside the holes in the wood to see whether the screws were well embedded.

There is nothing in this examination that demeans the witness's credentials or challenges his willingness to tell the truth. There is plenty in this examination that is helpful if the theory for this portion of the examination is that the wood is not the source of the problem. You do not have to be an expert to understand there was substantial force contained within that spring (actually potential energy, but who wants to try to teach the jurors the distinction?), and therefore the installers should have known they needed adequate screw connections. It is also nice to have the expert, for her own purposes, speak enthusiastically about the force of the released spring when you want the jurors to have that picture of the explosive release that caught the plaintiff in the face, with the bracket spinning wildly.

For another example, take a cross-examination of the damages expert in the employment case we used as an earlier example. A constructive to destructive approach of that expert might go like this:

Q: You would agree with me that you are projecting damages seven years into the future?

A: Yes.

Q: And, of course, this involves making a prediction?

A: Yes.

Q: And with all predicting you have to make assumptions?

A: Yes.

Q: You made an assumption about a discount rate?

A: Yes.

Q: And you agree with me, that the higher the discount rate, the lower total dollars will be paid in the future?

A: Yes.

Q: And selecting the right discount rate involves making a choice?

A: Yes.

Q: Some select discount rates that are drawn from published figures of the interest a person can make from investing in a reasonable safe security. You chose to use that rate, but then subtracted out an amount for inflation?

A: Yes.

Q: Some experts might select an interest rate appropriate for a particular type of business?

A: Yes.

Q: For example, if we were looking at trying to find a discount rate for wages being paid by a computer start-up company, we might have to discount wages in such a company by 50 percent, because of the competition in the market and the risk that the company would not be in existence in another two years, not to say seven years?

A: That's right, but I chose not to do that because Firm, Inc. had such an established track record.

Q: Yes, but that is an assumption on your part?

A: Yes.

[*Here your voice can take on more incredulity.*]

Q: You are aware that banks, for example, have data on discount rates they use when lending money?

A: Yes.

Q: They use these discount rates for various industries to determine how much money to lend, for how long, and what interest to charge?

A: Yes.

Q: Banks find it helpful to look at industry averages, to help them judge the risk of getting paid back sometime in the future?

A: I guess.

Q: You chose not to consult these rates for the purposes of doing your analysis?

A: That's correct. I did not.

13.4 Primacy v. Recency

Recall the earlier discussion of primacy and recency in this text. It conveys that a listener remembers best what she hears first and remembers second best what she hears last. In cross-examination, you want to lead with an important point and end with a point that is also important. You must take care to select points for these positions that are certain winners, because there is nothing worse than losing at the very beginning—except for losing at the very end.

Here is a candidate for the first position in the cross-examination of Dr. Nels Interwood, a point that is not overtly destructive, but is important enough to be a theme for your entire case:

Q: Dr. Interwood, good afternoon.

A: Good afternoon.

Q: Let's see if we can agree on a few things right off the bat. You agree with me that the holding power of a number 10 screw in wood is directly proportional to the length of the threaded portion in contact with the wood?

A: Yes . . . well, yes.

Q: So twice as much thread in the wood, twice as much holding power. It's that simple, isn't it?

A: Yes, other things being equal, that's correct.

Q: You know, as an expert, that the installation instructions for this spring and bracket assembly call for 2-1/2" number 10 wood screws?

A: Yes, I have seen those instructions.

Q: The head on a 2-1/2" number 10 wood screw is 1/8", right? [*Writing on the board to create and fill in a chart.*]

A: Yes, that is standard.

Q: And those 2-1/2" screws have shoulders that are 2/8"?

A: Yes, the shoulder dimension is the same until you get to much smaller screws.

Q: The tip, the pointed-end portion, is 1/8", just like the head?

A: Yes, 1/8".

Q: The remainder is threaded?

A: Yes, all the rest is the threaded portion, which actually holds in the wood.

Q: A 2-1/2" screw has a head, shoulder, and tip of 1/8", 2/8", and 1/8" that don't hold in the wood?

A: That's right.

Q: That's 1/2" that doesn't hold in the wood?

A: Right.

Q: So, with a 2-1/2" screw, like that called for in the installation instructions, 2" would be holding in the wood if it was correctly inserted all the way?

A: Well, yes, that's right. Two inches of threaded portion.

Q: The 1-1/4" screws that were used, they had these same head, shoulder, and tip portions?

A: The same dimensions, yes. The same length for each.

Q: So on the 1-1/4" screws that were actually used, 1/2" was the portion that didn't hold in the wood?

A: That's correct.

Q: That leaves 3/4" to hold in the wood, if it is properly inserted all the way?

A: Well, yes, that's right.

Q: The proper screw would have 2" of threaded screw in the wood; the ones used could only have 3/4". Have I got that right?

A: Well, yes, but there are other factors to consider.

Q: Yes, and we'll come to those, Dr. Interwood. But we have to take one step at a time. First tell me, is that right, that the screws called for in the instructions would have 2" of threaded screw in contact with the wood, and the ones actually used couldn't have more than 3/4"?

A: Yes, that's right.

Q: Now, there was wallboard installed over the wood header, wasn't there, Dr. Interwood?

A: Yes, but that really wasn't important in determining the holding power of the screws.

Q: It wasn't important because the wallboard does not hold onto the screws, does it? It just crumbles?

A: Yes, that is the kind of material it is. Like plaster, it turns to dust.

Q: It doesn't hold onto the screw, but the screw has to go through it, doesn't it?

A: Well, certainly. I don't know what you mean.

Q: Was this 3/8" wallboard, or 1/2" wallboard, Dr. Interwood?

A: Just 3/8".

Q: So, no matter what screw you used, the one from the instructions or the one the crew actually used, 3/8" of that screw was in the wallboard, not in the wood?

A: Yes, that would be correct, for either one.

Q: For the screw, the instructions said to use the 2-1/2" screw, we figured earlier (indicating the chart) that 2" would be in contact with the wood, threaded into the wood?

A: Yes, we made that note there.

Q: And considering the wallboard, that longer screw would now have only 1-5/8" of thread in contact with the wood?

A: Yes, 2" minus 3/8". Yes.

Q: The screws actually used, those had 3/4" of threaded portion available to contact the wood? (Indicating the chart.)

A: Yes, that's right.

Q: And now, considering the wallboard, we can agree the screws actually used by the Woodframe Construction crew had only 3/8" of threaded portion in actual contact with the wood? That's 3/4" minus 3/8", right?

A: Yes, that's right.

Q: One and five-eighths inches compared to 3/8". The proper screws, called for in the instructions, would have had more than four times as much threaded screw in contact with the wood, isn't that correct, Dr. Interwood?

A: Yes, that's correct, but there are other factors we haven't talked about yet.

Q: And we have already agreed that four times the length of thread in the wood means four times the holding power, haven't we?

A: Well, yes, I recall that is where we started today.

This point is so fundamental to the theory of the plaintiff's case that it is a logical candidate for the primary position, that lead-off position that uses the principle of primacy to make the greatest impression on the jurors. Your hope is that having heard it first, the jurors will be impressed most strongly by this point and will remember it regardless of what comes later in the cross-examination or the redirect. By the same principle of primacy, consider placing this point at the beginning of the closing argument as an important element in your statement of the theme of the case, which might be something like: "They didn't take the time to do the job right, even though everybody knew this spring was a potential killer that had to be controlled."

Now you should look for the solid point to place at the end of the cross-examination, to take advantage of the principle of recency, and also to guarantee that you can sit down on a winning point. (In choosing the final point on cross of an expert, avoiding a defeat is more important than ending with the best point available. If that best point has some risk of failure attached, put it in the middle somewhere, and go for the clear winner that may be slightly less valuable substantively.) In the hypothetical case presented here, without going through all of the mechanics of the questions and answers, a nice safe finishing point would be the fact if the 3/8" wallboard had been removed by the installers, according to instructions, the screw would have been inserted into the wood an additional 3/8", and the 1/4" removal by the homeowner would not have caused the failure. You wind up with a very succinct summary of your case, extracted from the opposing expert witness. Using your most incredulous tone, you might ask:

Q: In other words, if Woodframe Construction had just cut through the wallboard, there would have been no injury?

Q: And if Woodframe Construction had used screws that were just 1/4" longer, there would have been no injury?

This is a pretty good place to sit down.

13.5   Storytelling v. Fact-Gathering

In the above examples of cross-examination, care was taken to explain all of the logical connections between the facts and the expert's observations and opinions, so the trier of fact could appreciate the significance of the information being presented—a story was told through the mouth of the lawyer with the assent of the opposing expert. Presentations in a story format are remembered more clearly and have a more vivid impact than lists of facts or events. The story apparently provides a framework within which the jurors can organize the new information and remember the relationships among facts. If, however, you are faced with a less cooperative or less honest witness, who presents greater danger, or if time is short because the jurors are restless or the judge is impatient, you may have to use the *fact-gathering* format for your cross-examination.

Gathering facts through cross-examination does not require as much language facility as telling a story, but it does require more restraint on the part of the cross-examiner. As a trial lawyer, or oral advocate, you want to persuade people, to make them understand you are scoring points—important points, points they should notice. But with aggressive opposing experts or weary judges and jurors, you sometimes have to postpone the persuasive oral advocacy until your closing argument and satisfy yourself instead with merely extracting the facts you need for closing—storing up the bricks from which you will build a wall on closing. Consider this portion of the "primacy" cross-examination presented in storytelling from above, but now cut back to brick-gathering form:

Q: Dr. Interwood, the head of a number 10 screw is 1/8" thick?

A: Yes.

Q: The shoulder, the unthreaded portion, 2/8" long?

A: Yes, that's correct.

Q: These numbers are correct for all number 10 screws, whatever the total length of the screw?

A: Yes, those are standard, except for very small screws not relevant here.

Q: If a screw has twice as much contact with the wood, it holds twice as forcefully?

A: Well, in general that's correct if you are talking about contact of the threaded portion, the shank, of the screw.

Q: The instructions here, Plaintiff's Exhibit 17, tell Woodframe Construction to remove the wallboard or other covering over the header. Do you see that?

A: Yes, that's part of what it says.

Q: And the instructions tell Woodframe Construction to use 2-1/2" number 10 screws, don't they?

A: Yes, but they also point out that the homeowner should be advised not to attempt adjustment of the spring-bracket assembly himself— that he should call qualified installation experts.

That is another good place to stop. The expert understands the significance of the answers he is being forced to give, and he is beginning to fight back a bit too strenuously to safely engage in further questioning in this area. Using the fact-gathering mode, be sure you get in, get your facts, get out, and be satisfied that you will explain the significance of those facts—to assemble your jigsaw puzzle, to decorate your Christmas tree, to grind your sheaves into flour and bake your bread, to add the mortar and construct your wall—on closing argument when there is no one to interrupt you with disagreement—at least no one with advanced degrees in impressive fields of knowledge.

13.6 Substance v. Impeachment

Another dichotomy with which you must deal in facing an expert is when to engage in cross-examination to make substantive points and when to engage in cross-examination to impeachment. On first consideration, it might seem it would always be ideal to cross-examine with material that is both substantive and impeaching at the same time—in other words, to have as the goal questions such as:

Q: Dr. Interwood, despite your testimony to your lawyer this morning that the wallboard played no role in this spring-bracket failure, didn't you tell me, under oath at your deposition three months ago, you disapproved of the practice by many companies, including defendant Woodframe Construction, of installing the bracket on top of the wallboard?

Even if the question is broken into four or five bite-sized questions, to maintain control of the witness and to keep the jurors with the examination, this question or line of questions nevertheless presents the jurors with the difficulty of trying to remember (or to figure out as an initial matter) which version is supposed to be the truth; if the expert is a liar (or nonobjective, or an exaggerator, or unqualified), why should her statement from three months ago be believed? Is she a liar all of the time? Was she associated with the same lawyer and party three months ago? Does she have the same motivation for slanting her opinions?

These are fair questions. While you may have persuasive answers (e.g., as more problems with the client's position became clear after the deposition, the expert adjusted her opinions to try to avoid them), the logical process of absorbing those answers and evaluating the testimony (direct and cross) in light of those answers may consume the jurors' attention, so the substantive significance of the concessions contained in the impeaching material may be overlooked.

Where the substantive material is important to you and where it can be presented either in an impeachment or in some constructive way, the constructive way is preferable. There is no question about what the jurors are supposed to believe—they are supposed to believe the important substantive material on which you and the expert have just "agreed that you can agree." The dual purpose material, including examination using "learned treatise" material under Rule 803(18), should probably be planned to follow whatever purely constructive material you have in case the dual purpose material devolves into a destructive cross-examination involving impeachment.

Finally, conduct your more impeaching cross-examination, the destructive questioning intended to suggest that what the witness brought to the case (the "major premise": her intelligence, education, background, experience, integrity, objectivity, reputation) is somehow inadequate for the tests or what the case gave to the witness (the "minor premise": the facts, the issues, the witnesses, the budget, the time constraints, the necessary assumptions, the assistants, and the assistance) is somehow inadequate or inaccurate. From the spring-bracket case, you could find examples of purely impeaching cross-examination:

Q: Dr. Interwood, you did not conduct tests of the header and spring-bracket assembly, did you? [*Incredulity*].

A: No. I am familiar with the tests that were conducted, however.

Q: There were tests, but you weren't present for them?

A: That's correct. I studied videos of those tests.

Q: You were invited to attend?

A: Yes, but I saw no need to be there.

Q: Those tests were conducted by the garage door manufacturing company?

A: Yes, I believe that is correct.

Q: You did not select what tests were done?

A: No, that was decided by those other researchers.

Q: You did not decide how many tests to run?

A: No, as I said, that was decided by others.

Q: You don't know whether any pilot holes were drilled for the bracket screws, do you?

A: Well, I certainly know there were no oversized holes drilled, which would have been very poor practice because it reduces the purchase that the screw has in the wood.

Q: You don't know whether any pilot holes were drilled for the bracket screws, do you?

A: No, I don't—except if any were drilled, they were not oversized.

Q: They could have been smaller than the recommended size?

A: Yes, that's right.

Q: You don't know? [*Incredulity*].

A: I don't know.

While the adequacy of the tests and the size of the pilot holes may be important substantive questions, you would not be trying to obtain substantive statements on those subjects; instead, you are demonstrating that the witness should be considered less credible because she is willing to rely on tests done by others, over whom she had no control, or she is willing to proceed to a conclusion and opinion in the absence of apparently important information. Therefore, these are bald impeachments that challenge her competence and methodology. (Notice with respect to the tests on which Dr. Interwood relies, you would be careful not to denigrate them, since, on these facts, they were done under your supervision—shared with the garage door manufacturing company—and they probably underpin your own expert's testimony. You would not be impeaching Interwood for relying on those; you would be impeaching him for not being there, for not participating, for not doing his own work, and then coming to an opinion as an expert—in other words, for being inadequately committed to finding out the truth.)

13.7 Applying Control Techniques to Cross-Examination of Experts

Experts are expert. The opposing expert therefore will have some advantages over you, the cross-examining lawyer, and you have to be careful. The ability to manipulate jargon is a major advantage. The expert typically has spent years honing her ability to speak "in code," to make distinctions and connections that are not apparent to laypersons, and to correct innocent misuses of the language of her profession, much like a parent instinctively corrects a child's misuse of grammar.

Remember, however, that jurors also do not understand the distinctions or connections. You finds yourself on common ground with the jurors in this regard. Many jurors do not like the expert telling them how to think, and they enjoy seeing a self-possessed, somewhat arrogant intellectual being brought down a peg or two by the common sense and practical wisdom available to the everyday person. You should be able to take advantage of this anti-intellectual streak that runs deep in many of us.

If you can simply explain, narrow, and demystify the issues during the cross, you can score big points with the jury, especially where you will not call your own expert. On the other hand, where you will call your own witness and have tested this part of your cross on the expert during the deposition, you might start with a technique that combines enlistment with a narrowing of the issues.

13.7.1 Enlistment and Narrowing of Issues

Perhaps the best way to explain how enlistment can lead to narrowing the issues by getting the opposing expert to agree with your own expert is to give an example. Imagine cross-examining the opposing doctor at trial in the motorcycle accident case used earlier; the doctor, a neurologist, has opined that the client's epilepsy, which appeared shortly after the accident, is not causally related to the accident, but is idiopathic—that is, of unknown origin. The cross begins as follows:

Q: Dr. Rosenberg, you are a neurologist, right?

A: Yes.

Q: And you see patients?

A: Yes.

Q: You are, in fact, affiliated with a hospital?

A: Yes.

Q: And by "affiliated," that means the hospital has reviewed your credentials and your record and has authorized you to treat patients at its facility?

A: Yes.

Q: One hospital where you work is Nita General Hospital?

A: Yes.

Q: Dr. Barron, the treating physician, also has privileges at Nita General Hospital?

A: Yes.

Q: And you know Dr. Barron, at least by reputation?

A: Yes.

Q: You work together at the same hospital?

A: You could say that.

Q: And you know Dr. Barron has a very good reputation as a treating physician?

A: Well . . . I guess that's right.

Professionals (especially those affiliated in some way) who belong to the same professional organizations or work in the same community are often loath to speak badly of other similarly situated professionals. By enlisting the opposing expert in credentialing your own expert, your goal is at least to put your expert on a par with the opposition. To follow up, you might go on to legitimize the area of your witness's particular expertise. For example:

Q: Now, Dr. Rosenberg, not every physician is a specialist, correct?

A: Yes.

Q: And general practitioners, they see a lot of different kinds of patients, don't they?

A: That's right.

Q: They see people with everything from cancer to the common cold?

A: That's right.

Q: And one type of illness of particular relevance that general practitioners treat is epilepsy?

A: That's right.

Q: You have no quarrel with Dr. Barron's qualifications to treat epilepsy?

A: No.

Q: And you agree with his diagnosis of epilepsy in Jackie, don't you?

A: Yes.

Q: And, in fact, you agree with his treatment of Jackie for his epilepsy, don't you?

A: Yes.

By showing areas of agreement between the expert and the opposing expert, you can enlist the opposing expert to accredit your own expert's work. The jurors will also appreciate this effort, because you are narrowing the issues and simplifying the dispute for them. Now they do not have to worry that the doctors might disagree on diagnosis or treatment. You can use this technique in a variety of settings:

Accountants (cross-examining a "forensic economist" where the expert is an experienced auditor):

> Q: You agree that auditors examine companies to help determine if and what value the company has? . . . And you agree with (my expert's) math, and with his arithmetic? Your single disagreement with him is over the assumptions he made?

Chemist (in a criminal case):

> Q: You agree that what I have here in my hand is cocaine? And you agree that the chemist for the state used the correct method, the right test, to determine that the white powdery substance is cocaine? . . . You merely wonder whether it came from the defendant?

You can see that enlistment is closely related to a second friendly beginning point, narrowing the issues.

13.8   Macro v. Micro Cross-Examination

Remember the Alger Hiss case discussed earlier? Remember the choice the lawyer for Chambers made in cross-examining the psychologist who testified that Hiss was lying based on simply observing him in court? The lawyer tried to challenge the field of psychology, a challenge that was much too broad and complex and probably doomed to failure because of the expert's entrenched need to protect his raison d'être. Taking a lesson from that, before the jurors at trial, effective cross-examiners simplify, regardless of whether they are cross-examining psychologists, psychiatrists, accountants, defense medical malpractice experts, plaintiff causation experts, construction experts, or "human factors" experts. The place to challenge an entire field is in limine, in a *Daubert*-type challenge. Cross-examination in court is more often directed toward weight, not admissibility, but because the jurors are still asked to make credibility decisions (plus causation and damages decisions), they will appreciate any help you can provide on these matters.

If you go after the whole discipline and field, it is impossible for the jurors and the expert not to recognize the personal attack: "Your line of work is a fraud, worthless, not useful in daily life." The expert will fight you and fight you hard by discussing all of the people and institutions who rely on the opinions such experts give (whether an auditor who audits a business, a psychiatrist who evaluates the mentally ill to determine whether they should be let out on the streets, or Dr. Done of Benedectin fame who had worked for the Food and Drug Administration).

You are more likely to succeed in cross-examining the expert on the facts, Imwinkelreid's minor premise. In the Hiss case, it might have been more effective for Chambers's lawyer to question as follows:

Q: Now, Doctor, your psychiatric evaluation in this case is based on Mr. Chambers's language choice, eye movement, perspiration, and "body language"?

A: Taken together, yes.

Q: Well, let's take them one at a time for a moment. You would agree that a courtroom is in many ways unlike the surroundings in which you normally practice?

A: What do you mean?

Q: Well, here in the courtroom, there is an audience that is looking at the witness?

A: Yes.

Q: In this case, there is a jury trying to determine if the witness is telling the truth?

A: Yes.

Q: And the witness is allowed to talk only when asked a question?

A: Right.

Q: And the questioner often stands in a position that is away from the jury?

A: Yes.

Q: And the witness has to shift his eyes from looking at the jury to looking at the questioner and back?

A: Yes.

Q: And the press is here—the reporters, the camera crews?

A: Yes.

Q: They've asked for these bright lights to be used?

A: I guess.

Q: And they are bright?

A: Yes.

Q: And I'm told that if you look at them for more than a few seconds, they can damage your retinas. Did you know that?

A: No.

Q: And those lights are hot?

A: Now that you mention it, I do feel a little heat.

Q: So, a little sweat in such circumstances does not necessarily reveal a liar, does it?

A: Well, no.

Often, by crossing on the facts, you can challenge the expert and her specific opinions without conducting a broad frontal assault on her field. This is of great importance when you are also relying on an expert from the same field. Resist challenging the entire discipline; instead, focus your cross on the facts you need to discredit the particular expert's work in the case.

For example, Dr. Rosenberg and the motorcycle case—where simply calling the key facts to the attention of Dr. Rosenberg from the record he reviewed can be particularly devastating to his opinion.

Q: You reviewed the emergency room record?

A: Yes.

Q: You saw that it said he had been in a motorcycle accident?

A: Yes.

Q: That it said that he had been unconscious for thirty minutes?

A: Yes.

Q: That the police report said that he had come to rest seventy-five feet from where the Cadillac had pulled out?

A: Yes.

Q: That a witness has testified that he thought Jackie was dead?

A: No, I didn't know that.

Q: That in Dr. Barron's report, he believed from talking to the parents that Jackie may have suffered a petite mal seizure that same night after the accident?

A: I saw that.

Q: That he was dizzy and disoriented that night?

A: Yes.

Q: That he had a severe headache?

A: But he didn't come back to the hospital.

Q: You saw that Dr. Barron did report Jackie had a severe headache that night?

A: Yes.

Q: And in any event, it was just two weeks after this thirty minutes of being unconscious, after having been thrown seventy-five feet from the motorcycle—just two weeks after this that Jackie suffered his first grand mal seizure?

A: Yes.

The art here is juxtaposition. Juxtapose the facts and stack them for the jurors to consider. Make the dispute about what happened, an area that you control through your proof and your witnesses. You should normally conduct your cross on the micro-level of the minor premises, not on the macro-level of the major premises.

13.9   Demystify the Dispute—Analogies

One of the most effective ways of showing the expert that you are in control and of persuading the jurors that they can understand the dispute is to use analogies during the cross. For example, consider the following portion of the cross of Dr. Rosenberg:

Q: Dr. Rosenberg?

A: Yes.

Q: Sometime in your life you have ordered pizza and had it delivered?

A: Yes.

Q: When the pizza came, did you ever open the box and find that the pizza had slid all over the inside?

A: Yes.

Q: So the pizza wasn't quite round anymore—it had hit the box sides and lost its shape?

A: Yes, that's happened to me.

Q: Now the human brain is encased in the skull, right?

A: Yes.

Q: And the brain is soft, and the skull is hard?

A: Yes.

Q: And if something hits the human head really hard on one side, the brain inside can bounce or move around?

A: OK, that is one way to describe it.

Q: And sometimes the brain can actually hit the opposite side of the skull? I believe you call this a "contra coup" effect?

A: Yes.

Q: Now, Jackie hit the front right side of his head in the motorcycle accident—at least he had bumps and bruises on the front right side?

A: Yes.

Q: And his EEG showed irregularities in the back left part of his brain?

A: Yes.

Q: Exactly opposite where his head was hit?

A: That's correct.

The pizza analogy helps make the point and personalizes the cross-examiner to the jury. So you should work with your expert to come up with an analogy that not only teaches, but that you can control. Then even if the opposing expert refuses to cooperate, you can always have your expert use the analogy to teach the jurors what is going on. Not surprisingly, the more complex the subject, the more likely it is the expert has had to use analogies to explain to lay people what is going on. Remember, choose your own expert based partly on her teaching abilities; then use her to teach with analogies and examples on direct and enlist her help in developing analogies to use in the cross.

One of our favorite examples of using an analogy is from one of NITA's best teachers and trial lawyers, Keith Roberts. His demonstration cross of an actuarial economist started like this:

Q: Mr. Expert, you are projecting damages to the plaintiff out over thirty years?

A: Yes.

Q: Do you ever play golf?

A: Yes, I do.

Q: You a pretty good putter?

A: Yes, I'm pretty good.

Q: You agree with me that short putts are easier than long putts?

A: Yes.

Q: Short putts are easier because even if you are off just a little they can still sneak in the hole?

A: Yes.

Q: Long putts are tougher? True?

A: I guess.

Q: Well that's because of the all the breaks and undulations in the green?

A: I guess.

Q: In fact, if you are, say, a long way away from the hole, if you are off just a little at the start, your ball can end up a long way away from the hole?

A: Yes.

Q: Now, you are not standing feet away, your projections place you thirty years away from your target?

A: Yes.

Q: Let's look at your projections on earnings growth, and then look at the discount rate.

13.10 Corralling the Expert

Good cross-examiners will close the corral gate on the expert, particularly if they are going to take the expert on in her area of expertise. The examiner closes the gate by taking away places where the expert can escape. For example:

Q: Now, Dr. Rosenberg, today you've told us that you did a number of things before coming to your conclusion about Jackie's epilepsy?

A: Right.

Q: Let's just review those things you did. You consulted the following before arriving at your opinion.

[*Cross-examiner makes a chart, asks questions, and then writes only after the witness confirms.*]

Q: You read the emergency record of Jackie Fulbright for his treatment after the motorcycle accident, August 14, YR-2?

A: Yes.

Q: You examined the hospital discharge summary?

A: Yes.

Q: The EEG report relating to his first seizure and first hospitalization in September?

A: Yes.

Q: The report of Dr. Barron, dated October 2, YR-2?

A: Yes.

Q: And you also looked at the police report?

A: Yes.

Q: And read Jackie's deposition?

A: Yes.

Q: And that's it, right?

A: What do you mean?

Q: Well, before you met with the attorney and gave him your opinion, those [*points at the list*] are the only things you consulted in reaching your opinion?

A: That's right.

Now the expert has more difficulty pointing to other sources if the cross-examiner backs her into a corner. As a cross-examiner, you want to cut off any places where the expert can run and hide. Obviously, you must carefully set up this cross-examination at deposition or through analyzing other controlling materials, like the expert's report. At deposition, it is important to screen the objective from the expert by asking: "What did you do?" "What else did you do?" "Is there anything else that you did?," instead of asking: "You didn't do X"; "You didn't do Y?" By having the witness exhaustively list everything she did, you turn the impeachment into an impeachment by omission, which we discussed earlier. Although this impeachment is somewhat harder to set up at trial, the alternative presents the risk of tipping off the witness and her counsel at deposition about the line of cross-examination you intend ("things you did not do") and thus allow them to prepare for it. By focusing on what she did and exhausting the list of what she did, you may hide that objective and preserve his cross. For Rosenberg, you would not want him to add at trial that he talked to the nurses, the ambulance drivers, or consulted a particular text or treatise. You should be pretty safe here, especially under the Federal Rules of Civil Procedure, which put the expert under an affirmative obligation to identify in her report the bases of her opinion. In addition, she has an obligation to supplement her report and her deposition if she reaches further conclusions that are not present in either; if she does not supplement, she may lose her ability to refer to the report or to state those additional opinions or bases at trial.

One technique to keep the examination on reasonably friendly terms is to give the expert an out by allowing her to blame the lawyers for her incomplete examination of all the pertinent facts. For example:

Q: Now, Dr. Rosenberg, you didn't talk to the ambulance drivers who drove Jackie to the emergency room?

A: No.

Q: You didn't talk with the nurses?

A: No.

Q: Never talked with Dr. Barron, the treating physician?

A: No, there was no need.

Q: You never talked to the parents to determine what they recalled about Jackie's behavior?

A: No, I didn't need to because I had Dr. Barron's report of what he found relevant from his conversations with those people.

Q: Dr. Rosenberg, that was not my question. Are you saying that you did talk to Jackie's parents? (*Reverse repeat.*)

A: No.

Q: In any event, you wanted to do what the lawyers for Americraft Industries were asking you to do, and they didn't tell you that it was necessary for you to talk to the nurses?

A: No.

Q: Or to talk to the parents?

A: No.

Q: Or to examine Jackie yourself—they didn't give you that opportunity?

A: No.

Sometimes you will get more cooperation from the witness by allowing them to blame the lawyers for restricting her access. Again, this is why when you hire your own expert, you want to make certain she tells you what she needs as a professional to give an opinion. Then, if she sets the protocol, she is more likely to defend what she did, why she did it, and how it is customary in her field. Of course, the advantage to the cross-examining lawyer is that he does not care whether it is the lawyers' fault, as long as the jurors gets the point that Dr. Rosenberg had much less to go on than the treating physician.

13.11 Eighth-Grade Science Norms[1]

Think back to eighth-grade science. First, everybody learned about the scientific method. There were a couple of scientific principles everyone, including jurors, learned that are particularly useful to cross-examination of experts. The first is, to identify cause and effect, the scientist states a hypothesis and then tests his hypothesis with an experiment. The experiment was only valid if the scientist controlled all the important variables. For example, think of what you might say to Dr. Rosenberg, the expert who claims there is no knowable cause for Jackie Fulbright's epilepsy.

Q: Dr. Rosenberg, you do agree that Jackie has epilepsy, right?

A: Yes.

Q: And you agree that he suffers grand mal seizures from time to time?

A: He may.

Q: You agree that Jackie did not have epilepsy before the motorcycle accident?

A: That is right.

Q: But that he has it now?

A: Yes.

Q: You believe that his epilepsy is idiopathic?

A: Yes.

Q: That means your opinion is that you don't know the cause?

A: Yes.

Q: Then, really, your opinion is you have no opinion about what is the cause of Jackie's epilepsy?

A: I guess that's another way to say it.

Q: Now, you do agree that sometimes the cause of epilepsy is known?

A: Yes.

Q: That trauma can cause epilepsy?

A: Yes.

Q: But, as a matter of science, your hypothesis is that the cause was unknown—but was not traumatic?

A: Yes.

---

1. Frank Rothschild, an innovative and exciting NITA teacher from Hawaii, is the first person we heard using this phrase to teach about cross-examining an expert.

National Institute for Trial Advocacy

Q: So, let's look at what you did to test your hypothesis. You never talked to Jackie, did you?

A: No.

Q: You never talked to the ambulance attendant who treated Jackie immediately after the motorcycle accident?

A: No.

Q: You didn't see Jackie in the emergency room?

A: No.

Q: You never talked to the emergency room doctors who treated Jackie?

A: No.

Q: You never talked to his parents?

A: No. I read the records.

Q: That's right, you read the records and read the depositions, right?

A: Yes.

Q: And that's what you did to test your hypothesis that Jackie's epilepsy was not traumatic.

A: Yes.

A second violation of the scientific method occurs when the scientist fails to keep an open mind when bias or prejudice are introduced. All jurors understand the scientific method requires objective analysis of the data so the conclusions are not tainted. Researchers use placebos and blind studies in testing drugs because they do not want to affect the interpretations of the patients' symptoms by what either the doctors or patients expect. This principle of scientific independence also works against an expert, especially when the expert commits herself to her opinion too early in the case. (Consider the section on examination for financial or other bias.)

13.12 Expert Testimony on Reconstruction and Recreations

Come back with us now to a time many decades ago, to the wilds of northern Maine, in the middle of a stormy winter night, at Christmastime, when most people stayed snug in their homes wrapped in their cardigans and comforters, warming their hands in the glow of the 22" Sony Trinitron, in the days before the Internet had intruded into beautiful rugged country meant only for snowmobiles and four-footed creatures. On the road winding through the hills, the headlights of a small car pierce the darkness, lighting up the wall of falling snow until the curve of the road sends the lights blazing, useless, into the trees, leaving the driver blind to the full-grown male moose standing stock still in the center of the highway.

The collision is incredible. The moose lunges at the last moment and collides with the car at the roof pillar on the driver's side. The roof collapses, pinning the occupants into their seats until they can be cut out by the rescue squad—but only after waiting painful, freezing hours in the dark. Their injuries are severe, although the moose lumbered off into the winter night without apparent damage.

Their recovery takes months, and during that time they have but one thought running through their heads, a thought to which they finally give voice when they are once again healthy and whole: Who can we sue? Their lawyer quickly rules out the moose as a defendant; he fears identification problems in court, and he supposes, like most moose, this one will be judgment-proof. Besides, he never felt comfortable with those procedural rules about venue, service, and personal jurisdiction involving *ferae naturae*.

A lawsuit is filed[2] against the manufacturer of the car, a Subaru, alleging its roof pillars were not sufficiently strong or well-constructed to withstand foreseeable impacts, as impacts with a moose in Maine were alleged to be. Discovery proceeded, expert reports were exchanged, expert depositions were taken and defended, and then came the predictable barrage of motions from both sides: motions in limine; motions to preclude and exclude; motions to compel, dispel, and repel; and motions to supplement, strike, and redepose. When the smoke had cleared (and it was finally determined there was no fire), the court made several rulings, which remind us that, even in these sophisticated times of *Daubert* and *Kumho*, the basic elements of evidentiary foundation—like relevance and authenticity—maintain their importance.

13.12.1 The Recreation of Damage to the Roof of the Subaru

The plaintiff's expert intended to demonstrate the roof pillars of the Subaru were inadequately designed and constructed by hoisting a similar car upside down to a point eighteen inches above the concrete floor of the laboratory work space, releasing it suddenly, and then measuring the extent to which the roof and pillars were crushed toward the passenger compartment. When questioned at deposition about the choice of the eighteen-inch distance, the expert answered he had seen a description of procedures utilized by the Society of Automotive Engineers, an engineering group that used an inverted drop-test for purposes of assessing damage from rollovers, although he admitted that those purposes were not directly stated to be moose-related.

During pretrial, the court excluded the expert's testimony about this test and his results on the grounds of relevance because there was no showing by the plaintiffs' counsel that the damage caused by dropping a Subaru on its roof onto concrete was scientifically or logically related to the damage caused by a moose colliding with the front, left roof pillar. Indeed, the ability of the four roof pillars to withstand the

---

2. Brawn v. Fuji, 817 F. Supp. 192 (D. Me. 1993).

impact caused by the full weight of the car being dropped a distance of eighteen inches tells us nothing about the moose-car interaction. Presumably, the car weighs more than the moose, so the test damage might be greater; on the other hand, there are four pillars absorbing the impact, not just one, as in the original accident, so the test damage might be less. Therefore, the evidence does not help the jurors to resolve a fact in issue—it does not make a fact in issue more or less likely—the classic definition of relevance. Regardless of the sophistication of the methodology the expert employed; regardless of his credentials, lack of bias, or knowledge regarding "testability" or "known or knowable" error rate; regardless of any of the criteria or reliability, which the Supreme Court has invited trial lawyers and judges to use to assess the confidence they should place in expert methodologies; the simple fact remains that such testimony must be relevant if it is to be admissible.

The court also expressed concern the this evidence would confuse the jurors rather than help them understand the issues related to the roof's integrity in this accident. That possibility of confusion, of course, especially when amplified by the impressive credentials and presence of an expert, can be an independent basis for the exclusion of evidence under Rule 403—even of clearly relevant evidence.[3]

13.12.2 The Model of the Moose

In an attempt to demonstrate the moose-worthiness of the Subaru, the defendants' expert constructed a moose-model—a life-size model of the moose—from canvas sandbags, straps, and rope, and then weighted the moose-model by adding water to the sandbags as it hung in the laboratory. When it was hanging to her satisfaction, the defendants' expert had someone, presumably a properly qualified assistant, drive a similar Subaru into the strapped-up, rope-hung, water-weighted, canvas-sandbag moose-model, and then the expert measured the damage from the impact.

Plaintiffs' counsel, not wanting to appear immobile, moved to exclude this expert evidence on the grounds there had been no showing that the collision between the replacement Subaru and a canvas sandbag moose was sufficiently similar to the original collision between the original Subaru and the original moose. Without some basis for concluding that these events were similar, argued the plaintiffs' counsel, these hanging-canvas-sandbag moose tests were simply not relevant.

In this instance, the court ruled the model-moose test would only be relevant if a very specific collection of facts was found to have existed in the actual accident—facts that were then duplicated by this model-moose test. Scientific testimony must deal with some controversy or issue the jurors must resolve, and demonstrations

---

3. The court also noted the relevance problems caused by the absence of any standards against which to compare the damage caused by the upside-down drop test; that is, without knowledge of the extent of crush of an acceptable safe roof, how can the jurors determine the significance of the extent of crush that they see in the test?

or recreations must be sufficiently similar that observing such evidence will help the jurors do this job. Unless the test circumstances and the actual circumstances are very similar, there is no way to go from sandbag moose to actual moose without engaging in speculation and supposition that are unsupported by the evidence. However, the court ruled it was within the province of the jurors to determine whether the facts of the accident were, indeed, that set of facts that matched the model-moose test, and the test was admitted with plaintiffs' counsel perfectly free to attempt to persuade the jurors that no such similarity existed.[4]

The important lesson from both rulings is that relevance remains a supervening, absolutely essential element of foundation for expert testimony, and no amount of scientific sophistication or pseudoscientific legerdemain will substitute for a clear statement of the logical connection between the evidence being offered and the issues that must be resolved. Recreations and demonstrations must be substantially similar to the historic reality giving rise to the lawsuit or they will be excluded as irrelevant, regardless of the willingness of an expert to swear by the scientific reliability and validity of the methodologies employed.

13.12.3 The Roof Pillars that Were Not Roof Pillars

The defendants' expert also attempted to demonstrate that a heavier gauge of steel for the roof pillars—a gauge suggested by plaintiffs' expert—would not have prevented the injuries suffered in the accident. However, instead of testing actual roof pillars, or exemplar roof pillars constructed with the heavier gauge steel, the expert merely subjected pieces of steel of the different gauges to forces in an apparatus she designed herself and then concluded, based on the results of such deformation testing, that the heavier gauge steel would not have prevented any of the observed injuries. Based on her tests, the expert admitted that she could not say how either of these gauges of steel would perform as roof pillars in an impact. Based on this less-than-enthusiastic recommendation by the expert of her own tests, the court rejected them as being of no help to the jurors and as presenting an undue risk of confusion.[5]

13.12.4 Conclusions from the Moose Case for Direct and Cross-Examination

All of these problems are relevance problems—not *Daubert* problems, not *Kumho* problems, not specialized problems pertaining only to experts. Just plain relevance.

---

4. The model moose was not completely available to the plaintiffs' expert for tests to determine whether the results could be replicated—while the model had sat on the unheated, concrete patio outside the laboratory through the remainder of the Maine winter, some substantial parts of its moose-model anatomy froze to the floor and could not be saved. Nevertheless, the half-rumpled model and tests could still be admissible, said the court, because representative samples of its material were available to the plaintiffs, and nothing prevented them from repeating the tests that had been adequately described. *Id.* at 193.

5. *Id.*

When you are preparing your expert, when you are considering demonstrations and recreations, and when you are preparing to challenge the opposing expert, do not become so caught up in questions relating to the reliability of the scientific or other expert methodology being employed that you forget that the expert testimony must always satisfy the most fundamental of foundational requirements: relevance.

After *Daubert*, some commentators took to referring to the relevance component of expert testimony as "fit," perhaps so they could enjoy the alliteration of *fit and foundation*. Relevance-fit, however, is already part of foundation (which is comprised of relevance, authenticity, absence of privilege, absence of or exception from hearsay, and satisfaction of the original document rule; therefore, saying *fit and foundation* is redundant. *Relevance and reliability* provides the same element of alliteration and avoids redundancy. In this use, reliability is part of authentication— that is, "Is the preferred testimony what its proponent says she is offering?" In this context, is it specialized knowledge, which is sufficiently well-founded according to some appropriate measures (the four *Daubert* criteria or other indicia or reliability) that it should be admitted for the jurors' consideration and use?

In fairness to those who prefer *fit*, or some name other than simple relevance when discussing the admissibility of expert testimony, there is clearly some additional component to this relevance. With other evidence, it is relevant if it makes a matter in issue more or less likely than that matter would be without the preferred evidence; with expert testimony, however, it is relevant (or it fits) if it is relevant in the classic sense just stated and also if it is *helpful* to the jurors.[6]

This additional requirement of relevance comes from the phrase in Rule 702, "help the trier of fact to understand the evidence." Expert testimony is helpful if it presents information or knowledge to the jurors, or allows them access to methods of analysis, that they would not have on their own. To phrase this in the contrapositive, if expert testimony does nothing for the jurors that they could not do for itself, then it is by definition not *helpful* and should not be admitted, regardless of its relevance in the traditional sense. The idea of *fit* certainly is intended to embody this helpfulness concept; however, in place of creating a new category of foundation, it seems simpler merely to recognize that when relevance of expert testimony is discussed, testimony must be *help* the jurors resolve the question in issue, not merely be *related* to the matter at issue.

---

6. Federal Rule of Evidence 702 states:

> A witness who is qualified as an expert by knowledge, skill, experience, training, or education may testify in the form of opinion or otherwise if:
> (a)   the expert's scientific, technical, or other specialized knowledge will help the trier of fact to understand the evidence or to determine a fact in issue;
> (b)   the testimony is based on sufficient facts or data;
> (c)   the testimony is the product of reliable principles and methods; and
> (d)   the expert has reliably applied the principles and methods to the facts of the case.

CHAPTER FOURTEEN

CROSS-EXAMINING AN EXPERT WITNESS IN AN INTERNATIONAL COMMERCIAL ARBITRATION

(Significant comments and editorial contributions to this chapter were made by Peter R. Day[1])

Before a common-law trained trial lawyer conducts a cross-examination of an expert witness in an international commercial arbitration, such a lawyer must consider how he needs to change his approach to make sure he does not to lose the persuasive impact of the cross-examination.[2] Cross-examining an expert witness in an international arbitration involves lawyering skills and techniques that are both dissimilar and similar to those the advocate uses in the common-law courtroom. They are dissimilar because the advocate will have different materials available from which to prepare. His preparation will also be substantially different because the lawyer may have much less factual material than would be obtained from U.S. discovery. The skills required are also dissimilar because the arbitrators often come from civil-law countries, which have different expectations of the cross-examiner. In addition, in an international commercial arbitration, the expert witness usually has special obligations to be independent. These obligations will serve to discipline the expert's opinions differently from settings where the expert is more of an advocate. Also, the advocate in an international commercial arbitration is often under strict time constraints from the arbitrators, requiring much more pointed and concise questioning.

At the same time, it is important for the cross-examiner to be cognizant of the use of his traditional trial cross-examination techniques. The cross-examiner needs to have a clear idea of the purpose of his cross-examination, of what legal theory he is using, and must have an eye on how the cross-examination might fit his theme in the case. He must also be able to control the expert as in the court room to best

---

1. FCIArb; Principal, Mercer Island Arbitration Chambers International LLC.
2. This article grows out of the authors' (Zwier and Day) recent experience conducting a Cross-Examination Skills Training Programs for Chinese lawyers at the Beijing and Shanghai Arbitration Associations on December 9–10, and 14–15, 2012, respectively. The authors were inspired by their faculty colleagues, including Clarisse von Wunschheim; Franchi Nassim; Dan Tan; Christopher Moger; Bruce W Collins; Natalie Voser and U.S. faculty Hon. Mark Drummond; Hon. Hollis Hill; Vanessa Lee.

For the purposes of keeping the grammar from being too clunky, we again continue our practice of referring to the lawyer by the masculine pronoun, and the expert by the feminine pronoun.

advance his theories or themes. He must use questioning techniques designed to maximize his control of the witness. Moreover, the lawyer must have sourced his questions in the expert's report, or letters, or past expert opinions, or learned treatises, or his own experts' expertise, or in the facts from lay witnesses, to ensure that his cross-examination does not give the expert a second chance to advance the opposing theory in the case.

14.1 Dissimilarities in Skills and Techniques of Cross-Examination between an International Commercial Arbitration and Trial

14.1.1 General Discovery

A major difference between U.S. trials and international arbitration is the lack of U.S.-style discovery. In particular, in few if any circumstances would counsel be permitted to take a deposition of an expert witness before the hearing. If the IBA Rules on the Taking of Evidence in International Arbitration (the "IBA Rules") are followed, the production of documents or other tangible evidence is dramatically less than under the U.S. discovery. While this is another topic, Article 3 of the IBA Rules requires that a production request specify the document requested in great detail, and, most importantly, "(b) a statement as to how the documents requested are "relevant to the case and *material to its outcome*; . . ." (emphasis added). Thus large amounts of documents from the other party or from third parties are not likely to be available. While the IBA Rules are an attempt to seek common ground between the common-law and civil-law systems, many civil-law arbitrators will interpret the IBA Rules more restrictively than will common-law arbitrators.

14.1.2 Expert Reports

As we have discussed in earlier chapters, in federal court in the United States, experts are required to write reports that contain "all the facts or data the expert considered" in arriving at their opinion. Also in federal court, the expert's opinion can be challenged under Federal Rule of Evidence 702 for want of sufficient data or reliable methodology. In addition, the expert is required in a federal case to provide her résumé, her compensation information, her earlier court testimony, and earlier engagements as an expert.

With regard to experts in international arbitration, both the IBA Rules and the Chartered Institute of Arbitrators Protocol for the Use of Party-appointed Expert Witnesses in International Arbitration ("CIArb Protocol") require substantial disclosure of the assumptions, facts, methodology, etc., that are used in preparing an expert opinion. In addition, under both the IBA Rules and the CIArb Protocol, the tribunal may order the experts to confer prior to the hearing to identify areas of agreement and better define the areas of disagreement. (Article 6 of the CIArb

Protocol further requires, unless the tribunal orders otherwise, that the experts consult prior to formulating their opinions.) Thus, unlike the more limited opportunity to cross-examine fact witnesses based on depositions and access to volumes of the other parties' documents, if the tribunal follows the IBA Rules and/or CIArb Protocol, the advocate should have sufficient information to prepare and conduct an effective cross-examination.

Under the IBA Rules and the CIArb Protocol, one key principle will apply that can cast a flavor on the cross-examination of experts different from that in an American jury trial; the expert must certify that she is a neutral whose duty is to serve the tribunal rather than the party who engaged her. The CIArb Protocol requires that the expert's opinion include the affirmations in Article 8, the first two paragraphs of which are:

> I understand that my duty in giving evidence in this arbitration is to assist the arbitral tribunal decide the issues in respect of which expert evidence was adduced. I have complied with, and will continue to apply with, that duty.

> I confirm that this is my own, impartial, objective, unbiased opinion which has not been influenced by the pressures of the dispute resolution process or by any party to the arbitration.

As we will see, this may present special opportunities for the cross-examiner to expose the expert's lack of independence in a way that can limit the weight the tribunal will give the expert's testimony.

Thus, the overall approach is to avoid the "dueling gunfighter" approach to experts and seek an objective and consensus-seeking process.

Clearly, each party will still seek experts who support the theory of its case. Nevertheless, effective cross-examination should aim at focusing on the underlying facts supporting the opinion, the methodology and theories used, and the rationale of the opposing expert regarding those areas of disagreement. In addition, impeachment by means of inconsistent prior testimony, inconsistent publications, etc., should still be permissible, but care should be taken not to create an overly confrontational tone when doing so.

14.1.3 General Approach

Take the example of a damages expert in a commercial dispute involving a projection of loss to the claimant from respondent's unfair trade practices in denying claimant's ability to sell a new product. Claimant's expert might try to opine that claimant would have been able to duplicate respondent's profits if it had not been wrongfully denied it contract rights. Yet, of course, the respondent performed, and part of his profit may have been due to respondent's own unique abilities. How can the claimant fairly be said to have been able to do as well if the respondent never had sold this product before in this market?

If claimant's expert relies in part on her experience with the way most companies are able to adapt their advertising to the markets in which they seek to sell their goods, the respondent may challenge this basis as lacking sufficient data to support whether the claimant would have been able to do what experience tells the expert they would be able to do. The respondent might ask in federal court what steps the expert has taken to test whether claimant would have been able to duplicate what others had done in this market? What is the claimant's expert's confidence rate, or "error rate" in making his assumptions? Has anyone else been willing to use general experience about advertising ability in building a damages model like claimant's expert has?

In a federal court setting, respondent would challenge the expert's ability to testify at all. While in a U.S. court it may be a worthwhile attempt to seek to exclude the expert report, it is extremely rare that such a tactic would be considered in international arbitration. Since one of the relatively few grounds set forth in both the Convention on the Recognition and Enforcement of Foreign Arbitral Awards (the "New York Convention") and in the UNCITRAL Model Law on International Commercial Arbitration (which is increasingly adopted by countries as their domestic law governing international arbitrations) to have an award set aside at the seat of the arbitration or oppose enforcement of the award in another jurisdiction is that "a party was unable to present his case," the tendency of arbitrators is to accept into evidence whatever a party presents unless it is clearly duplicative or irrelevant rather than risk giving ammunition to the losing party to challenge the award.

Thus, in international commercial arbitration, the claimant's expert's opinion may be let in without discovery or testing of her basis—under the general approach that the arbitrators are not bound by the rules of evidence—and will be given whatever weight the arbitrators believe it is due. Of course, this makes sense, because there is less fear the arbitrators will give the expert's opinion too much credit, as might be the case in front of a jury. Still, the cross-examiner might have to challenge the sufficiency of the expert's basis to the arbitrators to flag to the arbitrators the unreliable nature of experts' assumptions. In a traditional federal court setting, such challenges would likely be made pretrial. Under the IBA Rules, if the tribunal wishes to appoint its own experts, the parties may challenge the expert's qualifications.

Note also that in a civil-law environment, there is often a bias toward written evidence. Article 6, subparagraph (f) of the CIArb Protocol and IBA Rule 5.3 permit additional reports to deal with matters raised in the written opinion of the other experts. In many cases then, the strongest argument to rebut the opposing experts' opinions might best be made in follow-up written submissions. Therefore, cross-examination should be carefully planned to highlight the most persuasive evidence challenging the opposing experts' opinion without becoming redundant.

In other words, in an arbitration setting, the cross-examining advocate often has more on his plate than if his challenges were limited to issues of credibility or to faulty applications of accepted methodologies to specific portions of the expert's analysis.

14.1.4 Researching the Expert's Qualifications

The skills needed to cross-examine an expert in a commercial arbitration setting also are dissimilar because they require the lawyer to prepare differently. The setting is more like what the advocate faces in many U.S. state courts. The advocate likely has not had a chance for any deposition of the expert's testimony. So the advocate will be required to take full advantage of his informal discovery of the opposing expert. Here the Internet can be particularly helpful. The advocate should be particularly careful to make thorough searches regarding expert's qualifications and her past relationships with counsel or opposing clients. This information might also be gleaned from other testimony the expert has given in another forum, such as a federal court. Trial testimony might reveal experience the witness has with either the counsel or client. This might then generate a request to the arbitrator for disclosure of the timing of the experts' arriving at their opinion, the role counsel played in shaping the opinion, and finally, production of any analysis of earlier opinions given by the experts in earlier cases that may show lack of independence.

The question of experts' qualifications is often overlooked. The advocate needs to take special care to examine the expert's past opinions to determine what different opinions the expert is going to give to this tribunal. Without the aid of the Federal Rule of Civil Procedure 26, the expert might not have listed each of her opinions. It is incumbent on the advocate to seek such a list. Then the advocate must examine the qualification to see if there is a match between the expert's opinions and her qualifications. For example, in the case of the damages expert we described above, if one of the expert's opinions is that the claimant would have been successful in advertising the product that is the basis of the dispute, what are the expert's qualifications to give such an opinion? Has she worked in advertising, done advertising in similar markets, or studied advertising in similar market conditions? The cross-examiner needs to be prepared to challenge the expert's opinions where she lacks the requisite expertise.

In particular, the expert's report needs careful examination for the hidden or unstated opinions and assumptions that form the basis of the expert's opinion. Where the expert is relying on "experience," such experience needs be examined to make sure that a criterion has been developed by the expert to guide her in how to apply her experience. Otherwise it can become her *ipse dixe*, or "Take my word for it. I am right."

14.1.5 Background of the Tribunal

The skills required for international arbitration are also dissimilar to those used during courtroom cross-examination, especially when the arbitrators come from civil-law countries and have different expectations of the cross-examiner. Civil-law arbitrators from Switzerland, Germany, France, or Eastern Europe are often frustrated by English-, Australian-, or United States-style cross-examinations of experts, as they often feel those types of examinations are not helpful and confuse more than clarify the issues before the tribunal. Asian arbitrators may share some of the same attitudes of arbitrators from these civil-law countries. On the other hand, some Asian arbitrators are influenced by Hong Kong-style arbitrations, which are in turn influenced by the British. As a result, it is important for advocates to examine the specific predilections of the arbitrators to best understand what attitudes they might hold and anticipate how the tribunal will react to their cross-examination.

It is important to examine these attitudes to determine whether the common-law advocate will accede to them or whether he will challenge the opposing expert, even in the face of these attitudes. Sometimes the arbitrators are chosen, in part, because of their expertise in the subject matter of the arbitration. In these cases, the experts may play less of a role in helping to educate the court. The arbitration process may be relying more on expertise from the tribunal itself than on the expert anyway. In the case of Asian arbitrators, it may be that experts are viewed as lacking importance and credibility because they are overly in the control of a particular party. These experts may be seen as undisciplined by any oath to tell the truth and so lacking in independence as to be almost shills for the parties. Testimony from these witnesses are often given little weight, and the cross-examination of these witnesses are seen as largely a waste of time, as their credibility is already so suspect.

Even with respect to party-appointed experts, many arbitrators may intervene with their own questions during the cross-examination. While this can adversely affect the advocates attempt to set up the expert with a series of questions fencing in the expert to arrive at the desired answer, it can also give the advocates an idea of what issues are most important of the tribunal.

14.1.6 Damages v. Other Issues

Damages experts may fit somewhere in between technical experts and experts who are seen as lay advocate witnesses. They might have some appearance of independence, and because of their heightened professional status, they might carry some extra weight with the arbitration tribunal. And so it is with damages experts that the advocate must take care to determine whether he might engage in a more vigorous cross-examination to challenge the expert about the underlying nature of her assumptions.

These are not trivial matters. Damages experts often come from litigation-support departments of major accounting firms. They often bear the credentials and experience of seasoned experts. In addition, they are skilled at making assumptions that can produce numbers at the extremes. It is not uncommon for damages models to produce outcomes that are hundreds of million dollars apart. It is in these cases that the advocate may know a great deal more about the nature of the expert's assumptions than do the arbitrators, so a good cross-examiner needs to rely on more traditional trial skills in conducting his cross-examination.

14.1.7 Time Constraints

The advocate in an international commercial arbitration is often under strict time constraints that require much more pointed and concise questioning. Such constraints can also create a way to discipline the expert to limit their answers in a way that will allow the advocate to comply with these time constraints. It is hard for the expert to convey independence if she keeps giving long answers and explanations where such answers repeat things she has said in her witness statement. The tribunal will lose patience with the expert, as opposed to the cross-examiner. This, however will only come to be the effect on the tribunal if the advocate uses the skills of a well-prepared trial cross-examiner. It is therefore important to remember what these skills are.

14.2 Trial Advocacy Cross-Examination Skills and Techniques for International Commercial Arbitrations

As in any trial, the cross-examiner needs to have a clear idea of the purpose of his cross-examination, of what legal theory he is using, and must have an eye on how the cross-examination might fit his theme in the case. His preparation and planning must start with an analysis of how he will seek to promote his theory and theme on closing argument. Because the expert is often very knowledgeable and is active on a playing field where she is more familiar, the cross-examining lawyer must take an attitude towards the expert like one might take toward handling a poisonous snake. He must be careful not to get bit. He must then cross-examine the expert only to the extent necessary to make his point on closing. This means that if he can make his points adequately during the examination of his own expert, then he does not need to make the points again during the cross-examination. On the other hand, where he can use the opposing expert's own admissions or reports to either narrow the nature of the dispute, or confirm theories his own expert has used, then the cross should make these take advantage of these opportunities.

Once the cross-examiner has determined which points he will make during his cross, he must arrange them with care for maximum impact. Three basic choices present themselves. The first is to organize the points by starting with the areas of agreement, and then moving to areas of disagreement, saving any bias points for places where the expert might not concede legitimate areas of agreement. Where the expert quarrels unnecessarily, she shows her lack of independence and loses credibility.

A second organizational principle would be to use the opportunity presented by expert testimony to remind the tribunal of the lawyer's overriding theme. In this case, the lawyer uses the expert's review of the file to remind the arbitrators of key facts that the expert has seen in the file that supports the lawyer's theory of the case. Focusing on the facts makes the expert play on the lawyer's field of advantage. The lawyer is likely to be able to present to the expert facts from witness statements that paint a picture of the world that is contrary to the world the expert may have assumed to be the case.

For example, in our discussion of a claimant's expert who assumes the ability of the claimant to have been able to sell a new product in a new market, the cross-examiner might make the points from the witness statements that claimant: 1) had never sold the product before; 2) had no offices in the new market; 3) had never hired advertiser there; 4) did not have experience with using TV, radio, or print advertising in that market; 5) had no existing personnel who even spoke the language spoken in those markets; and 6) wants hundreds of millions of dollars in an award where they have never sold even one product or expended any resources.

Finally, the advocate might try to limit himself to making three simple points, starting with his best point first, then his more risky point, and end with his second strongest point. This keeps the advocate focused on keeping maximum impact on the arbitrators without losing control; it relies on the theory of primacy and recency: that the arbitrators will remember best what they hear first and second best what they hear last, and so the points in between are lesser importance, and more likely to be ignored or forgotten.

14.2.1 Basic Techniques

As far as the question of techniques, the trial lawyer can rely on what has most impact at the hearing. He should remain focused on his audience. That is, he is not cross-examining the expert to get the expert to concede, but is cross-examining the expert to persuade the arbitrators of his theory of the case. His purpose is to talk to the arbitrators by making statements to the expert, which the expert will confirm to be the case. So for each question he must use the grammar he would use in making a statement: noun followed by verb. For example: "Ms. Expert, *you examined* the witness statements of the claimant's witnesses. *You saw* that claimant had no office in Greece?" The question in the statement will come in the tone of voice used by the advocate, and by his gestures. Using his hands, he will make a statement followed by gesturing with palms up, as if handing the expert the statement on a platter. The witness will inevitably respond by answering either "yes" or "no."

The cross-examiner must also be able to control the expert as in the courtroom to best advance his theories or themes. In other words, the cross-examiner must have sourced his questions in the expert's report—or letters, or past expert opinions, or learned treatises, or his own experts expertise, or in the facts from lay witnesses—to ensure that his cross-examination does not give the expert a second chance to advance the opposing theory in the case. This sourcing is vital to being able to bring the expert back to the lawyer's point by reading from the expert's report or source to confirm the fact the cross-examiner has put to the witness.

Finally, the control during cross will be enhanced if the cross-examiner can remember these fundamentals:

1. Try to keep questions short—best seven words or less.

2. Add one fact at a time to maintain control.

3. Edit the statements for adjectives or adverbs. Adjectives and adverbs are often wiggle words, or fighting words, as they give the expert a chance to wiggle or fight and give an explanation for why her theory still holds.

4. Use a tone of incredulity rather than an angry or fighting tone. An incredulous tone help the arbitrators understand the cross-examiner's point without being distracted by watching a fight.

5. Don't ask for explanations from the expert.

6. Never ask her to say why they did what they did.

Finally, as in trial it is still best to save the conclusion for closing. If the lawyer does not ask the concluding question—"So you have no basis to say that claimant will have been able to do as well in selling the product as did the respondent?"—the claimant's expert is not given a chance to restate or remember new reasons for why the claimant would have been able to sell as well as the respondent.

14.2.2 Additional Techniques

With respect to cross-examination, especially when dealing with arbitrators with a civil-law background, it is important not to create the impression that the witness is being badgered or the hearing is being delayed by over-questioning.

While this point applies to both jury trials and international arbitration, it is important that the very first questions posed in cross-examination of an expert demonstrate that the advocate is well prepared and has a thorough understanding of the subject matter. As previously stated, many international arbitrators are skeptical of cross-examination and fear 1) that it will be too long, 2) it will be a fishing expedition, 3) the witness will be unnecessarily embarrassed or insulted, and 4) it will not accomplish anything. If the first five minutes of questioning show the competence and preparation of the advocate and produce statements from the expert that are clearly supportive of the advocate's case, the advocate is more likely to be given wider latitude in completing his intended examination.

As a practical matter, it is very helpful to provide to the arbitrators, the expert, and other counsel a tabbed binder of key excerpts of those documents that will be used in cross-examination. Since time is often restricted at a hearing (some arbitrators choose a chess clock, i.e., a fixed, equal amount of time for each party to question the particular witness) and since many binders of documents are likely to submitted to the tribunal, being able to refer the expert witness, opposing counsel, and the tribunal to Tab X in the binder that contains the key pages of the document in question (and an accurate reference to the location of the complete document) can both save time and also give the impression of the competence and preparation of the advocate.

While seemingly an obvious point, it is important to listen carefully to the tribunal's questions to all fact witnesses and experts as well as its comments and reactions to the terms of reference given to the experts on all sides. Some arbitrators will interact actively with counsel, which gives counsel some insight into the arbitrators thinking—or at least which issues the arbitrator is focusing on.

14.2.3   Tribunal-Appointed Experts

Note that both the IBA Rules and the CIArb Protocol permit the tribunal to appoint its own experts. While generally the same requirements apply to what is provided to the parties with respect to the terms of reference, facts, assumptions, methodologies, etc., used by the tribunal-appointed expert, it is more likely that the tribunal may take the lead in questioning its own expert, changing the dynamic of the parties' cross-examination. In these situations, the common-law advocate may well limit his questioning to clarifications of the parts of the expert's opinion that support his side's case.

14.2.4   Witness Conferencing

There is also an emerging trend in international arbitration to use witness conferencing—or "hot tubbing"—where experts for both parties, and perhaps some fact witnesses, are examined together. Proponents argue that this is both more efficient in terms of time, but more importantly, allows definitional problems, semantic issues, and the like to be more quickly resolved. By permitting witnesses to hear each other's testimony, it may be easier and quicker to identify areas of agreement and better define areas of disagreement.

While done in different fashions, the chair of the tribunal usually takes an active, if not predominant, role in conducting examination to ensure it is done in an orderly manner. While counsel may also ask questions, the questioning is likely to be more restrictive than classic cross-examination.

14.3   Summary

Cross-examining an expert witness in an international arbitration is at least as difficult as doing so in court. The cross-examiner's job is further complicated by a setting where the panelists often expect independence from the expert, even though the independence may be somewhat suspect. Finally, the arbitrators expect that the cross-examiner will be brief and ask questions that are limited to topics salient to the expert's opinion, regardless of the examiner's overall persuasive theories. Still, if the cross-examiner prepares with these differences in mind and uses organizational and questioning techniques that work in a trial court room setting, the cross-examiner can still work the situation to his advantage. This is especially the case where the advocate's purpose is to help the arbitrators by narrowing the scope of the dispute, pointing out areas where the expert may lack independence, and reveal where the experts opinion may lack sufficient support and reliable methodologies.

CHAPTER FIFTEEN

DAUBERT TRILOGY

15.1   Daubert: **The Gathering Clouds**

A number of cases from the 1960s through the 1990s attempted to deal with what was perceived as the problem of "junk science." Raised in the public's awareness by mass tort product liability cases—such as the "Dalkon Shield" litigation, "saddlebag gas tank" litigation, the asbestos litigation, and the tobacco litigation—these multiforum lawsuits called on judges to determine whether expert testimony, most often going to the dispositive facts of the case, was sufficiently reliable to be presented to the jury—and to determine what weight to give to the experts' own testimony that their methodologies were reliable. Among the most famous of these product liability cases were those suing the providers of the morning sickness drug Bendectin, which was alleged to cause limb-reduction ("teratogenic") deformities in newborns.

In 1993, the Supreme Court ruled in *Daubert v. Merrell Dow Pharmaceuticals, Inc.*,[1] that trial courts had to make their own assessment of the reliability of such testimony and methodologies, and it articulated four criteria for consideration in that particular case and perhaps in others, while inviting the lower courts to identify and use others. As a result, the *Frye*[2] test (general acceptance in relevant scientific community) was no longer the law of the land, although it continues to play a somewhat undefined role as one of the criteria to be considered in appropriate cases. While recognizing the exclusion of expert testimony can have a dispositive impact, the Supreme Court in *General Electric v. Joiner*[3] instructed the lower courts that the standard of review for decision on evidentiary admissibility—even those excluding expert testimony—is "clear abuse of discretion."

In the late 1970s, a drug was being widely prescribed to women in their first trimester of pregnancy to reduce the incidence of morning sickness. Its manufacturer was Merrell Dow (which had several other names during the course of the cases that eventually arose), and the drug was called Bendectin. It seemed to be very effective, and its use became more and more widespread. But at some point, parents

---

1. 509 U.S. 579 (1993). *Daubert, Joiner,* and *Kumho Tire* are reproduced in Appendix C, respectively.
2. Frye v. United States 293 F. 1013 (D.C. Cir. 1923).
3. 522 U.S. 136 (1997).

and doctors noticed the occurrence of birth defects in children whose mothers had been taking the drug. And so there occurred a series of lawsuits—perhaps hundreds of lawsuits across the country—that sought damages from Merrell Dow (or its successors), claiming Bendectin was teratogenic. Through an interesting turn of events, which allows us to focus quite closely on a crucial expert issue, there arose in the District of Columbia two lawsuits involving Bendectin. The lawsuits were virtually identical: the two different plaintiffs were represented by the same plaintiff's law firm; the defendant was represented by the same defendant's law firm; the extent of the birth defects was similar; and the central expert witness was the same man, Dr. Done. However, one significant difference existed between the two cases: one case had been filed in the city courts, the Superior Court for the District of Columbia, and the other one had been filed in the Federal District Court for the District of Columbia, based on diversity. The two cases proceeded nearly simultaneously with essentially the same proof. In the expert phase of the plaintiffs' cases, Dr. Done testified twice that there had been a number of studies about the teratogenic effects of Bendectin—he recounted about five—and those studies involved epidemiological analyses of animal studies and clinical studies. He in turn had studied all the studies. He recognized in each of the studies the conclusion had been reached that for one reason or another the data were insufficient to allow a conclusion with a reasonable degree of epidemiological confidence that Bendectin was, in fact, the cause of birth defects.[4]

Dr. Done went on to testify, however, that he had agglomerated the data from these various studies, and using methodology he had developed, he had reanalyzed the combined data and was now able to conclude to his satisfaction as an expert that Bendectin was the cause of birth defects such as those observed with these children. In both courts, the cases were submitted to the jury. In the Superior Court for the District of Columbia, the jury returned a verdict of $1 million for the child and its parents, and the verdict was affirmed by the city Court of Appeals. In the Federal District Court, the jury returned a verdict of $1 million for the child and the parents, but the verdict was set aside by the trial judge, who entered judgment for the defendant corporation, a decision affirmed by the Court of Appeals for the District of Columbia Circuit. Thus, in one court $1 million was awarded to the afflicted child, and in the other court, nothing.

Why was there a different outcome? In the city court, Dr. Done's testimony was admitted based on a low threshold—his statements that the methodology he employed was scientifically valid and reliable. The court then allowed the jury to determine what weight to give the expert's testimony. In the federal court, the judge heard the same testimony from Dr. Done, but the judge concluded that the testimony did not support a preliminary finding of sufficient reliability so as to permit admission and submission to the jury. These two cases, occurring virtually

---

4. In fact, it remains true to this day that no epidemiological studies are able to conclude to an acceptable level of statistical certainty that Bendectin has ever caused birth defects.

simultaneously, turned on the issue of who determines whether expert testimony is sufficiently reliable to be admitted and on what evidence such a determination is made. They demonstrated, in a draconian way, the potential ramifications of such a decision.

Across the country, these conflicting outcomes were repeated. Indeed, Dr. Done testified from state to state in numerous cases, sometimes being accepted and sometimes being rejected, and the Bendectin cases became emblematic of this quandary in the law of expert evidence: Who decides reliability and on what basis?

15.2 *Daubert*: The Supreme Court, Gatekeepers, and Expert Reliability

It was in this context that the case of *Daubert v. Merrell Dow Pharmaceuticals* arose. In a federal court in Los Angeles, the parents of William Daubert filed suit against Merrell Dow, alleging that William's mother's use of Bendectin during her pregnancy had resulted in those same types of birth defects suffered by children across the country. The federal district court granted Merrell Dow's motion for summary judgment, concluding Dr. Done's testimony was inadmissible because it did not meet the *Frye* test of "general acceptance in the relevant (here epidemiological) scientific community."

The case went to the United States Court of Appeals for the Ninth Circuit on the *Frye* question, and the court of appeals upheld the district court, ruling in a two-page opinion by Judge Kozinski that the plaintiff's expert's approach was not generally accepted in the relevant scientific community. The court of appeals found the unpublished reanalysis studies were "particularly problematic in the light of the massive weight of the original published studies supporting the defendant's position, all of which had undergone full scrutiny from the scientific community." The court also stated any decision to include or exclude scientific evidence must be reviewed de novo on appeal because "the reliability of a scientific technique or process does not vary according to the circumstances of each case [and therefore is not] . . . within each trial judge's individual discretion."[5] The Supreme Court then granted certiorari in light of the sharp divisions among the circuits and the dispositive nature of the question.

Justice Blackmun, for a unanimous Court, held the *Frye* test was at odds with the "permissive backdrop" of the amended Federal Rules of Evidence. On the gatekeeping issue, a majority of the Court set out a two-prong test for the admissibility of scientific evidence, based on Rule 702, and assigned a "screening" or "gatekeeping" role to the trial judge. The Court said the trial judge must "insure that any and all testimony or evidence admitted is not only relevant, but reliable." The Court's two-prong test of

---

5. Daubert v. Merrell Dow Pharmaceuticals, Inc., 951 F.2d 1128, 1129–30 (9th Cir. 1991).

reliability of the evidence and helpfulness of the evidence to the jury was intended to guide the trial judge's gatekeeping decision.

Rule 702. Testimony by Experts

A witness who is qualified as an expert by knowledge, skill, experience, training, or education may testify in the form of opinion or otherwise if:

(a) the expert's scientific, technical, or other specialized knowledge will help the trier of fact to understand the evidence or to determine a fact in issue;

(b) the testimony is based on sufficient facts or data;

(c) the testimony is the product of reliable principles and methods; and

(d) the expert has reliably applied the principles and methods to the facts of the case.

The Court first defined reliability by interpreting the words "scientific knowledge" in Rule 702, holding 702 did not refer to "scientific certainty," but to knowledge that has a basis in the methods of science and is "supported by appropriate validation (i.e., 'good grounds' based on what is known)." In other words, the requirement that the expert's testimony pertain to "scientific knowledge" establishes a standard of evidentiary reliability. The trial judge must assess whether the reasoning or methodology underlying the testimony was scientifically valid. The Court insisted that "[t]he focus . . . must be solely on principals and methodology, not on the conclusion that they generate."

Second, the Supreme Court majority defined "helpfulness" by relying on the language of Rule 702: the evidence must help the trier of fact to understand the evidence or to determine a fact in issue. The Court said the evidence must have a "valid scientific connection to the pertinent inquiry as a precondition to admissibility." In other words, the Court said the helpfulness prong is one of "fit"—and the inquiry is whether the nexus between the expert testimony and the facts of the particular case is sufficient to assist the jury in resolving the dispute.

Apparently confident that the trial court would be able to conduct such reviews, the Court provided a list of illustrative factors to keep in mind when doing such an inquiry. The factors mentioned by the court were 1) whether the theory or technique can be or has been tested, 2) peer review and publication of the theory or technique, 3) the known or potential rate of error and the existence and maintenance of standards controlling the technique's operation, and 4) general acceptance of the methodology or technique in the scientific community (remember "PEAT": peer review, error rate, acceptance, and testability (meaning falsifiability and replicability)). Clearly, the court was indicating that the pursuit of science is an empirical endeavor—knowledge about the universe progresses by the development of scientific principals and theories capable of falsification.[6]

It is interesting to note the plaintiffs, on behalf of their afflicted children, were seeking the Supreme Court's approval of the proposition that the Federal Rules of Evidence had implicitly overruled *Frye* and therefore liberalized the restrictive view of admissibility taken by the Ninth Circuit and other courts. Ironically, while the plaintiffs won this battle—the court ruled the law was contained in the rules of evidence and not in *Frye*—that victory was completely hollow, because on remand the Ninth Circuit exercised its newly defined "gatekeeper function" and rejected the plaintiff's proffered scientific proof as failing to meet the *Daubert* criteria and other indicators of reliability.

On remand, Judge Kozinski used the court's newly strengthened discretion as a gatekeeper and applied Rule 702 as explained by the Supreme Court in *Daubert*. He said he now had to determine whether the plaintiff's expert testimony was "derived by the scientific method or . . . based on scientifically valid principals."[7] Kozinski determined the first prong of Rule 702 required some objective, independent validation of the expert's methodology. He felt the four factors did not constitute a definitive or exhaustive checklist and added two additional ways to satisfy the first prong of 702—either a) the expert's testimony must grow out of prelitigation research, or b) the expert's research in the case must have been subjected to peer review. Applying these additional factors, Kozinski held the plaintiff's experts did not satisfy the first prong of Rule 702 in either of the two ways suggested because their testimony was not based on prelitigation research and their work on Bendectin was not published in a peer-reviewed journal or subjected to any other formal review.

Judge Kozinski was not the only creative jurist to engraft branches onto the trunk of *Daubert*. Additional criteria for admissibility—*indicia* of reliability—created by the courts include the relationship of the methodology in question to other methods that have previously been established as reliable; the particular qualifications of the expert using the methodology; the internal, logical consistency of the methodology; the precision of the results generated by the methodology (as compared to less useful, broad generalizations); and the extent to which research preceded the development of any conclusions.

15.3 Post-*Daubert* Issues

In post-*Daubert* decisions, the courts seem to have done very well in applying *Daubert* where there are no studies in the scientific community that support

---

6. The concept of "falsification" requires that for a principle or theory to be accepted as useful, the attorney must be able to conceive of facts that if themselves true would make the principle or theory false; otherwise, the theory would not be testable, and we could not determine its truth or falsity—the principle or theory is dogma, belief accepted regardless of facts.
7. *Daubert*, 43 F.3d at 1316.

the proffered methodology. In situations where there are some studies, but those studies are not "widely accepted," the courts' analysis is more uneven. Some of the courts simply exclude the expert or her opinion altogether. Others have chosen to trust lay juries and their rough sense of justice where the scientific community is itself divided. (As a practice tip, one thing to look for in this time of post-*Daubert* decision-making is whether the cases come from the criminal arena or whether they come from the civil arena. Some commentators have noted a tendency in the courts not to apply *Daubert* as strictly where the party offering the expert testimony is the government in a criminal case.[8])

In some areas, defendants have been successful in barring plaintiff's experts from testifying by using *Daubert* challenges—and in others by even using new pleading requirements to bar the plaintiff's claim at the outset. This is particularly true in the area of antitrust litigation.[9]

As we discussed briefly in chapter one, some attorneys have attempted to avoid, rather than meet, the admissibility criteria presented by *Daubert* and its progeny by claiming that their witness testifies not as an expert under Rules 702 and 703, but rather as a lay witness with a relevant opinion presented under Rule 701. Most courts have rejected these attempts, and they will eventually be seen to be merely less-than-clever ruses.[10] Rule 701, permitting lay witness opinion testimony, was intended to authorize lay witnesses to express themselves in the sometimes conclusory or summary fashion normal people do (otherwise known in federal common law as the "collective facts" exception to the rule excluding opinion testimony from lay witnesses), so a lay witness could testify that "the man looked drunk" instead of having to engage in the awkward exercise of attempting to recite each and every fact of sight, sound, and, in this instance, smell, that led her to such a conclusion. Faced with the evidentiary objection that such testimony constituted an opinion, courts gave birth to the lay opinion doctrine.

Where the witness on the stand is being used to present opinion testimony—not as a means of facilitating her articulation of collective facts, but rather as a means of providing the jurors with her judgment on the significance of facts before

---

8. J. P. Kesan, "An Autopsy of Scientific Evidence in a Post-*Daubert* World," Georgetown L. J. (1985): 84.
9. *See* Verizon Communications Inc. v. Law Offices of Curtis V. Trinko, 540 U.S. 398 (2004); Bell Atl. Corp. v. Twombly, 550 U.S. 544 (2007); *see generally* James Langenfeld and Christoper Alexander, "*Daubert* and Other Gate-Keeping Challenges of Anti-Trust Experts, *http://www.americanbar.org/content/dam/aba/administrative/litigation/materials/sac_2012/18-1_b_daubert_and_other_gatekeeping_challenges_with_appendix_antitrust.authcheckdam.pdf*; John E Lopatka and William H. Page, "Economic Authority and the Limits of Expertise in Antitrust Cases," 90 CORNELL L. REV. 617 (2005).
10. In fairness, one man's ruse is another man's legitimate premise. Using the treating physician as an example, you could argue with some rationality that a witness's experience may be sufficiently broad that her own perceptions provide a sufficient basis for helpful testimony even if she is not presented as an expert, and therefore Rule 701 provides an avenue for the admission of such "experience-based" opinions quite separate from the Rules 702 and 703 based approach constrained by the *Daubert* doctrine. This "lay witness approach to avoiding *Daubert*" has not yet been sufficiently tested in the courts to determine its scope or its degree of acceptance.

them—the witness should be treated as an expert, and the admissibility of her testimony should be analyzed under Rules 702 and 703 rather than under the nonexpert Rule 701. (It seems a reasonably easy way to identify a "lay opinion witness" would be to recognize she is percipient—that is, she actually perceived the historical events involved in the lawsuit. If she is testifying about those perceptions, whether in the form of lay opinion, Rule 1006 summaries, or otherwise, *Daubert* should not apply.)

Other attorneys, particularly prosecutors in criminal cases, seem to be attempting to use "summary witnesses" to evade the *Daubert* requirements. Thus, drug enforcement officers are offered to talk about drug deals and IRS officers/computer specialists are offered to talk about tax fraud.[11] To prevent evasion of *Daubert* requirements, courts should be careful to restrict summary witnesses to testimony based on otherwise admissible voluminous facts. This will not include giving opinions about what the facts mean or opinions about causation or damages suffered.

An additional issue regarding the *Daubert* approach was resolved in the *Joiner* case,[12] in which the Supreme Court reviewed the lower appellate court's holding that a decision to exclude expert testimony under the *Daubert* criteria would be subjected to more intensive scrutiny on appellate review because of the likelihood that exclusion would have a substantial impact on the outcome of the case. The Supreme Court held decisions to admit or exclude expert testimony in the federal system should be reviewed by appellate courts using the same "abuse of discretion" standard that they use for all other questions of evidentiary admissibility. To the extent that the attempt by the lower court to impose greater review on the expert decision was based on a concern that the exclusion would have great impact on the case, the Supreme Court's decision is clearly sound in stating there are many items of evidence proffered and rejected that could have that same dispositive effect. To establish a rule of review that required the judge to estimate the impact of evidence on the eventual outcome of the case before determining its admissibility merely introduces greater uncertainty into the law of evidence.

---

11. United States v. Ganier, 468 F.3d 920, 926 (6th Cir. 2006). In *Ganier*, the court reasoned as follows:

> Because the categorization of computer-related testimony is a relatively new question, comparisons with other areas of expert testimony are instructive. Software programs such as Microsoft Word and Outlook may be as commonly used as home medical thermometers, but the forensic tests Drueck (government's expert) ran are more akin to specialized medical tests run by physician. (citations omitted). The average layperson today may be able to interpret the outputs of popular software programs as easily as he or she interprets everyday vernacular, but the interpretation Drueck needed to apply to make sense of the software reports is more similar to the specialized knowledge police officers use to interpret slang and code words used by drug dealers. (citations omitted).

(The Sixth Circuit goes on to say that one fact that is key is when the witness is doing his or her analysis. If done after the case has been brought, as opposed to while the expert is examining a patient, or witnessing an event, then the court is more likely to hold that the opinion is not based on personal experience, but based on specialized knowledge).

12. *General Electric Co. v. Joiner, supra* note 3.

A number of commentators, and some courts, had concluded after *Daubert* that the directions in that case applied only to "scientific" opinion testimony and not to opinion testimony presenting the "technical or other specialized knowledge" referred to in the remainder of the rule. Not only did this create an unacceptable breach in the circuits between the "all opinions" circuits and the "only scientific opinions" circuits, but the "only scientific opinions" circuits provided little guidance on how attorneys and judges were supposed to distinguish between scientific and nonscientific opinions. These distinctions have largely evaporated in the light shed by *Kumho Tire*, as discussed below.

15.4   *Daubert*: To *Kumho* and Beyond

In reviewing federal circuit court decisions that determine whether matters subject to the *Daubert* criteria for admissibility of scientific testimony, no clear pattern emerges across the circuits. For example, while you might arrange disciplines such as mechanical engineering, vocational aptitude counseling, social psychology, or underground construction engineering in some reasonably rational pattern across the spectrum ranging from less scientific to more scientific, the federal circuits have achieved no such rational arrangement. Close examination shows some of these decisions are ambiguous and do not provide sufficient information to determine that the expert opinion was rejected because it was thought to be scientific, but did not satisfy the *Daubert* criteria; or because it was nonscientific and therefore not subject to *Daubert*, but foundationally defective in some other way. It remains clear, however, that confusion across the circuits remained, at least in many areas of expert knowledge as to when *Daubert* was to be applied.

This problem of determining what was scientific and what was nonscientific has been resolved, however, because in *Kumho Tire Co., Ltd. v. Carmichael*, the Supreme Court ruled that the *Daubert* approach to assessing the reliability for expert testimony applied to all expert knowledge, whether it was scientific, technical, or "other specialized" knowledge. In an important sense, however, this decision was both the good news and the bad news. It was good news because trial lawyers and trial courts no longer needed to wonder whether particular expert testimony would or should be measured for reliability when it was offered—it should and would, regardless of the field of knowledge. Therefore, the "hard-soft" scientific spectrum, which seemed pertinent, but ambiguous after *Daubert*, could be discarded. *Kumho Tire* was the bad news in the sense that every expert is now likely to be subjected to challenge for reliability, even experts whose testimony had previously been routinely accepted.

For example, consider the testimony of economists and econometricians in antitrust cases. Putting aside their complex testimony about the existence of competition in a particular product or geographic market, consider merely the much simpler testimony about the existence of that product or geographic market.

- There is extensive literature on these questions in peer-reviewed publications, so one *Daubert* criterion may be satisfied by this economic testimony.

- No economist has data to show how many times she has been wrong, or economists generally have been wrong, in determining the relevant market. Indeed, if you use only contested cases as your sample, it would seem for every economist who is "right" on relevant market questions, there is one testifying for the other side who is "wrong." That leads to a 50 percent error rate, which clearly is not acceptable.

- With regard to "general acceptance in the relevant scientific field," there is substantial room for debate. The Merger Guidelines formulated by the Antitrust Division of the Justice Department provide a method for assessing relevant market questions, but it is hard to say this approach represents consensus in the field of antitrust economics; instead, it appears merely to be a pragmatic attempt to introduce some consistency into this area of litigation. Of course, the very fact that this approach was created for litigation purposes diminishes its reliability, as was recognized by the Ninth Circuit on the remand of the original *Daubert* case when it added "creation for non-litigation purposes" to the four criteria for reliability the Supreme Court had suggested.

- The approaches taken by economic experts on the question of relevant market may be testable, but it is unclear they have ever been tested because markets do not lend themselves to duplication in the laboratory or clinical examination in large numbers. There are many microeconomic studies of individual product and geographic markets, but the facts for each are so particularized that it is very difficult to conclude the results from one market prove a universal truth about all markets. What will you learn from studying the geographic market for cement (a very dense, expensive-to-transport, low-priced commodity) that will apply to generate accurate conclusions about the geographic market for pharmaceutical products (a very lightweight, inexpensive-to-transport, high-priced commodity)?

Obviously, additional analysis, applying criteria beyond those four or five from *Daubert*, would be necessary to determine whether such economic testimony should be admitted; though *Kumho* makes it very clear that such analysis is appropriate and such additional criteria may be identified and used, it does not provide much guidance to courts or trial lawyers in identifying those additional criteria.

What is known from the *Daubert* and *Kumho* cases is this: the Supreme Court has directed trial courts and trial counsel to look for evidence of reliability that is reasonably pertinent to the witness's area of activity (in *Daubert* it was statistical epidemiology; in *Kumho* it was mechanical engineering). Trial lawyers are not constrained by either the original four criteria or by any other list of criteria as they look for indications that the testimony is sufficiently reliable to be admissible. Under this approach, they will examine the cabinetmaker as well as the epidemiologist. The cabinetmaker's reliability might be adequately shown by her adherence to the traditional methods of her mother and grandmother; the treating physician's reliability might be adequately shown by her success in curing patients based on the conclusions she reached through intuition informed by experience; the forklift designer might be shown to be reliable based on her familiarity with the materials to be used, the distribution of forces through the machine, and her success in designing other heavy equipment. These experts are shown to be reliable, despite the fact not one of these "experts" used any pure form of the "scientific method" in coming to the conclusions for which his or her testimony is offered.

Because a determination of admissibility—that is, whether an item of evidence satisfies the appropriate foundational requirements—normally requires the application of a very low threshold of proof (for example, with respect to the authenticity of a signature, the question is merely, "Could a reasonable juror conclude on the proffered evidence that this is the authentic signature?"), it seems likely the important decision of whether expert information is sufficiently reliable to be considered will be made by the jurors.

Of course, matters could have become even more complicated if *Kumho* had not resolved the scientific/nonscientific quandary by teaching reliability testing was a necessary part of the gatekeeping function for district courts dealing with *all* expert testimony. Suppose, for example, an astrologer, a necromancer, or a palm reader were offered as an expert. A court might have concluded that such an "expert" was not offering scientific testimony and therefore was not subject to *Daubert* reliability testing, even though our visceral reaction to such pseudo-experts is they should be *more* clearly excluded for lack of reliability than most other categories of expert witnesses. Of course, the court would most likely exclude the testimony of the astrologer based on some pre-*Daubert* analysis, like lack of "general acceptance in the scientific community," conveniently stepping right over the question of which scientific community is appropriately consulted. Without going into this problem, it is interesting to observe that when you analyze the reliability of mechanical engineers or statistical epidemiologists, you are quite comfortable using standards from the fields of mechanical engineering and statistical epidemiology. When you look at the reliability and consequent admissibility of the testimony of chiropractors or acupuncturists, however, you tend to use standards from the field of Western medicine (and astrologers have no hope of being measured in court against the standards of the reasonable astrologer). These may be correct decisions; however, the interesting question is, can you articulate why they are correct, creating a standard approach for testing reliability of any discipline, new or old, that comes along?[13]

---

13. For a more extensive analysis of this issue, which includes proposals for methods of testing reliability that do not contain biases toward established beliefs and prejudices against new or imported fields of knowledge, *see* David M. Malone and Ryan M. Malone, "The Zodiac Expert: Reliability Beyond Kumho," TRIAL LAWYER (Fall 1999).

CHAPTER SIXTEEN

EXAMINING THE RELIABILITY OF EXPERT TESTIMONY

There are two ways that an opponent can challenge the reliability of an expert's testimony. One way is to diminish the persuasive impact of the experts opinion by trying to keep the jurors from hearing particular bases the expert relied on in arriving on her opinion. The second way we have already referred to, but now need to take a specific look at—namely, how an opponent might use the *Daubert* factors to try to keep the expert from testifying at all.

Rule 703 provides that an expert can rely on evidence as a bases for her opinion that was made known to the expert after the litigation was first brought, as long as it is of the type reasonably relied on by experts in that field. If the facts or data are otherwise inadmissible, then such facts or data will not be disclosed to the jurors unless the court determines their reliability outweighs the danger of unfair prejudice. So hearsay or otherwise *inadmissible* evidence may be disclosed to the jurors only if that *inadmissible* evidence is reliable. That raises the question of how can something the evidence rules hold is inadmissible (presumably because it is either irrelevant or unreliable) and yet be reliable enough to still be disclosed to the jurors.

We need to distinguish between a number of types of potentially inadmissible bases for experts opinions. First we need to review hearsay to see that what might first appear to be inadmissible bases are admissible because they are either defined by Rule 801 as not being hearsay at all or meet an exception to a hearsay rule. Second, we need to look at bases that do not meet an exception to the hearsay rule, but are made reliable by the expert's area of expertise. Often these are facts or data that are inadmissible as hearsay, but are facts that each side's expert relies on in reaching her opinions. These types of bases might be disclosed on direct examination, accompanied by a limiting instruction, or admitted on cross-examination where the opponent chooses to expose the lack of reliability or sufficiency of the data used by the expert. Third, we need to look at bases that if admitted would violate a defendant's confrontation clause rights.

16.1 Hearsay Exceptions and Admissibility of Bases

If an expert relies on statements made by others, the opposing side might object and claim that what the others told the expert is hearsay. Often, however, the statement is not be hearsay at all. For example, an statement a party makes in his deposition, called to the expert's attention, can be used to support an expert's opinion that a fact exists. Note that opposing party statements only apply to statements made by opposing parties used against that party. What if the opposing expert is using statements made by her side's client? Here, you might raise a valid objection that such a statement is inadmissible and shouldn't be disclosed to the jurors. If the party has already testified or was subjected to cross-examination of that fact at a deposition, the court might allow the expert to repeat such a fact as a reason for her opinion. As the opponent, you might ask for accompanying instruction from the judge that such facts are not to be considered true, but serve only to inform the jurors of the basis of the expert's opinion.

Or, for example, an expert might rely on hearsay that meets an exception based in a Rule 803(1) present sense impression, 803(2) excited utterance, 803(3) then existing state of mind, or 803(4) statement made for the purpose of medical diagnosis and treatment. As to the 803(4), an expert physician might rely on records made by the ambulance attendant or the emergency room physician and reveal that information while giving her testimony. Here again, the reliability of the facts is tested by the exceptions provided under the rule. Where contested, the opposing party, through counsel, can contest the facts during cross-examination of the expert. The expert can be "reminded" during cross-examination that the jury is free to disagree with him about whether that fact existed. Alternatively, the expert might be asked to admit that the expert did not test that fact independently to determine whether it did exist.

Finally, in civil cases, you might invoke 803(6)—the business records exception—as sufficiently establishing the reliability of the facts recorded in the such records. So a forensic economist might rely on an company's financial records to determine whether the company had been damaged by a particular event.

16.2 Confrontation Clause Challenges to Expert Bases in Criminal Cases

There is one important potential exception to the use of 803(6). In criminal cases, there may be confrontation clause problems if the defendant does not produce the business record and the business record is testimonial in nature. In such a case, the court might choose to not allow the jurors to hear the evidence because the witness has not appeared in court.[1] Otherwise the prosecution could call an expert

---

1. Melendez-Diaz v. Massachusetts, 557 U.S. 305 (2009); Bullcoming v. New Mexico, 131 S. Ct. 2705 (2011).

who could rely on witnesses against the defense as a back door way to getting the jurors to hear from these witnesses.[2]

16.3 Interviews, Market Information, or Research Produced by the Expert Herself to Test Her Opinion

If an expert conducts market research that may involve interviews or focus groups or conversations with the party's employees, the court may question whether it is fair for the expert to reveal such hearsay, especially where the opponent had little notice of such research or data. Again, if the opponent was on notice that the expert relied on this kind of research and had a full opportunity to depose the expert about the research, the court may determine that the reliability has been sufficiently tested and that the opposing side is not prejudiced if the jurors hear the results of the research.

Rule 803(18) provides that learned treatises can be admitted in court for their truth. Similarly, experts can rely on data compilations and market information without objection.

16.4 *Daubert* Challenges to the Reliability of the Expert's Opinion

A number of cases have created or applied criteria of reliability beyond those four presented in the original *Daubert* case, including the Ninth Circuit on the remand of *Daubert* itself. This chapter will list a number of such criteria and then come back to discuss each in some greater detail, giving examples where useful. In the Appendix we have also cited to and provided brief summaries of cases involving experts from important federal court of appeals cases. The Supreme Court, in both *Daubert* and *Kumho*, has emphasized that its listings of such useful criteria are not to be considered exhaustive and that no single criterion or group of criteria is either necessary in every case nor automatically sufficient in all cases.

The fact that a particular methodology has not been published at all does not render testimony based on that methodology inadmissible; consider, as an example, the race car driver's ability to control high-speed skids or the gymnast's ability to do double backflips. Nor does the fact that the methodology has been published widely and subjected to intense favorable peer review and critique establish the reliability of that methodology. Therefore, do not associate undue importance with the fact that, "Here is a list!" The criteria of reliability are as many and varied as the areas of human knowledge, and as Justice Breyer wrote in *Kumho*, the value of examining a number of such criteria is not so attorneys can know them all, but so that they can know how to know more of them. Where the approach to witness preparation,

---

2. *Cf.* Williams v. Illinois, 132 S. Ct. 2221 (2012), where Justice Alito, in a plurality opinion, held lab reports containing DNA results could be admitted and relied on by an expert because such lab results were not offered for the truth, but merely to support the expert's opinion.

presentation, deposition, or cross-examination on a particular criterion needs more elaboration, further discussion is provided.

1. Publication and peer critique.

2. Error rate that can be or is known.

3. Acceptance in the relevant scientific field.

4. Testability or replicability.

5. Preparation or creation for a purpose other than litigation.

6. Adequacy to explain important empirical data.

7. Basis in quantitatively sufficient data.

8. Basis in qualitatively acceptable data.

9. Consistency in methodology.

10. Consistency in this application.

11. Recognition in a body of literature.

12. Adequacy of the expert's credentials.

13. Derivation from mainstream approaches.

16.4.1 Publication and Peer Critique

This is one of the four criteria of reliability mentioned in *Daubert*, so it has the *imprimatur* of the Supreme Court. Unfortunately, it is one of the least useful because mere publication tells us little (e.g., consider the reliability of many of the stories in the *National Enquirer* and similar publications), and peer review suggests that review by others in the same field as the author is significant, which is very much like the old *Frye* test. Like *Frye*, general acceptance in the field only suggests that thousands of books and articles about astrology would be persuasive evidence of the reliability of that "science." At the least, such examples demonstrate the insufficiency of this single criterion as a basis for concluding that a methodology (or field) is sufficiently reliable to be accepted in court. Thus, like many of these criteria, the presence of years of publication and peer review may not be sufficient, and the absence of such publication may not be disqualifying. Both are factors that, in their specific context, you must consider.

However, if the methodology could logically have been published, but was in fact never published, that is some reason for concern. You may not discount the gymnast's expert testimony simply because she never published an article on the vaulting horse; but you may be skeptical of the methodology preferred by the statistical epidemiologist, someone who has read articles on the subject and published other articles of her own, if she has never published anything on this particular methodology in the seven years she claims to have been using it.

16.4.2 Error Rate that Can Be or Is Known

Your skepticism will increase if the purported expert cannot tell you with some reasonable certainty anything about the possibility that she is wrong in her opinions. If she claims never to be wrong, the court may use the testimony as a factor in determining whether the opinion is a gross overreach and whether it should reject the expert's opinions as unreliable; if the expert admits she is often wrong (unlikely), the court may applaud her honesty, but may reject her opinions nevertheless; and if she tells the court that she does not know how often she is wrong, the court may reject her opinions because it would not know how often or whether they were wrong.

16.4.3 Acceptance in the Relevant Scientific Field

This criterion of reliability is infected with some of the same deficiencies as "publication in a peer-reviewed journal." The definition of "relevant scientific field" is elusive and may not be accepted by the expert and those whom she considers to be peers. Nevertheless, there was little problem in examining the expert testimony of the statistical epidemiologist in *Daubert* under the magnifying glass of the scientific field of statistical epidemiology. There are general principles available in the field that you can use to measure the extent to which this expert has conformed her methodology. The greater the departure from those principles will lead to a greater feeling of unreliability, whereas the expert showing that she has adhered to those general principles provides some assurance that she (and you) have not gone too far out on a limb. Where the purported "scientific field" is unusual or unknown, you may need to refer to other indicia of reliability.

16.4.4 Testability or Replicability

If a belief or opinion has a foundation in evidence or is premised on sound theories, you will be able to identify those foundations in response to the question: "What would I have to show you to have you reject your current opinion?" For example, someone who believes in the Pythagorean Theorem might say: "If you can show me a right triangle where the sum of the squares of the lengths of the two other sides does not equal the square of the length of the hypotenuse, then I will reject this belief." By identifying what different facts would cause her to reject her belief, she articulates the factual foundation on which she relies. The facts can then be explored and, if they are different from those she relied on, her opinion or belief should be rejected. The Greeks' belief in Zeus was not testable because true believers would not identify facts, which, if controverted, would cause them to abandon their belief; therefore, expert testimony about the existence of Zeus should be ruled inadmissible. On the other hand, sometimes it is enough to simply say, "Because I saw soot on the sparkplugs, I knew the engine had not been maintained." The expert does not need to prove or test her theory. Sometimes, whether an expert must prove the safety of her proposed alternative design hangs on the applicable state tort law.[3]

16.4.5 Preparation or Creation for a Purpose Other Than Litigation

This criterion was grafted onto the *Daubert* case by the Ninth Circuit when the matter was reversed and remanded. The appellate court did so in response to the Supreme Court's invitation to the lower courts to add criteria beyond the "*Daubert* four" when examining reliability. In the *Daubert* case, the methodology proposed by the statistical epidemiologist, Dr. Done, had not been used for any regular epidemiological work, but only for the Bendectin litigation, in which he was an expert in a number of cases.

Note the question is not, "Was the methodology created for *this* litigation?", but rather, "Was the methodology created for any litigation?" Therefore, if the expert developed her approach for a different litigation, for a different party, in a different court, at a different time, to resolve different (although obviously related) issues, the reliability of that methodology is suspect. This is because of the possibility that the expert was functioning as an advocate rather than as an objective "scientist" pursuing the goals of her vocation.

When preparing the witness to testify—indeed, when selecting the witness initially—be sure the expert created the methodology during the course of the expert's normal pursuit of her nonlitigation, expert work—at least in its roots, if not in all of the adjustments and refinements that will need to be made for the particular litigation. In deposition, question the opposing expert carefully about the genesis of her methodology, going step by step from the first occasion on which she learned of the methodology, or attempted to use it, or began to develop it—up to the point it assumed the shape it takes in the current litigation. If the methodology changes substantially when litigation becomes the focus, then a motion in limine to exclude

---

3. *See* RESTATEMENT (THIRD) Section 2(b). RESTATEMENT (THIRD) Section 2(b), comment (e) notes that 2(b) does not itself require testability. It only requires plaintiff prove as a part of its prima facie case a reasonable alternative design. Comment e to Section 2(b) of the RESTATEMENT (THIRD) lists many of the issues on which the plaintiff must offer expert testimony:

- the instructions and warnings that might accompany the reasonable alternative design;
- how the design will satisfy consumer expectations;
- cost of producing the alternative design;
- the effect of the design on product function;
- the effect of the design on product longevity;
- the aesthetics of the proposed design; and
- the marketability of the design.

that testimony may be well-founded. Finally, on direct examination, show the court and jurors the clear foundations of your expert's methodology in established fields of knowledge unrelated to litigation: "Doctor Vytautas, tell us how you first came to use this procedure of data compilation in performing your statistical analyses of cancer metastasis."

16.4.6 Adequacy to Explain Important Empirical Data

In *Kumho*, the Supreme Court was concerned about the inability of the tire expert, using his "tactile and visual" methodology for analyzing tire failure (he touched and looked at the tire), to determine whether the tire had been driven only 10,000 miles or as much as 50,000 miles. The Court felt, based apparently on a priori beliefs, that distance traveled could be an important factor in causing the failure of a tire. When the expert's methodology cannot account for such presumptively significant data, the court is less willing to rely on such methodology.

Of course, the threshold decision that certain data is so significant it cannot logically be ignored embodies a priori beliefs about the field of knowledge that may not be accurate, so there is a real danger the court will be seriously mistaken. As a quick example, consider expert testimony before Galileo's time in which the expert states the speed of a falling feather would be the same as the speed of a falling cannonball in a vacuum. Under this adequacy criterion, the court might reject the expert's opinion because the expert had apparently ignored the most significant factor, the relative weights of the two objects. Based on post-Galileo knowledge, it is known that in a vacuum, the masses of the objects are irrelevant, so it can be concluded the earlier court rejected the testimony on spurious grounds.[4]

In actuality, it has not erred. If you were to take the time to state more fully the court's concern, you would recognize the court is not saying, "You, Dr. Volpicelli, have failed to consider one of the most significant pieces of empirical information, and therefore, your methodology is suspect," but rather, "You, Dr. Volpicelli, have failed to provide a satisfactory explanation of why your methodology does not take object weight or mass (or tire mileage) into consideration." In short, not "You should have," but rather, "You didn't tell us why you didn't need to."

Restating the criterion this way places a responsibility on the proponent to invite the expert to explain why omitted data is not significant; a responsibility on the court to ask about omitted data with which it is concerned; and a responsibility on the cross-examiner to bring salient items of omitted data to the attention of the court and the expert. When preparing an expert to testify at deposition and trial, you are advised to ask your consulting expert or graduate student assistants to brain-

---

4. *See, e.g.*, Holesapple v. Barrett, 5 Fed. App'x 177 (4th Cir. 2001); *cf.* Ford v. Nationwide Mutual 02-2115 (unpublished) (1st Cir. 2003) (where the court relies on cross-examination to test the inadequacy of explanations and holes in the underlying data in challenges to the testimony of an accident reconstruction expert).

storm on "data not used," so the expert can be drilled in her explanations for using this data, but not that data.

You can use that same brainstorming technique, with the help of your testifying expert, to identify areas for inquiry at the deposition and perhaps at trial. At a deposition of the opposing expert, if you believe you have a lead on data that should have been considered, be cautious in drawing attention to it and giving the opposing expert the opportunity after deposition and before trial to conduct further analysis and then supplementing her report, opinions, and bases. Instead, rely on questioning about "what was done," "what was considered," "is that all," "have you now told us everything that you considered?" Then, by implication, everything else was not considered, including your favorite significant data.

The risk you run it trying to lay this trap for trial is that you will miss hearing from the expert why she thought the data was insignificant or what other steps the expert took to insure the reliability in the absence of such data. Also note that it is likely that the opposing counsel will draw his expert's attention to your own expert's reliance on significant data. If in doubt at all about your theory, test it during the deposition rather than assume that at trial you will be able to discredit the opposing expert on her methodology.

16.4.7 Basis in Quantitatively Sufficient Data

Consider two cases: in the first, an expert in child abuse testifies she has interviewed more than 300 children who reported they were victims of abuse, and through that experience she has developed expertise in recognizing the signs and symptoms of such abuse. In the second, an expert in mechanical engineering testifies that in studying the causes of the collapse of an industrial conveyor system, she has examined three bolts from one portion of a large number of bolts, using the most sophisticated and well-accepted tests for tensile strength, compression strength, shear strength, and metal composition.

With the child abuse expert, you have no concern that 300 children were not enough children to comprise a large enough sample; you do not even insist on proof that 300 is a statistically significant sample to feel reasonably comfortable with that number. You may have other problems with this testimony (as will be discussed immediately below), but the *quantitative* adequacy is not one of those problems. With the conveyor testimony, however, you are concerned with the fact the expert looked at only three bolts, and those three were from only one portion (and therefore may have been from the same production lot of bolts, different from many of the other bolts). Three does not seem like a sufficiently large number when you may be dealing with hundreds or thousands. In both cases, therefore, it is appropriate to look at the quantitative adequacy of the data on which the experts are relying; here, you will come to different conclusions in the two cases.

Note that to a true scientist, data points are never sufficient. Milton Friedman may believe from his analysis of the data concerning the Great Depression that the government should have been more proactive in increasing the money supply based on his analysis of the data of how demand for money caused a death spiral between savings, interest rates, and employment. Friedman is quick to point out that while he sees evidence this happened in many businesses throughout the country, he is not confident he has sufficient data to know what the government might best do in a new setting. The one event, having many data points, tells us only what happened in the past, but is not necessarily sufficient for predicting what will happen in the future.

16.4.8 Basis in Qualitatively Acceptable Data

Now, again considering those same cases, look at the qualitative adequacy of the data employed. While 300 interviews are enough quantitatively, it should concern you that these are out-of-court interviews of impressionable children and that you only have the expert's own word about the avoidance of suggestion, the ability of the children to recall and recount, the understanding of the children of the concept of truthfulness and of the importance of telling the truth, and the appreciation of the children of the seriousness of the accusations they were making. Indeed, you may know almost nothing about the circumstances of each of those interviews, and to determine the reliability of the information obtained (assuming the expert is correctly reporting it), you would have to conduct "mini-trials" for each of the 300 inside the trial that you are actually concerned with. In other words, you have a problem with the *qualitative* acceptability of the data being used. With the conveyor expert, you were not happy with her examination of only three bolts from one section, but you have no concern that the tests that she performed were qualitatively adequate. In the case of causation of an illness, the court may require more than a physician's physical examination of patient.[5] When preparing an expert, you must examine both aspects of their bases and request the expert adjust her approach if you see weakness. When deposing an expert, you are likely to make more progress if you separate the two topics of quantitative and qualitative adequacy of data and question on them independently. When presenting cross-examination on these points at trial, be certain to separate them clearly, using graphics for each and clear transitions when you move from one to the other.

In their analyses, courts often commingle the sufficiency of underlying data as a qualitative matter with the testability and replicability factor. This commingling can lead to inconsistent applications. Looking just at situations in which the courts require testability, the following inconsistencies develop. In the criminal arena, there

---

5. *See* Black v. Food Lion, Inc., 171 F.3d 308, 310 (5th Cir. 1999) (where court requires more scientific proof that trauma can cause fibromyalgia); *see also* Bocanegra v. Vicmar Servs., 320 F.3d 581, 585 (5th Cir. 2003) (where it was enough to relate marijuana use to impaired driving based on studies of marijuana's effect on judgment).

are times the courts use general acceptance as a proxy for testability. Fingerprint evidence is a prime example; the court so readily concludes that the scientific community generally accepts the statistical validity of fingerprint identification that it does not require testimony on the underlying testability of the method. On the other hand, federal drug enforcement officers are allowed to give testimony as to the nature of a drug market,[6] or a drug importation scheme,[7] without describing any basis, statistical analysis, or study of verifiability for their opinions, other than the witnesses' experience. Moreover, in voice recognition cases[8] and with handwriting experts,[9] the courts are more skeptical of an expert's ability to give a helpful opinion, especially for the defense, and they cite as disqualifying factors the lack of testability and an insufficiency of data underlying the expert's method.

In 2005, prompted by a spate of reversals of convictions based on new evidence techniques, Congress commissioned the National Academy of Sciences (NAS) to undertake a study of the state of the forensic science in the United States. The task fell to the Committee on Identifying the Needs of the Forensic Sciences Community, cochaired by Judge Harry T. Edwards of the U.S. Court of Appeals for the D.C. Circuit and Constantine Galsonis, a Brown University biostatistics professor. In 2009, after four years, the committee's 300-page report finally appeared.[10] The NAS Report reviewed over a dozen fields, from DNA to such imprecise methods as those used to review bite marks and tire-tread analysis. Looking to determine whether the methods were based on science—except for DNA—the report concluded that the other methods did not prove worthy of the label of their being based on science. Shortcomings in the various fields included:

- the fields lacked a formal, standardized training program for its practitioners;

- practitioners often lacked an understanding of the scientific principles that underlay their work;

- testing facilities lacked accreditation and often were operated by law-enforcement agencies;

- no standardized protocols governed investigative tests;

- nor did standardized criteria guide analysis of results; and

- judges and lawyers often lacked the scientific training needed to evaluate the reliability of the resulting evidence.

---

6. *See, e.g.,* United States v. Ayala-Pizarro, 407 F.3d 25 (1st Cir. 2005).
7. *See, e.g.,* United States v. Lopez-Lopez, 282 F.3d 1, 22 (1st Cir. 2002).
8. *See, e.g.,* United States v. Salimonu, 182 F.3d 63, 73 (1st Cir. 1999).
9. *See, e.g.,* United States v. Mooney, 315 F.3d 54, 61 (1st Cir 2002).
10. *See* National Academy of Sciences, Strengthening Forensic Science in the United States: A Path Forward (2009) (NAS Report).

Criminal defense experts predicted that the report would support challenges, especially to fingerprint and firearms evidence because of their lack of empirical support for the underlying methodology. Barry Scheck, one of the founders of the Innocence Project, predicted that "[t]his is a major turning point in the history of forensic science in America."[11] As of 2013, however, it appears that the report has had little influence on admission of forensic testimony in the nation's courtrooms. Few prominent courts have acted to exclude forensic expertise because of the Academy's criticism.[12] The main reason seems to be that the courts are still relying on the personal vouching of the particular expert that her methods are reasonable and reliable. It seems that in criminal cases, the need for the testimony influences the court to weigh the *Daubert* factors in way that permits the evidence to be admitted.[13]

In contrast to the court's lenience in admitting forensic testimony offered by the prosecution, for plaintiff's experts in civil cases, courts are unwilling to accept an opinion about cause and effect of a product and disease,[14] a failure to treat,[15] opinion that a trauma during birth caused cerebral palsy,[16] or a physician's prediction of future development of injury without some scientific tests or replicability studies. In this last case, the expert's testimony was held to be unreliable even though he was relying on studies linking the baby's condition prebirth to the baby's condition afterward. The court held that his opinion failed because he had no studies connecting this baby's condition and situation to the harm in this case.

The courts are likewise uncertain about how much testability or replicability or data is required as sufficient to support an expert opinion about either the reason for disparity in treatment in employment or about future economic loss that resulted or will result from the defendant's conduct. For example, leeway seems to be granted an expert to pick a high figure to represent an employee's wages if that selection is backed by an explanation that is "within the common sense of the jury,"[17] whereas verification or testing of data needs to be done by an expert if the data comes from the parties themselves.[18] In addition, it is error for a court to exclude statistical evidence of a firm's disparity in hiring and promotion because such statistical evidence is relevant to a jury finding of discrimination;[19] on the other hand, it has been

---

11. Jason Felch & Mara Dolan, "The Science Behind Many Courtroom Claims about Forensic Evidence is Lacking, a National Panel Says," L. A. TIMES Feb. 19 2009, at A9

12. *See* GEORGE FISHER, EVIDENCE 884 (3rd ed. 2013).

13. *Cf,* United States v. Semrau, 693 F.3d 510 (6th Cir. 2013) (where the Sixth Circuit ruled it was not abuse of discretion for the district court to deny the opinion of an expert relying on a functional MRI to support the truthfulness of the defendant's version of his setting of prices).

14. *See, e.g.,* Allison v. McGhan Med. Corp., 184 F.3d 1300 (11th Cir. 1999) (silicone breast implants).

15. *See, e.g.,* McDowell v. Brown, 392 F.3d 1283, 1293 (11th Cir. 2004) (effect of a four-day failure to treat).

16. *See, e.g.,* Tanner v. Westbrook, 174 F.3d 542 (5th Cir. 1999).

17. Cummings v. Std. Register Co., 265 F.3d 56, 67 (2001).

18. *See, e.g.,* Cooper v. Travelers Indem. Co., No. 03-15551, D.C. No. CV-01-02400-VRW (2005) (unpublished opinion).

19. *See* Obrey v. Johnson, 400 F.3d 691, 693 (9th Cir. 2005).

held to be impermissible for an economist in a case of an alleged monopoly, where the expert predicts loss, to give an opinion or testify about his statistical evidence without using a regression analysis.[20] (Why wouldn't the statistical evidence be relevant despite the lack of a regression analysis? Doesn't the decision not to use regression analysis go to the weight of the evidence, not its admissibility?)

The evolution in social science of statistical methodologies has raised the question of how and when it is necessary to use regression analyses and multiple-regression analyses to support opinions on the cause of disparate treatment. Early courts were skeptical about the use of multiple-regression analyses for proving discrimination.[21] The important parts of the court's opinion in *Wilkins* are excerpted below.

> The thrust of our original opinion on faculty compensation remains unchanged: Plaintiffs have failed to demonstrate the validity of the multiple regression model as a whole. [Footnotes omitted.] As we stated in our original opinion, "Multiple regression analysis is a relatively sophisticated means of determining the effect that any number of different factors have on a particular variable." 654 F.2d at 402–03. Since multiple regression analysis is subject to misuse, courts cannot be expected to accept at face value conclusions derived from such a model absent expert testimony concerning the validity of the model itself. In this case, the class plaintiffs are attempting to use the university's own data to establish a case of discrimination in faculty compensation. At trial, however, only one expert attempted-on the university's behalf-to lay a foundation for the validity of the model used. As we have seen, the value of this expert's testimony is now doubtful at best. Yet when the class plaintiffs purported to use the university's statistics for their own purposes, they did not fulfill their burden of showing that the multiple regression analysis model employed was valid. Without guidance, this court cannot be expected to resolve in the class plaintiffs' favor fundamental questions relating to the model itself.

Other courts have seemed to require regression analysis.[22]

More recently, a Third Circuit district court found a way of reconciling the different approaches to requiring regression analysis by distinguishing situations where other data is just not available and where the questions of reliability go to weight as opposed to admissibility. The important parts of that opinion are excerpted below.

Background:

This action was filed on July 1, 1999. The complaint alleges that defendant engaged in a nationwide practice of terminating employees based on

---

20. *See* Zenith Elecs. Corp v. WH-TV Broad. Corp., 395 F.3d 416, 417 (7th Cir. 2005).

21. *See* Wilkins v. Univ. of Houston, 662 F.2d 1156 (5th Cir. 1981).

22. *See, e.g.*, Smith v. Xerox Corp., 196 F.3d 358, 362, 371 (2d Cir. 1999); Hollander v. Amer. Cyanamid, 172 F.3d 192, 202–03 (2d Cir. 1999); Raskin v. The Wyatt Co., 125 F.3d 55, 67–68 (2d Cir. 1997).

their age (over 40) during 1995, 1996, and 1997. (See Complaint P 8). To assist in the proof of its allegations, plaintiff has engaged the services of Janice Fanning Madden, Ph. D. ("Madden"), a statistician and sociology professor at the University of Pennsylvania. (See Declaration of Judy Keenan in Opposition to the Motion ("Keenan Decl."), Exh. 2). Madden submitted her first report in this case on December 20, 2000. (See Affidavit of Patrick Brady in Support of the Motion ("Brady Aff."), Exh. A), The purpose of the report was to "Evaluate whether the 1995, 1996, and 1997 Layoff Decisions at F.W. Woolworth Co., Inc. Were Age Neutral." (See Id.) The report examined how these layoffs affected workers over the age of 40, as well as those over 50, and concluded that both groups "experienced a statistically significant greater probability [sic] of being laid off than younger workers [who were] in the same Woolworth store," the same job category, and had the same work schedule. (Id. at 1).

On February 1, 2001, two expert witnesses retained by defendant submitted a review of Madden's report. (Brady Aff., Exh. F). This review cited "two major shortcomings" in Madden's analysis. (See Id. at 1). First, defendant's experts criticized the way that Madden grouped workers with "similar job duties" together for purposes of comparing layoff rates for different age groups. (See Id. at 1, 7). Madden grouped workers used the EEOC's job definition codes whereas the defense experts thought it would have been better to use the more specific "labor codes" that Woolworth used internally. Second, defendant's experts asserted that Madden failed to properly account for the fact that many of the younger workers she included in her analysis were part-time who were workers hired during the layoffs. According to defendant, these workers were not "exposed" to the layoffs, so including them in the age group comparison misleadingly increased the layoff rate disparity between older and younger workers. (See Brady Aff., Exh. F at 1, 7-9). On February 15, 2001, Madden submitted a rebuttal report in which she responds to defendant's expert's criticisms and maintains that her methodology was appropriate (Brady Aff., Exh. B). She also submitted a second rebuttal report, which was based on new data provided by the defendant. (See Brady Aff., Exh. D). This report re-assessed the age-neutrality of the layoffs (based on the new data) and also estimated the damages suffered by those affected by the discriminatory layoffs. (See Id.) At a hearing on April 17, 2001, the Court granted a motion by plaintiff to amend Madden's second rebuttal report. (See Record of Proceedings, April 17, 2001). The amended second rebuttal report was submitted by Madden on June 5, 2001, and contains revised estimates of both the number of layoffs attributable to a lack of age-neutrality and the amount of damages sustained by the alleged victims of Woolworth's age-discrimination (See

Keenan Decl., Exh. 3). Defendant moved to preclude Madden's reports and testimony on June 25, 2001.

Discussion:

Admission of expert testimony and reports is governed by Federal Rule of Evidence 702, as well as by the Supreme Court's holdings in Daubert v. Merrell Dow Pharmaceuticals, Inc., 509 U.S. 579, 125 L. Ed. 2d 469, 113 S. Ct. 2786 (1993) and Kumho Tire Co. v. Carmichael, 526 U.S. 137, 143 L. Ed. 2d 238, 119 S. Ct. 1167 (1999). Expert testimony will be admitted if it is based on reasonable scientific methodology and if it is relevant to the facts of the case. See FRE 702; Daubert, 509 U.S. at 589-92. Despite defendant's arguments to the contrary, Madden's reports, as well as testimony based on those reports, satisfy this standard for admissibility.

1. Multiple Regression Analysis

Multiple regression is a technique of data analysis that seeks to isolate the effect of several different "independent variables" on a particular result, or "dependent variable." By isolating several factors, statisticians can better understand which of those factors is most responsible for the given result. See Ottaviani v. State Univ. of New York, 875 F.2d 365, 366-67 (2d Cir.1989). In this case, defendant argues that Madden's reports are inadmissible because she did not employ multiple regression analysis in her examination of the Woolworth layoffs, and thus did not attempt to determine whether other factors (besides age) influenced the company's layoff decisions. In making this argument, defendant relies on three Second Circuit cases in which the plaintiffs' experts did not use multiple regression analysis and the reports were held to be inadmissible. See Smith v. Xerox Corp., 196 F.3d 358, 362, 371 (2d Cir. 1999); Amer. Cyanamid v. Hollander, 172 F.3d 192, 202-03 (2d Cir. 1999); Raskin v. Wyatt, 125 F.3d 55, 67-68 (2d Cir. 1997). However, although the Second Circuit certainly allows, and may even look approvingly upon, multiple regression analysis, it is not a prerequisite for the admission of statistical reports in cases such as this. As the Smith court itself said, statistics come in infinite varieties and their usefulness depends on the surrounding facts and circumstances; thus, statistics should be analyzed on a case-by-case basis. Smith 196 F.3d at 366, citing Watson v. Fort Worth Bank & Trust, 487 U.S. 977, 996 n.3, 101 L. Ed. 2d 827, 108 S. Ct. 2777 (1988). The prior cases cited by defendant all dealt with statistical reports that had fundamental problems beyond the fact that they did not employ multiple regression analysis. In Smith, the plaintiff's expert did not analyze the possible impact of employee performance evaluations on the layoff decisions. The numerical data from those evaluations could have easily been incorporated into a statistical analysis, but plaintiff's expert only analyzed whether chance could have been responsible for the age disparity in layoffs. This failure to include the evaluation numbers, coupled with the statistician's illogical groupings of employees for age comparison purposes, caused the court to deem the expert's report inadmissible. See Smith at 362, 371. In the case at bar, there were no numerical evaluations that Madden could have isolated in a regression. Some data regarding performance evaluations does exist, but defendant's own witness admitted that these records were incomplete. (See Keenan Decl., Exh. 11, Deposition of Mitchell Kosh at 279, 284-85). There are also some numerical rankings that were created as part of the 1997 layoff decision process, but since plaintiff alleges that the ranking process itself was tainted by age discrimination it would have made little sense to include those numbers in the analysis. And although there is some disagreement between the parties' experts over the pooling methods Madden used (see Section 2, infra), her groupings were not clearly inappropriate as in Smith.

* *See also* Bazemore v. Friday 478 U.S. 385, 400, 92 L. Ed. 2d 315, 106 S. Ct. 3000 (1986) (statistical analysis need not include all measurable variables to be admissible in employment discrimination cases; the omission of a particular variable affects the probativeness of the evidence, not its admissibility).

In Raskin, the plaintiff's expert failed to account for a company retirement plan that induced older workers to retire voluntarily (and thus caused the average age that people retired from the company to be lower than in the general population). Also, although the expert found that the defendant did not promote any employees over the age of 50 during a two-year period, his analysis was based only on the employees' ages at the beginning of that period and thus it failed to account for those employees who turned 50 during the two-year period and were then promoted. See Raskin, 125 F.3d at 67-68. Madden's report does not contain such fundamental flaws. Her analysis only includes those workers who were terminated for lack of work, not those who retired or left Woolworth for other reasons. (See Brady Aff., Exh A at 3 n.4). Her failure to use multiple regression analysis may affect the weight the fact-finder gives to her reports and testimony, but it does not dictate the exclusion of her reports and testimony. See Schanzer v. United Technologies Corp., 120 F. Supp. 2d 200, 203-07 (D.Conn. 2000).

2. Madden's Analytical Techniques

Defendant also criticizes several of the analytical decisions Madden made while performing her analysis. Defendant first takes issue with the way Madden grouped employees according to the EEOC's job codes, as opposed to the defendant's more specific internal "labor codes," and also included younger part-time workers in her analysis, despite defendant's assertion that these part-time workers were not subject to the layoffs. Madden's rebuttal report answers these criticisms, which were originally voiced by defendant's experts in their report of February 1, 2001. (See Brady Aff., Exh. F at 1, 7-9). In her rebuttal, Madden maintains that she only used the EEOC codes in her first report because defendant's database did not clearly indicate the 2-digit Woolworth labor code that applied to each employee (the 2-digits were part of a larger 14-digit ID number that was not clearly marked). Also, her 2nd rebuttal report analyzes the data using the labor codes and she still finds a statistically significant age disparity between those laid off and those retained (or hired). (See Brady Aff., Exh. D at 7-18). As to the younger workers not exposed to the layoffs, Madden argues in her rebuttal report that her inclusion of these workers in the analysis was reasonable because their hiring reflects the company's preference for younger workers. (See Brady Aff., Exh B at 9). However, she also maintains that even if these workers are not included in the analysis, the age disparities between those workers retained and those laid off are still significant. (See Id.) The Court need not resolve which side has the stronger argument on these two points, since that decision belongs to the fact-finder. Rather, the Court finds that since these particular analytical decisions by Madden do not constitute a basis to find her report and testimony to be inadmissible.

The same can be said of Madden's decision to analyze only those layoffs that occurred during three distinct layoff periods, as opposed to all layoffs that occurred between the summer of 1995 and the spring of 1997. Indeed, this decision seems completely logical given defendant's own characterization of the layoffs as having occurred during the three separate periods that Madden used in her analysis. (See Def. 56.1 Statement in Support of Partial Summary Judgment Motion as to Plaintiff's Pattern and Practice Claim, PP 1-11.)

Finally, defendant takes issue with the fact that Madden analyzed the age-neutrality of the layoffs with respect to both workers over 40 and workers over 50. Defendant argues that since workers over the age of 50 are not a specifically protected group under the ADEA, Madden's analysis of this group is irrelevant. H0owever, plaintiff is alleging that defendant engaged in a pattern of disparate treatment based on age, not simply that defendant's facially neutral policies had a disparate impact on older employees. Thus, since plaintiff alleges that the layoff decisions were made with an eye towards getting rid of older workers, data showing that a worker's chances of being laid off increased as he passed a particular age within the group protected by the ADEA is certainly relevant to plaintiff's allegations.

3. Damages Estimates

Defendant also argues that Madden's reports and testimony are inadmissible because the methodology she used to estimate the laid off employees' damages is flawed. Specifically, defendant takes issue with: Madden's estimation of the employees' back wages damages; her inclusion of prejudgment interest in her damages estimates; and the assumptions she makes regarding the mitigation of damages. Plaintiff answers these criticisms and offers a rational justification for each of Madden's assumptions. And as with Madden's analysis of the layoffs themselves, the Court cannot say that her group damages estimates are so fundamentally flawed as to preclude their admission as evidence. Also, as plaintiff correctly points out, if the Court grants plaintiff's motion to bifurcate the trial into separate liability and individual damages phases, in accordance with Int'l. Brotherhood of Teamsters v. United States, 431 U.S. 324, 52 L. Ed. 2d 396, 97 S. Ct. 1843 (1977), the group damages estimates contained in Madden's report will not even be offered at trial. Thus, whatever shortcomings these estimates may contain cannot justify a finding that all of Madden's reports and testimony are inadmissible.

4. Rule 403

Finally, defendant argues that under Rule 403 any probative value of Madden's testimony is substantially outweighed by its unduly prejudicial effect. This argument is predicated on defendant's primary argument that the statistical analysis conducted by Madden is not probative on the question of whether age-bias infected the layoff decision process. The Court has already rejected this argument (see supra); accordingly, Rule 403 does not provide grounds to exclude Madden's reports and testimony.

Conclusion:

For the reasons stated above, defendant's motion to exclude the statistical evidence contained in the reports and testimony of Dr. Madden is denied.[23]

16.4.9 Methodological Consistency

If someone encountered a mathematical system in which two plus two was sometimes four, but some other times was five, that person would not rely on it for any significant purposes. If the methodology employed does not consistently produce

---

23. EEOC v. Venator Group, 2002 U.S. Dist. LEXIS 1724, 88 Fair Empl. Prac. Cas. (BNA) 157 (SDNY 2002).

the same result for the same inputs, or consistent results for related inputs (if two plus two equals four, four plus four should equal eight), then it is reasonable to suspect the methodology is flawed. By analogy, if an expert's methodology contains inconsistencies, you should have the same suspicions. Suppose, for example, that within the econometrician's analytic framework there are several ways of determining the relevant geographic market—that is, the geographic area within which two companies compete with one another. If those different approaches lead to different conclusions—not just on whether the two companies compete in this particular town, but on significant conclusions like whether or not there is competition between them at all in a substantial portion of the purported market—that suggests unreliability.

Consistency, on the other hand, does not imply reliability, although it is certainly tempting to see it that way. The econometrician may be working with a methodology that is so insensitive to the particular details of a market that she finds competition (or absence of competition) everywhere. As has been written elsewhere,[24] a madman genuinely believing himself to be Napoleon could be entirely consistent, perceiving all elements of his modern surroundings as being correctly nineteenth century. A perfect liar would also, by definition, be perfectly consistent, as might Napoleon himself. Thus, inconsistency suggests unreliability, but consistency is ambiguous.

16.4.10 Consistency in This Application

If the expert's methodology is apparently consistent, it is still possible for the expert's application of that methodology to the particular case to be inconsistent. For example, the *Kumho Tire* expert said that if he found evidence that two of his four signs of tire abuse were present, he would conclude that the tire likely failed due to owner abuse. In the actual case, he did find evidence of two of those signs, but proceeded to minimize one and claimed that defect, not abuse, was the likely cause of failure. This inconsistency between his general statement of methodology and his actual application led the Supreme Court to conclude his method was unreliable. Indeed, when you find specific inconsistencies between what the methodology says should be done and what was actually done, you should suspect the expert has become an advocate and been result-oriented in her analysis.

This is precisely why it is important when deposing an opposing expert for you to ask first: "How do you do this?" "How do you determine relevant geographic market?" "How do you differentiate between failure of a tire due to defect and failure due to abuse?" In other words, ask: "What is the general approach, the general methodology?" After that general approach is a matter of record, ask: "How did you analyze this case?" "What did you do with this market?" "What did you touch and see with this tire?" If you ask about the specific application first and

---

24. David M. Malone and Ryan M. Malone, "The Zodiac Expert: Reliability Beyond *Kumho*," Trial Lawyer (Fall 1999).

then seek a description of the general methodology, it is more likely inconsistencies between the two will be hidden because the expert will have just reviewed, at his request, precisely what she did in the specific instance, and she will be alert to avoid inconsistencies.

16.4.11 *Recognition in a Body of Literature*

Regardless of whether the methodology being employed has been published in journals that require or invite peer review, that methodology will be seen as more reliable if there is a body of literature that recognizes the methodology exists. As with inconsistency and consistency, however, you will be more persuaded of its unreliability if the body of literature does not exist than you will be persuaded of its reliability if the body of literature does exist. For example, the prophecies of Nostradamus have inspired hundreds, if not thousands, of books and articles by people claiming to possess the "accurate" interpretation of those famous quatrains. Nevertheless, a court would be loath to accept such quatrains in evidence—for example, to explain an economic decline the defense claims was the actual cause of a bank's failure—because (as with the children who were interviewed by the child abuse expert) there is no reasonable way to determine the qualitative value of such literature in determining the reliability of the predictions.

On the other hand, the absence of a body of literature is some evidence the methodology has not obtained widespread use or acceptance. The court and the cross-examiner should view this absence of literature in the context of the opportunities for such literature to exist. For example, if there are several journals and texts that are concerned, at least in part, with the topic of analyzing tire failure, the failure of such publications even to mention "tactile and visual analysis" is obviously more persuasive evidence of the lack of acceptance of that methodology than if there were no such journals and texts.

16.4.12 *Adequacy of the Expert's Credentials*

In the concern with sophisticated bases in logic and the scientific method for evaluating the reliability of proffered expert testimony, do not overlook the fundamental proposition that an expert must have adequate credentials to present admissible testimony. Rule 702 says "a witness qualified as an expert by knowledge, skill, experience, training or education . . ." may testify to the expert knowledge being offered. Misuse or misapplication of an otherwise appropriate methodology would logically render the testimony just as unreliable as use of an inappropriate methodology.

Therefore, look for opportunities on direct examination to show the expert's familiarity and comfort with the methodology by referring to prior work, education, training, or publications that deal specifically with that methodology; try to discover in deposition and researching the opposing expert's background whether the expert has ever used this methodology previously or has any persuasive basis for familiarity with it. Do not confuse this concern with the challenge that arises because the methodology is new and untried; that is much more serious because an unproven methodology provides little basis for reliance, while a proven methodology may be so straightforward that even a neophyte can apply it properly. Nevertheless, make sure the trier of fact knows this analytic machine is in the hands of a neophyte.

16.4.13 Derivation from Mainstream Approaches

No doubt there are moments that provide inspirational insight into important truths; the story of Isaac Newton and the apple falling from the tree may be apocryphal, but it is instructive nevertheless. On a superficial level, this story appears to suggest momentous ideas can spring from accident alone, but it must be recognized Newton had been pondering the problem—the tendency of objects to move toward the earth without any apparent force acting on them—for some time, and he had filled his mind with explorations and experiments, examples and exceptions, so (assuming the truth of the apple story) he was prepared to "see in," to appreciate the insight for what it was and what it taught. He was ready and able to connect his perception of the falling apple through his theory to the old information and beliefs by showing where the old was incomplete or mistaken and where and why the new provided better answers. Thus, there was not a perception of a radical jump in Newton's recognition of gravitational force, as much as the bursting forth of a blossom from a well-nurtured plant.

People are delighted with the popular image of the Wright brothers as bicycle mechanics who were inspired to discover the secret of flight; they are less enthralled with the more truthful view that the brothers studied everything available about flight, building on the work of other inventors, testing, failing, testing again, and ultimately succeeding. This struggle to discover the next link in the bicycle chain through painstaking analysis of the previous links is the rule, while inspiration striking in the middle of the night is the exception. The story is that Thomas Edison tested thousands of different materials as filaments in his light bulbs before he settled on tungsten. Developments, discoveries, theories, and methodologies have precedents, connections to what went before. If the expert in litigation is espousing a methodology that has no such precedents, you and the court should be uneasy about relying on it.

In some cases, there are precedents and connections, and you must evaluate reliability through other means. *Daubert* itself is such a case: the methods of Dr. Done, the plaintiffs' statistical epidemiologist, were directly related to accepted statistical methods. He had, however, taken them one step further by agglomerating data sets that individually were too small to provide statistically significant bases for analysis. The concern with a logical derivation of the methodology does not help the analysis of reliability in such a case. But if you are confronted with the need to assess the reliability of astrology, you can ask at deposition: "What are the sciences or fields of knowledge to which astrology is connected?" If the witness answers, "astronomy," then you can ask how her theories and methodology are connected to those of astronomy; you can ask whether she can identify any astronomers who practice astrology or even believe in it; you can ask whether astrology has been the subject of any favorable comment in astronomy journals. In searching for a connection, you either find no connections, which makes you skeptical, or you find purported connections, which give you material for further exploration.

CHAPTER SEVENTEEN

CONCLUSION

In the preceding chapters, we have moved from the initial decision to hire an expert, through the search for the right expert, all the way through the various pretrial and trial activities for which experts—and attorneys—must be prepared. We have looked in detail both at the careful steps that must be undertaken in deposing experts and at the tools available for cross-examining the expert. We have seen the many opportunities for persuasion that are presented when conducting direct examination of the expert, and we have come to understand the extra work that is required to control the expert—compared to the lay witness—on cross-examination. Attention to detail, patience with follow-up, care in organization, avoidance of ego—you must develop and use all of these skills to present and to oppose experts effectively.

We have tried to emphasize throughout this book the need for you to treat the expert—consulting and testifying—as an integral part of the trial team. The shape of the case—as it is determined by the complaint and answer and early discovery—should reflect both your judgment and the expert's knowledge. If either is lacking, complex cases become very difficult cases. When disclosing material to the expert that may be subject to discovery, you must exercise care in avoiding waiver of work-product confidentiality or attorney-client privilege; at the same time, you must include the expert in discussions and decisions that shape the case and the expert's role. This difficult balance calls on the best of your skills.

As an understanding of the significance of the *Daubert* trilogy spreads through the bar and the bench, we anticipate that all of us, judges and lawyers, will become more sophisticated in understanding the many ways in which expert testimony should be assessed before a jury is exposed to its charm. Discovery of the opposing expert's methodology—through the report, the deposition, study of the literature, and work with your own expert—allows you to bring weaknesses and limitations to the court's attention during pretrial, so the jurors will not be misled by "junk" or misapplied science at trial.

You must understand the *Daubert* trilogy so you can help, or even direct, the court in its gatekeeping function of keeping unreliable expert testimony out of the record, which allows them to participate in the development of useful, additional criteria for assessing methodological reliability. The criteria already in use range from the mundane—did the expert follow her own normal procedures?—to the sublime—is the methodology *unfalsifiable* and, therefore, unacceptable? New criteria can therefore be expected to range across that same spectrum, and the cases in which they are articulated are similarly likely to be both mundane—*Kumho*'s tire failure—and sublime—*Daubert*'s statistical epidemiological analysis of pharmacological general causation of teratogenic birth defects. Abstracting from particular interests as plaintiff's or defendant's counsel in an expert case and viewing the role of attorneys as participants in a system that has justice as its end, all members of the bar should understand that delimiting the proper role of expert witnesses in trial is a responsibility shared by the legislature, the experts, the courts, and, perhaps most importantly, the trial lawyers.

With an expert, you have the opportunity to present a specially trained, highly articulate witness—one who possesses educational credentials far beyond those of anyone in the jury box, one who has written articles and books that the average juror has never considered being able to read, one whose presentation skills and persuasive abilities rival those of the best lawyers in the profession. When such a witness's powers are coupled with the tactical, procedural, and rhetorical skills of an experienced and zealous trial lawyer, the interests of justice may be wonderfully served or abysmally defeated. The use of the *Daubert* approach by courts to admit only reliable and relevant expert testimony must be supported by counsel as much as it is challenged by overstatements by expert witnesses. After all, there is no expert witness—who adjusted her methodology to obtain results for this case or who made a judgment to depart from the rigors of her normal approach or who intentionally understated the degree to which her methods departed from those used in the field generally—who was not presented and supported by trial counsel.

We therefore recommend that trial lawyers bring the same care to assessing the proper boundaries for their own experts' testimony as they apply to uncovering and presenting challenges to their opponents' experts. The tools presented in this book are, in general, ethically neutral, as are most of the skills taught in trial advocacy courses across the country. Thus, the use of an impeachment by prior inconsistent statement does not imply the impeaching attorney is right or wrong or the presenting attorney was wrong or right. Completely separate from whether such a skill is used effectively is the question of whether the information conveyed to the jury is informative, on the one hand, or misleading, on the other.

This ethical or normative note is a response in part to critics of trial advocacy skills training who charge that skills trainers emphasize effectiveness and trial success without attempting to instruct lawyers in fundamentals of ethics and fairness. The experience of the authors in working with hundreds of advocacy trainers across the country tells us these critics are largely ill-informed; most advocacy teachers go to great pains to incorporate ethical precepts into the fundamental rules of effective trial advocacy. Nevertheless, the point is taken: along with greater ability in the courtroom should come greater recognition of the obligation to succeed ethically.

Because of the enormous, even dispositive, impact an expert can have on a case, your obligation to avoid overstatement through expert testimony is substantial. We hope you will apply the lessons of this book to function at a higher level of advocacy on behalf of your clients—achieving success where justice is served by success—and that your enjoyment of the "charm and delight" intrinsic to expert practice is heightened by some of these lessons. We also hope these tools will be used to simplify our increasingly complex world of litigation so expert testimony will help jurors find the truth.

Appendix A

Selected Federal Rules of Evidence

Article VII

Opinions and Expert Testimony

Rule 701. Opinion Testimony by Lay Witnesses

If a witness is not testifying as an expert, testimony in the form of an opinion is limited to one that is:

(a) rationally based on the witness's perception;

(b) helpful to clearly understanding the witness's testimony or to determining a fact in issue; and

(c) not based on scientific, technical, or other specialized knowledge within the scope of Rule 702.

Rule 702. Testimony by Expert Witnesses

A witness who is qualified as an expert by knowledge, skill, experience, training, or education may testify in the form of an opinion or otherwise if:

(a) the expert's scientific, technical, or other specialized knowledge will help the trier of fact to understand the evidence or to determine a fact in issue;

(b) the testimony is based on sufficient facts or data;

(c) the testimony is the product of reliable principles and methods; and

(d) the expert has reliably applied the principles and methods to the facts of the case.

Rule 703. Bases of an Expert's Opinion Testimony

An expert may base an opinion on facts or data in the case that the expert has been made aware of or personally observed. If experts in the particular field would reasonably rely on those kinds of facts or data in forming an opinion on the subject, they need not be admissible for the opinion to be admitted. But if the facts or data would otherwise be inadmissible, the proponent of the opinion may disclose them to the jury only if their probative value in helping the jury evaluate the opinion substantially outweighs their prejudicial effect.

Rule 704.   Opinion on an Ultimate Issue

(a)   **In General—Not Automatically Objectionable.** An opinion is not objectionable just because it embraces an ultimate issue.

(b)   **Exception.** In a criminal case, an expert witness must not state an opinion about whether the defendant did or did not have a mental state or condition that constitutes an element of the crime charged or of a defense. Those matters are for the trier of fact alone.

Rule 705.   Disclosing the Facts or Data Underlying an Expert's Opinion

Unless the court orders otherwise, an expert may state an opinion—and give the reasons for it—without first testifying to the underlying facts or data. But the expert may be required to disclose those facts or data on cross-examination.

Rule 706.   Court-Appointed Expert Witnesses

(a)   **Appointment Process.** On a party's motion or on its own, the court may order the parties to show cause why expert witnesses should not be appointed and may ask the parties to submit nominations. The court may appoint any expert that the parties agree on and any of its own choosing. But the court may only appoint someone who consents to act.

(b)   **Expert's Role.** The court must inform the expert of the expert's duties. The court may do so in writing and have a copy filed with the clerk or may do so orally at a conference in which the parties have an opportunity to participate. The expert:

(1)   must advise the parties of any findings the expert makes;

(2)   may be deposed by any party;

(3)   may be called to testify by the court or any party; and

(4)   may be cross-examined by any party, including the party that called the expert.

(c) **Compensation.** The expert is entitled to a reasonable compensation, as set by the court. The compensation is payable as follows:

(1) in a criminal case or in a civil case involving just compensation under the Fifth Amendment, from any funds that are provided by law; and

(2) in any other civil case, by the parties in the proportion and at the time that the court directs—and the compensation is then charged like other costs.

(d) **Disclosing the Appointment to the Jury.** The court may authorize disclosure to the jury that the court appointed the expert.

(e) **Parties' Choice of Their Own Experts.** This rule does not limit a party in calling its own experts.

Article VIII

Hearsay

Rule 803. Exceptions to the Rule Against Hearsay—Regardless of Whether the Declarant Is Available as a Witness

The following are not excluded by the rule against hearsay, regardless of whether the declarant is available as a witness:

(18) ***Statements in Learned Treatises, Periodicals, or Pamphlets.*** A statement contained in a treatise, periodical, or pamphlet if:

(A) the statement is called to the attention of an expert witness on cross-examination or relied on by the expert on direct examination; and

(B) the publication is established as a reliable authority by the expert's admission or testimony, by another expert's testimony, or by judicial notice.

If admitted, the statement may be read into evidence but not received as an exhibit.

APPENDIX B

FEDERAL RULE OF CIVIL PROCEDURE 26
TITLE V. DISCLOSURES AND DISCOVERY

Rule 26. Duty to Disclose; General Provisions Governing Discovery

(a) **Required Disclosures.**

(1) *Initial Disclosure.*

    (A) *In General.* Except as exempted by Rule 26(a) (1)(B) or as otherwise stipulated or ordered by the court, a party must, without awaiting a discovery request, provide to the other parties:

        (i) the name and, if known, the address and telephone number of each individual likely to have discoverable information—along with the subjects of that information—that the disclosing party may use to support its claims or defenses, unless the use would be solely for impeachment;

        (ii) a copy—or a description by category and location—of all documents, electronically stored information, and tangible things that the disclosing party has in its possession, custody, or control and may use to support its claims or defenses, unless the use would be solely for impeachment;

        (iii) a computation of each category of damages claimed by the disclosing party—who must also make available for inspection and copying as under Rule 34 the documents or other evidentiary material, unless privileged or protected from disclosure, on which each computation is based, including materials bearing on the nature and extent of injuries suffered; and

(iv) for inspection and copying as under Rule 34, any insurance agreement under which an insurance business may be liable to satisfy all or part of a possible judgment in the action or to indemnify or reimburse for payments made to satisfy the judgment.

(B) *Proceedings Exempt from Initial Disclosure.* The following proceedings are exempt from initial disclosure:

(i) an action for review on an administrative record;

(ii) a forfeiture action in rem arising from a federal statute;

(iii) a petition for habeas corpus or any other proceeding to challenge a criminal conviction or sentence;

(iv) an action brought without an attorney by a person in the custody of the United States, a state, or a state subdivision;

(v) an action to enforce or quash an administrative summons or subpoena;

(vi) an action by the United States to recover benefit payments;

(vii) an action by the United States to collect on a student loan guaranteed by the United States;

(viii) a proceeding ancillary to a proceeding in another court; and

(ix) an action to enforce an arbitration award.

(C) *Time for Initial Disclosures—In General.* A party must make the initial disclosures at or within 14 days after the parties' Rule 26(f) conference unless a different time is set by stipulation or court order, or unless a party objects during the conference that initial disclosures are not appropriate in this action and states the objection in the proposed discovery plan. In ruling on the objection, the court must determine what disclosures, if any, are to be made and must set the time for disclosure.

(D) *Time for Initial Disclosures—For Parties Served or Joined Later.* A party that is first served or otherwise joined after the Rule 26(f) conference must make the initial disclosures within 30 days after being served or joined, unless a different time is set by stipulation or court order.

(E) *Basis for Initial Disclosure; Unacceptable Excuses.* A party must make its initial disclosures based on the information then reasonably available to it. A party is not excused from making its disclosures because it has not fully investigated the case or because it challenges the sufficiency of another party's disclosures or because another party has not made its disclosures.

(2) ***Disclosure of Expert Testimony.***

(A) *In General.* In addition to the disclosures required by Rule 26(a)(1), a party must disclose to the other parties the identity of any witness it may use at trial to present evidence under Federal Rule of Evidence 702, 703, or 705.

(B) *Witnesses Who Must Provide a Written Report.* Unless otherwise stipulated or ordered by the court, this disclosure must be accompanied by a written report—prepared and signed by the witness—if the witness is one retained or specially employed to provide expert testimony in the case or one whose duties as the party's employee regularly involve giving expert testimony. The report must contain:

(i) a complete statement of all opinions the witness will express and the basis and reasons for them;

(ii) the facts or data considered by the witness in forming them;

(iii) any exhibits that will be used to summarize or support them;

(iv) the witness's qualifications, including a list of all publications authored in the previous 10 years;

      (v)   a list of all other cases in which, during the previous 4 years, the witness testified as an expert at trial or by deposition; and

      (vi)   a statement of the compensation to be paid for the study and testimony in the case.

(C) *Witnesses Who Do Not Provide a Written Report.* Unless otherwise stipulated or ordered by the court, if the witness is not required to provide a written report, this disclosure must state:

      (i)   the subject matter on which the witness is expected to present evidence under Federal Rule of Evidence 702, 703, or 705; and

      (ii)   a summary of the facts and opinions to which the witness is expected to testify.

(D) *Time to Disclose Expert Testimony.* A party must make these disclosures at the times and in the sequence that the court orders. Absent a stipulation or a court order, the disclosures must be made:

      (i)   at least 90 days before the date set for trial or for the case to be ready for trial; or

      (ii)   if the evidence is intended solely to contradict or rebut evidence on the same subject matter identified by another party under Rule 26(a)(2)(B) or (C), within 30 days after the other party's disclosure.

(E) *Supplementing the Disclosure.* The parties must supplement these disclosures when required under Rule 26(e).

(3) ***Pretrial Disclosures.***

(A) *In General.* In addition to the disclosures required by Rule 26(a)(1) and (2), a party must provide to the other parties and promptly file the following information about the evidence that it may present at trial other than solely for impeachment:

      (i)   the name and, if not previously provided, the address and telephone number of each witness—separately identifying those the party expects to present and those it may call if the need arises;

(ii) the designation of those witnesses whose testimony the party expects to present by deposition and, if not taken stenographically, a transcript of the pertinent parts of the deposition; and

(iii) an identification of each document or other exhibit, including summaries of other evidence—separately identifying those items the party expects to offer and those it may offer if the need arises.

(B) Time for Pretrial Disclosures; Objections. Unless the court orders otherwise, these disclosures must be made at least 30 days before trial. Within 14 days after they are made, unless the court sets a different time, a party may serve and promptly file a list of the following objections: any objections to the use under Rule 32(a) of a deposition designated by another party under Rule 26(a)(3)(A) (ii); and any objection, together with the grounds for it, that may be made to the admissibility of materials identified under Rule 26(a)(3)(A)(iii). An objection not so made—except for one under Federal Rule of Evidence 402 or 403—is waived unless excused by the court for good cause.

(4) *Form of Disclosures.* Unless the court orders otherwise, all disclosures under Rule 26(a) must be in writing, signed, and served.

(b) Discovery Scope and Limits.

(1) *Scope in General.* Unless otherwise limited by court order, the scope of discovery is as follows: Parties may obtain discovery regarding any nonprivileged matter that is relevant to any party's claim or defense—including the existence, description, nature, custody, condition, and location of any documents or other tangible things and the identity and location of persons who know of any discoverable matter. For good cause, the court may order discovery of any matter relevant to the subject matter involved in the action. Relevant information need not be admissible at the trial if the discovery appears reasonably calculated to lead to the discovery of admissible evidence. All discovery is subject to the limitations imposed by Rule 26(b)(2)(C).

(2) ***Limitations on Frequency and Extent.***

  (A) *When Permitted.* By order, the court may alter the limits in these rules on the number of depositions and interrogatories or on the length of depositions under Rule 30. By order or local rule, the court may also limit the number of requests under Rule 36.

  (B) *Specific Limitations on Electronically Stored Information* A party need not provide discovery of electronically stored information from sources that the party identifies as not reasonably accessible because of undue burden or cost. On motion to compel discovery or for a protective order, the party from whom discovery is sought must show that the information is not reasonably accessible because of undue burden or cost. If that showing is made, the court may nonetheless order discovery from such sources if the requesting party shows good cause, considering the limitations of Rule 26(b)(2)(C). The court may specify conditions for the discovery.

  (C) *When Required.* On motion or on its own, the court must limit the frequency or extent of discovery otherwise allowed by these rules or by local rule if it determines that:

    (i) the discovery sought is unreasonably cumulative or duplicative, or can be obtained from some other source that is more convenient, less burdensome, or less expensive;

    (ii) the party seeking discovery has had ample opportunity to obtain the information by discovery in the action; or

    (iii) the burden or expense of the proposed discovery outweighs its likely benefit, considering the needs of the case, the amount in controversy, the parties' resources, the importance of the issues at stake in the action, and the importance of the discovery in resolving the issues.

(3) **Trial Preparation: Materials.**

    (A) *Documents and Tangible Things.* Ordinarily, a party may not discover documents and tangible things that are prepared in anticipation of litigation or for trial by or for another party or its representative (including the other party's attorney, consultant, surety, indemnitor, insurer, or agent). But, subject to Rule 26(b)(4), those materials may be discovered if:

        (i) they are otherwise discoverable under Rule 26(b)(1); and

        (ii) the party shows that it has substantial need for the materials to prepare its case and cannot, without undue hardship, obtain their substantial equivalent by other means.

    (B) *Protection Against Disclosure.* If the court orders discovery of those materials, it must protect against disclosure of the mental impressions, conclusions, opinions, or legal theories of a party's attorney or other representative concerning the litigation.

    (C) *Previous Statement.* Any party or other person may, on request and without the required showing, obtain the person's own previous statement about the action or its subject matter. If the request is refused, the person may move for a court order, and Rule 37(a)(5) applies to the award of expenses. A previous statement is either:

        (i) a written statement that the person has signed or otherwise adopted or approved; or

        (ii) a contemporaneous stenographic, mechanical, electrical, or other recording—or a transcription of it—that recites substantially verbatim the person's oral statement.

(4) **Trial Preparation: Experts.**

    (A) *Deposition of an Expert Who May Testify.* A party may depose any person who has been identified as an expert whose opinions may be presented at trial. If Rule 26(a)(2)(B) requires a report from the expert, the deposition may be conducted only after the report is provided.

(B) *Trial-Preparation Protection for Draft Reports or Disclosures.* Rules 26(b)(3)(A) and (B) protect drafts of any report or disclosure required under Rule 26(a) (2), regardless of the form in which the draft is recorded.

(C) *Trial-Preparation Protection for Communications Between a Party's Attorney and Expert Witnesses.* Rules 26(b)(3)(A) and (B) protect communications between the party's attorney and any witness required to provide a report under Rule 26(a)(2)(B), regardless of the form of the communications, except to the extent that the communications:

    (i) relate to compensation for the expert's study or testimony;

    (ii) identify facts or data that the party's attorney provided and that the expert considered in forming the opinions to be expressed; or

    (iii) identify assumptions that the party's attorney provided and that the expert relied on in forming the opinions to be expressed.

(D) *Expert Employed Only for Trial Preparation.* Ordinarily, a party may not, by interrogatories or deposition, discover facts known or opinions held by an expert who has been retained or specially employed by another party in anticipation of litigation or to prepare for trial and who is not expected to be called as a witness at trial. But a party may do so only:

    (i) as provided in Rule 35(b); or

    (ii) on showing exceptional circumstances under which it is impracticable for the party to obtain facts or opinions on the same subject by other means.

(E) Payment. Unless manifest injustice would result, the court must require that the party seeking discovery:

    (i) pay the expert a reasonable fee for time spent in responding to discovery under Rule 26(b)(4) (A) or (D); and

        (ii)   for discovery under (D), also pay the other party a fair portion of the fees and expenses it reasonably incurred in obtaining the expert's facts and opinions.

    (5)   ***Claiming Privilege or Protecting Trial-Preparation Materials.***

        (A) *Information Withheld.* When a party withholds information otherwise discoverable by claiming that the information is privileged or subject to protection as trial-preparation material, the party must:

            (i)   expressly make the claim; and

            (ii)   describe the nature of the documents, communications, or tangible things not produced or disclosed—and do so in a manner that, without revealing information itself privileged or protected, will enable other parties to assess the claim.

        (B) *Information Produced.* If information produced in discovery is subject to a claim of privilege or of protection as trial-preparation material, the party making the claim may notify any party that received the information of the claim and the basis for it. After being notified, a party must promptly return, sequester, or destroy the specified information and any copies it has; must not use or disclose the information until the claim is resolved; must take reasonable steps to retrieve the information if the party disclosed it before being notified; and may promptly present the information to the court under seal for a determination of the claim. The producing party must preserve the information until the claim is resolved.

(c) **Protective Orders.**

    (1) ***In General.*** A party or any person from whom discovery is sought may move for a protective order in the court where the action is pending—or as an alternative on matters relating to a deposition, in the court for the district where the deposition will be taken. The motion must include a certification that the movant has in good faith conferred or attempted to confer with other affected parties in an effort to resolve the dispute without court action. The court may, for good cause, issue an order to protect a party or person from annoyance, embarrassment, oppression, or undue burden or expense, including one or more of the following:

(A) forbidding the disclosure or discovery;

(B) specifying terms, including time and place, for the disclosure or discovery;

(C) prescribing a discovery method other than the one selected by the party seeking discovery;

(D) forbidding inquiry into certain matters, or limiting the scope of disclosure or discovery to certain matters;

(E) designating the persons who may be present while the discovery is conducted;

(F) requiring that a deposition be sealed and opened only on court order;

(G) requiring that a trade secret or other confidential research, development, or commercial information not be revealed or be revealed only in a specified way; and

(H) requiring that the parties simultaneously file specified documents or information in sealed envelopes, to be opened as the court directs.

(2) ***Ordering Discovery.*** If a motion for a protective order is wholly or partly denied, the court may, on just terms, order that any party or person provide or permit discovery.

(3) ***Awarding Expenses.*** Rule 37(a)(5) applies to the award of expenses.

(d) Timing and Sequence of Discovery.

(1) ***Timing.*** A party may not seek discovery from any source before the parties have conferred as required by Rule 26(f), except in a proceeding exempted from initial disclosure under Rule 26(a)(1)(B), or when authorized by these rules, by stipulation, or by court order.

(2) *Sequence.* Unless, on motion, the court orders otherwise for the parties' and witnesses' convenience and in the interests of justice:

(A) methods of discovery may be used in any sequence; and

(B) discovery by one party does not require any other party to delay its discovery.

(e) Supplementing Disclosures and Responses.

(1) *In General.* A party who has made a disclosure under Rule 26(a)—or who has responded to an interrogatory, request for production, or request for admission—must supplement or correct its disclosure or response:

(A) in a timely manner if the party learns that in some material respect the disclosure or response is incomplete or incorrect, and if the additional or corrective information has not otherwise been made known to the other parties during the discovery process or in writing; or

(B) as ordered by the court.

(2) *Expert Witness.* For an expert whose report must be disclosed under Rule 26(a)(2)(B), the party's duty to supplement extends both to information included in the report and to information given during the expert's deposition. Any additions or changes to this information must be disclosed by the time the party's pretrial disclosures under Rule 26(a)(3) are due.

(f) Conference of the Parties; Planning for Discovery.

(1) *Conference Timing.* Except in a proceeding exempted from initial disclosure under Rule 26(a)(1)(B) or when the court orders otherwise, the parties must confer as soon as practicable—and in any event at least 21 days before a scheduling conference is to be held or a scheduling order is due under Rule 16(b).

(2) *Conference Content; Parties' Responsibilities.* In conferring, the parties must consider the nature and basis of their claims and defenses and the possibilities for promptly settling or resolving the case; make or arrange for the disclosures required by Rule 26(a)(1); discuss any issues about preserving discoverable information; and develop a proposed discovery plan. The attorneys of record and all unrepresented parties that have appeared in the case are jointly responsible for arranging the conference, for attempting in good faith to agree on the proposed discovery plan, and for submitting to the court within 14 days after the conference a written report outlining the plan. The court may order the parties or attorneys to attend the conference in person.

(3) ***Discovery Plan.*** A discovery plan must state the parties' views and proposals on:

(A) what changes should be made in the timing, form, or requirement for disclosures under Rule 26(a), including a statement of when initial disclosures were made or will be made;

(B) the subjects on which discovery may be needed, when discovery should be completed, and whether discovery should be conducted in phases or be limited to or focused on particular issues;

(C) any issues about disclosure or discovery of electronically stored information, including the form or forms in which it should be produced;

(D) any issues about claims of privilege or of protection as trial-preparation materials, including—if the parties agree on a procedure to assert these claims after production—whether to ask the court to include their agreement in an order;

(E) what changes should be made in the limitations on discovery imposed under these rules or by local rule, and what other limitations should be imposed; and

(F) any other orders that the court should issue under Rule 26(c) or under Rule 16(b) and (c).

(4) ***Expedited Schedule.*** If necessary to comply with its expedited schedule for Rule 16(b) conferences, a court may by local rule:

(A) require the parties' conference to occur less than 21 days before the scheduling conference is held or a scheduling order is due under Rule 16(b); and

(B) require the written report outlining the discovery plan to be filed less than 14 days after the parties' conference, or excuse the parties from submitting a written report and permit them to report orally on their discovery plan at the Rule 16(b) conference.

(g) Signing Disclosures and Discovery Requests, Responses, and Objections.

(1) *Signature Required; Effect of Signature.* Every disclosure under Rule 26(a)(1) or (a)(3) and every discovery request, response, or objection must be signed by at least one attorney of record in the attorney's own name—or by the party personally, if unrepresented—and must state the signer's address, e-mail address, and telephone number. By signing, an attorney or party certifies that to the best of the person's knowledge, information, and belief formed after a reasonable inquiry:

(A) with respect to a disclosure, it is complete and correct as of the time it is made; and

(B) with respect to a discovery request, response, or objection, it is:

(i) consistent with these rules and warranted by existing law or by a nonfrivolous argument for extending, modifying, or reversing existing law, or for establishing new law;

(ii) not interposed for any improper purpose, such as to harass, cause unnecessary delay, or needlessly increase the cost of litigation; and

(iii) neither unreasonable nor unduly burdensome or expensive, considering the needs of the case, prior discovery in the case, the amount in controversy, and the importance of the issues at stake in the action.

(2) *Failure to Sign.* Other parties have no duty to act on an unsigned disclosure, request, response, or objection until it is signed, and the court must strike it unless a signature is promptly supplied after the omission is called to the attorney's or party's attention.

(3) ***Sanction for Improper Certification.*** If a certification violates this rule without substantial justification, the court, on motion or on its own, must impose an appropriate sanction on the signer, the party on whose behalf the signer was acting, or both. The sanction may include an order to pay the reasonable expenses, including attorney's fees, caused by the violation.

Appendix C
Selected Cases Supreme
Court of the United States

Daubert v. Merrell Dow Pharmaceuticals, Inc. 509 U.S. 579 (1993)

Petitioners, two minor children and their parents, alleged in their suit against respondent that the children's serious birth defects had been caused by the mothers' prenatal ingestion of Bendectin, a prescription drug marketed by respondent. The District Court granted respondent summary judgment based on a well-credentialed expert's affidavit concluding, upon reviewing the extensive published scientific literature on the subject, that maternal use of Bendectin has not been shown to be a risk factor for human birth defects. Although petitioners had responded with the testimony of eight other well-credentialed experts, who based their conclusion that Bendectin can cause birth defects on animal studies, chemical structure analyses, and the unpublished "reanalysis" of previously published human statistical studies, the court determined that this evidence did not meet the applicable "general acceptance" standard for the admission of expert testimony. The Court of Appeals agreed and affirmed, citing *Frye v. United States*, 54 App. D.C. 46, 47, 293 F. 1013, 1014, for the rule that expert opinion based on a scientific technique is inadmissible unless the technique is "generally accepted" as reliable in the relevant scientific community.

Held:

The Federal Rules of Evidence, not *Frye*, provide the standard for admitting expert scientific testimony in a federal trial.

(a) *Frye*'s "general acceptance" test was superseded by the Rules' adoption. The Rules occupy the field, *United States v. Abel*, 469 U.S. 45, 49, and, although the common law of evidence may serve as an aid to their application, *id.*, at 51–52, respondent's assertion that they somehow assimilated *Frye* is unconvincing. Nothing in the Rules as a whole or in the text and drafting history of Rule 702, which specifically governs expert testimony, gives any indication that "general acceptance" is a necessary precondition to the admissibility of scientific evidence. Moreover, such a rigid standard would be at odds with the Rules' liberal thrust and their general approach of relaxing the traditional barriers to "opinion" testimony.

(b)   The Rules—especially Rule 702—place appropriate limits on the admissibility of purportedly scientific evidence by assigning to the trial judge the task of ensuring that an expert's testimony both rests on a reliable foundation and is relevant to the task at hand. The reliability standard is established by Rule 702's requirement that an expert's testimony pertain to "scientific knowledge," since the adjective "scientific" implies a grounding in science's methods and procedures, while the word "knowledge" connotes a body of known facts or of ideas inferred from such facts or accepted as true on good grounds. The Rule's requirement that the testimony "assist the trier of fact to understand the evidence or to determine a fact in issue" goes primarily to relevance by demanding a valid scientific connection to the pertinent inquiry as a precondition to admissibility.

(c)   Faced with a proffer of expert scientific testimony under Rule 702, the trial judge, pursuant to Rule 104(a), must make a preliminary assessment of whether the testimony's underlying reasoning or methodology is scientifically valid and properly can be applied to the facts at issue. Many considerations will bear on the inquiry, including whether the theory or technique in question can be (and has been) tested, whether it has been subjected to peer review and publication, its known or potential error rate, and the existence and maintenance of standards controlling its operation, and whether it has attracted widespread acceptance within a relevant scientific community. The inquiry is a flexible one, and its focus must be solely on principles and methodology, not on the conclusions that they generate. Throughout, the judge should also be mindful of other applicable Rules.

(d)   Cross-examination, presentation of contrary evidence, and careful instruction on the burden of proof, rather than wholesale exclusion under an uncompromising "general acceptance" standard, is the appropriate means by which evidence based on valid principles may be challenged. That even limited screening by the trial judge, on occasion, will prevent the jury from hearing of authentic scientific breakthroughs is simply a consequence of the fact that the Rules are not designed to seek cosmic understanding but, rather, to resolve legal disputes.

951 F. 2d 1128, vacated and remanded.

BLACKMUN, J., delivered the opinion for a unanimous Court with respect to Parts I and II-A, and the opinion of the Court with respect to Parts II-B, II-C, III, and IV, in which WHITE, O'CONNOR, SCALIA, KENNEDY, SOUTER, and THOMAS, JJ., joined. REHNQUIST, C. J., filed an opinion concurring in part and dissenting in part, in which STEVENS, J., joined.

Opinion

JUSTICE BLACKMUN delivered the opinion of the Court.

In this case we are called upon to determine the standard for admitting expert scientific testimony in a federal trial.

I

Petitioners Jason Daubert and Eric Schuller are minor children born with serious birth defects. They and their parents sued respondent in California state court, alleging that the birth defects had been caused by the mothers' ingestion of Bendectin, a prescription anti-nausea drug marketed by respondent. Respondent removed the suits to federal court on diversity grounds.

After extensive discovery, respondent moved for summary judgment, contending that Bendectin does not cause birth defects in humans and that petitioners would be unable to come forward with any admissible evidence that it does. In support of its motion, respondent submitted an affidavit of Steven H. Lamm, physician and epidemiologist, who is a well-credentialed expert on the risks from exposure to various chemical substances[1] Doctor Lamm stated that he had reviewed all the literature on Bendectin and human birth defects—more than 30 published studies involving over 130,000 patients. No study had found Bendectin to be a human teratogen (i.e., a substance capable of causing malformations in fetuses). On the basis of this review, Doctor Lamm concluded that maternal use of Bendectin during the first trimester of pregnancy has not been shown to be a risk factor for human birth defects.

Petitioners did not (and do not) contest this characterization of the published record regarding Bendectin. Instead, they responded to respondent's motion with the testimony of eight experts of their own, each of whom also possessed impressive credentials.[2] These experts had concluded that Bendectin can cause birth defects. Their conclusions were based upon "in vitro" (test tube) and "in vivo" (live) animal studies that found a link between Bendectin and malformations; pharmacological

---

1. Doctor Lamm received his master's and doctor of medicine degrees from the University of Southern California. He has served as a consultant in birth-defect epidemiology for the National Center for Health Statistics and has published numerous articles on the magnitude of risk from exposure to various chemical and biological substances. App. 34–44.

2. For example, Shanna Helen Swan, who received a master's degree in biostatics from Columbia University and a doctorate in statistics from the University of California at Berkeley, is chief of the section of the California Department of Health and Services that determines causes of birth defects, and has served as a consultant to the World Health Organization, the Food and Drug Administration, and the National Institutes of Health. App. 113–114, 131–132. Stewart A. Newman, who received his master's and a doctorate in chemistry from Columbia University and the University of Chicago, respectively, is a professor at New York Medical College and has spent over a decade studying the effect of chemicals on limb development. App. 54–56. The credentials of the others are similarly impressive. *See* App. 61–66, 73–80, 148–153, 187–192, and Attachment to Petitioners' Opposition to Summary Judgment, Tabs 12, 20, 21, 26, 31, 32.

studies of the chemical structure of Bendectin that purported to show similarities between the structure of the drug and that of other substances known to cause birth defects; and the "reanalysis" of previously published epidemiological (human statistical) studies.

The District Court granted respondent's motion for summary judgment. The court stated that scientific evidence is admissible only if the principle upon which it is based is "'sufficiently established to have general acceptance in the field to which it belongs.'" 727 F. Supp. 570, 572 (SD Cal. 1989), *quoting United States v. Kilgus*, 571 F. 2d 508, 510 (CA9 1978). The court concluded that petitioners' evidence did not meet this standard. Given the vast body of epidemiological data concerning Bendectin, the court held, expert opinion which is not based on epidemiological evidence is not admissible to establish causation. 727 F. Supp., at 575. Thus, the animal-cell studies, live-animal studies, and chemical-structure analyses on which petitioners had relied could not raise by themselves a reasonably disputable jury issue regarding causation. *Ibid.* Petitioners' epidemiological analyses, based as they were on recalculations of data in previously published studies that had found no causal link between the drug and birth defects, were ruled to be inadmissible because they had not been published or subjected to peer review. *Ibid.*

The United States Court of Appeals for the Ninth Circuit affirmed. 951 F.2d 1128 (1991). Citing *Frye v. United States*, 54 App. D.C. 46, 47, 293 F. 1013, 1014 (1923), the court stated that expert opinion based on a scientific technique is inadmissible unless the technique is "generally accepted" as reliable in the relevant scientific community. 951 F. 2d, at 1129–1130. The court declared that expert opinion based on a methodology that diverges "significantly from the procedures accepted by recognized authorities in the field . . . cannot be shown to be 'generally accepted as a reliable technique.'" *Id.*, at 1130, quoting *United States v. Solomon*, 753 F. 2d 1522, 1526 (CA9 1985).

The court emphasized that other Courts of Appeals considering the risks of Bendectin had refused to admit reanalyses of epidemiological studies that had been neither published nor subjected to peer review. 951 F. 2d, at 1130–1131. Those courts had found unpublished reanalyses "particularly problematic in light of the massive weight of the original published studies supporting [respondent's] position, all of which had undergone full scrutiny from the scientific community." *Id.*, at 1130. Contending that reanalysis is generally accepted by the scientific community only when it is subjected to verification and scrutiny by others in the field, the Court of Appeals rejected petitioners' reanalyses as "unpublished, not subjected to the normal peer review process and generated solely for use in litigation." *Id.*, at 1131. The court concluded that petitioners' evidence provided an insufficient foundation to allow admission of expert testimony that Bendectin caused their injuries and, accordingly, that petitioners could not satisfy their burden of proving causation at trial.

We granted certiorari,_____U.S._____(1992), in light of sharp divisions among the courts regarding the proper standard for the admission of expert testimony. Compare, e.g., *United States v. Shorter*, 257 U.S. App. D.C. 358, 363–364, 809 F. 2d 54, 59–60 (applying the "general acceptance" standard), cert. denied, 484 U.S. 817 (1987), with *DeLuca v. Merrell Dow Pharmaceuticals, Inc.*, 911 F. 2d 941, 955 (CA3 1990) (rejecting the "general acceptance" standard).

II

A

In the 70 years since its formulation in the *Frye* case, the "general acceptance" test has been the dominant standard for determining the admissibility of novel scientific evidence at trial. *See* E. Green & C. Nesson, Problems, Cases, and Materials on Evidence 649 (1983). Although under increasing attack of late, the rule continues to be followed by a majority of courts, including the Ninth Circuit.[3]

The *Frye* test has its origin in a short and citation-free 1923 decision concerning the admissibility of evidence derived from a systolic blood pressure deception test, a crude precursor to the polygraph machine. In what has become a famous (perhaps infamous) passage, the then Court of Appeals for the District of Columbia described the device and its operation and declared:

"Just when a scientific principle or discovery crosses the line between the experimental and demonstrable stages is difficult to define. Somewhere in this twilight zone the evidential force of the principle must be recognized, and while courts will go a long way in admitting expert testimony deduced from a well-recognized scientific principle or discovery, the thing from which the deduction is made must be sufficiently established to have gained general acceptance in the particular field in which it belongs." 54 App. D.C., at 47, 293 F., at 1014 (emphasis added).

Because the deception test had "not yet gained such standing and scientific recognition among physiological and psychological authorities as would justify the courts in admitting expert testimony deduced from the discovery, development, and experiments thus far made," evidence of its results was ruled inadmissible. *Ibid.*

The merits of the *Frye* test have been much debated, and scholarship on its proper scope and application is legion.[4] Indeed, the debates over *Frye* are such a

---

3. For a catalogue of the many cases on either side of this controversy, *see* P. Gianelli & E. Imwinkelried, Scientific Evidence §1–5, pp. 10–14 (1986 & Supp. 1991).

4. *See, e.g.*, Green, Expert Witnesses and Sufficiency of Evidence in Toxic Substances Litigation: The Legacy of Agent Orange and Bendectin Litigation, 86 NW. U. L. Rev. 643 (1992) (hereinafter Green); Becker & Orenstein, The Federal Rules of Evidence After Sixteen Years—The Effect of "Plain Meaning" Jurisprudence, the Need for an Advisory Committee on the Rules of Evidence, and Suggestions for Selective Revision of the Rules, 60 Geo. Wash. L. Rev. 857, 876–885 (1992); Hanson, "James

well-established part of the academic landscape that a distinct term—"Frye-olo-gist"—has been advanced to describe those who take part. *See* Behringer, Intro-duction, Proposals for a Model Rule on the Admissibility of Scientific Evidence, 26 Jurimetrics J., at 239, *quoting* Lacey, Scientific Evidence, 24 Jurimetrics J. 254, 264 (1984). Petitioners' primary attack, however, is not on the content but on the continuing authority of the rule. They contend that the *Frye* test was superseded by the adoption of the Federal Rules of Evidence.[5] We agree.

We interpret the legislatively-enacted Federal Rules of Evidence as we would any statute. *Beech Aircraft Corp. v. Rainey*, 488 U.S. 153, 163 (1988). Rule 402 provides the baseline:

> "All relevant evidence is admissible, except as otherwise provided by the Constitution of the United States, by Act of Congress, by these rules, or by other rules prescribed by the Supreme Court pursuant to statutory authority. Evidence which is not relevant is not admissible."

> "Relevant evidence" is defined as that which has "any tendency to make the existence of any fact that is of consequence to the determination of the action more probable or less probable than it would be without the evidence." Rule 401. The Rule's basic standard of relevance thus is a liberal one.

Frye, of course, predated the Rules by half a century. In *United States v. Abel*, 469 U.S. 45 (1984), we considered the pertinence of background common law in interpreting the Rules of Evidence. We noted that the Rules occupy the field, *id.*, at 49, but, quoting Professor Cleary, the Reporter, explained that the common law nevertheless could serve as an aid to their application:

> "In principle, under the Federal Rules no common law of evidence remains. 'All relevant evidence is admissible, except as otherwise provided. . . .' In reality, of course, the body of common law knowledge continues

---

Alphonso Frye is Sixty-Five Years Old; Should He Retire?," 16 W. St. U. L. Rev. 357 (1989); Black, A Unified Theory of Scientific Evidence, 56 Ford. L. Rev. 595 (1988); Imwinkelried, The "Bases" of Expert Testimony: The Syllogistic Structure of Scientific Testimony, 67 N.C. L. Rev. 1 (1988); Proposals for a Model Rule on the Admissibility of Scientific Evidence, 26 Jurimetrics J. 235 (1986); Gianelli, The Admissibility of Novel Scientific Evidence: Frye v. United States, A Half-Century Later, 80 Colum. L. Rev. 1197 (1980); The Supreme Court, 1986 Term, 101 Harv. L. Rev. 7, 119, 125–127 (1987).

5. Like the question of *Frye*'s merit, the dispute over its survival has divided courts and commentators. *Compare, e.g.*, United States v. Williams, 583 F. 2d 1194 (CA2 1978), *cert. denied*, 439 U.S. 1117 (1979) (*Frye* is superseded by the Rules of Evidence), *with* Christopherson v. Allied-Signal Corp., 939 F. 2d 1106, 1111, 1115–1116 (CA5 1991) (en banc) (*Frye* and the Rules coexist), *cert. denied*, _____ U.S. _____ (1992), 3 J. Weinstein & M. Berger, Weinstein's Evidence ¶702[03], pp. 702–36 to 702–37 (1988) (hereinafter Weinstein & Berger) (*Frye* is dead), and M. Graham, Handbook of Federal Evidence §703.2 (2d ed. 1991) (*Frye* lives). *See generally* P. Gianelli & E. Imwinkelried, Scientific Evidence §1–5, pp. 28–29 (1986 & Supp. 1991) (citing authorities).

to exist, though in the somewhat altered form of a source of guidance in the exercise of delegated powers." *Id.*, at 51–52.

We found the common-law precept at issue in the *Abel* case entirely consistent with Rule 402's general requirement of admissibility, and considered it unlikely that the drafters had intended to change the rule. *Id.*, at 50–51. In *Bourjaily v. United States*, 483 U.S. 171 (1987), on the other hand, the Court was unable to find a particular common-law doctrine in the Rules, and so held it superseded.

Here there is a specific Rule that speaks to the contested issue. Rule 702, governing expert testimony, provides:

> "*If scientific*, technical, or other specialized *knowledge will assist the trier of fact* to understand the evidence or to determine a fact in issue, a witness qualified as an expert by knowledge, skill, experience, training, or education, may testify *thereto* in the form of an opinion or otherwise."

Nothing in the text of this Rule establishes "general acceptance" as an absolute prerequisite to admissibility. Nor does respondent present any clear indication that Rule 702 or the Rules as a whole were intended to incorporate a "general acceptance" standard. The drafting history makes no mention of *Frye*, and a rigid "general acceptance" requirement would be at odds with the "liberal thrust" of the Federal Rules and their "general approach of relaxing the traditional barriers to 'opinion' testimony." *Beech Aircraft Corp. v. Rainey*, 488 U.S., at 169 (citing Rules 701 to 705). *See also* Weinstein, Rule 702 of the Federal Rules of Evidence is Sound; It Should Not Be Amended, 138 F.R.D. 631, 631 (1991) ("The Rules were designed to depend primarily upon lawyer-adversaries and sensible triers of fact to evaluate conflicts"). Given the Rules' permissive backdrop and their inclusion of a specific rule on expert testimony that does not mention "general acceptance," the assertion that the Rules somehow assimilated *Frye* is unconvincing. *Frye* made 'general acceptance' the exclusive test for admitting expert scientific testimony. That austere standard, absent from and incompatible with the Federal Rules of Evidence, should not be applied in federal trials.[6]

B

That the *Frye* test was displaced by the Rules of Evidence does not mean, however, that the Rules themselves place no limits on the admissibility of purportedly scientific evidence.[7] Nor is the trial judge disabled from screening such evidence. To

---

6. Because we hold that *Frye* has been superseded and base the discussion that follows on the content of the congressionally-enacted Federal Rules of Evidence, we do not address petitioners' argument that application of the *Frye* rule in this diversity case, as the application of a judge-made rule affecting substantive rights, would violate the doctrine of *Erie R. Co. v. Tompkins*, 304 U.S. 64 (1938).
7. The Chief Justice "do[es] not doubt that Rule 702 confides to the judge some gatekeeping responsibility," but would neither say how it does so, nor explain what that role entails. We believe the better course is to note the nature and source of the duty.

the contrary, under the Rules the trial judge must ensure that any and all scientific testimony or evidence admitted is not only relevant, but reliable. The primary locus of this obligation is Rule 702, which clearly contemplates some degree of regulation of the subjects and theories about which an expert may testify. "If scientific, technical, or other specialized knowledge will assist the trier of fact to understand the evidence or to determine a fact in issue" an expert "may testify thereto." The subject of an expert's testimony must be "scientific . . . knowledge."[8] The adjective "scientific" implies a grounding in the methods and procedures of science. Similarly, the word "knowledge" connotes more than subjective belief or unsupported speculation. The term "applies to any body of known facts or to any body of ideas inferred from such facts or accepted as truths on good grounds." Webster's Third New International Dictionary 1252 (1986). Of course, it would be unreasonable to conclude that the subject of scientific testimony must be "known" to a certainty; arguably, there are no certainties in science. *See, e.g.*, Brief for Nicolaas Bloembergen et al. as *Amici Curiae* 9 ("Indeed, scientists do not assert that they know what is immutably 'true'—they are committed to searching for new, temporary theories to explain, as best they can, phenomena"); Brief for American Association for the Advancement of Science and the National Academy of Sciences as *Amici Curiae* 7–8 ("Science is not an encyclopedic body of knowledge about the universe. Instead, it represents a process for proposing and refining theoretical explanations about the world that are subject to further testing and refinement") (emphasis in original). But, in order to qualify as "scientific knowledge," an inference or assertion must be derived by the scientific method. Proposed testimony must be supported by appropriate validation—i.e., "good grounds," based on what is known. In short, the requirement that an expert's testimony pertain to "scientific knowledge" establishes a standard of evidentiary reliability.[9]

Rule 702 further requires that the evidence or testimony "assist the trier of fact to understand the evidence or to determine a fact in issue." This condition goes primarily to relevance. "Expert testimony which does not relate to any issue in the case is not relevant and, ergo, nonhelpful." 3 Weinstein & Berger ¶ 702[02], p. 702–18.

---

8. Rule 702 also applies to "technical, or other specialized knowledge." Our discussion is limited to the scientific context because that is the nature of the expertise offered here.

9. We note that scientists typically distinguish between "validity" (does the principle support what it purports to show?) and "reliability" (does application of the principle produce consistent results?). *See* Black, A Unified Theory of Scientific Evidence, 56 Ford. L. Rev. 595, 599 (1988). Although "the difference between accuracy, validity, and reliability may be such that each is distinct from the other by no more than a hen's kick," Starrs, *Frye v. United States* Restructured and Revitalized: A Proposal to Amend Federal Evidence Rule 702, 26 Jurimetrics J. 249, 256 (1986), our reference here is to evidentiary reliability—that is, trustworthiness. *Cf., e.g.*, Advisory Committee's Notes on Fed. Rule Evid. 602 ("'[T]he rule requiring that a witness who testifies to a fact which can be perceived by the senses must have had an opportunity to observe, and must have actually observed the fact' is a 'most pervasive manifestation' of the common law insistence upon 'the most reliable sources of information.'" (citation omitted)); Advisory Committee's Notes on Art. VIII of the Rules of Evidence (hearsay exceptions will be recognized only "under circumstances supposed to furnish guarantees of trustworthiness"). In a case involving scientific evidence, *evidentiary reliability* will be based upon *scientific validity*.

See also United States v. Downing, 753 F. 2d 1224, 1242 (CA3 1985) ("An additional consideration under Rule 702—and another aspect of relevancy—is whether expert testimony proffered in the case is sufficiently tied to the facts of the case that it will aid the jury in resolving a factual dispute"). The consideration has been aptly described by Judge Becker as one of "fit." *Ibid.* "Fit" is not always obvious, and scientific validity for one purpose is not necessarily scientific validity for other, unrelated purposes. *See* Starrs, *Frye v. United States* Restructured and Revitalized: A Proposal to Amend Federal Evidence Rule 702, and 26 Jurimetrics J. 249, 258 (1986). The study of the phases of the moon, for example, may provide valid scientific "knowledge" about whether a certain night was dark, and if darkness is a fact in issue, the knowledge will assist the trier of fact. However (absent creditable grounds supporting such a link), evidence that the moon was full on a certain night will not assist the trier of fact in determining whether an individual was unusually likely to have behaved irrationally on that night. Rule 702's "helpfulness" standard requires a valid scientific connection to the pertinent inquiry as a precondition to admissibility.

That these requirements are embodied in Rule 702 is not surprising. Unlike an ordinary witness, see Rule 701, an expert is permitted wide latitude to offer opinions, including those that are not based on firsthand knowledge or observation. *See* Rules 702 and 703. Presumably, this relaxation of the usual requirement of firsthand knowledge—a rule which represents "a 'most pervasive manifestation' of the common law insistence upon 'the most reliable sources of information,'" Advisory Committee's Notes on Fed. Rule Evid. 602 (citation omitted)—is premised on an assumption that the expert's opinion will have a reliable basis in the knowledge and experience of his discipline.

C

Faced with a proffer of expert scientific testimony, then, the trial judge must determine at the outset, pursuant to Rule 104(a),[10] whether the expert is proposing to testify to (1) scientific knowledge that (2) will assist the trier of fact to understand or determine a fact in issue.[11] This entails a preliminary assessment of whether the

---

10. Rule 104(a) provides:

> "Preliminary questions concerning the qualification of a person to be a witness, the existence of a privilege, or the admissibility of evidence shall be determined by the court, subject to the provisions of subdivision (b) [pertaining to conditional admissions]. In making its determination, it is not bound by the rules of evidence except those with respect to privileges."

These matters should be established by a preponderance of proof. *See Bourjaily v. United States*, 483 U.S. 171, 175–176 (1987).

11. Although the *Frye* decision itself focused exclusively on "novel" scientific techniques, we do not read the requirements of Rule 702 to apply specially or exclusively to unconventional evidence. Of course, well-established propositions are less likely to be challenged than those that are novel, and they are more handily defended. Indeed, theories that are so firmly established as to have attained the status of scientific law, such as the laws of thermodynamics, properly are subject to judicial notice under Fed. Rule Evid. 201.

---

reasoning or methodology underlying the testimony is scientifically valid and of whether that reasoning or methodology properly can be applied to the facts in issue. We are confident that federal judges possess the capacity to undertake this review. Many factors will bear on the inquiry, and we do not presume to set out a definitive checklist or test. But some general observations are appropriate.

Ordinarily, a key question to be answered in determining whether a theory or technique is scientific knowledge that will assist the trier of fact will be whether it can be (and has been) tested. "Scientific methodology today is based on generating hypotheses and testing them to see if they can be falsified; indeed, this methodology is what distinguishes science from other fields of human inquiry." *Green*, at 645. *See also* C. Hempel, Philosophy of Natural Science 49 (1966) ("[T]he statements constituting a scientific explanation must be capable of empirical test"); K. Popper, Conjectures and Refutations: The Growth of Scientific Knowledge 37 (5th ed. 1989) ("[T]he criterion of the scientific status of a theory is its falsifiability, or refutability, or testability").

Another pertinent consideration is whether the theory or technique has been subjected to peer review and publication. Publication (which is but one element of peer review) is not a sine qua non of admissibility; it does not necessarily correlate with reliability, *see* S. Jasanoff, The Fifth Branch: Science Advisors as Policymakers 61–76 (1990), and in some instances well-grounded but innovative theories will not have been published, *see* Horrobin, The Philosophical Basis of Peer Review and the Suppression of Innovation, 263 J. Am. Med. Assn. 1438 (1990). Some propositions, moreover, are too particular, too new, or of too limited interest to be published. But submission to the scrutiny of the scientific community is a component of "good science," in part because it increases the likelihood that substantive flaws in methodology will be detected. *See* J. Ziman, Reliable Knowledge: An Exploration of the Grounds for Belief in Science 130–133 (1978); Relman and Angell, How Good Is Peer Review?, 321 New Eng. J. Med. 827 (1989). The fact of publication (or lack thereof) in a peer-reviewed journal thus will be a relevant, though not dispositive, consideration in assessing the scientific validity of a particular technique or methodology on which an opinion is premised.

Additionally, in the case of a particular scientific technique, the court ordinarily should consider the known or potential rate of error, *see, e.g., United States v. Smith*, 869 F. 2d 348, 353–354 (CA7 1989) (surveying studies of the error rate of spectrographic voice identification technique), and the existence and maintenance of standards controlling the technique's operation. *See United States v. Williams*, 583 F. 2d 1194, 1198 (CA2 1978) (noting professional organization's standard governing spectrographic analysis), *cert. denied*, 439 U.S. 1117 (1979).

Finally, "general acceptance" can yet have a bearing on the inquiry. A "reliability assessment does not require, although it does permit, explicit identification of a relevant scientific community and an express determination of a particular degree of acceptance within that community." *United States v. Downing*, 753 F. 2d, at 1238. *See also* 3 Weinstein & Berger ¶ 702[03], pp. 702–41 to 702–42. Widespread acceptance can be an important factor in ruling particular evidence admissible, and "a known technique that has been able to attract only minimal support within the community," *Downing, supra*, at 1238, may properly be viewed with skepticism.

The inquiry envisioned by Rule 702 is, we emphasize, a flexible one.[12] Its over-arching subject is the scientific validity—and thus the evidentiary relevance and reliability—of the principles that underlie a proposed submission. The focus, of course, must be solely on principles and methodology, not on the conclusions that they generate.

Throughout, a judge assessing a proffer of expert scientific testimony under Rule 702 should also be mindful of other applicable rules. Rule 703 provides that expert opinions based on otherwise inadmissible hearsay are to be admitted only if the facts or data are "of a type reasonably relied upon by experts in the particular field in forming opinions or inferences upon the subject." Rule 706 allows the court at its discretion to procure the assistance of an expert of its own choosing. Finally, Rule 403 permits the exclusion of relevant evidence "if its probative value is substantially outweighed by the danger of unfair prejudice, confusion of the issues, or misleading the jury. . . ." Judge Weinstein has explained: "Expert evidence can be both powerful and quite misleading because of the difficulty in evaluating it. Because of this risk, the judge in weighing possible prejudice against probative force under Rule 403 of the present rules exercises more control over experts than over lay witnesses." Weinstein, 138 F.R.D., at 632.

VI

We conclude by briefly addressing what appear to be two underlying concerns of the parties and amici in this case. Respondent expresses apprehension that abandonment of "general acceptance" as the exclusive requirement for admission will result in a "free-for-all" in which befuddled juries are confounded by absurd and irrational pseudoscientific assertions. In this regard respondent seems to us to be overly pessimistic about the capabilities of the jury, and of the adversary system generally. Vigorous cross-examination, presentation of contrary evidence, and careful instruction on the burden of proof are the traditional and appropriate means of attacking shaky but admissible evidence. *See Rock v. Arkansas*, 483 U.S. 44, 61

---

12. A number of authorities have presented variations on the reliability approach, each with its own slightly different set of factors. *See, e.g., Downing*, 753 F. 2d 1238–1239 (on which our discussion draws in part); 3 Weinstein & Berger ¶702[03], pp. 702–41 to 702–42 (on which the *Downing* court in turn partially relied); McCormick, Scientific Evidence: Defining a New Approach to Admissibility, 67 Iowa L. Rev. 879, 911–912 (1982); and Symposium on Science and the Rules of Evidence, 99 F.R.D. 187, 231 (1983) (statement by Margaret Berger). To the extent that they focus on the reliability of evidence as ensured by the scientific validity of its underlying principles, all these versions may well have merit, although we express no opinion regarding any of their particular details.

(1987). Additionally, in the event the trial court concludes that the scintilla of evidence presented supporting a position is insufficient to allow a reasonable juror to conclude that the position more likely than not is true, the court remains free to direct a judgment, Fed. Rule Civ. Proc. 50 (a), and likewise to grant summary judgment, Fed. Rule Civ. Proc. 56. *Cf., e.g., Turpin v. Merrell Dow Pharmaceuticals, Inc.,* 959 F. 2d 1349 (CA6) (holding that scientific evidence that provided foundation for expert testimony, viewed in the light most favorable to plaintiffs, was not sufficient to allow a jury to find it more probable than not that defendant caused plaintiff's injury), *cert. denied,* 506 U.S._____(1992); *Brock v. Merrell Dow Pharmaceuticals, Inc.,* 874 F. 2d 307 (CA5 1989) (reversing judgment entered on jury verdict for plaintiffs because evidence regarding causation was insufficient), *modified,* 884 F. 2d 166 (CA5 1989), *cert. denied,* 494 U.S. 1046 (1990); *Green,* 680–681. These conventional devices, rather than wholesale exclusion under an uncompromising "general acceptance" test, are the appropriate safeguards where the basis of scientific testimony meets the standards of Rule 702.

Petitioners and, to a greater extent, their amici exhibit a different concern. They suggest that recognition of a screening role for the judge that allows for the exclusion of "invalid" evidence will sanction a stifling and repressive scientific orthodoxy and will be inimical to the search for truth. *See, e.g.,* Brief for Ronald Bayer et al. as *Amici Curiae.* It is true that open debate is an essential part of both legal and scientific analyses. Yet there are important differences between the quest for truth in the courtroom and the quest for truth in the laboratory. Scientific conclusions are subject to perpetual revision. Law, on the other hand, must resolve disputes finally and quickly. The scientific project is advanced by broad and wide-ranging consideration of a multitude of hypotheses, for those that are incorrect will eventually be shown to be so, and that in itself is an advance. Conjectures that are probably wrong are of little use, however, in the project of reaching a quick, final, and binding legal judgment—often of great consequence—about a particular set of events in the past. We recognize that in practice, a gatekeeping role for the judge, no matter how flexible, inevitably on occasion will prevent the jury from learning of authentic insights and innovations. That, nevertheless, is the balance that is struck by Rules of Evidence designed not for the exhaustive search for cosmic understanding but for the particularized resolution of legal disputes.[13]

VIII

To summarize: "general acceptance" is not a necessary precondition to the admissibility of scientific evidence under the Federal Rules of Evidence, but the Rules of

---

13. This is not to say that judicial interpretation, as opposed to adjudicative fact-finding, does not share basic characteristics of the scientific endeavor: "The work of a judge is in one sense enduring and in another ephemeral . . . . In the endless process of testing and retesting, there is a constant rejection of the dross and a constant retention of whatever is pure and sound and fine." B. Cardozo, The Nature of the Judicial Process 178, 179 (1921).

Evidence—especially Rule 702—do assign to the trial judge the task of ensuring that an expert's testimony both rests on a reliable foundation and is relevant to the task at hand. Pertinent evidence based on scientifically valid principles will satisfy those demands.

The inquiries of the District Court and the Court of Appeals focused almost exclusively on "general acceptance," as gauged by publication and the decisions of other courts. Accordingly, the judgment of the Court of Appeals is vacated and the case is remanded for further proceedings consistent with this opinion.

It is so ordered.

OPINION

Chief Justice Rehnquist, with whom Justice Stevens joins, concurring in part and dissenting in part.

The petition for certiorari in this case presents two questions: first, whether the rule of *Frye v. United States* 54 App. D.C. 46, 293 F.1013 (1923), remains good law after the enactment of the Federal Rules of Evidence; and second, if Frye remains valid, whether it requires expert scientific testimony to have been subjected to a peer-review process in order to be admissible. The Court concludes, correctly in my view, that the *Frye* rule did not survive the enactment of the Federal Rules of Evidence, and I therefore join Parts I and II–A of its opinion. The second question presented in the petition for certiorari necessarily is mooted by this holding, but the Court nonetheless proceeds to construe Rules 702 and 703 very much in the abstract, and then offers some "general observations."

> This Court customarily carry great weight with lower federal courts, but the ones offered here suffer from the flaw common to most such Observations—they are not applied to deciding whether or not particular testimony was or was not admissible, and therefore they tend to be not only general, but vague and abstract. This is particularly unfortunate in a case such as this, where the ultimate legal question depends on an appreciation of one or more bodies of knowledge not judicially noticeable, and subject to different interpretations in the briefs of the parties and their amici. Twenty-two amicus briefs have been filed in the case, and indeed the Court's opinion contains no less than 37 citations to amicus briefs and other secondary sources.

The various briefs filed in this case are markedly different from typical briefs, in that large parts of them do not deal with decided cases or statutory language—the sort of material we customarily interpret. Instead, they deal with definitions of scientific knowledge, scientific method, scientific validity, and peer review—in short, matters far afield from the expertise of judges. This is not to say that such materials are not useful or even necessary in deciding how Rule 703 should be applied; but it is to say that the unusual subject matter should cause us to proceed with great caution in deciding more than we have to, because our reach can so easily exceed our grasp.

But even if it were desirable to make "general observations" not necessary to decide the questions presented, I cannot subscribe to some of the observations made by the Court. In Part II–B, the Court concludes that reliability and relevancy are the touchstones of the admissibility of expert testimony. *Ante*, at 9. Federal Rule of Evidence 402 provides, as the Court points out, that "[e]vidence which is not relevant is not admissible." But there is no similar reference in the Rule to "reliability." The Court constructs its argument by parsing the language "[i]f scientific, technical, or other specialized knowledge will assist the trier of fact to understand the evidence or to determine a fact in issue . . . an expert . . . may testify thereto . . . ." Fed. Rule Evid. 702. It stresses that the subject of the expert's testimony must be "scientific . . . knowledge," and points out that "scientific" "implies a grounding in the methods and procedures of science," and that the word "knowledge" "connotes more than subjective belief or unsupported speculation." From this it concludes that "scientific knowledge" must be "derived by the scientific method." Proposed testimony, we are told, must be supported by "appropriate validation." Indeed, in footnote 9, the Court decides that "[i]n a case involving scientific evidence, evidentiary reliability will be based upon scientific validity."

Questions arise simply from reading this part of the Court's opinion, and countless more questions will surely arise when hundreds of district judges try to apply its teaching to particular offers of expert testimony. Does all of this dicta apply to an expert seeking to testify on the basis of "technical or other specialized knowledge"—the other types of expert knowledge to which Rule 702 applies—or are the "general observations" limited only to "scientific knowledge"? What is the difference between scientific knowledge and technical knowledge; does Rule 702 actually contemplate that the phrase "scientific, technical, or other specialized knowledge" be broken down into numerous subspecies of expertise, or did its authors simply pick general descriptive language covering the sort of expert testimony which courts have customarily received? The Court speaks of its confidence that federal judges can make a "preliminary assessment of whether the reasoning or methodology underlying the testimony is scientifically valid and of whether that reasoning or methodology properly can be applied to the facts in issue." The Court then states that a "key question" to be answered in deciding whether something is "scientific knowledge" "will be whether it can be (and has been) tested." Following this sentence are three quotations from treatises, which speak not only of empirical testing, but one of which states that "the criterion of the scientific status of a theory is its falsifiability, or refutability, or testability."

I defer to no one in my confidence in federal judges; but I am at a loss to know what is meant when it is said that the scientific status of a theory depends on its "falsifiability," and I suspect some of them will be, too.

I do not doubt that Rule 702 confides to the judge some gatekeeping responsibility in deciding questions of the admissibility of proffered expert testimony. But I do not think it imposes on them either the obligation or the authority to become amateur scientists in order to perform that role. I think the Court would be far better advised in this case to decide only the questions presented, and to leave the further development of this important area of the law to future cases.

GENERAL ELECTRIC CO. V. JOINER
522 U.S. 136 (1997)

After he was diagnosed with small-cell lung cancer, respondent Joiner sued in Georgia state court, alleging, inter alia, that his disease was "promoted" by his workplace exposure to chemical "PCBs" and derivative "furans" and "dioxins" that were manufactured by, or present in materials manufactured by, petitioners. Petitioners removed the case to federal court and moved for summary judgment. Joiner responded with the depositions of expert witnesses, who testified that PCBs, furans, and dioxins can promote cancer, and opined that Joiner's exposure to those chemicals was likely responsible for his cancer. The District Court ruled that there was a genuine issue of material fact as to whether Joiner had been exposed to PCBs, but granted summary Judgment for petitioners because (1) there was no genuine issue as to whether he had been exposed to furans and dioxins, and (2) his experts' testimony had failed to show that there was a link between exposure to PCBs and small-cell lung cancer and was therefore inadmissible because it did not rise above "subjective belief or unsupported speculation." In reversing, the Eleventh Circuit applied "a particularly stringent standard of review" to hold that the District Court had erred in excluding the expert testimony.

Held:

1. Abuse of discretion—the standard ordinarily applicable to review of evidentiary rulings—is the proper standard by which to review a district court's decision to admit or exclude expert scientific evidence. Contrary to the Eleventh Circuit's suggestion, *Daubert v. Merrell Dow Pharmaceuticals, Inc.*, 509 U.S. 579, did not somehow alter this general rule in the context of a district court's decision to exclude scientific evidence. *Daubert* did not address the appellate review standard for evidentiary rulings at all, but did indicate that, while the Federal Rules of Evidence allow district courts to admit a somewhat broader range of scientific testimony than did pre-existing law, they leave in place the trial judge's "gatekeeper" role of screening such evidence to ensure that it is not only relevant, but reliable. *Id.*, at 589. A court of appeals applying "abuse of discretion" review to such rulings may not categorically distinguish between rulings allowing expert testimony and rulings which disallow it. *Compare Beech Aircraft Corp. v. Rainey*, 488 U.S. 153, 172, with *United States v. Abel*, 469 U.S. 45, 54. This Court rejects Joiner's argument that because the granting of summary judgment in this case was "outcome determinative," it should have been subjected to a more searching standard of review. On a summary judgment motion, disputed issues of fact are resolved against the moving

party—here, petitioners. But the question of admissibility of expert testimony is not such an issue of fact, and is reviewable under the abuse of discretion standard. In applying an overly "stringent" standard, the Eleventh Circuit failed to give the trial court the deference that is the hallmark of abuse of discretion review.

2. A proper application of the correct standard of review indicates that the District Court did not err in excluding the expert testimony at issue. The animal studies cited by respondent's experts were so dissimilar to the facts presented here—i.e., the studies involved infant mice that developed alveologenic adenomas after highly concentrated, massive doses of PCBs were injected directly into their peritoneums or stomachs, whereas *Joiner* was an adult human whose small-cell carcinomas allegedly resulted from exposure on a much smaller scale—that it was not an abuse of discretion for the District Court to have rejected the experts' reliance on those studies. Nor did the court abuse its discretion in concluding that the four epidemiological studies on which *Joiner* relied were not a sufficient basis for the experts' opinions, since the authors of two of those studies ultimately were unwilling to suggest a link between increases in lung cancer and PCB exposure among the workers they examined, the third study involved exposure to a particular type of mineral oil not necessarily relevant here, and the fourth involved exposure to numerous potential carcinogens in addition to PCBs. Nothing in either *Daubert* or the Federal Rules of Evidence requires a district court to admit opinion evidence which is connected to existing data only by the *ipse dixit* of the expert.

3. These conclusions, however, do not dispose of the entire case. The Eleventh Circuit reversed the District Court's conclusion that Joiner had not been exposed to furans and dioxins. Because petitioners did not challenge that determination in their certiorari petition, the question whether exposure to furans and dioxins contributed to Joiner's cancer is still open.

78 F.3d 524, reversed and remanded.

REHNIQUIST, C. J., delivered the opinion for a unanimous Court with respect to Parts I and II, and the opinion of the Court with respect to Part III, in which O'CONNOR, SCALIA, KENNEDY, SOUTER, THOMAS, GINSBERG, and BREYER, JJ., joined. BREYER, J., filed a concurring opinion. STEVENS, J., filed an opinion concurring in part and dissenting in part.

OPINION

CHIEF JUSTICE REHNQUIST delivered the opinion of the Court.

We granted certiorari in this case to determine what standard an appellate court should apply in reviewing a trial court's decision to admit or exclude expert testimony under *Daubert v. Merrell Dow Pharmaceuticals, Inc.*, 509 U.S. 579 (1993). We hold that abuse of discretion is the appropriate standard. We apply this standard and conclude that the District Court in this case did not abuse its discretion when it excluded certain proffered expert testimony.

I

Respondent Robert Joiner began work as an electrician in the Water & Light Department of Thomasville, Georgia (City) in 1973. This job required him to work with and around the City's electrical transformers, which used a mineral-based dielectric fluid as a coolant. Joiner often had to stick his hands and arms into the fluid to make repairs. The fluid would sometimes splash onto him, occasionally getting into his eyes and mouth. In 1983 the City discovered that the fluid in some of the transformers was contaminated with polychlorinated biphenyls (PCBs). PCBs are widely considered to be hazardous to human health. Congress, with limited exceptions, banned the production and sale of PCBs in 1978. *See* 90 Stat. 2020, 15 U.S.C. § 2605(e)(2)(A).

Joiner was diagnosed with small cell lung cancer in 1991. He[1] sued petitioners in Georgia state court the following year. Petitioner Monsanto manufactured PCBs from 1935 to 1977; petitioners General Electric and Westinghouse Electric manufactured transformers and dielectric fluid. In his complaint Joiner linked his development of cancer to his exposure to PCBs and their derivatives, polychlorinated dibenzofurans (furans) and polychlorinated dibenzodioxins (dioxins). Joiner had been a smoker for approximately eight years, his parents had both been smokers, and there was a history of lung cancer in his family. He was thus perhaps already at a heightened risk of developing lung cancer eventually. The suit alleged that his exposure to PCBs "promoted" his cancer; had it not been for his exposure to these substances, his cancer would not have developed for many years, if at all. Petitioners removed the case to federal court. Once there, they moved for summary judgment. They contended that (1) there was no evidence that Joiner suffered significant exposure to PCBs, furans, or dioxins, and (2) there was no admissible scientific evidence that PCBs promoted Joiner's cancer. Joiner responded that there were numerous disputed factual issues that required resolution by a jury. He relied largely on the testimony of expert witnesses. In depositions, his experts had testified that PCBs alone can promote cancer and that furans and dioxins can also promote cancer. They opined that since Joiner had been exposed to PCBs, furans, and dioxins, such exposure was likely responsible for Joiner's cancer.

The District Court ruled that there was a genuine issue of material fact as to whether Joiner had been exposed to PCBs. But it nevertheless granted summary judgment for petitioners because (1) there was no genuine issue as to whether Joiner had been exposed to furans and dioxins, and (2) the testimony of Joiner's experts had failed to show that there was a link between exposure to PCBs and small cell

---

1. Joiner's wife was also a plaintiff in the suit and is a respondent here. For convenience, we refer to respondent in the singular.

lung cancer. The court believed that the testimony of respondent's experts to the contrary did not rise above "subjective belief or unsupported speculation." 864 F. Supp. 1310, 1329 (N.D. Ga. 1994). Their testimony was therefore inadmissible.

The Court of Appeals for the Eleventh Circuit reversed. 78 F.3d 524 (1996). It held that "[b]ecause the Federal Rules of Evidence governing expert testimony display a preference for admissibility, we apply a particularly stringent standard of review to the trial judge's exclusion of expert testimony." *Id.* at 529. Applying that standard, the Court of Appeals held that the District Court had erred in excluding the testimony of Joiner's expert witnesses. The District Court had made two fundamental errors. First, it excluded the experts' testimony because it "drew different conclusions from the research than did each of the experts." The Court of Appeals opined that a district court should limit its role to determining the "legal reliability of proffered expert testimony, leaving the jury to decide the correctness of competing expert opinions." *Id.* at 533. Second, the District Court had held that there was no genuine issue of material fact as to whether Joiner had been exposed to furans and dioxins. This was also incorrect, said the Court of Appeals, because testimony in the record supported the proposition that there had been such exposure.

We granted petitioners' petition for a writ of certiorari, 520 U.S.____(1997), and we now reverse.

II

Petitioners challenge the standard applied by the Court of Appeals in reviewing the District Court's decision to exclude respondent's experts' proffered testimony. They argue that that court should have applied traditional "abuse of discretion" review. Respondent agrees that abuse of discretion is the correct standard of review. He contends, however, that the Court of Appeals applied an abuse of discretion standard in this case. As he reads it, the phrase "particularly stringent" announced no new standard of review. It was simply an acknowledgment that an appellate court can and will devote more resources to analyzing district court decisions that are dispositive of the entire litigation. All evidentiary decisions are reviewed under an abuse of discretion standard. He argues, however, that it is perfectly reasonable for appellate courts to give particular attention to those decisions that are outcome-determinative.

We have held that abuse of discretion is the proper standard of review of a district court's evidentiary rulings. *Old Chief v. United States*, 519 U.S.____,____n. 1 (1997) (slip op., at 1–2, n.1), *United States v. Abel*, 469 U.S. 45, 54 (1984). Indeed, our cases on the subject go back as far as *Spring Co. v. Edgar*, 99 U.S. 645, 658 (1879) where we said that "cases arise where it is very much a matter of discretion with the court whether to receive or exclude the evidence; but the appellate court will not reverse in such a case, unless the ruling is manifestly erroneous." The Court of Appeals suggested that *Daubert* somehow altered this general rule in the context of a district court's decision to exclude scientific evidence. But *Daubert* did not address the standard of appellate review for evidentiary rulings at all. It did hold that the "austere" *Frye* standard of "general acceptance" had not been carried over into the Federal Rules of Evidence. But the opinion also said:

> That the *Frye* test was displaced by the Rules of Evidence does not mean, however, that the Rules themselves place no limits on the admissibility of purportedly scientific evidence. Nor is the trial judge disabled from screening such evidence. To the contrary, under the Rules the trial judge must ensure that any and all scientific testimony or evidence admitted is not only relevant, but reliable." 509 U.S., at 589 (footnote omitted).

Thus, while the Federal Rules of Evidence allow district courts to admit a somewhat broader range of scientific testimony than would have been admissible under *Frye*, they leave in place the "gatekeeper" role of the trial judge in screening such evidence. A court of appeals applying "abuse of discretion" review to such rulings may not categorically distinguish between rulings allowing expert testimony and rulings which disallow it. *Compare Beech Aircraft Corp v. Rainey*, 488 U.S. 153, 172 (1988) (applying abuse of discretion review to a lower court's decision to exclude evidence) *with United States v. Abel, supra* at 54 (applying abuse of discretion review to a lower court's decision to admit evidence). We likewise reject respondent's argument that because the granting of summary judgment in this case was "outcome determinative," it should have been subjected to a more searching standard of review. On a motion for summary judgment, disputed issues of fact are resolved against the moving party—here, petitioners. But the question of admissibility of expert testimony is not such an issue of fact, and is reviewable under the abuse of discretion standard.

We hold that the Court of Appeals erred in its review of the exclusion of Joiner's experts' testimony. In applying an overly "stringent" review to that ruling, it failed to give the trial court the deference that is the hallmark of abuse of discretion review. *See, e.g., Koon v. United States*, 518 U.S._____,_____(1996) (slip op., at 14–15).

III

We believe that a proper application of the correct standard of review here indicates that the District Court did not abuse its discretion. Joiner's theory of liability was that his exposure to PCBs and their derivatives "promoted" his development of small cell lung cancer. In support of that theory he proffered the deposition testimony of expert witnesses. Dr. Arnold Schecter testified that he believed it "more likely than not that Mr. Joiner's lung cancer was causally linked to cigarette smoking and PCB exposure." App. at 107. Dr. Daniel Teitelbaum testified that Joiner's "lung cancer was caused by or contributed to in a significant degree by the materials with which he worked." *Id.* at 140.

Petitioners contended that the statements of Joiner's experts regarding causation were nothing more than speculation. Petitioners criticized the testimony of the experts in that it was "not supported by epidemiological studies . . . [and was] based exclusively on isolated studies of laboratory animals." Joiner responded by claiming that his experts had identified "relevant animal studies which support their opinions." He also directed the court's attention to four epidemiological studies[2] on which his experts had relied.

The District Court agreed with petitioners that the animal studies on which respondent's experts relied did not support his contention that exposure to PCBs had contributed to his cancer. The studies involved infant mice that had developed cancer after being exposed to PCBs. The infant mice in the studies had had massive doses of PCBs injected directly into their peritoneums[3] or stomachs. Joiner was an adult human being whose alleged exposure to PCBs was far less than the exposure in the animal studies. The PCBs were injected into the mice in a highly concentrated form. The fluid with which Joiner had come into contact generally had a much smaller PCB concentration of between 0–500 parts per million. The cancer that these mice developed was alveologenic adenomas; Joiner had developed small-cell carcinomas. No study demonstrated that adult mice developed cancer after being exposed to PCBs. One of the experts admitted that no study had demonstrated that PCBs lead to cancer in any other species.

Respondent failed to reply to this criticism. Rather than explaining how and why the experts could have extrapolated their opinions from these seemingly far-removed animal studies, respondent chose "to proceed as if the only issue [was] whether animal studies can ever be a proper foundation for an expert's opinion." *Joiner*, 864 F. Supp. at 1324. Of course, whether animal studies can ever be a proper foundation for an expert's opinion was not the issue. The issue was whether these experts' opinions were sufficiently supported by the animal studies on which they purported to rely. The studies were so dissimilar to the facts presented in this litigation that it was not an abuse of discretion for the District Court to have rejected the experts' reliance on them.

The District Court also concluded that the four epidemiological studies on which respondent relied were not a sufficient basis for the experts' opinions. The first such study involved workers at an Italian capacitor[4] plant who had been exposed to PCBs. Bertazzi, Riboldi, Pesatori, Radice, & Zocchetti, Cancer Mortality of Capacitor Manufacturing Workers, 11 American Journal of Industrial Medicine 165 (1987). The authors noted that lung cancer deaths among ex-employees at the plant were higher than might have been expected, but concluded that "there were apparently no grounds for associating lung cancer deaths (although increased above expectations) and exposure in the plant." *Id.* at 172. Given that Bertazzi et al. were

---

2. Epidemiological studies examine the pattern of disease in human populations.
3. The peritoneum is the lining of the abdominal cavity.
4. A capacitor is an electrical component that stores an electric charge.

unwilling to say that PCB exposure had caused cancer among the workers they examined, their study did not support the experts' conclusion that Joiner's exposure to PCBs caused his cancer.

The second study followed employees who had worked at Monsanto's PCB production plant. J. Zack & D. Munsch, Mortality of PCB Workers at the Monsanto Plant in Sauget, Illinois (Dec. 14, 1979) (unpublished report), 3 Rec., Doc. Number 11. The authors of this study found that the incidence of lung cancer deaths among these workers was somewhat higher than would ordinarily be expected. The increase, however, was not statistically significant and the authors of the study did not suggest a link between the increase in lung cancer deaths and the exposure to PCBs.

The third and fourth studies were likewise of no help. The third involved workers at a Norwegian cable manufacturing company who had been exposed to mineral oil. Ronneberg, Andersen, Skyberg, Mortality and Incidence of Cancer Among Oil-Exposed Workers in a Norwegian Cable Manufacturing Company, 45 British Journal of Industrial Medicine 595 (1988). A statistically significant increase in lung cancer deaths had been observed in these workers. The study, however, (1) made no mention of PCBs and (2) was expressly limited to the type of mineral oil involved in that study, and thus did not support these experts' opinions. The fourth and final study involved a PCB-exposed group in Japan that had seen a statistically significant increase in lung cancer deaths. Kuratsune, Nakamura, Ikeda, & Hirohata, Analysis of Deaths Seen Among Patients with Yusho—A Preliminary Report, 16 Chemosphere, Nos. 8/9, 2085 (1987). The subjects of this study, however, had been exposed to numerous potential carcinogens, including toxic rice oil that they had ingested. Respondent points to *Daubert's* language that the "focus, of course, must be solely on principles and methodology, not on the conclusions that they generate." 509 U.S., at 595. He claims that because the District Court's disagreement was with the conclusion that the experts drew from the studies, the District Court committed legal error and was properly reversed by the Court of Appeals. But conclusions and methodology are not entirely distinct from one another. Trained experts commonly extrapolate from existing data. But nothing in either *Daubert* or the Federal Rules of Evidence requires a district court to admit opinion evidence which is connected to existing data only by the *ipse dixit* of the expert. A court may conclude that there is simply too great an analytical gap between the data and the opinion proffered. *See Turpin v. Merrell Dow Pharmaceuticals, Inc.*, 959 F.2d 1349, 1360 (CA 6), *cert. denied*, 506 U.S. 826 (1992). That is what the District Court did here, and we hold that it did not abuse its discretion in so doing.

We hold, therefore, that abuse of discretion is the proper standard by which to review a district court's decision to admit or exclude scientific evidence. We further hold that, because it was within the District Court's discretion to conclude that the studies upon which the experts relied were not sufficient, whether individually or in combination, to support their conclusions that Joiner's exposure to PCBs contributed to his cancer, the District Court did not abuse its discretion in excluding their testimony. These conclusions, however, do not dispose of this entire case.

Respondent's original contention was that his exposure to PCBs, furans, and dioxins contributed to his cancer. The District Court ruled that there was a genuine issue of material fact as to whether Joiner had been exposed to PCBs, but concluded that there was no genuine issue as to whether he had been exposed to furans and dioxins. The District Court accordingly never explicitly considered if there was admissible evidence on the question whether Joiner's alleged exposure to furans and dioxins contributed to his cancer. The Court of Appeals reversed the District Court's conclusion that there had been no exposure to furans and dioxins. Petitioners did not challenge this determination in their petition to this Court. Whether Joiner was exposed to furans and dioxins, and whether if there was such exposure, the opinions of Joiner's experts would then be admissible, remain open questions. We accordingly reverse the judgment of the Court of Appeals and remand this case for proceedings consistent with this opinion.

Opinion

JUSTICE BREYER, CONCURRING.

The Court's opinion, which I join, emphasizes *Daubert*'s statement that a trial judge, acting as "gatekeeper," must "'ensure that any and all scientific testimony or evidence admitted is not only relevant, but reliable.'" *Ante*, (quoting *Daubert v. Merrell Dow Pharmaceuticals, Inc.*, 509 U.S. 579, 589 (1993)). This requirement will sometimes ask judges to make subtle and sophisticated determinations about scientific methodology and its relation to the conclusions an expert witness seeks to offer—particularly when a case arises in an area where the science itself is tentative or uncertain, or where testimony about general risk levels in human beings or animals is offered to prove individual causation. Yet, as amici have pointed out, judges are not scientists and do not have the scientific training that can facilitate the making of such decisions. *See, e.g.*, Brief for Trial Lawyers for Public Justice as *Amicus Curiae* 15; Brief for The New England Journal of Medicine et al. as *Amici Curiae* 2 ("Judges . . . are generally not trained scientists").

Of course, neither the difficulty of the task nor any comparative lack of expertise can excuse the judge from exercising the "gatekeeper" duties that the Federal Rules impose—determining, for example, whether particular expert testimony is reliable and "will assist the trier of fact," Fed. Rule Evid. 702, or whether the "probative value" of testimony is substantially outweighed by risks of prejudice, confusion or waste of time. Fed. Rule Evid. 403. To the contrary, when law and science intersect, those duties often must be exercised with special care.

Today's toxic tort case provides an example. The plaintiff in today's case says that a chemical substance caused, or promoted, his lung cancer. His concern, and that of others, about the causes of cancer is understandable, for cancer kills over one in five Americans. *See* U.S. Dept. of Health and Human Services, National Center for Health Statistics, Health United States 1996–97 and Injury Chartbook 117 (1997) (23.3% of all deaths in 1995). Moreover, scientific evidence implicates some chemicals as potential causes of some cancers. *See, e.g.,* U.S. Dept. of Health and Human Services, Public Health Service, National Toxicology Program, 1 Seventh Annual Report on Carcinogens, pp. v–vi (1994). Yet modern life, including good health as well as economic well-being, depends upon the use of artificial or manufactured substances, such as chemicals. And it may, therefore, prove particularly important to see that judges fulfill their *Daubert* gatekeeping function, so that they help assure that the powerful engine of tort liability, which can generate strong financial incentives to reduce, or to eliminate, production, points towards the right substances and does not destroy the wrong ones. It is, thus, essential in this science-related area that the courts administer the Federal Rules of Evidence in order to achieve the "end[s]" that the Rules themselves set forth, not only so that proceedings may be "justly determined," but also so "that the truth may be ascertained." Fed. Rule Evid. 102.

I therefore want specially to note that, as cases presenting significant science-related issues have increased in number, *see* Judicial Conference of the United States, Report of the Federal Courts Study Committee 97 (Apr. 2, 1990) ("Economic, statistical, technological, and natural and social scientific data are becoming increasingly important in both routine and complex litigation"), judges have increasingly found in the Rules of Evidence and Civil Procedure ways to help them overcome the inherent difficulty of making determinations about complicated scientific or otherwise technical evidence. Among these techniques are an increased use of Rule 16's pretrial conference authority to narrow the scientific issues in dispute, pretrial hearings where potential experts are subject to examination by the court, and the appointment of special masters and specially trained law clerks. *See* J. Cecil & T. Willging, Court-Appointed Experts: Defining the Role of Experts Appointed Under Federal Rule of Evidence 706, pp. 83–88 (1993); J. Weinstein, Individual Justice in Mass Tort Litigation 107–110 (1995); *cf.* Kaysen, In Memoriam: Charles E. Wyzanski, Jr., 100 Harv. L. Rev. 713, 713–715 (1987) (discussing a judge's use of an economist as a law clerk in *United States v. United Shoe Machinery Corp.*, 110 F. Supp. 295 (D Mass 1953), *aff'd*, 347 U.S. 521 (1954)).

In the present case, the New England Journal of Medicine has filed an *amici* brief "in support of neither petitioners nor respondents" in which the Journal writes:

> "[A] judge could better fulfill this gatekeeper function if he or she had help from scientists. Judges should be strongly encouraged to make greater use of their inherent authority . . . to appoint experts . . . . Reputable experts could be recommended to courts by established scientific organizations, such as the National Academy of Sciences or the American Association for the Advancement of Science."

Brief for The New England Journal of Medicine 18–19; *cf.* Fed. Rule Evid. 706 (court may "on its own motion or on the motion of any party" appoint an expert to serve on behalf of the court, and this expert may be selected as "agreed upon by the parties" or chosen by the court); *see also* Weinstein, *supra*, at 116 (a court should sometimes "go beyond the experts proffered by the parties" and "utilize its powers to appoint independent experts under Rule 706 of the Federal Rules of Evidence"). Given this kind of offer of cooperative effort, from the scientific to the legal community, and given the various Rules-authorized methods for facilitating the courts' task, it seems to me that *Daubert's* gatekeeping requirement will not prove inordinately difficult to implement; and that it will help secure the basic objectives of the Federal Rules of Evidence; which are, to repeat, the ascertainment of truth and the just determination of proceedings. Fed. Rule Evid. 102.

Opinion

JUSTICE STEVENS, concurring in part and dissenting in part.

The question that we granted certiorari to decide is whether the Court of Appeals applied the correct standard of review. That question is fully answered in Parts I and II of the Court's opinion. Part III answers the quite different question whether the District Court properly held that the testimony of plaintiff's expert witnesses was inadmissible. Because I am not sure that the parties have adequately briefed that question, or that the Court has adequately explained why the Court of Appeals' disposition was erroneous, I do not join Part III. Moreover, because a proper answer to that question requires a study of the record that can be performed more efficiently by the Court of Appeals than by the nine members of this Court, I would remand the case to that court for application of the proper standard of review.

One aspect of the record will illustrate my concern. As the Court of Appeals pointed out, Joiner's experts relied on "the studies of at least thirteen different researchers, and referred to several reports of the World Health Organization that address the question of whether PCBs cause cancer." 78 F.3d 524, 533 (CA11 1996). Only one of those studies is in the record, and only six of them were discussed in the District Court opinion. Whether a fair appraisal of either the methodology or the conclusions of Joiner's experts can be made on the basis of such an incomplete record is a question that I do not feel prepared to answer.

It does seem clear, however, that the Court has not adequately explained why its holding is consistent with Federal Rule of Evidence702,[5] as interpreted in *Daubert v.*

---

5. Rule 702 states: "If scientific, technical, or other specialized knowledge will assist the trier of fact to understand the evidence or to determine a fact in issue, a witness qualified as an expert by knowledge, skill, experience, training, or education, may testify thereto in the form of an opinion or otherwise."

Merrell Dow Pharmaceuticals, Inc., 509 U.S. 579 (1993).[6] In general, scientific testimony that is both relevant and reliable must be admitted and testimony that is irrelevant or unreliable must be excluded. *Id.*, at 597. In this case, the District Court relied on both grounds for exclusion.

The relevance ruling was straightforward. The District Court correctly reasoned that an expert opinion that exposure to PCBs, "furans" and "dioxins" together may cause lung cancer would be irrelevant unless the plaintiff had been exposed to those substances. Having already found that there was no evidence of exposure to furans and dioxins, 864 F. Supp. 1310, 1318–1319 (N.D. Ga. 1994), it necessarily followed that this expert opinion testimony was inadmissible. Correctly applying *Daubert*, the District Court explained that the experts' testimony "manifestly does not fit the facts of this case, and is therefore inadmissible." 864 F. Supp., at 1322. Of course, if the evidence raised a genuine issue of fact on the question of Joiner's exposure to furans and dioxins—as the Court of Appeals held that it did—then this basis for the ruling on admissibility was erroneous, but not because the district judge either abused her discretion or misapplied the law.[7]

The reliability ruling was more complex and arguably is not faithful to the statement in *Daubert* that "[t]he focus, of course, must be solely on principles and methodology, not on the conclusions that they generate." 509 U.S., at 595. Joiner's experts used a "weight of the evidence" methodology to assess whether Joiner's exposure to transformer fluids promoted his lung cancer.[8] They did not suggest that any one study provided adequate support for their conclusions, but instead relied on all the studies taken together (along with their interviews of Joiner and their review of his medical records). The District Court, however, examined the studies one by one and concluded that none was sufficient to show a link between PCBs and lung

---

6. The specific question on which the Court granted certiorari in *Daubert* was whether the rule of *Frye v. United States*, 54 App. D.C. 46, 293 F. 1013 (1923), remained valid after the enactment of the Federal Rules of Evidence, but the Court went beyond that issue and set forth alternative requirements for admissibility in place of the *Frye* test. Even though the *Daubert* test was announced in dicta, *see* 509 U.S., at 598–601 (Rehnquist, C. J., concurring in part and dissenting in part), we should not simply ignore its analysis in reviewing the District Court's rulings.

7. Petitioners do not challenge the Court of Appeals' straightforward review of the District Court's summary judgment ruling on exposure to furans and dioxins. As today's opinion indicates, it remains an open question on remand whether the District Court should admit expert testimony that PCBs, furans and dioxins together promoted Joiner' cancer.

8. Dr. Daniel Teitelbaum elaborated on that approach in his deposition testimony: "[A]s a toxicologist when I look at a study, I am going to require that that study meet the general criteria for methodology and statistical analysis, but that when all of that data is collected and you ask me as a patient, 'Doctor, have I got a risk of getting cancer from this?' That those studies don't answer the question, that I have to put them all together in my mind and look at them in relation to everything I know about the substance and everything I know about the exposure and come to a conclusion. I think when I say, 'To a reasonable medical probability as a medical toxicologist, this substance was a contributing cause,' . . . to his cancer, that that is a valid conclusion based on the totality of the evidence presented to me. And I think that that is an appropriate thing for a toxicologist to do, and it has been the basis of diagnosis for several hundred years, anyway." Supp. App. to Brief for Respondents 19.

---

cancer. 864 F. Supp., at 1324–1326. The focus of the opinion was on the separate studies and the conclusions of the experts, not on the experts' methodology. *Id.*, at 1322 ("Defendants . . . persuade the court that Plaintiffs' expert testimony would not be admissible . . . by attacking the conclusions that Plaintiffs' experts draw from the studies they cite").

Unlike the District Court, the Court of Appeals expressly decided that a "weight of the evidence" methodology was scientifically acceptable.[9] To this extent, the Court of Appeals' opinion is persuasive. It is not intrinsically "unscientific" for experienced professionals to arrive at a conclusion by weighing all available scientific evidence—this is not the sort of "junk science" with which *Daubert* was concerned.[10] After all, as *Joiner* points out, the Environmental Protection Agency (EPA) uses the same methodology to assess risks, albeit using a somewhat different threshold than that required in a trial. Brief for Respondents 40–41 (quoting EPA, Guidelines for Carcinogen Risk Assessment, 51 Fed. Reg. 33992, 33996 (1986)). Petitioners' own experts used the same scientific approach as well.[11] And using this methodology, it would seem that an expert could reasonably have concluded that the study of workers at an Italian capacitor plant, coupled with data from Monsanto's study and other studies, raises an inference that PCBs promote lung cancer.[12]

The Court of Appeals' discussion of admissibility is faithful to the dictum in *Daubert* that the reliability inquiry must focus on methodology, not conclusions. Thus, even though I fully agree with both the District Court's and this Court's explanation of why each of the studies on which the experts relied was by itself unpersuasive, a critical question remains unanswered: When qualified experts have reached relevant conclusions on the basis of an acceptable methodology, why are their opinions inadmissible?

---

9. The court explained: "Opinions of any kind are derived from individual pieces of evidence, each of which by itself might not be conclusive, but when viewed in their entirety are the building blocks of a perfectly reasonable conclusion, one reliable enough to be submitted to a jury along with the tests and criticisms cross-examination and contrary evidence would supply." 78 F.3d 524, 532 (CA11 1996).

10. An example of "junk science" that should be excluded under *Daubert* as too unreliable would be the testimony of a phrenologist who would purport to prove a defendant's future dangerousness based on the contours of the defendant's skull.

11. *See, e.g.*, Deposition of Dr. William Charles Bailey, Supp. App. to Brief for Respondents 56 ("I've just reviewed a lot of literature and come to some conclusions . . .").

12. The Italian capacitor plant study found that workers exposed to PCBs had a higher-than-expected rate of lung cancer death, though "the numbers were small [and] the value of the risk estimate was not statistically significant." 864 F. Supp. 1310, 1324 (ND Ga. 1994). The Monsanto study also found a correlation between PCB exposure and lung cancer death, but the results were not statistically significant. *Id.*, at 1325. Moreover, it should be noted that under Georgia law, which applies in this diversity suit, Joiner need only show that his exposure to PCBs "promoted" his lung cancer, not that it was the sole cause of his cancer. Brief for Respondents 7, n. 16 (quoting Brief for Appellants in No. 94—9131 (CA 11), pp. 7–10).

Daubert quite clearly forbids trial judges from assessing the validity or strength of an expert's scientific conclusions, which is a matter for the jury.[13] Because I am persuaded that the difference between methodology and conclusions is just as categorical as the distinction between means and ends, I do not think the statement that "conclusions and methodology are not entirely distinct from one another" is either accurate or helps us answer the difficult admissibility question presented by this record.

In any event, it bears emphasis that the Court has not held that it would have been an abuse of discretion to admit the expert testimony. The very point of today's holding is that the abuse of discretion standard of review applies whether the district judge has excluded or admitted evidence. And nothing in either *Daubert* or the Federal Rules of Evidence requires a district judge to reject an expert's conclusions and keep them from the jury when they fit the facts of the case and are based on reliable scientific methodology.

Accordingly, while I join Parts I and II of the Court's opinion, I do not concur in the judgment or in Part III of its opinion.

---

13. The Court stated in *Daubert*: "Vigorous cross-examination, presentation of contrary evidence, and careful instruction on the burden of proof are the traditional and appropriate means of attacking shaky but admissible evidence . . . Additionally, in the event the trial court concludes that the scintilla of evidence presented supporting a position is insufficient to allow a reasonable juror to conclude that the position more likely than not is true, the court remains free to direct a judgment, Fed. Rule Civ. Proc. 50(a), and likewise to grant summary judgment, Fed. Rule Civ. Proc. 56 . . . These conventional devices, rather than wholesale exclusion under an uncompromising 'general acceptance' test, are the appropriate safeguards where the basis of scientific testimony meets the standards of Rule 702." 509 U.S., at 596.

KUMHO TIRE COMPANY, LTD. V. CARMICHAEL
526 U.S. 137 (1999)

When a tire on the vehicle driven by Patrick Carmichael blew out and the vehicle overturned, one passenger died and the others were injured. The survivors and the decedent's representative, respondents here, brought this diversity suit against the tire's maker and its distributor (collectively *Kumho Tire*), claiming that the tire that failed was defective. They rested their case in significant part upon the depositions of a tire failure analyst, Dennis Carlson, Jr., who intended to testify that, in his expert opinion, a defect in the tire's manufacture or design caused the blow out. That opinion was based upon a visual and tactile inspection of the tire and upon the theory that in the absence of at least two of four specific, physical symptoms indicating tire abuse, the tire failure of the sort that occurred here was caused by a defect. *Kumho Tire* moved to exclude Carlson's testimony on the ground that his methodology failed to satisfy Federal Rule of Evidence 702, which says: "If scientific, technical, or other specialized knowledge will assist the trier of fact . . . , a witness qualified as an expert . . . may testify thereto in the form of an opinion." Granting the motion (and entering summary judgment for the defendants), the District Court acknowledged that it should act as a reliability "gatekeeper" under *Daubert v. Merrell Dow Pharmaceuticals, Inc.*, 509 U.S. 579, 589, in which this Court held that Rule 702 imposes a special obligation upon a trial judge to ensure that scientific testimony is not only relevant, but reliable. The court noted that *Daubert* discussed four factors—testing, peer review, error rates, and "acceptability" in the relevant scientific community—which might prove helpful in determining the reliability of a particular scientific theory or technique, *id.*, at 593–594, and found that those factors argued against the reliability of Carlson's methodology. On the plaintiffs' motion for reconsideration, the court agreed that *Daubert* should be applied flexibly, that its four factors were simply illustrative, and that other factors could argue in favor of admissibility. However, the court affirmed its earlier order because it found insufficient indications of the reliability of Carlson's methodology. In reversing, the Eleventh Circuit held that the District Court had erred as a matter of law in applying *Daubert*. Believing that *Daubert* was limited to the scientific context, the court held that the *Daubert* factors did not apply to Carlson's testimony, which it characterized as skill- or experience-based.

Held:

1.   The *Daubert* factors may apply to the testimony of engineers and other experts who are not scientists.

(a)   The *Daubert* "gatekeeping" obligation applies not only to "scientific" testimony, but to all expert testimony. Rule 702 does not distinguish between "scientific" knowledge and "technical" or "other specialized" knowledge, but makes clear that any such knowledge might become the subject of expert testimony. It is the Rule's word "knowledge," not the words (like "scientific") that modify that word, that establishes a standard of evidentiary reliability. 509 U.S., at 589–590. *Daubert* referred only to "scientific" knowledge because that was the nature of the expertise there at issue. *Id.*, at 590, n. 8. Neither is the evidentiary rationale underlying *Daubert*'s "gatekeeping" determination limited to "scientific" knowledge. Rules 702 and 703 grant all expert witnesses, not just "scientific" ones, testimonial latitude unavailable to other witnesses on the assumption that the expert's opinion will have a reliable basis in the knowledge and experience of his discipline. *Id.*, at 592. Finally, it would prove difficult, if not impossible, for judges to administer evidentiary rules under which a "gatekeeping" obligation depended upon a distinction between "scientific" knowledge and "technical" or "other specialized" knowledge, since there is no clear line dividing the one from the others and no convincing need to make such distinctions.

(b)   A trial judge determining the admissibility of an engineering expert's testimony may consider one or more of the specific *Daubert* factors. The emphasis on the word "may" reflects *Daubert*'s description of the Rule 702 inquiry as "a flexible one." 509 U.S., at 594. The *Daubert* factors do not constitute a definitive checklist or test, *id.*, at 593, and the gatekeeping inquiry must be tied to the particular facts, *id.*, at 591. Those factors may or may not be pertinent in assessing reliability, depending on the nature of the issue, the expert's particular expertise, and the subject of his testimony. Some of those factors may be helpful in evaluating the reliability even of experience-based expert testimony, and the Court of Appeals erred insofar as it ruled those factors out in such cases. In determining whether particular expert testimony is reliable, the trial court should consider the specific *Daubert* factors where they are reasonable measures of reliability.

(c)   The court of appeals must apply an abuse-of-discretion standard when it reviews the trial court's decision to admit or exclude expert testimony. *General Electric Co. v. Joiner*, 522 U.S. 136, 138–139. That standard applies as much to the trial court's decisions about how to determine reliability as to its ultimate conclusion. Thus, whether *Daubert*'s specific factors are, or are not, reasonable measures of reliability in a particular case is a matter that the law grants the trial judge broad latitude to determine. *See id.*, at 143. The Eleventh Circuit erred insofar as it held to the contrary.

2. Application of the foregoing standards demonstrates that the District Court's decision not to admit Carlson's expert testimony was lawful. The District Court did not question Carlson's qualifications, but excluded his testimony because it initially doubted his methodology and then found it unreliable after examining the transcript in some detail and considering respondents' defense of it. The doubts

that triggered the court's initial inquiry were reasonable, as was the court's ultimate conclusion that Carlson could not reliably determine the cause of the failure of the tire in question. The question was not the reliability of Carlson's methodology in general, but rather whether he could reliably determine the cause of failure of the particular tire at issue. That tire, Carlson conceded, had traveled far enough so that some of the tread had been worn bald, it should have been taken out of service, it had been repaired (inadequately) for punctures, and it bore some of the very marks that he said indicated, not a defect, but abuse. Moreover, Carlson's own testimony cast considerable doubt upon the reliability of both his theory about the need for at least two signs of abuse and his proposition about the significance of visual inspection in this case. Respondents stress that other tire failure experts, like Carlson, rely on visual and tactile examinations of tires. But there is no indication in the record that other experts in the industry use Carlson's particular approach or that tire experts normally make the very fine distinctions necessary to support his conclusions, nor are there references to articles or papers that validate his approach. Respondents' argument that the District Court too rigidly applied *Daubert* might have had some validity with respect to the court's initial opinion, but fails because the court, on reconsideration, recognized that the relevant reliability inquiry should be "flexible," and ultimately based its decision upon Carlson's failure to satisfy either *Daubert*'s factors or any other set of reasonable reliability criteria.

131 F. 3d 1433, reversed.

BREYER, J., delivered the opinion of the Court, in which REHNQUIST, C. J., and O'CONNOR, SCALIA, KENNEDY, SOUTER, THOMAS, and GINSBURG, JJ., joined, and in which STEVENS, J., joined as to Parts I and II. SCALIA, J., filed a concurring opinion, in which O'CONNOR and THOMAS, JJ., joined. STEVENS, J., filed an opinion concurring in part and dissenting in part.

Opinion

JUSTICE BREYER delivered the opinion of the Court.

In *Daubert v. Merrell Dow Pharmaceuticals, Inc.*, 509 U.S. 579 (1993), this Court focused upon the admissibility of scientific expert testimony. It pointed out that such testimony is admissible only if it is both relevant and reliable. And it held that the Federal Rules of Evidence "assign to the trial judge the task of ensuring that an expert's testimony both rests on a reliable foundation and is relevant to the task at hand." *Id.*, at 597. The Court also discussed certain more specific factors, such as testing, peer review, error rates, and "acceptability" in the relevant scientific community, some or all of which might prove helpful in determining the reliability of a particular scientific "theory or technique." *Id.*, at 593–594.

This case requires us to decide how *Daubert* applies to the testimony of engineers and other experts who are not scientists. We conclude that *Daubert*'s general holding—

setting forth the trial judge's general "gatekeeping" obligation—applies not only to testimony based on "scientific" knowledge, but also to testimony based on "technical" and "other specialized" knowledge. *See* Fed. Rule Evid. 702. We also conclude that a trial court may consider one or more of the more specific factors that *Daubert* mentioned when doing so will help determine that testimony's reliability. But, as the Court stated in *Daubert,* the test of reliability is "flexible," and *Daubert's* list of specific factors neither necessarily nor exclusively applies to all experts or in every case. Rather, the law grants a district court the same broad latitude when it decides how to determine reliability as it enjoys in respect to its ultimate reliability determination. *See General Electric Co. v. Joiner,* 522 U.S. 136, 143 (1997) (courts of appeals are to apply "abuse of discretion" standard when reviewing district court's reliability determination).

Applying these standards, we determine that the District Court's decision in this case—not to admit certain expert testimony—was within its discretion and therefore lawful.

I

On July 6, 1993, the right rear tire of a minivan driven by Patrick Carmichael blew out. In the accident that followed, one of the passengers died, and others were severely injured. In October 1993, the Carmichaels brought this diversity suit against the tire's maker and its distributor, whom we refer to collectively as Kumho Tire, claiming that the tire was defective. The plaintiffs rested their case in significant part upon deposition testimony provided by an expert in tire failure analysis, Dennis Carlson, Jr., who intended to testify in support of their conclusion.

Carlson's depositions relied upon certain features of tire technology that are not in dispute. A steel-belted radial tire like the Carmichaels' is made up of a "carcass" containing many layers of flexible cords, called "plies," along which (between the cords and the outer tread) are laid steel strips called "belts." Steel wire loops, called "beads," hold the cords together at the plies' bottom edges. An outer layer, called the "tread," encases the carcass, and the entire tire is bound together in rubber, through the application of heat and various chemicals. *See generally, e.g.,* J. Dixon, Tires, Suspension and Handling 68–72 (2d ed. 1996). The bead of the tire sits upon a "bead seat," which is part of the wheel assembly. That assembly contains a "rim flange," which extends over the bead and rests against the side of the tire. *See* M. Mavrigian, Performance Wheels & Tires 81, 83 (1998) (illustrations).

[Graphic omitted.] A. Markovich, How To Buy and Care For Tires 4 (1994).

Carlson's testimony also accepted certain background facts about the tire in question. He assumed that before the blowout the tire had traveled far. (The tire was made in 1988 and had been installed some time before the Carmichaels bought the used minivan in March 1993; the Carmichaels had driven the van approximately 7,000 additional miles in the two months they had owned it.) Carlson noted that the tire's tread depth, which was 11/32 of an inch when new, App. 242, had been worn down to depths that ranged from 3/32 of an inch along some parts of the tire, to nothing at all along others. *Id.*, at 287. He conceded that the tire tread had at least two punctures which had been inadequately repaired. *Id.*, at 258–261, 322. Despite the tire's age and history, Carlson concluded that a defect in its manufacture or design caused the blow-out. He rested this conclusion in part upon three premises which, for present purposes, we must assume are not in dispute: First, a tire's carcass should stay bound to the inner side of the tread for a significant period of time after its tread depth has worn away. *Id.*, at 208–209. Second, the tread of the tire at issue had separated from its inner steel-belted carcass prior to the accident. *Id.*, at 336. Third, this "separation" caused the blowout. *Ibid.*

Carlson's conclusion that a defect caused the separation, however, rested upon certain other propositions, several of which the defendants strongly dispute. First, Carlson said that if a separation is not caused by a certain kind of tire misuse called "overdeflection" (which consists of underinflating the tire or causing it to carry too much weight, thereby generating heat that can undo the chemical tread/carcass bond), then, ordinarily, its cause is a tire defect. *Id.*, at 193–195, 277–278. Second, he said that if a tire has been subject to sufficient overdeflection to cause a separation, it should reveal certain physical symptoms. These symptoms include (a) tread wear on the tire's shoulder that is greater than the tread wear along the tire's center, *id.*, at 211; (b) signs of a "bead groove," where the beads have been pushed too hard against the bead seat on the inside of the tire's rim, *id.*, at 196–197; (c) sidewalls of the tire with physical signs of deterioration, such as discoloration, *id.*, at 212; and/or (d) marks on the tire's rim flange, *id.*, at 219–220. Third, Carlson said that where he does not find at least two of the four physical signs just mentioned (and presumably where there is no reason to suspect a less common cause of separation), he concludes that a manufacturing or design defect caused the separation. *Id.*, at 223–224.

Carlson added that he had inspected the tire in question. He conceded that the tire to a limited degree showed greater wear on the shoulder than in the center, some signs of "bead groove," some discoloration, a few marks on the rim flange, and inadequately filled puncture holes (which can also cause heat that might lead to separation). *Id.*, at 256–257, 258–261, 277, 303–304, 308. But, in each instance, he testified that the symptoms were not significant, and he explained why he believed that they did not reveal overdeflection. For example, the extra shoulder wear, he said, appeared primarily on one shoulder, whereas an overdeflected tire would reveal equally abnormal wear on both shoulders. *Id.*, at 277. Carlson concluded that the tire did not bear at least two of the four overdeflection symptoms, nor was there any less obvious cause of separation; and since neither overdeflection nor the punctures caused the blowout, a defect must have done so.

Kumho Tire moved the District Court to exclude Carlson's testimony on the ground that his methodology failed Rule 702's reliability requirement. The court agreed with Kumho that it should act as a *Daubert*-type reliability "gatekeeper," even though one might consider Carlson's testimony as "technical," rather than "scientific." *See Carmichael v. Samyang Tires, Inc.*, 923 F. Supp. 1514, 1521–1522 (SD Ala. 1996). The court then examined Carlson's methodology in light of the reliability-related factors that *Daubert* mentioned, such as a theory's testability, whether it "has been a subject of peer review or publication," the "known or potential rate of error," and the "degree of acceptance . . . within the relevant scientific community." 923 F. Supp., at 1520 (*citing Daubert*, 509 U.S., at 592–594). The District Court found that all those factors argued against the reliability of Carlson's methods, and it granted the motion to exclude the testimony (as well as the defendants' accompanying motion for summary judgment).

The plaintiffs, arguing that the court's application of the *Daubert* factors was too "inflexible," asked for reconsideration. And the Court granted that motion. *Carmichael v. Samyang Tires, Inc.*, Civ. Action No. 93-0860-CB-S (SD Ala., June 5, 1996), App. to Pet. for Cert. 1c. After reconsidering the matter, the court agreed with the plaintiffs that *Daubert* should be applied flexibly, that its four factors were simply illustrative, and that other factors could argue in favor of admissibility. It conceded that there may be widespread acceptance of a "visual-inspection method" for some relevant purposes. But the court found insufficient indications of the reliability of:

> the component of Carlson's tire failure analysis which most concerned the Court, namely, the methodology employed by the expert in analyzing the data obtained in the visual inspection, and the scientific basis, if any, for such an analysis. *Id.*, at 6c.

It consequently affirmed its earlier order declaring Carlson's testimony inadmissible and granting the defendants' motion for summary judgment.

The Eleventh Circuit reversed. *See Carmichael v. Samyang Tire, Inc.*, 131 F.3d 1433 (1997). It "review[ed] . . . de novo" the "district court's legal decision to apply *Daubert*." *Id.*, at 1435. It noted that "the Supreme Court in *Daubert* explicitly limited its holding to cover only the 'scientific context,'" adding that "a *Daubert* analysis" applies only where an expert relies "on the application of scientific principles," rather than "on skill- or experience-based observation." *Id.*, at 1435–1436. It concluded that Carlson's testimony, which it viewed as relying on experience, "falls outside the scope of *Daubert*," that "the district court erred as a matter of law by applying *Daubert* in this case," and that the case must be remanded for further (non-*Daubert*-type) consideration under Rule 702. *Id.*, at 1436.

Kumho Tire petitioned for certiorari, asking us to determine whether a trial court "may" consider Daubert's specific "factors" when determining the "admissibility of an engineering expert's testimony." Pet. for Cert. i. We granted certiorari in light of uncertainty among the lower courts about whether, or how, *Daubert* applies to expert testimony that might be characterized as based not upon "scientific" knowledge, but rather upon "technical" or "other specialized" knowledge. Fed. Rule Evid.

702; *compare, e.g., Watkins v. Telsmith, Inc.*, 121 F.3d 984, 990–991 (CA5 1997), *with, e.g., Compton v. Subaru of America, Inc.*, 82 F.3d 1513, 1518–1519 (CA10), *cert. denied*, 519 U.S. 1042 (1996).

II

A

In *Daubert*, this Court held that Federal Rule of Evidence 702 imposes a special obligation upon a trial judge to "ensure that any and all scientific testimony . . . is not only relevant, but reliable." 509 U.S., at 589. The initial question before us is whether this basic gatekeeping obligation applies only to "scientific" testimony or to all expert testimony. We, like the parties, believe that it applies to all expert testimony. *See* Brief for Petitioners 19; Brief for Respondents 17.

For one thing, Rule 702 itself says:

> "If scientific, technical, or other specialized knowledge will assist the trier of fact to understand the evidence or to determine a fact in issue, a witness qualified as an expert by knowledge, skill, experience, training, or education, may testify thereto in the form of an opinion or otherwise."

This language makes no relevant distinction between "scientific" knowledge and "technical" or "other specialized" knowledge. It makes clear that any such knowledge might become the subject of expert testimony. In *Daubert*, the Court specified that it is the Rule's word "knowledge," not the words (like "scientific") that modify that word, that "establishes a standard of evidentiary reliability." 509 U.S., at 589–590. Hence, as a matter of language, the Rule applies its reliability standard to all "scientific," "technical," or "other specialized" matters within its scope. We concede that the Court in *Daubert* referred only to "scientific" knowledge. But as the Court there said, it referred to "scientific" testimony "because that [wa]s the nature of the expertise" at issue. *Id.*, at 590, n. 8.

Neither is the evidentiary rationale that underlay the Court's basic *Daubert* "gatekeeping" determination limited to "scientific" knowledge. *Daubert* pointed out that Federal Rules 702 and 703 grant expert witnesses testimonial latitude unavailable to other witnesses on the "assumption that the expert's opinion will have a reliable basis in the knowledge and experience of his discipline." *Id.*, at 592 (pointing out that experts may testify to opinions, including those that are not based on firsthand knowledge or observation). The Rules grant that latitude to all experts, not just to "scientific" ones.

Finally, it would prove difficult, if not impossible, for judges to administer evidentiary rules under which a gatekeeping obligation depended upon a distinction between "scientific" knowledge and "technical" or "other specialized" knowledge. There is no clear line that divides the one from the others. Disciplines such as engineering rest upon scientific knowledge. Pure scientific theory itself may depend for its development upon observation and properly engineered machinery. And conceptual efforts to distinguish the two are unlikely to produce clear legal lines capable of application in particular cases. *Cf.* Brief for National Academy of Engineering as *Amicus Curiae* 9 (scientist seeks to understand nature while the engineer seeks nature's modification); Brief for Rubber Manufacturers Association as *Amicus Curiae* 14–16 (engineering, as an "applied science," relies on "scientific reasoning and methodology"); Brief for John Allen et al. as *Amici Curiae* 6 (engineering relies upon "scientific knowledge and methods").

Neither is there a convincing need to make such distinctions. Experts of all kinds tie observations to conclusions through the use of what Judge Learned Hand called "general truths derived from . . . specialized experience." Hand, Historical and Practical Considerations Regarding Expert Testimony, 15 Harv. L. Rev. 40, 54 (1901). And whether the specific expert testimony focuses upon specialized observations, the specialized translation of those observations into theory, a specialized theory itself, or the application of such a theory in a particular case, the expert's testimony often will rest "upon an experience confessedly foreign in kind to [the jury's] own." *Ibid.* The trial judge's effort to assure that the specialized testimony is reliable and relevant can help the jury evaluate that foreign experience, whether the testimony reflects scientific, technical, or other specialized knowledge.

We conclude that *Daubert's* general principles apply to the expert matters described in Rule 702. The Rule, in respect to all such matters, "establishes a standard of evidentiary reliability." 509 U.S., at 590. It "requires a valid . . . connection to the pertinent inquiry as a precondition to admissibility." *Id.*, at 592. And where such testimony's factual basis, data, principles, methods, or their application are called sufficiently into question, see Part III, *infra*, the trial judge must determine whether the testimony has "a reliable basis in the knowledge and experience of [the relevant] discipline." 509 U.S., at 592.

B

The petitioners ask more specifically whether a trial judge determining the "admissibility of an engineering expert's testimony" may consider several more specific factors that *Daubert* said might "bear on" a judge's gate-keeping determination. These factors include:

- Whether a "theory or technique . . . can be (and has been) tested";

- Whether it "has been subjected to peer review and publication";

- Whether, in respect to a particular technique, there is a high "known or potential rate of error" and whether there are "standards controlling the technique's operation"; and

– Whether the theory or technique enjoys "general acceptance" within a "relevant scientific community." 509 U.S., at 592–594.

Emphasizing the word "may" in the question, we answer that question yes.

Engineering testimony rests upon scientific foundations, the reliability of which will be at issue in some cases. *See, e.g.*, Brief for Stephen Bobo et al. as *Amici Curiae* 23 (stressing the scientific bases of engineering disciplines). In other cases, the relevant reliability concerns may focus upon personal knowledge or experience. As the Solicitor General points out, there are many different kinds of experts, and many different kinds of expertise. *See* Brief for United States as *Amicus Curiae* 18–19, and n. 5 (citing cases involving experts in drug terms, handwriting analysis, criminal modus operandi, land valuation, agricultural practices, railroad procedures, attorney's fee valuation, and others). Our emphasis on the word "may" thus reflects *Daubert's* description of the Rule 702 inquiry as "a flexible one." 509 U.S., at 594. *Daubert* makes clear that the factors it mentions do not constitute a "definitive checklist or test." *Id.*, at 593. And *Daubert* adds that the gatekeeping inquiry must be "'tied to the facts'" of a particular "case." *Id.*, at 591 (quoting *United States v. Downing*, 753 F.2d 1224, 1242 (CA3 1985)). We agree with the Solicitor General that "[t]he factors identified in *Daubert* may or may not be pertinent in assessing reliability, depending on the nature of the issue, the expert's particular expertise, and the subject of his testimony." Brief for United States as *Amicus Curiae* 19. The conclusion, in our view, is that we can neither rule out, nor rule in, for all cases and for all time the applicability of the factors mentioned in *Daubert*, nor can we now do so for subsets of cases categorized by category of expert or by kind of evidence. Too much depends upon the particular circumstances of the particular case at issue.

Daubert itself is not to the contrary. It made clear that its list of factors was meant to be helpful, not definitive. Indeed, those factors do not all necessarily apply even in every instance in which the reliability of scientific testimony is challenged. It might not be surprising in a particular case, for example, that a claim made by a scientific witness has never been the subject of peer review, for the particular application at issue may never previously have interested any scientist. Nor, on the other hand, does the presence of *Daubert's* general acceptance factor help show that an expert's testimony is reliable where the discipline itself lacks reliability, as, for example, do theories grounded in any so-called generally accepted principles of astrology or necromancy. At the same time, and contrary to the Court of Appeals' view, some of *Daubert's* questions can help to evaluate the reliability even of experience-based testimony. In certain cases, it will be appropriate for the trial judge to ask, for example, how often an engineering expert's experience-based methodology has produced erroneous results, or whether such a method is generally accepted in the relevant engineering community. Likewise, it will at times be useful to ask even of a witness whose expertise is based purely on experience, say, a perfume tester able to distinguish among 140 odors at a sniff, whether his preparation is of a kind that others in the field would recognize as acceptable.

We must therefore disagree with the Eleventh Circuit's holding that a trial judge may ask questions of the sort *Daubert* mentioned only where an expert "relies on the application of scientific principles," but not where an expert relies "on skill- or experience-based observation." 131 F.3d, at 1435. We do not believe that Rule 702 creates a schematism that segregates expertise by type while mapping certain kinds of questions to certain kinds of experts. Life and the legal cases that it generates are too complex to warrant so definitive a match.

To say this is not to deny the importance of *Daubert*'s gatekeeping requirement. The objective of that requirement is to ensure the reliability and relevancy of expert testimony. It is to make certain that an expert, whether basing testimony upon professional studies or personal experience, employs in the courtroom the same level of intellectual rigor that characterizes the practice of an expert in the relevant field. Nor do we deny that, as stated in *Daubert*, the particular questions that it mentioned will often be appropriate for use in determining the reliability of challenged expert testimony. Rather, we conclude that the trial judge must have considerable leeway in deciding in a particular case how to go about determining whether particular expert testimony is reliable. That is to say, a trial court should consider the specific factors identified in *Daubert* where they are reasonable measures of the reliability of expert testimony.

C

The trial court must have the same kind of latitude in deciding how to test an expert's reliability, and to decide whether or when special briefing or other proceedings are needed to investigate reliability, as it enjoys when it decides whether that expert's relevant testimony is reliable. Our opinion in *Joiner* makes clear that a court of appeals is to apply an abuse-of-discretion standard when it "review[s] a trial court's decision to admit or exclude expert testimony." 522 U.S., at 138–139. That standard applies as much to the trial court's decisions about how to determine reliability as to its ultimate conclusion. Otherwise, the trial judge would lack the discretionary authority needed both to avoid unnecessary "reliability" proceedings in ordinary cases where the reliability of an expert's methods is properly taken for granted, and to require appropriate proceedings in the less usual or more complex cases where cause for questioning the expert's reliability arises. Indeed, the Rules seek to avoid "unjustifiable expense and delay" as part of their search for "truth" and the "jus[t] determin[ation]" of proceedings. Fed. Rule Evid. 102. Thus, whether *Daubert*'s specific factors are, or are not, reasonable measures of reliability in a particular case is a matter that the law grants the trial judge broad latitude to determine. *See Joiner, supra*, at 143. And the Eleventh Circuit erred insofar as it held to the contrary.

III

We further explain the way in which a trial judge "may" consider *Daubert's* factors by applying these considerations to the case at hand, a matter that has been briefed exhaustively by the parties and their 19 *amici*. The District Court did not doubt Carlson's qualifications, which included a masters degree in mechanical engineering, 10 years' work at Michelin America, Inc., and testimony as a tire failure consultant in other tort cases. Rather, it excluded the testimony because, despite those qualifications, it initially doubted, and then found unreliable, "the methodology employed by the expert in analyzing the data obtained in the visual inspection, and the scientific basis, if any, for such an analysis." Civ. Action No. 93-0860-CB-S (SD Ala., June 5, 1996), App. to Pet. for Cert. 6c. After examining the transcript in "some detail," 923 F. Supp., at 1518–519, n. 4, and after considering respondents' defense of Carlson's methodology, the District Court determined that Carlson's testimony was not reliable. It fell outside the range where experts might reasonably differ, and where the jury must decide among the conflicting views of different experts, even though the evidence is "shaky." *Daubert*, 509 U.S., at 596. In our view, the doubts that triggered the District Court's initial inquiry here were reasonable, as was the court's ultimate conclusion.

For one thing, and contrary to respondents' suggestion, the specific issue before the court was not the reasonableness in general of a tire expert's use of a visual and tactile inspection to determine whether overdeflection had caused the tire's tread to separate from its steel-belted carcass. Rather, it was the reasonableness of using such an approach, along with Carlson's particular method of analyzing the data thereby obtained, to draw a conclusion regarding the particular matter to which the expert testimony was directly relevant. That matter concerned the likelihood that a defect in the tire at issue caused its tread to separate from its carcass. The tire in question, the expert conceded, had traveled far enough so that some of the tread had been worn bald; it should have been taken out of service; it had been repaired (inadequately) for punctures; and it bore some of the very marks that the expert said indicated, not a defect, but abuse through overdeflection. *See supra*, at 3–5; App. 293–294. The relevant issue was whether the expert could reliably determine the cause of this tire's separation.

Nor was the basis for Carlson's conclusion simply the general theory that, in the absence of evidence of abuse, a defect will normally have caused a tire's separation. Rather, the expert employed a more specific theory to establish the existence (or absence) of such abuse. Carlson testified precisely that in the absence of at least two of four signs of abuse (proportionately greater tread wear on the shoulder; signs of grooves caused by the beads; discolored sidewalls; marks on the rim flange) he concludes that a defect caused the separation. And his analysis depended upon acceptance of a further implicit proposition, namely, that his visual and tactile inspection could determine that the tire before him had not been abused despite some evidence of the presence of the very signs for which he looked (and two punctures).

For another thing, the transcripts of Carlson's depositions support both the trial court's initial uncertainty and its final conclusion. Those transcripts cast considerable doubt upon the reliability of both the explicit theory (about the need for two signs of abuse) and the implicit proposition (about the significance of visual inspection in this case). Among other things, the expert could not say whether the tire had traveled more than 10, or 20, or 30, or 40, or 50 thousand miles, adding that 6,000 miles was "about how far" he could "say with any certainty." *Id.*, at 265. The court could reasonably have wondered about the reliability of a method of visual and tactile inspection sufficiently precise to ascertain with some certainty the abuse-related significance of minute shoulder/center relative tread wear differences, but insufficiently precise to tell "with any certainty" from the tread wear whether a tire had traveled less than 10,000 or more than 50,000 miles. And these concerns might have been augmented by Carlson's repeated reliance on the "subjective[ness]" of his mode of analysis in response to questions seeking specific information regarding how he could differentiate between a tire that actually had been overdeflected and a tire that merely looked as though it had been. *Id.*, at 222, 224–225, 285–286. They would have been further augmented by the fact that Carlson said he had inspected the tire itself for the first time the morning of his first deposition, and then only for a few hours. (His initial conclusions were based on photographs.) *Id.*, at 180.

Moreover, prior to his first deposition, Carlson had issued a signed report in which he concluded that the tire had "not been . . . overloaded or underinflated," not because of the absence of "two of four" signs of abuse, but simply because "the rim flange impressions . . . were normal." *Id.*, at 335–336. That report also said that the "tread depth remaining was 3/32 inch," *id.*, at 336, though the opposing expert's (apparently undisputed) measurements indicate that the tread depth taken at various positions around the tire actually ranged from 5/32 of an inch to 4/32 of an inch, with the tire apparently showing greater wear along both shoulders than along the center, *id.*, at 432–433.

Further, in respect to one sign of abuse, bead grooving, the expert seemed to deny the sufficiency of his own simple visual-inspection methodology. He testified that most tires have some bead groove pattern, that where there is reason to suspect an abnormal bead groove he would ideally "look at a lot of [similar] tires" to know the grooving's significance, and that he had not looked at many tires similar to the one at issue. *Id.*, at 212–213, 214, 217.

Finally, the court, after looking for a defense of Carlson's methodology as applied in these circumstances, found no convincing defense. Rather, it found (1) that "none" of the *Daubert* factors, including that of "general acceptance" in the relevant expert community, indicated that Carlson's testimony was reliable, 923 F. Supp., at 1521; (2) that its own analysis "revealed no countervailing factors operating in favor of admissibility which could outweigh those identified in *Daubert*," App. to Pet. for Cert. 4c; and

(3) that the "parties identified no such factors in their briefs," *ibid.* For these three reasons taken together, it concluded that Carlson's testimony was unreliable.

Respondents now argue to us, as they did to the District Court, that a method of tire failure analysis that employs a visual/tactile inspection is a reliable method, and they point both to its use by other experts and to Carlson's long experience working for Michelin as sufficient indication that that is so. But no one denies that an expert might draw a conclusion from a set of observations based on extensive and specialized experience. Nor does anyone deny that, as a general matter, tire abuse may often be identified by qualified experts through visual or tactile inspection of the tire. *See* Affidavit of H. R. Baumgardner 1–2, cited in Brief for National Academy of Forensic Engineers as *Amici Curiae* 16 (Tire engineers rely on visual examination and process of elimination to analyze experimental test tires). As we said before, *supra*, at 14, the question before the trial court was specific, not general. The trial court had to decide whether this particular expert had sufficient specialized knowledge to assist the jurors "in deciding the particular issues in the case." 4 J. McLaughlin, Weinstein's Federal Evidence ¶702.05[1], p. 702–33 (2d ed. 1998); *see also* Advisory Committee's Note on Proposed Fed. Rule Evid. 702, Preliminary Draft of Proposed Amendments to the Federal Rules of Civil Procedure and Evidence: Request for Comment 126 (1998) (stressing that district courts must "scrutinize" whether the "principles and methods" employed by an expert "have been properly applied to the facts of the case").

The particular issue in this case concerned the use of Carlson's two-factor test and his related use of visual/tactile inspection to draw conclusions on the basis of what seemed small observational differences. We have found no indication in the record that other experts in the Industry use Carlson's two-factor test or that tire experts such as Carlson normally make the very fine distinctions about, say, the symmetry of comparatively greater shoulder tread wear that were necessary, on Carlson's own theory, to support his conclusions. Nor, despite the prevalence of tire testing, does anyone refer to any articles or papers that validate Carlson's approach. *Compare* Bobo, Tire Flaws and Separations, in Mechanics of Pneumatic Tires 636–637 (S. Clark ed. 1981); C. Schnuth et al., Compression Grooving and Rim Flange Abrasion as Indicators of Over-Deflected Operating Conditions in Tires, presented to Rubber Division of the American Chemical Society, Oct. 21–24, 1997; J. Walter & R. Kiminecz, Bead Contact Pressure Measurements at the Tire-Rim Interface, presented to Society of Automotive Engineers, Feb. 24–28, 1975. Indeed, no one has argued that Carlson himself, were he still working for Michelin, would have concluded in a report to his employer that a similar tire was similarly defective on grounds identical to those upon which he rested his conclusion here. Of course, Carlson himself claimed that his method was accurate, but, as we pointed out in *Joiner*, "nothing in either *Daubert* or the Federal Rules of Evidence requires a district court to admit opinion evidence that is connected to existing data only by the *ipse dixit* of the expert." 522 U.S., at 146.

Respondents additionally argue that the District Court too rigidly applied *Daubert's* criteria. They read its opinion to hold that a failure to satisfy any one of those criteria automatically renders expert testimony inadmissible. The District Court's initial opinion might have been vulnerable to a form of this argument. There, the court, after rejecting respondents' claim that Carlson's testimony was "exempted from *Daubert*-style scrutiny" because it was "technical analysis" rather than "scientific evidence," simply added that "none of the four admissibility criteria outlined by the *Daubert* court are satisfied." 923 F. Supp., at 1522. Subsequently, however, the court granted respondents' motion for reconsideration. It then explicitly recognized that the relevant reliability inquiry "should be 'flexible,'" that its "'overarching subject [should be] . . . validity' and reliability," and that "*Daubert* was intended neither to be exhaustive nor to apply in every case." App. to Pet. for Cert. 4c (quoting *Daubert*, 509 U.S., at 594–595). And the court ultimately based its decision upon Carlson's failure to satisfy either *Daubert's* factors or any other set of reasonable reliability criteria. In light of the record as developed by the parties, that conclusion was within the District Court's lawful discretion. In sum, Rule 702 grants the district judge the discretionary authority, reviewable for its abuse, to determine reliability in light of the particular facts and circumstances of the particular case. The District Court did not abuse its discretionary authority in this case. Hence, the judgment of the Court of Appeals is

Reversed.

JUSTICE SCALIA, with whom JUSTICE O'CONNOR and JUSTICE THOMAS join, concurring.

I join the opinion of the Court, which makes clear that the discretion it endorses—trial-court discretion in choosing the manner of testing expert reliability—is not discretion to abandon the gatekeeping function. I think it worth adding that it is not discretion to perform the function inadequately. Rather, it is discretion to choose among reasonable means of excluding expertise that is fausse and science that is junky. Though, as the Court makes clear today, the *Daubert* factors are not holy writ, in a particular case the failure to apply one or another of them may be unreasonable, and hence an abuse of discretion.

OPINION

JUSTICE STEVENS, concurring in part and dissenting in part.

The only question that we granted certiorari to decide is whether a trial judge "[m]ay . . . consider the four factors set out by this Court in *Daubert v. Merrill Dow Pharmaceuticals, Inc.*, 509 U.S. 579 (1993), in a Rule 702 analysis of admissibility of an engineering expert's testimony." Pet. for Cert. i. That question is fully and correctly answered in Parts I and II of the Court's opinion, which I join.

Part III answers the quite different question whether the trial judge abused his discretion when he excluded the testimony of Dennis Carlson. Because a proper answer to that question requires a study of the record that can be performed more efficiently by the Court of Appeals than by the nine Members of this Court, I would remand the case to the Eleventh Circuit to perform that task. There are, of course, exceptions to most rules, but I firmly believe that it is neither fair to litigants nor good practice for this Court to reach out to decide questions not raised by the certiorari petition. *See General Electric Co. v. Joiner*, 522 U.S. 136, 150–151 (1997) (Stevens, J., concurring in part and dissenting in part).

Accordingly, while I do not feel qualified to disagree with the well-reasoned factual analysis in Part III of the Court's opinion, I do not join that Part, and I respectfully dissent from the Court's disposition of the case.

MELENDEZ-DIAZ V. MASSACHUSETTS
577 U.S. 305 (2009)

At petitioner's state-court drug trial, the prosecution introduced certificates of state laboratory analysts stating that material seized by police and connected to petitioner was cocaine of a certain quantity. As required by Massachusetts law, the certificates were sworn to before a notary public and were submitted as prima facie evidence of what they asserted. Petitioner objected, asserting that *Crawford v. Washington*, 541 U.S. 36, required the analysts to testify in person. The trial court disagreed, the certificates were admitted, and petitioner was convicted. The Massachusetts Appeals Court affirmed, rejecting petitioner's claim that the certificates' admission violated the Sixth Amendment.

Held:

The admission of the certificates violated petitioner's Sixth Amendment right to confront the witnesses against him.

(a) Under *Crawford*, a witness's testimony against a defendant is inadmissible unless the witness appears at trial or, if the witness is unavailable, the defendant had a prior opportunity for cross-examination. 541 U.S., at 54. The certificates here are affidavits, which fall within the "core class of testimonial statements" covered by the Confrontation Clause, *id.*, at 51. They asserted that the substance found in petitioner's possession was, as the prosecution claimed, cocaine of a certain weight—the precise testimony the analysts would be expected to provide if called at trial. Not only were the certificates made, as *Crawford* required for testimonial statements, "under circumstances which would lead an objective witness reasonably to believe that the statement would be available for use at a later trial," *id.*, at 52, but under the relevant Massachusetts law their *sole purpose* was to provide prima facie evidence of the substance's composition, quality, and net weight. Petitioner was entitled to "be confronted with" the persons giving this testimony at trial.

(b) The arguments advanced to avoid this rather straightforward application of *Crawford* are rejected. Respondent's claim that the analysts are not subject to confrontation because they are not "accusatory" witnesses finds no support in the Sixth Amendment's text or in this Court's case law. The affiants' testimonial statements were not "nearly contemporaneous" with their observations, nor, if they had been, would that fact alter the statements' testimonial character. There is no support for the proposition that witnesses who testify regarding facts other than those observed at the crime scene are exempt from confrontation. The absence of interrogation is irrelevant; a witness who volunteers his testimony is no less a witness for Sixth Amendment purposes. The affidavits do not qualify as traditional official or business records. The argument that the analysts should not be subject to confrontation because their statements result from neutral scientific testing is little more than an invitation to return to the since-overruled decision in *Ohio v. Roberts*, 448 U.S. 56, 66, which held that evidence with "particularized guarantees of trustworthiness" was admissible without confrontation. Petitioner's power to subpoena the analysts is no substitute for the right of confrontation. Finally, the requirements of the Confrontation Clause may not be relaxed because they make the prosecution's task burdensome. In any event, the practice in many States already accords with today's decision, and the serious disruption predicted by respondent and the dissent has not materialized.

Reversed and remanded.

Opinion

JUSTICE SCALIA delivered the opinion of the Court.

The Massachusetts courts in this case admitted into evidence affidavits reporting the results of forensic analysis which showed that material seized by the police and connected to the defendant was cocaine. The question presented is whether those affidavits are "testimonial," rendering the affiants "witnesses" subject to the defendant's right of confrontation under the Sixth Amendment.

I

In 2001, Boston police officers received a tip that a Kmart employee, Thomas Wright, was engaging in suspicious activity. The informant reported that Wright repeatedly received phone calls at work, after each of which he would be picked up in front of the store by a blue sedan, and would return to the store a short time later. The police set up surveillance in the Kmart parking lot and witnessed this precise sequence of events. When Wright got out of the car upon his return, one of the officers detained and searched him, finding four clear white plastic bags containing a substance resembling cocaine. The officer then signaled other officers on the scene to arrest the two men in the car—one of whom was petitioner Luis Melendez-Diaz. The officers placed all three men in a police cruiser.

During the short drive to the police station, the officers observed their passengers fidgeting and making furtive movements in the back of the car. After depositing the men at the station, they searched the police cruiser and found a plastic bag containing 19 smaller plastic bags hidden in the partition between the front and back seats. They submitted the seized evidence to a state laboratory required by law to conduct chemical analysis upon police request. Mass. Gen. Laws, ch. 111, § 12 (West 2006).

Melendez-Diaz was charged with distributing cocaine and with trafficking in cocaine in an amount between 14 and 28 grams. At trial, the prosecution placed into evidence the bags seized from Wright and from the police cruiser. It also submitted three "certificates of analysis" showing the results of the forensic analysis performed on the seized substances. The certificates reported the weight of the seized bags and stated that the bags "[h]a[ve] been examined with the following results: The substance was found to contain: Cocaine." App. to Pet. for Cert. 24a, 26a, 28a. The certificates were sworn to before a notary public by analysts at the State Laboratory Institute of the Massachusetts Department of Public Health, as required under Massachusetts law. Mass. Gen. Laws, ch. 111, § 13.

Petitioner objected to the admission of the certificates, asserting that our Confrontation Clause decision in *Crawford v. Washington*, 541 U.S. 36 (2004), required the analysts to testify in person. The objection was overruled, and the certificates were admitted pursuant to state law as "prima facie evidence of the composition, quality, and the net weight of the narcotic . . . analyzed." Mass. Gen. Laws, ch. 111, § 13.

The jury found Melendez-Diaz guilty. He appealed, contending, among other things, that admission of the certificates violated his Sixth Amendment right to be confronted with the witnesses against him. The Appeals Court of Massachusetts rejected the claim, affirmance order, 870 N.E.2d (July 31, 2007), relying on the Massachusetts Supreme Judicial Court's decision in *Commonwealth v. Verde*, 827 N.E.2d 701 (2005), which held that the authors of certificates of forensic analysis are not subject to confrontation under the Sixth Amendment. The Supreme Judicial Court denied review. 874 N.E.2d 407 (2007). We granted certiorari. 552 U.S. 1256 (2008).

II

The Sixth Amendment to the United States Constitution, made applicable to the States via the Fourteenth Amendment, *Pointer v. Texas*, 380 U.S. 400 (1965), provides that "[i]n all criminal prosecutions, the accused shall enjoy the right . . . to be confronted with the witnesses against him." In *Crawford*, after reviewing the Clause's historical underpinnings, we held that it guarantees a defendant's right to confront those "who 'bear testimony'" against him. 541 U.S., at 51. A witness's testimony against a defendant is thus inadmissible unless the witness appears at trial or, if the witness is unavailable, the defendant had a prior opportunity for cross-examination. *Id.*, at 54.

Our opinion described the class of testimonial statements covered by the Confrontation Clause as follows:

Various formulations of this core class of testimonial statements exist: *ex parte* in-court testimony or its functional equivalent—that is, material such as affidavits, custodial examinations, prior testimony that the defendant was unable to cross-examine, or similar pretrial statements that declarants would reasonably expect to be used prosecutorially; extrajudicial statements . . . contained in formalized testimonial materials, such as affidavits, depositions, prior testimony, or confessions; statements that were made under circumstances which would lead an objective witness reasonably to believe that the statement would be available for use at a later trial." *Id.,* at 51–52 (internal quotation marks and citations omitted).

There is little doubt that the documents at issue in this case fall within the "core class of testimonial statements" thus described. Our description of that category mentions affidavits twice. *See also White v. Illinois,* 502 U.S. 346 (1992) (Thomas, J., concurring in part and concurring in judgment) ("[T]he Confrontation Clause is implicated by extrajudicial statements only insofar as they are contained in formalized testimonial materials, such as affidavits, depositions, prior testimony, or confessions"). The documents at issue here, while denominated by Massachusetts law "certificates," are quite plainly affidavits: "declaration[s] of facts written down and sworn to by the declarant before an officer authorized to administer oaths." Black's Law Dictionary 62 (8th ed. 2004). They are incontrovertibly a "'solemn declaration or affirmation made for the purpose of establishing or proving some fact.'" *Crawford, supra,* at 51 (quoting 2 N. Webster, An American Dictionary of the English Language (1828)). The fact in question is that the substance found in the possession of Melendez-Diaz and his codefendants was, as the prosecution claimed, cocaine—the precise testimony the analysts would be expected to provide if called at trial. The "certificates" are functionally identical to live, in-court testimony, doing "precisely what a witness does on direct examination." *Davis v. Washington,* 547 U.S. 813 (2006) (emphasis deleted).

Here, moreover, not only were the affidavits "'made under circumstances which would lead an objective witness reasonably to believe that the statement would be available for use at a later trial,'" *Crawford, supra,* at 52, but under Massachusetts law the *sole purpose* of the affidavits was to provide "prima facie evidence of the composition, quality, and the net weight" of the analyzed substance, Mass. Gen. Laws, ch. 111, § 13. We can safely assume that the analysts were aware of the affidavits' evidentiary purpose, since that purpose—as stated in the relevant state-law provision—was reprinted on the affidavits themselves. *See* App. to Pet. for Cert. 25a, 27a, 29a.

In short, under our decision in *Crawford* the analysts' affidavits were testimonial statements, and the analysts were "witnesses" for purposes of the Sixth Amendment. Absent a showing that the analysts were unavailable to testify at trial *and* that petitioner had a prior opportunity to cross-examine them, petitioner was entitled to "'be confronted with'" the analysts at trial. *Crawford, supra*, at 54.[1]

III

Respondent and the dissent advance a potpourri of analytic arguments in an effort to avoid this rather straightforward application of our holding in *Crawford*. Before addressing them, however, we must assure the reader of the falsity of the dissent's opening alarum that we are "sweep[ing] away an accepted rule governing the admission of scientific evidence" that has been "established for at least 90 years" and "extends across at least 35 States and six Federal Courts of Appeals."

The vast majority of the state-court cases the dissent cites in support of this claim come not from the last 90 years, but from the last 30, and not surprisingly nearly all of them rely on our decision in *Ohio v. Roberts*, 448 U.S. 56 (1980), or its since-rejected theory that unconfronted testimony was admissible as long as it bore indicia of reliability, *id.*, at 66.[2] As for the six Federal Courts of Appeals cases cited by the dissent, five of them postdated and expressly relied on *Roberts*. The sixth predated *Roberts* but relied entirely on the same erroneous theory. *See Kay v. United States*, 255 F.2d 476 (CA4 1958) (rejecting Confrontation Clause challenge "where there is reasonable necessity for [the evidence] and where . . . the evidence has those qualities of reliability and trustworthiness").

A review of cases that predate the *Roberts* era yields a mixed picture. As the dissent notes, three State Supreme Court decisions from the early 20th century denied confrontation with respect to certificates of analysis regarding a substance's alcohol content. *See post* (citing cases from Massachusetts, Connecticut, and Virginia). But other state courts in the same era reached the opposite conclusion. *See Torres v. State*, 18 S.W.2d 179, 180 (Tex. Crim. App. 1929); *Volrich v. State*, 4 Ohio Law Abs. 253, 1925 WL 2473 (App. 1925) (per curiam). At least this much is entirely clear: In faithfully applying *Crawford* to the facts of this case, we are not overruling

---

1. Contrary to the dissent's suggestion, *post* (opinion of Kennedy, J.), we do not hold, and it is not the case, that anyone whose testimony may be relevant in establishing the chain of custody, authenticity of the sample, or accuracy of the testing device, must appear in person as part of the prosecution's case. While the dissent is correct that "[it] is the obligation of the prosecution to establish the chain of custody," this does not mean that everyone who laid hands on the evidence must be called. As stated in the dissent's own quotation, *ibid.*, from *United States v. Lott*, 854 F.2d 244, 250 (CA7 1988), "gaps in the chain [of custody] normally go to the weight of the evidence rather than its admissibility." It is up to the prosecution to decide what steps in the chain of custody are so crucial as to require evidence; but what testimony *is* introduced must (if the defendant objects) be introduced live. Additionally, documents prepared in the regular course of equipment maintenance may well qualify as nontestimonial records. *See infra*.

2. The exception is a single pre-*Roberts* case that relied on longstanding Massachusetts precedent. *See Commonwealth v. Harvard*, 356 Mass. 452, 462 (1969). Others are simply irrelevant, since they involved medical reports created for treatment purposes, which would not be testimonial under our decision today. *See, e.g., Baber v. State*, 775 So. 2d 258 (Fla. 2000); *State v. Garlick*, 313 Md. 209, 223–225 (1988).

90 years of settled jurisprudence. It is the dissent that seeks to overturn precedent by resurrecting *Roberts* a mere five years after it was rejected in *Crawford*.

We turn now to the various legal arguments raised by respondent and the dissent.

A

Respondent first argues that the analysts are not subject to confrontation because they are not "accusatory" witnesses, in that they do not directly accuse petitioner of wrongdoing; rather, their testimony is inculpatory only when taken together with other evidence linking petitioner to the contraband. *See* Brief for Respondent 10. This finds no support in the text of the Sixth Amendment or in our case law.

The Sixth Amendment guarantees a defendant the right "to be confronted with the witnesses against him." (Emphasis added.) To the extent the analysts were witnesses (a question resolved above), they certainly provided testimony against petitioner, proving one fact necessary for his conviction—that the substance he possessed was cocaine. The contrast between the text of the Confrontation Clause and the text of the adjacent Compulsory Process Clause confirms this analysis. While the Confrontation Clause guarantees a defendant the right to be confronted with the witnesses "against him," the Compulsory Process Clause guarantees a defendant the right to call witnesses "in his favor." U.S. Const., Amdt. 6. The text of the Amendment contemplates two classes of witnesses—those against the defendant and those in his favor. The prosecution must produce the former;[3] the defendant may call the latter. Contrary to respondent's assertion, there is not a third category of witnesses, helpful to the prosecution, but somehow immune from confrontation.

It is often, indeed perhaps usually, the case that an adverse witness's testimony, taken alone, will not suffice to convict. Yet respondent fails to cite a single case in which such testimony was admitted absent a defendant's opportunity to cross-examine.[4] Unsurprisingly, since such a holding would be contrary to longstanding case law. In *Kirby v. United States*, 174 U.S. 47 (1899), the Court considered Kirby's conviction for receiving stolen property, the evidence for which consisted, in part, of the records of conviction of three individuals who were found guilty of stealing the relevant property. *Id.*, at 53. Though this evidence proved only that the property was stolen, and not that Kirby received it, the Court nevertheless ruled that admission

3. The right to confrontation may, of course, be waived, including by failure to object to the offending evidence; and States may adopt procedural rules governing the exercise of such objections. *See infra.*
4. Respondent cites our decision in *Gray v. Maryland*, 523 U.S. 185 (1998). That case did indeed distinguish between evidence that is "incriminating on its face" and evidence "bec[omes] incriminating . . . only when linked with evidence introduced later at trial," *id.* at 191 (internal quotation marks omitted). But it did so for the entirely different purpose of determining when a nontestifying codefendant's confession, redacted to remove all mention of the defendant, could be admitted into evidence with instruction for the jury not to consider the confession as evidence against the nonconfessor. The very premise of the case was that, without the limiting instruction even admission of a redacted confession containing evidence of the latter sort *would have* violated the defendant's Sixth Amendment rights. *See id.* at 190–191,

of the records violated Kirby's rights under the Confrontation Clause. *Id.*, at 55. *See also King v. Turner*, 1 Mood. 347, 168 Eng. Rep. 1298 (1832) (confession by one defendant to having stolen certain goods could not be used as evidence against another defendant accused of receiving the stolen property).

B

Respondent and the dissent argue that the analysts should not be subject to confrontation because they are not "conventional" (or "typical" or "ordinary") witnesses of the sort whose *ex parte* testimony was most notoriously used at the trial of Sir Walter Raleigh. *Post*; Brief for Respondent 28. It is true, as the Court recognized in *Crawford*, that *ex parte* examinations of the sort used at Raleigh's trial have "long been thought a paradigmatic confrontation violation." 541 U.S., at 52. But the paradigmatic case identifies the core of the right to confrontation, not its limits. The right to confrontation was not invented in response to the use of the *ex parte* examinations in *Raleigh's Case*, 2 How. St. Tr. 1 (1603). That use provoked such an outcry precisely because it flouted the deeply rooted common-law tradition "of live testimony in court subject to adversarial testing." *Crawford, supra,* at 43 (citing 3 W. Blackstone, Commentaries on the Laws of England 373–374. *See also Crawford, supra,* at 43–47.

In any case, the purported distinctions respondent and the dissent identify between this case and Sir Walter Raleigh's "conventional" accusers do not survive scrutiny. The dissent first contends that a "conventional witness recalls events observed in the past, while an analyst's report contains near-contemporaneous observations of the test." It is doubtful that the analyst's reports in this case could be characterized as reporting "near-contemporaneous observations"; the affidavits were completed almost a week after the tests were performed. *See* App. to Pet. for Cert. 24a–29a (the tests were performed on November 28, 2001, and the affidavits sworn on December 4, 2001). But regardless, the dissent misunderstands the role that "near-contemporaneity" has played in our case law. The dissent notes that that factor was given "substantial weight" in *Davis*, but in fact that decision *disproves* the dissent's position. There the Court considered the admissibility of statements made to police officers responding to a report of a domestic disturbance. By the time officers arrived the assault had ended, but the victim's statements—written and oral—were sufficiently close in time to the alleged assault that the trial court admitted her affidavit as a "present sense impression." *Davis*, 547 U.S., at 820 (internal quotation marks omitted). Though the witness's statements in *Davis* were "near-contemporaneous" to the events she reported, we nevertheless held that they could *not* be admitted absent an opportunity to confront the witness. *Id.*, at 830.

A second reason the dissent contends that the analysts are not "conventional witnesses" (and thus not subject to confrontation) is that they "observe[d] neither the crime nor any human action related to it." The dissent provides no authority for this particular limitation of the type of witnesses subject to confrontation. Nor is it conceivable that all witnesses who fit this description would be outside the scope of the Confrontation Clause. For example, is a police officer's investigative report describing the crime scene admissible absent an opportunity to examine the officer? The dissent's novel exception from coverage of the Confrontation Clause would exempt all expert witnesses—a hardly "unconventional" class of witnesses.

A third respect in which the dissent asserts that the analysts are not "conventional" witnesses and thus not subject to confrontation is that their statements were not provided in response to interrogation. *See also* Brief for Respondent 29. As we have explained, "[t]he Framers were no more willing to exempt from cross-examination volunteered testimony or answers to open-ended questions than they were to exempt answers to detailed interrogation." *Davis, supra*, at 822–823, n 1. Respondent and the dissent cite no authority, and we are aware of none, holding that a person who volunteers his testimony is any less a "'witness against' the defendant," Brief for Respondent 26, than one who is responding to interrogation. In any event, the analysts' affidavits in this case *were* presented in response to a police request. *See* Mass. Gen. Laws, ch. 111, §§ 12–13. If an affidavit submitted in response to a police officer's request to "write down what happened" suffices to trigger the Sixth Amendment's protection (as it apparently does, *see Davis*, 547 U.S., at 819–820 (Thomas, J., concurring in judgment in part and dissenting in part)), then the analysts' testimony should be subject to confrontation as well.

C

Respondent claims that there is a difference, for Confrontation Clause purposes, between testimony recounting historical events, which is "prone to distortion or manipulation," and the testimony at issue here, which is the "resul[t] of neutral, scientific testing." Brief for Respondent 29. Relatedly, respondent and the dissent argue that confrontation of forensic analysts would be of little value because "one would not reasonably expect a laboratory professional . . . to feel quite differently about the results of his scientific test by having to look at the defendant." *Id.,* at 31 (internal quotation marks omitted).

This argument is little more than an invitation to return to our over-ruled decision in *Roberts*, 448 U.S. 56, which held that evidence with "particularized guarantees of trustworthiness" was admissible notwithstanding the Confrontation Clause. *Id.*, at 66. What we said in *Crawford* in response to that argument remains true:

"To be sure, the Clause's ultimate goal is to ensure reliability of evidence, but it is a procedural rather than a substantive guarantee. It commands, not that evidence be reliable, but that reliability be assessed in a particular manner: by testing in the crucible of cross-examination. . . .

Dispensing with confrontation because testimony is obviously reliable is akin to dispensing with jury trial because a defendant is obviously guilty. This is not what the Sixth Amendment prescribes." 541 U.S., at 61–62.

Respondent and the dissent may be right that there are other ways—and in some cases better ways—to challenge or verify the results of a forensic test.[5] But the Constitution guarantees one way: confrontation. We do not have license to suspend the Confrontation Clause when a preferable trial strategy is available.

Nor is it evident that what respondent calls "neutral scientific testing" is as neutral or as reliable as respondent suggests. Forensic evidence is not uniquely immune from the risk of manipulation. According to a recent study conducted under the auspices of the National Academy of Sciences, "[t]he majority of [laboratories producing forensic evidence] are administered by law enforcement agencies, such as police departments, where the laboratory administrator reports to the head of the agency." National Research Council of the National Academies, Strengthening Forensic Science in the United States: A Path Forward 183 (2009) (hereinafter National Academy Report). And "[b]ecause forensic scientists often are driven in their work by a need to answer a particular question related to the issues of a particular case, they sometimes face pressure to sacrifice appropriate methodology for the sake of expediency." *Id.*, at 23–24. A forensic analyst responding to a request from a law enforcement official may feel pressure—or have an incentive—to alter the evidence in a manner favorable to the prosecution.

Confrontation is one means of assuring accurate forensic analysis. While it is true, as the dissent notes, that an honest analyst will not alter his testimony when forced to confront the defendant, *post*, the same cannot be said of the fraudulent analyst. *See* Brief for National Innocence Network as *Amicus Curiae* 15–17 (discussing cases of documented "drylabbing" where forensic analysts report results of tests that were never performed); National Academy Report 44–48 (discussing documented cases of fraud and error involving the use of forensic evidence). Like the eyewitness who has fabricated his account to the police, the analyst who provides false results may, under oath in open court, reconsider his false testimony. *See Coy v. Iowa*, 487 U.S. 1012 (1988). And, of course, the prospect of confrontation will deter fraudulent analysis in the first place.

Confrontation is designed to weed out not only the fraudulent analyst, but the incompetent one as well. Serious deficiencies have been found in the forensic evidence used in criminal trials. One commentator asserts that "[t]he legal community now concedes, with varying degrees of urgency, that our system produces erroneous convictions based on discredited forensics." Metzger, Cheating the Constitution, 59 Vand. L. Rev. 475, 491 (2006). One study of cases in which exonerating evidence resulted in the overturning of criminal convictions concluded that invalid

---

5. Though surely not always. Some forensic analyses, such as autopsies and breathalyzer tests, cannot be repeated, and the specimens used for other analyses have often been lost or degraded.

forensic testimony contributed to the convictions in 60% of the cases. Garrett & Neufeld, Invalid Forensic Science Testimony and Wrongful Convictions, 95 Va. L. Rev. 1, 14 (2009). And the National Academy Report concluded:

> "The forensic science system, encompassing both research and practice, has serious problems that can only be addressed by a national commitment to overhaul the current structure that supports the forensic science community in this country." National Academy Report, at *xx*.[6]

Like expert witnesses generally, an analyst's lack of proper training or deficiency in judgment may be disclosed in cross-examination.

This case is illustrative. The affidavits submitted by the analysts contained only the bare-bones statement that "[t]he substance was found to contain: Cocaine." App. to Pet. for Cert. 24a, 26a, 28a. At the time of trial, petitioner did not know what tests the analysts performed, whether those tests were routine, and whether interpreting their results required the exercise of judgment or the use of skills that the analysts may not have possessed. While we still do not know the precise tests used by the analysts, we are told that the laboratories use "methodology recommended by the Scientific Working Group for the Analysis of Seized Drugs," App. to Brief for Petitioner 1a–2a. At least some of that methodology requires the exercise of judgment and presents a risk of error that might be explored on cross-examination. *See* 2 P. Giannelli & E. Imwinkelried, Scientific Evidence § 23.03[c], pp 532–533, and ch. 23A, p 607 (4th ed. 2007) (identifying four "critical errors" that analysts may commit in interpreting the results of the commonly used gas chromatography/mass spectrometry analysis); Shellow, The Application of Daubert to the Identification of Drugs, 2 Shepard's Expert & Scientific Evidence Quarterly 593, 600 (1995) (noting that while spectrometers may be equipped with computerized matching systems, "forensic analysts in crime laboratories typically do not utilize this feature of the instrument, but rely exclusively on their subjective judgment").

The same is true of many of the other types of forensic evidence commonly used in criminal prosecutions. "[T]here is wide variability across forensic science disciplines with regard to techniques, methodologies, reliability, types and numbers of potential errors, research, general acceptability, and published material." National Academy Report 6–7. *See also id.*, at 138–139, 142–143, 154–155 (discussing problems of subjectivity, bias, and unreliability of common forensic tests such as latent fingerprint analysis, pattern/impression analysis, and toolmark and firearms analysis). Contrary to respondent's and the dissent's suggestion, there is little reason

---

6. Contrary to the dissent's suggestion, we do not "rel[y] in such great measure" on the deficiencies of crime-lab analysts shown by this report to resolved the constitutional question presented in this case. The analysts who swore the affidavits provided testimony against Melendez-Diaz, and they are therefore subject to confrontation; we would reach the same conclusion if all analysts always possessed the scientific acumen of Mme. Curie and the veracity of Mother Theresa. We discuss the report only to refute the suggestion that this category of evidence is uniquely reliable and that cross-examination of the analysts would be an empty formalism.

to believe that confrontation will be useless in testing analysts' honesty, proficiency, and methodology—the features that are commonly the focus in the cross-examination of experts.

D

Respondent argues that the analysts' affidavits are admissible without confrontation because they are "akin to the types of official and business records admissible at common law." Brief for Respondent 35. But the affidavits do not qualify as traditional official or business records, and even if they did, their authors would be subject to confrontation nonetheless.

Documents kept in the regular course of business may ordinarily be admitted at trial despite their hearsay status. *See* Fed. Rule Evid. 803(6). But that is not the case if the regularly conducted business activity is the production of evidence for use at trial. Our decision in *Palmer v. Hoffman*, 318 U.S. 109 (1943), made that distinction clear. There we held that an accident report provided by an employee of a railroad company did not qualify as a business record because, although kept in the regular course of the railroad's operations, it was "calculated for use essentially in the court, not in the business." *Id.*, at 114.[7] The analysts' certificates—like police reports generated by law enforcement officials—do not qualify as business or public records for precisely the same reason. *See* Rule 803(8) (defining public records as "excluding, however, in criminal cases matters observed by police officers and other law enforcement personnel").

Respondent seeks to rebut this limitation by noting that at common law the results of a coroner's inquest were admissible without an opportunity for confrontation. But as we have previously noted, whatever the status of coroner's reports at common law in England, they were not accorded any special status in American practice. *See Crawford*, 541 U.S., at 47, n. 2; *Giles v. California*, 554 U.S. 353, 399–400 (2008) (Breyer, J., dissenting); Note, Evidence—Official Records—Coroner's Inquest, 65 U. Pa. L. Rev. 290 (1917).

The dissent identifies a single class of evidence which, though prepared for use at trial, was traditionally admissible: a clerk's certificate authenticating an official record—or a copy thereof—for use as evidence. But a clerk's authority in that regard was narrowly circumscribed. He was permitted "to certify to the correctness of a copy of a record kept in his office," but had "no authority to furnish, as evidence for the trial of a lawsuit, his interpretation of what the record contains or shows, or to certify to its substance or effect." *State v. Wilson*, 75 So. 95, 97 (La. 1917). *See also State v. Champion*, 21 S. E. 700, 700–701 (NC 1895); 5 J. Wigmore, Evidence

---

7. The early common-law cases likewise involve records prepared for the administration of an entity's affairs, and not for use in litigation. *See, e.g., King v. Rhodes*, 1 Leach 24 (1742) (admitting into evidence ship's muster book); *King v. Martin*, 2 Camp. 100, 101 (1809) (vestry book); *King v. Aickles*, 1 Leach 390, 391–392 (1785) (prison logbook).

§ 1678 (3d ed. 1940). The dissent suggests that the fact that this exception was "'narrowly circumscribed'" makes no difference. To the contrary, it makes all the difference in the world. It shows that even the line of cases establishing the one narrow exception the dissent has been able to identify simultaneously vindicates the general rule applicable to the present case. A clerk could by affidavit authenticate or provide a copy of an otherwise admissible record, but could not do what the analysts did here: create a record for the sole purpose of providing evidence against a defendant.[8]

Far more probative here are those cases in which the prosecution sought to admit into evidence a clerk's certificate attesting to the fact that the clerk had searched for a particular relevant record and failed to find it. Like the testimony of the analysts in this case, the clerk's statement would serve as substantive evidence against the defendant whose guilt depended on the nonexistence of the record for which the clerk searched. Although the clerk's certificate would qualify as an official record under respondent's definition—it was prepared by a public officer in the regular course of his official duties—and although the clerk was certainly not a "conventional witness" under the dissent's approach, the clerk was nonetheless subject to confrontation. *See People v. Bromwich*, 93 N. E. 933, 934, (NY 1911); *People v. Goodrode*, 94 N. W. 14, 16 (Mich. 1903); Wigmore, *supra*, § 1678.[9]

Respondent also misunderstands the relationship between the business-and-official-records hearsay exceptions and the Confrontation Clause. As we stated in Crawford: "Most of the hearsay exceptions covered statements that by their nature were not testimonial—for example, business records or statements in furtherance of a conspiracy." 541 U.S., at 56. Business and public records are generally admissible absent confrontation not because they qualify under an exception to the hearsay rules, but because—having been created for the administration of an entity's affairs and not for the purpose of establishing or proving some fact at trial—they are not testimonial. Whether or not they qualify as business or official records, the analysts' statements here—prepared specifically for use at petitioner's trial—were testimony against petitioner, and the analysts were subject to confrontation under the Sixth Amendment.

---

8. The dissent's reliance on our decision in *Dowdell v. United States*, 221 U.S. 325 (1911) is similarly misplaced. As the opinion stated in *Dowdell*—and as this Court noted in *Davis v. Washington*, 547 U.S. 813, 825 (2006)—the judge and clerk who made the statements at issue in *Dowdell* were not witnesses for purposes of the Confrontation Clause because their statements concerned only the conduct of the defendants' prior to trial, not any facts regarding defendants' guilt or innocence. 221 U.S. at 330–331.
9. An earlier line of 19th century state-court cases also supports the notion that forensic analysts' certificates were not admitted into evidence as pubic or business records. *See Commonwealth v. Waite*, 93 Mass. 264 (1865); *Shivers v. Newton*, 45 N.J.L. 469, 476 (Sup. Ct. 1883); *State v. Campbell*, 64 N.H. 402, 403 (1888). In all three cases, defendants—who were prosecuted for selling adulterated milk—objected to the admission of the state chemists' certificates of analysis. In all three cases, the objection was defeated because the chemist testified live at trial. That the prosecution came forward with live witnesses in all three cases suggests doubt as to the admissibility of the certificates without opportunity for cross-examination.

E

Respondent asserts that we should find no Confrontation Clause violation in this case because petitioner had the ability to subpoena the analysts. But that power—whether pursuant to state law or the Compulsory Process Clause—is no substitute for the right of confrontation. Unlike the Confrontation Clause, those provisions are of no use to the defendant when the witness is unavailable or simply refuses to appear. *See, e.g., Davis,* 547 U.S., at 820 ("[The witness] was subpoenaed, but she did not appear at . . . trial"). Converting the prosecution's duty under the Confrontation Clause into the defendant's privilege under state law or the Compulsory Process Clause shifts the consequences of adverse-witness no-shows from the State to the accused. More fundamentally, the Confrontation Clause imposes a burden on the prosecution to present its witnesses, not on the defendant to bring those adverse witnesses into court. Its value to the defendant is not replaced by a system in which the prosecution presents its evidence via ex parte affidavits and waits for the defendant to subpoena the affiants if he chooses.

F

Finally, respondent asks us to relax the requirements of the Confrontation Clause to accommodate the "'necessities of trial and the adversary process.'" Brief for Respondent 59. It is not clear whence we would derive the authority to do so. The Confrontation Clause may make the prosecution of criminals more burdensome, but that is equally true of the right to trial by jury and the privilege against self-incrimination. The Confrontation Clause—like those other constitutional provisions—is binding, and we may not disregard it at our convenience.

We also doubt the accuracy of respondent's and the dissent's dire predictions. The dissent, respondent, and its amici highlight the substantial total number of controlled-substance analyses performed by state and federal laboratories in recent years. But only some of those tests are implicated in prosecutions, and only a small fraction of those cases actually proceed to trial. *See* Brief for Law Professors as Amici Curiae 7–8 (nearly 95% of convictions in state and federal courts are obtained via guilty plea).[10]

Perhaps the best indication that the sky will not fall after today's decision is that it has not done so already. Many States have already adopted the constitutional rule

---

10. The dissent provides some back-of-the-envelope calculations regarding the number of court appearances that will result from today's ruling. Those numbers rely on various unfounded assumptions: that the prosecution will place into evidence a drug analysis certificate in every case; that the defendant will never stipulate to the nature of the controlled substance; that even where no such stipulation is made, every defendant will object to the evidence or otherwise demand the appearance of the analyst. These assumptions are wildly unrealistic, and, as discussed below, the figures they produce do not reflect what has in fact occurred in those jurisdictions that have already adopted the rule we announce today.

we announce today,[11] while many others permit the defendant to assert (or forfeit by silence) his Confrontation Clause right after receiving notice of the prosecution's intent to use a forensic analyst's report, *id.*, at 13–15 (cataloging such state laws). Despite these widespread practices, there is no evidence that the criminal justice system has ground to a halt in the States that, one way or another, empower a defendant to insist upon the analyst's appearance at trial. Indeed, in Massachusetts itself, a defendant may subpoena the analyst to appear at trial, *see* Brief for Respondent 57, and yet there is no indication that obstructionist defendants are abusing the privilege.

The dissent finds this evidence "far less reassuring than promised." But its doubts rest on two flawed premises. First, the dissent believes that those state statutes "requiring the defendant to give early notice of his intent to confront the analyst," are "burden-shifting statutes [that] may be invalidated by the Court's reasoning." That is not so. In their simplest form, notice-and-demand statutes require the prosecution to provide notice to the defendant of its intent to use an analyst's report as evidence at trial, after which the defendant is given a period of time in which he may object to the admission of the evidence absent the analyst's appearance live at trial. *See, e.g.,* Ga. Code Ann. § 35-3-154.1 (2006); Tex. Code Crim. Proc. Ann., Art. 38.41, § 4 (Vernon 2005); Ohio Rev. Code Ann. § 2925.51(C) (Lexis 2006). Contrary to the dissent's perception, these statutes shift no burden whatever. The defendant always has the burden of raising his Confrontation Clause objection; notice-and-demand statutes simply govern the time within which he must do so. States are free to adopt procedural rules governing objections. *See Wainwright v. Sykes*, 433 U.S. 72, 86–87 (1977). It is common to require a defendant to exercise his rights under the Compulsory Process Clause in advance of trial, announcing his intent to present certain witnesses. *See* Fed. Rules Crim. Proc. 12.1(a), (e), 16(b)(1)(C); Comment: Alibi Notice Rules: The Preclusion Sanction as Procedural Default, 51 U. Chi. L. Rev. 254, 254–255, 281–285 (1984) (discussing and cataloguing State notice-of-alibi rules); *Taylor v. Illinois*, 484 U.S. 400, 411 (1988); *Williams v. Florida*, 399 U.S. 78, 81–82 (1970). There is no conceivable reason why he cannot similarly be compelled to exercise his Confrontation Clause rights before trial. *See Hinojos-Mendoza v. People*, 169 P. 3d 662, 670 (Colo. 2007) (discussing and approving Colorado's notice-and-demand

---

11. *State v. Johnson*, 982 So. 2d 672, 680–681 (Fla. 2008); *Hinojos-Mendoza v. People*, 169 P. 3d 662, 666–667 (Colo. 2007); *State v. Birchfield*, 342 Ore. 624, 631–632 (2007); *State v. March*, 216 S.W.3d 663, 666–667 (Mo. 2007); *Thomas v. United States*, 914 A.2d 1, 12–13 (D.C. 2006); *State v. Caulfield*, 722 N.W.2d 304, 310 (Minn. 2006); *Las Vegas v. Walsh*, 124 P. 3d 203, 207–208 (Nev. 2005); *People v. McClanahan*, 729 N.E.2d 470, 474–475 (Ill. 2000); *Miller v. State*, 472 S.E.2d 74, 78–79 (Ga. 1996); *Barnette v. State*, 481 So. 2d 788, 792 (Miss. 1985).

provision). Today's decision will not disrupt criminal prosecutions in the many large States whose practice is already in accord with the Confrontation Clause.[12]

Second, the dissent notes that several of the state-court cases that have already adopted this rule did so pursuant to our decision in *Crawford*, and not "independently . . . as a matter of state law." That may be so. But in assessing the likely practical effects of today's ruling, it is irrelevant why those courts adopted this rule; it matters only that they did so. It is true that many of these decisions are recent, but if the dissent's dire predictions were accurate, and given the large number of drug prosecutions at the state level, one would have expected immediate and dramatic results. The absence of such evidence is telling.

But it is not surprising. Defense attorneys and their clients will often stipulate to the nature of the substance in the ordinary drug case. It is unlikely that defense counsel will insist on live testimony whose effect will be merely to highlight rather than cast doubt upon the forensic analysis. Nor will defense attorneys want to antagonize the judge or jury by wasting their time with the appearance of a witness whose testimony defense counsel does not intend to rebut in any fashion.[13] The amicus brief filed by District Attorneys in Support of the Commonwealth in the Massachusetts Supreme Court case upon which the Appeals Court here relied said that "it is almost always the case that [analysts' certificates] are admitted without objection. Generally, defendants do not object to the admission of drug certificates most likely because there is no benefit to a defendant from such testimony." Brief for District Attorneys in Support of the Commonwealth in No. SJC-09320 (Mass.), p 7 (footnote omitted). Given these strategic considerations, and in light of the experience in those States that already provide the same or similar protections to defendants, there is little reason to believe that our decision today will commence the parade of horribles respondent and the dissent predict.

This case involves little more than the application of our holding in *Crawford v. Washington*, 541 U.S. 36. The Sixth Amendment does not permit the prosecution to prove its case via ex parte out-of-court affidavits, and the admission of such

---

12. As the dissent notes, *some* state statutes, "require[e] defense counsel to subpoena the analyst, to show good cause for demanding the analyst's presence, or even to affirm under oath an intent to cross-examine the analyst." We have no occasion today to pass on the constitutionality of every variety of statute commonly given the notice-and-demand label. It suffices to say that what we have referred to as the "simplest form [of] notice-and-demand statutes," is constitutional; that such provisions are in place in a number of States; and that in those States, and in other States that required confrontation with notice-and-demand, there is no indication that the dire consequences predicted by the dissent have materialized.

13. Contrary to the dissent's suggestion, we do not cast aspersion on trial judges, who we trust will not be antagonized by good-faith requests for analysts' appearance at trial. Nor do we expect defense attorneys to refrain from zealous representation of their clients. We simply do not expect defense attorneys to believe that their client's interests (or their own) are furthered by objections to analysts' reports whose conclusions counsel have no intention of challenging.

evidence against Melendez-Diaz was error.[14] We therefore reverse the judgment of the Appeals Court of Massachusetts and remand the case for further proceedings not inconsistent with this opinion.

It is so ordered.

JUSTICE THOMAS, **CONCURRING.**

I write separately to note that I continue to adhere to my position that "the Confrontation Clause is implicated by extrajudicial statements only insofar as they are contained in formalized testimonial materials, such as affidavits, depositions, prior testimony, or confessions." *White v. Illinois*, 502 U.S. 346, 365 (1992) (opinion concurring in part and concurring in judgment); *see also Giles v. California*, 554 U.S. 353, 378 (2008) (concurring opinion) (characterizing statements within the scope of the Confrontation Clause to include those that are "sufficiently formal to resemble the Marian examinations" because they were Mirandized or custodial or "accompanied by [a] similar indicia of formality" (internal quotation marks omitted)); *Davis v. Washington*, 547 U.S. 813, 836 (2006) (opinion concurring in judgment in part and dissenting in part) (reiterating that the Clause encompasses extrajudicial statements contained in the types of formalized materials listed in *White, supra*, at 365 (opinion of Thomas, J.)). I join the Court's opinion in this case because the documents at issue in this case "are quite plainly affidavits." As such, they "fall within the core class of testimonial statements" governed by the Confrontation Clause. *Ibid.* (internal quotation marks omitted).

DISSENT BY: KENNEDY

DISSENT

JUSTICE KENNEDY, with whom THE CHIEF JUSTICE, JUSTICE BREYER, AND JUSTICE ALITO join, dissenting.

The Court sweeps away an accepted rule governing the admission of scientific evidence. Until today, scientific analysis could be introduced into evidence without testimony from the "analyst" who produced it. This rule has been established for at least 90 years. It extends across at least 35 States and six Federal Courts of Appeals. Yet the Court undoes it based on two recent opinions that say nothing about forensic analysts: *Crawford v. Washington*, 541 U.S. 36 (2004) and *Davis v. Washington*, 547 U.S. 813 (2006).

---

14. We of course express no view as to whether the error was harmless. The Appeals Court of Massachusetts did not reach that question and we decline to address it in the first instance. *Cf. Coy v. Iowa*, 487 U.S. 1012, 1021–1022 (1988). In connection with that determination, however, we disagree with the dissent's contention that "only an analyst's testimony suffices to prove [the] fact" that "the substance is cocaine." Today's opinion, while insisting upon retention of the confrontation requirement, in no way alters the type of evidence (including circumstantial evidence) sufficient to sustain a conviction.

It is remarkable that the Court so confidently disregards a century of jurisprudence. We learn now that we have misinterpreted the Confrontation Clause—hardly an arcane or seldom-used provision of the Constitution—for the first 218 years of its existence. The immediate systemic concern is that the Court makes no attempt to acknowledge the real differences between laboratory analysts who perform scientific tests and other, more conventional witnesses—"witnesses" being the word the Framers used in the Confrontation Clause.

Crawford and *Davis* dealt with ordinary witnesses—women who had seen, and in two cases been the victim of, the crime in question. Those cases stand for the proposition that formal statements made by a conventional witness—one who has personal knowledge of some aspect of the defendant's guilt—may not be admitted without the witness appearing at trial to meet the accused face to face. But *Crawford* and *Davis* do not say—indeed, could not have said, because the facts were not before the Court—that anyone who makes a testimonial statement is a witness for purposes of the Confrontation Clause, even when that person has, in fact, witnessed nothing to give them personal knowledge of the defendant's guilt.

Because *Crawford* and *Davis* concerned typical witnesses, the Court should have done the sensible thing and limited its holding to witnesses as so defined. Indeed, as Justice Thomas warned in his opinion in *Davis*, the Court's approach has become "disconnected from history and unnecessary to prevent abuse." 547 U.S., at 838 (opinion concurring in judgment in part and dissenting in part). The Court's reliance on the word "testimonial" is of little help, of course, for that word does not appear in the text of the Clause.

The Court dictates to the States, as a matter of constitutional law, an as-yet-undefined set of rules governing what kinds of evidence may be admitted without in-court testimony. Indeed, under today's opinion the States bear an even more onerous burden than they did before *Crawford*. Then, the States at least had the guidance of the hearsay rule and could rest assured that "where the evidence f[ell] within a firmly rooted hearsay exception," the Confrontation Clause did not bar its admission. *Ohio v. Roberts*, 448 U.S. 56 (1980) (overruled by *Crawford*). Now, without guidance from any established body of law, the States can only guess what future rules this Court will distill from the sparse constitutional text. *See, e.g., Mendez, Crawford v. Washington*: A Critique, 57 Stan. L. Rev. 569, 586–593 (2004) (discussing unanswered questions regarding testimonial statements).

The Court's opinion suggests this will be a body of formalistic and wooden rules, divorced from precedent, common sense, and the underlying purpose of the Clause. Its ruling has vast potential to disrupt criminal procedures that already give ample protections against the misuse of scientific evidence. For these reasons, as more fully explained below, the Court's opinion elicits my respectful dissent.

I

A

1

The Court says that, before the results of a scientific test may be introduced into evidence, the defendant has the right to confront the "analysts." One must assume that this term, though it appears nowhere in the Confrontation Clause, nevertheless has some constitutional substance that now must be elaborated in future cases. There is no accepted definition of analyst, and there is no established precedent to define that term.

Consider how many people play a role in a routine test for the presence of illegal drugs. One person prepares a sample of the drug, places it in a testing machine, and retrieves the machine's printout—often, a graph showing the frequencies of radiation absorbed by the sample or the masses of the sample's molecular fragments. *See* 2 P. Giannelli & E. Imwinkelried, Scientific Evidence § 23.03 (4th ed. 2007) (describing common methods of identifying drugs, including infrared spectrophotometry, nuclear magnetic resonance, gas chromatography, and mass spectrometry). A second person interprets the graph the machine printsout—perhaps by comparing that printout with published, standardized graphs of known drugs. *Ibid.* Meanwhile, a third person—perhaps an independent contractor—has calibrated the machine and, having done so, has certified that the machine is in good working order. Finally, a fourth person—perhaps the laboratory's director—certifies that his subordinates followed established procedures.

It is not at all evident which of these four persons is the analyst to be confronted under the rule the Court announces today. If all are witnesses who must appear for in-court confrontation, then the Court has, for all practical purposes, forbidden the use of scientific tests in criminal trials. As discussed further below, requiring even one of these individuals to testify threatens to disrupt if not end many prosecutions where guilt is clear but a newly found formalism now holds sway. *See* Part I-C, *infra*.

It is possible to read the Court's opinion, however, to say that all four must testify. Each one has contributed to the test's result and has, at least in some respects, made a representation about the test. Person One represents that a pure sample, properly drawn, entered the machine and produced a particular printout. Person Two represents that the printout corresponds to a known drug. Person Three represents that the machine was properly calibrated at the time. Person Four represents that all the others performed their jobs in accord with established procedures.

And each of the four has power to introduce error. A laboratory technician might adulterate the sample. The independent contractor might botch the machine's calibration. And so forth. The reasons for these errors may range from animus against the particular suspect or all criminal suspects to unintentional oversight; from gross negligence to good-faith mistake. It is no surprise that a plausible case can be made for deeming each person in the testing process an analyst under the Court's opinion.

Consider the independent contractor who has calibrated the testing machine. At least in a routine case, where the machine's result appears unmistakable, that result's accuracy depends entirely on the machine's calibration. The calibration, in turn, can be proved only by the contractor's certification that he or she did the job properly. That certification appears to be a testimonial statement under the Court's definition: It is a formal, out-of-court statement, offered for the truth of the matter asserted, and made for the purpose of later prosecution. It is not clear, under the Court's ruling, why the independent contractor is not also an analyst.

Consider the person who interprets the machine's printout. His or her interpretation may call for the exercise of professional judgment in close cases. *See* Giannelli & Imwinkelried, *supra*. If we assume no person deliberately introduces error, this interpretive step is the one most likely to permit human error to affect the test's result. This exercise of judgment might make this participant an analyst. The Court implies as much.

And we must yet consider the laboratory director who certifies the ultimate results. The director is arguably the most effective person to confront for revealing any ambiguity in findings, variations in procedures, or problems in the office, as he or she is most familiar with the standard procedures, the office's variations, and problems in prior cases or with particular analysts. The prosecution may seek to introduce his or her certification into evidence. The Court implies that only those statements that are actually entered into evidence require confrontation. This could mean that the director is also an analyst, even if his or her certification relies upon or restates work performed by subordinates.

The Court offers no principles or historical precedent to determine which of these persons is the analyst. All contribute to the test result. And each is equally remote from the scene, has no personal stake in the outcome, does not even know the accused, and is concerned only with the performance of his or her role in conducting the test.

It could be argued that the only analyst who must testify is the person who signed the certificate. Under this view, a laboratory could have one employee sign certificates and appear in court, which would spare all the other analysts this burden. But the Court has already rejected this arrangement. The Court made clear in *Davis* that it will not permit the testimonial statement of one witness to enter into evidence through the in-court testimony of a second:

> "[W]e do not think it conceivable that the protections of the Confrontation Clause can readily be evaded by having a note-taking policeman [here, the laboratory employee who signs the certificate] recite the unsworn

hearsay testimony of the declarant [here, the analyst who performs the actual test], instead of having the declarant sign a deposition. Indeed, if there is one point for which no case—English or early American, state or federal—can be cited, that is it." 547 U.S., at 826.

Under this logic, the Court's holding cannot be cabined to the person who signs the certificates. If the signatory is restating the testimonial statements of the true analysts—whoever they might be—then those analysts, too, must testify in person.

Today's decision demonstrates that even in the narrow category of scientific tests that identify a drug, the Court cannot define with any clarity who the analyst is. Outside this narrow category, the range of other scientific tests that may be affected by the Court's new confrontation right is staggering. *See, e.g.*, Comment, Toward a Definition of "Testimonial": How Autopsy Reports Do Not Embody the Qualities of a Testimonial Statement, 96 Cal. L. Rev. 1093, 1094, 1115 (2008) (noting that every court post-*Crawford* has held that autopsy reports are not testimonial, and warning that a contrary rule would "effectively functio[n] as a statute of limitations for murder").

2

It is difficult to confine at this point the damage the Court's holding will do in other contexts. Consider just two—establishing the chain of custody and authenticating a copy of a document.

It is the obligation of the prosecution to establish the chain of custody for evidence sent to testing laboratories—that is, to establish "the identity and integrity of physical evidence by tracing its continuous whereabouts." 23 C. J. S., Criminal Law § 1142, p 66 (2006). Meeting this obligation requires representations—that one officer retrieved the evidence from the crime scene, that a second officer checked it into an evidence locker, that a third officer verified the locker's seal was intact, and so forth. The iron logic of which the Court is so enamored would seem to require in-court testimony from each human link in the chain of custody. That, of course, has never been the law. *See, e.g., United States v. Lott*, 854 F.2d 244, 250 (CA7 1988) ("[G]aps in the chain [of custody] normally go to the weight of the evidence rather than its admissibility"); 29A Am. Jur. 2d, Evidence § 962, p 269 (2008) ("The fact that one of the persons in control of a fungible substance does not testify at trial does not, without more, make the substance or testimony relating to it inadmissible"); C. J. S., *supra*, § 1142, at 67 ("It is generally not necessary that every witness who handled the evidence testify").

It is no answer for the Court to say that "[i]t is up to the prosecution to decide what steps in the chain of custody are so crucial as to require evidence." The case itself determines which links in the chain are crucial—not the prosecution. In any number of cases, the crucial link in the chain will not be available to testify and so the evidence will be excluded for lack of a proper foundation.

Consider another context in which the Court's holding may cause disruption: The long-accepted practice of authenticating copies of documents by means of a certificate from the document's custodian stating that the copy is accurate. *See, e.g.,* Fed. Rule Evid. 902(4) (in order to be self-authenticating, a copy of a public record must be "certified as correct by the custodian"); Rule 902(11) (business record must be "accompanied by a written declaration of its custodian"). Under one possible reading of the Court's opinion, recordkeepers will be required to testify. So far, courts have not read *Crawford* and *Davis* to impose this largely meaningless requirement. *See, e.g., United States v. Adefehinti*, 510 F.3d 319, 327–328 (CADC 2008) (certificates authenticating bank records may be admitted without confrontation); *United States v. Ellis*, 460 F.3d 920, 927 (CA7 2006) (certificate authenticating hospital records). But the breadth of the Court's ruling today, and its undefined scope, may well be such that these courts now must be deemed to have erred. The risk of that consequence ought to tell us that something is very wrong with the Court's analysis.

Because the Court is driven by nothing more than a wooden application of the *Crawford* and *Davis* definition of "testimonial," divorced from any guidance from history, precedent, or common sense, there is no way to predict the future applications of today's holding. Surely part of the justification for the Court's formalism must lie in its predictability. There is nothing predictable here, however, other than the uncertainty and disruption that now must ensue.

B

With no precedent to guide us, let us assume that the Court's analyst is the person who interprets the machine's printout. This result makes no sense. The Confrontation Clause is not designed, and does not serve, to detect errors in scientific tests. That should instead be done by conducting a new test. Or, if a new test is impossible, the defendant may call his own expert to explain to the jury the test's flaws and the dangers of relying on it. And if, in an extraordinary case, the particular analyst's testimony is necessary to the defense, then, of course, the defendant may subpoena the analyst. The Court frets that the defendant may be unable to do so "when the [analyst] is unavailable or simply refuses to appear." But laboratory analysts are not difficult to locate or to compel. As discussed below, analysts already devote considerable time to appearing in court when subpoenaed to do so. *See* Part I-C, *infra*; *see also* Brief for State of Alabama et al. as *Amici Curiae* 26–28. Neither the Court, petitioner, nor amici offer any reason to believe that defendants have trouble subpoenaing analysts in cases where the analysts' in-court testimony is necessary.

The facts of this case illustrate the formalistic and pointless nature of the Court's reading of the Clause. Petitioner knew, well in advance of trial, that the Commonwealth would introduce the tests against him. The bags of cocaine were in court, available for him to test, and entered into evidence. Yet petitioner made no effort, before or during trial, to mount a defense against the analysts' results. Petitioner could have challenged the test's reliability by seeking discovery concerning the testing methods used or the qualifications of the laboratory analysts. *See* Mass. Rule Crim. Proc. 14(a)(2) (2009). He did not do so. Petitioner could have sought to conduct his own test. *See* Rule 41. Again, he did not seek a test; indeed, he did not argue that the drug was not cocaine. Rather than dispute the authenticity of the samples tested or the accuracy of the tests performed, petitioner argued to the jury that the prosecution had not shown that he had possessed or dealt in the drugs.

Despite not having prepared a defense to the analysts' results, petitioner's counsel made what can only be described as a pro forma objection to admitting the results without in-court testimony, presumably from one particular analyst. Today the Court, by deciding that this objection should have been sustained, transforms the Confrontation Clause from a sensible procedural protection into a distortion of the criminal justice system.

It is difficult to perceive how the Court's holding will advance the purposes of the Confrontation Clause. One purpose of confrontation is to impress upon witnesses the gravity of their conduct. *See Coy v. Iowa*, 487 U.S. 1012, 1019–1020 (1988). A witness, when brought to face the person his or her words condemn, might refine, reformulate, reconsider, or even recant earlier statements. *See ibid.* A further purpose is to alleviate the danger of one-sided interrogations by adversarial government officials who might distort a witness testimony. The Clause guards against this danger by bringing the interrogation into the more neutral and public forum of the courtroom. *See Maryland v. Craig*, 497 U.S. 836, 869–870 (1990) (Scalia, J., dissenting) (discussing the "value of the confrontation right in guarding against a child's distorted or coerced recollections"); *see also* Comment, 96 Cal. L. Rev., at 1120–1122 ("During private law-enforcement questioning, police officers or prosecutors can exert pressure on the witness without a high risk of being discovered. Courtroom questioning, in contrast, is public and performed in front of the jury, judge and defendant. Pressure is therefore harder to exert in court").

But neither purpose is served by the rule the Court announces today. It is not plausible that a laboratory analyst will retract his or her prior conclusion upon catching sight of the defendant the result condemns. After all, the analyst is far removed from the particular defendant and, indeed, claims no personal knowledge of the defendant's guilt. And an analyst performs hundreds if not thousands of tests each year and will not remember a particular test or the link it had to the defendant.

This is not to say that analysts are infallible. They are not. It may well be that if the State does not introduce the machine printout or the raw results of a laboratory analysis; if it does not call an expert to interpret a test, particularly if that test is complex or little known; if it does not establish the chain of custody and the reliability of the laboratory; then the State will have failed to meet its burden of proof. That result follows because the State must prove its case beyond a reasonable doubt, without relying on presumptions, unreliable hearsay, and the like. *See United States v. United States Gypsum Co.*, 438 U.S. 422, 446 (1978) (refusing to permit a "'conclusive presumption [of intent],'" which "'would effectively eliminate intent as an ingredient of the offense'" (quoting *Morissette v. United States*, 342 U.S. 246, 275 (1952)). The State must permit the defendant to challenge the analyst's result. *See Holmes v. South Carolina*, 547 U.S. 319, 331 (2006) (affirming the defendant's right to "have a meaningful opportunity to present a complete defense" (internal quotation marks omitted)). The rules of evidence, including those governing reliability under hearsay principles and the latitude to be given expert witnesses; the rules against irrebutable presumptions; and the overriding principle that the prosecution must make its case beyond a reasonable doubt—all these are part of the protections for the accused. The States, however, have some latitude in determining how these rules should be defined.

The Confrontation Clause addresses who must testify. It simply does not follow, however, that this clause, in lieu of the other rules set forth above, controls who the prosecution must call on every issue. Suppose, for instance, that the defense challenges the procedures for a secure chain of custody for evidence sent to a lab and then returned to the police. The defense has the right to call its own witnesses to show that the chain of custody is not secure. But that does not mean it can demand that, in the prosecution's case in chief, each person who is in the chain of custody—and who had an undoubted opportunity to taint or tamper with the evidence—must be called by the prosecution under the Confrontation Clause. And the same is true with lab technicians.

The Confrontation Clause is simply not needed for these matters. Where, as here, the defendant does not even dispute the accuracy of the analyst's work, confrontation adds nothing.

C

For the sake of these negligible benefits, the Court threatens to disrupt forensic investigations across the country and to put prosecutions nationwide at risk of dismissal based on erratic, all-too-frequent instances when a particular laboratory technician, now invested by the Court's new constitutional designation as the analyst, simply does not or cannot appear.

Consider first the costs today's decision imposes on criminal trials. Our own Court enjoys weeks, often months, of notice before cases are argued. We receive briefs well in advance. The argument itself is ordered. A busy trial court, by contrast, must consider not only attorneys' schedules but also those of witnesses and juries. Trial courts have huge caseloads to be processed within strict time limits. Some cases may unexpectedly plead out at the last minute; others, just as unexpectedly, may not. Some juries stay out longer than predicted; others must be reconstituted. An analyst cannot hope to be the trial court's top priority in scheduling. The analyst must instead face the prospect of waiting for days in a hallway outside the courtroom before being called to offer testimony that will consist of little more than a rote recital of the written report. *See* Part I-B, *supra*.

As matters stood before today's opinion, analysts already spent considerable time appearing as witnesses in those few cases where the defendant, unlike petitioner in this case, contested the analyst's result and subpoenaed the analyst. *See* Brief for State of Alabama et al. as *Amici Curiae* 26–28 (testifying takes time); *ante*, (before today's opinion, it was "'almost always the case that analysts' certificates [we]re admitted without objection'" in Massachusetts courts). By requiring analysts also to appear in the far greater number of cases where defendants do not dispute the analyst's result, the Court imposes enormous costs on the administration of justice.

Setting aside, for a moment, all the other crimes for which scientific evidence is required, consider the costs the Court's ruling will impose on state drug prosecutions alone. In 2004, the most recent year for which data are available, drug possession and trafficking resulted in 362,850 felony convictions in state courts across the country. *See* Dept. of Justice, Bureau of Justice Statistics, M. Durose & P. Langan, Felony Sentences in State Courts 2004, p 2 (July 2007). Roughly 95% of those convictions were products of plea bargains, *see id.*, at 1, which means that state courts saw more than 18,000 drug trials in a single year.

The analysts responsible for testing the drugs at issue in those cases now bear a crushing burden. For example, the district attorney in Philadelphia prosecuted 25,000 drug crimes in 2007. Brief for National Dist. Attorneys Association et al. as *Amici Curiae* 12–13. Assuming that number remains the same, and assuming that 95% of the cases end in a plea bargain, each of the city's 18 drug analysts, *ibid.*, will be required to testify in more than 69 trials next year. Cleveland's district attorney prosecuted 14,000 drug crimes in 2007. *Ibid.* Assuming that number holds, and that 95% of the cases end in a plea bargain, each of the city's 6 drug analysts (2 of whom work only part time) must testify in 117 drug cases next year. *Id.*, at 13.

The Federal Government may face even graver difficulties than the States because its operations are so widespread. For example, the Federal Bureau Investigation (FBI) laboratory at Quantico, Virginia, supports federal, state, and local investigations across the country. Its 500 employees conduct over 1 million scientific tests each year. Dept. of Justice, Federal Bureau of Investigation Laboratory 2007, Message from the FBI Laboratory Director, http://www.fbi.gov/hq/lab/lab2007/labannual07.pdf (as visited June 22, 2009, and available in Clerk of Court's case file). The Court's decision means that before any of those million tests reaches a jury, at least one of the laboratory's analysts must board a plane, find his or her way to an unfamiliar courthouse, and sit there waiting to read aloud notes made months ago.

The Court purchases its meddling with the Confrontation Clause at a dear price, a price not measured in taxpayer dollars alone. Guilty defendants will go free, on the most technical grounds, as a direct result of today's decision, adding nothing to the truth-finding process. The analyst will not always make it to the courthouse in time. He or she may be ill; may be out of the country; may be unable to travel because of inclement weather; or may at that very moment be waiting outside some other courtroom for another defendant to exercise the right the Court invents today. If for any reason the analyst cannot make it to the courthouse in time, then, the Court holds, the jury cannot learn of the analyst's findings (unless, by some unlikely turn of events, the defendant previously cross-examined the analyst). The result, in many cases, will be that the prosecution cannot meet its burden of proof, and the guilty defendant goes free on a technicality that, because it results in an acquittal, cannot be reviewed on appeal.

The Court's holding is a windfall to defendants, one that is unjustified by any demonstrated deficiency in trials, any well-understood historical requirement, or any established constitutional precedent.

II

All of the problems with today's decision—the imprecise definition of "analyst," the lack of any perceptible benefit, the heavy societal costs—would be of no moment if the Constitution did, in fact, require the Court to rule as it does today. But the Constitution does not.

The Court's fundamental mistake is to read the Confrontation Clause as referring to a kind of out-of-court statement—namely, a testimonial statement—that must be excluded from evidence. The Clause does not refer to kinds of statements. Nor does the Clause contain the word "testimonial." The text, instead, refers to kinds of persons, namely, to "witnesses against" the defendant. Laboratory analysts are not "witnesses against" the defendant as those words would have been understood at the framing. There is simply no authority for this proposition.

Instead, the Clause refers to a conventional "witness"—meaning one who witnesses (that is, perceives) an event that gives him or her personal knowledge of some aspect of the defendant's guilt. Both *Crawford* and *Davis* concerned just this kind of ordinary witness—and nothing in the Confrontation Clause's text, history, or precedent justifies the Court's decision to expand those cases.

A

The Clause states: "In all criminal prosecutions, the accused shall enjoy the right . . . to be confronted with the witnesses against him." U.S. Const., Amdt. 6. Though there is "virtually no evidence of what the drafters of the Confrontation Clause intended it to mean," *White v. Illinois*, 502 U.S. 346, 359 (1992) (Thomas, J., concurring in part and concurring in judgment), it is certain the Framers did not contemplate that an analyst who conducts a scientific test far removed from the crime would be considered a "witnes[s] against" the defendant.

The Framers were concerned with a typical witness—one who perceived an event that gave rise to a personal belief in some aspect of the defendant's guilt. There is no evidence that the Framers understood the Clause to extend to unconventional witnesses. As discussed below, there is significant evidence to the contrary. *See* Part II-B, *infra*. In these circumstances, the historical evidence in support of the Court's position is "'too meager . . . to form a solid basis in history, preceding and contemporaneous with the framing of the Constitution.'" (2008) (quoting *Reid v. Covert*, 354 U.S. 1, 64 (1957) (Frankfurter, J., concurring in result)). The Court goes dangerously wrong when it bases its constitutional interpretation upon historical guesswork.

The infamous treason trial of Sir Walter Raleigh provides excellent examples of the kinds of witnesses to whom the Confrontation Clause refers. Raleigh's Case, 2 How. St. Tr. 1 (1603); *see Crawford*, 541 U.S., at 44–45 (Raleigh's trial informs our understanding of the Clause because it was, at the time of the framing, one of the "most notorious instances" of the abuse of witnesses' out-of-court statements). Raleigh's accusers claimed to have heard Raleigh speak treason, so they were witnesses in the conventional sense. We should limit the Confrontation Clause to witnesses like those in Raleigh's trial.

The Court today expands the Clause to include laboratory analysts, but analysts differ from ordinary witnesses in at least three significant ways. First, a conventional witness recalls events observed in the past, while an analyst's report contains near-contemporaneous observations of the test. An observation recorded at the time it is made is unlike the usual act of testifying. A typical witness must recall a previous event that he or she perceived just once, and thus may have misperceived or misremembered. But an analyst making a contemporaneous observation need not rely on memory; he or she instead reports the observations at the time they are made. We gave this consideration substantial weight in *Davis*. There, the "primary purpose" of the victim's 911 call was "to enable police assistance to meet an ongoing emergency," rather than "to establish or prove past events potentially relevant to later criminal prosecution." 547 U.S., at 822, 827. *See also People v. Geier*, 161 P. 3d 104, 139–141 (Cal. 2007). The Court cites no authority for its holding that an observation recorded at the time it is made is an act of "witness[ing]" for purposes of the Confrontation Clause.

Second, an analyst observes neither the crime nor any human action related to it. Often, the analyst does not know the defendant's identity, much less have personal knowledge of an aspect of the defendant's guilt. The analyst's distance from the crime and the defendant, in both space and time, suggests the analyst is not a witness against the defendant in the conventional sense.

Third, a conventional witness responds to questions under interrogation. *See, e.g.*, Raleigh's Case, *supra*, at 15–20. But laboratory tests are conducted according to scientific protocols; they are not dependent upon or controlled by interrogation of any sort. Put differently, out-of-court statements should only "require confrontation if they are produced by, or with the involvement of, adversarial government officials responsible for investigating and prosecuting crime." Comment, 96 Cal. L. Rev., at 1118. There is no indication that the analysts here—who work for the State Laboratory Institute, a division of the Massachusetts Department of Public Health—were adversarial to petitioner. Nor is there any evidence that adversarial officials played a role in formulating the analysts' certificates.

Rather than acknowledge that it expands the Confrontation Clause beyond conventional witnesses, the Court relies on our recent opinions in *Crawford* and *Davis*. The Court assumes, with little analysis, that *Crawford* and *Davis* extended the Clause to any person who makes a "testimonial" statement. But the Court's confident tone cannot disguise the thinness of these two reeds. Neither *Crawford* nor *Davis* considered whether the Clause extends to persons far removed from the crime who have no connection to the defendant. Instead, those cases concerned conventional witnesses. *Davis, supra*, at 826–830 (witnesses were victims of defendants' assaults); *Crawford, supra*, at 38 (witness saw defendant stab victim).

It is true that *Crawford* and *Davis* employed the term "testimonial," and thereby suggested that any testimonial statement, by any person, no matter how distant from the defendant and the crime, is subject to the Confrontation Clause. But that suggestion was not part of the holding of *Crawford* or *Davis*. Those opinions used the adjective "testimonial" to avoid the awkward phrasing required by reusing the noun "witness." The Court today transforms that turn of phrase into a new and sweeping legal rule, by holding that anyone who makes a formal statement for the purpose of later prosecution—no matter how removed from the crime—must be considered a "witnes[s] against" the defendant. The Court cites no authority to justify this expansive new interpretation.

B

No historical evidence supports the Court's conclusion that the Confrontation Clause was understood to extend beyond conventional witnesses to include analysts who conduct scientific tests far removed from the crime and the defendant. Indeed, what little evidence there is contradicts this interpretation.

Though the Framers had no forensic scientists, they did use another kind of unconventional witness—the copyist. A copyist's work may be as essential to a criminal prosecution as the forensic analyst's. To convict a man of bigamy, for example, the State often requires his marriage records. *See, e.g., Williams v. State*, 54 Ala. 131, 134, 135 (1875); *State v. Potter*, 52 Vt. 33, 38 (1879). But if the original records cannot be taken from the archive, the prosecution must rely on copies of those records, made for the purpose of introducing the copies into evidence at trial. *See ibid.* In that case, the copyist's honesty and diligence are just as important as the analyst's here. If the copyist falsifies a copy, or even misspells a name or transposes a date, those flaws could lead the jury to convict. Because so much depends on his or her honesty and diligence, the copyist often prepares an affidavit certifying that the copy is true and accurate.

Such a certificate is beyond question a testimonial statement under the Court's definition: It is a formal out-of-court statement offered for the truth of two matters (the copyist's honesty and the copy's accuracy), and it is prepared for a criminal prosecution.

During the Framers' era copyists' affidavits were accepted without hesitation by American courts. *See, e.g., United States v. Percheman,* 32 U.S. 51, (1833) (opinion for the Court by Marshall, C. J.); *see also* Advisory Committee's Note on Fed. Rule Evid. 902(4), 28 U.S.C. App., p 390 ("The common law . . . recognized the procedure of authenticating copies of public records by certificate"); 5 J. Wigmore, Evidence §§ 1677, 1678 (J. Chadbourn rev. 1974). And courts admitted copyists' affidavits in criminal as well as civil trials. *See Williams, supra; Potter, supra.* This demonstrates that the framing generation, in contrast to the Court today, did not consider the Confrontation Clause to require in-court confrontation of unconventional authors of testimonial statements.

The Court attempts to explain away this historical exception to its rule by noting that a copyist's authority is "narrowly circumscribed." But the Court does not explain why that matters, nor, if it does matter, why laboratory analysts' authority should not also be deemed "narrowly circumscribed" so that they, too, may be excused from testifying. And drawing these fine distinctions cannot be squared with the Court's avowed allegiance to formalism. Determining whether a witness' authority is "narrowly circumscribed" has nothing to do with *Crawford*'s testimonial framework. It instead appears much closer to the pre-*Crawford* rule of *Ohio v. Roberts,* under which a statement could be admitted without testimony if it "bears adequate indicia of reliability." 448 U.S., at 66 (internal quotation marks omitted).

In keeping with the traditional understanding of the Confrontation Clause, this Court in *Dowdell v. United States,* 221 U.S. 325 (1911), rejected a challenge to the use of certificates, sworn out by a clerk of court, a trial judge, and a court reporter, stating that defendants had been present at trial. Those certificates, like a copyist's certificate, met every requirement of the Court's current definition of "testimonial." In rejecting the defendants' claim that use of the certificates violated the Confrontation Clause, the Court in *Dowdell* explained that the officials who executed the certificates "were not witnesses against the accused" because they "were not asked to testify to facts concerning [the defendants'] guilt or innocence." *Id.,* at 330. Indeed, as recently as *Davis,* the Court reaffirmed *Dowdell.* 547 U.S., at 825.

By insisting that every author of a testimonial statement appear for confrontation, on pain of excluding the statement from evidence, the Court does violence to the Framers' sensible, and limited, conception of the right to confront "witnesses against" the defendant.

C

In addition to lacking support in historical practice or in this Court's precedent, the Court's decision is also contrary to authority extending over at least 90 years, 35 States, and six Federal Courts of Appeals.

Almost 100 years ago three state supreme courts held that their state constitutions did not require analysts to testify in court. In a case much like this one, the Massachusetts Supreme Judicial Court upheld the admission of a certificate stating that the liquid seized from the defendant contained alcohol, even though the author of the certificate did not testify. *Commonwealth v. Slavski*, 140 N. E. 465, 467 (Mass. 1923). The highest courts in Connecticut and Virginia reached similar conclusions under their own constitutions. *State v. Torello*, 131 A. 429 (Conn. 1925); *Bracy v. Commonwealth*, 89 S.E. 144 (Va. 1916). Just two state courts appear to have read a state constitution to require a contrary result. *State v. Clark*, 964 P.2d 766, 770–772 (Mont. 1998) (laboratory drug report requires confrontation under Montana's Constitution, which is "[u]nlike its federal counterpart"); *State v. Birchfield*, 157 P. 3d 216 (Ore. 2007), *but see id.*, at 220 (suggesting that a "typical notice requirement" would be lawful).

As for the Federal Constitution, before *Crawford* the authority was stronger still: The Sixth Amendment does not require analysts to testify in court. All Federal Courts of Appeals to consider the issue agreed. *Sherman v. Scott*, 62 F.3d 136, 139–142 (CA5 1995); *Minner v. Kerby*, 30 F.3d 1311, 1313–1315 (CA10 1994); *United States v. Baker*, 855 F.2d 1353, 1359–1360 (CA8 1988); *Reardon v. Manson*, 806 F.2d 39 (CA2 1986); *Kay v. United States*, 255 F.2d 476, 480–481 (CA4 1958); *see also Manocchio v. Moran*, 919 F.2d 770, 777–782 (CA1 1990) (autopsy report stating cause of victim's death). Some 24 state courts, and the Court of Appeals for the Armed Forces, were in accord. *See Appendix A, infra.* (Some cases cited in the appendixes concern doctors, coroners, and calibrators rather than laboratory analysts, but their reasoning is much the same.) Eleven more state courts upheld burden-shifting statutes that reduce, if not eliminate, the right to confrontation by requiring the defendant to take affirmative steps prior to trial to summon the analyst. *See ibid.* Because these burden-shifting statutes may be invalidated by the Court's reasoning, these 11 decisions, too, appear contrary to today's opinion. *See* Part III-B, *infra.* Most of the remaining States, far from endorsing the Court's view, appear not to have addressed the question prior to *Crawford.* Against this weight of authority, the Court proffers just two cases from intermediate state courts of appeals.

On a practical level, today's ruling would cause less disruption if the States' hearsay rules had already required analysts to testify. But few States require this. At least 16 state courts have held that their evidentiary rules permit scientific test results, calibration certificates, and the observations of medical personnel to enter evidence without in-court testimony. *See* Appendix B, *infra.* The Federal Courts of Appeals have reached the same conclusion in applying the federal hearsay rule. United States v. Garnett, 122 F.3d 1016, 1018-1019 (CA11 1997) (per curiam); *United States v. Gilbert*, 774 F.2d 962, 965 (CA9 1985) (per curiam); *United States v. Ware*, 247 F.2d 698, 699–700 (CA7 1957); *but see United States v. Oates*, 560 F.2d 45, 82 (CA2 1977) (report prepared by law enforcement not admissible under public-records or business-records exceptions to federal hearsay rule).

The modern trend in the state courts has been away from the Court's rule and toward the admission of scientific test results without testimony—perhaps because the States have recognized the increasing reliability of scientific testing. *See* Appendix B, *infra* (citing cases from three States overruling or limiting previous precedents that had adopted the Court's rule as a matter of state law). It appears that a mere six courts continue to interpret their States' hearsay laws to require analysts to testify. *See ibid.* And, of course, where courts have grounded their decisions in state law, rather than the Constitution, the legislatures in those States have had, until now, the power to abrogate the courts' interpretation if the costs were shown to outweigh the benefits. Today the Court strips that authority from the States by carving the minority view into the constitutional text.

State legislatures, and not the Members of this Court, have the authority to shape the rules of evidence. The Court therefore errs when it relies in such great measure on the recent report of the National Academy of Sciences. That report is not directed to this Court, but rather to the elected representatives in Congress and the state legislatures, who, unlike Members of this Court, have the power and competence to determine whether scientific tests are unreliable and, if so, whether testimony is the proper solution to the problem.

The Court rejects the well-established understanding—extending across at least 90 years, 35 States, and six Federal Courts of Appeals—that the Constitution does not require analysts to testify in court before their analysis may be introduced into evidence. The only authority on which the Court can rely is its own speculation on the meaning of the word "testimonial," made in two recent opinions that said nothing about scientific analysis or scientific analysts.

III

In an attempt to show that the "sky will not fall after today's decision," the Court makes three arguments, none of which withstands scrutiny.

A

In an unconvincing effort to play down the threat that today's new rule will disrupt or even end criminal prosecutions, the Court professes a hope that defense counsel will decline to raise what will soon be known as the *Melendez-Diaz* objection. The Court bases this expectation on its understanding that defense attorneys surrender constitutional rights because the attorneys do not "want to antagonize the judge or jury by wasting their time." *Ibid.*

The Court's reasoning is troubling on at least two levels. First, the Court's speculation rests on the apparent belief that our Nation's trial judges and jurors are unwilling to accept zealous advocacy and that, once "antagonize[d]" by it, will punish such advocates with adverse rulings. *Ibid.* The Court offers no support for this stunning slur on the integrity of the Nation's courts. It is commonplace for the defense to request, at the conclusion of the prosecution's opening case, a directed verdict of acquittal. If the prosecution has failed to prove an element of the crime—even an element that is technical and rather obvious, such as movement of a car in interstate commerce—then the case must be dismissed. Until today one would not have thought that judges should be angered at the defense for making such motions, nor that counsel has some sort of obligation to avoid being troublesome when the prosecution has not done all the law requires to prove its case.

Second, even if the Court were right to expect trial judges to feel "antagonize[d]" by *Melendez-Diaz* objections and to then vent their anger by punishing the lawyer in some way, there is no authority to support the Court's suggestion that a lawyer may shirk his or her professional duties just to avoid judicial displeasure. There is good reason why the Court cites no authority for this suggestion—it is contrary to what some of us, at least, have long understood to be defense counsel's duty to be a zealous advocate for every client. This Court has recognized the bedrock principle that a competent criminal defense lawyer must put the prosecution to its proof:

> "[T]he adversarial process protected by the Sixth Amendment requires that the accused have 'counsel acting in the role of an advocate.' *Anders v. California*, 386 U.S. 738, 743 (1967). The right to the effective assistance of counsel is thus the right of the accused to require the prosecution's case to survive the crucible of meaningful adversarial testing. When a true adversarial criminal trial has been conducted . . . the kind of testing envisioned by the Sixth Amendment has occurred. But if the process loses its character as a confrontation between adversaries, the constitutional guarantee is violated." *United States v. Cronic*, 466 U.S. 648, 656–657 (1984) (footnotes omitted).

See also ABA Model Code of Professional Responsibility, Canon 7-1, in ABA Compendium of Professional Responsibility Rules and Standards (2008) ("The duty of a lawyer, both to his client and to the legal system, is to represent his client zealously within the bounds of the law . . ." (footnotes omitted)).

The instant case demonstrates how zealous defense counsel will defend their clients. To convict, the prosecution must prove the substance is cocaine. Under the Court's new rule, apparently only an analyst's testimony suffices to prove that fact. (Of course there will also be a large universe of other crimes, ranging from homicide to robbery, where scientific evidence is necessary to prove an element.) In cases where scientific evidence is necessary to prove an element of the crime, the Court's rule requires the prosecution to call the person identified as the analyst; this requirement has become a new prosecutorial duty linked with proving the State's case beyond a reasonable doubt. Unless the Court is ashamed of its new rule, it is inexplicable that the Court seeks to limit its damage by hoping that defense counsel will be derelict in their duty to insist that the prosecution prove its case. That is simply not the way the adversarial system works.

In any event, the Court's hope is sure to prove unfounded. The Court surmises that "[i]t is unlikely that defense counsel will insist on live testimony whose effect will be merely to highlight rather than cast doubt upon the forensic analysis." This optimistic prediction misunderstands how criminal trials work. If the defense does not plan to challenge the test result, "highlight[ing]" that result through testimony does not harm the defense as the Court supposes. If the analyst cannot reach the courtroom in time to testify, however, a *Melendez-Diaz* objection grants the defense a great windfall: The analyst's work cannot come into evidence. Given the prospect of such a windfall (which may, in and of itself, secure an acquittal) few zealous advocates will pledge, prior to trial, not to raise a *Melendez-Diaz* objection. Defense counsel will accept the risk that the jury may hear the analyst's live testimony, in exchange for the chance that the analyst fails to appear and the government's case collapses. And if, as here, the defense is not that the substance was harmless, but instead that the accused did not possess it, the testimony of the technician is a formalism that does not detract from the defense case.

In further support of its unlikely hope, the Court relies on the Brief for Law Professors as *Amici Curiae* 7–8, which reports that nearly 95% of convictions are obtained via guilty plea and thus do not require in-court testimony from laboratory analysts. What the Court does not consider is how its holding will alter these statistics. The defense bar today gains the formidable power to require the government to transport the analyst to the courtroom at the time of trial. Zealous counsel will insist upon concessions: a plea bargain, or a more lenient sentence in exchange for relinquishing this remarkable power.

B

As further reassurance that the "sky will not fall after today's decision," *ibid.*, the Court notes that many States have enacted burden-shifting statutes that require the defendant to assert his Confrontation Clause right prior to trial or else "forfeit" it "by silence." The Court implies that by shifting the burden to the defendant to take affirmative steps to produce the analyst, these statutes reduce the burden on the prosecution.

The Court holds that these burden-shifting statutes are valid because, in the Court's view, they "shift no burden whatever." While this conclusion is welcome, the premise appears flawed. Even what the Court calls the "simplest form" of burden-shifting statutes do impose requirements on the defendant, who must make a formal demand, with proper service, well before trial. Some statutes impose more requirements, for instance by requiring defense counsel to subpoena the analyst, to show good cause for demanding the analyst's presence, or even to affirm under oath an intent to cross-examine the analyst. *See generally* Metzger, Cheating the Constitution, 59 Vand. L. Rev. 475, 481–485 (2006). In a future case, the Court may find that some of these more onerous burden-shifting statutes violate the Confrontation Clause because they "impos[e] a burden . . . on the defendant to bring . . . adverse witnesses into court."

The burden-shifting statutes thus provide little reassurance that this case will not impose a meaningless formalism across the board.

C

In a further effort to support its assessment that today's decision will not cause disruption, the Court cites 10 decisions from States that, the Court asserts, "have already adopted the constitutional rule we announce today." The Court assures us that "there is no evidence that the criminal justice system has ground to a halt in the[se] States."

On inspection, the citations prove far less reassuring than promised. Seven were decided by courts that considered themselves bound by *Crawford*. These cases thus offer no support for the Court's assertion that the state jurists independently "adopted" the Court's interpretation as a matter of state law. Quite the contrary, the debate in those seven courts was over just how far this Court intended *Crawford* to sweep. *See, e.g., State v. Belvin*, 986 So. 2d 516, 526 (Fla. 2008) (Wells, J., concurring in part and dissenting in part) ("I believe that the majority has extended the *Crawford* and *Davis* decisions beyond their intended reach" (citations omitted)). The Court should correct these courts' overbroad reading of *Crawford*, not endorse it. Were the Court to do so, these seven jurisdictions might well change their position.

Moreover, because these seven courts only "adopted" the Court's position in the wake of *Crawford*, their decisions are all quite recent. These States have not yet been subject to the widespread, adverse results of the formalism the Court mandates today.

The citations also fail to reassure for a different reason. Five of the Court's ten citations—including all three pre-*Crawford* cases—come from States that have reduced the confrontation right. Four States have enacted a burden-shifting statute requiring the defendant to give early notice of his intent to confront the analyst. *See* Part III-B, *supra*; Colorado: *Hinojos-Mendoza v. People*, 169 P. 3d 662, 668–671 (Colo. 2007), Colo. Rev. Stat. Ann. § 16-3-309 (2008) (defendant must give notice 10 days before trial); Georgia: *Compare Miller v. State*, 472 S. E. 2d 74, 78–79

(Ga. 1996) (striking down earlier notice statute requiring defendant to show good cause, prior to trial, to call the analyst), *with* Ga. Code Ann. § 35-3-154.1 (2006) (defendant must give notice 10 days before trial); Illinois: *People v. McClanahan*, 729 N.E.2d 470, 474–475 (Ill. 2000), Ill. Comp. Stat., ch. 725, § 5/115-15 (West 2006) (defendant must give notice "within 7 days" of "receipt of the report"); Oregon: *State v. Birchfield*, 342 Ore., at 631–632, 157 P. 3d, at 220 (suggesting that a "typical notice requirement" would be lawful), *see* Ore. Rev. Stat. § 475.235 (2007) (defendant must give notice 15 days before trial). A fifth State, Mississippi, excuses the prosecution from producing the analyst who conducted the test, so long as it produces someone. *Compare Barnette v. State*, 481 So. 2d 788, 792 (Miss. 1985) (cited by the Court), *with McGowen v. State*, 859 So. 2d 320, 339–340 (Miss. 2003) (the Sixth Amendment does not require confrontation with the particular analyst who conducted the test). It is possible that neither Mississippi's practice nor the burden-shifting statutes can be reconciled with the Court's holding. *See* Part III-B, *supra*. The disruption caused by today's decision has yet to take place in these States.

* * *

Laboratory analysts who conduct routine scientific tests are not the kind of conventional witnesses to whom the Confrontation Clause refers. The judgment of the Appeals Court of Massachusetts should be affirmed.

APPENDIXES

A

The following authorities held, prior to *Crawford*, that the Confrontation Clause does not require confrontation of the analyst who conducted a routine scientific test: *United States v. Vietor*, 10 M. J. 69, 72 (Ct. Mil. App. 1980) (laboratory drug report); *State v. Cosgrove*, 436 A.2d 33, 40–41 (Conn. 1980) (same); *Howard v. United States*, 473 A.2d 835, 838–839 (D. C. 1984) (same); *Baber v. State*, 775 So. 2d 258 (Fla. 2000) (blood-alcohol test); *Commonwealth v. Harvard*, 253 N.E.2d 346 (Mass. 1969) (laboratory drug report); *DeRosa v. First Judicial Dist. Court of State ex rel. Carson City*, 985 P.2d 157, 162 (Nev. 1999) (per curiam) (blood-alcohol test); *State v. Coombs*, 821 A.2d 1030, 1032 (N.H. 2003) (blood-alcohol test); *State v. Fischer*, 459 N.W.2d 818 (N. D. 1990) (laboratory drug report); *Commonwealth v. Carter*, 932 A.2d 1261 (Pa. 2007) (laboratory drug report; applying pre-*Crawford* law); *State v. Tavares*, 590 A.2d 867, 872–873 (R. I. 1991) (laboratory analysis of victim's bodily fluid); *State v. Hutto*, 481 S. E. 2d 432, 436 (S.C. 1997) (footprint); *State v. Best*, 703 P.2d 548, 550–551 (Ariz. App. 1985) (fingerprint); *State v. Christian*, 895 P.2d 676 (N.M. App. 1995) (blood-alcohol test); *State v. Sosa*, 59 Wn. App. 678, 684-687, 800 P.2d 839, 843-844 (1990) (laboratory drug report).

The following authorities held, prior to *Crawford*, that the Confrontation Clause does not require confrontation of the results of autopsy and hospital reports describing the victim's injuries: *People v. Clark*, 833 P.2d 561, 627–628 (Calif. 1992) (autopsy report); *Henson v. State*, 332 A.2d 773, 774–776 (Del. 1975) (treating physician's report of victim's injuries, with medical conclusions redacted); *Collins v. State*, 369 N.E.2d 422, 423 (Ind. 1977) (autopsy report); *State v. Wilburn*, 198 So. 765, 765–766 (La. 1940) (hospital record stating victim's cause of death (citing *State v. Parker*, 7 La. Ann. 83 (1852) (coroner's written inquest stating cause of death))); *State v. Garlick*, 545 A.2d 27, 34 (Md. 1988) (blood test showing presence of illegal drug); *People v. Kirtdoll*, 217 N.W.2d 37, 46-48 (Mich. 1974) (treating physician's report describing victim's injuries); *State v. Spikes*, 423 N.E.2d 1122, 1128–1130 (Ohio 1981) (treating physician's report of defendant's injuries); *State v. Kreck*, 542 P.2d 782, 786–787 (Wn. 1975) (laboratory report stating that murder victim's blood contained poison).

The following authorities held, prior to *Crawford*, that the Confrontation Clause does not require confrontation of certificates stating that instruments were in good working order at the time of a test: *State v. Ing*, 497 P.2d 575, 577–579 (Haw. 1972) (certificate that police car's speedometer was in working order), *accord, State v. Ofa*, 828 P.2d 813, 817–818 (Haw. App. 1992) (per curiam) (certificate that breathalyzer was in working order); *State v. Ruiz*, 903 P.2d 845 (N.M. App. 1995) (same); *State v. Dilliner*, 569 S. E. 2d 211, 217–218 (W. Va. 2002) (same); *State v. Huggins*, 659 P.2d 613, 616–617 (Alaska App. 1982) (same); *State v. Conway*, 690 P.2d 1128 (Ore. 1984) (same).

The following decisions reduced the right to confront the results of scientific tests by upholding burden-shifting statutes that require the defendant to take affirmative steps prior to trial to summon the analyst: *Johnson v. State*, 792 S.W.2d 863, 866–867 (Ark. 1990) (defendant must give notice 10 days before trial); *State v. Davison*, 245 N.W.2d 321 (Iowa 1976) Iowa Code § 749A.2 (1975), now codified as Iowa Code Ann. § 691.2 (2009) (same); *State v. Crow*, 974 P.2d 100 (Kan. 1999) (defendant must give notice within 10 days of receiving the result and must show that the result will be challenged at trial); *State v. Christianson*, 404 A.2d 999 (Me. 1979) (defendant must give notice 10 days before trial); *State v. Miller*, 790 A.2d 144, 156 (N.J. 2002) (defendant must give notice within 10 days of receiving the result and must show that the result will be challenged at trial); *State v. Smith*, 323 S. E. 2d 316, 328 (N.C. 1984) (defendant must subpoena analyst); *State v. Hancock*, 854 P.2d 926, 928–930 (Ore. 1993) (same), *but see State v. Birchfield*, 157 P. 3d 216 (Ore.) (reducing defendant's burden); *State v. Hughes*, 713 S.W.2d 58 (Tenn. 1986) (defendant must subpoena analyst); *Magruder v. Commonwealth*, 657 S. E. 2d 113, 119–121 (Va. 2008) (defendant must "'call the person performing such analysis,'" at the State's expense); *People v. Mayfield-Ulloa*, 817 P.2d 603 (Colo. App. 1991) (defendant must give notice to State and the analyst 10 days before trial);

State v. Matthews, 632 So. 2d 294, 300–302 (La. App. 1993) (defendant must give notice five days before trial).

B

The following authorities hold that State Rules of Evidence permit the results of routine scientific tests to be admitted into evidence without confrontation: *State v. Torres*, 589 P.2d 83 (Haw. 1978) (X-ray of victim's body); *State v. Davis*, 269 N.W.2d 434, 440 (Iowa 1978) (laboratory analysis of victim's bodily fluid); *State v. Taylor*, 486 S.W.2d 239, 241–243 (Mo. 1972) (microscopic comparison of wood chip retrieved from defendant's clothing with wood at crime scene); *State v. Snider*, 541 P.2d 1204, 1210 (Mont. 1975) (laboratory drug report); *People v. Porter*, 362 N. Y. S. 2d 249, 255-256 (1974) (blood-alcohol report); *Robertson v. Commonwealth*, 175 S. E. 2d 260, 262–264 (Va. 1970) (laboratory analysis of victim's bodily fluid); *Kreck, supra*, at 542 P.2d, 786–787 (laboratory report stating that murder victim's blood contained poison).

The following authorities hold that State Rules of Evidence permit autopsy and hospital reports to be admitted into evidence without confrontation: *People v. Williams*, 345 P.2d 47, 63-64 (Cal. 1959) (autopsy report); *Henson*, 332 A.2d, at 775–776 (report of physician who examined victim); *Wilburn*, 198 So., at 765–766 (hospital record stating victim's cause of death); *Garlick, supra*, at 545 A. 2d, at 34 (blood test); *State v. Reddick*, 248 A.2d 425, 426–427 (N.J. 1968) (per curiam) (autopsy report stating factual findings, but not opinions, of medical examiner); *People v. Nisonoff*, 59 N.E.2d 420 (N.Y. 1944) (same).

The following authorities hold that State Rules of Evidence permit certificates, which state that scientific instruments were in good working order, to be admitted into evidence without confrontation: *Wester v. State*, 528 P.2d 1179, 1183 (Alaska 1974) (certificate stating that breathalyzer machine was in working order); *Best v. State*, 328 A.2d 141, 143 (Del. 1974) (certificate that breathalyzer was in working order); *State v. Rines*, 269 A.2d 9, 13–15 (Me. 1970) (manufacturer's certificate stating that blood-alcohol test kit was in working order admissible under the business-records exception); *McIlwain v. State*, 700 So. 2d 586, 590–591 (Miss. 1997) (same).

Taking the minority view, the following authorities interpret state hearsay rules to require confrontation of the results of routine scientific tests or observations of medical personnel: *State v. Sandoval-Tena*, 71 P. 3d 1055, 1059 (Idaho 2003) (laboratory drug report inadmissible under state hearsay rule); *Spears v. State*, 241 So. 2d 148 (Miss. 1970) (nurse's observation of victim inadmissible under state hearsay rule and constitution); *State v. James*, 179 S.E. 2d 41 (S.C. 1971) (chemical analysis of victim's bodily fluid inadmissible under state hearsay rule); *Cole v. State*, 839 S.W.2d 798 (Tex. Crim. App. 1990) (laboratory drug report inadmissible under state hearsay rule); *State v. Workman*, 122 P. 3d 639, 642–643 (same); *State v. Williams*, 2002

WI 58, PP32-62, 253 Wis. 2d 99, 118–127, 644 N.W.2d 919, 928–932 (same), *but see id.*, at 109–117, 644 N. W. 2d, at 924–927 (no confrontation violation where expert testified based on test results prepared by an out-of-court analyst).]

This summary does not include decisions that find test results inadmissible because the State failed to lay a proper foundation. Rather than endorse the minority view, those cases merely reaffirm the government's burden to prove the authenticity of its evidence and the applicability of an exception to the state hearsay rule. *See, e.g., State v. Fisher*, 178 N.W.2d 380 (Iowa 1970) (laboratory test of victim's bodily fluid inadmissible under business-records exception because the prosecution did not show that it was kept in regular course of business); *State v. Foster*, 422 P.2d 964 (Kan. 1967) (no foundation laid for introduction of blood-alcohol test because the prosecution did not show that the test was conducted in the usual course of business); *Moon v. State*, 478 A.2d 695, 702–703 (Md. 1984) (blood alcohol test inadmissible because insufficient foundational evidence that the test was conducted in a reliable manner); *cf. Davis, supra*, at 440 (laboratory test of victim's bodily fluid admitted under business-records exception to state hearsay rule); *Garlick*, 545 A. 2d, at 30, n. 2, 34 (laboratory test of defendant's blood falls within "firmly rooted" hearsay exception).

Three States once espoused the minority view but appear to have changed course to some degree: *People v. Lewis*, 293 N. W. 907 (Mich. 1940) (hospital record describing victim's injuries inadmissible hearsay), *overruled by Kirtdoll*, 217 N. W. 2d, at 39 (noting that "in its 35 year long history, Lewis . . . has never been relied upon to actually deny admission into evidence of a business entry record in a criminal case"), *but see People v. McDaniel*, 670 N.W.2d 659 (Mich. 2003) (per curiam) (police laboratory report inadmissible hearsay); *State v. Tims*, 224 N.E.2d 348, 350 (Ohio 1967) (hospital record describing victim's injuries inadmissible hearsay), *overruled by Spikes*, 423 N. E. 2d, at 1128-1130; *State v. Henderson*, 554 S.W.2d 117 (Tenn. 1977) (laboratory drug report inadmissible absent confrontation), *abrogated by statute as recognized by Hughes*, 713 S.W.2d 58 (statute permitted defendant to subpoena analyst who prepared blood alcohol report; by not doing so, defendant waived his right to confront the analyst).

BULLCOMING V. NEW MEXICO
131 S. CT. 2705 (2011)

The Sixth Amendment's Confrontation Clause gives the accused "[i]n all criminal prosecutions, . . . the right . . . to be confronted with the witnesses against him." In *Crawford v. Washington*, 541 U.S. 36, 59, this Court held that the Clause permits admission of "[t]estimonial statements of witnesses absent from trial . . . only where the declarant is unavailable, and only where the defendant has had a prior opportunity to cross-examine." Later, in *Melendez-Diaz v. Massachusetts*, 557 U.S. 305, the Court declined to create a "forensic evidence" exception to *Crawford*, holding that a forensic laboratory report, created specifically to serve as evidence in a criminal proceeding, ranked as "testimonial" for Confrontation Clause purposes. Absent stipulation, the Court ruled, the prosecution may not introduce such a report without offering a live witness competent to testify to the truth of the report's statements. 557 U.S., at_____, 129 S. Ct. 2527.

Petitioner Bullcoming's jury trial on charges of driving while intoxicated (DWI) occurred after *Crawford*, but before *Melendez-Diaz*. Principal evidence against him was a forensic laboratory report certifying that his blood-alcohol concentration was well above the threshold for aggravated DWI. Bullcoming's blood sample had been tested at the New Mexico Department of Health, Scientific Laboratory Division (SLD), by a forensic analyst named Caylor, who completed, signed, and certified the report. However, the prosecution neither called Caylor to testify nor asserted he was unavailable; the record showed only that Caylor was placed on unpaid leave for an undisclosed reason. In lieu of Caylor, the State called another analyst, Razatos, to validate the report. Razatos was familiar with the testing device used to analyze Bullcoming's blood and with the laboratory's testing procedures, but had neither participated in nor observed the test on Bullcoming's blood sample. Bullcoming's counsel objected, asserting that introduction of Caylor's report without his testimony would violate the Confrontation Clause, but the trial court overruled the objection, admitted the SLD report as a business record, and permitted Razatos to testify. Bullcoming was convicted, and, while his appeal was pending before the New Mexico Supreme Court, this Court decided *Melendez-Diaz*. The state high court acknowledged that the SLD report qualified as testimonial evidence under *Melendez-Diaz*, but held that the report's admission did not violate the Confrontation Clause because: (1) certifying analyst Caylor was a mere scrivener who simply transcribed machine-generated test results, and (2) SLD analyst Razatos, although he did not participate in testing Bullcoming's blood, qualified as an expert witness with respect to the testing machine and SLD procedures. The court affirmed Bullcoming's conviction.

Held:

The judgment is reversed, and the case is remanded.

Justice Ginsburg delivered the opinion of the Court with respect to all but Part IV and footnote 6. The Confrontation Clause, the opinion concludes, does not permit the prosecution to introduce a forensic laboratory report containing a testimonial certification, made in order to prove a fact at a criminal trial, through the in-court testimony of an analyst who did not sign the certification or personally perform or observe the performance of the test reported in the certification. The accused's right is to be confronted with the analyst who made the certification, unless that analyst is unavailable at trial, and the accused had an opportunity, pretrial, to cross-examine that particular scientist.

(a) If an out-of-court statement is testimonial, it may not be introduced against the accused at trial unless the witness who made the statement is unavailable and the accused has had a prior opportunity to confront that witness.

(i) Caylor's certification reported more than a machine-generated number: It represented that he received Bullcoming's blood sample intact with the seal unbroken; that he checked to make sure that the forensic report number and the sample number corresponded; that he performed a particular test on Bullcoming's sample, adhering to a precise protocol; and that he left the report's remarks section blank, indicating that no circumstance or condition affected the sample's integrity or the analysis' validity. These representations, relating to past events and human actions not revealed in raw, machine-produced data, are meat for cross-examination. The potential ramifications of the state court's reasoning, therefore, raise red flags. Most witnesses testify to their observations of factual conditions or events. Where, for example, a police officer's report recorded an objective fact such as the read-out of a radar gun, the state court's reasoning would permit another officer to introduce the information, so long as he or she was equipped to testify about the technology the observing officer deployed and the police department's standard operating procedures. As, e.g., *Davis v. Washington*, 547 U.S. 813, 826, makes plain, however, such testimony would violate the Confrontation Clause. The comparative reliability of an analyst's testimonial report does not dispense with the Clause. *Crawford*, 541 U.S., at 62. The analysts who write reports introduced as evidence must be made available for confrontation even if they have "the scientific acumen of Mme. Curie and the veracity of Mother Teresa." *Melendez-Diaz*, 129 S. Ct. 2527.

(ii) Nor was Razatos an adequate substitute witness simply because he qualified as an expert with respect to the testing machine and the SLD's laboratory procedures. Surrogate testimony of the kind Razatos was equipped to give could not convey what Caylor knew or observed about the events he certified, nor expose any lapses or lies on Caylor's part. Significantly, Razatos did not know why Caylor had been placed on unpaid leave. With Caylor on the stand, Bullcoming's counsel could have asked Caylor questions designed to reveal whether Caylor's incompetence, evasiveness, or dishonesty accounted for his removal from work. And the State did not assert that Razatos had any independent opinion concerning Bullcoming's blood alcohol content. More fundamentally, the Confrontation Clause does not tolerate dispensing with confrontation simply because the court believes that questioning one witness about another's testimonial statements provides a fair enough opportunity for cross-examination. Although the purpose of Sixth Amendment rights is to ensure a fair trial, it does not follow that such rights can be disregarded because, on the whole, the trial is fair. *United States v. Gonzalez-Lopez*, 548 U.S. 140, 145. If a "particular guarantee" is violated, no substitute procedure can cure the violation. *Id.*, at 146.

(b) *Melendez-Diaz* precluded the State's argument that introduction of the SLD report did not implicate the Confrontation Clause because the report is nontestimonial. Like the certificates in *Melendez-Diaz*, the SLD report is undoubtedly an "affirmation made for the purpose of establishing or proving some fact" in a criminal proceeding. 557 U.S., at_____. Created solely for an "evidentiary purpose," *id.*, at_____, the report ranks as testimonial. In all material respects, the SLD report resembles the certificates in *Melendez-Diaz*. Here, as there, an officer provided seized evidence to a state laboratory required by law to assist in police investigations. Like the *Melendez-Diaz* analysts, Caylor tested the evidence and prepared a certificate concerning the result of his analysis. And like the *Melendez-Diaz* certificates, Caylor's report here is "formalized" in a signed document, *Davis*, 547 U.S., at 837, n. 2. Also noteworthy, the SLD report form contains a legend referring to municipal and magistrate courts' rules that provide for the admission of certified blood-alcohol analyses. Thus, although the SLD report was not notarized, the formalities attending the report were more than adequate to qualify Caylor's assertions as testimonial.

GINSBERG, J., delivered the opinion of the Court, except as to Part IV and footnote 6. SCALIA, J., joined that opinion in full, SOTOMAYOR and KAGAN, JJ., joined as to all but Part IV, and THOMAS, J., joined as to all but Part IV and footnote 6. Sotomayor, J., filed an opinion concurring in part. KENNEDY, J., filed a dissenting opinion, in which ROBERTS, C. J., and BREYER and ALITO, JJ., joined.

Opinion

In *Melendez-Diaz v. Massachusetts*, 557 U.S. 305 (2009), this Court held that a forensic laboratory report stating that a suspect substance was cocaine ranked as testimonial for purposes of the Sixth Amendment's Confrontation Clause. The report had been created specifically to serve as evidence in a criminal proceeding. Absent stipulation, the Court ruled, the prosecution may not introduce such a report without offering a live witness competent to testify to the truth of the statements made in the report.

In the case before us, petitioner Donald Bullcoming was arrested on charges of driving while intoxicated (DWI). Principal evidence against Bullcoming was a forensic laboratory report certifying that Bullcoming's blood-alcohol concentration was well above the threshold for aggravated DWI. At trial, the prosecution did not call as a witness the analyst who signed the certification. Instead, the State called another analyst who was familiar with the laboratory's testing procedures, but had neither participated in nor observed the test on Bullcoming's blood sample. The New Mexico Supreme Court determined that, although the blood-alcohol analysis was "testimonial," the Confrontation Clause did not require the certifying analyst's in-court testimony. Instead, New Mexico's high court held, live testimony of another analyst satisfied the constitutional requirements.

The question presented is whether the Confrontation Clause permits the prosecution to introduce a forensic laboratory report containing a testimonial certification—made for the purpose of proving a particular fact—through the in-court testimony of a scientist who did not sign the certification or perform or observe the test reported in the certification. We hold that surrogate testimony of that order does not meet the constitutional requirement. The accused's right is to be confronted with the analyst who made the certification, unless that analyst is unavailable at trial, and the accused had an opportunity, pretrial, to cross-examine that particular scientist.

I

A

In August 2005, a vehicle driven by petitioner Donald Bullcoming rear-ended a pick-up truck at an intersection in Farmington, New Mexico. When the truckdriver exited his vehicle and approached Bullcoming to exchange insurance information, he noticed that Bullcoming's eyes were bloodshot. Smelling alcohol on Bullcoming's breath, the truckdriver told his wife to call the police. Bullcoming left the scene before the police arrived, but was soon apprehended by an officer who observed his performance of field sobriety tests. Upon failing the tests, Bullcoming was arrested for driving a vehicle while "under the influence of intoxicating liquor" (DWI), in violation of N.M. Stat. Ann. § 66-8-102 (2004).

Because Bullcoming refused to take a breath test, the police obtained a warrant authorizing a blood-alcohol analysis. Pursuant to the warrant, a sample of Bullcoming's blood was drawn at a local hospital. To determine Bullcoming's blood-alcohol concentration (BAC), the police sent the sample to the New Mexico Department of Health, Scientific Laboratory Division (SLD). In a standard SLD form titled "Report of Blood Alcohol Analysis," participants in the testing were identified, and the forensic analyst certified his finding. App. 62.

SLD's report contained in the top block "information . . . filled in by [the] arresting officer." *Ibid.* (capitalization omitted). This information included the "reason [the] suspect [was] stopped" (the officer checked "Accident"), and the date ("8.14.05") and time ("18:25 PM") the blood sample was drawn. *Ibid.* (capitalization omitted). The arresting officer also affirmed that he had arrested Bullcoming and witnessed the blood draw. *Ibid.* The next two blocks contained certifications by the nurse who drew Bullcoming's blood and the SLD intake employee who received the blood sample sent to the laboratory. *Ibid.*

Following these segments, the report presented the "certificate of analyst," *ibid.* (capitalization omitted), completed and signed by Curtis Caylor, the SLD forensic analyst assigned to test Bullcoming's blood sample. *Id.*, at 62, 64–65. Caylor recorded that the BAC in Bullcoming's sample was 0.21 grams per hundred milliliters, an inordinately high level. *Id.*, at 62. Caylor also affirmed that "[t]he seal of th[e] sample was received intact and broken in the laboratory," that "the statements in [the analyst's block of the report] asre correct," and that he had "followed the procedures set out on the reverse of th[e] report." *Ibid.* Those "procedures" instructed analysts, inter alia, to "retai[n] the sample container and the raw data from the analysis," and to "not[e] any circumstance or condition which might affect the integrity of the sample or otherwise affect the validity of the analysis." *Id.*, at 65. Finally, in a block headed "certificate of reviewer," the SLD examiner who reviewed Caylor's analysis certified that Caylor was qualified to conduct the BAC test, and that the "established procedure" for handling and analyzing Bullcoming's sample "ha[d] been followed." *Id.*, at 62 (capitalization omitted).

SLD analysts use gas chromatograph machines to determine BAC levels. Operation of the machines requires specialized knowledge and training. Several steps are involved in the gas chromatograph process, and human error can occur at each step.[1]

---

1. Gas chromatography is a widely used scientific method of quantitatively analyzing the constituents of a mixture. *See generally* H. McNair & J. Miller, Basic Gas Chromatography (2d ed. 2009) (hereinafter McNair). Under SLD's standard testing protocol, the analyst extracts two blood samples and inserts them into vials containing an "internal standard"—a chemical additive. App. 53. *See* McNair 141–142. The analyst then "cap[s] the [two] sample[s]," "crimp[s] them with an aluminum top," and places the vials into the gas chromatograph machine. App. 53–54. Within a few hours, this device produces a printed graph—a chromatogram—along with calculations representing a software-generated interpretation of the data. *See* Brief for State of New Mexico Dept. of Health, SLD as *Amicus Curiae* 16–17. Although the State presented testimony that obtaining an accurate BAC measurement merely entails "look[ing] at the [gas chromatograph] machine and record[ing] the results," App. 54, authoritative sources reveal that the matter is not so simple or certain. "In order to perform quantitative analyses satisfactorily and . . . support the results under rigorous examination in court, the analyst must be aware of, an adhere to, good analytical practices and understand what is being done and why." Stafford, Chromatography, in Principles of Forensic Toxicology 92, 114 (B. Levine 2d ed. 2006). *See also* McNair 137 ("Errors that occur in any step can invalidate the best chromatographic analysis, so attention must be paid to all steps."); D. Bartell, M. McMurray, & A. ImObersteg, Attacking and Defending Drunk Driving Tests § 16:80 (2d revision 2010) (stating that 93% of errors in laboratory tests for BAC levels are human errors that occur either before or after machines analyze samples). Even after the machine has produced its printed result, a review of the chromatogram may indicate that the test was not valid. *See* McNair 207–214. Nor is the risk of human error so remote

Caylor's report that Bullcoming's BAC was 0.21 supported a prosecution for aggravated DWI, the threshold for which is a BAC of 0.16 grams per hundred milliliters, § 66-8-102(D)(1). The State accordingly charged Bullcoming with this more serious crime.

B

The case was tried to a jury in November 2005, after our decision in *Crawford v. Washington*, 541 U.S. 36 (2004), but before *Melendez-Diaz*. On the day of trial, the State announced that it would not be calling SLD analyst Curtis Caylor as a witness because he had "very recently [been] put on unpaid leave" for a reason not revealed. 2010-NMSC-007, P8, 2010 NMSC 7, 147 N.M. 487, 226 P.3d 1, 6 (internal quotation marks omitted); App. 58. A startled defense counsel objected. The prosecution, she complained, had never disclosed, until trial commenced, that the witness "out there . . . [was] not the analyst [of Bullcoming's sample]." *Id.*, at 46. Counsel stated that, "had [she] known that the analyst [who tested Bullcoming's blood] was not available," her opening, indeed, her entire defense "may very well have been dramatically different." *Id.*, at 47. The State, however, proposed to introduce Caylor's finding as a "business record" during the testimony of Gerasimos Razatos, an SLD scientist who had neither observed nor reviewed Caylor's analysis. *Id.*, at 44.

Bullcoming's counsel opposed the State's proposal. *Id.*, at 44–45. Without Caylor's testimony, defense counsel maintained, introduction of the analyst's finding would violate Bullcoming's Sixth Amendment right "to be confronted with the witnesses against him." *Ibid.*[2] The trial court overruled the objection, *id.*, at 46–47, and admitted the SLD report as a business record, *id.*, at 44–46, 57.[3] The jury convicted Bullcoming of aggravated DWI, and the New Mexico Court of Appeals upheld the conviction, concluding that "the blood alcohol report in the present case was non-testimonial and prepared routinely with guarantees of trustworthiness." 2008-NMCA-097, § 17, 189 P.3d 679, 685.

---

as to be negligible. Amici inform us, for example, that in neighboring Colorado, a single forensic laboratory produced at least 206 flawed blood-alcohol readings over a three-year span, prompting the dismissal of several criminal prosecutions. *See* Brief for National Association of Criminal Defense Lawyers et al. as Amici Curiae 32–33. An analyst had used improper amounts of the internal standard, causing the chromatograph machine systematically to inflate BAC measurements. The analyst's error, a supervisor said, was "fairly complex." Ensslin, Final Tally on Flawed DUI: 206 Errors, 9 Tossed or Reduced, Colorado Springs Gazette, Apr. 19, 2010, p. 1 (internal quotation marks omitted), available at http://gazette.com/articles/report-97354-police-discuss.html. (all Internet materials as visited June 21, 2011, and included in Clerk of Court's case file).

2. The State called as witnesses the arresting officer and the nurse who drew Bullcoming's blood. Bullcoming did not object to the State's failure to call the SLD intake employee or the reviewing analyst. "It is up to the prosecution," the Court observed in *Melendez-Diaz v. Massachusetts*, 577 U.S. 305, 311 (2009), "to decide what steps in the chain of custody are so crucial as to require evidence; but what testimony is introduced must (if the defendant objects) be introduced live."

3. The trial judge noted that, when he started out in law practice, "there were no breath tests or blood tests. They just brought in the cop, and the cop said, 'Yeah, he was drunk.'" App. 47.

C

While Bullcoming's appeal was pending before the New Mexico Supreme Court, this Court decided *Melendez-Diaz*. In that case, "[t]he Massachusetts courts [had] admitted into evidence affidavits reporting the results of forensic analysis which showed that material seized by the police and connected to the defendant was cocaine." 557 U.S., at 307. Those affidavits, the Court held, were "'testimonial,' rendering the affiants 'witnesses' subject to the defendant's right of confrontation under the Sixth Amendment." *Ibid.*

In light of *Melendez-Diaz*, the New Mexico Supreme Court acknowledged that the blood-alcohol report introduced at Bullcoming's trial qualified as testimonial evidence. Like the affidavits in *Melendez-Diaz*, the court observed, the report was "functionally identical to live, in-court testimony, doing precisely what a witness does on direct examination." 226 P.3d, at 8 (quoting *Melendez-Diaz*, 557 U.S., at 310).[4] Nevertheless, for two reasons, the court held that admission of the report did not violate the Confrontation Clause.

First, the court said certifying analyst Caylor "was a mere scrivener," who "simply transcribed the results generated by the gas chromatograph machine." 226 P.3d, at 8–9. Second, SLD analyst Razatos, although he did not participate in testing Bullcoming's blood, "qualified as an expert witness with respect to the gas chromatograph machine." *Id.*, at 9. "Razatos provided live, in-court testimony," the court stated, "and, thus, was available for cross-examination regarding the operation of the . . . machine, the results of [Bullcoming's] BAC test, and the SLD's established laboratory procedures." *Ibid.* Razatos' testimony was crucial, the court explained, because Bullcoming could not cross-examine the machine or the written report. *Id.*, at 10. But "[Bullcoming's] right of confrontation was preserved," the court concluded, because Razatos was a qualified analyst, able to serve as a surrogate for Caylor. *Ibid.*

We granted certiorari to address this question: Does the Confrontation Clause permit the prosecution to introduce a forensic laboratory report containing a testimonial certification, made in order to prove a fact at a criminal trial, through the in-court testimony of an analyst who did not sign the certification or personally perform or observe the performance of the test reported in the certification. 561 U.S.____, 131 S. Ct. 62, 177 L. Ed. 2d 1152 (2010). Our answer is in line with controlling precedent: As a rule, if an out-of-court statement is testimonial in nature, it may not be introduced against the accused at trial unless the witness who made the statement is unavailable and the accused has had a prior opportunity to confront that witness. Because the New Mexico Supreme Court permitted the testimonial statement of one witness, i.e., Caylor, to enter into evidence through the in-court testimony of a second person, i.e., Razatos, we reverse that court's judgment.

---

4. In so ruling, the New Mexico Supreme Court explicitly overruled *State v. Dedman*, 102 P.3d 628 (N.M. 2004), which had classified blood-alcohol reports as public records neither "investigative nor prosecutorial" in nature. 226 P.3d, at 7–8.

II

The Sixth Amendment's Confrontation Clause confers upon the accused "[i]n all criminal prosecutions, . . . the right . . . to be confronted with the witnesses against him." In a pathmarking 2004 decision, *Crawford v. Washington*, we overruled *Ohio v. Roberts*, 448 U.S. 56 (1980), which had interpreted the Confrontation Clause to allow admission of absent witnesses' testimonial statements based on a judicial determination of reliability. *See Roberts*, 448 U.S., at 66. Rejecting *Roberts'* amorphous notions of 'reliability,' *Crawford*, 541 U.S., at 61, *Crawford* held that fidelity to the Confrontation Clause permitted admission of "[t]estimonial statements of witnesses absent from trial . . . only where the declarant is unavailable, and only where the defendant has had a prior opportunity to cross-examine," *id.*, at 59. *See Michigan v. Bryant*, 131 S. Ct. 1143 (2011) ("[F]or testimonial evidence to be admissible, the Sixth Amendment 'demands what the common law required: unavailability [of the witness] and a prior opportunity for cross-examination.'" (quoting *Crawford*, 541 U.S., at 68). *Melendez-Diaz*, relying on *Crawford*'s rationale, refused to create a "forensic evidence" exception to this rule.[5] An analyst's certification prepared in connection with a criminal investigation or prosecution, the Court held, is "testimonial," and therefore within the compass of the Confrontation Clause. *Id.*, 129 S. Ct. 2527.[6]

The State in the instant case never asserted that the analyst who signed the certification, Curtis Caylor, was unavailable. The record showed only that Caylor was placed on unpaid leave for an undisclosed reason. Nor did Bullcoming have an opportunity to cross-examine Caylor. *Crawford* and *Melendez-Diaz*, therefore, weigh heavily in Bullcoming's favor. The New Mexico Supreme Court, however, although recognizing that the SLD report was testimonial for purposes of the Confrontation Clause, considered SLD analyst Razatos an adequate substitute for Caylor. We explain first why Razatos' appearance did not meet the Confrontation Clause requirement. We next address the State's argument that the SLD report ranks as "nontestimonial," and therefore "[was] not subject to the Confrontation Clause in the first place. Brief for Respondent 7 (capitalization omitted).

---

5. The dissent makes plain that its objections is less to the application of the Court's decisions in *Crawford* and *Melendez-Diaz* to this case than to those pathmarking decisions themselves. *See post* (criticizing the "*Crawford* line of cases" for rejecting "reliable evidence") (deploring "*Crawford's* rejection of the [reliability-centered] regime of *Ohio v. Roberts*").

6. To rank as "testimonial," a statement must have a "primary purpose" of "establish[ing] or prov[ing] past events potentially relevant to later criminal prosecution." *Davis v. Washington*, 547 U.S. 813 (2006). *See also Bryant*, 562 U.S. at __. Elaborating on the purpose for which a "testimonial report" is created, we observed in *Melendez-Diaz* that business and public records "are generally admissible absent confrontation . . . because—having been created for the administration of an entity's affairs and not for the purpose of establishing or proving some fact at trial—they are not testimonial." 557 U.S., at 324.

A

The New Mexico Supreme Court held surrogate testimony adequate to satisfy the Confrontation Clause in this case because analyst Caylor "simply transcribed the resul[t] generated by the gas chromatograph machine," presenting no interpretation and exercising no independent judgment. 226 P.3d, at 8. Bullcoming's "true 'accuser,'" the court said, was the machine, while testing analyst Caylor's role was that of "mere scrivener." *Id.*, at 9. Caylor's certification, however, reported more than a machine-generated number.

Caylor certified that he received Bullcoming's blood sample intact with the seal unbroken, that he checked to make sure that the forensic report number and the sample number "correspond[ed]," and that he performed on Bullcoming's sample a particular test, adhering to a precise protocol. App. 62–65. He further represented, by leaving the "[r]emarks" section of the report blank, that no "circumstance or condition . . . affect[ed] the integrity of the sample or . . . the validity of the analysis." *Id.*, at 62, 65. These representations, relating to past events and human actions not revealed in raw, machine-produced data, are meet for cross-examination.

The potential ramifications of the New Mexico Supreme Court's reasoning, furthermore, raise red flags. Most witnesses, after all, testify to their observations of factual conditions or events, e.g., "the light was green," "the hour was noon." Such witnesses may record, on the spot, what they observed. Suppose a police report recorded an objective fact—Bullcoming's counsel posited the address above the front door of a house or the read-out of a radar gun. *See* Brief for Petitioner 35. Could an officer other than the one who saw the number on the house or gun present the information in court—so long as that officer was equipped to testify about any technology the observing officer deployed and the police department's standard operating procedures? As our precedent makes plain, the answer is emphatically "No." *See Davis v. Washington*, 547 U.S. 813 (2006) (Confrontation Clause may not be "evaded by having a note-taking police[officer] recite the . . . testimony of the declarant" (emphasis deleted)); *Melendez-Diaz*, 557 U.S., at 335 (Kennedy, J., dissenting) ("The Court made clear in *Davis* that it will not permit the testimonial statement of one witness to enter into evidence through the in-court testimony of a second.").

The New Mexico Supreme Court stated that the number registered by the gas chromatograph machine called for no interpretation or exercise of independent judgment on Caylor's part. 226 P.3d, at 8–9. We have already explained that Caylor certified to more than a machine-generated number. In any event, the comparative reliability of an analyst's testimonial report drawn from machine-produced data does not overcome the Sixth Amendment bar. This Court settled in *Crawford* that the "obviou[s] reliab[ility]" of a testimonial statement does not dispense with the Confrontation Clause. 541 U.S., at 62; *see id.*, at 61 (Clause "commands, not that evidence be reliable, but that reliability be assessed in a particular manner: by testing [the evidence] in the crucible of cross-examination"). Accordingly, the analysts who write reports that the prosecution introduces must be made available for confrontation even if they possess "the scientific acumen of Mme. Curie and the veracity of Mother Teresa." *Melendez-Diaz*, 557 U.S., at 319, n. 6.

B

Recognizing that admission of the blood-alcohol analysis depended on "live, in-court testimony [by] a qualified analyst," 226 P.3d, at 10, the New Mexico Supreme Court believed that Razatos could substitute for Caylor because Razatos "qualified as an expert witness with respect to the gas chromatograph machine and the SLD's laboratory procedures," *id.*, at 9. But surrogate testimony of the kind Razatos was equipped to give could not convey what Caylor knew or observed about the events his certification concerned, i.e., the particular test and testing process he employed.[7] Nor could such surrogate testimony expose any lapses or lies on the certifying analyst's part.[8] Significant here, Razatos had no knowledge of the reason why Caylor had been placed on unpaid leave. With Caylor on the stand, Bullcoming's counsel could have asked questions designed to reveal whether incompetence, evasiveness, or dishonesty accounted for Caylor's removal from his work station. Notable in this regard, the State never asserted that Caylor was "unavailable"; the prosecution conveyed only that Caylor was on uncompensated leave. Nor did the State assert that Razatos had any "independent opinion" concerning Bullcoming's BAC. *See* Brief for Respondent 58, n. 15. In this light, Caylor's live testimony could hardly be typed "a hollow formality."

More fundamentally, as this Court stressed in *Crawford*,] "[t]he text of the Sixth Amendment does not suggest any open-ended exceptions from the confrontation requirement to be developed by the courts." 541 U.S., at 54. Nor is it "the role of courts to extrapolate from the words of the [Confrontation Clause] to the values behind it, and then to enforce its guarantees only to the extent they serve (in the courts' views) those underlying values." *Giles v. California*, 554 U.S. 353, 375 (2008). Accordingly, the Clause does not tolerate dispensing with confrontation simply because the court believes that questioning one witness about another's testimonial statements provides a fair enough opportunity for cross-examination.

A recent decision involving another Sixth Amendment right—the right to counsel—is instructive. In *United States v. Gonzalez-Lopez*, 548 U.S. 140 (2006), the Government argued that illegitimately denying a defendant his counsel of choice

---

7. We do not question that analyst Caylor, in common with other analysts employed by SLD, likely would not recall a particular test, given the number of tests each analyst conducts and the standard procedure followed in testing. Even so, Caylor's testimony under oath would have enabled Bullcoming's counsel to raise before a jury questions concerning Caylor's proficiency, the care he took in performing his work, and his veracity. In particular, Bullcoming's counsel likely would have inquired on cross-examination why Caylor hand been placed on unpaid leave.

8. At Bullcoming's trial, Razatos acknowledged that "you don't know unless you actually observe the analysis that someone else conducts, whether they followed th[e] protocol in every instance." App. 59.

did not violate the Sixth Amendment where "substitute counsel's performance" did not demonstrably prejudice the defendant. *Id.*, at 144–145. This Court rejected the Government's argument. "[T]rue enough," the Court explained, "the purpose of the rights set forth in [the Sixth] Amendment is to ensure a fair trial; but it does not follow that the rights can be disregarded so long as the trial is, on the whole, fair." *Id.*, at 145. If a "particular guarantee" of the Sixth Amendment is violated, no substitute procedure can cure the violation, and "[n]o additional showing of prejudice is required to make the violation 'complete.' *Id.*, at 146. If representation by substitute counsel does not satisfy the Sixth Amendment, neither does the opportunity to confront a substitute witness.

In short, when the State elected to introduce Caylor's certification, Caylor became a witness Bullcoming had the right to confront. Our precedent cannot sensibly be read any other way. *See* Melendez-Diaz, 129 S. Ct. 2527, 2545 (Kennedy, J., dissenting) (Court's holding means "the . . . analyst who must testify is the person who signed the certificate").

III

We turn, finally, to the State's contention that the SLD's blood-alcohol analysis reports are nontestimonial in character, therefore no Confrontation Clause question even arises in this case. *Melendez-Diaz* left no room for that argument, the New Mexico Supreme Court concluded, *see* 226 P.3d, at 7–8, a conclusion we find inescapable.

In *Melendez-Diaz*, a state forensic laboratory, on police request, analyzed seized evidence (plastic bags) and reported the laboratory's analysis to the police (the substance found in the bags contained cocaine). 129 S. Ct. 2527, 2533. The "certificates of analysis" prepared by the analysts who tested the evidence in *Melendez-Diaz*, this Court held, were "incontrovertibly . . . affirmation[s] made for the purpose of establishing or proving some fact" in a criminal proceeding. *Id.*, at 129 S. Ct. 2527, 2540, (internal quotation marks omitted). The same purpose was served by the certificate in question here.

The State maintains that the affirmations made by analyst Caylor were not "adversarial" or "inquisitorial," Brief for Respondent 27–33; instead, they were simply observations of an "independent scientis[t]" made "according to a non-adversarial public duty," *id.*, at 32–33. That argument fares no better here than it did in *Melendez-Diaz*. A document created solely for an "evidentiary purpose," *Melendez-Diaz* clarified, made in aid of a police investigation, ranks as testimonial. 129 S. Ct. 2527 (forensic reports available for use at trial are "testimonial statements" and certifying analyst is a "'witness' for purposes of the Sixth Amendment).

Distinguishing Bullcoming's case from *Melendez-Diaz*, where the analysts' findings were contained in certificates "sworn to before a notary public," *id.*, at 129 S. Ct.

2527, 2531, the State emphasizes that the SLD report of Bullcoming's BAC was "unsworn." Brief for Respondent 13; ("only sworn statement" here was that of Razatos, "who was present and [did] testif[y]"). As the New Mexico Supreme Court recognized, "'the absence of [an] oath [i]s not dispositive' in determining if a statement is testimonial." 226 P.3d, at 8 (quoting *Crawford*, 541 U.S., at 52). Indeed, in *Crawford*, this Court rejected as untenable any construction of the Confrontation Clause that would render inadmissible only sworn ex parte affidavits, while leaving admission of formal, but unsworn statements "perfectly OK." *Id.*, at 52–53, n. 3. Reading the Clause in this "implausible" manner, *ibid.*, the Court noted, would make the right to confrontation easily erasable. *See Davis*, 547 U.S., at 830–831, n. 5; *id.*, at 838 (Thomas, J., concurring in judgment in part and dissenting in part).

In all material respects, the laboratory report in this case resembles those in *Melendez-Diaz*. Here, as in *Melendez-Diaz*, a law-enforcement officer provided seized evidence to a state laboratory required by law to assist in police investigations, N.M. Stat. Ann. § 29-3-4 (2004). Like the analysts in *Melendez-Diaz*, analyst Caylor tested the evidence and prepared a certificate concerning the result of his analysis. App. 62. Like the *Melendez-Diaz* certificates, Caylor's certificate is "formalized" in a signed document, *Davis*, 547 U.S., at 837, n. 2 (opinion of Thomas, J.), headed a "report," App. 62. Noteworthy as well, the SLD report form contains a legend referring to municipal and magistrate courts' rules that provide for the admission of certified blood-alcohol analyses.

In sum, the formalities attending the "report of blood alcohol analysis" are more than adequate to qualify Caylor's assertions as testimonial. The absence of notarization does not remove his certification from Confrontation Clause governance. The New Mexico Supreme Court, guided by *Melendez-Diaz*, correctly recognized that Caylor's report "fell within the core class of testimonial statements" 226 P.3d, at 7, described in this Court's leading Confrontation Clause decisions: *Melendez-Diaz*, 129 S. Ct. 2527; *Davis*, 547 U.S., at 830; *Crawford*, 541 U.S., at 51–52.

IV

The State and its amici urge that unbending application of the Confrontation Clause to forensic evidence would impose an undue burden on the prosecution. This argument, also advanced in the dissent, largely repeats a refrain rehearsed and rejected in *Melendez-Diaz*. *See* 129 S. Ct. 2527, 2540. The constitutional requirement, we reiterate, "may not [be] disregard[ed] . . . at our convenience," *id.*, at 129 S. Ct. 2527, and the predictions of dire consequences, we again observe, are dubious, see *id.*, at 129 S. Ct. 2527.

New Mexico law, it bears emphasis, requires the laboratory to preserve samples, which can be retested by other analysts, see N.M. Admin. Code § 7.33.2.15(A)(4)–(6) (2010), available at http://www.nmcpr.state.nm.us/nmac/_title07/T07C033.htm, and neither party questions SLD's compliance with that requirement. Retesting "is almost always an option . . . in [DWI] cases," Brief for Public Defender Service for District of Columbia et al. as *Amici Curiae* 25 (hereinafter PDS Brief), and the State had that option here: New Mexico could have avoided any Confrontation Clause problem by asking Razatos to retest the sample, and then testify to the results of his retest rather than to the results of a test he did not conduct or observe.

Notably, New Mexico advocates retesting as an effective means to preserve a defendant's confrontation right "when the [out-of-court] statement is raw data or a mere transcription of raw data onto a public record." Brief for Respondent 53–54. But the State would require the defendant to initiate retesting. *Id.*, at 55; (defense "remains free to . . . . call and examine the technician who performed a test"), ("free retesting" is available to defendants). The prosecution, however, bears the burden of proof. *Melendez-Diaz*, 129 S. Ct. 2527 ("[T]he Confrontation Clause imposes a burden on the prosecution to present its witnesses, not on the defendant to bring those adverse witnesses into court."). Hence the obligation to propel retesting when the original analyst is unavailable is the State's, not the defendant's. *See Taylor v. Illinois*, 484 U.S. 400, 410, n. 14 (1988) (Confrontation Clause's requirements apply "in every case, whether or not the defendant seeks to rebut the case against him or to present a case of his own").

Furthermore, notice-and-demand procedures, long in effect in many jurisdictions, can reduce burdens on forensic laboratories. Statutes governing these procedures typically "render . . . otherwise hearsay forensic reports admissible[,]while specifically preserving a defendant's right to demand that the prosecution call the author/analyst of [the] report." PDS Brief 9; *see Melendez-Diaz*, 129 S. Ct. 2527 (observing that notice-and-demand statutes "permit the defendant to assert (or forfeit by silence) his Confrontation Clause right after receiving notice of the prosecution's intent to use a forensic analyst's report").

Even before this Court's decision in *Crawford*, moreover, it was common prosecutorial practice to call the forensic analyst to testify. Prosecutors did so "to bolster the persuasive power of [the State's] case[,] . . . [even] when the defense would have preferred that the analyst did not testify." PDS Brief 8.

We note also the "small fraction of . . . cases" that "actually proceed to trial." *Melendez-Diaz*, 129 S. Ct. 2527, 2540 (citing estimate that "nearly 95% of convictions in state and federal courts are obtained via guilty plea"). And, "when cases in which forensic analysis has been conducted [do] go to trial," defendants "regularly . . . [stipulate] to the admission of [the] analysis." PDS Brief 20. "[A]s a result, analysts testify in only a very small percentage of cases," *id.*, at 21, for "[i]t is unlikely that defense counsel will insist on live testimony whose effect will be merely to highlight rather than cast doubt upon the forensic analysis." *Melendez-Diaz*, 129 S. Ct. 2527, 2556.[9]

---

9. The dissent argues otherwise, reporting and 71% increase, from 2008 to 2010, in the number of subpoenas for New Mexico analysts' testimony in impaired-driving cases. The dissent is silent,

Tellingly, in jurisdictions in which "it is the [acknowledged] job of . . . analysts to testify in court . . . about their test results," the sky has not fallen. PDS Brief 23. State and municipal laboratories "make operational and staffing decisions" to facilitate analysts' appearance at trial. *Ibid.* Prosecutors schedule trial dates to accommodate analysts' availability, and trial courts liberally grant continuances when unexpected conflicts arise. *Id.*, at 24–25. In rare cases in which the analyst is no longer employed by the laboratory at the time of trial, "the prosecution makes the effort to bring that analyst . . . to court." *Id.*, at 25. And, as is the practice in New Mexico, *see supra*, laboratories ordinarily retain additional samples, enabling them to run tests again when necessary.[10]

* * *

For the reasons stated, the judgment of the New Mexico Supreme Court is reversed, and the case is remanded for further proceedings not inconsistent with this opinion.[11]

CONCUR

JUSTICE SOTOMAYOR, concurring in part.

I agree with the Court that the trial court erred by admitting the blood alcohol concentration (BAC) report. I write separately first to highlight why I view the report at issue to be testimonial—specifically because its "primary purpose" is evidentiary—and second to emphasize the limited reach of the Court's opinion.

---

however, on the number of instances in which subpoenaed analysts in fact testify, i.e., the figure that would reveal the actual burden of courtroom testimony. Moreover, New Mexico's Department of Health, Scientific Laboratory Division, has attributed the "chaotic" conditions noted by the dissent, *ibid.*, to several factors, among them, staff attrition, a state hiring freeze, a 15% increase in the number of blood samples received for testing, and "wildly" divergent responses by New Mexico District Attorneys to *Melendez-Diaz.* Brief for State of New Mexico Dept. of Health, SLD as *Amicus Curiae* 2–5. Some New Mexico District Attorneys' offices, we are informed, "subpen[a] every analyst with any connection to a blood sample," *id.*, at 5, and exorbitant practice that undoubtedly inflates the number of subpoenas issued.

10. The dissent refers, selectively, to experience in Los Angeles, but overlooks experience documented in Michigan. In that State, post-*Melendez-Diaz*, the increase in in-court analyst testimony has been slight. Compare PDS Brief 21 (in 2006, analysts provided testimony for only 0.7% of all tests), with Michigan State Police, Forensic Science Division, available at http://www.michigan.gov/msp/0,1607,7-123-1493_3800-15910-,00.html (in 2010, analysts provided testimony for approximately 1% of all tests).

11. As in *Melendez-Diaz*, 129 S. Ct. 2527, we express no view on whether the Confrontation Clause error in this case was harmless. The New Mexico Supreme Court did not reach that question, *see* Brief for Respondent 59–60, and nothing in this opinion impedes a harmless-error inquiry on remand.

I

A

Under our precedents, the New Mexico Supreme Court was correct to hold that the certified BAC report in this case is testimonial. 226 P.3d 1, 8.

To determine if a statement is testimonial, we must decide whether it has "a primary purpose of creating an out-of-court substitute for trial testimony." *Michigan v. Bryant*, 131 S. Ct. 1143, 1155 (2011). When the "primary purpose" of a statement is "not to create a record for trial," *ibid.*, "the admissibility of [the] statement is the concern of state and federal rules of evidence, not the Confrontation Clause," *id.*, at S. Ct. 1143.

This is not the first time the Court has faced the question of whether a scientific report is testimonial. As the Court explains, in *Melendez-Diaz v. Massachusetts*, 557 U.S. 305 (2009), we held that "certificates of analysis," completed by employees of the State Laboratory Institute of the Massachusetts Department of Public Health, *id.*, at 129 S. Ct. 2527, were testimonial because they were "incontrovertibly . . . "'solemn declaration[s] or affirmation[s] made for the purpose of establishing or proving some fact,'" *id.*, at 129 S. Ct. 2527 (quoting *Crawford v. Washington*, 541 U.S. 36, 51 (2004), in turn quoting 2 N. Webster, An American Dictionary of the English Language (1828)).

As we explained earlier this Term in *Michigan v. Bryant*, 131 S. Ct. 1143 (2010), "[i]n making the primary purpose determination, standard rules of hearsay . . . will be relevant." *Id.*, at 131 S. Ct. 1143.[1] As applied to a scientific report, *Melendez-Diaz* explained that pursuant to Federal Rule of Evidence 803, "[d]ocuments kept in the regular course of business may ordinarily be admitted at trial despite their hearsay status," except "if the regularly conducted business activity is the production of evidence for use at trial." 129 S. Ct. 2527 (citing Fed. Rule Evid. 803(6)). In that circumstance, the hearsay rules bar admission of even business records. Relatedly, in the Confrontation Clause context, business and public records "are generally admissible absent confrontation . . . because—having been created for the administration of an entity's affairs and not for the purpose of establishing or proving some fact at trial—they are not testimonial." *Melendez-Diaz*, 129 S. Ct. 2527. We concluded, therefore, that because the purpose of the certificates of analysis was use at trial, they were not properly admissible as business or public records under the hearsay rules, *id.*, 129 S. Ct. 2527, nor were they admissible under the Confrontation Clause, *id.*, at 129 S. Ct. 2527. The hearsay rule's recognition of the certificates' evidentiary purpose thus confirmed our decision that the certificates were testimonial under

---

1. Contrary to the dissent's characterization, Bryant deemed reliability, as reflected in the hearsay rules, to be "relevant," 131 S. Ct. 1143, not "essential," (opinion of Kennedy, J.). The rules of evidence, not the Confrontation Clause, are designed primarily to police reliability; the purpose of the Confrontation Clause is to determine whether statements are testimonial and therefore require confrontation.

the primary purpose analysis required by the Confrontation Clause. *See id.*, at 129 S. Ct. 2527 (explaining that under Massachusetts law not just the purpose but the "sole purpose of the affidavits was to provide" evidence).

Similarly, in this case, for the reasons the Court sets forth the BAC report and Caylor's certification on it clearly have a "primary purpose of creating an out-of-court substitute for trial testimony." *Bryant*, 131 S. Ct. 1143. The Court also explains why the BAC report is not materially distinguishable from the certificates we held testimonial in *Melendez-Diaz*. *See* 129 S. Ct. 2527.[2]

The formality inherent in the certification further suggests its evidentiary purpose. Although "[f]ormality is not the sole touchstone of our primary purpose inquiry," a statement's formality or informality can shed light on whether a particular statement has a primary purpose of use at trial. *Bryant*, 131 S. Ct. 1143.[3] I agree with the Court's assessment that the certificate at issue here is a formal statement, despite the absence of notarization. *Crawford*, 541 U.S., at 52, 124 S. Ct. 1354, 158 L. Ed. 2d 177 ("[T]he absence of [an] oath [is] not dispositive"). The formality derives from the fact that the analyst is asked to sign his name and "certify" to both the result and the statements on the form. A "certification" requires one "[t]o attest" that the accompanying statements are true. Black's Law Dictionary 258 (9th ed. 2009) (definition of "certify"); *see also id.*, at 147 (defining "attest" as "[t]o bear witness; testify," or "[t]o affirm to be true or genuine; to authenticate by signing as a witness").

In sum, I am compelled to conclude that the report has a "primary purpose of creating an out-of-court substitute for trial testimony," *Bryant*, 131 S. Ct. 1143, which renders it testimonial.

B

After holding that the report was testimonial, the New Mexico Supreme Court nevertheless held that its admission was permissible under the Confrontation Clause

---

2. This is not to say, however, that every person noted on the BAC report must testify. As we explained in *Melendez-Diaz*, it is not the case "that anyone whose testimony may be relevant in establishing the chain of custody, authenticity of the sample, or accuracy of the testing device, must appear in person as part of the prosecution's case . . . . It is up to the prosecution to decide what steps in the chain of custody are so crucial as to require evidence . . . ." 129 S. Ct. 2527.

3. By looking at the formality of the statement, we do not "trea[t] the reliability of evidence as a reason to exclude it." Although in some instances formality could signal reliability, the dissent's argument fails to appreciate that, under our Confrontation Clause precedents, formality is primarily an indicator of testimonial purpose. Formality is not the sole indicator of the testimonial nature of a statement because it is too easily evaded. *See Davis v. Washington*, 547 U.S. 813, 838 (2006) (Thomas, J. concurring in judgment in part and dissenting in part). Nonetheless formality has long been a hallmark of testimonial statements because formality suggests that the statement is intended for use a trial. As we explained in *Bryant*, informality, on the other hand, "does not necessarily indicate . . . lack of testimonial intent." 131 S. Ct. 1143. The dissent itself recognizes the relevance of formality to the testimonial inquiry when it notes the formality of the problematic unconfronted statements in Sir Walter Raleigh's trial.

for two reasons: because Caylor was a "mere scrivener," and because Razatos could be cross-examined on the workings of the gas chromatograph and laboratory procedures. 226 P.3d, at 8–10. The Court convincingly explains why those rationales are incorrect. Therefore, the New Mexico court contravened our precedents in holding that the report was admissible via Razatos' testimony.

II

Although this case is materially indistinguishable from the facts we considered in *Melendez-Diaz*, I highlight some of the factual circumstances that this case does not present.

First, this is not a case in which the State suggested an alternate purpose, much less an alternate primary purpose, for the BAC report. For example, the State has not claimed that the report was necessary to provide Bullcoming with medical treatment. *See Bryant*, 131 S. Ct. 1143 (listing "Statements for Purposes of Medical Diagnosis or Treatment" under Federal Rule of Evidence 803(4) as an example of statements that are "by their nature, made for a purpose other than use in a prosecution"); *Melendez-Diaz*, 129 S. Ct. 2527, 2533 ("[M]edical reports created for treatment purposes . . . would not be testimonial under our decision today"); *Giles v. California*, 554 U.S. 353, 376 (2008) ("[S]tatements to physicians in the course of receiving treatment would be excluded, if at all, only by hearsay rules").

Second, this is not a case in which the person testifying is a supervisor, reviewer, or someone else with a personal, albeit limited, connection to the scientific test at issue. Razatos conceded on cross-examination that he played no role in producing the BAC report and did not observe any portion of Curtis Caylor's conduct of the testing. App. 58. The court below also recognized Razatos' total lack of connection to the test at issue. 226 P.3d, at 6. It would be a different case if, for example, a supervisor who observed an analyst conducting a test testified about the results or a report about such results. We need not address what degree of involvement is sufficient because here Razatos had no involvement whatsoever in the relevant test and report.

Third, this is not a case in which an expert witness was asked for his independent opinion about underlying testimonial reports that were not themselves admitted into evidence. *See* Fed. Rule Evid. 703 (explaining that facts or data of a type upon which experts in the field would reasonably rely in forming an opinion need not be admissible in order for the expert's opinion based on the facts and data to be admitted). As the Court notes, the State does not assert that Razatos offered an independent, expert opinion about Bullcoming's blood alcohol concentration. Rather, the State explains, "[a]side from reading a report that was introduced as an exhibit, Mr. Razatos offered no opinion about Petitioner's blood alcohol content. . . ." Brief for Respondent 58, n. 15 (citation omitted). Here the State offered the BAC report, including Caylor's testimonial statements, into evidence. We would face a different question if asked to determine the constitutionality of allowing an expert witness to discuss others' testimonial statements if the testimonial statements were not themselves admitted as evidence.

Finally, this is not a case in which the State introduced only machine-generated results, such as a printout from a gas chromatograph. The State here introduced Caylor's statements, which included his transcription of a blood alcohol concentration, apparently copied from a gas chromatograph printout, along with other statements about the procedures used in handling the blood sample; App. 62 ("I certify that I followed the procedures set out on the reverse of this report, and the statements in this block are correct"). Thus, we do not decide whether, as the New Mexico Supreme Court suggests, 226 P.3d, at 10, a State could introduce (assuming an adequate chain of custody foundation) raw data generated by a machine in conjunction with the testimony of an expert witness. *See* Reply Brief for Petitioner 16, n. 5.

This case does not present, and thus the Court's opinion does not address, any of these factual scenarios.

* * *

As in *Melendez-Diaz*, the primary purpose of the BAC report is clearly to serve as evidence. It is therefore testimonial, and the trial court erred in allowing the State to introduce it into evidence via Razatos' testimony. I respectfully concur.

DISSENT

JUSTICE KENNEDY, with whom the CHIEF JUSTICE, JUSTICE BREYER, and JUSTICE ALITO join, dissenting.

The Sixth Amendment Confrontation Clause binds the States and the National Government. *Pointer v. Texas*, 380 U.S. 400, 403 (1965). Two Terms ago, in a case arising from a state criminal prosecution, the Court interpreted the Clause to mandate exclusion of a laboratory report sought to be introduced based on the authority of that report's own sworn statement that a test had been performed yielding the results as shown. *Melendez-Diaz v. Massachusetts*, 129 S. Ct. 2527 (2009). The Court's opinion in that case held the report inadmissible because no one was present at trial to testify to its contents.

Whether or not one agrees with the reasoning and the result in *Melendez-Diaz*, the Court today takes the new and serious misstep of extending that holding to instances like this one. Here a knowledgeable representative of the laboratory was present to testify and to explain the lab's processes and the details of the report; but because he was not the analyst who filled out part of the form and transcribed onto it the test result from a machine printout, the Court finds a confrontation violation. Some of the principal objections to the Court's underlying theory have been set out earlier and need not be repeated here. *See id.*, at 129 S. Ct. 2527 (Kennedy, J., dissenting). Additional reasons, applicable to the extension of that doctrine and to the new ruling in this case, are now explained in support of this respectful dissent.

I

Before today, the Court had not held that the Confrontation Clause bars admission of scientific findings when an employee of the testing laboratory authenticates the findings, testifies to the laboratory's methods and practices, and is cross-examined at trial. Far from replacing live testimony with "systematic" and "extrajudicial" examinations, *Davis v. Washington*, 547 U.S. 813, 835, 836, (2006) (Thomas, J., concurring in judgment in part and dissenting in part) (emphasis deleted and internal quotation marks omitted), these procedures are fully consistent with the Confrontation Clause and with well-established principles for ensuring that criminal trials are conducted in full accord with requirements of fairness and reliability and with the confrontation guarantee. They do not "resemble Marian proceedings." *Id.*, at 837.

The procedures followed here, but now invalidated by the Court, make live testimony rather than the "solemnity" of a document the primary reason to credit the laboratory's scientific results. *Id.*, at 838. Unlike *Melendez-Diaz*, where the jury was asked to credit a laboratory's findings based solely on documents that were "quite plainly affidavits," 129 S. Ct. 2527 (Thomas, J., concurring) (internal quotation marks omitted), here the signature, heading, or legend on the document were routine authentication elements for a report that would be assessed and explained by in-court testimony subject to full cross-examination. The only sworn statement at issue was that of the witness who was present and who testified.

The record reveals that the certifying analyst's role here was no greater than that of anyone else in the chain of custody. App. 56 (laboratory employee's testimony agreeing that "once the material is prepared and placed in the machine, you don't need any particular expertise to record the results"). The information contained in the report was the result of a scientific process comprising multiple participants' acts, each with its own evidentiary significance. These acts included receipt of the sample at the laboratory; recording its receipt; storing it; placing the sample into the testing device; transposing the printout of the results of the test onto the report; and review of the results. *See id.*, at 48–56; *see also* Brief for State of New Mexico Dept. of Health Scientific Laboratory Division as *Amicus Curiae* 4 (hereinafter New Mexico Scientific Laboratory Brief) ("Each blood sample has original testing work by . . . as many as seve[n] analysts. . . ."); App. 62 (indicating that this case involved three laboratory analysts who, respectively, received, analyzed, and reviewed analysis of the sample); *cf.* Brief for State of Indiana et al. as *Amici Curiae* in *Briscoe v. Vir-*

ginia, O. T. 2009, No. 07-11191, p. 10 (hereinafter Indiana Brief) (explaining that DNA analysis can involve the combined efforts of up to 40 analysts).

In the New Mexico scientific laboratory where the blood sample was processed, analyses are run in batches involving 40–60 samples. Each sample is identified by a computer-generated number that is not linked back to the file containing the name of the person from whom the sample came until after all testing is completed. *See* New Mexico Scientific Laboratory Brief 26. The analysis is mechanically performed by the gas chromatograph, which may operate—as in this case—after all the laboratory employees leave for the day. *See id.*, at 17. And whatever the result, it is reported to both law enforcement and the defense. *See id.*, at 36.

The representative of the testing laboratory whom the prosecution called was a scientific analyst named Mr. Razatos. He testified that he "help[ed] in overseeing the administration of these programs throughout the State," and he was qualified to answer questions concerning each of these steps. App. 49. The Court has held that the government need not produce at trial "everyone who laid hands on the evidence," *Melendez-Diaz, supra*, at 129 S. Ct. 2527. Here, the defense used the opportunity in cross-examination to highlight the absence at trial of certain laboratory employees. Under questioning by Bullcoming's attorney, Razatos acknowledged that his name did not appear on the report; that he did not receive the sample, perform the analysis, or complete the review; and that he did not know the reason for some personnel decisions. App. 58. After weighing arguments from defense counsel concerning these admissions, and after considering the testimony of Mr. Razatos, who knew the laboratory's protocols and processes, the jury found no reasonable doubt as to the defendant's guilt.

In these circumstances, requiring the State to call the technician who filled out a form and recorded the results of a test is a hollow formality. The defense remains free to challenge any and all forensic evidence. It may call and examine the technician who performed a test. And it may call other expert witnesses to explain that tests are not always reliable or that the technician might have made a mistake. The jury can then decide whether to credit the test, as it did here. The States, furthermore, can assess the progress of scientific testing and enact or adopt statutes and rules to ensure that only reliable evidence is admitted. Rejecting these commonsense arguments and the concept that reliability is a legitimate concern, the Court today takes a different course. It once more assumes for itself a central role in mandating detailed evidentiary rules, thereby extending and confirming *Melendez-Diaz's* "vast potential to disrupt criminal procedures." 129 S. Ct. 2527 (Kennedy, J., dissenting).

II

The protections in the Confrontation Clause, and indeed the Sixth Amendment in general, are designed to ensure a fair trial with reliable evidence. But the *Crawford v. Washington*, 541 U.S. 36, (2004), line of cases has treated the reliability of evidence as a reason to exclude it. *Id.*, at 61–62. Today, for example, the Court bars admission of a lab report because it "is formalized in a signed document." The Court's unconventional and unstated premise is that the State—by acting to ensure a statement's reliability—makes the statement more formal and therefore less likely to be admitted. Park, Is Confrontation the Bottom Line? 19 Regent U. L. Rev. 459, 461 (2007). That is so, the Court insists, because reliability does not animate the Confrontation Clause; *Melendez-Diaz, supra*, at 129 S. Ct. 2527; *Crawford, supra*, at 61–62. Yet just this Term the Court ruled that, in another confrontation context, reliability was an essential part of the constitutional inquiry. *See Michigan v. Bryant*, 131 S. Ct. 1143 (2010).

Like reliability, other principles have weaved in and out of the *Crawford* jurisprudence. Solemnity has sometimes been dispositive, *see Melendez-Diaz*, 129 S. Ct. 2527; *id.*, at 129 S. Ct. 2527 (Thomas, J., concurring), and sometimes not, *see Davis*, 547 U.S., at 834–837, 841 (Thomas, J., concurring in judgment in part and dissenting in part). So, too, with the elusive distinction between utterances aimed at proving past events, and those calculated to help police keep the peace. *Compare Davis, supra*, and *Bryant*, 131 S. Ct. 1143, *with id.*, at 131 S. Ct. 1143 (Scalia, J., dissenting).

It is not even clear which witnesses' testimony could render a scientific report admissible under the Court's approach. *Melendez-Diaz* stated an inflexible rule: Where "analysts' affidavits" included "testimonial statements," defendants were "entitled to be confronted with the analysts" themselves. 129 S. Ct. 2527 (internal quotation marks omitted). Now, the Court reveals, this rule is either less clear than it first appeared or too strict to be followed. A report is admissible, today's opinion states, if a "live witness competent to testify to the truth of the statements made in the report" appears. Such witnesses include not just the certifying analyst, but also any "scientist who . . . perform[ed] or observe[d] the test reported in the certification."

Today's majority is not committed in equal shares to a common set of principles in applying the holding of *Crawford*. *Compare Davis, supra* (opinion for the Court by Scalia, J.), *with id.*, at 126 S. Ct. 2266 (Thomas, J., concurring in judgment in part and dissenting in part); *and Bryant, supra*, (opinion for the Court by Sotomayor, J.), *with id.*, at 131 S. Ct. 1143 (Thomas, J., concurring in judgment), *and id.*, at 131 S. Ct. 1143 (Scalia, J., dissenting), *and id.*, at 131 S. Ct. 1143 (Ginsburg, J., dissenting). That the Court in the wake of *Crawford* has had such trouble fashioning a clear vision of that case's meaning is unsettling; for *Crawford* binds every judge in every criminal trial in every local, state, and federal court in the Nation. This Court's prior decisions leave trial judges to "guess what future rules this Court will distill from the sparse constitutional text," *Melendez-Diaz, supra,* at 129 S. Ct. 2527 (Kennedy, J., dissenting), or to struggle to apply an "amorphous, if not entirely subjective," "highly context-dependent inquiry" involving "open-ended balancing." *Bryant, supra,* at 131 S. Ct. 1143 (Scalia, J., dissenting) (internal quotation marks omitted) (listing 11 factors relevant under the majority's approach).

The persistent ambiguities in the Court's approach are symptomatic of a rule not amenable to sensible applications. Procedures involving multiple participants illustrate the problem. In *Melendez-Diaz* the Court insisted that its opinion did not require everyone in the chain of custody to testify but then qualified that "what testimony is introduced must . . . be introduced live." 129 S. Ct. 2527. This could mean that a statement that evidence remained in law-enforcement custody is admissible if the statement's maker appears in court. If so, an intern at police headquarters could review the evidence log, declare that chain of custody was retained, and so testify. The rule could also be that that the intern's statement—which draws on statements in the evidence log—is inadmissible unless every officer who signed the log appears at trial. That rule, if applied to this case, would have conditioned admissibility of the report on the testimony of three or more identified witnesses. *See* App. 62. In other instances, 7 or even 40 witnesses could be required. The court has thus—in its fidelity to *Melendez-Diaz*—boxed itself into a choice of evils: render the Confrontation Clause pro forma or construe it so that its dictates are unworkable.

III

Crawford itself does not compel today's conclusion. It is true, as *Crawford* confirmed, that the Confrontation Clause seeks in part to bar the government from replicating trial procedures outside of public view. *See* 541 U.S., at 50; *Bryant, supra,* at 131 S. Ct. 1143. *Crawford* explained that the basic purpose of the Clause was to address the sort of abuses exemplified at the notorious treason trial of Sir Walter Raleigh. 541 U.S., at 51. On this view the Clause operates to bar admission of out-of-court statements obtained through formal interrogation in preparation for trial. The danger is that innocent defendants may be convicted on the basis of unreliable, untested statements by those who observed—or claimed to have observed—preparation for or commission of the crime. And, of course, those statements might not have been uttered at all or—even if spoken—might not have been true.

A rule that bars testimony of that sort, however, provides neither cause nor necessity to impose a constitutional bar on the admission of impartial lab reports like the instant one, reports prepared by experienced technicians in laboratories that follow professional norms and scientific protocols. In addition to the constitutional right to call witnesses in his own defense, the defendant in this case was already protected by checks on potential prosecutorial abuse such as free retesting for defendants;

result-blind issuance of reports; testing by an independent agency; routine processes performed en masse, which reduce opportunities for targeted bias; and labs operating pursuant to scientific and professional norms and oversight. *See* Brief for Respondent 5, 14–15, 41, 54; New Mexico Scientific Laboratory Brief 2, 26.

In addition to preventing the State from conducting ex parte trials, *Crawford*'s rejection of the regime of *Ohio v. Roberts*, 448 U.S. 56 (1980), seemed to have two underlying jurisprudential objectives. One was to delink the intricacies of hearsay law from a constitutional mandate; and the other was to allow the States, in their own courts and legislatures and without this Court's supervision, to explore and develop sensible, specific evidentiary rules pertaining to the admissibility of certain statements. These results were to be welcomed, for this Court lacks the experience and day-to-day familiarity with the trial process to suit it well to assume the role of national tribunal for rules of evidence. Yet far from pursuing these objectives, the Court rejects them in favor of their opposites.

Instead of freeing the Clause from reliance on hearsay doctrines, the Court has now linked the Clause with hearsay rules in their earliest, most rigid, and least refined formulations. *See, e.g.*, Mosteller, Remaking Confrontation Clause and Hearsay Doctrine Under the Challenge of Child Sexual Abuse Prosecutions, 1993 U. Ill. L. Rev. 691, 739–740, 742, 744–746; Gallanis, The Rise of Modern Evidence Law, 84 Iowa L. Rev. 499, 502–503, 514–515, 533–537 (1999). In cases like *Melendez-Diaz* and this one, the Court has tied the Confrontation Clause to 18th century hearsay rules unleavened by principles tending to make those rules more sensible. Sklansky, Hearsay's Last Hurrah, 2009 S. Ct. Rev. 1, 5–6, 36. As a result, the Court has taken the Clause far beyond its most important application, which is to forbid sworn, ex parte, out-of-court statements by unconfronted and available witnesses who observed the crime and do not appear at trial.

Second, the States are not just at risk of having some of their hearsay rules reviewed by this Court. They often are foreclosed now from contributing to the formulation and enactment of rules that make trials fairer and more reliable. For instance, recent state laws allowing admission of well-documented and supported reports of abuse by women whose abusers later murdered them must give way, unless that abuser murdered with the specific purpose of foreclosing the testimony. *Giles v. California*, 554 U.S. 353 (2008); Sklansky, *supra*, at 14–15. Whether those statutes could provide sufficient indicia of reliability and other safeguards to comply with the Confrontation Clause as it should be understood is, to be sure, an open question. The point is that the States cannot now participate in the development of this difficult part of the law.

In short, there is an ongoing, continued, and systemic displacement of the States and dislocation of the federal structure. *Cf. Melendez-Diaz, supra*, at 129 S. Ct. 2527. If this Court persists in applying wooden formalism in order to bar reliable testimony offered by the prosecution—testimony thought proper for many decades in state and federal courts committed to devising fair trial processes—then the States might find it necessary and appropriate to enact statutes to accommodate this new, intrusive federal regime. If they do, those rules could remain on State statute books for decades, even if subsequent decisions of this Court were to better implement the objectives of *Crawford*. This underscores the disruptive, long-term structural consequences of decisions like the one the Court announces today.

States also may decide it is proper and appropriate to enact statutes that require defense counsel to give advance notice if they are going to object to introduction of a report without the presence in court of the technician who prepared it. Indeed, today's opinion relies upon laws of that sort as a palliative to the disruption it is causing. It is quite unrealistic, however, to think that this will take away from the defense the incentives to insist on having the certifying analyst present. There is in the ordinary case that proceeds to trial no good reason for defense counsel to waive the right of confrontation as the Court now interprets it.

Today's opinion repeats an assertion from *Melendez-Diaz* that its decision will not "impose an undue burden on the prosecution." But evidence to the contrary already has begun to mount. *See, e.g.*, Brief for State of California et al. as *Amici Curiae* 7 (explaining that the 10 toxicologists for the Los Angeles Police Department spent 782 hours at 261 court appearances during a 1-year period); Brief for National District Attorneys Association et al. as *Amici Curiae* 23 (observing that each blood-alcohol analyst in California processes 3,220 cases per year on average). New and more rigorous empirical studies further detailing the unfortunate effects of *Melendez-Diaz* are sure to be forthcoming.

In the meantime, New Mexico's experience exemplifies the problems ahead. From 2008 to 2010, subpoenas requiring New Mexico analysts to testify in impaired-driving cases rose 71%, to 1,600—or 8 or 9 every workday. New Mexico Scientific Laboratory Brief 2. In a State that is the Nation's fifth largest by area and that employs just 10 total analysts, *id.*, at 3, each analyst in blood alcohol cases recently received 200 subpoenas per year, *id.*, at 33. The analysts now must travel great distances on most working days. The result has been, in the laboratory's words, "chaotic." *Id.*, at 5. And if the defense raises an objection and the analyst is tied up in another court proceeding; or on leave; or absent; or delayed in transit; or no longer employed; or ill; or no longer living, the defense gets a windfall. As a result, good defense attorneys will object in ever-greater numbers to a prosecution failure or inability to produce laboratory analysts at trial. The concomitant increases in subpoenas will further impede the state laboratory's ability to keep pace with its obligations. Scarce state resources could be committed to other urgent needs in the criminal justice system.

* * *

Seven years after its initiation, it bears remembering that the *Crawford* approach was not preordained. This Court's missteps have produced an interpretation of the word "witness" at odds with its meaning elsewhere in the Constitution, including elsewhere in the Sixth Amendment, *see* Amar, Sixth Amendment First Principles, 84 Geo. L. J. 641, 647, 691–696 (1996), and at odds with the sound administration of justice. It is time to return to solid ground. A proper place to begin that return is to decline to extend *Melendez-Diaz* to bar the reliable, commonsense evidentiary framework the State sought to follow in this case.

Williams v. Illinois
132 S. Ct. 2221 (2012)

ALITO, J., announced the judgment of the Court and delivered an opinion, in which ROBERTS, C.J., and KENNEDY, and BREYER, J.J., joined. BREYER, J. filed a concurring opinion. THOMAS, J., filed an opinion concurring in the judgment. KAGAN, J., filed a dissenting opinion, in which SCALIA, GINSBURG, and SOTOMAYOR, J.J., joined.

Opinion

JUSTICE ALITO announced the judgment of the Court and delivered an opinion, which the CHIEF JUSTICE, JUSTICE KENNEDY, and JUSTICE BREYER join.

In this case, we decide whether *Crawford v. Washington*, 541 U.S. 36, 50 (2004), precludes an expert witness from testifying in a manner that has long been allowed under the law of evidence. Specifically, does *Crawford* bar an expert from expressing an opinion based on facts about a case that have been made known to the expert but about which the expert is not competent to testify? We also decide whether *Crawford* substantially impedes the ability of prosecutors to introduce DNA evidence and thus may effectively relegate the prosecution in some cases to reliance on older, less reliable forms of proof.

In petitioner's bench trial for rape, the prosecution called an expert who testified that a DNA profile produced by an outside laboratory, Cellmark, matched a profile produced by the state police lab using a sample of petitioner's blood. On direct examination, the expert testified that Cellmark was an accredited laboratory and that Cellmark provided the police with a DNA profile. The expert also explained the notations on documents admitted as business records, stating that, according to the records, vaginal swabs taken from the victim were sent to and received back from Cellmark. The expert made no other statement that was offered for the purpose of identifying the sample of biological material used in deriving the profile or for the purpose of establishing how Cellmark handled or tested the sample. Nor did the expert vouch for the accuracy of the profile that Cellmark produced. Nevertheless, petitioner contends that the expert's testimony violated the Confrontation Clause as interpreted in *Crawford*.

Petitioner's main argument is that the expert went astray when she referred to the DNA profile provided by Cellmark as having been produced from semen found on the victim's vaginal swabs. But both the Illinois Appellate Court and the Illinois Supreme Court found that this statement was not admitted for the truth of the matter asserted, and it is settled that the Confrontation Clause does not bar the admission of such statements. *See id.*, at 59–60, n. 9 (citing *Tennessee v. Street*, 471 U.S. 409 (1985)). For more than 200 years, the law of evidence has permitted the sort of testimony that was given by the expert in this case. Under settled evidence law, an expert may express an opinion that is based on facts that the expert assumes, but does not know, to be true. It is then up to the party who calls the expert to introduce other evidence establishing the facts assumed by the expert. While it was once the practice for an expert who based an opinion on assumed facts to testify in the form of an answer to a hypothetical question, modern practice does not demand this formality and, in appropriate cases, permits an expert to explain the facts on which his or her opinion is based without testifying to the truth of those facts. *See* Fed. Rule Evid. 703. That is precisely what occurred in this case, and we should not lightly "swee[p] away an accepted rule governing the admission of scientific evidence." *Melendez-Diaz v. Massachusetts*, 557 U.S. 305, 330 (2009) (Kennedy, J., dissenting).

We now conclude that this form of expert testimony does not violate the Confrontation Clause because that provision has no application to out-of-court statements that are not offered to prove the truth of the matter asserted. When an expert testifies for the prosecution in a criminal case, the defendant has the opportunity to cross-examine the expert about any statements that are offered for their truth. Out-of-court statements that are related by the expert solely for the purpose of explaining the assumptions on which that opinion rests are not offered for their truth and thus fall outside the scope of the Confrontation Clause. Applying this rule to the present case, we conclude that the expert's testimony did not violate the Sixth Amendment.

As a second, independent basis for our decision, we also conclude that even if the report produced by Cellmark had been admitted into evidence, there would have been no Confrontation Clause violation. The Cellmark report is very different from the sort of extrajudicial statements, such as affidavits, depositions, prior testimony, and confessions, that the Confrontation Clause was originally understood to reach. The report was produced before any suspect was identified. The report was sought not for the purpose of obtaining evidence to be used against petitioner, who was not even under suspicion at the time, but for the purpose of finding a rapist who was on the loose. And the profile that Cellmark provided was not inherently inculpatory. On the contrary, a DNA profile is evidence that tends to exculpate all but one of the more than 7 billion people in the world today. The use of DNA evidence to exonerate persons who have been wrongfully accused or convicted is well known. If DNA profiles could not be introduced without calling the technicians who participated in the preparation of the profile, economic pressures would encourage prosecutors to forgo DNA testing and rely instead on older forms of evidence, such as eyewitness identification, that are less reliable. *See Perry v. New Hampshire*, 565 U.S._____,

132 S. Ct. 716 (2012). The Confrontation Clause does not mandate such an undesirable development. This conclusion will not prejudice any defendant who really wishes to probe the reliability of the DNA testing done in a particular case because those who participated in the testing may always be subpoenaed by the defense and questioned at trial.

I

A

On February 10, 2000, in Chicago, Illinois, a young woman, L. J., was abducted while she was walking home from work. The perpetrator forced her into his car and raped her, then robbed her of her money and other personal items and pushed her out into the street. L. J. ran home and reported the attack to her mother, who called the police. An ambulance took L. J. to the hospital, where doctors treated her wounds and took a blood sample and vaginal swabs for a sexual-assault kit. A Chicago Police detective collected the kit, labeled it with an inventory number, and sent it under seal to the Illinois State Police (ISP) lab.

At the ISP lab, a forensic scientist received the sealed kit. He conducted a chemical test that confirmed the presence of semen on the vaginal swabs, and he then resealed the kit and placed it in a secure evidence freezer.

During the period in question, the ISP lab often sent biological samples to Cellmark Diagnostics Laboratory in Germantown, Maryland, for DNA testing. There was evidence that the ISP lab sent L. J.'s vaginal swabs to Cellmark for testing and that Cellmark sent back a report containing a male DNA profile produced from semen taken from those swabs. At this time, petitioner was not under suspicion for L. J.'s rape.

Sandra Lambatos, a forensic specialist at the ISP lab, conducted a computer search to see if the Cellmark profile matched any of the entries in the state DNA database. The computer showed a match to a profile produced by the lab from a sample of petitioner's blood that had been taken after he was arrested on unrelated charges on August 3, 2000.

On April 17, 2001, the police conducted a lineup at which L. J. identified petitioner as her assailant. Petitioner was then indicted for aggravated criminal sexual assault, aggravated kidnaping, and aggravated robbery. In lieu of a jury trial, petitioner chose to be tried before a state judge.

B

Petitioner's bench trial began in April 2006. In open court, L. J. again identified petitioner as her attacker. The State also offered three expert forensic witnesses to link petitioner to the crime through his DNA. First, Brian Hapack, an ISP forensic scientist, testified that he had confirmed the presence of semen on the vaginal swabs taken from L. J. by performing an acid phosphatase test. After performing this test, he testified, he resealed the evidence and left it in a secure freezer at the ISP lab.

Second, Karen Abbinanti, a state forensic analyst, testified that she had used Polymerase Chain Reaction (PCR) and Short Tandem Repeat (STR) techniques to develop a DNA profile from a blood sample that had been drawn from petitioner after he was arrested in August 2000. She also stated that she had entered petitioner's DNA profile into the state forensic database.

Third, the State offered Sandra Lambatos as an expert witness in forensic biology and forensic DNA analysis. On direct examination, Lambatos testified about the general process of using the PCR and STR techniques to generate DNA profiles from forensic samples such as blood and semen. She then described how these DNA profiles could be matched to an individual based on the individual's unique genetic code. In making a comparison between two DNA profiles, Lambatos stated, it is a "commonly accepted" practice within the scientific community for "one DNA expert to rely on the records of another DNA expert." App. 51. Lambatos also testified that Cellmark was an "accredited crime lab" and that, in her experience, the ISP lab routinely sent evidence samples via Federal Express to Cellmark for DNA testing in order to expedite the testing process and to "reduce [the lab's] backlog." *Id.*, at 49–50. To keep track of evidence samples and preserve the chain of custody, Lambatos stated, she and other analysts relied on sealed shipping containers and labeled shipping manifests, and she added that experts in her field regularly relied on such protocols. *Id.*, at 50–51.

Lambatos was shown shipping manifests that were admitted into evidence as business records, and she explained what they indicated, namely, that the ISP lab had sent L. J.'s vaginal swabs to Cellmark, and that Cellmark had sent them back, along with a deduced male DNA profile. *Id.*, at 52–55. The prosecutor asked Lambatos whether there was "a computer match" between "the male DNA profile found in semen from the vaginal swabs of [L. J.]" and "[the] male DNA profile that had been identified" from petitioner's blood sample. *Id.*, at 55.

The defense attorney objected to this question for "lack of foundation," arguing that the prosecution had offered "no evidence with regard to any testing that's been done to generate a DNA profile by another lab to be testified to by this witness." *Ibid.*

The prosecutor responded: "I'm not getting at what another lab did." *Id.*, at 56. Rather, she said, she was simply asking Lambatos about "her own testing based on [DNA] information" that she had received from Cellmark. *Ibid.* The trial judge agreed, noting, "If she says she didn't do her own testing and she relied on a test of another lab and she's testifying to that, we will see what she's going to say." *Ibid.*

The prosecutor then proceeded, asking Lambatos, "Did you compare the semen that had been identified by Brian Hapack from the vaginal swabs of [L. J.] to the male DNA profile that had been identified by Karen [Abbinanti] from the blood of [petitioner]?" *Ibid.*

Lambatos answered "Yes." *Ibid.* Defense counsel lodged an objection "to the form of the question," but the trial judge overruled it. *Ibid.* Lambatos then testified that, based on her own comparison of the two DNA profiles, she "concluded that [petitioner] cannot be excluded as a possible source of the semen identified in the vaginal swabs," and that the probability of the profile's appearing in the general population was "1 in 8.7 quadrillion black, 1 in 390 quadrillion white, or 1 in 109 quadrillion Hispanic unrelated individuals." *Id.*, at 57. Asked whether she would "call this a match to [petitioner]," Lambatos answered yes, again over defense counsel's objection. *Id.*, at 58.

The Cellmark report itself was neither admitted into evidence nor shown to the factfinder. Lambatos did not quote or read from the report; nor did she identify it as the source of any of the opinions she expressed.

On cross-examination, Lambatos confirmed that she did not conduct or observe any of the testing on the vaginal swabs, and that her testimony relied on the DNA profile produced by Cellmark. *Id.*, at 59. She stated that she trusted Cellmark to do reliable work because it was an accredited lab, but she admitted she had not seen any of the calibrations or work that Cellmark had done in deducing a male DNA profile from the vaginal swabs. *Id.*, at 59–62.

Asked whether the DNA sample might have been degraded before Cellmark analyzed it, Lambatos answered that, while degradation was technically possible, she strongly doubted it had occurred in this case. She gave two reasons. First, the ISP lab likely would have noticed the degradation before sending the evidence off to Cellmark. Second, and more important, Lambatos also noted that the data making up the DNA profile would exhibit certain telltale signs if it had been deduced from a degraded sample: The visual representation of the DNA sequence would exhibit "specific patterns" of degradation, and she "didn't see any evidence" of that from looking at the profile that Cellmark produced. *Id.*, at 81–82.

When Lambatos finished testifying, the defense moved to exclude her testimony "with regards to testing done by [Cellmark]" based on the Confrontation Clause. *Id.*, at 90. Defense counsel argued that there was "no evidence with regards to . . . any work done by [Cellmark] to justify testimony coming into this case with regard to their analysis." *Ibid.* Thus, while defense counsel objected to and sought the exclusion of Lambatos' testimony insofar as it implicated events at the Cellmark lab, defense counsel did not object to or move for the exclusion of any other portion of Lambatos' testimony, including statements regarding the contents of the shipment sent to or received back from Cellmark. *See id.*, at 55, 56, 90. *See also*

895 N.E.2d 961, 968 (Ill. 2008) (chain-of-custody argument based on shipping manifests waived).

The prosecution responded that petitioner's Confrontation Clause rights were satisfied because he had the opportunity to cross-examine the expert who had testified that there was a match between the DNA profiles produced by Cellmark and Abbinanti. App. 91. Invoking Illinois Rule of Evidence 703,[1] the prosecutor argued that an expert is allowed to disclose the facts on which the expert's opinion is based even if the expert is not competent to testify to those underlying facts. She further argued that any deficiency in the foundation for the expert's opinion "[d]oesn't go to the admissibility of [that] testimony," but instead "goes to the weight of the testimony." App. 91.

The trial judge agreed with the prosecution and stated that "the issue is . . . what weight do you give the test, not do you exclude it." *Id.*, at 94. Accordingly, the judge stated that he would not exclude Lambatos' testimony, which was "based on her own independent testing of the data received from [Cellmark]." *Id.*, at 94–95 (alteration in original).

The trial court found petitioner guilty of the charges against him. The state court of appeals affirmed in relevant part, concluding that Lambatos' testimony did not violate petitioner's confrontation rights because the Cellmark report was not offered into evidence to prove the truth of the matter it asserted. *See* 895 N.E.2d, at 969–970 ("Cellmark's report was not offered for the truth of the matter asserted; rather, it was offered to provide a basis for Lambatos' opinion") The Supreme Court of Illinois also affirmed. 238 939 N.E.2d 268, 345 (Ill. 2010). Under state law, the court noted, the Cellmark report could not be used as substantive evidence. When Lambatos referenced the report during her direct examination, she did so "for the limited purpose of explaining the basis for [her expert opinion]," not for the purpose of showing "the truth of the matter asserted" by the report. *Id.*, at 282. Thus, the report was not used to establish its truth, but only "to show the underlying facts and data Lambatos used before rendering an expert opinion." *Id.*, at 279.

We granted certiorari. 564 U.S._____, 131 S. Ct. 3090, 180 L. Ed. 2d 911 (2011).

---

1. Consistent with the Federal Rules, Illinois Rule of Evidence 703 provides as follows:

   "The facts or data in the particular case upon which an expert bases an opinion or inference may be those perceived by or made known to the expert at or before the hearing. If of a type reasonably relied upon by experts in the particular field in forming opinions or inferences upon the subject, the facts or data need not be admissible in evidence."

II

A

The Confrontation Clause of the Sixth Amendment provides that, "[i]n all criminal prosecutions, the accused shall enjoy the right . . . to be confronted with the witnesses against him." Before *Crawford*, this Court took the view that the Confrontation Clause did not bar the admission of an out-of-court statement that fell within a firmly rooted exception to the hearsay rule, *see Ohio v. Roberts*, 448 U.S. 56, 66 (1980), but in *Crawford*, the Court adopted a fundamentally new interpretation of the confrontation right, holding that "[t]estimonial statements of witnesses absent from trial [can be] admitted only where the declarant is unavailable, and only where the defendant has had a prior opportunity to cross-examine." 541 U.S., at 59. *Crawford* has resulted in a steady stream of new cases in this Court. *See Bullcoming v. New Mexico*, 564 U.S._____, 131 S. Ct. 2705, 180 L. Ed. 2d 610 (2011); *Michigan v. Bryant*, 562 U.S._____, 131 S. Ct. 1143, 179 L. Ed. 2d 93 (2011); *Melendez-Diaz*, 557 U.S. 305; *Giles v. California*, 554 U.S. 353 (2008); *Indiana v. Edwards*, 554 U.S. 164 (2008); *Davis v. Washington*, 547 U.S. 813 (2006).

Two of these decisions involved scientific reports. In *Melendez-Diaz*, the defendant was arrested and charged with distributing and trafficking in cocaine. At trial, the prosecution introduced bags of a white powdery substance that had been found in the defendant's possession. The trial court also admitted into evidence three "certificates of analysis" from the state forensic laboratory stating that the bags had been "examined with the following results: The substance was found to contain: Cocaine." 557 U.S., at 308 (internal quotation marks omitted).

The Court held that the admission of these certificates, which were executed under oath before a notary, violated the Sixth Amendment. They were created for "the sole purpose of providing evidence against a defendant," *id.*, at 323, and were "'quite plainly affidavits,'" *id.*, at 330 (Thomas, J., concurring). The Court emphasized that the introduction of the report to prove the nature of the substance found in the defendant's possession was tantamount to "live, in-court testimony" on that critical fact and that the certificates did "precisely what a witness does on direct examination." *Id.*, at 311 (internal quotation marks omitted). There was no doubt that the certificates were used to prove the truth of the matter they asserted. Under state law, "the sole purpose of the affidavits was to provide prima facie evidence of the composition, quality, and the net weight of the analyzed substance." *Ibid.* (internal quotation marks omitted and emphasis deleted). On these facts, the Court said, it was clear that the certificates were "testimonial statements" that could not be introduced unless their authors were subjected to the "'crucible of cross-examination.'" *Id.*, at 311 (quoting *Crawford, supra*, at 61).

In *Bullcoming*, we held that another scientific report could not be used as substantive evidence against the defendant unless the analyst who prepared and certified the report was subject to confrontation. The defendant in that case had been convicted of driving while intoxicated. At trial, the court admitted into evidence a forensic report certifying that a sample of the defendant's blood had an alcohol concentration of 0.21 grams per hundred milliliters, well above the legal limit. Instead of calling the analyst who signed and certified the forensic report, the prosecution called another analyst who had not performed or observed the actual analysis, but was only familiar with the general testing procedures of the laboratory. The Court declined to accept this surrogate testimony, despite the fact that the testifying analyst was a "knowledgeable representative of the laboratory" who could "explain the lab's processes and the details of the report." 564 U.S., at_____, 131 S. Ct. 2705 (Kennedy, J., dissenting). The Court stated simply: "The accused's right is to be confronted with the analyst who made the certification." *Id.*, at_____, 131 S. Ct. 2705.

Just as in *Melendez-Diaz*, the forensic report that was "introduce[d]" in *Bullcoming* "contain[ed] a testimonial certification, made in order to prove a fact at a criminal trial." 564 U.S., at_____-_____, 131 S. Ct. 2705. The report was signed by the nontestifying analyst who had authored it, stating, "I certify that I followed the procedures set out on the reverse of this report, and the statements in this block are correct. The concentration of alcohol in this sample is based on the grams of alcohol in one hundred milliliters of blood." App. in *Bullcoming*, O. T. 2010, No. 09-10876, p. 62. Critically, the report was introduced at trial for the substantive purpose of proving the truth of the matter asserted by its out-of-court author—namely, that the defendant had a blood-alcohol level of 0.21. This was the central fact in question at the defendant's trial, and it was dispositive of his guilt.

In concurrence, Justice Sotomayor highlighted the importance of the fact that the forensic report had been admitted into evidence for the purpose of proving the truth of the matter it asserted. She emphasized that "this [was] not a case in which an expert witness was asked for his independent opinion about underlying testimonial reports that were not themselves admitted into evidence." 564 U.S., at_____, 131 S. Ct. 2705 (opinion concurring in part) (citing Fed. Rule Evid. 703). "We would face a different question," she observed, "if asked to determine the constitutionality of allowing an expert witness to discuss others' testimonial statements if the testimonial statements were not themselves admitted as evidence." *Id.*, at_____, 131 S. Ct. 2705.

We now confront that question.

B

It has long been accepted that an expert witness may voice an opinion based on facts concerning the events at issue in a particular case even if the expert lacks first-hand knowledge of those facts.

At common law, courts developed two ways to deal with this situation. An expert could rely on facts that had already been established in the record. But because it was not always possible to proceed in this manner, and because record evidence was often disputed, courts developed the alternative practice of allowing an expert to testify in the form of a "hypothetical question." Under this approach, the expert would be asked to assume the truth of certain factual predicates, and was then asked to offer an opinion based on those assumptions. *See* 1 K. Broun, McCormick on Evidence § 14, p. 87 (6th ed. 2006); 1 J. Wigmore, Evidence § 677, p. 1084 (2d ed. 1923) ("If the witness is skilled enough, his opinion may be adequately obtained upon hypothetical data alone; and it is immaterial whether he has ever seen the person, place or thing in question" (citation omitted)). The truth of the premises could then be established through independent evidence, and the factfinder would regard the expert's testimony to be only as credible as the premises on which it was based.

An early example of this approach comes from the English case of *Beckwith v. Sydebotham*, 1 Camp. 116, 170 Eng. Rep. 897 (K. B. 1807), where a party sought to prove the seaworthiness of a ship, the Earl of Wycombe, by calling as witnesses "several eminent surveyors of ships who had never seen the 'Earl of Wycombe.'" *Ibid.* The opposing party objected to the testimony because it relied on facts that were not known to be true, but the judge disagreed. Because the experts were "peculiarly acquainted" with "a matter of skill or science," the judge said, the "jury might be assisted" by their hypothetical opinion based on certain assumed facts. *Id.*, at 117, 170 Eng. Rep., at 897. The judge acknowledged the danger of the jury's being unduly prejudiced by wrongly assuming the truth of the hypothetical facts, but the judge noted that the experts could be asked on cross-examination what their opinion of the ship's seaworthiness would be if different hypothetical facts were assumed. If the party that had called the experts could not independently prove the truth of the premises they posited, then the experts' "opinion might not go for much; but still it was admissible evidence." *Ibid.*

There is a long tradition of the use of hypothetical questions in American courts. In 1887, for example, this Court indicated its approval of the following jury instruction:

> "As to the questions, you must understand that they are not evidence; they are mere statements to these witnesses . . . and, upon the hypothesis or assumption of these questions the witnesses are asked to give their [opinion]. You must readily see that the value of the answers to these questions depends largely, if not wholly, upon the fact whether the statements made in these questions are sustained by the proof. If the statements in these questions are not supported by the proof, then the answers to the questions are entitled to no weight, because based upon false assumptions or statements of facts." Forsyth v. Doolittle, 120 U.S. 73, 77 (internal quotation marks omitted).

Modern rules of evidence continue to permit experts to express opinions based on facts about which they lack personal knowledge, but these rules dispense with the need for hypothetical questions. Under both the Illinois and the Federal Rules of Evidence, an expert may base an opinion on facts that are "made known to the expert at or before the hearing," but such reliance does not constitute admissible evidence of this underlying information. Ill. Rule Evid. 703; Fed. Rule Evid. 703. Accordingly, in jury trials, both Illinois and federal law generally bar an expert from disclosing such inadmissible evidence.[2] In bench trials, however, both the Illinois and the Federal Rules place no restriction on the revelation of such information to the factfinder. When the judge sits as the trier of fact, it is presumed that the judge will understand the limited reason for the disclosure of the underlying inadmissible information and will not rely on that information for any improper purpose. As we have noted, "[i]n bench trials, judges routinely hear inadmissible evidence that they are presumed to ignore when making decisions." *Harris v. Rivera*, 454 U.S. 339, 346 (1981) (per curiam). There is a "well-established presumption" that "the judge [has] adhered to basic rules of procedure," when the judge is acting as a factfinder. *Id.*, at 346-347 (emphasis added). *See also Gentile v. State Bar of Nev.*, 501 U.S. 1030, 1078 (1991) (Rehnquist, C. J., dissenting).

This feature of Illinois and federal law is important because *Crawford*, while departing from prior Confrontation Clause precedent in other respects, took pains to reaffirm the proposition that the Confrontation Clause "does not bar the use of testimonial statements for purposes other than establishing the truth of the matter asserted." 541 U.S., at 59–60, n. 9 (*citing Tennessee v. Street*, 471 U.S. 409). In *Street*, the defendant claimed that the police had coerced him into adopting the confession of his alleged accomplice. The prosecution sought to rebut this claim by showing that the defendant's confession differed significantly from the accomplice's. Although the accomplice's confession was clearly a testimonial statement, the Court held that the jurors could hear it as long as they were instructed to consider that confession not for its truth, but only for the "distinctive and limited purpose" of comparing it to the defendant's confession, to see whether the two were identical. *Id.*, at 417.

---

2. But disclosure of these facts or data to the jury is permitted if the value of disclosure "substantially outweighs [any] prejudicial effect," Fed. Rule Evid. 703, or "the probative value . . . outweighs the risk of unfair prejudice." People v. Pasch, 604 N.E.2d 294, 333 (Ill. 1992). When this disclosure occurs, "the underlying facts" are revealed to the jury "for the limited purpose of explaining the basis for [the expert's] opinion" and not "for the truth of the matter asserted." *Id.*, at 311.

III

A

In order to assess petitioner's Confrontation Clause argument, it is helpful to inventory exactly what Lambatos said on the stand about Cellmark. She testified to the truth of the following matters: Cellmark was an accredited lab, App. 49; the ISP occasionally sent forensic samples to Cellmark for DNA testing, *ibid.*; according to shipping manifests admitted into evidence, the ISP lab sent vaginal swabs taken from the victim to Cellmark and later received those swabs back from Cellmark, *id.*, at 52–55; and, finally, the Cellmark DNA profile matched a profile produced by the ISP lab from a sample of petitioner's blood, *id.*, at 55–56. Lambatos had personal knowledge of all of these matters, and therefore none of this testimony infringed petitioner's confrontation right.

Lambatos did not testify to the truth of any other matter concerning Cellmark. She made no other reference to the Cellmark report, which was not admitted into evidence and was not seen by the trier of fact. Nor did she testify to anything that was done at the Cellmark lab, and she did not vouch for the quality of Cellmark's work.

B

The principal argument advanced to show a Confrontation Clause violation concerns the phrase that Lambatos used when she referred to the DNA profile that the ISP lab received from Cellmark. This argument is developed most fully in the dissenting opinion, and therefore we refer to the dissent's discussion of this issue.

In the view of the dissent, the following is the critical portion of Lambatos' testimony, with the particular words that the dissent finds objectionable italicized:

> "Q Was there a computer match generated of the male DNA profile found in semen from the vaginal swabs of [L.J.] to a male DNA profile *that had been identified as having originated from Sandy Williams?*
>
> "A Yes, there was."

According to the dissent, the italicized phrase violated petitioner's confrontation right because Lambatos lacked personal knowledge that the profile produced by Cellmark was based on the vaginal swabs taken from the victim, L. J. As the dissent acknowledges, there would have been "nothing wrong with Lambatos's testifying that two DNA profiles—the one shown in the Cellmark report and the one derived from Williams's blood—matched each other; that was a straightforward application of Lambatos's expertise." Thus, if Lambatos' testimony had been slightly modified as follows, the dissent would see no problem:

"Q Was there a computer match generated of the male DNA profile produced by Cellmark to a male DNA profile that had been identified as having originated from Sandy Williams?

"A Yes, there was."[3]

The defect in this argument is that under Illinois law (like federal law) it is clear that the putatively offending phrase in Lambatos' testimony was not admissible for the purpose of proving the truth of the matter asserted—i.e., that the matching DNA profile was "found in semen from the vaginal swabs." Rather, that fact was a mere premise of the prosecutor's question, and Lambatos simply assumed that premise to be true when she gave her answer indicating that there was a match between the two DNA profiles. There is no reason to think that the trier of fact took Lambatos' answer as substantive evidence to establish where the DNA profiles came from.

The dissent's argument would have force if petitioner had elected to have a jury trial. In that event, there would have been a danger of the jury's taking Lambatos' testimony as proof that the Cellmark profile was derived from the sample obtained from the victim's vaginal swabs. Absent an evaluation of the risk of juror confusion and careful jury instructions, the testimony could not have gone to the jury.

This case, however, involves a bench trial and we must assume that the trial judge understood that the portion of Lambatos' testimony to which the dissent objects was not admissible to prove the truth of the matter asserted.[4] The dissent, on the other hand, reaches the truly remarkable conclusion that the wording of Lambatos' testimony confused the trial judge. Were it not for that wording, the argument goes, the judge might have found that the prosecution failed to introduce sufficient admissible evidence to show that the Cellmark profile was derived from the sample taken from the victim, and the judge might have disregarded the DNA evidence. This argument reflects a profound lack of respect for the acumen of the trial judge.[5]

---

3. The small difference between what Lambatos actually said on the stand and the slightly revised version that the dissent would find unobjectionable shows that, despite the dissent's rhetoric, its narrow argument would have little practical effect in future cases. Prosecutors would be allowed to do exactly what the prosecution did in this case so long as their testifying experts' testimony was slightly modified along the lines shown above. Following that course presumably would not constitute a "prosecutorial dodge," "subterfuge," "indirection," the "neat trick" of "sneak[ing]" in evidence, or the countenancing of constitutional violations with "a wink and a nod." *See post* (opinion of KAGAN, J.).

4. We do not suggest that the Confrontation Clause applies differently depending on the identity of the factfinder. *Cf. post*, (opinion of KAGAN, J.). Instead, our point is that the identity of the factfinder makes a big difference in evaluating the likelihood that the factfinder mistakenly based its decision on inadmissible evidence.

5. *See post*, (opinion of KAGAN, J.) ("I do not doubt that a judge typically will do better than a jury in excluding such inadmissible evidence from his decisionmaking process. Perhaps the judge did so here" (emphasis added)).

To begin, the dissent's argument finds no support in the trial record. After defense counsel objected to Lambatos' testimony, the prosecutor made clear that she was asking Lambatos only about "her own testing based on [DNA] information" that she had received from Cellmark. App. 56. Recognizing that Lambatos' testimony would carry weight only if the underlying premises could be established, the judge noted that "the issue is . . . what weight do you give the test [performed by Lambatos], not do you exclude it." *Id.*, at 94. This echoes the old statement in *Beckwith* that an expert's opinion based on disputed premises "might not go for much; but still it [is] admissible evidence." 1 Camp., at 117, 170 Eng. Rep., at 897. Both the Illinois Appellate Court and the Illinois Supreme Court viewed the record in this way, and we see no ground for disagreement.[6]

Second, it is extraordinarily unlikely that any trial judge would be confused in the way that the dissent posits. That Lambatos was not competent to testify to the chain of custody of the sample taken from the victim was a point that any trial judge or attorney would immediately understand. Lambatos, after all, had absolutely nothing to do with the collection of the sample from the victim, its subsequent handling or preservation by the police in Illinois, or its shipment to and receipt by Cellmark. No trial judge would take Lambatos' testimony as furnishing "the missing link" in the State's evidence regarding the identity of the sample that Cellmark tested.

Third, the admissible evidence left little room for argument that the sample tested by Cellmark came from any source other than the victim's vaginal swabs.[7] This is so because there is simply no plausible explanation for how Cellmark could have produced a DNA profile that matched Williams' if Cellmark had tested any sample other than the one taken from the victim. If any other items that might have contained Williams' DNA had been sent to Cellmark or were otherwise in Cellmark's possession, there would have been a chance of a mix-up or of cross-contamination. *See District Attorney's Office for Third Judicial Dist. v. Osborne*, 557 U.S. 52, 80 (2009) (Alito, J., concurring). But there is absolutely nothing to suggest that Cellmark had any such items. Thus, the fact that the Cellmark profile matched Williams—the very man whom the victim identified in a lineup and at trial as her

---

6. The dissent finds evidence of the trial judge's confusion in his statement that petitioner is "'the guy whose DNA, *according to the evidence from the experts*, is in the semen recovered from the victim's vagina.'" *Post*, (opinion of KAGAN, J.) (emphasis added). The dissent interprets the phrase "according to the evidence from the experts" as a reference to what one expert, Lambatos, said about the origin of the sample that Cellmark tested. In context, however, the judge's statement is best understood as attributing to Lambatos nothing more than the conclusion that there was a match between the two DNA profiles that were compared. The foundational facts, that one of the profiles came from the defendant and that the other came from "'the semen recovered from the victim's vagina,'" were established not by expert testimony but by ordinary chain-of-custody evidence.

7. Our point is not that admissible evidence regarding the identity of the sample that Cellmark tested excuses the admission of testimonial hearsay on this matter. *Compare post*, (THOMAS, J., concurring in judgment), *with post*, (KAGAN, J., dissenting). Rather, our point is that, because there was substantial (albeit circumstantial) evidence on this matter, there is no reason to infer that the trier of fact must have taken Lambatos' statement as providing "the missing link."

attacker—was itself striking confirmation that the sample that Cellmark tested was the sample taken from the victim's vaginal swabs. For these reasons, it is fanciful to suggest that the trial judge took Lambatos' testimony as providing critical chain-of-custody evidence.

C

Other than the phrase that Lambatos used in referring to the Cellmark profile, no specific passage in the trial record has been identified as violating the Confrontation Clause, but it is nevertheless suggested that the State somehow introduced "the substance of Cellmark's report into evidence." The main impetus for this argument appears to be the (erroneous) view that unless the substance of the report was sneaked in, there would be insufficient evidence in the record on two critical points: first, that the Cellmark profile was based on the semen in the victim's vaginal swabs and, second, that Cellmark's procedures were reliable. This argument is both legally irrelevant for present purposes and factually incorrect.

As to legal relevance, the question before us is whether petitioner's Sixth Amendment confrontation right was violated, not whether the State offered sufficient foundational evidence to support the admission of Lambatos' opinion about the DNA match. In order to prove these underlying facts, the prosecution relied on circumstantial evidence, and the Illinois courts found that this evidence was sufficient to satisfy state-law requirements regarding proof of foundational facts. *See* 895 N.E.2d, at 967–968. We cannot review that interpretation and application of Illinois law. Thus, even if the record did not contain any evidence that could rationally support a finding that Cellmark produced a scientifically reliable DNA profile based on L. J.'s vaginal swab, that would not establish a Confrontation Clause violation. If there were no proof that Cellmark produced an accurate profile based on that sample, Lambatos' testimony regarding the match would be irrelevant, but the Confrontation Clause, as interpreted in *Crawford*, does not bar the admission of irrelevant evidence, only testimonial statements by declarants who are not subject to cross-examination.[8]

It is not correct, however, that the trial record lacks admissible evidence with respect to the source of the sample that Cellmark tested or the reliability of the Cellmark profile. As to the source of the sample, the State offered conventional chain-of-custody evidence, namely, the testimony of the physician who obtained the vaginal swabs, the testimony of the police employees who handled and kept custody of that evidence until it was sent to Cellmark, and the shipping manifests,

---

8. Applying the Due Process Clause, we have held that a federal court may determine whether a rational trier of fact could have found the existence of all the elements needed for conviction for a state offense. *Jackson v. Virginia*, 443 U.S. 307, 314 (1979), but petitioner has not raised a due process claim. And in any event, L.J.'s identification of petitioner as her assailant would be sufficient to defeat any such claim.

which provided evidence that the swabs were sent to Cellmark and then returned to the ISP lab. In addition, as already discussed, the match between the Cellmark profile and petitioner's profile was itself telling confirmation that the Cellmark profile was deduced from the semen on the vaginal swabs.

This match also provided strong circumstantial evidence regarding the reliability of Cellmark's work. Assuming (for the reasons discussed above) that the Cellmark profile was based on the semen on the vaginal swabs, how could shoddy or dishonest work in the Cellmark lab[9] have resulted in the production of a DNA profile that just so happened to match petitioner's? If the semen found on the vaginal swabs was not petitioner's and thus had an entirely different DNA profile, how could sloppy work in the Cellmark lab have transformed that entirely different profile into one that matched petitioner's? And without access to any other sample of petitioner's DNA (and recall that petitioner was not even under suspicion at this time), how could a dishonest lab technician have substituted petitioner's DNA profile? Under the circumstances of this case, it was surely permissible for the trier of fact to infer that the odds of any of this were exceedingly low.

This analysis reveals that much of the dissent's argument rests on a very clear error. The dissent argues that Lambatos' testimony could be "true" only if the predicate facts asserted in the Cellmark report were true, and therefore Lambatos' reference to the report must have been used for the purpose of proving the truth of those facts. But the truth of Lambatos' testimony, properly understood, was not dependent on the truth of any predicate facts. Lambatos testified that two DNA profiles matched. The correctness of this expert opinion, which the defense was able to test on cross-examination, was not in any way dependent on the origin of the samples from which the profiles were derived. Of course, Lambatos' opinion would have lacked probative value if the prosecution had not introduced other evidence to establish the provenance of the profiles, but that has nothing to do with the truth of her testimony.

The dissent is similarly mistaken in its contention that the Cellmark report "was offered for its truth because that is all such 'basis evidence' can be offered for." *See post* (Thomas, J., concurring in judgment) ("[S]tatements introduced to explain the basis of an expert's opinion are not introduced for a plausible nonhearsay purpose"). This view is directly contrary to the current version of Rule 703 of the Federal Rules of Evidence, which this Court approved and sent to Congress in 2000. Under that Rule, "basis evidence" that is not admissible for its truth may be disclosed even in a jury trial under appropriate circumstances. The purpose for allowing this disclosure is that it may "assis[t] the jury to evaluate the expert's opinion." Advisory Committee's 2000 Notes on Fed. Rule Evid. 703, 28 U.S.C. App., p. 361. The Rule 703 approach, which was controversial when adopted,[10] is based on the idea that the

---

9. *See post,* (KAGAN, J., dissenting).
10. *See* Advisory Committee's 2000 Notes on Rule 703, at 361.

disclosure of basis evidence can help the factfinder understand the expert's thought process and determine what weight to give to the expert's opinion. For example, if the factfinder were to suspect that the expert relied on factual premises with no support in the record, or that the expert drew an unwarranted inference from the premises on which the expert relied, then the probativeness or credibility of the expert's opinion would be seriously undermined. The purpose of disclosing the facts on which the expert relied is to allay these fears—to show that the expert's reasoning was not illogical, and that the weight of the expert's opinion does not depend on factual premises unsupported by other evidence in the record—not to prove the truth of the underlying facts.

Perhaps because it cannot seriously dispute the legitimate nonhearsay purpose of illuminating the expert's thought process, the dissent resorts to the last-ditch argument that, after all, it really does not matter whether Lambatos' statement regarding the source of the Cellmark report was admitted for its truth. The dissent concedes that "the trial judge might have ignored Lambatos's statement about the Cellmark report," but nonetheless maintains that "the admission of that statement violated the Confrontation Clause even if the judge ultimately put it aside." But in a bench trial, it is not necessary for the judge to stop and make a formal statement on the record regarding the limited reason for which the testimony is admitted. If the judge does not consider the testimony for its truth, the effect is precisely the same. Thus, if the trial judge in this case did not rely on the statement in question for its truth, there is simply no way around the proviso in *Crawford* that the Confrontation Clause applies only to out-of-court statements that are "use[d]" to "establis[h]" the truth of the matter asserted." 541 U.S., at 59–60, n. 9 (*citing Street*, 471 U.S. 409).

For all these reasons, we conclude that petitioner's Sixth Amendment confrontation right was not violated.

D

This conclusion is entirely consistent with *Bullcoming* and *Melendez-Diaz*. In those cases, the forensic reports were introduced into evidence, and there is no question that this was done for the purpose of proving the truth of what they asserted: in *Bullcoming* that the defendant's blood alcohol level exceeded the legal limit and in *Melendez-Diaz* that the substance in question contained cocaine. Nothing comparable happened here. In this case, the Cellmark report was not introduced into evidence. An expert witness referred to the report not to prove the truth of the matter asserted in the report, i.e., that the report contained an accurate profile of the perpetrator's DNA, but only to establish that the report contained a DNA profile that matched the DNA profile deduced from petitioner's blood. Thus, just as in *Street*, the report was not to be considered for its truth but only for the "distinctive and limited purpose" of seeing whether it matched something else. 471 U.S., at 417. The relevance of the match was then established by independent circumstantial evidence showing that the Cellmark report was based on a forensic sample taken from the scene of the crime.

Our conclusion will not open the door for the kind of abuses suggested by some of petitioner's amici and the dissent. *See* Brief for Richard D. Friedman as *Amicus Curiae* 20–21. In the hypothetical situations posited, an expert expresses an opinion based on factual premises not supported by any admissible evidence, and may also reveal the out-of-court statements on which the expert relied.[11] There are at least four safeguards to prevent such abuses. First, trial courts can screen out experts who would act as mere conduits for hearsay by strictly enforcing the requirement that experts display some genuine "scientific, technical, or other specialized knowledge [that] will help the trier of fact to understand the evidence or to determine a fact in issue." Fed. Rule Evid. 702(a). Second, experts are generally precluded from disclosing inadmissible evidence to a jury. *See* Fed. Rule Evid. 703; *People v. Pasch*, 604 N.E.2d 294, 310–311 (Ill. 1992). Third, if such evidence is disclosed, the trial judges may and, under most circumstances, must, instruct the jury that out-of-court statements cannot be accepted for their truth, and that an expert's opinion is only as good as the independent evidence that establishes its underlying premises. *See* Fed. Rules Evid. 105, 703; *People v. Scott*, 594 N.E.2d 217, 236–237 (Ill. 1992). And fourth, if the prosecution cannot muster any independent admissible evidence to prove the foundational facts that are essential to the relevance of the expert's testimony, then the expert's testimony cannot be given any weight by the trier of fact.[12]

---

11. Both Justice THOMAS and Justice KAGAN quote statements in D. Kaye, D. Bernstein, & J. Mnookin, The New Wigmore: Expert Evidence § 4.10.1, pp. 196–197 (2d ed.2011) (hereinafter New Wigmore), that are critical of the theory that an expert, without violating the Confrontation Clause, may express an opinion that is based on testimonial hearsay and may, in some circumstances, disclose that testimonial hearsay to the trier of fact. The principal basis for this criticism seems to be the fear that juries, even if given limiting instructions, will view the disclosed hearsay as evidence of the truth of the matter asserted. *See id.*, at 196, n. 36 (referring reader to the more detailed discussion in Mnookin, Expert Evidence and the Confrontation Clause After *Crawford v. Washington*, 15 J.L. & Pol'y 791 (2007)); New Wigmore 197, and n. 39 (citing jury cases); *Mnookin, supra*, at 802–804, 811–813. This argument plainly has no application in a case like this one, in which a judge sits as the trier of fact. In the 2012 Supplement of The New Wigmore, the authors discuss the present case and criticize the reasoning of the Illinois courts as follows:

> "The problem with [the not-for-the-truth-of-the-matter argument accepted by the Illinois courts] is that Lambatos had to rely on the truth of the statements in the Cellmark report to reach her own conclusion. The claim that evidence that the jury must credit in order to credit the conclusion of the expert is introduced for something other than its truth is sheer fiction." New Wigmore § 4.11.6, at 24 (2012 Supp.) (emphasis added).

This discussion is flawed. It overlooks the fact that there was no jury in this case, and as we have explained, the trier of fact did not have to rely on any testimonial hearsay in order to find that Lambatos' testimony about the DNA match was supported by adequate foundational evidence and was thus probative.

12. Our discussion of the first ground for our decision cannot conclude without commenting on the *Kocak* case, which dramatically appears at the beginning of the dissent. In that case, a Cellmark lab analyst realized while testifying at a pretrial hearing that there was an error in the lab's report and that the DNA profile attributed to the accused was actually that of the victim. The lesson of this cautionary tale is nothing more than the truism that it is possible for an apparently incriminating DNA profile

IV

A

Even if the Cellmark report had been introduced for its truth, we would nevertheless conclude that there was no Confrontation Clause violation. The Confrontation Clause refers to testimony by "witnesses against" an accused. Both the noted evidence scholar James Henry Wigmore and Justice Harlan interpreted the Clause in a strictly literal sense as referring solely to persons who testify in court, but we have not adopted this narrow view. It has been said that "[t]he difficulty with the Wigmore-Harlan view in its purest form is its tension with much of the apparent history surrounding the evolution of the right of confrontation at common law." *White v. Illinois*, 502 U.S. 346, 360 (1992) (Thomas, J., concurring). "[T]he principal evil at which the Confrontation Clause was directed," the Court concluded in *Crawford*, "was the civil-law mode of criminal procedure, and particularly its use of ex parte examinations as evidence against the accused." 541 U.S., at 50. "[I]n England, pretrial examinations of suspects and witnesses by government officials 'were sometimes read in court in lieu of live testimony.' *Bryant*, 562 U.S., at____, 131 S. Ct. 1143 (quoting *Crawford, supra*, at 43. The Court has thus interpreted the Confrontation Clause as prohibiting modern-day practices that are tantamount to the abuses that gave rise to the recognition of the confrontation right. But any further expansion would strain the constitutional text.

The abuses that the Court has identified as prompting the adoption of the Confrontation Clause shared the following two characteristics: (a) they involved out-of-court statements having the primary purpose of accusing a targeted individual of engaging in criminal conduct and (b) they involved formalized statements such as affidavits, depositions, prior testimony, or confessions. In all but one of the post-*Crawford* cases[13] in which a Confrontation Clause violation has been found, both of these characteristics were present. *See Bullcoming*, 564 U.S., at 308 (certified lab report having purpose of showing that defendant's blood-alcohol level exceeded

---

to be mistakenly attributed to an accused. But requiring that the lab analyst or analysts who produced the DNA profile be called as prosecution witnesses is neither sufficient nor necessary to prevent such errors. Since samples may be mixed up or contaminated at many points along the way from a crime scene to the lab, calling one or more lab analysts will not necessarily catch all such mistakes. For example, a mistake might be made by a clerical employee responsible for receiving shipments of samples and then providing them to the lab's technicians. What is needed is for the trier of fact to make sure that the evidence, whether direct or circumstantial, rules out the possibility of such mistakes at every step along the way. And in the usual course of authentication, defense counsel will have access to sufficient information to inquire into, question, or challenge the procedures used by a laboratory if this seems to be a prudent and productive strategy.

13. Experience might yet show that the holdings in those cases should be reconsidered for the reasons, among others, expressed in the dissents the decisions produced. Those decisions are not challenged in this case and are to be deemed binding precedents, but they can and should be distinguished on the facts here.

legal limit); *Melendez-Diaz*, 557 U.S., at 308 (certified lab report having purpose of showing that substance connected to defendant contained cocaine); *Crawford, supra*, at 38 (custodial statement made after *Miranda* warnings that shifted blame from declarant to accused).[14] The one exception occurred in *Hammon v. Indiana*, 547 U.S. 813, 829–832 (2006), which was decided together with *Davis v. Washington*, but in *Hammon* and every other post-*Crawford* case in which the Court has found a violation of the confrontation right, the statement at issue had the primary purpose of accusing a targeted individual.

B

In *Hammon*, the one case in which an informal statement was held to violate the Confrontation Clause, we considered statements elicited in the course of police interrogation. We held that a statement does not fall within the ambit of the Clause when it is made "under circumstances objectively indicating that the primary purpose of the interrogation is to enable police assistance to meet an ongoing emergency." 547 U.S., at 822. In *Bryant*, another police-interrogation case, we explained that a person who makes a statement to resolve an ongoing emergency is not acting like a trial witness because the declarant's purpose is not to provide a solemn declaration for use at trial, but to bring an end to an ongoing threat. *See* 562 U.S., at_____,_____, 131 S. Ct. 1143. We noted that "the prospect of fabrication . . . is presumably significantly diminished" when a statement is made under such circumstances, *id.*, at_____, 131 S. Ct. 1143, and that reliability is a salient characteristic of a statement that falls outside the reach of the Confrontation Clause, *id.*, at_____-_____, 131 S. Ct. 1143. We emphasized that if a statement is not made for "the primary purpose of creating an out-of-court substitute for trial testimony," its admissibility "is the concern of state and federal rules of evidence, not the Confrontation Clause." *Id.*, at_____-_____, 131 S. Ct. 1143.

In *Melendez-Diaz* and *Bullcoming*, the Court held that the particular forensic reports at issue qualified as testimonial statements, but the Court did not hold that all forensic reports fall into the same category. Introduction of the reports in those cases ran afoul of the Confrontation Clause because they were the equivalent of affidavits made for the purpose of proving the guilt of a particular criminal defendant at trial. There was nothing resembling an ongoing emergency, as the suspects in both cases had already been captured, and the tests in question were relatively simple and can generally be performed by a single analyst. In addition, the technicians who prepared the reports must have realized that their contents (which reported an elevated blood-alcohol level and the presence of an illegal drug) would be incriminating.

---

14. With respect to *Crawford, see Davis*, 547 U.S., at 840 (THOMAS, J., concurring in judgment in part and dissenting in part).

C

The Cellmark report is very different. It plainly was not prepared for the primary purpose of accusing a targeted individual. In identifying the primary purpose of an out-of-court statement, we apply an objective test. *Bryant,* 562 U.S., at_____, 131 S. Ct. 1143. We look for the primary purpose that a reasonable person would have ascribed to the statement, taking into account all of the surrounding circumstances. *Ibid.*

Here, the primary purpose of the Cellmark report, viewed objectively, was not to accuse petitioner or to create evidence for use at trial. When the ISP lab sent the sample to Cellmark, its primary purpose was to catch a dangerous rapist who was still at large, not to obtain evidence for use against petitioner, who was neither in custody nor under suspicion at that time. Similarly, no one at Cellmark could have possibly known that the profile that it produced would turn out to inculpate petitioner—or for that matter, anyone else whose DNA profile was in a law enforcement database. Under these circumstances, there was no "prospect of fabrication" and no incentive to produce anything other than a scientifically sound and reliable profile. *Id.,* at_____, 131 S. Ct. 1143.

The situation in which the Cellmark technicians found themselves was by no means unique. When lab technicians are asked to work on the production of a DNA profile, they often have no idea what the consequences of their work will be. In some cases, a DNA profile may provide powerful incriminating evidence against a person who is identified either before or after the profile is completed. But in others, the primary effect of the profile is to exonerate a suspect who has been charged or is under investigation. The technicians who prepare a DNA profile generally have no way of knowing whether it will turn out to be incriminating or exonerating—or both.

It is also significant that in many labs, numerous technicians work on each DNA profile. *See* Brief for New York County District Attorney's Office et al. as *Amici Curiae* 6 (New York lab uses at least 12 technicians for each case); *People v. Johnson,* 906 N.E.2d 70, 79 (Ill. App. 2009) ("[A]pproximately 10 Cellmark analysts were involved in the laboratory work in this case"). When the work of a lab is divided up in such a way, it is likely that the sole purpose of each technician is simply to perform his or her task in accordance with accepted procedures.

Finally, the knowledge that defects in a DNA profile may often be detected from the profile itself provides a further safeguard. In this case, for example, Lambatos testified that she would have been able to tell from the profile if the sample used by Cellmark had been degraded prior to testing. As noted above, moreover, there is no real chance that "sample contamination, sample switching, mislabeling, [or] fraud" could have led Cellmark to produce a DNA profile that falsely matched petitioner. At the time of the testing, petitioner had not yet been identified as a suspect, and there is no suggestion that anyone at Cellmark had a sample of his DNA to swap in by malice or mistake. And given the complexity of the DNA molecule, it is inconceivable that shoddy lab work would somehow produce a DNA profile that just so happened to have the precise genetic makeup of petitioner, who just so happened to be picked out of a lineup by the victim. The prospect is beyond fanciful.

In short, the use at trial of a DNA report prepared by a modern, accredited laboratory "bears little if any resemblance to the historical practices that the Confrontation Clause aimed to eliminate." *Bryant, supra*, at_____, 131 S. Ct. 1143 (Thomas, J., concurring).

* * *

For the two independent reasons explained above, we conclude that there was no Confrontation Clause violation in this case. Accordingly, the judgment of the Supreme Court of Illinois is affirmed.

CONCUR BY: BREYER; THOMAS

CONCUR

JUSTICE BREYER, concurring.

This case raises a question that I believe neither the plurality nor the dissent answers adequately: How does the Confrontation Clause apply to the panoply of crime laboratory reports and underlying technical statements written by (or otherwise made by) laboratory technicians? In this context, what, if any, are the outer limits of the "testimonial statements" rule set forth in *Crawford v. Washington*, 541 U.S. 36 (2004)? Because I believe the question difficult, important, and not squarely addressed either today or in our earlier opinions, and because I believe additional briefing would help us find a proper, generally applicable answer, I would set this case for reargument. In the absence of doing so, I adhere to the dissenting views set forth in *Melendez-Diaz v. Massachusetts*, 557 U.S. 305 (2009), and *Bullcoming v. New Mexico*, 564 U.S._____, 131 S. Ct. 2705 (2011). I also join the plurality's opinion.

I

A

This case is another in our series involving the intersection of the Confrontation Clause and expert testimony. Before trial, the prosecution's expert, Sandra Lambatos, received a copy of a report prepared by Cellmark Diagnostics Laboratory. That report reflected the fact that Cellmark technicians had received material from a vaginal swab taken from the crime victim, had identified semen in that material, and had derived a profile of the male DNA that the semen contained. Lambatos then entered that profile into an Illinois State Police Crime Laboratory computerized database, which contained, among many other DNA profiles, a profile derived by the crime laboratory from Williams' blood (taken at an earlier time). The computer she was using showed that the two profiles matched. Lambatos then confirmed the match.

Later, Lambatos testified at trial, where the prosecutor asked her three relevant questions. First, the prosecutor asked whether there was "a computer match generated of the male DNA profile [derived by Cellmark] found in [the] semen from the vaginal swabs . . . to [the] male DNA profile [found in the database] that had been identified as having originated from Sandy Williams"? App. 56. Since the computer had shown such a match, Lambatos answered affirmatively. *Ibid.*

Second, the prosecutor asked whether Lambatos had independently "compare[d the DNA profile that Cellmark had derived from] the semen that had been identified . . . from the vaginal swabs of [the victim] to the male DNA profile [found in the database] that had been [derived] . . . from the blood of Sandy Williams." Ibid. Lambatos again answered affirmatively. *Ibid.*

Third, the prosecutor asked whether, in Lambatos' expert opinion, the DNA profile derived from the semen identified in the vaginal swabs of the victim was "a match to Sandy Williams." *Id.*, at 58. Lambatos again answered affirmatively. *Ibid.*

The Confrontation Clause problem lies in the fact that Lambatos did not have personal knowledge that the male DNA profile that Cellmark said was derived from the crime victim's vaginal swab sample was in fact correctly derived from that sample. And no Cellmark expert testified that it was true. Rather, she simply relied for her knowledge of the fact upon Cellmark's report. And the defendant Williams had no opportunity to cross-examine the individual or individuals who produced that report.

In its first conclusion, the plurality explains why it finds that admission of Lambatos' testimony nonetheless did not violate the Confrontation Clause. That Clause concerns out-of-court statements admitted for their truth. Lambatos' testimony did not introduce the Cellmark report (which other circumstantial evidence supported) for its truth. Rather, Lambatos used the Cellmark report only to indicate the underlying factual information upon which she based her independent expert opinion. Under well-established principles of evidence, experts may rely on otherwise inadmissible out-of-court statements as a basis for forming an expert opinion if they are of a kind that experts in the field normally rely upon. *See* Fed. Rule Evid. 703; Ill. Rule Evid. 703. Nor need the prosecution enter those out-of-court statements into evidence for their truth. That, the Illinois courts held, is just what took place here.

The dissent would abandon this well-established rule. It would not permit Lambatos to offer an expert opinion in reliance on the Cellmark report unless the prosecution also produces one or more experts who wrote or otherwise produced the report. I am willing to accept the dissent's characterization of the present rule as artificial, but I am not certain that the dissent has produced a workable alternative, *see Bullcoming, supra*, at_____, 131 S. Ct. 2705 (Kennedy, J., dissenting) (expressing similar view).

Once one abandons the traditional rule, there would seem often to be no logical stopping place between requiring the prosecution to call as a witness one of the laboratory experts who worked on the matter and requiring the prosecution to call all of the laboratory experts who did so. Experts—especially laboratory experts—regularly rely on the technical statements and results of other experts to form their own opinions. The reality of the matter is that the introduction of a laboratory report involves layer upon layer of technical statements (express or implied) made by one expert and relied upon by another. Hence my general question: How does the Confrontation Clause apply to crime laboratory reports and underlying technical statements made by laboratory technicians?

B

The general question is not easy to answer. The California case described at the outset of the dissenting opinion helps to illustrate the difficulty. In that example, Cellmark, the very laboratory involved in this case, tested a DNA sample taken from the crime scene. A laboratory analyst, relying upon a report the laboratory had prepared, initially stated (at a pretrial hearing about admissibility) that the laboratory had found that the crime-scene DNA sample matched a sample of the defendant's DNA. But during the hearing and after reviewing the laboratory's notes, the laboratory analyst realized that the written report was mistaken. In fact, the testing showed only that the crime-scene DNA matched a sample of the victim's DNA, not the defendant's DNA. At some point during the writing of the report, someone, perhaps the testifying analyst herself, must have misread the proper original sample labeling. Upon discovering the error, the analyst corrected her testimony.

The example is useful, not simply because as adapted it might show the importance of cross-examination (an importance no one doubts), but also because it can reveal the nature of the more general question before us. When the laboratory in the example received the DNA samples, it labeled them properly. The laboratory's final report mixed up the labels. Any one of many different technicians could be responsible for an error like that. And the testifying analyst might not have reviewed the underlying notes and caught the error during direct examination (or for that matter, during cross-examination).

Adapting the example slightly, assume that the admissibility of the initial laboratory report into trial had been directly at issue. Who should the prosecution have had to call to testify? Only the analyst who signed the report noting the match? What if the analyst who made the match knew nothing about either the laboratory's underlying procedures or the specific tests run in the particular case? Should

the prosecution then have had to call all potentially involved laboratory technicians to testify? Six to twelve or more technicians could have been involved. Some
or all of the words spoken or written by each technician out of court might well
have constituted relevant statements offered for their truth and reasonably relied on
by a supervisor or analyst writing the laboratory report. Indeed, petitioner's amici
argue that the technicians at each stage of the process should be subject to cross-
examination. *See* Brief for Innocence Network as *Amicus Curiae* 13–23 (hereinafter
Innocence Network Brief).

And as is true of many hearsay statements that fall within any of the 20 or more
hearsay exceptions, cross-examination could sometimes significantly help to elicit
the truth. *See* Fed. Rule Evid. 803 (listing 24 hearsay exceptions). The Confrontation Clause as interpreted in *Crawford* recognizes, as a limitation upon a pure
"testimonial statement" requirement, circumstances where the defendant had an
adequate "prior opportunity to cross-examine." 541 U.S., at 59. To what extent
might the "testimonial statements" requirement embody one or more (or modified
versions) of these traditional hearsay exceptions as well?

Lower courts and treatise writers have recognized the problem. And they have
come up with a variety of solutions. The New Wigmore, for example, lists several
nonexclusive approaches to when testifying experts may rely on testing results or
reports by nontestifying experts (i.e., DNA technicians or analysts), including:
(1) "the dominant approach," which is simply to determine the need to testify
by looking "the quality of the nontestifying expert's report, the testifying expert's
involvement in the process, and the consequent ability of the testifying expert to
use independent judgment and interpretive skill"; (2) permitting "a substitute
expert to testify about forensic science results only when the first expert is unavailable" (irrespective of the lack of opportunity to cross-examine the first expert,
cf. Crawford, supra, at 59; (3) permitting "a substitute expert" to testify if "the
original test was documented in a thorough way that permits the substitute expert
to evaluate, assess, and interpret it"; (4) permitting a DNA analyst to introduce
DNA test results at trial without having "personally perform[ed] every specific
aspect of each DNA test in question, provided the analyst was present during the
critical stages of the test, is familiar with the process and the laboratory protocol
involved, reviews the results in proximity to the test, and either initials or signs
the final report outlining the results"; (5) permitting the introduction of a crime
laboratory DNA report without the testimony of a technician where the "testing
in its preliminary stages" only "requires the technician simply to perform largely
mechanical or ministerial tasks . . . absent some reason to believe there was error
or falsification"; and (6) permitting introduction of the report without requiring
the technicians to testify where there is a showing of "genuine unavailability."
See D. Kaye, D. Bernstein, & J. Mnookin, The New Wigmore: Expert Evidence,
§§4.10.2, 4.10.3, pp. 202, 204, 206 (2d ed. 2010) (internal quotation marks and
footnote omitted); *id.,* §4.11.6, at 24 (Supp. 2012).

Some of these approaches seem more readily compatible with *Crawford* than others. Some seem more easily considered by a rules committee (or by state courts) than by this Court. Nonetheless, all assume some kind of *Crawford* boundary—some kind of limitation upon the scope of its application—though they reflect different views as to just how and when that might be done.

Answering the underlying general question just discussed, and doing so soon, is important. Trial judges in both federal and state courts apply and interpret hearsay rules as part of their daily trial work. The trial of criminal cases makes up a large portion of that work. And laboratory reports frequently constitute a portion of the evidence in ordinary criminal trials. Obviously, judges, prosecutors, and defense lawyers have to know, in as definitive a form as possible, what the Constitution requires so that they can try their cases accordingly.

The several different opinions filed today embody several serious, but different, approaches to the difficult general question. Yet none fully deals with the underlying question as to how, after *Crawford*, Confrontation Clause "testimonial statement" requirements apply to crime laboratory reports. Nor can I find a general answer in *Melendez-Diaz* or *Bullcoming*. While, as a matter of pure logic, one might use those cases to answer a narrowed version of the question presented here, those cases do not fully consider the broader evidentiary problem presented. I consequently find the dissent's response, "Been there, done that," unsatisfactory.

Under these circumstances, I would have this case reargued. I would request the parties and amici to focus specifically upon the broader "limits" question. And I would permit them to discuss, not only the possible implications of our earlier post-*Crawford* opinions, but also any necessary modifications of statements made in the opinions of those earlier cases.

II

In the absence of reargument, I adhere to the dissenting view set forth in *Melendez-Diaz* and *Bullcoming*, under which the Cellmark report would not be considered "testimonial" and barred by the Confrontation Clause. That view understands the Confrontation Clause as interpreted in *Crawford* to bar the admission of "*[t]estimonial*" statements made out of court unless the declarant is unavailable and the defendant had a prior opportunity to cross-examine. 541 U.S., at 59 (emphasis added). It also understands the word "testimonial" as having outer limits and *Crawford* as describing a constitutional heartland. And that view would leave the States with constitutional leeway to maintain traditional expert testimony rules as well as hearsay exceptions where there are strong reasons for doing so and *Crawford*'s basic rationale does not apply.

In particular, the States could create an exception that presumptively would allow introduction of DNA reports from accredited crime laboratories. The defendant would remain free to call laboratory technicians as witnesses. Were there significant reason to question a laboratory's technical competence or its neutrality, the presumptive exception would disappear, thereby requiring the prosecution to produce any relevant technical witnesses. Such an exception would lie outside *Crawford*'s constitutional limits.

Consider the report before us. Cellmark's DNA report embodies technical or professional data, observations, and judgments; the employees who contributed to the report's findings were professional analysts working on technical matters at a certified laboratory; and the employees operated behind a veil of ignorance that likely prevented them from knowing the identity of the defendant in this case. Statements of this kind fall within a hearsay exception that has constituted an important part of the law of evidence for decades. *See* Fed. Rule Evid. 803(6) ("Records of Regularly Conducted Activity"); 2 J. Wigmore, Evidence §§1517–1533, pp. 1878–1899 (1904) ("Regular Entries"). And for somewhat similar reasons, I believe that such statements also presumptively fall outside the category of "testimonial" statements that the Confrontation Clause makes inadmissible.

As the plurality points out, the introduction of statements of this kind does not risk creating the "principal evil at which the Confrontation Clause was directed." *Crawford*, 541 U.S., at 50. That evil consists of the pre-Constitution practice of using "ex parte examinations as evidence against the accused." *Ibid.* Sir Walter Raleigh's case illustrates the point. State authorities questioned Lord Cobham, the key witness against Raleigh, outside his presence. They then used those testimonial statements in court against Raleigh. And when Raleigh asked to face and to challenge his accuser, he was denied that opportunity. *See id.*, at 44.

The Confrontation Clause prohibits the use of this kind of evidence because allowing it would deprive a defendant of the ability to cross-examine the witness. *Id.*, at 61–62; *Mattox v. United States*, 156 U.S. 237, 242–243 (1895). That deprivation would prevent a defendant from confronting the witness. And it would thereby prevent a defendant from probing the witness' perception, memory, narration, and sincerity. *See, e.g.*, 2 K. Broun et al., McCormick on Evidence § 245, p. 125 (6th ed. 2006); E. Morgan, Some Problems of Proof Under the Anglo-American System of Litigation 119–127 (1956); 30 C. Wright & K. Graham, Federal Practice and Procedure § 6324, pp. 44–49 (1997); *see also* M. Hale, History of the Common Law of England 258 (1713) (explaining virtues of confronting witness); 3 W. Blackstone, Commentaries on the Laws of England 373 (1768) (same). But the need for cross-examination is considerably diminished when the out-of-court statement was made by an accredited laboratory employee operating at a remove from the investigation in the ordinary course of professional work.

For one thing, as the hearsay exception itself reflects, alternative features of such situations help to guarantee its accuracy. An accredited laboratory must satisfy well-established professional guidelines that seek to ensure the scientific reliability of the laboratory's results. App. 59–60, 74, 86–87; *see* Brief for National District Attorneys Assn. et al. *as Amici Curiae* 25, n. 5 (hereinafter NDAA Brief) (noting that the standards date back 30 years); Giannelli, Regulating Crime Laboratories: The Impact of DNA Evidence, 15 J. L. & Pol'y 59, 72–76 (2007). For example, forensic DNA testing laboratories permitted to access the FBI's Combined DNA Index System must adhere to standards governing, among other things, the organization and management of the laboratory; education, training, and experience requirements for laboratory personnel; the laboratory's physical facilities and security measures; control of physical evidence; validation of testing methodologies; procedures for analyzing samples, including the reagents and controls that are used in the testing process; equipment calibration and maintenance; documentation of the process used to test each sample handled by the laboratory; technical and administrative review of every case file; proficiency testing of laboratory; personnel; corrective action that addresses any discrepancies in proficiency tests and casework analysis; internal and external audits of the laboratory; environmental health and safety; and outsourcing of testing to vendor laboratories. *See* Brief for New York County District Attorney's Office et al. as *Amici Curiae* 4, n. 4 (hereinafter NY County DAO Brief); *see also* App. to NY County DAO Brief A22–A49.

These standards are not foolproof. Nor are they always properly applied. It is not difficult to find instances in which laboratory procedures have been abused. *See, e.g.,* Innocence Network Brief 6–11; App. to Brief for Public Defender Service for the District of Columbia et al. as *Amici Curiae* 1a–12a; *cf.* Giannelli, The Abuse of Scientific Evidence in Criminal Cases: The Need for Independent Crime Laboratories, 4 Va. J. Soc. Pol'y & L. 439 (1997). Moreover, DNA testing itself has exonerated some defendants who previously had been convicted in part upon the basis of testimony by laboratory experts. *See Melendez-Diaz v. Massachusetts*, 557 U.S., at 319 (citing Garrett & Neufeld, Invalid Forensic Science Testimony and Wrongful Convictions, 95 Va. L. Rev. 1 (2009)).

But if accreditation did not prevent admission of faulty evidence in some of those cases, neither did cross-examination. In the wrongful-conviction cases to which this Court has previously referred, the forensic experts all testified in court and were available for cross-examination. Sklansky, Hearsay's Last Hurrah, 2009 S. Ct. Rev. 1, 72–73 (cited study "did not identify any cases in which hearsay from forensic analysts contributed to the conviction of innocent defendants"); *see* Garrett & Neufeld, *supra*, at 10–12, 84, 89 (noting that cross-examination was rarely effective); *see also* Murphy, The New Forensics: Criminal Justice, False Certainty, and the Second Generation of Scientific Evidence, 95 Cal. L. Rev. 721, 785–786 (2007) (suggesting need for greater reliance upon accreditation and oversight of accredited laboratories); Sklansky, *supra*, at 74 (same). Similarly, the role of cross-examination is ambiguous in the laboratory example that the dissent describes. (Apparently, the report's error came to light and was corrected after cross-examination had concluded, *see* Thompson, Taroni, & Aitken, Author's Response, 49 J. Forensic Sci.

1202 (2003), and in any event all parties had received the correctly labeled underlying laboratory data, *see* Clarke, Commentary, *id.*, at 1201).

For another thing, the fact that the laboratory testing takes place behind a veil of ignorance makes it unlikely that a particular researcher has a defendant-related motive to behave dishonestly, say, to misrepresent a step in an analysis or otherwise to misreport testing results. *Cf. Michigan v. Bryant*, 562 U.S._____,_____, 131 S. Ct. 1143 (2011)) (discussing the "prospect of fabrication" as a factor in whether the Confrontation Clause requires statements "to be subject to the crucible of cross-examination"). The laboratory here, for example, did not know whether its test results might help to incriminate a particular defendant. *Cf. Melendez-Diaz, supra*, at 310–311; *Bullcoming*, 564 U.S., at_____, 131 S. Ct. 2705.

Further, the statements at issue, like those of many laboratory analysts, do not easily fit within the linguistic scope of the term "testimonial statement" as we have used that term in our earlier cases. As the plurality notes, in every post-*Crawford* case in which the Court has found a Confrontation Clause violation, the statement at issue had the primary purpose of accusing a targeted individual. *See, e.g., Davis v. Washington*, 547 U.S. 813, 822 (2006) ("primary purpose . . . is to establish or prove past events potentially relevant to later criminal prosecution"); *Bryant, supra*, at_____-_____, 131 S. Ct. 1143 ("primary purpose of creating an out-of-court substitute for trial testimony"). The declarant was essentially an adverse witness making an accusatory, testimonial statement—implicating the core concerns of the Lord Cobham-type affidavits. But here the DNA report sought, not to accuse petitioner, but instead to generate objectively a profile of a then-unknown suspect's DNA from the semen he left in committing the crime.

Finally, to bar admission of the out-of-court records at issue here could undermine, not fortify, the accuracy of factfinding at a criminal trial. Such a precedent could bar the admission of other reliable case-specific technical information such as, say, autopsy reports. Autopsies, like the DNA report in this case, are often conducted when it is not yet clear whether there is a particular suspect or whether the facts found in the autopsy will ultimately prove relevant in a criminal trial. Autopsies are typically conducted soon after death. And when, say, a victim's body has decomposed, repetition of the autopsy may not be possible. What is to happen if the medical examiner dies before trial? *E.g.*, State v. Lackey, 120 P. 3d 332, 341 (Kan. 2005); *see also People v. Geier*, 161 P. 3d 104, 136–137 (Cal. 2007). Is the Confrontation Clause "'effectively'" to function "'as a statute of limitations for murder'"? *Melendez-Diaz, supra*, at 335 (Kennedy, J., dissenting) (quoting Comment, Toward a Definition of "Testimonial": How Autopsy Reports Do Not Embody the Qualities of a Testimonial Statement, 96 Cal. L. Rev. 1093, 1115 (2008)).

In general, such a holding could also increase the risk of convicting the innocent. The New York County District Attorney's Office and the New York City Office of the Chief Medical Examiner tell us that the additional cost and complexity involved in requiring live testimony from perhaps dozens of ordinary laboratory technicians who participate in the preparation of a DNA profile may well force a laboratory "to reduce the amount of DNA testing it conducts, and force prosecutors to forgo forensic DNA analysis in cases where it might be highly probative. In the absence of DNA testing, defendants might well be prosecuted solely on the basis of eyewitness testimony, the reliability of which is often questioned." NY County DAO Brief 10 (*citing United States v. Wade*, 388 U.S. 218, 229 (1967)); *see also* NDAA Brief 26 (such a holding "will also impact the innocent who may wait to be cleared from suspicion or exonerated from mistaken conviction"). I find this plausible. *But cf.* Innocence Network Brief 3. An interpretation of the Clause that risks greater prosecution reliance upon less reliable evidence cannot be sound. *Cf. Maryland v. Craig*, 497 U.S. 836, 845 (1990) ("The central concern of the Confrontation Clause is to ensure the reliability of the evidence against a criminal defendant").

Consequently, I would consider reports such as the DNA report before us presumptively to lie outside the perimeter of the Clause as established by the Court's precedents. Such a holding leaves the defendant free to call the laboratory employee as a witness if the employee is available. Moreover, should the defendant provide good reason to doubt the laboratory's competence or the validity of its accreditation, then the alternative safeguard of reliability would no longer exist and the Constitution would entitle defendant to Confrontation Clause protection. Similarly, should the defendant demonstrate the existence of a motive to falsify, then the alternative safeguard of honesty would no longer exist and the Constitution would entitle the defendant to Confrontation Clause protection. *Cf.* 2 [**125] Wigmore, Evidence §1527, at 1892 (in respect to the business records exception, "there must have been no motive to misrepresent"). Thus, the defendant would remain free to show the absence or inadequacy of the alternative reliability/honesty safeguards, thereby rebutting the presumption and making the Confrontation Clause applicable. No one has suggested any such problem in respect to the Cellmark Report at issue here.

Because the plurality's opinion is basically consistent with the views set forth here, I join that opinion in full.

CONCUR

JUSTICE THOMAS, concurring in the judgment.

I agree with the plurality that the disclosure of Cellmark's out-of-court statements through the expert testimony of Sandra Lambatos did not violate the Confrontation Clause. I reach this conclusion, however, solely because Cellmark's statements lacked the requisite "formality and solemnity" to be considered "'testimonial'" for purposes of the Confrontation Clause. *See Michigan v. Bryant*, 562 U.S._____,_____, 131 S. Ct. 1143 (2011) (Thomas, J., concurring in judgment). As I explain below, I share the dissent's view of the plurality's flawed analysis.

The threshold question in this case is whether Cellmark's statements were hearsay at all. As the Court has explained, "[t]he [Confrontation] Clause . . . does not bar the use of testimonial statements for purposes other than establishing the truth of the matter asserted." *See Crawford v. Washington*, 541 U.S. 36, 60, n. 9 (2004) (*citing Tennessee v. Street*, 471 U.S. 409, 414 (1985)). Here, the State of Illinois contends that Cellmark's statements—that it successfully derived a male DNA profile and that the profile came from L. J.'s swabs—were introduced only to show the basis of Lambatos' opinion, and not for their truth. In my view, however, there was no plausible reason for the introduction of Cellmark's statements other than to establish their truth.

A

Illinois Rule of Evidence 703 (2011) and its federal counterpart permit an expert to base his opinion on facts about which he lacks personal knowledge and to disclose those facts to the trier of fact. Relying on these Rules, the State contends that the facts on which an expert's opinion relies are not to be considered for their truth, but only to explain the basis of his opinion. *See People v. Pasch*, 604 N.E.2d 294, 311 (Ill. 1992) ("By allowing an expert to reveal the information for this purpose alone, it will undoubtedly aid the jury in assessing the value of his opinion"); *see also* Advisory Committee's Notes on Fed. Rule Evid. 703, 28 U.S.C. App., p. 361 (stating that expert basis testimony is admissible "only for the purpose of assisting the jury in evaluating an expert's opinion"). Accordingly, in the State's view, the disclosure of expert "basis testimony" does not implicate the Confrontation Clause.

I do not think that rules of evidence should so easily trump a defendant's confrontation right. To be sure, we should not "lightly swee[p] away an accepted rule" of federal or state evidence law when applying the Confrontation Clause. "Rules of limited admissibility are commonplace in evidence law." Mnookin, Expert Evidence and the Confrontation Clause after *Crawford v. Washington*, 15 J. L. & Pol'y 791, 812 (2007). And, we often presume that courts and juries follow limiting instructions. *See, e.g., Street, supra*, at 415, n. 6. But we have recognized that concepts central to the application of the Confrontation Clause are ultimately matters of federal constitutional law that are not dictated by state or federal evidentiary rules. *See Barber v. Page*, 390 U.S. 719, 724–725 (1968) (defining a constitutional standard for whether a witness is "unavailable" for purposes of the Confrontation Clause); *see also Ohio v. Roberts*, 448 U.S. 56, 76 (1980) (recognizing that *Barber* "explored the issue of constitutional unavailability" (emphasis added)). Likewise, we have held that limiting instructions may be insufficient in some circumstances to protect against violations of the Confrontation Clause. *See Bruton v. United States*, 391 U.S. 123 (1968).

Of particular importance here, we have made sure that an out-of-court statement was introduced for a "legitimate, nonhearsay purpose" before relying on the not-for-its-truth rationale to dismiss the application of the Confrontation Clause. *See Street*, 471 U.S., at 417 (emphasis added). In *Street*, the defendant testified that he gave a false confession because police coerced him into parroting his accomplice's confession. *Id.*, at 411. On rebuttal, the prosecution introduced the accomplice's confession to demonstrate to the jury the ways in which the two confessions differed. *Id.*, at 411–412. Finding no Confrontation Clause problem, this Court held that the accomplice's out-of-court confession was not introduced for its truth, but only to impeach the defendant's version of events. *Id.*, at 413–414. Although the Court noted that the confession was not hearsay "under traditional rules of evidence," *id.*, at 413, the Court did not accept that nonhearsay label at face value. Instead, the Court thoroughly examined the use of the out-of-court confession and the efficacy of a limiting instruction before concluding that the Confrontation Clause was satisfied "[i]n this context." *Id.*, at 417.

Unlike the confession in *Street*, statements introduced to explain the basis of an expert's opinion are not introduced for a plausible nonhearsay purpose. There is no meaningful distinction between disclosing an out-of-court statement so that the factfinder may evaluate the expert's opinion and disclosing that statement for its truth. "To use the inadmissible information in evaluating the expert's testimony, the jury must make a preliminary judgment about whether this information is true." D. Kaye, D. Bernstein, & J. Mnookin, The New Wigmore: A Treatise on Evidence: Expert Evidence §4.10.1, p. 196 (2d ed. 2011) (hereinafter Kaye). "If the jury believes that the basis evidence is true, it will likely also believe that the expert's reliance is justified; inversely, if the jury doubts the accuracy or validity of the basis evidence, it will be skeptical of the expert's conclusions." *Ibid.*[1]

Contrary to the plurality's suggestion, this common-sense conclusion is not undermined by any longstanding historical practice exempting expert basis testimony from the rigors of the Confrontation Clause. Prior to the adoption of the Federal Rules of Evidence in 1975, an expert could render an opinion based only on facts that the expert had personally perceived or facts that the expert learned at trial, either by listening to the testimony of other witnesses or through a hypothetical question based on facts in evidence. *See* Advisory Committee's Notes on Fed. Rule Evid. 703, 28 U.S.C. App., p. 361; 29 C. Wright & V. Gold, Federal Practice and Procedure § 6271, pp. 300–301 (1997) (hereinafter Wright); 1 K. Broun et al., McCormick on Evidence § 14, p. 86 (6th ed. 2006) (hereinafter Broun); Kaye § 4.6, at 156–157. In those situations, there was little danger that the expert would

---

1. The plurality relies heavily on the fact that this case involved a bench trial, emphasizing that a judge sitting as factfinder is presumed—more so than a jury—to "understand the limited reason for the disclosure" of basis testimony and to "not rely on that information for any improper purpose." Even accepting that presumption, the point is not that the factfinder is unable to understand the restricted purpose for basis testimony. Instead, the point is that the purportedly "limited reason" for such testimony—to aid the factfinder in evaluating the expert's opinion—necessarily entails an evaluation of whether the basis testimony is true.

rely on testimonial hearsay that was not subject to confrontation because the expert and the witnesses on whom he relied were present at trial. It was not until 1975 that the universe of facts upon which an expert could rely was expanded to include facts of the case that the expert learned out of court by means other than his own perception. 1 Broun § 14, at 87; Kaye § 4.6, at 157. It is the expert's disclosure of those facts that raises Confrontation Clause concerns.[2]

B

Those concerns are fully applicable in this case. Lambatos opined that petitioner's DNA profile matched the male profile derived from L. J.'s vaginal swabs. In reaching that conclusion, Lambatos relied on Cellmark's out-of-court statements that the profile it reported was in fact derived from L. J.'s swabs, rather than from some other source. Thus, the validity of Lambatos' opinion ultimately turned on the truth of Cellmark's statements. The plurality's assertion that Cellmark's statements were merely relayed to explain "the assumptions on which [Lambatos'] opinion rest[ed]" overlooks that the value of Lambatos' testimony depended on the truth of those very assumptions.[3]

It is no answer to say that other nonhearsay evidence established the basis of the expert's opinion. Here, Lambatos disclosed Cellmark's statements that it generated a male DNA profile from L. J.'s swabs, but other evidence showed that L. J.'s swabs contained semen and that the swabs were shipped to and received from Cellmark. That evidence did not render Cellmark's statements superfluous. Of course, evidence that Cellmark received L. J.'s swabs and later produced a DNA profile is some indication that Cellmark in fact generated the profile from those swabs, rather than from some other source (or from no source at all). *Cf. Melendez-Diaz v. Massachusetts*, 557 U.S. 305, 319 (2009) (citing brief that describes "cases of documented 'drylabbing' where forensic analysts report results of tests that were never performed," including DNA tests). But the only direct evidence to that effect was

---

2. In its discussion of history, the plurality relies on *Beckwith v. Sydebotham*, 1 Camp. 116, 170 Eng. Rep. 897 (K.B.1807). In that case, experts were asked to render opinions on a ship's seaworthiness based on facts read into court from the sworn ex parte deposition of a witness who purported to have seen the ship's deficiencies. To be sure, *Beckwith* involved expert reliance on testimonial hearsay. But *Beckwith* was an English case decided after the ratification of the Confrontation Clause, and this form of expert testimony does not appear to have been a common feature of early American evidentiary practice. *See* 29 Wright § 6271, at 300–301; 1 Broun § 14, at 86–87; Kaye § 4.6, at 156–157.

3. Cellmark's statements were not introduced for the nonhearsay purpose of showing their effect on Lambatos i.e., to explain what prompted her to search the DNA database for a match. *See, e.g.,* 30B M. Graham, Federal Practice and Procedure § 7034.1, pp. 521–529 (interim ed. 2011) (noting that out-of-court statements introduced for their effect on listener do not implicate the Confrontation Clause). The statements that Lambatos conveyed went well beyond what was necessary to explain why she performed the search. Lambatos did not merely disclose that she received a DNA profile from Cellmark. Rather, she further disclosed Cellmark's statements that the profile was "male" and that it was "found in semen from the vaginal swabs of [L.J.]." App. 56. Those facts had nothing to do with her decision to conduct a search. They were introduced for their truth.

Cellmark's statement, which Lambatos relayed to the factfinder. In any event, the factfinder's ability to rely on other evidence to evaluate an expert's opinion does not alter the conclusion that basis testimony is admitted for its truth. The existence of other evidence corroborating the basis testimony may render any Confrontation Clause violation harmless, but it does not change the purpose of such testimony and thereby place it outside of the reach of the Confrontation Clause.[4] I would thus conclude that Cellmark's statements were introduced for their truth.

C

The plurality's contrary conclusion may seem of little consequence to those who view DNA testing and other forms of "hard science" as intrinsically reliable. *But see Melendez-Diaz, supra,* at 318 ("Forensic evidence is not uniquely immune from the risk of manipulation"). Today's holding, however, will reach beyond scientific evidence to ordinary out-of-court statements. For example, it is not uncommon for experts to rely on interviews with third parties in forming their opinions. *See, e.g., People v. Goldstein,* 843 N.E.2d 727, 729–730 (N.Y. 2005) (psychiatrist disclosed statements made by the defendant's acquaintances as part of the basis of her opinion that the defendant was motivated to kill by his feelings of sexual frustration).

It is no answer to say that "safeguards" in the rules of evidence will prevent the abuse of basis testimony. To begin with, courts may be willing to conclude that an expert is not acting as a "mere condui[t]" for hearsay as long as he simply provides some opinion based on that hearsay. *See* Brief for Respondent 18, n. 4 (collecting cases). In addition, the hearsay may be the kind of fact on which experts in a field reasonably rely. *See* Fed. Rule Evid. 703; *Goldstein, supra,* at 731 (evidence showed that reputable psychiatrists relied upon third-party interviews in forming their opinions). Of course, some courts may determine that hearsay of this sort is not substantially more probative than prejudicial and therefore should not be disclosed under Rule 703. But that balancing test is no substitute for a constitutional provision that has already struck the balance in favor of the accused. *See Crawford,* 541 U.S., at 61 ("[The Confrontation Clause] commands, not that evidence be reliable, but that reliability be assessed in a particular manner: by testing in the crucible of cross-examination").

---

4. The plurality concludes that the Confrontation Clause would not be implicated here "even if the record did not contain any [other] evidence that could rationally support a finding that Cellmark produced a scientifically reliable DNA profile based on L.J.'s vaginal swab." But, far from establishing a "legitimate" nonhearsay purpose for Cellmark's statements, *Tennessee v. Street,* 471 U.S. 409, 417 (1985), a complete lack of other evidence tending to prove the facts conveyed by Cellmark's statements would completely refute the not-for-its-truth rationale. The trial court, in announcing its verdict, expressly concluded that petitioner's DNA matched the "DNA . . . in the semen recovered from the victim's vagina." 4 R. JJJ151. Absent other evidence, it would have been impossible for the trial court to reach that conclusion without relying on the truth of Cellmark's statement that its test results were based on the semen from L.J.'s swabs.

II

A

Having concluded that the statements at issue here were introduced for their truth, I turn to whether they were "testimonial" for purposes of the Confrontation Clause. In *Crawford*, the Court explained that "[t]he text of the Confrontation Clause . . . applies to 'witnesses' against the accused—in other words, those who 'bear testimony.' *Id.*, at 51 (quoting 2 N. Webster, An American Dictionary of the English Language (1828)). "'Testimony,'" in turn, is "'[a] solemn declaration or affirmation made for the purpose of establishing or proving some fact.' 541 U.S., at 51. In light of its text, I continue to think that the Confrontation Clause regulates only the use of statements bearing "indicia of solemnity." *Davis v. Washington*, 547 U.S. 813, 836–837 (2006) (Thomas, J., concurring in judgment in part and dissenting in part). This test comports with history because solemnity marked the practices that the Confrontation Clause was designed to eliminate, namely, the ex parte examination of witnesses under the English bail and committal statutes passed during the reign of Queen Mary. *See id.*, at 835; *Bryant*, 562 U.S., at____, 131 S. Ct. 1143 (Thomas, J., concurring in judgment); *Crawford, supra*, at 43–45. Accordingly, I have concluded that the Confrontation Clause reaches "'formalized testimonial materials,'" such as depositions, affidavits, and prior testimony, or statements resulting from "'formalized dialogue,'" such as custodial interrogation. *Bryant, supra*, at____, 131 S. Ct. 1143; *see also Davis, supra*, at 836–837.[5]

Applying these principles, I conclude that Cellmark's report is not a statement by a "witnes[s]" within the meaning of the Confrontation Clause. The Cellmark report lacks the solemnity of an affidavit or deposition, for it is neither a sworn nor a certified declaration of fact. Nowhere does the report attest that its statements accurately reflect the DNA testing processes used or the results obtained. *See* Report of Laboratory Examination, Lodging of Petitioner. The report is signed by two "reviewers," but they neither purport to have performed the DNA testing nor certify the accuracy of those who did. *See ibid.* And, although the report was produced at the request of law enforcement, it was not the product of any sort of formalized dialogue resembling custodial interrogation.

The Cellmark report is distinguishable from the laboratory reports that we determined were testimonial in *Melendez-Diaz*, 557 U.S. 305, and in *Bullcoming v. New Mexico*, 564 U.S.____, 131 S. Ct. 2705 (2011). In *Melendez-Diaz*, the reports in question were "sworn to before a notary public by [the] analysts" who

---

5. In addition, I have stated that, because the Confrontation Clause "sought to regulate prosecutorial abuse occurring through use of ex parte statements," it "also reaches the use of technically informal statements when used to evade the formalized process." *Davis*, 547 U.S., at 838 (opinion concurring in judgment in part and dissenting in part). But, in this case, there is no indication that Cellmark's statements were offered "in order to evade confrontation." *Id.*, at 840.

tested a substance for cocaine. 557 U.S., at 308. In *Bullcoming*, the report, though unsworn, included a "Certificate of Analyst" signed by the forensic analyst who tested the defendant's blood sample. 564 U.S., at_____, 131 S. Ct. 2705. The analyst "affirmed that '[t]he seal of th[e] sample was received intact and broken in the laboratory,' that 'the statements in [the analyst's block of the report] are correct,' and that he had 'followed the procedures set out on the reverse of th[e] report.'" *Ibid.*

The dissent insists that the *Bullcoming* report and Cellmark's report are equally formal, separated only by such "minutia" as the fact that Cellmark's report "is not labeled a 'certificate.'" To the contrary, what distinguishes the two is that Cellmark's report, in substance, certifies nothing. That distinction is constitutionally significant because the scope of the confrontation right is properly limited to extrajudicial statements similar in solemnity to the *Marian* examination practices that the Confrontation Clause was designed to prevent. *See Davis, supra*, at 835–836 (opinion of Thomas, J.). By certifying the truth of the analyst's representations, the unsworn *Bullcoming* report bore "a 'striking resemblance,'" 547 U.S., at 837 (*quoting Crawford*, 541 U.S., at 52), to the *Marian* practice in which magistrates examined witnesses, typically on oath, and "certif[ied] the results to the court." *Id.*, at 44. And, in *Melendez-Diaz*, we observed that "'certificates' are functionally identical to live, in-court testimony, doing precisely what a witness does on direct examination." 557 U.S., at 310–311. Cellmark's report is marked by no such indicia of solemnity.

Contrary to the dissent's suggestion, acknowledging that the Confrontation Clause is implicated only by formalized statements that are characterized by solemnity will not result in a prosecutorial conspiracy to elude confrontation by using only informal extrajudicial statements against an accused. As I have previously noted, the Confrontation Clause reaches bad-faith attempts to evade the formalized process. Moreover, the prosecution's use of informal statements comes at a price. As the dissent recognizes, such statements are "less reliable" than formalized statements and therefore less persuasive to the factfinder. *Cf. post* (arguing that prosecutors are unlikely to "forgo DNA evidence in favor of less reliable eyewitness testimony" simply because the defendant is entitled to confront the DNA analyst). But, even assuming that the dissent accurately predicts an upswing in the use of "less reliable" informal statements, that result does not "turn the Confrontation Clause upside down." The Confrontation Clause does not require that evidence be reliable, *Crawford, supra*, at 61, but that the reliability of a specific "class of testimonial statements"—formalized statements bearing indicia of solemnity—be assessed through cross-examination. *See Melendez-Diaz*, 557 U.S., at 309–310.

B

Rather than apply the foregoing principles, the plurality invokes its "primary purpose" test. The original formulation of that test asked whether the primary purpose of an extrajudicial statement was "to establish or prove past events potentially relevant to later criminal prosecution." *Davis, supra*, at 822. I agree that, for a statement to be testimonial within the meaning of the Confrontation Clause, the declarant must primarily intend to establish some fact with the understanding that his statement may be used in a criminal prosecution. *See Bryant*, 562 U.S., at_____, 131 S. Ct. 1143 (Scalia, J., dissenting). But this necessary criterion is not sufficient, for it sweeps into the ambit of the Confrontation Clause statements that lack formality and solemnity and is thus "disconnected from history." *Davis, supra*, at 838–842 (opinion concurring in judgment in part and dissenting in part); *Bryant, supra*, at_____, 131 S. Ct. 1143 (opinion concurring in judgment). In addition, a primary purpose inquiry divorced from solemnity is unworkable in practice. *Davis, supra*, at 839; *Bryant, supra*, at_____, 131 S. Ct. 1143. Statements to police are often made both to resolve an ongoing emergency and to establish facts about a crime for potential prosecution. The primary purpose test gives courts no principled way to assign primacy to one of those purposes. *Davis, supra*, at 839. The solemnity requirement is not only true to the text and history of the Confrontation Clause, but goes a long way toward resolving that practical difficulty. If a statement bears the formality and solemnity necessary to come within the scope of the Clause, it is highly unlikely that the statement was primarily made to end an ongoing emergency.

The shortcomings of the original primary purpose test pale in comparison, however, to those plaguing the reformulated version that the plurality suggests today. The new primary purpose test asks whether an out-of-court statement has "the primary purpose of accusing a targeted individual of engaging in criminal conduct." That test lacks any grounding in constitutional text, in history, or in logic.

The new test first requires that an out-of-court statement be made "for the purpose of proving the guilt of a particular criminal defendant." Under this formulation, statements made "before any suspect was identified" are beyond the scope of the Confrontation Clause. There is no textual justification, however, for limiting the confrontation right to statements made after the accused's identity became known. To be sure, the Sixth Amendment right to confrontation attaches "[i]n . . . criminal prosecutions," at which time the accused has been identified and apprehended. But the text of the Confrontation Clause does not constrain the time at which one becomes a "witnes[s]." Indeed, we have previously held that a declarant may become a "witnes[s]" before the accused's prosecution. *See Crawford*, 541 U.S., at 50–51 (rejecting the view that the Confrontation Clause applies only to in-court testimony).

Historical practice confirms that a declarant could become a "witnes[s]" before the accused's identity was known. As previously noted, the confrontation right was a response to ex parte examinations of witnesses in 16th-century England. Such examinations often occurred after an accused was arrested or bound over for trial, but some examinations occurred while the accused remained "unknown or fugitive." J. Langbein, Prosecuting Crime in the Renaissance 90 (1974) (describing examples, including the deposition of a victim who was swindled out of 20 shillings by a "'cunning man'"); *see also* 1 J. Stephen, A History of the Criminal Law of England 217–218 (1883) (describing the sworn examinations of witnesses by coroners, who were charged with investigating suspicious deaths by asking local citizens if they knew "who [was] culpable either of the act or of the force" (internal quotation marks omitted)).

There is also little logical justification for the plurality's rule. The plurality characterizes Cellmark's report as a statement elicited by police and made by Cellmark not "to accuse petitioner or to create evidence for use at trial," but rather to resolve the ongoing emergency posed by "a dangerous rapist who was still at large." But, as I have explained, that distinction is unworkable in light of the mixed purposes that often underlie statements to the police. The difficulty is only compounded by the plurality's attempt to merge the purposes of both the police and the declarant. *See Bryant, supra,* at_____-_____, 131 S. Ct. 1143 (majority opinion).

But if one purpose must prevail, here it should surely be the evidentiary one, whether viewed from the perspective of the police, Cellmark, or both. The police confirmed the presence of semen on L. J.'s vaginal swabs on February 15, 2000, placed the swabs in a freezer, and waited until November 28, 2000, to ship them to Cellmark. App. 30–34, 51–52. Cellmark, in turn, did not send its report to the police until April 3, 2001, *id.*, at 54, over a year after L. J.'s rape. Given this timeline, it strains credulity to assert that the police and Cellmark were primarily concerned with the exigencies of an ongoing emergency, rather than with producing evidence in the ordinary course.

In addition to requiring that an out-of-court statement "targe[t]" a particular accused, the plurality's new primary purpose test also considers whether the statement is so "inherently inculpatory" that the declarant should have known that his statement would incriminate the accused. In this case, the plurality asserts that "[t]he technicians who prepare a DNA profile generally have no way of knowing whether it will turn out to be incriminating or exonerating—or both," and thus "no one at Cellmark could have possibly known that the profile that it produced would turn out to inculpate petitioner."

Again, there is no textual justification for this limitation on the scope of the Confrontation Clause. In *Melendez-Diaz*, we held that "[t]he text of the [Sixth] Amendment contemplates two classes of witnesses—those against the defendant and those in his favor." 557 U.S., at 313–314. We emphasized that "there is not a third category of witnesses, helpful to the prosecution, but somehow immune from confrontation." *Id.*, at 314. Thus, the distinction between those who make "inherently inculpatory" statements and those who make other statements that are merely "helpful to the prosecution" has no foundation in the text of the Amendment.

It is also contrary to history. The 16th-century *Marian* statutes instructed magistrates to transcribe any information by witnesses that "'shall be material to prove the felony.'" *See, e.g.,* 1 *Stephen, supra,* at 219 (quoting 1 & 2 Phil. & Mary, ch. 13

(1554)). Magistrates in the 17th and 18th centuries were also advised by practice manuals to take the ex parte examination of a witness even if his evidence was "weak" or the witness was "unable to inform any material thing against" an accused. J. Beattie, Crime and the Courts in England: 1660–1800, p. 272 (1986) (internal quotation marks omitted). Thus, neither law nor practice limited ex parte examinations to those witnesses who made "inherently inculpatory" statements.

This requirement also makes little sense. A statement that is not facially inculpatory may turn out to be highly probative of a defendant's guilt when considered with other evidence. Recognizing this point, we previously rejected the view that a witness is not subject to confrontation if his testimony is "inculpatory only when taken together with other evidence." *Melendez-Diaz, supra*, at 313. I see no justification for reviving that discredited approach, and the plurality offers none.[6]

* * *

Respondent and its amici have emphasized the economic and logistical burdens that would be visited upon States should every analyst who reports DNA results be required to testify at trial. These burdens are largely the product of a primary purpose test that reaches out-of-court statements well beyond the historical scope of the Confrontation Clause and thus sweeps in a broad range of sources on which modern experts regularly rely. The proper solution to this problem is not to carve out a Confrontation Clause exception for expert testimony that is rooted only in legal fiction. Nor is it to create a new primary purpose test that ensures that DNA evidence is treated differently. *See ibid.* Rather, the solution is to adopt a reading of the Confrontation Clause that respects its historically limited application to a narrow class of statements bearing indicia of solemnity. In forgoing that approach, today's decision diminishes the Confrontation Clause's protection in cases where experts convey the contents of solemn, formalized statements to explain the bases for their opinions. These are the very cases in which the accused should "enjoy the right . . . to be confronted with the witnesses against him."

DISSENT BY: KAGAN

DISSENT

JUSTICE KAGAN, with whom JUSTICE SCALIA, JUSTICE GINSBURG, and JUSTICE SOTOMAYOR join, dissenting.

---

6. The plurality states that its test "will not prejudice any defendant who really wishes to probe the reliability" of out-of-court statements introduced in his case because the person or persons who made the statements "may always be subpoenaed by the defense and questioned at trial." *Melendez–Diaz* rejected this reasoning as well, holding that the defendant's subpoena power "is no substitute for the right of confrontation." 557 U.S., at 324.

National Institute for Trial Advocacy

Some years ago, the State of California prosecuted a man named John Kocak for rape. At a preliminary hearing, the State presented testimony from an analyst at the Cellmark Diagnostics Laboratory—the same facility used to generate DNA evidence in this case. The analyst had extracted DNA from a bloody sweatshirt found at the crime scene and then compared it to two control samples—one from Kocak and one from the victim. The analyst's report identified a single match: As she explained on direct examination, the DNA found on the sweatshirt belonged to Kocak. But after undergoing cross-examination, the analyst realized she had made a mortifying error. She took the stand again, but this time to admit that the report listed the victim's control sample as coming from Kocak, and Kocak's as coming from the victim. So the DNA on the sweatshirt matched not Kocak, but the victim herself. *See* Tr. in No. SCD110465 (Super. Ct. San Diego Cty., Cal., Nov. 17, 1995), pp. 3–4 ("I'm a little hysterical right now, but I think . . . the two names should be switched"), online at http: //www.nlada.org/forensics/for_lib/Documents/1037341561.0/JohnIvanKocak.pdf (as visited June 15, 2012, and available in Clerk of Court's case file). In trying Kocak, the State would have to look elsewhere for its evidence.

Our Constitution contains a mechanism for catching such errors—the Sixth Amendment's Confrontation Clause. That Clause, and the Court's recent cases interpreting it, require that testimony against a criminal defendant be subject to cross-examination. And that command applies with full force to forensic evidence of the kind involved in both the Kocak case and this one. In two decisions issued in the last three years, this Court held that if a prosecutor wants to introduce the results of forensic testing into evidence, he must afford the defendant an opportunity to cross-examine an analyst responsible for the test. Forensic evidence is reliable only when properly produced, and the Confrontation Clause prescribes a particular method for determining whether that has happened. The Kocak incident illustrates how the Clause is designed to work: Once confronted, the analyst discovered and disclosed the error she had made. That error would probably not have come to light if the prosecutor had merely admitted the report into evidence or asked a third party to present its findings. Hence the genius of an 18th-century device as applied to 21st-century evidence: Cross-examination of the analyst is especially likely to reveal whether vials have been switched, samples contaminated, tests incompetently run, or results inaccurately recorded.

Under our Confrontation Clause precedents, this is an open-and-shut case. The State of Illinois prosecuted Sandy Williams for rape based in part on a DNA profile created in Cellmark's laboratory. Yet the State did not give Williams a chance to question the analyst who produced that evidence. Instead, the prosecution introduced the results of Cellmark's testing through an expert witness who had no idea how they were generated. That approach—no less (perhaps more) than the confrontation-free methods of presenting forensic evidence we have formerly banned—deprived Williams of his Sixth Amendment right to "confron[t] . . . the witnesses against him."

The Court today disagrees, though it cannot settle on a reason why. Justice Alito, joined by three other Justices, advances two theories—that the expert's summary of the Cellmark report was not offered for its truth, and that the report is not the kind of statement triggering the Confrontation Clause's protection. In the pages that follow, I call Justice Alito's opinion "the plurality," because that is the conventional term for it. But in all except its disposition, his opinion is a dissent: Five Justices specifically reject every aspect of its reasoning and every paragraph of its explication. Justice Thomas, for his part, contends that the Cellmark report is nontestimonial on a different rationale. But no other Justice joins his opinion or subscribes to the test he offers.

That creates five votes to approve the admission of the Cellmark report, but not a single good explanation. The plurality's first rationale endorses a prosecutorial dodge; its second relies on distinguishing indistinguishable forensic reports. Justice Thomas's concurrence, though positing an altogether different approach, suffers in the end from similar flaws. I would choose another path—to adhere to the simple rule established in our decisions, for the good reasons we have previously given. Because defendants like Williams have a constitutional right to confront the witnesses against them, I respectfully dissent from the Court's fractured decision.

I

Our modern Confrontation Clause doctrine began with *Crawford v. Washington*, 541 U.S. 36 (2004). About a quarter century earlier, we had interpreted the Clause to allow the admission of any out-of-court statement falling within a "firmly rooted hearsay exception" or carrying "particularized guarantees of trustworthiness." *Ohio v. Roberts*, 448 U.S. 56, 66 (1980). But in *Crawford*, we concluded that our old approach was misguided. Drawing on historical research about the Clause's purposes, we held that the prosecution may not admit "testimonial statements of a witness who [does] not appear at trial unless he [is] unavailable to testify, and the defendant . . . had a prior opportunity for cross-examination." 541 U.S., at 53–54. That holding has two aspects. First, the Confrontation Clause applies only to out-of-court statements that are "testimonial." Second, where the Clause applies, it guarantees to a defendant just what its name suggests—the opportunity to cross-examine the person who made the statement. *See id.*, at 59.

A few years later, we made clear that *Crawford*'s rule reaches forensic reports. In *Melendez-Diaz v. Massachusetts*, 557 U.S. 305 (2009), the Commonwealth introduced a laboratory's "'certificates of analysis'" stating that a substance seized from the defendant was cocaine. *Id.*, at 308. We held that the certificates fell within the Clause's "'core class of testimonial statements'" because they had a clear "evidentiary purpose": They were "'made under circumstances which would lead an objective witness reasonably to believe that [they] would be available for use at a later trial.'" *Id.*, at 310–311, (quoting *Crawford*, 541 U.S., at 51–52). Accordingly, we ruled, the defendant had a right to cross-examine the analysts who had authored them. In reaching that conclusion, we rejected the Commonwealth's argument that the Confrontation Clause should not apply because the statements resulted from "'neutral scientific testing,'" and so were presumptively reliable. 557 U.S., at 318. The Clause, we noted, commands that "'reliability be assessed in a particular manner'"—through "'testing in the crucible of cross-examination.'" *Id.*, at 317 (*quoting Crawford*, 541 U.S., at 61). Further, we doubted that the testing summarized in the certificates was "as neutral or as reliable" as the Commonwealth suggested. Citing chapter and verse from various studies, we concluded that "[f]orensic evidence is not uniquely immune from the risk of manipulation" and mistake. 557 U.S., at 318; *see id.*, at 319.

And just two years later (and just one year ago), we reiterated *Melendez-Diaz's* analysis when faced with a State's attempt to evade it. In *Bullcoming v. New Mexico,* 564 U.S._____, 131 S. Ct. 2705 (2011), a forensic report showed the defendant's blood-alcohol concentration to exceed the legal limit for drivers. The State tried to introduce that finding through the testimony of a person who worked at the laboratory but had not performed or observed the blood test or certified its results. We held that *Melendez-Diaz* foreclosed that tactic. The report, we stated, resembled the certificates in *Melendez-Diaz* in "all material respects," 564 U.S., at_____, 131 S. Ct. 2705: Both were signed documents providing the results of forensic testing designed to "'prov[e] some fact' in a criminal proceeding," *id.*, at_____, 131 S. Ct. 2705 (quoting *Melendez-Diaz*, 557 U.S., at 310). And the State's resort to a "surrogate" witness, in place of the analyst who produced the report, did not satisfy the Confrontation Clause. *Bullcoming*, 564 U.S., at_____, 131 S. Ct. 2705. Only the presence of "that particular scientist," we reasoned, would enable *Bullcoming's* counsel to ask "questions designed to reveal whether incompetence . . . or dishonesty" had tainted the results. *Id.*, at_____,_____, 131 S. Ct. 2705. Repeating the refrain of *Melendez-Diaz*, we held that "[t]he accused's right is to be confronted with" the actual analyst, unless he is unavailable and the accused "had an opportunity, pretrial, to cross-examine" him. *Bullcoming*, 564 U.S., at_____, 131 S. Ct. 2705.

This case is of a piece. The report at issue here shows a DNA profile produced by an analyst at Cellmark's laboratory, allegedly from a vaginal swab taken from a young woman, L. J., after she was raped. That report is identical to the one in *Bullcoming* (and *Melendez-Diaz*) in "all material respects." 564 U.S., at_____, 131 S. Ct. 2705. Once again, the report was made to establish "'some fact' in a criminal proceeding"—here, the identity of L. J.'s attacker. *Id.*, at_____, 131 S. Ct. 2705 (quoting *Melendez-Diaz*, 557 U.S., at 310). And once again, it details the results of forensic testing on evidence gathered by the police. Viewed side-by-side with the *Bullcoming* report, the Cellmark analysis has a comparable title; similarly describes the relevant samples, test methodology, and results; and likewise includes the signatures of laboratory officials. *Compare* Cellmark Diagnostics Report of Laboratory Examination (Feb. 15, 2001), Lodging of Petitioner with App. in *Bullcoming v.*

New Mexico, O. T. 2010, No. 09-10876, pp. 62–65. So under this Court's prior analysis, the substance of the report could come into evidence only if Williams had a chance to cross-examine the responsible analyst.

But that is not what happened. Instead, the prosecutor used Sandra Lambatos—a state-employed scientist who had not participated in the testing—as the conduit for this piece of evidence. Lambatos came to the stand after two other state analysts testified about forensic tests they had performed. One recounted how she had developed a DNA profile of Sandy Williams from a blood sample drawn after his arrest. And another told how he had confirmed the presence of (unidentified) semen on the vaginal swabs taken from L. J. All this was by the book: Williams had an opportunity to cross-examine both witnesses about the tests they had run. But of course, the State still needed to supply the missing link—it had to show that DNA found in the semen on L. J.'s vaginal swabs matched Williams's DNA. To fill that gap, the prosecutor could have called the analyst from Cellmark to testify about the DNA profile she had produced from the swabs. But instead, the State called Lambatos as an expert witness and had her testify that the semen on those swabs contained Sandy Williams's DNA:

> "Q Was there a computer match generated of the male DNA profile found in semen from the vaginal swabs of [L. J.] to a male DNA profile that had been identified as having originated from Sandy Williams?
>
> "A Yes, there was.
>
> "Q Did you compare the semen . . . from the vaginal swabs of [L. J.] to the male DNA profile . . . from the blood of Sandy Williams?
>
> "A Yes, I did.
>
> . . . . .
>
> "Q [I]s the semen identified in the vaginal swabs of [L. J.] consistent with having originated from Sandy Williams?
>
> "A Yes." App. 56–57.

And so it was Lambatos, rather than any Cellmark employee, who informed the trier of fact that the testing of L. J.'s vaginal swabs had produced a male DNA profile implicating Williams.

Have we not already decided this case? Lambatos's testimony is functionally identical to the "surrogate testimony" that New Mexico proffered in *Bullcoming*, which did nothing to cure the problem identified in *Melendez-Diaz* (which, for its part, straightforwardly applied our decision in *Crawford*). Like the surrogate witness in *Bullcoming*, Lambatos "could not convey what [the actual analyst] knew or observed about the events . . ., i.e., the particular test and testing process he employed." *Bullcoming*, 564 U.S., at_____, 131 S. Ct. 2705. "Nor could such surrogate testimony expose any lapses or lies" on the testing analyst's part. *Ibid.* Like the lawyers in *Melendez-Diaz* and *Bullcoming*, Williams's attorney could not ask questions about that analyst's "proficiency, the care he took in performing his work, and his veracity." 564 U.S., at_____, n. 7, 131 S. Ct. 2705. He could not probe whether the analyst had tested the wrong vial, inverted the labels on the samples, committed some more technical error, or simply made up the results. *See* App. to Brief for Public Defender Service for the District of Columbia et al. as *Amici Curiae* 5a, 11a (describing mistakes and fraud at Cellmark's laboratory). Indeed, Williams's lawyer was even more hamstrung than *Bullcoming*'s. At least the surrogate witness in *Bullcoming* worked at the relevant laboratory and was familiar with its procedures. That is not true of Lambatos: She had no knowledge at all of Cellmark's operations. Indeed, for all the record discloses, she may never have set foot in Cellmark's laboratory.

Under our case law, that is sufficient to resolve this case. "[W]hen the State elected to introduce" the substance of Cellmark's report into evidence, the analyst who generated that report "became a witness" whom Williams "had the right to confront." *Bullcoming*, 564 U.S., at_____, 131 S. Ct. 2705. As we stated just last year, "Our precedent[s] cannot sensibly be read any other way." *Ibid.*

II

The plurality's primary argument to the contrary tries to exploit a limit to the Confrontation Clause recognized in *Crawford*. "The Clause," we cautioned there, "does not bar the use of testimonial statements for purposes other than establishing the truth of the matter asserted." 541 U.S., at 59–60, n. 9 (*citing Tennessee v. Street*, 471 U.S. 409, 414 (1985)). The Illinois Supreme Court relied on that statement in concluding that Lambatos's testimony was permissible. On that court's view, "Lambatos disclosed the underlying facts from Cellmark's report" not for their truth, but "for the limited purpose of explaining the basis for her [expert] opinion," so that the factfinder could assess that opinion's value. 939 N.E.2d 268, 282. The plurality wraps itself in that holding, similarly asserting that Lambatos's recitation of Cellmark's findings, when viewed through the prism of state evidence law, was not introduced to establish "the truth of any . . . matter concerning [the] Cellmark" report. But five Justices agree, in two opinions reciting the same reasons, that this argument has no merit: Lambatos's statements about Cellmark's report went to its truth, and the State could not rely on her status as an expert to circumvent the Confrontation Clause's requirements.

To see why, start with the kind of case *Crawford* had in mind. In acknowledging the not-for-the-truth carveout from the Clause, the Court cited *Tennessee v. Street* as exemplary. *See Crawford*, 541 U.S., at 59–60, n. 9. There, Street claimed that his stationhouse confession of murder was a sham: A police officer, he charged, had read aloud his alleged accomplice's confession and forced him to repeat it. To help rebut that defense, the State introduced the other confession into the record, so the

jury could see how it differed from Street's. This Court rejected Street's Confrontation Clause claim because the State had offered the out-of-court statement not to
prove "the truth of [the accomplice's] assertions" about the murder, but only to
disprove Street's claim of how the police elicited his confession. *Street*, 471 U.S.,
at 413. Otherwise said, the truth of the admitted statement was utterly immaterial;
the only thing that mattered was that the statement (whether true or false) varied
from Street's.

The situation could not be more different when a witness, expert or otherwise,
repeats an out-of-court statement as the basis for a conclusion, because the statement's utility is then dependent on its truth. If the statement is true, then the conclusion based on it is probably true; if not, not. So to determine the validity of
the witness's conclusion, the factfinder must assess the truth of the out-of-court
statement on which it relies. That is why the principal modern treatise on evidence
variously calls the idea that such "basis evidence" comes in not for its truth, but only
to help the factfinder evaluate an expert's opinion "very weak," "factually implausible," "nonsense," and "sheer fiction." D. Kaye, D. Bernstein, & J. Mnookin, The
New Wigmore: Expert Evidence §4.10.1, pp. 196–197 (2d ed. 2011); *id.*, §4.11.6,
at 24 (Supp. 2012). "One can sympathize," notes that treatise, "with a court's desire
to permit the disclosure of basis evidence that is quite probably reliable, such as a
routine analysis of a drug, but to pretend that it is not being introduced for the
truth of its contents strains credibility." *Id.*, §4.10.1, at 198 (2d ed. 2011); *see also,
e.g., People v. Goldstein*, 843 N.E.2d 727, 732–733 (N.Y. 2005) ("The distinction
between a statement offered for its truth and a statement offered to shed light on an
expert's opinion is not meaningful"). Unlike in *Street*, admission of the out-of-court
statement in this context has no purpose separate from its truth; the factfinder can
do nothing with it except assess its truth and so the credibility of the conclusion it
serves to buttress.[1]

Consider a prosaic example not involving scientific experts. An eyewitness tells
a police officer investigating an assault that the perpetrator had an unusual, star-
shaped birthmark over his left eye. The officer arrests a person bearing that birthmark (let's call him Starr) for committing the offense. And at trial, the officer takes
the stand and recounts just what the eyewitness told him. Presumably the plurality
would agree that such testimony violates the Confrontation Clause unless the eyewitness is unavailable and the defendant had a prior opportunity to cross-examine
him. Now ask whether anything changes if the officer couches his testimony in the
following way: "I concluded that Starr was the assailant because a reliable eyewit-

---

1. In responding to this reasoning, the plurality confirms it. According to the plurality, basis evidence
supports the "credibility of the expert's opinion" by showing that he has relied on, and drawn logical inferences from, sound "factual premises." Quite right. And that process involves assessing such
premises' truth: If they are, as the majority puts it, "unsupported by other evidence in the record" or
otherwise baseless, they will not "allay [a factfinder's] fears" about an "expert's reasoning." I could not
have said it any better.

ness told me that the assailant had a star-shaped birthmark and, look, Starr has one just like that." Surely that framing would make no constitutional difference, even though the eyewitness's statement now explains the basis for the officer's conclusion. It remains the case that the prosecution is attempting to introduce a testimonial statement that has no relevance to the proceedings apart from its truth—and that the defendant cannot cross-examine the person who made it. Allowing the admission of this evidence would end-run the Confrontation Clause, and make a parody of its strictures.

And that example, when dressed in scientific clothing, is no different from this case. The Cellmark report identified the rapist as having a particular DNA profile (think of it as the quintessential birthmark). The Confrontation Clause prevented the State from introducing that report into evidence except by calling to the stand the person who prepared it. *See Melendez-Diaz*, 557 U.S., at 310–311; *Bullcoming*, 564 U.S., at_____, 131 S. Ct. 2705. So the State tried another route—introducing the substance of the report as part and parcel of an expert witness's conclusion. In effect, Lambatos testified (like the police officer above): "I concluded that Williams was the rapist because Cellmark, an accredited and trustworthy laboratory, says that the rapist has a particular DNA profile and, look, Williams has an identical one." And here too, that form of testimony should change nothing. The use of the Cellmark statement remained bound up with its truth, and the statement came into evidence without any opportunity for Williams to cross-examine the person who made it. So if the plurality were right, the State would have a ready method to bypass the Constitution (as much as in my hypothetical case); a wink and a nod, and the Confrontation Clause would not pose a bar to forensic evidence.

The plurality tries to make plausible its not-for-the-truth rationale by rewriting Lambatos's testimony about the Cellmark report. According to the plurality, Lambatos merely "assumed" that Cellmark's DNA profile came from L. J.'s vaginal swabs, accepting for the sake of argument the prosecutor's premise. But that is incorrect. Nothing in Lambatos's testimony indicates that she was making an assumption or considering a hypothesis. To the contrary, Lambatos affirmed, without qualification, that the Cellmark report showed a "male DNA profile found in semen from the vaginal swabs of [L. J.]." App. 56. Had she done otherwise, this case would be different. There was nothing wrong with Lambatos's testifying that two DNA profiles—the one shown in the Cellmark report and the one derived from Williams's blood—matched each other; that was a straightforward application of Lambatos's expertise. Similarly, Lambatos could have added that if the Cellmark report resulted from scientifically sound testing of L. J.'s vaginal swab, then it would link Williams to the assault. What Lambatos could not do was what she did: indicate that the Cellmark report was produced in this way by saying that L. J.'s vaginal swab contained DNA matching Williams's.[2] By testifying in that manner, Lambatos became

---

2. The plurality suggests that Lambatos's testimony is merely a modern, streamlined way of answering hypothetical questions and therefore raises no constitutional issue; similarly, the plurality contends that

just like the surrogate witness in *Bullcoming*—a person knowing nothing about "the particular test and testing process," but vouching for them regardless. 564 U.S., at_____, 131 S. Ct. 2705. We have held that the Confrontation Clause requires something more.

The plurality also argues that Lambatos's characterization of the Cellmark report did not violate the Confrontation Clause because the case "involve[d] a bench trial." I welcome the plurality's concession that the Clause might forbid presenting Lambatos's statement to a jury; it indicates that the plurality realizes that her testimony went beyond an "assumption." But the presence of a judge does not transform the constitutional question. In applying the Confrontation Clause, we have never before considered relevant the decisionmaker's identity. *See, e.g., Davis v. Washington*, 547 U.S. 813 (2006). And this case would be a poor place to begin. Lambatos's description of the Cellmark report was offered for its truth because that is all such "basis evidence" can be offered for; as described earlier, the only way the factfinder could consider whether that statement supported her opinion (that the DNA on L. J.'s swabs came from Williams) was by assessing the statement's truth. That is so, as a simple matter of logic, whether the factfinder is a judge or a jury. And thus, in either case, admission of the statement, without the opportunity to cross-examine, violates the Confrontation Clause. *See ante*, (opinion of Thomas, J.).

In saying that much, I do *not* doubt that a judge typically will do better than a jury in excluding such inadmissible evidence from his decisionmaking process. Perhaps the judge did so here; perhaps, as the plurality thinks, he understood that he could not consider Lambatos's representation about the Cellmark report, and found that other, "circumstantial evidence" established "the source of the sample that Cellmark tested" and "the reliability of the Cellmark profile." Some indications are to the contrary: In delivering his verdict, the judge never referred to the circumstantial evidence the plurality marshals, but instead focused only on Lambatos's testimony. *See* 4 Record JJJ151 (calling Lambatos "the best DNA witness I have ever heard" and referring to Williams as "the guy whose DNA, according to the evidence from the experts, is in the semen recovered from the victim's vagina"). But I take the plurality's point that when read "[i]n context" the judge's statements might be "best

---

the difference between what Lambatos said and what I would allow involves only "slightly revis[ing]" her testimony and so can be of no consequence. But the statement "if X is true, then Y follows" differs materially—and constitutionally—from the statement "Y is true because X is true (according to Z)." The former statement is merely a logical proposition, whose validity the defendant can contest by questioning the speaker. And then, assuming the prosecutor tries to prove the statement's premise through some other witness, the defendant can rebut that effort through cross-examination. By contrast, the latter statement as well contains a factual allegation (that X is true), which the defendant can only effectively challenge by confronting the person who made it (Z). That is why recognizing the difference between these two forms of testimony is not to insist on an archaism or a formality, but to ensure, in line with the Constitution, that defendants have the ability to confront their accusers. And if prosecutors can easily conform their conduct to that constitutional directive, as the plurality suggests, so much the better: I would not have thought it a ground of complaint that the Confrontation Clause, properly understood, manages to protect defendants without overly burdening the State.

understood" as meaning something other than what they appear to say. Still, that point suggests only that the admission of Lambatos's statement was harmless—that the judge managed to put it out of mind. After all, whether a factfinder is confused by an error is a separate question from whether an error has occurred. So the plurality's argument does not answer the only question this case presents: whether a constitutional violation happened when Lambatos recited the Cellmark report's findings.[3]

At bottom, the plurality's not-for-the-truth rationale is a simple abdication to state-law labels. Although the utility of the Cellmark statement that Lambatos repeated logically depended on its truth, the plurality thinks this case decided by an Illinois rule holding that the facts underlying an expert's opinion are not admitted for that purpose. See *People v. Pasch*, 604 N.E.2d 294, 311 (Ill. 1992). But we do not typically allow state law to define federal constitutional requirements. And needless to say (or perhaps not), the Confrontation Clause is a constitutional rule like any other. As Justice Thomas observes, even before *Crawford*, we did not allow the Clause's scope to be "dictated by state or federal evidentiary rules." Indeed, in *Street*, we independently reviewed whether an out-of-court statement was introduced for its truth—the very question at issue in this case. See 471 U.S., at 413–416. And in *Crawford*, we still more firmly disconnected the Confrontation Clause inquiry from state evidence law, by overruling an approach that looked in part to whether an out-of-court statement fell within a "'firmly rooted hearsay exception.'" 541 U.S., at 60 (quoting *Roberts*, 448 U.S., at 66). That decision made clear that the Confrontation Clause's protections are not coterminous with rules of evidence. So the plurality's state-law-first approach would be an about-face.

Still worse, that approach would allow prosecutors to do through subterfuge and indirection what we previously have held the Confrontation Clause prohibits. Imagine for a moment a poorly trained, incompetent, or dishonest laboratory analyst. (The analyst in *Bullcoming*, placed on unpaid leave for unknown reasons, might qualify.) Under our precedents, the prosecutor cannot avoid exposing that analyst to

---

3. The plurality asserts (without citation) that I am "reach[ing] the truly remarkable conclusion that the wording of Lambatos' testimony confused the trial judge," and then spends three pages explaining why that conclusion is wrong. But the plurality is responding to an argument of its own imagining, because I reach no such conclusion. As I just stated, the trial judge might well have ignored Lambatos's statement about the Cellmark report and relied on other evidence to conclude that "the Cellmark profile was derived from the sample taken from the victim." All I am saying is that the admission of that statement violated the Confrontation Clause even if the judge ultimately put it aside, because it came into evidence for nothing other than its truth. Similarly, the plurality claims (still without citation) that I think the other evidence about the Cellmark report insufficient. But once again, the plurality must be reading someone else's opinion. I express no view on sufficiency of the evidence because it is irrelevant to the Confrontation Clause issue we took this case to decide. It is the plurality that wrongly links the two, spending another five pages trumpeting the strength of the Cellmark report. But the plurality cannot properly decide whether a Confrontation Clause violation occurred at Williams's trial by determining that Williams was guilty. The American criminal justice system works the opposite way: determining guilt by holding trials in accord with constitutional requirements.

cross-examination simply by introducing his report. *See Melendez-Diaz*, 557 U.S., at 311. Nor can the prosecutor escape that fate by offering the results through the testimony of another analyst from the laboratory. *See Bullcoming*, 564 U.S., at_____, 131 S. Ct. 2705. But under the plurality's approach, the prosecutor could choose the analyst-witness of his dreams (as the judge here said, "the best DNA witness I have ever heard"), offer her as an expert (she knows nothing about the test, but boasts impressive degrees), and have her provide testimony identical to the best the actual tester might have given ("the DNA extracted from the vaginal swabs matched Sandy Williams's")—all so long as a state evidence rule says that the purpose of the testimony is to enable the factfinder to assess the expert opinion's basis. (And this tactic would not be confined to cases involving scientific evidence. As Justice Thomas points out, the prosecutor could similarly substitute experts for all kinds of people making out-of-court statements.) The plurality thus would countenance the Constitution's circumvention. If the Confrontation Clause prevents the State from getting its evidence in through the front door, then the State could sneak it in through the back. What a neat trick—but really, what a way to run a criminal justice system. No wonder five Justices reject it.

III

The plurality also argues, as a "second, independent basis" for its decision, that the Cellmark report falls outside the Confrontation Clause's ambit because it is nontestimonial. The plurality tries out a number of supporting theories, but all in vain: Each one either conflicts with this Court's precedents or misconstrues this case's facts. Justice Thomas rejects the plurality's views for similar reasons as I do, thus bringing to five the number of Justices who repudiate the plurality's understanding of what statements count as testimonial. Justice Thomas, however, offers a rationale of his own for deciding that the Cellmark report is nontestimonial. I think his essay works no better. When all is said and done, the Cellmark report is a testimonial statement.

A

According to the plurality, we should declare the Cellmark report nontestimonial because "the use at trial of a DNA report prepared by a modern, accredited laboratory 'bears little if any resemblance to the historical practices that the Confrontation Clause aimed to eliminate.'" *Ante*, (quoting *Michigan v. Bryant*, 562 U.S._____,_____, 131 S. Ct. 1143 (2011) (Thomas, J., concurring in judgment)). But we just last year treated as testimonial a forensic report prepared by a "modern, accredited laboratory"; indeed, we declared that the report at issue "fell within the core class of testimonial statements" implicating the Confrontation Clause. *Bullcoming*, 564 U.S., at_____, 131 S. Ct. 2705 (internal quotation marks omitted); *see* Brief for New Mexico Department of Health, Scientific Laboratory

Division as *Amicus Curiae* in *Bullcoming*, O. T. 2010, No. 09-10786, p. 1 (discussing accreditation). And although the plurality is close, it is not quite ready (or able) to dispense with that decision. *See ante*, ("Experience might yet show that the holdings in [*Bullcoming* and other post-*Crawford*] cases should be reconsidered"). So the plurality must explain: What could support a distinction between the laboratory analysis there and the DNA test in this case?[4]

As its first stab, the plurality states that the Cellmark report was "not prepared for the primary purpose of accusing a targeted individual." Where that test comes from is anyone's guess. Justice Thomas rightly shows that it derives neither from the text nor from the history of the Confrontation Clause. And it has no basis in our precedents. We have previously asked whether a statement was made for the primary purpose of establishing "past events potentially relevant to later criminal prosecution"—in other words, for the purpose of providing evidence. *Davis*, 547 U.S., at 822; *see also Bullcoming*, 564 U.S., at_____, 131 S. Ct. 2705; *Bryant*, 562 U.S., at_____,_____, 131 S. Ct. 1143; *Melendez-Diaz*, 557 U.S., at 310–311; *Crawford*, 541 U.S., at 51–52. None of our cases has ever suggested that, in addition, the statement must be meant to accuse a previously identified individual; indeed, in *Melendez-Diaz*, we rejected a related argument that laboratory "analysts are not subject to confrontation because they are not 'accusatory' witnesses." 557 U.S., at 313.

Nor does the plurality give any good reason for adopting an "accusation" test. The plurality apparently agrees with Justice Breyer that prior to a suspect's identification, it will be "unlikely that a particular researcher has a defendant-related motive to behave dishonestly. But surely the typical problem with laboratory analyses—and the typical focus of cross-examination—has to do with careless or incompetent work, rather than with personal vendettas. And as to that predominant concern, it makes not a whit of difference whether, at the time of the laboratory test, the police already have a suspect.[5]

---

4. Justice BREYER does not attempt to distinguish our precedents, opting simply to adhere to "the dissenting view set forth in *Melendez–Diaz* and *Bullcoming*." He principally worries that under those cases, a State will have to call to the witness stand "[s]ix to twelve or more technicians" who have worked on a report. But none of our cases—including this one—has presented the question of how many analysts must testify about a given report. (That may suggest that in most cases a lead analyst is readily identifiable.) The problem in the cases—again, including this one—is that no analyst came forward to testify. In the event that some future case presents the multiple-technician issue, the Court can focus on "the broader 'limits' question" that troubles Justice BREYER. But the mere existence of that question is no reason to wrongly decide the case before us—which, it bears repeating, involved the testimony of not twelve or six or three or one, but zero Cellmark analysts.
5. Neither can the plurality gain any purchase from the idea that a DNA profile is not "inherently inculpatory" because it "tends to exculpate all but one of the more than 7 billion people in the world today." All evidence shares this feature: the more inculpatory it is of a single person, the more exculpatory it is of the rest of the world. The one is but the flipside of the other. But no one has ever before suggested that this logical corollary provides a reason to ignore the Constitution's efforts to ensure the reliability of evidence.

The plurality next attempts to invoke our precedents holding statements nontestimonial when made "to respond to an 'ongoing emergency,'" rather than to create evidence for trial, *Bryant*, 562 U.S., at_____, 131 S. Ct. 1143; here, the plurality insists, the Cellmark report's purpose was "to catch a dangerous rapist who was still at large." But that is to stretch both our "ongoing emergency" test and the facts of this case beyond all recognition. We have previously invoked that test to allow statements by a woman who was being assaulted and a man who had just been shot. In doing so, we stressed the "informal [and] harried" nature of the statements, *Bryant*, 562 U.S., at_____, 131 S. Ct. 1143—that they were made as, or "minutes" after, *id.*, at_____, 131 S. Ct. 1143, the events they described "actually happen[ed]," *Davis*, 547 U.S., at 827 (emphasis deleted), by "frantic" victims of criminal attacks, *ibid.*, to officers trying to figure out "what had . . . occurred" and what threats remained, *Bryant*, 562 U.S., at_____, 131 S. Ct. 1143 (internal quotation marks omitted). On their face, the decisions have nothing to say about laboratory analysts conducting routine tests far away from a crime scene. And this case presents a peculiarly inapt set of facts for extending those precedents. Lambatos testified at trial that "all reports in this case were prepared for this criminal investigation . . . [a]nd for the purpose of the eventual litigation," App. 82—in other words, for the purpose of producing evidence, not enabling emergency responders. And that testimony fits the relevant timeline. The police did not send the swabs to Cellmark until November 2008—nine months after L. J.'s rape—and did not receive the results for another four months. *See id.*, at 30–34, 51–52, 54. That is hardly the typical emergency response.

Finally, the plurality offers a host of reasons for why reports like this one are reliable: "[T]here [i]s no prospect of fabrication"; multiple technicians may "work on each DNA profile"; and "defects in a DNA profile may often be detected from the profile itself." But once again: Been there, done that. In *Melendez-Diaz*, this Court rejected identical arguments, noting extensive documentation of "[s]erious deficiencies . . . in the forensic evidence used in criminal trials." 557 U.S., at 319; *see also Bullcoming*, 564 U.S., at_____, n. 1, 131 S. Ct. 2705 (citing similar errors in laboratory analysis); Brief for Public Defender Service for the District of Columbia et al. as *Amici Curiae* 13 (discussing "[s]ystemic problems," such as sample contamination, sample switching, mislabeling, and fraud, at " 'flagship' DNA labs"). Scientific testing is "technical," to be sure, but it is only as reliable as the people who perform it. That is why a defendant may wish to ask the analyst a variety of questions: How much experience do you have? Have you ever made mistakes in the past? Did you test the right sample? Use the right procedures? Contaminate the sample in any way? Indeed, as scientific evidence plays a larger and larger role in criminal prosecutions, those inquiries will often be the most important in the case.[6]

---

6. Both the plurality and Justice BREYER warn that if we require analysts to testify, we will encourage prosecutors to forgo DNA evidence in favor of less reliable eyewitness testimony and so "increase the risk of convicting the innocent." Neither opinion provides any evidence, even by way of anecdote,

And *Melendez-Diaz* made yet a more fundamental point in response to claims of the uber alles reliability of scientific evidence: It is not up to us to decide, *ex ante*, what evidence is trustworthy and what is not. *See* 557 U.S., at 317–318; *see also Bullcoming*, 564 U.S., at_____, 131 S. Ct. 2705. That is because the Confrontation Clause prescribes its own "procedure for determining the reliability of testimony in criminal trials." *Crawford*, 541 U.S., at 67. That procedure is cross-examination. And "[d]ispensing with [it] because testimony is obviously reliable is akin to dispensing with jury trial because a defendant is obviously guilty." *Id.*, at 62.

So the plurality's second basis for denying Williams's right of confrontation also fails. The plurality can find no reason consistent with our precedents for treating the Cellmark report as nontestimonial. That is because the report is, in every conceivable respect, a statement meant to serve as evidence in a potential criminal trial. And that simple fact should be sufficient to resolve the question.

B

Justice Thomas's unique method of defining testimonial statements fares no better. On his view, the Confrontation Clause "regulates only the use of statements bearing 'indicia of solemnity.'" And Cellmark's report, he concludes, does not qualify because it is "neither a sworn nor a certified declaration of fact." But Justice Thomas's approach grants constitutional significance to minutia, in a way that can only undermine the Confrontation Clause's protections.

To see the point, start with precedent, because the Court rejected this same kind of argument, as applied to this same kind of document, at around this same time just last year. In *Bullcoming*, the State asserted that the forensic report at issue was nontestimonial because—unlike the report in *Melendez-Diaz*—it was not sworn before a notary public. We responded that applying the Confrontation Clause only to a sworn forensic report "would make the right to confrontation easily erasable"— next time, the laboratory could file the selfsame report without the oath. 564 U.S., at_____, 131 S. Ct. 2705. We then held, as noted earlier, that "[i]n all material respects," the forensic report in *Bullcoming* matched the one in *Melendez-Diaz*. 564 U.S., at_____, 131 S. Ct. 2705. First, a law enforcement officer provided evidence to a state laboratory assisting in police investigations. *See* 564 U.S., at_____,

---

for that view, and I doubt any exists. DNA evidence is usually the prosecutor's most powerful weapon, and a prosecutor is unlikely to relinquish it just because he must bring the right analyst to the stand. Consider what Lambatos told the factfinder here: The DNA in L.J.'s vaginal swabs matched Williams's DNA and would match only "1 in 8.7 quadrillion black, 1 in 390 quadrillion white, or 1 in 109 quadrillion Hispanic unrelated individuals." App. 56–57. No eyewitness testimony could replace that evidence. I note as well that the Innocence Network—a group particularly knowledgeable about the kinds of evidence that produce erroneous convictions—disagrees with the plurality's and Justice BREYER's view. It argues here that "[c]onfrontation of the analyst . . . is essential to permit proper adversarial testing" and so to decrease the risk of convicting the innocent. Brief for the Innocence Network as Amicus Curiae 3, 7.

131 S. Ct. 2705. Second, the analyst tested the evidence and "prepared a certificate concerning the result[s]." *Ibid.* Third, the certificate was "formalized in a signed document . . . headed a 'report.'" *Ibid.* (some internal quotation marks omitted). That was enough.

Now compare that checklist of "material" features to the report in this case. The only differences are that Cellmark is a private laboratory under contract with the State (which no one thinks relevant), and that the report is not labeled a "certificate." That amounts to (maybe) a nickel's worth of difference: The similarities in form, function, and purpose dwarf the distinctions. Each report is an official and signed record of laboratory test results, meant to establish a certain set of facts in legal proceedings. Neither looks any more "formal" than the other; neither is any more formal than the other. *See ibid.* The variances are no more (probably less) than would be found if you compared different law schools' transcripts or different companies' cash flow statements or different States' birth certificates. The difference in labeling—a "certificate" in one case, a "report of laboratory examination" in the other—is not of constitutional dimension.

Indeed, Justice Thomas's approach, if accepted, would turn the Confrontation Clause into a constitutional gee-gaw—nice for show, but of little value. The prosecution could avoid its demands by using the right kind of forms with the right kind of language. (It would not take long to devise the magic words and rules—principally, never call anything a "certificate.")[7] And still worse: The new conventions, precisely by making out-of-court statements less "solem[n]," would also make them less reliable—and so turn the Confrontation Clause upside down. *See Crawford*, 541 U.S., at 52–53, n. 3 ("We find it implausible that a provision which concededly condemned trial by sworn ex parte affidavit thought trial by unsworn ex parte affidavit perfectly OK"). It is not surprising that no other Member of the Court has adopted this position. To do so, as Justice Thomas rightly says of the plurality's decision, would be to "diminis[h] the Confrontation Clause's protection" in "the very cases in which the accused should 'enjoy the right . . . to be confronted with the witnesses against him.'"

IV

Before today's decision, a prosecutor wishing to admit the results of forensic testing had to produce the technician responsible for the analysis. That was the result of not one, but two decisions this Court issued in the last three years. But that clear rule is clear no longer. The five Justices who control the outcome of today's case agree on very little. Among them, though, they can boast of two accomplishments. First, they have approved the introduction of testimony at Williams's trial that the

---

7. Justice THOMAS asserts there is no need to worry, because "the Confrontation Clause reaches bad-faith attempts to evade the formalized process." I hope he is right. But Justice THOMAS provides scant guidance on how to conduct this novel inquiry into motive.

Confrontation Clause, rightly understood, clearly prohibits. Second, they have left significant confusion in their wake. What comes out of four Justices' desire to limit *Melendez-Diaz* and *Bullcoming* in whatever way possible, combined with one Justice's one-justice view of those holdings, is—to be frank—who knows what. Those decisions apparently no longer mean all that they say. Yet no one can tell in what way or to what extent they are altered because no proposed limitation commands the support of a majority.

The better course in this case would have been simply to follow *Melendez-Diaz* and *Bullcoming*. Precedent-based decisionmaking provides guidance to lower court judges and predictability to litigating parties. Today's plurality and concurring opinions, and the uncertainty they sow, bring into relief that judicial method's virtues. I would decide this case consistently with, and for the reasons stated by, *Melendez-Diaz* and *Bullcoming*. And until a majority of this Court reverses or confines those decisions, I would understand them as continuing to govern, in every particular, the admission of forensic evidence.

I respectfully dissent.

BELL ATLANTIC CORP. V. TWOMBY
550 U.S. 544 (2007)

The 1984 divestiture of the American Telephone & Telegraph Company's (AT&T) local telephone business left a system of regional service monopolies, sometimes called Incumbent Local Exchange Carriers (ILECs), and a separate long-distance market from which the ILECs were excluded. The Telecommunications Act of 1996 withdrew approval of the ILECs' monopolies, "fundamentally restructur[ing] local telephone markets" and "subject[ing] [ILECs] to a host of duties intended to facilitate market entry." *AT&T Corp. v. Iowa Utilities Bd.*, 525 U.S. 366, 371. It also authorized them to enter the long-distance market. "Central to the [new] scheme [was each ILEC's] obligation . . . to share its network with" competitive local exchange carriers (CLECs). *Verizon Communications Inc. v. Law Offices of Curtis V. Trinko, LLP*, 540 U.S. 398, 402.

Respondents (hereinafter plaintiffs) represent a class of subscribers of local telephone and/or high speed Internet services in this action against petitioner ILECs for claimed violations of § 1 of the Sherman Act, which prohibits "[e]very contract, combination in the form of trust or otherwise, or conspiracy, in restraint of trade or commerce among the several States, or with foreign nations." The complaint alleges that the ILECs conspired to restrain trade (1) by engaging in parallel conduct in their respective service areas to inhibit the growth of upstart CLECs; and (2) by agreeing to refrain from competing against one another, as indicated by their common failure to pursue attractive business opportunities in contiguous markets and by a statement by one ILEC's chief executive officer that competing in another ILEC's territory did not seem right. The District Court dismissed the complaint, concluding that parallel business conduct allegations, taken alone, do not state a claim under § 1; plaintiffs must allege additional facts tending to exclude independent self-interested conduct as an explanation for the parallel actions. Reversing, the Second Circuit held that plaintiffs' parallel conduct allegations were sufficient to withstand a motion to dismiss because the ILECs failed to show that there is no set of facts that would permit plaintiffs to demonstrate that the particular parallelism asserted was the product of collusion rather than coincidence.

Held:

1. Stating a § 1 claim requires a complaint with enough factual matter (taken as true) to suggest that an agreement was made. An allegation of parallel conduct and a bare assertion of conspiracy will not suffice.

(a) Because § 1 prohibits "only restraints effected by a contract, combination, or conspiracy," *Copperweld Corp. v. Independence Tube Corp.*, 467 U.S. 752, 775, "[t]he crucial question" is whether the challenged anticompetitive conduct "stem[s] from independent decision or from an agreement," *Theatre Enterprises, Inc. v. Paramount Film Distributing Corp.*, 346 U.S. 537, 540. While a showing of parallel "business behavior is admissible circumstantial evidence from which" agreement may be inferred, it falls short of "conclusively establish[ing] agreement or . . . itself constitut[ing] a Sherman Act offense." *Id.*, at 540–541, 540. The inadequacy of showing parallel conduct or interdependence, without more, mirrors the behavior's ambiguity: consistent with conspiracy, but just as much in line with a wide swath of rational and competitive business strategy unilaterally prompted by common perceptions of the market. Thus, this Court has hedged against false inferences from identical behavior at a number of points in the trial sequence, e.g., at the summary judgment stage, *see Matsushita Elec. Industrial Co. v. Zenith Radio Corp.*, 475 U.S. 574.

(b) This case presents the antecedent question of what a plaintiff must plead in order to state a § 1 claim. Federal Rule of Civil Procedure 8(a)(2) requires only "a short and plain statement of the claim showing that the pleader is entitled to relief," in order to "give the defendant fair notice of what the . . . claim is and the grounds upon which it rests," *Conley v. Gibson*, 355 U.S. 41, 47. While a complaint attacked by a Rule 12(b)(6) motion to dismiss does not need detailed factual allegations, *ibid.*, a plaintiff's obligation to provide the "grounds" of his "entitle[ment] to relief" requires more than labels and conclusions, and a formulaic recitation of a cause of action's elements will not do. Factual allegations must be enough to raise a right to relief above the speculative level on the assumption that all of the complaint's allegations are true. Applying these general standards to a § 1 claim, stating a claim requires a complaint with enough factual matter to suggest an agreement. Asking for plausible grounds does not impose a probability requirement at the pleading stage; it simply calls for enough fact to raise a reasonable expectation that discovery will reveal evidence of illegal agreement. The need at the pleading stage for allegations plausibly suggesting (not merely consistent with) agreement reflects Rule 8(a)(2)'s threshold requirement that the "plain statement" possess enough heft to "sho[w] that the pleader is entitled to relief." A parallel conduct allegation gets the § 1 complaint close to stating a claim, but without further factual enhancement it stops short of the line between possibility and plausibility. The requirement of allegations suggesting an agreement serves the practical purpose of preventing a plaintiff with "'a largely groundless claim'" from "'tak[ing] up the time of a number of other people, with the right to do so representing an *in terrorem* increment of the settlement value.'" *Dura Pharms., Inc. v. Broudo*, 544 U.S. 336, 347. It is one thing to be cautious before dismissing an antitrust complaint in advance of discovery, but quite another to forget that proceeding to antitrust discovery can be expensive. That potential expense is obvious here, where plaintiffs represent a putative class of at least 90 percent of subscribers to local telephone or high-speed Internet service in an action against America's largest telecommunications firms for unspecified instances of antitrust violations that allegedly occurred over a 7-year period. It is no answer to say that a claim just shy of plausible entitlement can be weeded out early in the discovery process, given the common lament that the success of judicial supervision in checking discovery abuse has been modest. Plaintiffs' main argument against the plausibility standard at the pleading stage is its ostensible conflict with a literal reading of Conley's statement construing Rule 8: "a complaint should not be dismissed for failure to state a claim unless it appears beyond doubt that the plaintiff can prove no set of facts in support of his claim which would entitle him to relief." 355 U.S., at 45–46. The "no set of facts" language has been questioned, criticized, and explained away long enough by courts and commentators, and is best forgotten as an incomplete, negative gloss on an accepted pleading standard: once a claim has been stated adequately, it may be supported by showing any set of facts consistent with the allegations in the complaint. Conley described the breadth of opportunity to prove what an adequate complaint claims, not the minimum standard of adequate pleading to govern a complaint's survival.

2. Under the plausibility standard, plaintiffs' claim of conspiracy in restraint of trade comes up short. First, the complaint leaves no doubt that plaintiffs rest their § 1 claim on descriptions of parallel conduct, not on any independent allegation of actual agreement among the ILECs. The nub of the complaint is the ILECs' parallel behavior, and its sufficiency turns on the suggestions raised by this conduct when viewed in light of common economic experience. Nothing in the complaint invests either the action or inaction alleged with a plausible conspiracy suggestion. As to the ILECs' supposed agreement to disobey the 1996 Act and thwart the CLECs' attempts to compete, the District Court correctly found that nothing in the complaint intimates that resisting the upstarts was anything more than the natural, unilateral reaction of each ILEC intent on preserving its regional dominance. The complaint's general collusion premise fails to answer the point that there was no need for joint encouragement to resist the 1996 Act, since each ILEC had reason to try to avoid dealing with CLECs and would have tried to keep them out, regardless of the other ILECs' actions. Plaintiffs' second conspiracy theory rests on the competitive reticence among the ILECs themselves in the wake of the 1996 Act to enter into their competitors' territories, leaving the relevant market highly compartmentalized geographically, with minimal competition. This parallel conduct did not suggest conspiracy, not if history teaches anything. Monopoly was the norm in telecommunications, not the exception. Because the ILECs were born in that world, doubtless liked it, and surely knew the adage about him who lives by the sword, a natural explanation for the noncompetition is that the former Government-sanctioned monopolists were sitting tight, expecting their neighbors to do the same. Antitrust conspiracy was not suggested by the facts adduced under either theory of the complaint, which thus fails to state a valid § 1 claim. This analysis does not run counter to *Swierkiewicz v. Sorema N. A.*, 534 U.S. 506, 508, which held that "a complaint in an employment discrimination lawsuit [need] not contain

specific facts establishing a prima facie case of discrimination." Here, the Court is not requiring heightened fact pleading of specifics, but only enough facts to state a claim to relief that is plausible on its face. Because the plaintiffs here have not nudged their claims across the line from conceivable to plausible, their complaint must be dismissed.

425 F.3d 99, reversed and remanded.

SOUTER, J., delivered the opinion of the Court, in which ROBERTS, C. J., and SCALIA, KENNEDY, THOMAS, BREYER, and ALITO, JJ., joined. STEVENS, J., filed a dissenting opinion, in which GINSBURG, J., joined, except as to Part IV.

Opinion

JUSTICE SOUTER delivered the opinion of the Court.

Liability under § 1 of the Sherman Act, 15 U.S.C. § 1, requires a "contract, combination . . ., or conspiracy, in restraint of trade or commerce." The question in this putative class action is whether a § 1 complaint can survive a motion to dismiss when it alleges that major telecommunications providers engaged in certain parallel conduct unfavorable to competition, absent some factual context suggesting agreement, as distinct from identical, independent action. We hold that such a complaint should be dismissed.

I

The upshot of the 1984 divestiture of the American Telephone & Telegraph Company's (AT&T) local telephone business was a system of regional service monopolies (variously called "Regional Bell Operating Companies," "Baby Bells," or "Incumbent Local Exchange Carriers" (ILECs)), and a separate, competitive market for long-distance service from which the ILECs were excluded. More than a decade later, Congress withdrew approval of the ILECs' monopolies by enacting the Telecommunications Act of 1996 (1996 Act), 110 Stat. 56, which "fundamentally restructure[d] local telephone markets" and "subject[ed] [ILECs] to a host of duties intended to facilitate market entry." *AT&T Corp. v. Iowa Utilities Bd.*, 525 U.S. 366, 371 (1999). In recompense, the 1996 Act set conditions for authorizing ILECs to enter the long-distance market. *See* 47 U.S.C. § 271.

"Central to the [new] scheme [was each ILEC's] obligation . . . to share its network with competitors," *Verizon Communications Inc. v. Law Offices of Curtis V. Trinko, LLP*, 540 U.S. 398, 402 (2004), which came to be known as "competitive local exchange carriers" (CLECs), Pet. for Cert. 6, n 1. A CLEC could make use of an ILEC's network in any of three ways: by (1) "purchas[ing] local telephone services at wholesale rates for resale to end users," (2) "leas[ing] elements of the [ILEC's] network 'on an unbundled basis,'" or (3) "interconnect[ing] its own facilities with the [ILEC's] network." *Iowa Utilities Bd., supra,* at 371 (quoting 47 U.S.C. § 251(c)). Owing to the "considerable expense and effort" required to make unbundled network elements available to rivals at wholesale prices, *Trinko, supra,* at 410, the ILECs vigorously litigated the scope of the sharing obligation imposed by the 1996 Act, with the result that the Federal Communications Commission (FCC) three times revised its regulations to narrow the range of network elements to be shared with the CLECs. *See Covad Communs. Co. v. FCC,* 450 F.3d 528, 533–534 (CADC 2006) (summarizing the 10-year-long regulatory struggle between the ILECs and CLECs).

Respondents William Twombly and Lawrence Marcus (hereinafter plaintiffs) represent a putative class consisting of all "subscribers of local telephone and/or high speed internet services . . . from February 8, 1996 to present." Amended Complaint in No. 02 CIV. 10220 (GEL) (SDNY) P 53, App. 28 (hereinafter Complaint). In this action against petitioners, a group of ILECs,[1] plaintiffs seek treble damages and declaratory and injunctive relief for claimed violations of § 1 of the Sherman Act, ch. 647, 26 Stat. 209, as amended, 15 U.S.C. § 1, which prohibits "[e]very contract, combination in the form of trust or otherwise, or conspiracy, in restraint of trade or commerce among the several States, or with foreign nations."

The complaint alleges that the ILECs conspired to restrain trade in two ways, each supposedly inflating charges for local telephone and high-speed Internet services. Plaintiffs say, first, that the ILECs "engaged in parallel conduct" in their respective service areas to inhibit the growth of upstart CLECs. Complaint P 47, App. 23–26. Their actions allegedly included making unfair agreements with the CLECs for access to ILEC networks, providing inferior connections to the networks, overcharging, and billing in ways designed to sabotage the CLECs' relations with their own customers. *Ibid.* According to the complaint, the ILECs' "compelling common motivatio[n]" to thwart the CLECs' competitive efforts naturally led them to form a conspiracy; "[h]ad any one [ILEC] not sought to prevent CLECs . . . from competing effectively . . ., the resulting greater competitive inroads into that [ILEC's] territory would have revealed the degree to which competitive entry by CLECs would have been successful in the other territories in the absence of such conduct." *Id.,* P 50, App. 26–27.

Second, the complaint charges agreements by the ILECs to refrain from competing against one another. These are to be inferred from the ILECs' common failure "meaningfully [to] pursu[e]" "attractive business opportunit[ies]" in contiguous markets where they possessed "substantial competitive advantages," *id.,* PP 40–41,

---

1. The 1984 divestiture of AT&T's local telephone service created seven Regional Bell Operating Companies. Through a series of mergers and acquisitions, those seven companies were consolidated into the four ILECs named in this suit: BellSouth Corporation, Qwest Communications International, Inc., SBC Communications, Inc., and Verizon Communications, Inc. (successor-in-interest to Bell Atlantic Corporation). Complaint P 21, App. 16. Together, these ILECs allegedly control 90 percent or more of the market for local telephone service in the 48 contiguous states. *Id.* P 48, App. 26.

App. 21–22, and from a statement of Richard Notebaert, chief executive officer (CEO) of the ILEC Qwest, that competing in the territory of another ILEC " 'might be a good way to turn a quick dollar but that doesn't make it right,' " *id.*, P 42, App. 22.

The complaint couches its ultimate allegations this way:

> "In the absence of any meaningful competition between the [ILECs] in one another's markets, and in light of the parallel course of conduct that each engaged in to prevent competition from CLECs within their respective local telephone and/or high speed internet services markets and the other facts and market circumstances alleged above, Plaintiffs allege upon information and belief that [the ILECs] have entered into a contract, combination or conspiracy to prevent competitive entry in their respective local telephone and/or high speed internet services markets and have agreed not to compete with one another and otherwise allocated customers and markets to one another." *Id.*, P 51, App. 27.[2]

The United States District Court for the Southern District of New York dismissed the complaint for failure to state a claim upon which relief can be granted. The District Court acknowledged that "plaintiffs may allege a conspiracy by citing instances of parallel business behavior that suggest an agreement," but emphasized that "while '[c]ircumstantial evidence of consciously parallel behavior may have made heavy inroads into the traditional judicial attitude toward conspiracy [, . . .] "conscious parallelism" has not yet read conspiracy out of the Sherman Act entirely.'" 313 F. Supp. 2d 174, 179 (2003) (*quoting Theatre Enterprises, Inc. v. Paramount Film Distributing Corp.*, 346 U.S. 537, 541 (1954); alterations in original). Thus, the District Court understood that allegations of parallel business conduct, taken alone, do not state a claim under § 1; plaintiffs must allege additional facts that "ten[d] to exclude independent self-interested conduct as an explanation for defendants' parallel behavior." 313 F. Supp. 2d, at 179. The District Court found plaintiffs' allegations of parallel ILEC actions to discourage competition inadequate because "the behavior of each ILEC in resisting the incursion of CLECs is fully explained by the ILEC's own interests in defending its individual territory." *Id.*, at 183. As to the ILECs' supposed agreement against competing with each other, the District Court found that the complaint does not "alleg[e] facts . . . suggesting that refraining from competing in other territories as CLECs was contrary to [the ILECs'] apparent economic interests, and consequently [does] not rais[e] an inference that [the ILECs'] actions were the result of a conspiracy." *Id.*, at 188.

---

2. In setting forth the grounds for §1 relief, the complaint repeats these allegations in substantially similar language:"Beginning at least as early as February 6, 1996, and continuing to the present, the exact dates being unknown to Plaintiffs, Defendants and their co-conspirators engaged in a contract, combination or conspiracy to prevent competitive entry in their respective local telephone and/or high speed internet services market by, among other things, agreeing not to compete with one another and to stifle attempts by others to compete with them and otherwise allocating customers and markets to one another in violation of Section 1 of the Sherman Act." *Id.*, P 64, App. 30–31.

The Court of Appeals for the Second Circuit reversed, holding that the District Court tested the complaint by the wrong standard. It held that "plus factors are not required to be pleaded to permit an antitrust claim based on parallel conduct to survive dismissal." 425 F.3d 99, 114 (2005) (emphasis in original). Although the Court of Appeals took the view that plaintiffs must plead facts that "include conspiracy among the realm of 'plausible' possibilities in order to survive a motion to dismiss," it then said that "to rule that allegations of parallel anticompetitive conduct fail to support a plausible conspiracy claim, a court would have to conclude that there is no set of facts that would permit a plaintiff to demonstrate that the particular parallelism asserted was the product of collusion rather than coincidence." *Ibid.*

We granted certiorari to address the proper standard for pleading an antitrust conspiracy through allegations of parallel conduct, 548 U.S. 903 (2006), and now reverse.

II

A

Because § 1 of the Sherman Act "does not prohibit [all] unreasonable restraints of trade . . . but only restraints effected by a contract, combination, or conspiracy," *Copperweld Corp. v. Independence Tube Corp.*, 467 U.S. 752, 775 (1984), "[t]he crucial question" is whether the challenged anticompetitive conduct "stem[s] from independent decision or from an agreement, tacit or express," *Theatre Enterprises*, 346 U.S., at 540. While a showing of parallel "business behavior is admissible circumstantial evidence from which the fact finder may infer agreement," it falls short of "conclusively establish[ing] agreement or . . . itself constitut[ing] a Sherman Act offense." *Id.*, at 540–541. Even "conscious parallelism," a common reaction of "firms in a concentrated market [that] recogniz[e] their shared economic interests and their interdependence with respect to price and output decisions" is "not in itself unlawful." *Brooke Group Ltd. v. Brown & Williamson Tobacco Corp.*, 509 U.S. 209, 227 (1993); *see* 6 P. Areeda & H. Hovenkamp, Antitrust Law P 1433a, p 236 (2d ed. 2003) (hereinafter Areeda & Hovenkamp) ("The courts are nearly unanimous in saying that mere interdependent parallelism does not establish the contract, combination, or conspiracy required by Sherman Act § 1"); Turner, The Definition of Agreement Under the Sherman Act: Conscious Parallelism and Refusals to Deal, 75 Harv. L. Rev. 655, 672 (1962) ("[M]ere interdependence of basic price decisions is not conspiracy").

The inadequacy of showing parallel conduct or interdependence, without more, mirrors the ambiguity of the behavior: consistent with conspiracy, but just as much in line with a wide swath of rational and competitive business strategy unilaterally prompted by common perceptions of the market. *See, e.g.*, AEI-Brookings Joint Center for Regulatory Studies, Epstein, Motions to Dismiss Antitrust Cases:

Separating Fact from Fantasy, Related Publication 06-08, pp 3–4 (2006) (discussing problem of "false positives" in § 1 suits). Accordingly, we have previously hedged against false inferences from identical behavior at a number of points in the trial sequence. An antitrust conspiracy plaintiff with evidence showing nothing beyond parallel conduct is not entitled to a directed verdict, *see Theatre Enterprises, supra*; proof of a § 1 conspiracy must include evidence tending to exclude the possibility of independent action, *see Monsanto Co. v. Spray-Rite Service Corp.*, 465 U.S. 752 (1984); and at the summary judgment stage a § 1 plaintiff's offer of conspiracy evidence must tend to rule out the possibility that the defendants were acting independently, *see Matsushita Elec. Industrial Co. v. Zenith Radio Corp.*, 475 U.S. 574 (1986).

B

This case presents the antecedent question of what a plaintiff must plead in order to state a claim under § 1 of the Sherman Act. Federal Rule of Civil Procedure 8(a)(2) requires only "a short and plain statement of the claim showing that the pleader is entitled to relief," in order to "give the defendant fair notice of what the . . . claim is and the grounds upon which it rests," *Conley v. Gibson*, 355 U.S. 41, 47 (1957). While a complaint attacked by a Rule 12(b)(6) motion to dismiss does not need detailed factual allegations, *ibid.*; *Sanjuan v. American Bd. of Psychiatry and Neurology, Inc.*, 40 F.3d 247, 251 (CA7 1994), a plaintiff's obligation to provide the "grounds" of his "entitle[ment] to relief" requires more than labels and conclusions, and a formulaic recitation of the elements of a cause of action will not do, *see Papasan v. Allain*, 478 U.S. 265, 286 (1986) (on a motion to dismiss, courts "are not bound to accept as true a legal conclusion couched as a factual allegation"). Factual allegations must be enough to raise a right to relief above the speculative level, *see* 5 C. Wright & A. Miller, Federal Practice and Procedure § 1216, pp 235–236 (3d ed. 2004) (hereinafter Wright & Miller) ("[T]he pleading must contain something more . . . than . . . a statement of facts that merely creates a suspicion [of] a legally cognizable right of action"),[3] on the assumption that all the allegations in the complaint are true (even if doubtful in fact), *see, e.g., Swierkiewicz v. Sorema N. A.*, 534 U.S. 506, 508, n. 1 (2002); *Neitzke v. Williams*, 490 U.S. 319, 327 (1989)

---

3. The dissent greatly oversimplifies matters by suggesting that the Federal Rules somehow dispensed with the pleading of facts altogether (opinion of Stevens, J.) (pleading standard of Federal Rules "does not require, or even invite, the pleading of facts"). While, for most types of cases, the Federal Rules eliminated the cumbersome requirement that a claimant "set out *in detail* the facts upon which he bases his claim," *Conley v. Gibson*, 355 U.S. 41, 47 (1957) (emphasis added), Rule 8(a)(2) still requires a "showing," rather than a blanket assertion, of entitlement to relief. Without some factual allegation in the complaint, it is hard to see how a claimant could satisfy the requirement of providing not only "fair notice" of the nature of the claim, but also "grounds" on which the claim rests. See 5 Wright & Miller § 1202, at 94, 95 (Rule 8(a) "contemplate[s] the statement of circumstances, occurrences, and events in support of the claim presented" and does not authorize a pleader's "bare averment that he wants relief and is entitled to it.").

("Rule 12(b)(6) does not countenance . . . dismissals based on a judge's disbelief of a complaint's factual allegations"); *Scheuer v. Rhodes*, 416 U.S. 232, 236 (1974) (a well-pleaded complaint may proceed even if it appears "that a recovery is very remote and unlikely").

In applying these general standards to a § 1 claim, we hold that stating such a claim requires a complaint with enough factual matter (taken as true) to suggest that an agreement was made. Asking for plausible grounds to infer an agreement does not impose a probability requirement at the pleading stage; it simply calls for enough fact to raise a reasonable expectation that discovery will reveal evidence of illegal agreement.[4] And, of course, a well-pleaded complaint may proceed even if it strikes a savvy judge that actual proof of those facts is improbable, and "that a recovery is very remote and unlikely." *Ibid.* In identifying facts that are suggestive enough to render a § 1 conspiracy plausible, we have the benefit of the prior rulings and considered views of leading commentators, already quoted, that lawful parallel conduct fails to bespeak unlawful agreement. It makes sense to say, therefore, that an allegation of parallel conduct and a bare assertion of conspiracy will not suffice. Without more, parallel conduct does not suggest conspiracy, and a conclusory allegation of agreement at some unidentified point does not supply facts adequate to show illegality. Hence, when allegations of parallel conduct are set out in order to make a § 1 claim, they must be placed in a context that raises a suggestion of a preceding agreement, not merely parallel conduct that could just as well be independent action.

The need at the pleading stage for allegations plausibly suggesting (not merely consistent with) agreement reflects the threshold requirement of Rule 8(a)(2) that the "plain statement" possess enough heft to "sho[w] that the pleader is entitled to relief." A statement of parallel conduct, even conduct consciously undertaken, needs some setting suggesting the agreement necessary to make out a § 1 claim; without that further circumstance pointing toward a meeting of the minds, an account of a defendant's commercial efforts stays in neutral territory. An allegation of parallel conduct is thus much like a naked assertion of conspiracy in a § 1 complaint: it gets the complaint close to stating a claim, but without some further factual enhancement it stops short of the line between possibility and plausibility of "entitle[ment]

---

4. Commentators have offered several examples of parallel conduct allegations that would state a § 1 claim under this standard. *See, e.g.*, 6 Areeda & Hovenkamp P1425, at 167–185 (discussing "parallel behavior that would probably not result from chance, coincidence, independent responses to common stimuli, or mere interdependence unaided by an advance understanding among the parties"); Blechman, Conscious Parallelism, Signalling and Facilitating Devices: The Problem of Tacit Collusion Under the Antitrust Laws, 24 N.Y.L.S.L. Rev. 881, 899 (1979) (describing "conduct [that] indicates the sort of restricted freedom of action and sense of obligation that one generally associates with agreement"). The parties in this case agree that "complex and historically unprecedented changes in pricing structure made at the very same time by multiple competitors, and made for no other discernible reason," would support a plausible inference of conspiracy. Brief for Respondents 37; *see also* Reply Brief for Petitioners 12.

to relief." *Cf. DM Research, Inc. v. College of Am. Pathologists*, 170 F.3d 53, 56 (CA1 1999) ("[T]erms like 'conspiracy,' or even 'agreement,' are border-line: they might well be sufficient in conjunction with a more specific allegation—for example, identifying a written agreement or even a basis for inferring a tacit agreement, . . . but a court is not required to accept such terms as a sufficient basis for a complaint").[5]

We alluded to the practical significance of the Rule 8 entitlement requirement in *Dura Pharms., Inc. v. Broudo*, 544 U.S. 336 (2005), when we explained that something beyond the mere possibility of loss causation must be alleged, lest a plaintiff with "'a largely groundless claim'" be allowed to "'take up the time of a number of other people, with the right to do so representing an in terrorem increment of the settlement value.'" *Id.*, at 347 (*quoting Blue Chip Stamps v. Manor Drug Stores*, 421 U.S. 723 (1975)). So, when the allegations in a complaint, however true, could not raise a claim of entitlement to relief, "this basic deficiency should . . . be exposed at the point of minimum expenditure of time and money by the parties and the court." 5 Wright & Miller § 1216, at 233–234 (*quoting Daves v. Hawaiian Dredging Co.*, 114 F. Supp. 643, 645 (Haw. 1953)); *see also Dura, supra*, at 346; *Asahi Glass Co. v. Pentech Pharmaceuticals, Inc.*, 289 F. Supp. 2d 986, 995 (ND Ill. 2003) (Posner, J., sitting by designation) ("[S]ome threshold of plausibility must be crossed at the outset before a patent antitrust case should be permitted to go into its inevitably costly and protracted discovery phase").

Thus, it is one thing to be cautious before dismissing an antitrust complaint in advance of discovery, *cf. Poller v. Columbia Broadcasting System, Inc.*, 368 U.S. 464, 473 (1962), but quite another to forget that proceeding to antitrust discovery can be expensive. As we indicated over 20 years ago in *Associated Gen. Contractors of Cal., Inc. v. Carpenters*, 459 U.S. 519, 528, n. 17 (1983), "a district court must retain the power to insist upon some specificity in pleading before allowing a potentially massive factual controversy to proceed." *See also Car Carriers, Inc. v. Ford Motor Co.*, 745 F.2d 1101, 1106 (CA7 1984) ("[T]he costs of modern federal antitrust litigation and the increasing caseload of the federal courts counsel against sending the parties into discovery when there is no reasonable likelihood that the plaintiffs can construct a claim from the events related in the complaint"); Note, Modeling the Effect of One-Way Fee Shifting on Discovery Abuse in Private Antitrust Litigation, 78 N. Y. U. L. Rev. 1887, 1898–1899 (2003) (discussing the unusually high cost of discovery in antitrust cases); Manual for Complex Litigation, Fourth, § 30, p. 519 (2004) (describing extensive scope of discovery in antitrust cases); Memorandum from Paul V. Niemeyer, Chair, Advisory Committee on Civil Rules, to Hon. Anthony J. Scirica, Chair, Committee on Rules of Practice and Procedure (May 11, 1999), 192 F.R.D. 354, 357 (2000) (reporting that discovery accounts for as much as 90 percent of litigation costs when discovery is actively employed).

---

5. The border of *DM Research* was the line between the conclusory and the factual. Here it lies between the factually neutral and the factually suggestive. Each must be crossed to enter the realm of plausible liability.

That potential expense is obvious enough in the present case: plaintiffs represent a putative class of at least 90 percent of all subscribers to local telephone or high-speed Internet service in the continental United States, in an action against America's largest telecommunications firms (with many thousands of employees generating reams and gigabytes of business records) for unspecified (if any) instances of antitrust violations that allegedly occurred over a period of seven years.

It is no answer to say that a claim just shy of a plausible entitlement to relief can, if groundless, be weeded out early in the discovery process through "careful case management," given the common lament that the success of judicial supervision in checking discovery abuse has been on the modest side. *See, e.g.*, Easterbrook, Discovery as Abuse, 69 B. U. L. Rev. 635, 638 (1989) ("Judges can do little about impositional discovery when parties control the legal claims to be presented and conduct the discovery themselves"). And it is self-evident that the problem of discovery abuse cannot be solved by "careful scrutiny of evidence at the summary judgment stage," much less "lucid instructions to juries"; the threat of discovery expense will push cost-conscious defendants to settle even anemic cases before reaching those proceedings. Probably, then, it is only by taking care to require allegations that reach the level suggesting conspiracy that we can hope to avoid the potentially enormous expense of discovery in cases with no "'reasonably founded hope that the [discovery] process will reveal relevant evidence'" to support a § 1 claim. *Dura*, 544 U.S., at 347 (*quoting Blue Chip Stamps, supra*, at 741, 95 S. Ct. 1917, 44 L. Ed. 2d 539; alteration in *Dura*).[6]

Plaintiffs do not, of course, dispute the requirement of plausibility and the need for something more than merely parallel behavior explained in *Theatre Enterprises,*

---

6. The dissent takes heart in the reassurances of plaintiff's counsel that discovery would be "phased" and "limited to the existence of the alleged conspiracy and class certification." But determining whether some illegal agreement may have taken place between unspecified persons at different ILECs (each a multibillion dollar corporation with legions of management level employees) at some point over seven years is a sprawling, costly, and hugely time-consuming undertaking not easily susceptible to the kind of line-drawing and case management that the dissent envisions. Perhaps the best answer to the dissent's optimism that antitrust discovery is open to effective judicial control is a more extensive quotation of the authority just cited, a judge with a background in antitrust law. Given the system that we have, the hope of effective judicial supervision is slim: "The timing is all wrong. The plaintiff files a sketch complaint (the Rules of Civil Procedure discourage fulsome documents), and discovery is launched. The judicial officer always knows less than the parties, and the parties themselves may not know very well where they are going or what they expect to find. A magistrate supervising discovery does not—cannot—know the expected productivity of a given request, because the nature of the requester's claim and the contents of the files (or head) of the adverse party are unknown. Judicial officers cannot measure the costs and benefits to the requester and so cannot isolate impositional requests. Requesters have no reason to disclose their own estimates because they gain from imposing costs on rivals (and may lose from an improvement in accuracy). The portions of the Rules of Civil Procedure calling on judges to trim back excessive demands, therefore, have been, and are doomed to be, hollow. We cannot prevent what we cannot detect; we cannot detect what we cannot define; we cannot define 'abusive' discovery except in theory, because in practice we lack essential information." Easterbrook, Discovery as Abuse, 60 B. U. L. Rev. 635, 638–639 (1989) (footnote omitted).

Monsanto, and *Matsushita*, and their main argument against the plausibility standard at the pleading stage is its ostensible conflict with an early statement of ours construing Rule 8. Justice Black's opinion for the Court in *Conley v. Gibson* spoke not only of the need for fair notice of the grounds for entitlement to relief but of "the accepted rule that a complaint should not be dismissed for failure to state a claim unless it appears beyond doubt that the plaintiff can prove no set of facts in support of his claim which would entitle him to relief." 355 U.S., at 45–46. This "no set of facts" language can be read in isolation as saying that any statement revealing the theory of the claim will suffice unless its factual impossibility may be shown from the face of the pleadings; and the Court of Appeals appears to have read *Conley* in some such way when formulating its understanding of the proper pleading standard, *see* 425 F.3d at 106, 114 (invoking *Conley*'s "no set of facts" language in describing the standard for dismissal).[7]

On such a focused and literal reading of *Conley*'s "no set of facts," a wholly conclusory statement of claim would survive a motion to dismiss whenever the pleadings left open the possibility that a plaintiff might later establish some "set of [undisclosed] facts" to support recovery. So here, the Court of Appeals specifically found the prospect of unearthing direct evidence of conspiracy sufficient to preclude dismissal, even though the complaint does not set forth a single fact in a context that suggests an agreement. 425 F.3d, at 106, 114. It seems fair to say that this approach to pleading would dispense with any showing of a "'reasonably founded hope'" that a plaintiff would be able to make a case, *see Dura*, 544 U.S., at 347 (*quoting Blue Chip Stamps*, 421 U.S., at 741); Mr. Micawber's optimism would be enough.

Seeing this, a good many judges and commentators have balked at taking the literal terms of the *Conley* passage as a pleading standard. *See, e.g., Car Carriers*, 745 F.2d at 1106 ("*Conley* has never been interpreted literally" and, "[i]n practice, a complaint . . . must contain either direct or inferential allegations respecting all the material elements necessary to sustain recovery under some viable legal theory" (internal quotation marks omitted; emphasis and omission in original); *Ascon Properties, Inc. v. Mobil Oil Co.*, 866 F.2d 1149, 1155 (CA9 1989) (tension between *Conley*'s "no set of facts" language and its acknowledgment that a plaintiff must provide the "grounds" on which his claim rests); *O'Brien v. Di Grazia*, 544 F.2d 543, 546, n. 3 (CA1 1976) ("[W]hen a plaintiff . . . supplies facts to support his claim, we do not think that Conley imposes a duty on the courts to conjure up unpleaded

---

7. The Court of Appeals also relied on Chief Judge Clark's suggestion in *Nagler v. Admiral Corp.*, 248 F.2d 319 (CA2 1957), that facts indicating parallel conduct alone suffice to state a claim under § 1. 425 F.3d at 114 (citing *Nagler, supra*, at 325). But *Nagler* gave no explanation for citing *Theatre Enterprises* (which upheld a denial of a directed verdict for plaintiff on the ground that proof of parallelism was not proof of conspiracy) as authority that pleading parallel conduct sufficed to plead a Sherman Act conspiracy. Now that *Monsanto Co. v. Spray-Rite Service Corp.*, 465 U.S. 752 (1984), and *Matsushita Elec. Industrial Co. v. Zenith Radio Corp.*, 475 U.S. 574 (1986), have made it clear that neither parallel conduct or conscious parallelism, taken alone, raise the necessary implication of conspiracy, it is time for a fresh look at adequacy of pleading when a claim rests on parallel action.

facts that might turn a frivolous claim of unconstitutional . . . action into a substantial one"); *McGregor v. Industrial Excess Landfill, Inc.*, 856 F.2d 39, 42–43 (CA6 1988) (quoting *O'Brien*'s analysis); Hazard, From Whom No Secrets Are Hid, 76 Texas L. Rev. 1665, 1685 (1998) (describing *Conley* as having "turned Rule 8 on its head"); Marcus, The Revival of Fact Pleading Under the Federal Rules of Civil Procedure, 86 Colum. L. Rev. 433, 463–465 (1986) (noting tension between *Conley* and subsequent understandings of Rule 8).

We could go on, but there is no need to pile up further citations to show that *Conley*'s "no set of facts" language has been questioned, criticized, and explained away long enough. To be fair to the *Conley* Court, the passage should be understood in light of the opinion's preceding summary of the complaint's concrete allegations, which the Court quite reasonably understood as amply stating a claim for relief. But the passage so often quoted fails to mention this understanding on the part of the Court, and after puzzling the profession for 50 years, this famous observation has earned its retirement. The phrase is best forgotten as an incomplete, negative gloss on an accepted pleading standard: once a claim has been stated adequately, it may be supported by showing any set of facts consistent with the allegations in the complaint. *See Sanjuan*, 40 F.3d at 251 (once a claim for relief has been stated, a plaintiff "receives the benefit of imagination, so long as the hypotheses are consistent with the complaint"); *accord, Swierkiewicz*, 534 U.S., at 514; *National Organization for Women, Inc. v. Scheidler*, 510 U.S. 249, 256 (1994); *H. J. Inc. v. Northwestern Bell Telephone Co.*, 492 U.S. 229, 249–250 (1989); *Hishon v. King & Spalding*, 467 U.S. 69, 73 (1984). *Conley*, then, described the breadth of opportunity to prove what an adequate complaint claims, not the minimum standard of adequate pleading to govern a complaint's survival.[8]

---

8. Because *Conley*'s "'no set of facts'" language was one of our earliest statements about pleading under the Federal Rules, it is no surprise that it has since been "cited as authority" by this Court and others. Although we have not previously explained the circumstances and rejected the literal reading of the passage embraced by the Court of Appeals, our analysis comports with this Court's statements in the years since *Conley. See Dura Pharmaceuticals, Inc. v. Broudo*, 544 U.S., at 336, 347 (2005) (requiring "'reasonably founded hope that the [discovery] process will reveal relevant evidence'" to support the claim (alteration in *Dura*) (quoting *Blue Chip Stamps v. Manor Drug Stores*, 421 U.S. 723, 741 (1975); alteration in *Dura*)); *Associated Gen. Contractors of Cal., Inc. v. Carpenters*, 459 U.S. 519, 526 (1983) ("It is not . . . proper to assume that [the plaintiff] can prove facts that it has not alleged or that the defendants have violated the antitrust law in ways that have not been alleged"); *Wilson v. Schnettler*, 365 U.S. 381, 383 (1961) ("In absence of . . . an allegation [that the arrest was made without probable cause] the courts below could not, nor can we, assume that respondents arrested petitioner without probable cause to believe that he had committed . . . a narcotics offense"). Nor are we reaching out to decide this issue in a case where the matter was not raised by the parties, since both the ILECs and the Government highlight the problems stemming from a literal interpretation of *Conley*'s "no set of facts" language and seek clarification of the standard. Brief for Petitioners 27–28; Brief for United States as *Amicus Curiae* 22–25; *see also* Brief for Respondents 17 (describing "[p]etitioners and their amici" as mounting an "attack on *Conley*'s 'no set of facts' standard").

The dissent finds relevance in Court of Appeals precedents from the 1940s, which allegedly gave rise to *Conley*'s "no set of facts" language. Even indulging this line of analysis, these cases do not challenge the understanding that, before proceeding to discovery, a complaint must allege facts suggestive

III

When we look for plausibility in this complaint, we agree with the District Court that plaintiffs' claim of conspiracy in restraint of trade comes up short. To begin with, the complaint leaves no doubt that plaintiffs rest their § 1 claim on descriptions of parallel conduct and not on any independent allegation of actual agreement among the ILECs. *Supra*, at 550–551. Although in form a few stray statements speak directly of agreement,[9] on fair reading these are merely legal conclusions resting on the prior allegations. Thus, the complaint first takes account of the alleged "absence of any meaningful competition between [the ILECs] in one another's markets," "the parallel course of conduct that each [ILEC] engaged in to prevent competition from CLECs," "and the other facts and market circumstances alleged [earlier]"; "in light of" these, the complaint concludes "that [the ILECs] have entered into a contract, combination or conspiracy to prevent competitive entry into their . . . markets and have agreed not to compete with one another." Complaint P 51, App. 27.[10] The nub of the complaint, then, is the ILECs' parallel behavior, consisting of steps to keep the CLECs out and manifest disinterest in becoming CLECs themselves, and its sufficiency turns on the suggestions raised by this conduct when viewed in light of common economic experience.[11]

---

of illegal conduct. *See, e.g., Leimer v. State Mut. Life Assurance Co. of Worcester, Mass.,* 108 F.2d 302, 305 (CA8 1940) ("'[I]f, in view of what is alleged, it can reasonably be conceived that the plaintiffs . . . could, upon a trial, establish a case which would entitle them to . . . relief, the motion to dismiss should not have been granted'"); *Continental Collieries, Inc. v. Shober,* 130 F.2d 631, 635 (CA3 1942) ("No matter how likely it may seem that the pleader will be unable to prove his case, he is entitled, upon averring a claim, to an opportunity to try to prove it"). Rather, these cases stand for the unobjectionable proposition that, when a complaint adequately states a claim, it may not be dismissed based on a district court's assessment that the plaintiff will fail to find evidentiary support for his allegation or prove his claim to the satisfaction of the factfinder. *Cf. Scheuer v. Rhodes,* 416 U.S. 232, 236 (1974) (a district court weighing a motion to dismiss asks "not whether the plaintiff will ultimately prevail but whether the claimant is entitled to offer evidence to support the claims").

9. *See* Complaint PP 51, 64, App. 27, 30–31 (alleging that ILECs engaged in a "contract, combination or conspiracy" and agreed not to compete with one another.

10. If the complaint had not explained that the claim of agreement rested on the parallel conduct described, we doubt that the complaint's references to an agreement among the ILECs would have given the notice required by Rule 8. Apart from identifying a 7-year span in which the § 1 violations were supposed to have occurred (i.e., "[b]eginning at least as early as February 6, 1996, and continuing to the present," *id.,* P 64, App. 30), the pleadings mentioned no specific time, place, or person involved in the alleged conspiracies. This lack of notice contrasts sharply with the model form for pleading negligence, Form 9, which the dissent says exemplifies the kind of "bare allegation" that survives a motion to dismiss. Whereas the model form alleges that the defendant struck the plaintiff with his car while plaintiff was crossing a particular highway at a specified date and time, the complaint here furnishes no clue as to which of the four ILECs (much less which of their employees) supposedly agreed, or when and where the illicit agreement took place. A defendant wishing to prepare an answer in the simple fact pattern laid out in Form 9 would know what to answer; a defendant seeking to respond to plaintiffs' conclusory allegations in the § 1 context would have little idea where to begin.

11. The dissent's quotations from the complaint leave the impression that plaintiffs directly allege illegal agreement; in fact, they proceed exclusively via allegations of parallel conduct, as both the District Court and Court of Appeals recognized. *See* 313 F. Supp. 2d 174, 182 (SDNY 2003); 425 F.3d 90, 102–104 (CA2 2005).

We think that nothing contained in the complaint invests either the action or inaction alleged with a plausible suggestion of conspiracy. As to the ILECs' supposed agreement to disobey the 1996 Act and thwart the CLECs' attempts to compete, we agree with the District Court that nothing in the complaint intimates that the resistance to the upstarts was anything more than the natural, unilateral reaction of each ILEC intent on keeping its regional dominance. The 1996 Act did more than just subject the ILECs to competition; it obliged them to subsidize their competitors with their own equipment at wholesale rates. The economic incentive to resist was powerful, but resisting competition is routine market conduct, and even if the ILECs flouted the 1996 Act in all the ways the plaintiffs allege, *see id.*, P 47, App. 23–24, there is no reason to infer that the companies had agreed among themselves to do what was only natural anyway; so natural, in fact, that if alleging parallel decisions to resist competition were enough to imply an antitrust conspiracy, pleading a § 1 violation against almost any group of competing businesses would be a sure thing.

The complaint makes its closest pass at a predicate for conspiracy with the claim that collusion was necessary because success by even one CLEC in an ILEC's territory "would have revealed the degree to which competitive entry by CLECs would have been successful in the other territories." *Id.*, P 50, App. 26–27. But, its logic aside, this general premise still fails to answer the point that there was just no need for joint encouragement to resist the 1996 Act; as the District Court said, "each ILEC has reason to want to avoid dealing with CLECs" and "each ILEC would attempt to keep CLECs out, regardless of the actions of the other ILECs." 313 F. Supp. 2d, at 184; *cf. Kramer v. Pollock-Krasner Foundation*, 890 F. Supp. 250, 256 (SDNY 1995) (while the plaintiff "may believe the defendants conspired . . . , the defendants' allegedly conspiratorial actions could equally have been prompted by lawful, independent goals which do not constitute a conspiracy").[12]

Plaintiffs' second conspiracy theory rests on the competitive reticence among the ILECs themselves in the wake of the 1996 Act, which was supposedly passed in the "'hop[e] that the large incumbent local monopoly companies . . . might attack their neighbors' service areas, as they are the best situated to do so.'" Complaint P 38, App. 20 (quoting Consumer Federation of America, Lessons from 1996 Telecommunications Act: Deregulation Before Meaningful Competition Spells Consumer Disaster, p 12 (Feb. 2000)). Contrary to hope, the ILECs declined "'to enter each other's service territories in any significant way,'" Complaint P 38, App. 20, and the local telephone and high speed Internet market remains highly compartmentalized

---

12. From the allegation that the ILECs belong to the various trade associations, *see* Complaint P 46, App. 23, the dissent playfully suggests that they conspired to restrain trade, an inference said to be "buttressed by the common sense of Adam Smith." If Adam Smith is peering down today, he may be surprised to learn that his tongue-in-cheek remark would be authority to force his famous pinmaker to devote financial and human capital to hire lawyers, prepare depositions, and otherwise fend off allegations of conspiracy; all this just because he belonged to the same trade guild as one of his competitors when their pins carried the same price tag.

geographically, with minimal competition. Based on this state of affairs, and perceiving the ILECs to be blessed with "especially attractive business opportunities" in surrounding markets dominated by other ILECs, the plaintiffs assert that the ILECs' parallel conduct was "strongly suggestive of conspiracy." *Id.*, P 40, App. 21.

But it was not suggestive of conspiracy, not if history teaches anything. In a traditionally unregulated industry with low barriers to entry, sparse competition among large firms dominating separate geographical segments of the market could very well signify illegal agreement, but here we have an obvious alternative explanation. In the decade preceding the 1996 Act and well before that, monopoly was the norm in telecommunications, not the exception. *See Verizon Communs., Inc. v. FCC*, 535 U.S. 467, 477–478 (2002) (describing telephone service providers as traditional public monopolies). The ILECs were born in that world, doubtless liked the world the way it was, and surely knew the adage about him who lives by the sword. Hence, a natural explanation for the noncompetition alleged is that the former Government-sanctioned monopolists were sitting tight, expecting their neighbors to do the same thing.

In fact, the complaint itself gives reasons to believe that the ILECs would see their best interests in keeping to their old turf. Although the complaint says generally that the ILECs passed up "especially attractive business opportunit[ies]" by declining to compete as CLECs against other ILECs, Complaint P 40, App. 21, it does not allege that competition as CLECs was potentially any more lucrative than other opportunities being pursued by the ILECs during the same period,[13] and the complaint is replete with indications that any CLEC faced nearly insurmountable barriers to profitability owing to the ILECs' flagrant resistance to the network sharing requirements of the 1996 Act, *id.*, P 47, App. 23–26. Not only that, but even without a monopolistic tradition and the peculiar difficulty of mandating shared networks, "[f]irms do not expand without limit and none of them enters every market that an outside observer might regard as profitable, or even a small portion of such markets." Areeda & Hovenkamp P 307d, at 155 (Supp. 2006) (commenting on the case at bar). The upshot is that Congress may have expected some ILECs to become CLECs in the legacy territories of other ILECs, but the disappointment does not make conspiracy plausible. We agree with the District Court's assessment

---

13. The complaint quoted a reported statement of Qwest's CEO, Richard Notebaert, to suggest that the ILECs declined to compete against each other despite recognizing that it "might be a good way to turn a quick dollar." P 42, App. 22 (quoting Chicago Tribune, Oct. 31, 2002, Business section, p1). This was only part of what he reportedly said, however, and the District Court was entitled to take notice of the full contents of the published articles referenced in the complaint, from which the truncated quotations were drawn. *See* Fed. Rule Evid. 201. Notebaert was also quoted as saying that entering new markets as a CLEC would not be "a sustainable economic model" because the CLEC pricing model is "just . . . nuts." Chicago Tribune, Oct. 31, 2002, Business Section, p1 (cited in Compliant P 42, App. 22). Another source cited in the complaint quotes Notebaert as saying he thought it "unwise" to "base a business plain" on the privileges accorded to CLECs under the 1996 Act because the regulatory environment was too unstable. Chicago Tribune, Dec. 19, 2002, Business Section, p2 (cited at Complaint P 45, App. 23).

that antitrust conspiracy was not suggested by the facts adduced under either theory of the complaint, which thus fails to state a valid § 1 claim.[14]

Plaintiffs say that our analysis runs counter to *Swierkiewicz v. Sorema N. A.*, 534 U.S. at 508, which held that "a complaint in an employment discrimination lawsuit [need] not contain specific facts establishing a prima facie case of discrimination under the framework set forth in *McDonnell Douglas Corp. v. Green*, 411 U.S. 792 (1973)." They argue that just as the prima facie case is a "flexible evidentiary standard" that "should not be transposed into a rigid pleading standard for discrimination cases," *Swierkiewicz, supra,* at 512, "transpos[ing] 'plus factor' summary judgment analysis woodenly into a rigid Rule 12(b)(6) pleading standard . . . would be unwise," Brief for Respondents 39. As the District Court correctly understood, however, "*Swierkiewicz* did not change the law of pleading, but simply re-emphasized . . . that the Second Circuit's use of a heightened pleading standard for Title VII cases was contrary to the Federal Rules' structure of liberal pleading requirements." 313 F. Supp. 2d, at 181 (citation and footnote omitted). Even though *Swierkiewicz*'s pleadings "detailed the events leading to his termination, provided relevant dates, and included the ages and nationalities of at least some of the relevant persons involved with his termination," the Court of Appeals dismissed his complaint for failing to allege certain additional facts that *Swierkiewicz* would need at the trial stage to support his claim in the absence of direct evidence of discrimination. *Swierkiewicz*, 534 U.S., at 514. We reversed on the ground that the Court of Appeals had impermissibly applied what amounted to a heightened pleading requirement by insisting that *Swierkiewicz* allege "specific facts" beyond those necessary to state his claim and the grounds showing entitlement to relief. *Id.*, at 508.

Here, in contrast, we do not require heightened fact pleading of specifics, but only enough facts to state a claim to relief that is plausible on its face. Because the plaintiffs here have not nudged their claims across the line from conceivable to plausible, their complaint must be dismissed.

* * *

The judgment of the Court of Appeals for the Second Circuit is reversed, and the case is remanded for further proceedings consistent with this opinion.

It is so ordered.

---

14. In reaching this conclusion, we do not apply any "heighted" pleading standard, nor do we seek to broaden the scope of Federal Rule of Civil Procedure 9, which can only be accomplished "'by the process of amending the Federal Rules, and not by judicial interpretation.'" *Swierkiewicz v. Sorema N.A.*, 534 U.S. 506, 515 (2002) (*quoting Leatherman v. Tarrant County Narcotics Intelligence and Coordination Unit*, 507 U.S. 163, 168 (1993)). On certain subjects understood to raise a high risk of abusive litigation, a plaintiff must state factual allegations with greater particularity than Rule 8 requires. Fed. Rules Civ. Proc. 9(b)–(c). Here, our concern is not that the allegations in the complaint were insufficiently "particular[ized]," *ibid.*; rather, the complaint warranted dismissal because it failed *in toto* to render plaintiff's entitlement to relief possible.

DISSENT

JUSTICE STEVENS, with whom JUSTICE GINSBURG joins except as to Part IV, dissenting.

In the first paragraph of its 23-page opinion the Court states that the question to be decided is whether allegations that "major telecommunications providers engaged in certain parallel conduct unfavorable to competition" suffice to state a violation of § 1 of the Sherman Act. The answer to that question has been settled for more than 50 years. If that were indeed the issue, a summary reversal citing *Theatre Enterprises, Inc. v. Paramount Film Distributing Corp.*, 346 U.S. 537 (1954), would adequately resolve this case. As *Theatre Enterprises* held, parallel conduct is circumstantial evidence admissible on the issue of conspiracy, but it is not itself illegal. *Id.*, at 540–542.

Thus, this is a case in which there is no dispute about the substantive law. If the defendants acted independently, their conduct was perfectly lawful. If, however, that conduct is the product of a horizontal agreement among potential competitors, it was unlawful. The plaintiffs have alleged such an agreement and, because the complaint was dismissed in advance of answer, the allegation has not even been denied. Why, then, does the case not proceed? Does a judicial opinion that the charge is not "plausible" provide a legally acceptable reason for dismissing the complaint? I think not.

Respondents' amended complaint describes a variety of circumstantial evidence and makes the straightforward allegation that petitioners "entered into a contract, combination or conspiracy to prevent competitive entry in their respective local telephone and/or high speed internet services markets and have agreed not to compete with one another and otherwise allocated customers and markets to one another." Amended Complaint in No. 02 CIV. 10220 (GEL) (SDNY) P 51, App. 27 (hereinafter Complaint).

The complaint explains that, contrary to Congress' expectation when it enacted the 1996 Telecommunications Act, and consistent with their own economic self-interests, petitioner Incumbent Local Exchange Carriers (ILECs) have assiduously avoided infringing upon each other's markets and have refused to permit nonincumbent competitors to access their networks. The complaint quotes Richard Notebaert, the former chief executive officer of one such ILEC, as saying that competing in a neighboring ILEC's territory "'might be a good way to turn a quick dollar but that doesn't make it right.'" *Id.*, P 42, App. 22. Moreover, respondents allege that petitioners "communicate amongst themselves" through numerous industry associations. *Id.*, P 46, App. 23. In sum, respondents allege that petitioners entered into an agreement that has long been recognized as a classic per se violation of the Sherman Act. *See* Report of the Attorney General's National Committee to Study the Antitrust Laws 26 (1955).

Under rules of procedure that have been well settled since well before our decision in *Theatre Enterprises*, a judge ruling on a defendant's motion to dismiss a complaint "must accept as true all of the factual allegations contained in the complaint." *Swierkiewicz v. Sorema N. A.*, 534 U.S. 506, 508, n. 1 (2002); *see Overstreet v. North Shore Corp.*, 318 U.S. 125, 127 (1943). But instead of requiring knowledgeable executives such as Notebaert to respond to these allegations by way of sworn depositions or other limited discovery—and indeed without so much as requiring petitioners to file an answer denying that they entered into any agreement—the majority permits immediate dismissal based on the assurances of company lawyers that nothing untoward was afoot. The Court embraces the argument of those lawyers that "there is no reason to infer that the companies had agreed among themselves to do what was only natural anyway," that "there was just no need for joint encouragement to resist the 1996 Act," and that the "natural explanation for the noncompetition alleged is that the former Government-sanctioned monopolists were sitting tight, expecting their neighbors to do the same thing."

The Court and petitioners' legal team are no doubt correct that the parallel conduct alleged is consistent with the absence of any contract, combination, or conspiracy. But that conduct is also entirely consistent with the presence of the illegal agreement alleged in the complaint. And the charge that petitioners "agreed not to compete with one another" is not just one of "a few stray statements," it is an allegation describing unlawful conduct. As such, the Federal Rules of Civil Procedure, our longstanding precedent, and sound practice mandate that the District Court at least require some sort of response from petitioners before dismissing the case.

Two practical concerns presumably explain the Court's dramatic departure from settled procedural law. Private antitrust litigation can be enormously expensive, and there is a risk that jurors may mistakenly conclude that evidence of parallel conduct has proved that the parties acted pursuant to an agreement when they in fact merely made similar independent decisions. Those concerns merit careful case management, including strict control of discovery, careful scrutiny of evidence at the summary judgment stage, and lucid instructions to juries; they do not, however, justify the dismissal of an adequately pleaded complaint without even requiring the defendants to file answers denying a charge that they in fact engaged in collective decisionmaking. More importantly, they do not justify an interpretation of Federal Rule of Civil Procedure 12(b)(6) that seems to be driven by the majority's appraisal of the plausibility of the ultimate factual allegation rather than its legal sufficiency.

I

Rule 8(a)(2) of the Federal Rules requires that a complaint contain "a short and plain statement of the claim showing that the pleader is entitled to relief." The Rule did not come about by happenstance, and its language is not inadvertent. The English experience with Byzantine special pleading rules—illustrated by the hypertechnical *Hilary* rules of 1834[1]—made obvious the appeal of a pleading standard that was easy for the common litigant to understand and sufficed to put the defendant on notice as to the nature of the claim against him and the relief sought. Stateside, David Dudley Field developed the highly influential New York Code of 1848, which required "[a] statement of the facts constituting the cause of action, in ordinary and concise language, without repetition, and in such a manner as to enable a person of common understanding to know what is intended." An Act to Simplify and Abridge the Practice, Pleadings and Proceedings of the Courts of this State, ch. 379, § 120(2), 1848 N. Y. Laws pp. 497, 521. Substantially similar language appeared in the Federal Equity Rules adopted in 1912. *See* Fed. Equity Rule 25 (requiring "a short and simple statement of the ultimate facts upon which the plaintiff asks relief, omitting any mere statement of evidence").

A difficulty arose, however, in that the Field Code and its progeny required a plaintiff to plead "facts" rather than "conclusions," a distinction that proved far easier to say than to apply. As commentators have noted,

> "it is virtually impossible logically to distinguish among 'ultimate facts,' 'evidence,' and 'conclusions.' Essentially any allegation in a pleading must be an assertion that certain occurrences took place. The pleading spectrum, passing from evidence through ultimate facts to conclusions, is largely a continuum varying only in the degree of particularity with which the occurrences are described." Weinstein & Distler, Comments on Procedural Reform: Drafting Pleading Rules, 57 Colum. L. Rev. 518, 520–521 (1957).

See also Cook, Statements of Fact in Pleading Under the Codes, 21 Colum. L. Rev. 416, 417 (1921) (hereinafter Cook) ("[T]here is no logical distinction between statements which are grouped by the courts under the phrases 'statements of fact' and 'conclusions of law'"). Rule 8 was directly responsive to this difficulty. Its drafters intentionally avoided any reference to "facts" or "evidence" or "conclusions." *See* 5 C. Wright & A. Miller, Federal Practice and Procedure § 1216, p 207 (3d ed. 2004) (hereinafter Wright & Miller) ("The substitution of 'claim showing that the pleader is entitled to relief' for the code formulation of the 'facts' constituting a 'cause of action' was intended to avoid the distinctions drawn under the codes among 'evidentiary facts,' 'ultimate facts,' and 'conclusions' . . .").

Under the relaxed pleading standards of the Federal Rules, the idea was not to keep litigants out of court but rather to keep them in. The merits of a claim would be sorted out during a flexible pretrial process and, as appropriate, through the crucible of trial. *See Swierkiewicz*, 534 U.S., at 514 ("The liberal notice pleading of Rule 8(a) is the starting point of a simplified pleading system, which was adopted

---

1. *See* 9 W. Holdsworth, History of English Law 324–327 (1926).

to focus litigation on the merits of a claim"). Charles E. Clark, the "principal drafts-man" of the Federal Rules,[2] put it thus:

> "Experience has shown . . . that we cannot expect the proof of the case to be made through the pleadings, and that such proof is really not their function. We can expect a general statement distinguishing the case from all others, so that the manner and form of trial and remedy expected are clear, and so that a permanent judgment will result." The New Federal Rules of Civil Procedure: The Last Phase—Underlying Philosophy Embodied in Some of the Basic Provisions of the New Procedure, 23 A. B. A. J. 976, 977 (1937) (hereinafter Clark, New Federal Rules).

The pleading paradigm under the new Federal Rules was well illustrated by the inclusion in the appendix of Form 9, a complaint for negligence. As relevant, the Form 9 complaint states only: "On June 1, 1936, in a public highway called Boylston Street in Boston, Massachusetts, defendant negligently drove a motor vehicle against plaintiff who was then crossing said highway." Form 9, Complaint for Negligence, Forms App., Fed. Rules Civ. Proc., 28 U.S.C. App., p 829 (hereinafter Form 9). The complaint then describes the plaintiff's injuries and demands judgment. The asserted ground for relief—namely, the defendant's negligent driving—would have been called a "'conclusion of law'" under the code pleading of old. *See, e.g.,* Cook 419. But that bare allegation suffices under a system that "restrict[s] the pleadings to the task of general notice-giving and invest[s] the deposition-discovery process with a vital role in the preparation for trial."[3] *Hickman v. Taylor*, 329 U.S. 495, 501 (1947); *see also Swierkiewicz*, 534 U.S., at 513, n. 4 (citing Form 9 as an example of "'the simplicity and brevity of statement which the rules contemplate'"); *Thomson v. Washington*, 362 F.3d 969, 970 (CA7 2004) (Posner, J.) ("The federal rules replaced fact pleading with notice pleading").

II

It is in the context of this history that *Conley v. Gibson*, 355 U.S. 41 (1957), must be understood. The *Conley* plaintiffs were black railroad workers who alleged that their union local had refused to protect them against discriminatory discharges, in violation of the National Railway Labor Act. The union sought to dismiss the complaint on the ground that its general allegations of discriminatory treatment by the defendants lacked sufficient specificity. Writing for a unanimous Court, Justice Black rejected the union's claim as foreclosed by the language of Rule 8. *Id.,* at 47–48. In the course of doing so, he articulated the formulation the Court rejects

---

2. *Gulfstream Aerospace Corp. v. Mayacamas Corp.*, 485 U.S. 271, 283 (1988).

3. The Federal Rules do impose a "particularity" requirement of "all averments of fraud or mistake," Fed. Rule Civ. Proc. 9(b), neither of which has been alleged in this case. We have recognized that the canon of *expression unius est exclusion alterius* applies to Rule 9(b). *See Leatherman v. Tarrant County Narcotics Intelligence and Coordination Unit*, 507 U.S. 163 (1993).

today: "In appraising the sufficiency of the complaint we follow, of course, the accepted rule that a complaint should not be dismissed for failure to state a claim unless it appears beyond doubt that the plaintiff can prove no set of facts in support of his claim which would entitle him to relief." *Id.*, at 45–46.

Consistent with the design of the Federal Rules, *Conley's* "no set of facts" formulation permits outright dismissal only when proceeding to discovery or beyond would be futile. Once it is clear that a plaintiff has stated a claim that, if true, would entitle him to relief, matters of proof are appropriately relegated to other stages of the trial process. Today, however, in its explanation of a decision to dismiss a complaint that it regards as a fishing expedition, the Court scraps *Conley's* "no set of facts " language. Concluding that the phrase has been "questioned, criticized, and explained away long enough," the Court dismisses it as careless composition.

If *Conley's* "no set of facts" language is to be interred, let it not be without a eulogy. That exact language, which the majority says has "puzzl[ed] the profession for 50 years," has been cited as authority in a dozen opinions of this Court and four separate writings.[4] In not one of those 16 opinions was the language "questioned," "criticized," or "explained away." Indeed, today's opinion is the first by any Member of this Court to express any doubt as to the adequacy of the *Conley* formulation. Taking their cues from the federal courts, 26 States and the District of Columbia utilize as their standard for dismissal of a complaint the very language the majority repudiates: whether it appears "beyond doubt" that "no set of facts" in support of the claim would entitle the plaintiff to relief.[5]

---

4. *SEC v. Zandford*, 535 U.S. 813 (2002); *Davis v. Monroe County Bd. of Ed.*, 526 U.S. 629 (1999); *Hartford Fire Ins. Co. v. California*, 509 U.S. 764 (1993); *Brower v. County of Inyo*, 489 U.S. 593 (1989); *Hughes v. Rowe*, 449 U.S. 5, 10 (1980) (per curiam); *McLain v. Real Estate Bd. of New Orleans, Inc.*, 444 U.S. 232, 246 (1980); *Estelle v. Gamble*, 429 U.S. 97, 106 (1976); *Hospital Building Co. v. Trustees of Rex Hospital*, 425 U.S. 738, 746 (1976); *Scheuer v. Rhodes*, 416 U.S. 232, 236 (1974); *Cruz v. Beto*, 405 U.S. 319, 322 (1972) (per curiam); *Haines v. Kerner*, 404 U.S. 519, 521 (1972) (per curiam); *Jenkins v. McKeithen*, 395 U.S. 411, 422 (1969) (plurality opinion); *see also Cleveland Bd. of Ed. v. Loudermill*, 470 U.S. 532, 554 (1985) (Brennan, J., concurring in part and dissenting in part); *Hoover v. Ronwin*, 466 U.S. 558, 587 (1984) (STEVENS, J., dissenting); *United Air Lines, Inc. v. Evans*, 431 U.S. 553, 561, n. 1 (1977) (Marshall, J., dissenting); *Simon v. Eastern Ky. Welfare Rights Organization*, 426 U.S. 26, 55, n. 6 (1976) (Brennan, J., concurring in judgment).

5. *See, e.g., EB Invs., LLC v. Atlantis Development, Inc.*, 930 So. 2d 502, 507 (Ala. 2005); *Department of Health & Social Servs. v. Native Village of Curyung*, 151 P. 3d 388, 396 (Alaska 2006); *Newman v. Maricopa* Cty., 808 P. 2d 1253, 1255 (Ariz. App. 1991); *Public Serv. Co. of Colo. v. Van Wyk*, 27 P. 3d 377, 385–386 (Colo. 2001) (en banc); *Clawson v. St. Louis Post-Dispatch, LLC*, 906 A. 2d 308, 312 (D. C. 2006); *Hillman Constr. Corp. v. Wainer*, 636 So. 2d 576, 578 (Fla. App. 1994); *Kaplan v. Kaplan*, 469 S. E. 2d 198, 199 (Ga. 1996); *Wright v. Home Depot U.S.A.*, 142 P. 3d 265, 270 (Haw. 2006); *Taylor v. Maile*, 127 P. 3d 156, 160 (Idaho 2005); *Fink v. Bryant*, 2001.CC.0987, p. 4 (La. 11/28/01), 801 So. 2d 346, 349; *Gagne v. Cianbro Corp.*, 431 A. 2d 1313, 1318–1319 (Me. 1981); *Gasior v. Massachusetts Gen. Hospital*, 846 N. E. 2d 1133, 1135 (Mass. 2006); *Ralph Walker, Inc. v. Gallagher*, 926 So. 2d 890, 893 (Miss. 2006); *Jones v. Montana Univ. System*, 337 Mont. 1, 7, 155 P. 3d 1247, _____ (2007); *Johnston v. Nebraska Dept. of Correctional Servs.*, 709 N. W. 2d 321, 324 (Neb. 2006); *Blackjack Bonding v. Las Vegas Munic. Ct.*, 14 P. 3d 1275, 1278 (Nev. 2000); *Shepard v. Ocwen Fed. Bank*, 638 S. E. 2d 197, 199 (N.C. 2006); *Rose v. United Equitable Ins. Co.*,

Petitioners have not requested that the *Conley* formulation be retired, nor have any of the six amici who filed briefs in support of petitioners. I would not rewrite the Nation's civil procedure textbooks and call into doubt the pleading rules of most of its States without far more informed deliberation as to the costs of doing so. Congress has established a process—a rulemaking process—for revisions of that order. *See* 28 U. S. C. §§2072.2074 (2000 ed. and Supp. IV).

Today's majority calls *Conley's* "'no set of facts'" language "an incomplete, negative gloss on an accepted pleading standard: once a claim has been stated adequately, it may be supported by showing any set of facts consistent with the allegations in the complaint." This is not and cannot be what the *Conley* Court meant. First, as I have explained, and as the *Conley* Court well knew, the pleading standard the Federal Rules meant to codify does not require, or even invite, the pleading of facts.[6] The "pleading standard" label the majority gives to what it reads into the *Conley* opinion—a statement of the permissible factual support for an adequately

---

632 N. W. 2d 429, 434 (N.D. 2001); *State ex rel. Turner v. Houk*, 862 N. E. 2d 104, 105 (Ohio 2007) (per curiam); *Moneypenney v. Dawson*, 2006 OK 53, ¶2, 141 P. 3d 549, 551; *Gagnon v. State*, 570 A. 2d 656, 659 (R. I. 1990); *Osloond v. Farrier*, 2003 SD 28, ¶4, 659 N. W. 2d 20, 22 (per curiam); *Smith v. Lincoln Brass Works*, Inc., 712 S. W. 2d 470, 471 (Tenn. 1986); *Association of Haystack Property Owners v. Sprague*, 494 A. 2d 122, 124 (Vt. 1985); *In re Coday*, 156 Wash. 2d 485, 497, 30 P. 3d 809, 815 (Wash. 2006) (en banc); *Haines v. Hampshire Cty. Comm.n*, 607 S. E. 2d 828, 831 (W. Va. 2004); *Warren v. Hart*, 747 P. 2d 511, 512 (Wyo. 1987); *see also Malpiede v. Townson*, 780 A. 2d 1075, 1082–1083 (Del. 2001) (permitting dismissal only "where the court determines with reasonable certainty that the plaintiff could prevail on no set of facts that may be inferred from the well-pleaded allegations in the complaint" (internal quotation marks omitted)); *Canel v. Topinka*, 818 N. E. 2d 311, 317 (Ill. 2004) (replacing "appears beyond doubt" in the *Conley* formulation with "is clearly apparent"); *In re Young*, 522 N. E. 2d 386, 388 (Ind. 1988) (per curiam) (replacing "appears beyond doubt" with "appears to a certainty"); *Barkema v. Williams Pipeline Co.*, 666 N. W. 2d 612, 614 (Iowa 2003) (holding that a motion to dismiss should be sustained "only when there exists no conceivable set of facts entitling the non-moving party to relief"); *Pioneer Village v. Bullitt Cty.*, 104 S. W. 3d 757, 759 (Ky. 2003) (holding that judgment on the pleadings should be granted "if it appears beyond doubt that the nonmoving party cannot prove any set of facts that would entitle him/her to relief"); *Corley v. Detroit Bd. of Ed.*, 681 N. W. 2d 342, 345 (Mich. 2004) (per curiam) (holding that a motion for judgment on the pleadings should be granted only "'if no factual development could possibly justify recovery'"); *Oberkramer v. Ellisville*, 706 S. W. 2d 440, 441 (Mo. 1986) (en banc) (omitting the words "beyond doubt" from the *Conley* formulation); *Colman v. Utah State Land Bd.*, 795 P. 2d 622, 624 (Utah 1990) (holding that a motion to dismiss is appropriate "only if it clearly appears that [the plaintiff] can prove no set of facts in support of his claim"); *NRC Management Servs. Corp. v. First Va. Bank-Southwest*, 63 Va. Cir. 68, 70 (2003) ("The Virginia standard is identical [to the *Conley* formulation], though the Supreme Court of Virginia may not have used the same words to describe it").

6. The majority is correct to say that what the Federal Rules require is a "'showing'" of entitlement to relief. Whether and to what extent that "showing" requires allegations of fact will depend on the particulars of the claim. For example, had the amended complaint in this case alleged *only* parallel conduct, it would not have made the required "showing." *See supra*, at 1. Similarly, had the pleadings contained only an allegation of agreement, without specifying the nature or object of that agreement, they would have been susceptible to the charge that they did not provide sufficient notice that the defendants may answer intelligently. Omissions of that sort instance the type of "bareness" with which the Federal Rules are concerned. A plaintiff's inability to persuade a district court that the allegations actually included in her complaint are "plausible" is an altogether different kind of failing, and one that should not be fatal at the pleading stage.

pleaded complaint—would not, therefore, have impressed the *Conley* Court itself. Rather, that Court would have understood the majority's remodeling of its language to express an evidentiary standard, which the *Conley* Court had neither need nor want to explicate. Second, it is pellucidly clear that the *Conley* Court was interested in what a complaint must contain, not what it may contain. In fact, the Court said without qualification that it was "appraising the sufficiency of the complaint." 355 U.S., at 45 (emphasis added). It was, to paraphrase today's majority, describing "the minimum standard of adequate pleading to govern a complaint's survival."

We can be triply sure as to *Conley*'s meaning by examining the three Court of Appeals cases the *Conley* Court cited as support for the "accepted rule" that "a complaint should not be dismissed for failure to state a claim unless it appears beyond doubt that the plaintiff can prove no set of facts in support of his claim which would entitle him to relief." 355 U.S., at 45–46. In the first case, *Leimer v. State Mut. Life Assurance Co. of Worcester, Mass.*, 108 F.2d 302 (CA8 1940), the plaintiff alleged that she was the beneficiary of a life insurance plan and that the insurance company was wrongfully withholding proceeds from her. In reversing the District Court's grant of the defendant's motion to dismiss, the Eighth Circuit noted that court's own longstanding rule that, to warrant dismissal, "'it should appear from the allegations that a cause of action does not exist, rather than that a cause of action has been defectively stated.'" *Id.*, at 305 (quoting Winget v. Rockwood, 69 F.2d 326, 329 (CA8 1934)).

The *Leimer* court viewed the Federal Rules—specifically Rules 8(a)(2), 12(b)(6), 12(e) (motion for a more definite statement), and 56 (motion for summary judgment—as reinforcing the notion that "there is no justification for dismissing a complaint for insufficiency of statement, except where it appears to a certainty that the plaintiff would be entitled to no relief under any state of facts which could be proved in support of the claim." 108 F.2d at 306. The court refuted in the strongest terms any suggestion that the unlikelihood of recovery should determine the fate of a complaint: "No matter how improbable it may be that she can prove her claim, she is entitled to an opportunity to make the attempt, and is not required to accept as final a determination of her rights based upon inferences drawn in favor of the defendant from her amended complaint." *Ibid.*

The Third Circuit relied on *Leimer*'s admonition in *Continental Collieries, Inc. v. Shober*, 130 F.2d 631 (1942), which the *Conley* Court also cited in support of its "no set of facts" formulation. In a diversity action the plaintiff alleged breach of contract, but the District Court dismissed the complaint on the ground that the contract appeared to be unenforceable under state law. The Court of Appeals reversed, concluding that there were facts in dispute that went to the enforceability of the contract, and that the rule at the pleading stage was as in *Leimer*: "No matter how likely it may seem that the pleader will be unable to prove his case, he is entitled, upon averring a claim, to an opportunity to try to prove it." 130 F.2d at 635.

The third case the *Conley* Court cited approvingly was written by Judge Clark himself. In *Dioguardi v. Durning*, 139 F.2d 774 (CA2 1944), the pro se plaintiff, an importer of "tonics," charged the customs inspector with auctioning off the plaintiff's former merchandise for less than was bid for it—and indeed for an amount equal to the plaintiff's own bid—and complained that two cases of tonics went missing three weeks before the sale. The inference, hinted at by the averments but never stated in so many words, was that the defendant fraudulently denied the plaintiff his rightful claim to the tonics, which, if true, would have violated federal law. Writing six years after the adoption of the Federal Rules he held the lead rein in drafting, Judge Clark said that the defendant

> "could have disclosed the facts from his point of view, in advance of a trial if he chose, by asking for a pre-trial hearing or by moving for a summary judgment with supporting affidavits. But, as it stands, we do not see how the plaintiff may properly be deprived of his day in court to show what he obviously so firmly believes and what for present purposes defendant must be taken as admitting." *Id.*, at 775.

As any civil procedure student knows, Judge Clark's opinion disquieted the defense bar and gave rise to a movement to revise Rule 8 to require a plaintiff to plead a "'cause of action.'" *See* 5 Wright & Miller § 1201, at 86–87. The movement failed, *see ibid.*; *Dioguardi* was explicitly approved in *Conley*; and "[i]n retrospect the case itself seems to be a routine application of principles that are universally accepted," 5 Wright & Miller § 1220, at 284–285.

In light of *Leimer, Continental Collieries*, and *Dioguardi, Conley*'s statement that a complaint is not to be dismissed unless "no set of facts" in support thereof would entitle the plaintiff to relief is hardly "puzzling." It reflects a philosophy that, unlike in the days of code pleading, separating the wheat from the chaff is a task assigned to the pretrial and trial process. *Conley*'s language, in short, captures the policy choice embodied in the Federal Rules and binding on the federal courts.

We have consistently reaffirmed that basic understanding of the Federal Rules in the half century since *Conley*. For example, in *Scheuer v. Rhodes*, 416 U.S. 232 (1974), we reversed the Court of Appeals' dismissal on the pleadings when the respondents, the Governor and other officials of the State of Ohio, argued that the petitioners' claims were barred by sovereign immunity. In a unanimous opinion by then-Justice Rehnquist, we emphasized:

> "[W]hen a federal court reviews the sufficiency of a complaint, before the reception of any evidence either by affidavit or admissions, its task is necessarily a limited one. The issue is not whether a plaintiff will ultimately prevail but whether the claimant is entitled to offer evidence to support the claims. Indeed it may appear on the face of the pleadings that a recovery is very remote and unlikely but that is not the test." *Id.*, at 236 (emphasis added).

The *Rhodes* plaintiffs had "alleged generally and in conclusory terms" that the defendants, by calling out the National Guard to suppress the Kent State University student protests, "were guilty of wanton, wilful and negligent conduct." *Krause v. Rhodes*, 471 F.2d 430, 433 (CA6 1972). We reversed the Court of Appeals on the ground that "[w]hatever the plaintiffs may or may not be able to establish as to the merits of their allegations, their claims, as stated in the complaints, given the favorable reading required by the Federal Rules of Civil Procedure," were not barred by the Eleventh Amendment because they were styled as suits against the defendants in their individual capacities. 416 U.S., at 238.

We again spoke with one voice against efforts to expand pleading requirements beyond their appointed limits in *Leatherman v. Tarrant County Narcotics Intelligence and Coordination Unit*, 507 U.S. 163 (1993). Writing for the unanimous Court, Chief Justice Rehnquist rebuffed the Fifth Circuit's effort to craft a standard for pleading municipal liability that accounted for "the enormous expense involved today in litigation," *Leatherman v. Tarrant County Narcotics Intelligence and Coordination Unit*, 954 F.2d 1054, 1057 (1992) (internal quotation marks omitted), by requiring a plaintiff to "state with factual detail and particularity the basis for the claim which necessarily includes why the defendant-official cannot successfully maintain the defense of immunity," 507 U.S., at 167 (internal quotation marks omitted). We found this language inconsistent with Rules 8(a)(2) and 9(b) and emphasized that motions to dismiss were not the place to combat discovery abuse: "In the absence of [an amendment to Rule 9(b)], federal courts and litigants must rely on summary judgment and control of discovery to weed out unmeritorious claims sooner rather than later." *Id.*, at 168–169.

Most recently, in *Swierkiewicz*, 534 U.S. 506, we were faced with a case more similar to the present one than the majority will allow. In discrimination cases, our precedents require a plaintiff at the summary judgment stage to produce either direct evidence of discrimination or, if the claim is based primarily on circumstantial evidence, to meet the shifting evidentiary burdens imposed under the framework articulated in *McDonnell Douglas Corp. v. Green*, 411 U.S. 792 (1973). *See, e.g., Trans World Airlines, Inc. v. Thurston*, 469 U.S. 111 (1985). Swierkiewicz alleged that he had been terminated on account of national origin in violation of Title VII of the Civil Rights Act of 1964. The Second Circuit dismissed the suit on the pleadings because he had not pleaded a prima facie case of discrimination under the McDonnell Douglas standard.

We reversed in another unanimous opinion, holding that "under a notice pleading system, it is not appropriate to require a plaintiff to plead facts establishing a prima facie case because the *McDonnell Douglas* framework does not apply in every employment discrimination case." *Swierkiewicz*, 534 U.S., at 511. We also observed that Rule 8(a)(2) does not contemplate a court's passing on the merits of a litigant's claim at the pleading stage. Rather, the "simplified notice pleading standard" of the Federal Rules "relies on liberal discovery rules and summary judgment motions to define disputed facts and issues and to dispose of unmeritorious claims." *Id.*, at 512; *see* Brief for United States et al. as *Amici Curiae* in *Swierkiewicz v. Sorema N. A.*, O. T. 2001, No. 00-1853, p 10 (stating that a Rule 12(b)(6) motion is not "an appropriate device for testing the truth of what is asserted or for determining whether a plaintiff has any evidence to back up what is in the complaint" (internal quotation marks omitted)).[7]

As in the discrimination context, we have developed an evidentiary framework for evaluating claims under § 1 of the Sherman Act when those claims rest on entirely circumstantial evidence of conspiracy. *See Matsushita Elec. Industrial Co. v. Zenith Radio Corp.*, 475 U.S. 574 (1986). Under *Matsushita*, a plaintiff's allegations of an illegal conspiracy may not, at the summary judgment stage, rest solely on the inferences that may be drawn from the parallel conduct of the defendants. In order to survive a Rule 56 motion, a § 1 plaintiff "must present evidence 'that tends to exclude the possibility' that the alleged conspirators acted independently.'" *Id.*, at 588 (*quoting Monsanto Co. v. Spray-Rite Service Corp.*, 465 U.S. 752, 764 (1984)). That is, the plaintiff "must show that the inference of conspiracy is reasonable in light of the competing inferences of independent action or collusive action." 475 U.S., at 588.

Everything today's majority says would therefore make perfect sense if it were ruling on a Rule 56 motion for summary judgment and the evidence included nothing more than the Court has described. But it should go without saying in the wake of *Swierkiewicz* that a heightened production burden at the summary judgment stage does not translate into a heightened pleading burden at the complaint stage. The majority rejects the complaint in this case because—in light of the fact that the parallel conduct alleged is consistent with ordinary market behavior—the claimed conspiracy is "conceivable" but not "plausible." I have my doubts about the majority's assessment of the plausibility of this alleged conspiracy. *See* Part III, *infra*. But even if the majority's speculation is correct, its "plausibility" standard is irreconcilable with Rule 8 and with our governing precedents. As we made clear in *Swierkiewicz* and *Leatherman*, fear of the burdens of litigation does not justify factual conclusions supported only by lawyers' arguments rather than sworn denials or admissible evidence.

This case is a poor vehicle for the Court's new pleading rule, for we have observed that "in antitrust cases, where 'the proof is largely in the hands of the alleged conspirators,' . . . dismissals prior to giving the plaintiff ample opportunity for discovery should be granted very sparingly." *Hospital Building Co. v. Trustees of Rex*

---

7. *See also* 5 Wright & Miller §1202, at 89–90 ("[P]leadings under the rules simply may be a general summary of the party's position that is sufficient to advise the other party of the event being sued upon, to provide some guidance in a subsequent proceeding as to what was decided for purposes of res judicata and collateral estoppel, and to indicate whether the case should be tried to the court or to a jury. No more is demanded of the pleadings than this; indeed, history shows that no more can be performed successfully by the pleadings" (footnotes omitted)).

Hospital, 425 U.S. 738, 746 (1976) (*quoting Poller v. Columbia Broadcasting System, Inc.*, 368 U.S. 464, 473 (1962)); *see also Knuth v. Erie-Crawford Dairy Cooperative Asso.*, 395 F.2d 420, 423 (CA3 1968) ("The 'liberal' approach to the consideration of antitrust complaints is important because inherent in such an action is the fact that all the details and specific facts relied upon cannot properly be set forth as part of the pleadings"). Moreover, the fact that the Sherman Act authorizes the recovery of treble damages and attorney's fees for successful plaintiffs indicates that Congress intended to encourage, rather than discourage, private enforcement of the law. *See Radovich v. National Football League*, 352 U.S. 445, 454 (1957) ("Congress itself has placed the private antitrust litigant in a most favorable position. . . . In the face of such a policy this Court should not add requirements to burden the private litigant beyond what is specifically set forth by Congress in those laws"). It is therefore more, not less, important in antitrust cases to resist the urge to engage in armchair economics at the pleading stage.

The same year we decided *Conley*, Judge Clark wrote, presciently,

> "I fear that every age must learn its lesson that special pleading cannot be made to do the service of trial and that live issues between active litigants are not to be disposed of or evaded on the paper pleadings, i.e., the formalistic claims of the parties. Experience has found no quick and easy short cut for trials in cases generally and antitrust cases in particular." Special Pleading in the "Big Case"? in Procedure—The Handmaid of Justice 147, 148 (C. Wright & H. Reasoner eds. 1965) (hereinafter Clark, Special Pleading in the Big Case) (emphasis added).

In this "Big Case," the Court succumbs to the temptation that previous Courts have steadfastly resisted.[8] While the majority assures us that it is not applying any "'heightened'" pleading standard, I shall now explain why I have a difficult time understanding its opinion any other way.

---

8. Our decision in *Dura Pharmaceuticals, Inc. v. Broudo*, 544 U.S. 336 (2005), is not to the contrary. There, the plaintiffs failed adequately to allege loss causation, a required element in a private securities fraud action. Because it alleged nothing more than that the prices of the securities the plaintiffs purchased were artificially inflated, the *Dura* complaint failed to "provide the defendants with notice of what the relevant economic loss might be or of what the causal connection might be between that loss and the [alleged] misrepresentation." *Id.*, at 347. Here, the failure the majority identifies is not a failure of notice—which "notice pleading" rightly condemns—but rather a failure to satisfy the Court that the agreement alleged might plausibly have occurred. That being a question not of notice but of proof, it should not be answered without first hearing from the defendants (as apart from their lawyers).

Similarly, in *Associated Gen. Contractors of Cal., Inc. v. Carpenters*, 459 U.S. 519 (1983), in which we also found an antitrust complaint wanting, the problem was not that the injuries the plaintiffs alleged failed to satisfy some threshold of plausibility, but rather that the injuries as alleged were not "the type that the antitrust statute was intended to forestall." *Id.*, at 540; *see id.*, at 526 ("As the case comes to us, we must assume that the Union can prove the facts alleged in its amended complaint. It is not, however, proper to assume that the Union can prove facts that it has not alleged or that the defendants have violated the antitrust laws in ways that have not been alleged").

III

The Court does not suggest that an agreement to do what the plaintiffs allege would be permissible under the antitrust laws, *see, e.g., Associated Gen. Contractors of Cal., Inc. v. Carpenters*, 459 U.S. 519, 526–527 (1983). Nor does the Court hold that these plaintiffs have failed to allege an injury entitling them to sue for damages under those laws, *see Brunswick Corp. v. Pueblo Bowl-O-Mat, Inc.*, 429 U.S. 477, 489–490 (1977). Rather, the theory on which the Court permits dismissal is that, so far as the Federal Rules are concerned, no agreement has been alleged at all. This is a mind-boggling conclusion.

As the Court explains, prior to the enactment of the Telecommunications Act of 1996 the law prohibited the defendants from competing with each other. The new statute was enacted to replace a monopolistic market with a competitive one. The Act did not merely require the regional monopolists to take affirmative steps to facilitate entry to new competitors, *see Verizon Communications Inc. v. Law Offices of Curtis v. Trinko, LLP*, 540 U.S. 398, 402 (2004); it also permitted the existing firms to compete with each other and to expand their operations into previously forbidden territory. *See* 47 U.S.C. § 271. Each of the defendants decided not to take the latter step. That was obviously an extremely important business decision, and I am willing to presume that each company acted entirely independently in reaching that decision. I am even willing to entertain the majority's belief that any agreement among the companies was unlikely. But the plaintiffs allege in three places in their complaint, PP 4, 51, 64, App. 11, 27, 30, that the ILECs did in fact agree both to prevent competitors from entering into their local markets and to forgo competition with each other. And as the Court] recognizes, at the motion to dismiss stage, a judge assumes "that all the allegations in the complaint are true (even if doubtful in fact)."

The majority circumvents this obvious obstacle to dismissal by pretending that it does not exist. The Court admits that "in form a few stray statements in the complaint speak directly of agreement," but disregards those allegations by saying that "on fair reading these are merely legal conclusions resting on the prior allegations" of parallel conduct. The Court's dichotomy between factual allegations and "legal conclusions" is the stuff of a bygone era. That distinction was a defining feature of code pleading, *see generally* Clark, The Complaint in Code Pleading, 35 Yale L. J. 259 (1925–1926), but was conspicuously abolished when the Federal Rules were enacted in 1938. *See United States v. Employing Plasterers Ass'n*, 347 U.S. 186, 188 (1954) (holding, in an antitrust case, that the Government's allegations of effects on interstate commerce must be taken into account in deciding whether to dismiss the complaint "[w]hether these charges be called 'allegations of fact' or 'mere conclusions of the pleader'"); *Brownlee v. Conine*, 957 F.2d 353, 354 (CA7 1992) ("The Federal Rules of Civil Procedure establish a system of notice pleading rather than of fact pleading, . . . so the happenstance that a complaint is 'conclusory,' whatever exactly that overused lawyers' cliche means, does not automatically condemn it");

Walker Distributing Co. v. Lucky Lager Brewing Co., 323 F.2d 1, 3–4 (CA9 1963) ("[O]ne purpose of Rule 8 was to get away from the highly technical distinction between statements of fact and conclusions of law . . ."); *Oil, Chemical & Atomic Workers Int'l Union v. Delta*, 277 F.2d 694, 697 (CA6 1960) ("Under the notice system of pleading established by the Rules of Civil Procedure, . . . the ancient distinction between pleading 'facts' and 'conclusions' is no longer significant"); 5 Wright & Miller § 1218, at 267 ("[T]he federal rules do not prohibit the pleading of facts or legal conclusions as long as fair notice is given to the parties"). "Defendants entered into a contract" is no more a legal conclusion than "defendant negligently drove," *see* Form 9. Indeed it is less of one.[9]

Even if I were inclined to accept the Court's anachronistic dichotomy and ignore the complaint's actual allegations, I would dispute the Court's suggestion that any inference of agreement from petitioners' parallel conduct is "implausible." Many years ago a truly great economist perceptively observed that "[p]eople of the same trade seldom meet together, even for merriment and diversion, but the conversation ends in a conspiracy against the public, or in some contrivance to raise prices." A. Smith, An Inquiry Into the Nature and Causes of the Wealth of Nations, in 39 Great Books of the Western World 55 (R. Hutchins & M. Adler eds. 1952). I am not so cynical as to accept that sentiment at face value, but I need not do so here. Respondents' complaint points not only to petitioners' numerous opportunities to meet with each other, Complaint P 46, App. 23,[10] but also to Notebaert's curious statement that encroaching on a fellow incumbent's territory "might be a good way to turn a quick dollar but that doesn't make it right," *id.*, P 42, App. 22. What did he mean by that? One possible (indeed plausible) inference is that he meant that while it would be in his company's economic self-interest to compete with its brethren, he had agreed with his competitors not to do so. According to the complaint, that is how the Illinois Coalition for Competitive Telecom construed Notebaert's statement, *id.*, P 44, App. 22 (calling the statement "evidence of potential collusion among regional Bell phone monopolies to not compete against one another and kill off potential competitors in local phone service"), and that is how Members of

---

9. The Court suggests that the allegation of an agreement, even if credited, might not give the notice required by Rule 8 because it lacks specificity. The remedy for an allegation lacking sufficient specificity to provide adequate notice is, of course, a Rule 12(e) motion for a more definite statement. *See Swierkiewicz v. Sorema N. A.*, 534 U.S. 506, 514 (2002). Petitioners made no such motion and indeed have conceded that "[o]ur problem with the current complaint is not a lack of specificity, it's quite specific." Tr. of Oral Arg. 14. Thus, the fact that "the pleadings mentioned no specific time, place, or persons involved in the alleged conspiracies," is, for our purposes, academic.

10. The Court describes my reference to the allegation that the defendants belong to various trade associations as "playfully" suggesting that the defendants conspired to restrain trade. Quite the contrary: an allegation that competitors meet on a regular basis, like the allegations of parallel conduct, is consistent with—though not sufficient to prove—the plaintiffs' entirely serious and unequivocal allegation that the defendants entered into an unlawful agreement. Indeed, if it were true that the plaintiffs "rest their §1 claim on descriptions of parallel conduct and not on any independent allegation of actual agreement among the ILECs," there would have been no purpose in including a reference to the trade association meetings in the amended complaint.

Congress construed his company's behavior, *id.*, P 45, App. 23 (describing a letter to the Justice Department requesting an investigation into the possibility that the ILECs'"very apparent non-competition policy'" was coordinated).

Perhaps Notebaert meant instead that competition would be sensible in the short term but not in the long run. That's what his lawyers tell us anyway. *See* Brief for Petitioners 36. But I would think that no one would know better what Notebaert meant than Notebaert himself. Instead of permitting respondents to ask Notebaert, however, the Court looks to other quotes from that and other articles and decides that what he meant was that entering new markets as a competitive local exchange carrier would not be a "'sustainable economic model.'" Never mind that—as anyone ever interviewed knows—a newspaper article is hardly a verbatim transcript; the writer selects quotes to package his story, not to record a subject's views for posterity. But more importantly the District Court was required at this stage of the proceedings to construe Notebaert's ambiguous statement in the plaintiffs' favor.[11] *See Allen v. Wright*, 468 U.S. 737, 767–768, n. 1 (1984) (Brennan, J., dissenting). The inference the statement supports—that simultaneous decisions by ILECs not even to attempt to poach customers from one another once the law authorized them to do so were the product of an agreement—sits comfortably within the realm of possibility. That is all the Rules require.

To be clear, if I had been the trial judge in this case, I would not have permitted the plaintiffs to engage in massive discovery based solely on the allegations in this complaint. On the other hand, I surely would not have dismissed the complaint without requiring the defendants to answer the charge that they "have agreed not to compete with one another and otherwise allocated customers and markets to one another."[12] Complaint, P 51, App. 27. Even a sworn denial of that charge would not justify a summary dismissal without giving the plaintiffs the opportunity to take depositions from Notebaert and at least one responsible executive representing each of the other defendants.

Respondents in this case proposed a plan of "'phased discovery'" limited to the existence of the alleged conspiracy and class certification. Brief for Respondents 25–26. Two petitioners rejected the plan. *Ibid.* Whether or not respondents' proposed plan

---

11. It is ironic that the Court seeks to justify its decision to draw factual inferences in the defendants' favor at the pleading stage by citing to a rule of evidence. Under Federal Rule of Evidence 201(b), a judicially noticed fact "must be one not subject to reasonable dispute in that it is either (1) generally known within the territorial jurisdiction of the trial court or (2) capable of accurate and ready determination by resort to sources whose accuracy cannot reasonably be questioned." Whether Notebaert's statements constitute evidence of a conspiracy is hardly beyond reasonable dispute.

12. The Court worries that a defendant seeking to respond to this "conclusory" allegation "would have little idea where to begin." A defendant could, of course, begin by either denying or admitting the charge.

was sensible, it was an appropriate subject for negotiation.[13] Given the charge in the complaint—buttressed by the common sense of Adam Smith—I cannot say that the possibility that joint discussions and perhaps some agreements played a role in petitioners' decision-making process is so implausible that dismissing the complaint before any defendant has denied the charge is preferable to granting respondents even a minimal opportunity to prove their claims. *See* Clark, New Federal Rules 977 ("[T]hrough the weapons of discovery and summary judgment we have developed new devices, with more appropriate penalties to aid in matters of proof, and do not need to force the pleadings to their less appropriate function").

I fear that the unfortunate result of the majority's new pleading rule will be to invite lawyers' debates over economic theory to conclusively resolve antitrust suits in the absence of any evidence. It is no surprise that the antitrust defense bar—among whom "lament" as to inadequate judicial supervision of discovery is most "common"—should lobby for this state of affairs. But "we must recall that their primary

---

13. The potential for "sprawling, costly, and hugely time-consuming" discovery is no reason to throw the baby out with the bathwater. The Court vastly underestimates a district court's case-management arsenal. Before discovery even begins, the court may grant a defendant's Rule 12(e) motion; Rule 7(a) permits a trial court to order a plaintiff to reply to a defendant's answer, *see Crawford-El v. Britton*, 523 U.S. 574, 598 (1998); and Rule 23 requires "rigorous analysis" to ensure that class certification is appropriate, *General Telephone Co. of Southwest v. Falcon*, 457 U.S. 147, 160 (1982); *see In re Initial Public Offering Securities Litigation*, 471 F. 3d 24 (CA2 2006) (holding that a district court may not certify a class without ruling that each Rule 23 requirement is met, even if a requirement overlaps with a merits issue). Rule 16 invests a trial judge with the power, backed by sanctions, to regulate pretrial proceedings via conferences and scheduling orders, at which the parties may discuss, inter alia, "the elimination of frivolous claims or defenses," Rule 16(c)(1); "the necessity or desirability of amendments to the pleadings," Rule 16(c)(2); "the control and scheduling of discovery," Rule 16(c)(6); and "the need for adopting special procedures for managing potentially difficult or protracted actions that may involve complex issues, multiple parties, difficult legal questions, or unusual proof problems," Rule 16(c)(12).

Subsequently, Rule 26 confers broad discretion to control the combination of interrogatories, requests for admissions, production requests, and depositions permitted in a given case; the sequence in which such discovery devices may be deployed; and the limitations imposed upon them. *See* 523 U.S., at 598–599. Indeed, Rule 26(c) specifically permits a court to take actions "to protect a party or person from annoyance, embarrassment, oppression, or undue burden or expense" by, for example, disallowing a particular discovery request, setting appropriate terms and conditions, or limiting its scope. In short, the Federal Rules contemplate that pretrial matters will be settled through a flexible process of give and take, of proffers, stipulations, and stonewalls, not by having trial judges screen allegations for their plausibility *vel non* without requiring an answer from the defendant. *See Societe Internationale pour Participations Industrielles et Commerciales, S. A. v. Rogers*, 357 U.S. 197, 206 (1958) ("Rule 34 is sufficiently flexible to be adapted to the exigencies of particular litigation"). And should it become apparent over the course of litigation that a plaintiff's filings bespeak an *in terrorem* suit, the district court has at its call its own *in terrorem* device, in the form of a wide array of Rule 11 sanctions. See Rules 11(b), (c) (authorizing sanctions if a suit is presented "for any improper purpose, such as to harass or to cause unnecessary delay or needless increase in the cost of litigation"); *see Business Guides, Inc. v. Chromatic Communications Enterprises, Inc.,* 498 U.S. 533 (1991) (holding that Rule 11 applies to a represented party who signs a pleading, motion, or other papers, as well as to attorneys); *Atkins v. Fischer,* 232 F. R. D. 116, 126 (DC 2005) ("As possible sanctions pursuant to Rule 11, the court has an arsenal of options at its disposal").

responsibility is to win cases for their clients, not to improve law administration for the public." Clark, Special Pleading in the Big Case 152. As we did in our prior decisions, we should have instructed them that their remedy was to seek to amend the Federal Rules—not our interpretation of them.[14] *See Swierkiewicz*, 534 U.S., at 515; *Crawford-El v. Britton*, 523 U.S. 574, 595 (1998); *Leatherman*, 507 U.S., at 168.

IV

Just a few weeks ago some of my colleagues explained that a strict interpretation of the literal text of statutory language is essential to avoid judicial decisions that are not faithful to the intent of Congress. *Zuni Pub. Sch. Dist. No. 89 v. Dep't of Educ.* (Scalia, J., dissenting). I happen to believe that there are cases in which other tools of construction are more reliable than text, but I agree of course that congressional intent should guide us in matters of statutory interpretation. This is a case in which the intentions of the drafters of three important sources of law—the Sherman Act, the Telecommunications Act of 1996, and the Federal Rules of Civil Procedure—all point unmistakably in the same direction, yet the Court marches resolutely the other way. Whether the Court's actions will benefit only defendants in antitrust treble-damages cases, or whether its test for the sufficiency of a complaint will inure to the benefit of all civil defendants, is a question that the future will answer. But that the Court has announced a significant new rule that does not even purport to respond to any congressional command is glaringly obvious.

The transparent policy concern that drives the decision is the interest in protecting antitrust defendants—who in this case are some of the wealthiest corporations in our economy—from the burdens of pretrial discovery. Even if it were not apparent that the legal fees petitioners have incurred in arguing the merits of their Rule 12(b) motion have far exceeded the cost of limited discovery, or that those discovery costs would burden respondents as well as petitioners,[15] that concern would not provide an adequate justification for this law-changing decision. For in the final analysis it is only a lack of confidence in the ability of trial judges to control discovery, buttressed

---

14. Given his "background in antitrust law," Judge Easterbrook has recognized that the most effective solution to discovery abuse lies in the legislative and rulemaking arenas. He has suggested that the remedy for the ills he complains of requires a revolution in the rules of civil procedure:

"Perhaps a system in which judges pare away issues and focus on investigation is too radical to contemplate in this country—although it prevailed here before 1938, when the Federal Rules of Civil Procedure were adopted. The change could not be accomplished without abandoning notice pleading, increasing the number of judicial officers, and giving them more authority . . . . If we are to rule out judge-directed discovery, however, we must be prepared to pay the piper. Part of the price is the high cost of unnecessary discovery—impositional and otherwise." Discovery as Abuse, 69 B. U. L. Rev. 635, 645 (1989).

15. It would be quite wrong, of course, to assume that dismissal of an antitrust case after discovery is costless to plaintiffs. *See* Fed. Rule Civ. Proc. 54(d)(1) ("[C]osts other than attorneys' fees shall be allowed as of course to the prevailing party unless the court otherwise directs").

by appellate judges' independent appraisal of the plausibility of profoundly serious factual allegations, that could account for this stark break from precedent.

If the allegation of conspiracy happens to be true, today's decision obstructs the congressional policy favoring competition that undergirds both the Telecommunications Act of 1996 and the Sherman Act itself. More importantly, even if there is abundant evidence that the allegation is untrue, directing that the case be dismissed without even looking at any of that evidence marks a fundamental—and unjustified—change in the character of pretrial practice.

Accordingly, I respectfully dissent.

APPENDIX D

COURT OF APPEALS CASES

Antitrust Experts

Daubert *and Other Gatekeeping Challenges of Antitrust Experts*

James Langenfeld and Christopher Alexander

Antitrust, Vol. 25, No. 3, Summer 2011

http://www.americanbar.org/content/dam/aba/administrative/litigation/materials/
sac_2012/18-1_b_daubert_and_other_gatekeeping_challenges_with_appendix_
antitrust.authcheckdam.pdf

INDEX

A

Admissibility, additional criteria, 15.2

Analogies, 13.9

Arbitration. *See* International commercial arbitration

B

Bases of opinion, 6.1, 16.1
    confrontation clause challenges in criminal cases, 16.2
    Beauty contests, 5.5

Brainstorming, 6.3.1

Burton, Richard Francis, 8.3

C

Camera/video-to-monitor, 10.7

Care of experts, 3.1

Chambers, Whittaker, 9.1

Chart cross-examination, 12.1

Closed questions, guidance in answering, 8.3

Computer graphics, 10.2.2

Computer-to-display screen, 10.7

Confidentiality, 2.3, 5.6.1

Confrontation clause
    Expert bases in criminal cases, 16.2
    Control
    corralling the expert, 13.10
    expert's report, 12.4
    form of question, 11.1
    repeating the question, 11.2.1, 11.2.2
    scientific method principles, use of, 13.11
    techniques, 11.2, 13.7

Cross-examination
    analogies, 13.9
    anticipating, 9.4.7

bias, 12.5
    constructive, 13.3
    control, 11.1
    control of. *See* Control
    destructive, 13.3
    enlistment, 13.7.1
    eyes, cross-examination with, 11.2.3
    fact-gathering, 13.5
    impeachment, 12.1, 13.6
    international commercial arbitration. *See* International commercial arbitration
    macro, 13.8
    micro, 13.8
    organizational choices, 13.1–13.6
    primacy, 13.4
    recency, 13.4
    reconstruction and recreations, 13.12, 13.12.1–13.12.4
    run-on witness, 11.2
    storytelling, 13.5
    substance, 13.6

D

Daubert v. Merrill Dow Pharmaceuticals, Inc., 7.2, 15.1–15.4, 16.4, 16.4.1– 16.4.13

Deposition
    brainstorming, 6.3.1
    discovery, 6.1
    document review, 6.3.3
    goals, 6.3.3
    learned treatises, 8.2
    location, 6.2
    preparation, 6.3, 8.3
    strategies, 7.1, 7.2
    tactics, 8.1–8.4
    timeline, 6.3.2

Direct examination
    analyzing testimony, 9.1
    anticipating cross, 9.4.7
    bases, 9.4.6
    ending strong, 9.4.8
    general discussion, 9.3

opinions, 9.4.5
outline of testimony, 9.4
preparation, 9.2
qualifying the expert, 9.4.3
redirect, 9.4.8
tender, 9.4.4
tickler, 9.4.2

Discovery
beauty contests, 5.5
communications, 5.6
consulting expert, 5.2
expert, 6.1
international commercial arbitration,
    14.1.1
nonconsulting expert, 5.3
nondeposition, 5.1
protective orders, 5.4

Documents, handling, 10.7

E

Enlistment, 13.7.1

Evidence camera (Elmo), 10.7

Exhibits
computer graphics, 10.2.2
demonstrative, 10.2.2
evidentiary foundations, 10.1
evidentiary hurdles, 10.1.1
foundations for, 10.2
gold and dross rule, 10.9
handling documents, 10.7
hearsay hurdles, 10.1.2
illustrative, 10.1.1
mandatory disclosure, 4.4
medium and occasion, 10.8
misleading labels, 10.5.1
movies, 10.2.2
persuasive foundation, 10.9
photographs, 10.2.1
pretrial conference, 10.3
sightlines, 10.7
summaries, 10.1.1
ten tips for visuals, 10.7
three-step exhibit circuit, 10.7

Expert fees, 2.4

Experts
advantages, 7.1
caring for, 3.1
confidentiality, 2.3

fees, 2.4
finding, 2.1
inside experts, 2.1.1
nontestifying experts, ch.1, 2.1.2, 4.4
outside experts, 2.1.2, 2.2
testimony, ch.1, 10.1, 16.1
things to avoid. *See* Care of experts
vulnerabilities, 7.1

Expert's report
control asserted with, 12.4
destruction of records, 5.6.1.1
early filing, 4.4
indicia of reliability, 5.6.1.2
international commercial arbitration,
    14.1.2
preparation by, 5.6.1.2
rebuttal disclosure, 4.4
requirements, 4.3

F

Fact witnesses, 2.1.1, 4.4

Finding experts, 2.1
graduate students, 2.1, 6.1
inside experts, 2.1.1
Internet directories, 2.2
local institutions, 2.2
national institutions, 2.2
outside experts, 2.1.2, 2.2

Fit. *See* **Relevance**

Foundation. *See* **Reliability criteria**

Four Cs, 12.1

Frye v. United States, **15.1**

Funnel technique, Ch.8 Introduction

G

General Electric v. Joiner, **15.1**

H

Hearsay
exhibits, 10.1.2
opinion based on statements of others, 16.1

Hiss, Alger, 9.1

Huddleston v. United States, **12.6**

National Institute for Trial Advocacy

I

Impeachment
bias, 12.5
expert's report, 12.4
learned treatise, 12.3
omission, 12.2
prior bad acts, 12.6
prior inconsistent statements, 12.1

Imwinkelreid, Edward J.
major premise, 9.1
minor premise, 9.1

International commercial arbitration
appointed experts, 14.2.3
approach, 14.1.3
damages, 14.1.6
discovery, 14.1.1
expert reports, 14.1.2
general discussion, 14.3
qualifications of expert, researching,
14.1.4
time constraints, 14.1.7
trial advocacy cross-examination
skills and techniques, 14.2,
14.2.1–14.2.4
tribunal's background, 14.1.5
Witness conferencing, 14.2.4

K

Kumho Tire Co., Ltd. v. Carmichael, 15.4

L

Lay opinion doctrine, 15.3
Learned treatise, 8.2, 12.3

M

Misleading icons, 10.5.1
Movies, 10.2.2

N

Narrowing the issues, 13.7.1
Nguyen v. IBP, Inc., 4.3

O

Opinions and bases, 7.1

Organizational choices in cross-
examination, 13.1–13.6

P

Pennzoil Co. v. Texaco, Inc., 2.1.2, 7.1

Photographs, 10.2.1

Post-*Daubert* issues, 15.3

PowerPoint, 10.9

Preparation
deposition, 8.3
direct examination, 9.2
role-playing, 8.3

Pretrial conference
exhibits, 10.3
opposing graphic evidence, 10.6
OPRAH, 10.4
organization, 10.4

Primacy versus recency, 13.4

Protective orders, 5.4

Protector of fairness, 10.5

Q

Qualifying the expert
direct examination, 9.4.3
international commercial arbitration,
14.1.4

R

Rebuttal disclosure, 4.4

Reconstruction and recreations, 13.12,
13.12.1–13.12.4

Relevance, 13.12.4

Reliability criteria
acceptance in relevant scientific field,
16.4.3
adequacy of credentials, 16.4.12
confrontation clause challenges to expert
bases in criminal cases, 16.2

consistency in application, 16.4.10
consistency in methodology, 16.4.9
derivation from mainstream approaches,
    16.4.13
empirical data, 16.4.6
error rate, 16.4.2
hearsay exceptions and admissibility of
    bases, 16.1
peer critique, 16.4.1
preparation for a purpose other than
    litigation, 16.4.5
publication, 16.4.1
qualitatively acceptable data, 16.4.8
quantitatively sufficient data, 16.4.7
recognition in body of literature,
    16.4.11
testability, 16.4.4
testing of expert's own opinion, 16.3

Reliability of methodology, 16.4.9

Reverse repeat, 11.2.2

S

Speke, John Hanning, 8.3

Storytelling versus fact-gathering, 13.5

Substance versus impeachment, 13.6

T

Theory, testing, 6.3.3

Three-step exhibit circuit, 10.7

Tigar, Michael, Ch.1

Timelines
    defendant's expert, 4.2
    deposition timeline, 6.3.2
    expert's report, 4.3
    plaintiff's expert, 4.1
    rebuttal disclosure, 4.4

U

U.S. v. Tranowski, 9.3

V

Voluntary disclosures, 4.4, 5.6.1.2

NITA covers the key areas of trial advocacy.

Skills-based focus gives you the insight and experience necessary to take your advocacy to the next level.

Our publications are designed to help lawyers develop and refine their advocacy skills in every stage of litigation. Whether it's written discovery, e-discovery, deposition, trial preparation, appeals, or alternative dispute resolution, our books give you the tools to do it all with confidence.

If you're looking for practical skills advice, we have books ranging from how to handle an administrative agency case to preparing trial notebooks to winning appeals.

Modern Trial Advocacy

The Effective Deposition

Problems in Trial Advocacy

Statutory Interpretation

Effective Courtroom Advocacy

Federal Rules of Evidence with Objections

Winning on Appeal: Better Briefs & Oral Argument

Winning At Trial

Visit our online bookstore for the complete NITA collection.

Made in United States
North Haven, CT
20 January 2023

31343945R00265